PRINCIPLES OF CANADIAN INCOME TAX LAW

Seventh Edition

PETER W. HOGG
Professor Emeritus, Osgoode Hall Law School
York University, Toronto
Scholar in Residence
Blake, Cassels & Graydon LLP,
Toronto

JOANNE E. MAGEE
Director, School of
Public Policy and Administration
York University, Toronto

and

JINYAN LI
Professor, Osgoode Hall Law School,
York University, Toronto

CARSWELL®

Library and Archives Canada has catalogued this publication as follows:

ISSN 1493-4760
ISBN 978-0-7798-2852-4 (7th edition)

Printed in Canada by Thomson Reuters.

THOMSON REUTERS

CARSWELL, A DIVISION OF THOMSON REUTERS CANADA LIMITED

One Corporate Plaza
2075 Kennedy Road
Toronto, Ontario
M1T 3V4

Customer Relations
Toronto 1-416-609-3800
Elsewhere in Canada/U.S. 1-800-387-5164
Fax 1-416-298-5082
www.carswell.com
E-mail www.carswell.com/email

PREFACE

This is the seventh edition of *Principles of Canadian Income Tax Law*. The sixth edition was published in 2007 and the usual pace of change in the world of income tax has necessitated a further revision of the text.

The book originated as a set of lecture notes prepared by Professor Hogg for his course in Income Tax Law at the Osgoode Hall Law School of York University. The notes were handed out to students, and were revised from time to time. In order to help convert the notes into a book, Professor Hogg enlisted the aid of Professor Magee, who teaches income tax to accounting students at the Faculty of Liberal Arts and Professional Studies of York University. She joined the project in 1994, and participated in an extensive rewriting. The final versions of the first and second editions were a joint product.

Professor Hogg has not been able to continue as an active participant in the writing of subsequent editions. In the third edition, Ted Cook, now a Senior Rulings Officer for international tax with the Canada Revenue Agency in Ottawa became a co-author. Since the fourth edition, Jinyan Li has been a co-author and has undertaken significant restructuring and rewriting of the book.

This seventh edition covers several new topics and has been updated and rewritten to improve its usefulness to readers: students, professors, lawyers and the judiciary. Although some of the material is new, much of the material in earlier editions is retained and the book remains faithful to its original objectives.

The book covers personal income tax, with single chapters on corporations, partnerships, and trusts. The book is designed for students doing their first course in income tax law. It should also be useful for lawyers who need a refresher in the basic principles of personal income tax. We hope as well that it will be useful to courts, especially when they have to deal with fundamental issues, and we have been delighted that it has been cited in a number of decisions of the Supreme Court of Canada.

As the title indicates, the emphasis of the book is on the principles of income tax law. That means the ideas of the income tax system, the policies that underlie the system, and the major features of the system. Income tax law is portrayed as a rational system. There is a reason for everything, and we always try to explain what that reason is. The law is never portrayed as a set of purposeless technicalities. The approach is not merely descriptive. Alternative ideas and policies are examined, and the provisions of the Act and the case law are evaluated critically in light of our conceptions of sound tax policy.

The book is progressive. The early chapters assume an intelligent reader who has no knowledge of tax concepts or accounting concepts, and little of commercial matters. As ideas are explained and information provided, the chapters become more demanding. The book is intended to be an aid to learning rather than a reference work. However, the detailed table of contents, the table of cases and the index should make it easy for the non-continuous reader to find what he or she is looking for.

We have tried to avoid the complex abstractions with which the *Income Tax Act* is replete. Our language is as simple, concrete and non-technical as our capability and the nature of the subject permitted. Obviously, a lot of detail is unavoidable, but the minutiae of the subject are avoided or, where they are necessary for accuracy, are relegated to footnotes. Difficult numerical examples are avoided, although simple numerical examples are used from time to time to explain a concept. The book is designed to be easy to read.

The authors have had the good fortune to work in environments that encourage and facilitate the writing of a book such as this one. In preparing this book, we have been helped by comments from Larry Chapman, Thaddeus Hwong, Pearl Schusheim, Sandra Scott, Scott Wilkie, Brian Arnold, Bob Beam, Neil Brooks, Doug Hartkorn, Warren Grover, John Macintosh, Alan Macnaughton, Lisa Philipps, Lee St. Aubin, Graham Turner, David Spiro, Rick Krever, Denise Elliott, Joel Nitikman, Joe Frankovic, Aihua (Charlotte) Wu, Joanne Gort and Simon Leith. The editing, printing and production of this edition went smoothly thanks to Heather Cant and Beth Lariviere of Carswell.

The authors dedicate their contributions to this book to their spouses and children.

Toronto
March 31, 2010

Peter W. Hogg
Joanne E. Magee
Jinyan Li

Summary of Chapters

For detailed table of contents, see page vii.

CONTENTS

TABLE OF CASES

References are to section.

1
INCOME TAX LAW

1.1 — Introduction

"A tax is a levy, enforceable by law imposed under the authority of a legislature, imposed by a public body and levied for a public purpose."[1] "Income tax, if I may be pardoned for saying so, is a tax on income."[2]

This chapter provides an overview of the key functions of income tax, the sources of income tax law, the principles of statutory interpretation, the basic structure of the income tax system, and some basic income tax terminology and concepts.

1.2 — Roles of the income tax

(a) — Revenue

The main purpose of the income tax is to raise revenue to finance government spending. This is, of course, the purpose of every tax, but the income tax is the most important source of government revenue. In the 2010-2011 fiscal year, federal income tax is projected to yield 50.6 per cent of the federal government's revenue. The next most important sources of revenue are the federal goods and services tax

[1] *Kempe v. R.* (2000), [2001] 1 C.T.C. 2060 (T.C.C. [Informal Procedure]).

[2] *London County Council v. Attorney General* (1899), 4 T.C. 265 (England P.C.) (per Lord Macnaghten of the Privy Council).

("GST") (11.8 per cent), corporate income taxes (11 per cent) and employment insurance premiums (7.6 per cent).[3] The income tax is the most important source of revenue for the provinces as well. Provincial income taxes (on personal and corporate income) yielded 29.4 per cent of all provincial governments' revenues in 2007-08. This is followed by provincial sales taxes (18.4 per cent) and federal transfer payments (18.1 per cent).[4]

Income tax is also an important source of revenue in other developed countries, but to a lesser degree. Canada's income taxes amounted to 16.7% of gross domestic product (GDP) in 2007, higher than most of the 30 OECD member countries.[5] However, the overall tax-to-GDP ratio in Canada (33.3%) is lower than the average of OECD countries (35.9%), although higher than the United States (28.3%).

(b) — Redistribution of income

The income tax serves several other important functions in addition to raising revenue. These include the mitigation of unequal distribution of income in society through redistribution, the regulation of private economic activity and the promotion of social policies.

In Canada and other Western democracies, income is primarily distributed through market exchanges. The outcome of such distribution is considered "unjust" or "unfair" for a modern society. Income tax, especially personal income tax, was originally designed to redistribute social income in order to mitigate the unequal distribution. Taxes are collected from high-income earners at progressive rates (i.e., the higher the income, the higher the tax rate) and used to finance social programs. The extent of the redistribution is such that, in 2007, the share of federal personal income taxes paid by the top 10% of income earners (earning 35% of total income) was estimated to be 53% of all personal income tax collected and the corresponding figure for the top 50% (earning 86% of total income) was 96%.[6] Although the appropriate level of redistribution can be debated theoretically and politically, there is no denial that personal income tax is the only tax in Canada that is progressive and functions as the main instrument of redistribution.

---

[3]Department of Finance, Budget 2010, March 4, 2010, page 176. The figures are as follows in billions: total revenues ($231.3); personal income tax ($117.0), GST ($27.3), corporate income tax ($25.5) and EI ($17.6). Non-resident income taxes ($5.5), a combination of personal and corporate taxes, are disclosed separately from personal and corporate income taxes.

[4]Treff and Perry, *Finances of the Nation 2008* (Can. Tax Foundation, 2009), Table A.7 which is the most recent edition at the time of writing (March 2010).

[5]*OECD Factbook* 2009 at http://puck.sourceoecd.org/vl=4475360/cl=29/nw=1/rpsv/factbook2009/10/04/01/index.htm. Budget 2010 projections, note 3 above, are noticeably lower than 16.7% of GDP for 2008-2009 and subsequent years (for which there are no OECD figures) and are around 10 to 11%.

[6]http://www2.parl.gc.ca/content/LOP/ResearchPublications/prb0707-e.htm

(c) — Regulation of private activity

All governments use tax policy to regulate private activities in order to promote certain economic and social policies. This is evident during election campaigns and budget debates. Fundamental social and economic judgments are made in deciding who to tax, what to tax, and when. Tax subsidies are used to specifically promote activities, such as environmental protection, home ownership, retirement savings, post-secondary education and entrepreneurship. These tax subsidies are referred to as "tax expenditures" because they are government expenditures on programs which are delivered through tax reductions and exemptions. The tax revenue forfeited is the "tax expenditure". As with the redistribution function, the regulatory function of taxation is controversial and discussed further in Chapter 2.

1.3 — Income tax law

(a) — The *Income Tax Act*

(i) — History

The Canadian federal income tax is imposed by the *Income Tax Act* (the "Act").[7] The federal government first imposed an income tax in 1917 during World War I. The tax was supposed to be a temporary wartime measure because it was accepted that the field of direct taxation should be left to the provinces. But as the income tax was proven to be a reliable source of government revenue, the temporary tax became permanent after the war: in 1948, the word "War" was dropped and the Act was renamed "The Income Tax Act". The current Act was enacted in 1971,[8] and came into force at the beginning of 1972.

The original income tax legislation and supporting regulations introduced in 1917 comprised a mere 20 pages. The current Act (including historical references, various annotations, including proposed amendments) runs for about 1500 pages (in small print and on 2-column pages).[9] When supporting regulations are added, the legislation comprises some 2500 pages.[10] It weighs more than a kilogram![11]

In addition to an increase in length and resulting complexity, there have also been major changes in the style of legislative drafting. The 1917 legislation was drafted in broad, generally-worded provisions. The 1972 tax reform[12] and subsequent amendments reflect a high degree of detail and technical complexity. Recent legis-

---

[7]R.S.C. 1985 (5th Supp.), c. 1.

[8]S.C. 1970-71-72, c. 63 (Royal Assent December 23, 1971) enacted the substance of the Act, although it did not wholly repeal the previous Act. As explained under heading 1.6 below, the first federal income tax was introduced in 1917.

[9]For example, *The Practitioner's Income Tax Act* (37th, 2010).

[10]*Ibid.*

[11]*Ipsco Inc. v. R.*, [2002] 2 C.T.C. 2907, 2002 D.T.C. 1421 (T.C.C. [General Procedure]) at para. 26.

[12]See heading 2.2(e), "Tax reform of 1971 and the Carter Report", below.

lative drafting has also included the use of algebraic formulae. The change in statutory style has been caused by several factors, including: an increase in the complexity of income-earning transactions because of growth in cross-border activities, the rise of e-commerce, and advances in technology; the use of income tax legislation by the government as a fiscal policy instrument; legislative overrule of judicial interpretation of the Act; and the use of statutory anti-avoidance rules as new avoidance transactions become known to the government.

(ii) — Current structure

The Act is divided into parts: Part I contains the provisions that levy the ordinary income tax on individuals, corporations, trusts, and partnerships; Parts I.1 to XIV levy a variety of special taxes that supplement or complement the ordinary income tax; Part XV provides for administration and enforcement; Parts XVI and XVI.1 deal with tax avoidance; and Part XVII addresses interpretation, providing definitions of many of the terms used in the Act.

Part I is further divided into 10 "Divisions", identified by capital letters A to J. Division B and Division E are separated yet further into "Subdivisions", identified by lower case letters. The basic provisions are contained in Divisions A to E. Division A (headed "Liability for Tax") consists of a single section (section 2).

Division B (headed "Computation of Income") prescribes the rules for the measurement of a taxpayer's "income", which is commonly described as net income because it is net of deductions (other than the Division C deductions). Division B starts with section 3, which defines the income of a taxpayer for a taxation year as including, among other things, the taxpayer's "income for the year from each office, employment, business and property" (paragraph 3(a)). Division B then goes on to supply detailed rules for the computation of income from these sources: subdivision a provides the rules for income from "an office or employment"; subdivision b provides the rules for income from a business or property; subdivision c provides the rules for capital gains; and subdivisions d and e provide for a miscellaneous group of "other sources of income" and other deductions. There are several further subdivisions, each of which will be addressed in due course.

Division C sets forth rules for the determination of "taxable income". Taxable income is calculated by taking a taxpayer's income under Division B and subtracting the deductions and adding the additions allowed by Division C. Division C deductions include those for social assistance receipts, certain employee stock option benefits, part of the benefit arising from home relocation loans, charitable donations made by a corporation, exempt capital gains on qualified farm properties and shares of qualified small business corporations, losses incurred in other years, inter-corporate dividends, and income of part-time residents. Most individuals have no Division C deductions, which means that their "income" is the same as their "taxable income".

Division D prescribes the rules for the determination of taxable income earned in Canada by non-residents. Division E prescribes the rules for the computation of tax, including tax rates and credits.

Tax practitioners commonly refer to some specific areas of the Act by their Part, Division, or subdivisions. Some of the more common designations include "Division C" (deductions in computing taxable income), "subdivision e" (statutory deductions in computing income), "Part I" tax (basic income tax), and "Part XIII" tax (withholding taxes imposed on investment income earned in Canada by non-residents).

The Act contains over 260 sections. Sections are often further broken down into subsections, paragraphs, subparagraphs, clauses, and subclauses. A unique numbering system is used to refer to each layer of the hierarchy. This is illustrated by subclause 44(1)(e)(i)(A)(I) which is in subdivision c, Division B of Part I:

Part	I	(Roman numerals)
Division	B	(capital letters)
Subdivision	c	(lower case letters)
Section	44	(Arabic numerals)
Subsection	(1)	(Arabic numbers in brackets)
Paragraph	(e)	(lower case letters in brackets)
Subparagraph	(i)	(small Roman numerals in brackets)
Clause	(A)	(capital letters in brackets)
Subclause	(I)	(Roman numbers in brackets)

In referring to a provision of the Act, the key is usually the section number. For example, the above mentioned provision could be cited as section 44(1)(e)(i)(A)(I). Alternatively, it could be cited as subclause 44(1)(e)(i)(A)(I). Where a section is cited, it is unnecessary to include Parts, Divisions, and subdivisions, since the section numbers run consecutively and do not begin again with each new subdivision, Division, or Part.

(iii) — Legislative process

The Department of Finance is responsible for tax policy, which includes formulating amendments to the Act. Amendments are introduced into Parliament by the Minister of Finance. These amendments are not necessarily announced in the Minister's annual budget. Recent practice has been for the Minister to introduce a separate technical bill at least once a year dealing with technical deficiencies in the Act and areas of perceived abuse. Press releases sometimes announce changes to the Act when a single area is being targeted and there is a need for immediate action. Sometimes these technical changes are significant changes of policy, but, for the most part, they deal with particular fact situations and small numbers of taxpayers. It is usually the budget that is the source of major policy initiatives and substantive changes to the Act.

The Minister of Finance presents a budget to Parliament each year, usually in February. The budget provides an estimate of the government's revenues and expenditures for the next financial year, which starts on April 1. Because of the significance of income taxes for the revenue side, the budget usually proposes a set of changes to the Act. These proposals, along with the rest of the budget, are held in strict secrecy until the date of the Minister's presentation of the budget to Parliament. The reason for secrecy is to prevent taxpayers from anticipating the changes and taking avoidance measures or otherwise profiting from the proposals. When the budget is presented, the changes in the Act are normally proposed to be effective from the date of the budget, so that taxpayers have no incentive to take avoidance measures during the hiatus between the date of the budget and the date of the enactment of implementing legislation. Then, when the legislation is enacted, most of the changes are made retroactive to the date of the budget.

The Department of Finance is also responsible for starting the legislative process in amending the Act. The Act is amended frequently. A "notice of ways and means motion to amend the *Income Tax Act*" is prepared by the Department of Finance. This document lists and describes all of the amendments to the Act that have been proposed. The notice of ways and means motion is followed by legislation in draft form. Since 1983, the Department of Finance has followed the practice of issuing "explanatory notes" or "technical notes" to accompany the draft legislation. This material is helpful in explaining the purpose of amendments, which are often exceedingly difficult (even for tax professionals) to understand on their own. The purpose of issuing the legislation initially in draft form is to provide an opportunity for the tax community to comment on the legislation. In fact, commentary is received and sometimes does lead to changes in the legislation.

Eventually, a bill amending the Act is introduced into the House of Commons by the Minister of Finance. That bill then follows the normal legislative process, which includes scrutiny by standing committees of both the House of Commons and the Senate, and in due course the bill is enacted into law. The amending Act will usually make many of its provisions retroactive to the date when the changes were first publicly announced (in the budget or elsewhere).

Although it is generally accepted that it is unfair to apply a new law to transactions that were complete by the time of the law's announcement, the government has made a few amendments retroactively as a legislative response to a court decision that it did not agree with.[13] For example, a series of amendments to the general anti-avoidance rule (GAAR) in section 245 were announced in 2004 and enacted in 2005 but were effective retroactively to September 12, 1988, which was the effective date of GAAR.[14] Since the time elapsed from the date of the budget or other announcement to the date of enactment is sometimes more than a year, the tax proposals of one budget may not be implemented by the time of the next budget (usually 12 months later). When amendments that are proposed to be retroactive to

[13]For example, s. 10(1.01) was announced on December 20, 1995 as the legislative response to *Friesen v. R.*, (sub nom. *Friesen v. Canada)* [1995] 2 C.T.C. 369, 95 D.T.C. 5551 (S.C.C.).

[14]They were a legislative response to *Rousseau-Houle c. R.* (2001), (sub nom. *Rousseau-Houle v. R.)* 2001 D.T.C. 250 (Fr.), 2006 D.T.C. 3181 (Eng.) (T.C.C. [General Procedure]) and *Fredette c. R.*, [2001] 3 C.T.C. 2468, 2001 D.T.C. 621 (Eng.), (sub nom. *Fredette v. R.)* 2001 D.T.C. 263 (Fr.) (T.C.C. [General Procedure]).

the date of the budget have not been enacted by the time that the income tax return forms have to be printed, the proposed changes are simply incorporated into the forms on the (normally safe) assumption that the changes will eventually be enacted[15] and will be retroactive. The taxpayer is, of course, not legally bound to comply with amendments that have not been enacted by the time that a return is filed, but compliance is the course of prudence that is followed by nearly all taxpayers. The Department also prepares Income Tax Regulations (the "Regulations"). The Regulations are made by the cabinet (the Governor in Council), under the authority conferred by section 221 of the Act.

While the Act is the primary source of tax law there are other sources[16] of tax law as well. These sources help establish the meaning of provisions of the Act or the implementation of the Act. The Canada Revenue Agency (CRA)[17] also publishes administrative interpretation and commentary on the law, which is not a source of law but very useful to taxpayers.

(b) — Income tax application rules

The *Income Tax Application Rules, 1971*[18] (ITARs), were enacted in 1971, along with the present Act. They consist of transitional rules, which were needed to shift from the old Act to the new one. As time passes, the ITARs steadily lose their significance, but some of the rules are still relevant. For example, the ITARs have to be used in order to calculate a capital gain on the disposition of property that was acquired before 1972 (which was the year when capital gains first became taxable).

(c) — Income tax regulations

The Regulations are introduced under authority conferred by section 221 of the Act. Section 221 provides, among other things, that the Governor in Council may make regulations "prescribing anything that, by this Act, is to be prescribed or is to be determined or regulated by regulation". The Act makes frequent reference to "prescribed forms", "prescribed amounts", and so on. The word "prescribed" is the signal to look for in a regulation.

The Regulations contain much of the detail of income tax law. As regulations, they are made by Cabinet (the Governor in Council). Since they do not have to be enacted by Parliament, they can be changed much more easily than the Act. However, they have the same force of law as the Act itself.

---

[15] This assumption does not necessarily hold in the case of a minority government.

[16] Several publishers have searchable electronic databases which include the various sources of law as well as commentary by the CRA and others. These databases are updated daily.

[17] The CRA is discussed in more detail under heading 1.6(e)(i), The CRA, below.

[18] R.S.C. 1985 (5th Supp.), c. 2.

(d) — Tax treaties

Tax treaties are agreements entered into by Canada with other countries to coordinate the tax treatment of cross-border transactions. Canada has entered into tax treaties with more than 80 countries; tax haven countries account for most of the major exceptions. The most important tax treaty is the Canada-United States Tax Convention which was signed in 1980, came into effect in 1984 and has been amended by several protocols.

Under Canadian constitutional law, a treaty does not have the force of law unless and until it is implemented by legislation. After each treaty has been ratified by both countries, the Canadian Parliament implements the treaty by enacting a short statute which provides that the treaty has the force of law in Canada; the full text of the treaty is appended to the statute as a schedule.[19]

The purpose of each tax treaty is to avoid double taxation and to prevent fiscal evasion. Treaties are "relieving" in nature as they reduce taxes imposed under domestic law. Each treaty makes some changes to the Act in its application to taxpayers covered by the treaty. In the event of any domestic inconsistency between the treaty and law (other than the *Income Tax Conventions Interpretation Act*) the terms of the treaty are to prevail. The *Income Tax Conventions Interpretation Act* is a domestic statute that governs the interpretation of Canadian tax treaties.

(e) — Case law

Case law is an important source of tax law. Income tax liability is created solely by statute and many of the provisions of the Act have never been the subject of any judicial decision. However, there are topics upon which the Act is silent, incomplete, or unclear and which have given rise to many judicial decisions. The most frequently litigated issues include: (1) whether a person is a resident of Canada; (2) whether income is from employment or from a business; (3) whether a profit on the sale of property is a capital gain or income from a business; (4) whether certain types of expenses are deductible from income; (5) whether losses from unprofitable ventures are fully deductible from other income; (6) whether generally accepted accounting principles apply to the computation of income from a business; (7) whether an interest expense is currently deductible; and (8) whether any anti-avoidance rules are applicable.

(f) — Provincial income tax statutes

Each province also has an income tax act, and provincial income taxes are a significant impost, typically adding about 50 per cent to an individual's tax bill, depending on the province. The federal government has entered into tax collection agreements with most provinces. Under these agreements, the federal government collects the provincial tax, and, in return, each province agrees to accept most of the rules of the federal Act for the measurement of income (or the "tax base") and

---

[19]E.g., *Canada-United States Tax Convention Act, 1984*, S.C. 1984, c. 20.

sets its own provincial rates of tax and tax credits for its residents. Therefore, provincial income tax acts are generally quite short and simple (and uninformative). A province that has not entered into a tax collection agreement needs to provide for the collection of the provincial tax by the provincial government. With respect to the personal income tax, all provinces except for Quebec have entered into tax collection agreements. At the time of writing (March 2010), all provinces except for Quebec and Alberta have entered into corporate tax collection agreements.

(g) — Private law

The Act relies implicitly on the general law, especially the law of contract and property. For example, the person who is liable to pay tax on income is normally the person who has the legal right to receive the income; the existence and nature of that right will depend upon the law of the province in which the income is payable. Whether a person is an employee, independent contractor, partner, agent, beneficiary of a trust or shareholder of a corporation will usually have an effect on tax liability and will turn on concepts contained in general law. A tax problem often contains issues of federal income tax law combined with issues of general law.

(h) — Administrative publications

The CRA issues the forms and various publications, including information circulars,[20] interpretation bulletins, technical news and advance tax rulings, which cumulatively constitute an extensive and valuable commentary on the law.[21] Aside from some of the forms, which are prescribed by regulation, these publications do not have the force of law, but they are exceptionally valuable secondary sources of the law.

(i) — Information circulars

Information Circulars (ICs) are designed to provide information on administrative and procedural matters. They cover the CRA's organization and procedures and other useful information.[22] The first information circular, issued in 1970, announced the program of issuing information circulars and interpretation bulletins.[23]

---

[20]Some information circulars and interpretation bulletins have been revised and any revision is indicated by "R" after the original number of the circular or bulletin.

[21]These publications are available on the CRA website at http://www.cra-arc.gc.ca/formspubs/menu-e.html.

[22]Notable exceptions are Information Circular 88-2, "General Anti-Avoidance Rule" (1988), which explains the CRA's policy with respect to the general anti-avoidance rule (GAAR) (s. 245), and Information Circular 01-1, "Third-Party Civil Penalties" (2001), which explains the CRA's policy with respect to third-party civil penalty rules (s. 163.2). Both these information circulars are detailed commentaries on the law that are primarily addressed to tax specialists.

[23]Information Circular 70-1, "Information Circulars and Interpretation Bulletins" (1970).

Since 1970, several hundred circulars and bulletins have been issued, constituting an exceedingly valuable account of much taxation law and practice.

(ii) — Interpretation bulletins

Interpretation Bulletins (ITs) explain the CRA's interpretations of many of the provisions of the Act. Needless to say, the CRA's policy is to assess taxpayers in accordance with the legal opinions expressed in its publications. When the CRA wants to announce its opinion on a new provision of the Act or a recent judicial decision or wants to announce a change in its interpretation of an existing provision, it often does so at public conferences (such as the Canadian Tax Foundation's annual conference), by press release and/or in the CRA's Income Tax Technical News, which is published on an ad hoc basis.[24] Eventually this change will result in a new or revised interpretation bulletin and several interpretation bulletins have been revised a number of times.

In practice, the taxpayer is usually safe in relying upon an opinion contained in a CRA publication as being an accurate and up-to-date account of the CRA's view of the law. However, CRA publications are not like regulations, which are authorized by the Act and accordingly have the force of law. The Act is silent about them and it is clear that they do not have the force of law. In the past, the courts have looked at interpretation bulletins as a persuasive aid to interpretation,[25] but the courts are not bound by the CRA's opinions, and do not always follow them.[26]

Even the CRA itself is not bound to follow its own publications, although it nearly always does so. It is well established that the doctrine of estoppel does not preclude the CRA from issuing an assessment that is inconsistent with a previously published statement, or with a previous assessment, even when the taxpayer has relied upon the CRA's opinions as to the legal position.[27] In the rare case where the CRA departs from its own interpretation bulletin in assessing a return, the court will uphold the assessment if it concludes that the assessment is correct in law, notwithstanding the inconsistency.[28] In *Stickel v. M.N.R.* (1973),[29] the Minister had assessed the taxpayer on a basis that contradicted the applicable interpretation bulletin, upon which the taxpayer had relied. The Federal Court — Trial Division

---

[24]Interpretations published in Income Tax Technical News carry the same weight as those in the Interpretation Bulletins: Information Circular 70-6R5, "Advance Income Tax Ruling" (2002), para. 27.

[25]E.g., *Nowegijick v. R.*, [1983] C.T.C. 20 at 24, 83 D.T.C. 5041 5044 (S.C.C.).

[26]E.g., *Southside Car Market v. R.*, [1982] C.T.C. 214, 82 D.T.C. 6179 (Fed. T.D.).

[27]*Liberty & Co. v. C.I.R.* (1924), 12 T.C. 630 639; *Woon v. M.N.R.*, [1950] C.T.C. 263, 50 D.T.C. 871 (Ex. Ct.); *M.N.R. v. Inland Industries* (1971), [1972] C.T.C. 27, 72 D.T.C. 6013 (S.C.C.); and *Gibbon v. R.*, [1977] C.T.C. 334, 77 D.T.C. 5193 (Fed. T.D.).

[28]E.g., *74712 Alberta v. R.*, [1994] 2 C.T.C. 191, 94 D.T.C. 6392 (Fed. T.D.).

[29][1973] C.T.C. 202, 73 D.T.C. 5178 (Fed. C.A.); affirmed [1974] C.T.C. 416, 74 D.T.C. 6268 (S.C.C.).

rejected the taxpayer's argument that the Crown was estopped, and upheld the assessment.[30] On appeal, the Federal Court of Appeal reversed, not on the ground of estoppel, but on the ground that the interpretation bulletin, not the assessment, was the correct interpretation of the law.

(iii) — Advance rulings

An advance income tax ruling is issued at the request of a taxpayer, who pays a fee for the service. The purpose of a ruling is to explain to the taxpayer how the CRA will assess a transaction that is contemplated by the taxpayer.[31] In this way, the taxpayer obtains a secure opinion as to the precise tax consequences of a proposed transaction. If the tax consequences are sufficiently unfavourable, the transaction might be abandoned, although sometimes a restructuring is possible to avoid some of the bad consequences. In any event, it is always helpful to be aware of the tax consequences before a transaction is consummated.

The formal procedure of issuing advance income tax rulings was started in 1970, although informal rulings were sometimes given before then. At the inception of the formal advance income tax ruling program in 1970, it was announced that an advance income tax ruling "will be regarded as binding on the Department [now CRA]."[32] The current consensus is that an advance ruling is generally binding as to the application of a particular section of the Act other than whether the expense is reasonable under section 67. However, in the unlikely event that the CRA did decide to assess a taxpayer in violation of a ruling, the *Woon v. M.N.R.* (1950)[33] case probably states the legal position: the CRA would not be estopped by its ruling. In this case, the taxpayer had obtained an informal ruling as to the tax consequences of a dividend-stripping scheme. In reliance on the ruling, the taxpayer carried out the scheme, but the Minister assessed him for a tax liability far in excess of that stipulated in the ruling. The Court held that the assessment was correct in law, and that the Minister could not be estopped by the earlier ruling from applying the law correctly.

The CRA releases all of the advance income tax rulings in "severed form", that is, with names and other details omitted to preserve the anonymity of the taxpayer.[34] Taxpayers have to exercise caution in relying on published rulings, even if the facts of a particular ruling appear to be identical to a taxpayer's situation. It must be

---

[30][1972] C.T.C. 210, 72 D.T.C. 6178 (Fed. T.D.).

[31]The details of the CRA's policy respecting advance rulings, including the procedure for obtaining rulings, are set out in Information Circular 70-6R5, note 24, above.

[32]See Information Circular 70-6R5, *ibid.*, para. 6. Some special situations are contemplated by Information Circular 70-6R3, *ibid.*, paras. 10-14, such as misrepresentation of the applicable facts or amendment of the applicable law.

[33][1950] C.T.C. 263, 50 D.T.C. 871 (Ex. Ct.).

[34]The policy with respect to publication is described in Information Circular 70-6R5. Note 24, above, paras. 16(m), 21, 24-25 and Appendix A.

remembered that material facts may have been severed from the published version. Also, the CRA's view of the law may have changed since the ruling was given.

1.4 — Interpreting the Act

(a) — Statutory interpretation

As mentioned above, income tax law is entirely statutory in origin and the Act is the primary tax statute. Case law is important to the understanding of the meaning of provisions of the Act, but it does not create any tax liability. Moreover, some decisions have been immediately overruled by statutory amendments.[35] As detailed as the provisions of the Act are, the meaning of these provisions is often unclear or open to different interpretations. Thus learning to interpret the Act is crucial to understanding tax law.

The skill of statutory interpretation is crucial not only to lawyers practicing tax law, but also lawyers in general. Statutory interpretation skills are important to the practice of law, as most lawyers spend much more time working with legislative materials and judicial treatment of those materials than working with common law jurisprudence. Since the Act is one of the most complex statutes in the land, tax law is perfect for learning the skill of statutory interpretation.

The general principle of statutory interpretation is that "the words of an Act are to be read in their entire context and in their grammatical and ordinary sense harmoniously with the scheme of the Act, the object of the Act, and the intention of Parliament".[36] As discussed in more detail in Chapter 19 of this book, the Supreme Court of Canada refers to this as the "textual, contextual and purposive" approach.

(b) — Statutory language

The language of the Act is often difficult to comprehend fully. Contrary to many people's suspicions, the Act is not written deliberately to confuse. Unfortunately, though, it often has that effect. There are several factors that contribute to the difficulty in understanding the Act:

1. The sheer size of the Act. This fact alone makes its interpretation a daunting task. There are also many cross-references and related provisions that add further complexity.

2. The lack of statutory definitions. Although the Act contains some definitions, the meaning of the majority of words is undefined and their meaning has to be found in non-tax law and/or in judicial decisions.

---

[35] See, for example, *Friesen v. R.*, note 13, above; *Shell Canada Ltd. v. R.* (1999), (sub nom. *Shell Canada Ltd. v. Canada)* [1999] 3 S.C.R. 622, 99 D.T.C. 5669 (Eng.), 99 D.T.C. 5682 (Fr.), [1999] 4 C.T.C. 313 (S.C.C.); and *Royal Bank v. Sparrow Electric Corp.*, [1997] 1 S.C.R. 411, (sub nom. *R. v. Royal Bank)* 97 D.T.C. 5089 (S.C.C.).

[36] Driedger's *Construction of Statutes* (2nd ed.), at 87, cited in *Stubart Investments Ltd v. R.*, [1984] 1 S.C.R. 536 578, [1984] C.T.C. 294 316, 84 D.T.C. 6305 6323 (S.C.C.).

3. Taxes are imposed on a commercial and social reality that is often complex. The legal, commercial, accounting, and social circumstances in which income is earned must be examined in order to understand the tax implications.

4. The doctrine of supremacy of legislature. The overriding attitude of the judiciary is that the Act comes first. Even when a provision of the Act is unworkable or undesirable from a policy perspective, the court will not rewrite the law. The Supreme Court of Canada has stated in several cases that it is the Supreme Court, not the supreme legislature.[37]

5. Elusive legislative intent. Where legislative intent is relevant to the interpretation of a provision, such intent is often difficult to be discerned by simply reading the statute.

6. The use of precise language. The Act is intended to apply to more than 20 million taxpayers, many of whom are willing to exploit any linguistic imprecision to their benefit — to find a "loophole" in popular parlance. The drafters of the Act attempt to use precise language in order to minimize loopholes. Many of the provisions in the Act are limitations or restrictions involving two or more variables. Expressing such concepts algebraically would be more direct; using words to accomplish this task instead is often quite cumbersome.

7. Drafting conventions. Each provision (expressed in a subsection or section) is one sentence long. This convention causes difficulty in statutory interpretation. For example, the one sentence in subsection 95(2) (which deems income from the specified activities as either falling within the foreign accrual property income regime or falling outside it) has over 6000 words, and comprises more than seven pages.

(c) — Interpretation tips

The best way of learning how to interpret the Act is of course to read the Act. Reading the Act is not easy, and often intimidating. It is thus tempting to turn to secondary sources for help. Although sometimes useful, this is not a sufficient substitute for understanding the Act, given the number and breadth of amendments and revisions to the Act each year. Some interpretation tips might be helpful. These include:

1. *Keep in mind the following presumptions*: every word has a meaning; the same words have the same meaning(s); and different words have different meanings.

2. *Be familiar with the context.* When reading a provision of the Act, one should always observe where it is located in the structure of the Act. There is a basic logic to the structure of the Act, and a familiarity with this structure greatly assists in understanding individual provisions. Also, when reading a provision, always start from the beginning of the subsection or section where the complete sentence begins. One should also note the various levels of

[37]See *Friesen*, note 13, above.

paragraphing within each provision, their relationship to one another, and the functions they serve. Read the provision completely; do not jump to conclusions.

3. *Be familiar with defined terms.* When reading the Act, it is important to watch for defined terms. They are found in subsection 248(1) and many other places of the Act. A defined meaning trumps an ordinary meaning. Some terms are defined for the purpose of the Act. Other terms are defined for the purpose of a particular segment of the Act. The scope of a definition is limited by the words introducing it. Therefore, definitional provisions should be read very carefully. In addition, it is important to be alert for hidden definitions; terms in a particular section may be defined in the same section, or in a separate section or part of the Act.

4. *Learn the word patterns.* There are some commonly used words and phrases in the Act. Examples include "the total of [A] and [B]" (indicating addition), "the amount by which [A] exceeds [B]" (indicating subtraction), "that proportion of . . . that is [A] is of [B]" (expressing a fraction A/B), "the lesser of [A] and [B]" (indicating a maximum limit), "the greater of [A] and [B]" (indicating a minimum). These word patterns are used to give structure to the provision.[38]

5. *Do not overlook small words such as "and" and "or".* There is a world of difference between these two words. The word "and" is used as a conjunctive. Where "and" is used in respect of tests that must be satisfied, all of the tests must be satisfied before the resulting rules apply. In contrast, the word "or" is used as a disjunctive. If any one of the conditions set out is met, the resulting rules will apply. However, in certain contexts, the word "or" can also be a conjunctive. An example is the use of "or" between paragraphs 6(6)(a) and (b). The resulting rules (tax-free treatment of payment in respect of employment at special work site or remote locations) apply if the condition in one or both (a) and (b) are met.

6. *Skip over non-essential words.* Words in each provision of the Act generally fall into one of two categories: essential, operative words that give rise to the rule; and non-essential words that are simply verbiage used to make the legislation consistent and airtight. Being able to skip over the non-essential words makes it easier to understand the provision. The best way of doing this is to scan the whole provision first and then highlight the essential words.

7. *Find the basic rule.* The provisions of the Act often have limitations and exceptions, but every provision has a basic rule. It is thus important to extract the basic rule from the provision and know what limitations and exceptions should be taken into account in a particular factual context. One should guard against permitting the language of the provision to carry greater or lesser weight than was intended.

---

[38]For further detail, see Sherman, *Canadian Tax Research: A Practical Guide* (3rd ed., 1997), at 149–52.

1.5 — Structure of the income tax

The Act is structured to deal with five basic questions: (1) Who is subject to tax (liability for tax); (2) What is subject to tax (tax base); (3) When is tax payable (timing and accounting period); (4) How much tax is payable (rates and credits); and (5) How are taxes collected (tax administration)? Tax policy decisions affect the answer to each of these questions and are discussed in more detail in chapter 2.

(a) — Liability for tax

(i) — "Person"

Subsection 2(1) provides: "An income tax shall be paid, as required by this Act, on the taxable income for each taxation year of every person resident in Canada at any time in the year". A taxpayer under the Act is thus a "person", not a family or a marital unit. Subsection 248(1) defines a "person" to include a corporation and "executors, administrators or other legal representative of such a person" and defines a "taxpayer" to include "any person whether or not liable to pay tax". Because an "individual" is defined in s. 248(1) to mean "a person other than a corporation" and a trust is taxed as an individual under s. 104(2), an individual for income tax purposes includes a trust as well as a human being. In other words, human beings, trusts and corporations are all persons, and thus taxpayers under the Act. A partnership, on the other hand, is a legal entity that is not a "person" or "taxpayer" under the Act.

(ii) — Tax unit

Taxing individuals as a taxation unit has equity implications.[39] One large income bears a heavier tax load than it would if split into two or more smaller incomes. For example, in 2010 in Ontario, an individual earning $100,000 would pay (combined federal and provincial) tax of $28,405 (assuming the taxpayer claims only the basic personal credit). An individual earning $50,000 would pay tax of $9,777.[40] Thus, two incomes of $50,000 would attract a tax liability of $19,544, which is $8,851 less than the tax liability of a single income of $100,000. There are two reasons for this result. First, under the graduated rate structure in the Act (and its provincial counterpart), a substantial part of the income of $100,000 is taxed at higher rates than those applicable to the incomes of $50,000. As well, each taxpayer is entitled to a basic personal credit. The two incomes of $50,000 enjoy the benefit of two basic personal credits, while the one income of $100,000 will benefit from only one such credit.

---

[39] S. 117(2). See heading 14.6, "Tax rates", below.

[40] These amounts include the Ontario personal health premium which is based on a taxpayer's taxable income: $750 for a taxpayer with a taxable income of $100,000 and $600 for a taxpayer with a taxable income of $50,000. Federal and Ontario income tax rates are set out in a chart under heading 14.6, *ibid.*

The discrepancy in tax liability between one large income and two smaller incomes is the inevitable result of a progressive tax system. Whether an individual should be the taxation unit is an important policy question. The policy implications, and the pros and cons of the current system are discussed in chapter 13 below.

(iii) — Residence

The notion of "residence" is crucial to the determination of a person's tax liability under the Act. Whether a person is a Canadian resident determines whether the person is taxable in Canada on income earned from outside Canada. Only Canadian residents are liable to tax on their "worldwide" income and non-residents are taxable only on their "Canadian source" income. Furthermore, the residence status of an individual determines whether income from investment (such as dividends, interest and rents) is taxable at progressive rates (in the case of residents) or flat rate (in the case of non-residents).

(b) — Tax base

(i) — Concept of income

A "tax base" is the base upon which a tax is levied. Technically, the tax base under the Act is "taxable income" (subsections 2(1) and (2)). Taxable income, in turn, is based on "income" as computed under section 3 (sometimes called Division B "net income") because a taxpayer's "taxable income" is the taxpayer's "income" minus the deductions permitted by Division C of Part I of the Act.

"Income" is not a defined term, and the question of what items constitute income for tax purposes and thereby form part of the tax base is one of the major problems of income tax policy. As discussed in Chapter 4, not all economic gains or receipts are income. Inheritances, personal gifts, and gambling winnings are not taxed as income, whereas wages, business profits, and income from investments (such as dividends, interest and rents) are taxable.

(ii) — Measurement of income

The measurement of income consumes most of Part I of the Act. Division B contains these specific rules. In general, in the absence of statutory overrides, accounting principles are relevant in determining when an item is included or deducted in computing "income" from a business or property which is the main type of income earned by corporations and partnerships.

Tax accounting is thus important because, ultimately, taxpayers need to determine a specific number for their tax liability. Complex tax rules and policies must be reduced to a number. Many law students may regard tax accounting problems as merely mechanical exercises necessary to calculate profit. Accounting problems, however, frequently present some of the most difficult theoretical and policy issues in income taxation. Two taxpayers who have the same economic income and who engage in the same transactions may have different taxable income and tax liabilities, depending *only* on how they account the income.

(iii) — Assignment of income

Whose income is it? This is an important question because the Act imposes tax on each individual at progressive rates. Taxpayers can achieve significant tax savings through shifting income from high-tax family members to low-tax individuals by way of intra-family gifts or using an entity, such as a corporation.

In general, the question "whose income is it?" is easily answered: (a) income from personal services (e.g. wages, salaries, service fees) is earned by the person who renders the services; (b) income from property (e.g., dividend, interest, rent, and royalties) is earned by the owner of the property; (c) income from the sale of property is earned by the owner of the property; and (d) income from a business is earned by the owner of the business. When income is assigned or redirected to another person, the Act contains a number of anti-avoidance rules that may apply. These rules are further discussed in chapter 13, below.

(c) — Timing and accounting period

(i) — "Taxation year"

Income tax is calculated and paid annually, on the basis of a taxpayer's income for a "taxation year". Subsection 249(1) defines "taxation year" as "(a) in the case of a corporation, a fiscal period, and (b) in the case of an individual, a calendar year". This definition introduces the concept of a "fiscal period", which is the taxation year of a corporation.[41] A fiscal period can be any twelve-month period, thus, it may not be the calendar year. The taxation year of an individual is a "calendar year". Unlike a corporation, an individual has no choice as to the period for which income is to be reported for tax purposes: the period from January 1 to December 31 is the taxation year.[42]

---

[41]The meaning of taxation year for corporations, partnerships and trusts is discussed in chapters 15 to 17, below.

[42]Subject to ss. 34.1 and 34.2, which were introduced to apply to 1995 and subsequent years, an individual is allowed to select a fiscal period other than the calendar year for the calculation of business income (but not other types of income). However, in each calendar year the taxpayer would report the business income for the fiscal period ending and adjust the business income to a calendar-year basis using the formulas set out in subsections 34.1(1) and 34.1(3). The intent is to permit individuals who operate businesses to adopt an off-calendar year-end, where that makes business sense, but not to allow the off-calendar year-end to be used as a tax-postponement measure. The off-calendar year option is available because the government was convinced that off-calendar years should be allowed for business reasons. However, because there is no tax-postponement, very few individuals choose this option, perhaps (in part) because of its complexity. Before 1995 when section 34.1 was enacted, it was possible for individuals to postpone recognition of business income, with a consequent postponement of tax liability. For example, an individual who selected January 31 as the year-end for his or her business would report only the business income earned to January 31, 1993 in his or her income tax return for 1993; the business income earned from February 1, 1993 to December 31, 1993 did not have to be reported until calendar year 1994.

(ii) — Income fluctuation

When a taxpayer's income fluctuates from year to year, the progressive rate structure exacts a heavier total tax than it does from the same total amount of income earned in a multi-year period in fairly even annual amounts. For example, taxpayer A, who earns $20,000 in year one and $70,000 in year two, will find that his or her tax bill for the two years is more than $1,000 higher than taxpayer B, who earns $45,000 in year one and $45,000 in year two. Yet both taxpayers have earned the same amount of income, namely, $90,000, in the two-year period. The discrepancy in tax treatment arises from the measurement of income in annual periods. If income were measured in two-year periods, then the amount of tax payable by each taxpayer would be the same.

There are two possible measures of relief available to taxpayers with fluctuating income. One measure is averaging which (generally speaking) takes the change in income and allocates it over a period of years. Averaging was allowed under the Act until 1988. The rationale for abolishing averaging was that the broader tax brackets and lower rates of tax that were introduced in the tax reform of 1988 would diminish the adverse impact of fluctuating income, and the Act would be simpler without such complexities.

Another measure of relief is loss carryovers. Since 1988, this has been the only relief available. Loss carryover rules in the Act form an exception to the annual measurement of income because they enable a taxpayer who has incurred a loss in one year to carry the loss over to another year and deduct it against the income for that year. The policy reason for loss carryovers is much the same as the policy reason for averaging. There is no magic to the requirement that income be measured in watertight annual compartments, and there is force in the argument that only net income over a reasonable period of years should be taxed.[43]

(d) — Tax payable

(i) — Rates

Once a taxpayer's annual taxable income is computed, the next issue is the application of the applicable rates to this amount in order to calculate the taxpayer's tax payable. Sections 117 and 123 set out the rates applicable to individuals and corporations, respectively. The rates of personal income tax are progressive (15 to 29 per cent), whereas the rate of corporate income tax is flat (18% for 2010).[44]

Taxable bracket	Tax rate
$40,970 or less	15%
$40,971 to $81,941	22%
$81,942 to $127,021	26%

[43]For a discussion of loss deductions and carryovers, see headings 14.3 to 14.5, below.

[44]For a discussion of tax rates, see headings 14.6, "Tax rates", and 15.5(b), "Tax rates" (for corporations), below.

Taxable bracket	**Tax rate**
$127,022 or more	29%

The rates of tax imposed by the Act are rates of federal income tax, but taxpayers must pay provincial income tax as well. Provinces set their own rates, but most use a tax base very similar to that determined under the federal Act.

(ii) — Credits

A tax credit is a deduction in computing tax payable. Tax credits are used to provide incentives on grounds of social and economic policy. Personal tax credits are provided in sections 118 to 118.95 of the Act. The three most significant credits are the basic personal credit, the spouse or common-law partner credit and the equivalent to spouse (or eligible dependent) credit. Other personal credits include credits for other dependants, for tuition and education expenses, medical expenses and charitable donations. The Act also provides credits for corporations.[45] Tax policy debate on the use of tax credits and a more detailed description of the major credits are found in chapter 14, below.

(iii) — Computation of tax liability

The computation of federal tax liability involves four basic steps. (1) Compute income from each source, namely, income from an office or employment, income from business, income from property, income from other sources, and taxable capital gains (net of any allowable capital losses). Costs and expenses incurred in earning income are deductible. (2) Compute net income under section 3. At this stage, income from each of the sources is added together. From the aggregated amount, the following deductions are allowed: subdivision e amounts, current year losses from an office and employment, business or property, as well as investment business losses. (3) Compute taxable income under subsection 2(2) by deducting additional amounts specified in Division C from section 3 net income. (4) Finally, compute tax payable by multiplying applicable rates to taxable income and subtracting tax credits.

The following chart summarizes the computation of net income, taxable income, and tax for individuals:

[45]For a further discussion, see chapter 15, Corporations and Shareholders, below.

Exhibit 1-2

OVERVIEW OF COMPUTATION OF NET INCOME, TAXABLE INCOME AND TAX FOR INDIVIDUALS

Subdivision a: Income from an office or employment
+ Subdivision b: Income from a business or property
+ Subdivision c: Net taxable capital gains
+ Subdivision d: Other sources of income
- Subdivision e: Other deductions

Division B Net Income
- Division C Deductions

Taxable Income
× Tax Rates (4)

Tax
- Tax Credits

Basic Federal Tax
- Other federal tax credits

Part I Federal Tax
+ Provincial Income Tax

Total Income Tax

For example, consider Margo Barreto, a single taxpayer, who earned the following amounts in 2010: $50,000 of income from employment, $500 of interest income (income from property) and $500 in net taxable capital gains from a mutual fund investment. She also has $11,000 in other deductions ($8,000 for child care expenses for two children, ages 8 and 10, and her $3,000 for an RRSP contribution) and a $200 net capital loss carryforward (from a bad investment she sold in 2007).

Based on these facts, Margo's tax liability is computed as follows:

- Net income under Division B is $39,000 ($50,000 + $500 + $500 minus $11,000).

- Taxable income under Division C is $38,800 ($39,000 minus $200 of the net capital loss carryforward).

- Federal tax payable is $5,820: $38,800 × 15% (because her taxable income is $40,970 or less).

- Assuming she is eligible for $3,000 of federal tax credits, her net federal tax is $2,820 ($5,820 minus $3,000).

- Assuming Margo is a resident of Ontario and is eligible for $1,500 in Ontario tax credits, her net provincial income tax is $529, which is $2,029 (5.05% of first $37,106 plus 9.16% of the next $1,694) minus $1,500.

- Total income tax is therefore $3,349 (i.e., $2,820 of federal income tax and $529 of Ontario income tax).[46]

(iv) — Alternative minimum tax

The alternative minimum tax (AMT) is "alternative", because taxpayers must calculate both the amount of their AMT and their "ordinary tax", and then pay whichever figure is greater. As many of the tax preferences are available only to wealthy individuals, higher-income taxpayers are sometimes able to avail themselves of sufficient tax preferences to reduce their tax liability to an extremely low figure. Indeed, it became apparent in the mid-1980s that tax preferences enabled a few wealthy individuals to escape the bite of tax altogether. The ensuing public protest caused the enactment in 1986 of the alternative minimum tax (AMT) under section 127.5 of the Act. In light of the purpose of this tax, individuals whose main source of income is employment are not the targets of the AMT.

(e) — Tax administration

(i) — The CRA

The CRA[47] is responsible for the collection of income tax, and issues the forms and guides that are necessary to prepare an income tax return. The agency was established "in an effort to provide better, more cost-effective and responsive tax, customs and trade administration services to the public, the provinces and territories and Canadian business". The federal government oversees the CRA through a management board composed of private sector representatives nominated by the provinces and territories but the Minister of National Revenue is still accountable to Parliament for the delivery of tax, customs and trade programmes.

The administration of the Act involves the collection of tax through the system of tax returns, assessments, source deductions, refunds, audits and enforcement. The Act itself always describes its administrator as "the Minister", which is defined in subsection 248(1) as the Minister of National Revenue, but, in practice, of course, nearly all of the Minister's functions are performed by officials in the CRA.

The CRA also has the authority to enter into new partnerships with the provinces, territories and other government bodies to administer taxes and provide other services. The CRA has its headquarters in Ottawa. The headquarters develops policies for the CRA in all its areas of activity; it issues information circulars, interpretation

---

[46]This calculation ignores the Ontario tax reduction and the Ontario Health Premium.

[47]The CRA is formerly known as "Revenue Canada" and "Canada Customs and Revenue Agency". Before 1999, Revenue Canada (or the Department of National Revenue) administered the Act. In 1999, the functions of Revenue Canada were taken over by the Canada Customs and Revenue Agency (CCRA). In 2003, the Canada Border Service Agency was created and customs administration was moved to this new agency. Without "Customs", the CCRA became the CRA. The CRA is accountable to the Minister of National Revenue. In tax cases, the CRA is represented by the Minister of National Revenue.

bulletins and advance tax rulings; and it deals with some individual files that are in the appeal process. The CRA has several taxation centres, which are controlled by six regional offices. Taxpayers send their returns to the nearest taxation centre. The taxation centres process the returns and issue notices of assessment; when the process is complete, the taxation centres store the files.

(ii) — The self-assessment system

The income tax system is based on voluntary compliance or self-assessment. As discussed in more detail in chapter 18, the Act requires all taxpayers to file an annual tax return reporting their income and expenses accurately, together with a calculation of the amount of tax owing. The primary rationale for self-assessment is cost effectiveness.

The self-assessment system is supported by: (1) an extensive information reporting system under which payers of interest, dividends, income from partnerships or trusts must report to the CRA on the recipient of the income; (2) source withholding of taxes by employers and residents making payments to non-residents; (3) CRA's audit processes and enforcement powers; and (4) penalties for non-compliance. When all of these mechanisms are considered, compliance with the tax law is not exactly voluntary. Tax procedures and penalties are discussed in more detail in chapter 18.

(iii) — Resolution of tax disputes

A tax dispute between a taxpayer and the CRA is resolved through administrative appeals and/or judicial appeals. The process begins with a notice of objection filed by a taxpayer who disagrees with the CRA's assessment. The notice of objection is considered by the Appeals Branch of the CRA, which may confirm, vary or vacate the assessment. If the assessment is confirmed or varied in a manner that is unsatisfactory to the taxpayer, the taxpayer may appeal to the courts.

All income tax appeals are heard in the first instance by the Tax Court of Canada. The judgment of the Tax Court may be appealed to the Federal Court of Appeal,[48] and from there (with leave) to the Supreme Court of Canada. In all appeals, the taxpayer bears the burden to disprove any factual assumptions on which the CRA's assessment was based.

Litigation in the Tax Court, Federal Court, and Supreme Court of Canada on behalf of the Minister of National Revenue is conducted by counsel in the Tax Law section of the Department of Justice, which is located in the head office and each of the regional offices of the Department of Justice. Prosecutions of tax evaders in the provincial courts are conducted by criminal prosecutions counsel in the head or regional offices of the Department of Justice or by private lawyers employed as agents by the Department of Justice.

---

[48] If the case is tried under the informal procedure at the Tax Court, there is no further right of appeal, although the Court's decision is subject to judicial review by the Federal Court of Appeal. The appeal process is discussed in greater detail in chapter 18, below.

Taxpayers are aided by tax practitioners. Tax law has grown to the point where no one can possibly know all of the rules and approaches to various business and personal planning problems. Tax practitioners (lawyers and accountants) thus play an important role in advising clients. Although the judicial attitude towards tax avoidance and the plain meaning approach to statutory interpretation have provided ample room for creative and innovative tax planning, there remains a line between ethical and unethical tax planning. Tax lawyers are subject to ethical standards, which are discussed in more detail in chapter 18 of this book.

1.6 — Income tax terminology and concepts

(a) — Terminology

There are some basic income tax terminology and concepts used in this book. It is important for students to be familiar with them. Some of these terms have already been mentioned in the previous section, such as "tax base", "income", "capital gains" and "capital losses", "taxable income", "person", "corporation", "source of income", "deductions", and "credits." This section reviews some other terms and concepts.

(i) — Realization and recognition

Realization and recognition are important terms of art in income tax law. The Act does not generally recognize a gain or loss until it is "realized". In computing a gain or loss, a revenue receipt is generally recognized when it is "earned", which generally means when the taxpayer has acquired the legal right to be paid, or when it is "received". A cost or expense is generally recognized when it become "payable" or is "paid". These concepts are further discussed in chapters 5 to 8. A discussed in chapter 10, capital gains or losses are recognized when a capital property is "disposed of" (mostly by way of a sale).

(ii) — Cost and expense

Cost of property and expenses are generally recognized in tax law by way of a deduction in computing income or loss. However, whether the cost is immediately deductible in full depends on the purpose of incurring the cost (or the use of the property) and the characterization of the cost as "capital" or "current". As further discussed in chapters 9 and 10, if a car dealer buys a car for sale, the car is "inventory" and its cost is fully deductible when the car is sold. If a taxi driver buys a car for his business, the car is a "capital property" and the cost can only be "depreciated" (deducted) over a period of several years. If a law professor buys a car for commuting between her home and the law school, the cost of the car is not recognized at all (unless in the rare event that the value of the car increases and a gain is realized when she sells the car. In such case, the cost is deductible in computing the gain).

(iii) — Business entities

Business entities are legal devices for carrying business and investment activities. Different types of entities are taxed differently. A corporation is a legal device for organizing economic activities and is treated as a separate taxpaying entity. As discussed in chapter 15, corporations compute the amount of their income, for the most part, according to the same rules as those applicable to the business activities of individuals. Unlike individuals, however, corporations pay income tax at a flat rate. In order to minimize double taxation of income earned through corporations, the Act provides some "integration" of corporate tax and personal income tax payable by shareholders.

A trust is a legal device by which one person, the trustee, holds and invests property for the benefit of another person, the beneficiary. The Act treats a trust as a "flow-through" or "conduit" in certain circumstances and a separate taxpaying entity in other circumstances. Chapter 17 explains the taxation of a trust in more detail.

A partnership is a legal arrangement through which two or more people carry on a business for profit in common (or as co-owners). The Act does not treat a partnership as a separate taxpaying entity. Instead, the income or loss of a partnership must be allocated to its partners (individuals or corporations) for tax purposes. Chapter 16 discusses this "flow-through" treatment in more detail.

A sole proprietor is a person who owns a business solely and directly, that is, without having any partners or other co-owners and using any legal device. Any income or loss of the business is treated for tax purposes as the income or loss of the sole proprietor.

(b) — Characterization

"Character may or may not determine fate"[49] but character determines the tax consequences. As you have seen from the treatment of entities, the tax character of an amount or transaction is very important in tax law. For example, a receipt or gain is taxable only if it has the character of income for the purposes of income tax law. As discussed further in Chapter 4, a windfall, personal gift, punitive damage or strike pay does not have the character of income and is thus tax-free. The Act does not tax all income the same. Subsequent chapters of this book will explain how employment income is taxed differently from business income and investment income and how "regular" income is taxed differently from capital gains. The flip side of "income" or "gain" is "loss" and loss must be characterized as well. While "regular" losses are fully deductible against other income, "capital losses" are partially deductible and only against capital gains.

Costs and expenses must be characterized for tax purposes in determining their recognition in tax law. For example, if an expense has the character of a "current expense", it is fully deductible when it is paid or payable, whereas a "capital ex-

---

[49] "Character is Fate, said Novalis. . ." Hardy, *The Mayor of Casterbridge*, chapter 17.

pense" can only be "amortized" (or deducted) over a period of time. Similarly, a "personal expense" is not deductible in computing income, whereas a "business expense" or "income-earning expense" is.

Drawing the line between the different characters for tax law purposes is sometimes difficult and arbitrary. The Act rarely provides a "bright-line" test, so the issue is left to case law. Canadian case law heavily relies on the legal arrangement by the taxpayer in determining the character. Chapter 19 discusses the statutory interpretation approach that places value on "legal form" over the "substance" of a transaction.

Where a different character of an amount results in different tax consequences, it is natural for taxpayers to "structure" their transactions to benefit from the tax-favoured characterization. For example, if non-compete payment is not taxable, taxpayers would structure the sale of a business by including a portion of the sale price as "non-compete payment". Similarly, if income trust is treated as a "flow-through" entity and pays no entity-level income tax, taxpayers will carry on business activities through an income trust as opposed to a corporation in order to avoid double taxation (corporate income tax and personal income tax on the investor). In cases where taxpayers' ability to avoid tax through structuring threatens the integrity of the income tax system or violates fundamental policies, Parliament introduces specific and general anti-avoidance rules. Many specific anti-avoidance rules strive to align the "legal form" with the "economic substance" of the transaction.

(c) — Timing

Timing is everything. This is definitely true in tax law. By controlling the timing of the recognition of revenue and expenses in computing income, income and, therefore, the tax on such income can be deferred. Tax deferred is tax saved (for the year in question). In order to achieve a tax deferral, taxpayers must be able to accelerate the deduction of expenses or delay the inclusion of revenues.

There are two general timing methods for tax accounting: the "cash method" and "accrual method". Under the cash method, an item of revenue is included in income when received and an expense is deducted when paid. As explained in Chapters 5 and 6, this method is used to compute income from employment, office, property, and income from the business of farming. Under the accrual method, an item of revenue is included in computing income when it is receivable (i.e., the taxpayer has the legal right to be paid), and an expense is deductible when it is payable (i.e., the taxpayer has the legal obligation to pay the amount). The accrual method is the standard method for computing income from a business. Capital gains and capital losses are also generally recognized when a capital property is disposed of and the proceeds are receivable.

The Act also contains many exceptions to the general rules listed above. These exceptions include specific rules designed to: (1) promote certain socially and economically desirable activities (e.g., saving for retirement, the transfer of property between spouses, employee participation in employer stock option plans and investment in environmental protection); (2) conform with commercial accounting principles (e.g., the rules for doubtful debt reserves and prepaid expenses); or (3) to control undesirable tax deferral (e.g., the recognition of interest income on long-term investments). Overall, there are many opportunities for tax planning to achieve tax deferral.

(d) — Time value of money

Timing is important because of the time value of money. This reflects the idea that a sum of money that is due to be received in the future is worth less than the same sum of money that is due to be received immediately. The assumption underlying the time value of money is that a sum of money on hand today could be invested at compound interest, which over a period of time would cause it to grow. The longer the period of compounding, and the higher the rate of interest, the more the sum will grow. A useful guide is the rule of 72: money invested at compound interest will double in the number of years obtained by dividing 72 by the after-tax rate of interest. Thus, a sum invested inside a registered retirement savings plan (where income is untaxed) at a rate of 7.2 per cent compound interest will double in ten years; a sum invested at 10 per cent compound interest will double in 7.2 years.

Another way of expressing the idea of the time value of money is by reference to the "present value" of a sum of money to be received in the future. Determining the present value of a future obligation is known as "discounting", and it is simply the reverse of compounding. The present value of a future obligation decreases as (1) the payment date extends further into the future, and (2) the discount rate increases. For example (recalling our rule of 72), the present value of $1,000 to be received in ten years' time is $500, using an after-tax discount rate of 7.2 per cent. If a discount rate of 15 per cent were used, instead of 7.2 per cent, the present value of the $1,000 to be received in ten years' time would shrink to $247. This is the same as saying that $247 invested at 15 per cent compound interest would grow to $1,000 in ten years. The practical consequence of the present value concept is that, when the applicable rate of return stands at 15 per cent, a rational person ought to be indifferent as between (1) paying (or receiving) $247 now, and (2) paying (or receiving) $1,000 in ten years' time.

From the standpoint of the taxpayer, the longer that an obligation to pay tax can legally be put off, the more the present value of the obligation shrinks. A very simple concrete example will illustrate the point. Suppose that T, who pays tax at a rate of 50 per cent, has received a sum of $1,000 that he or she can either (a) recognize as taxable income in the current year, or (b) not recognize until a future year. Assume that he or she invests the $1,000 income at 7.2 per cent. Consider alternatives (a) and (b) after ten years:

(a) If he or she pays tax immediately:

Income		$1,000
Less: tax on $1,000 in year 1		(500)
Total available for investment		500
Add: Interest over ten years	500	

Less: tax on interest	250	250
Net result of investment		$750

(b) If he or she postpones payment of tax for ten years:

Income	$1,000
Less: tax on $1,000 in year 1	Nil
Total available for investment	1,000
Add: Interest over ten years	1,000
Total before tax	2,000
Less: tax on $2,000 in year 10	(1,000)
Net result of investment	$1,000

The net result of the investment in example (b) (postponement) is $250 more than in example (a) - a difference of one-third. This substantial gain is entirely the result of the postponement of tax. Notice that in example (b), the postponement case, there is no actual saving of tax. On the contrary, the taxpayer pays one-third more tax, $1,000 instead of $750. But the net result is still more favourable to the taxpayer because the total taxable income is also one-third more. What has happened in example (b) is that the money which would otherwise have been paid in tax ($500) has also been earning income ($500 in all), and only half of that extra income ($250) is paid in tax by T (who pays tax at a rate of 50 per cent).

(e) — Tax deferral

Understanding timing and tax deferral is key to understanding the determination of the tax base (especially the timing of recognition of income and expenses), the concept of annual taxation, and tax planning. Tax deferral is one of the most important objectives in tax planning. The Act provides many opportunities for deferral,[50] but in the meantime contains rules to curb deferral.[51]

The primary advantage to the taxpayer is that the taxpayer retains the use of money that would otherwise have to be paid to the government in tax. This is an obvious benefit to the taxpayer who needs extra cash, for example, for working capital in a business, and who would otherwise have to borrow the money at current interest rates. But even a taxpayer who has no special need of the money will benefit by having extra funds available for investment. Tax postponed is like an interest-free

[50]Some examples were discussed earlier in this chapter. Other examples of tax postponement will be encountered as we move through this book. For example, in chapter 9, Income from Business or Property: Capital Expenditures below, we shall see that the advantage of the deduction of capital cost allowances (the term in the Act for depreciation charges) that are higher than the actual decline in value of capital assets is that it causes a postponement of tax.

[51]See chapters 7 and 8, below.

loan from the government to the taxpayer. In other words, the taxpayers take advantage of the time value of money. The above example demonstrates that the advantages of tax postponement are so substantial that even if the taxpayer has moved into a higher tax bracket during the period of postponed liability (ten years in our example) he or she would still make more money by postponing tax. But a taxpayer with the means of deferring taxable income may be able to recognize that income in a year, or over a period of years, when his or her other income has fallen and taken the taxpayer down into a lower tax bracket. This is a great feature of the registered pension plans and registered retirement savings plans that are permitted by the Act. Contributions to these plans are deductible from income (subject to certain limits) so that the contributor is in effect investing not only the money he or she would have been able to save after the payment of tax, but also the money he or she would have paid in tax. This means that the fund invested will grow very much larger than would a fund built up solely of the money saved from after-tax dollars. Moreover, the income of the fund is not taxed as it is earned. The money in the fund is taxed when it is paid to the taxpayer in his or her years of retirement. In retirement, other income has normally fallen off, and the pension receipts, swollen by their years of tax-sheltered growth, are accordingly taxed at lower rates than would have been applicable in the years when the contributions were actually earned.[52]

Sometimes there are other advantages of tax postponement. Occasionally, something "turns up" which unexpectedly diminishes the taxpayer's liability. One way in which this may occur is that the law may change in the taxpayer's favour. Another way in which postponed tax liabilities may be reduced is where a taxpayer's personal circumstances change to his or her advantage. For example, the taxpayer may incur a business loss in a particular year which would make it advantageous to recognize some of the deferred income. Or a taxpayer may become a non-resident of Canada, and be able to recognize the deferred income at a low 15 per cent rate of withholding tax (where there is a tax treaty) that is applicable to much of the income of a non-resident. In other words, the old adage that one should not put off until tomorrow what one can do today is one that only the CRA can be expected to endorse. For the taxpayer, there are bound to be economic gains in tax postponement. And, occasionally, the predictable economic gains are further sweetened by an unpredictable windfall.

(f) — Tax minimization

Taxpayers regularly organize their transactions so that they can minimize the tax they pay. Sometimes the generous tax treatment results from the way that the transaction is characterized for the purposes of the Act and sometimes the generous tax treatment result from the way in which a particular statutory provision is interpreted. It is natural that taxpayers will structure their transactions to take advantage

[52]These retirement savings plans are discussed under heading 12.4, "Tax assisted private pension plans", below.

of any inconsistency, ambiguity, "loophole", or tax incentive in order to minimize their tax burden. A taxpayer's right to tax planning and tax avoidance has been well recognized in the Canadian income tax system and Lord Tomlin's famous statement from the *Duke of Westminster* (1936)[53] is considered to be "deeply entrenched in our tax law",[54] that is:

> Every man is entitled if he can to order his affairs so as that the tax attaching under the appropriate Acts is less than it otherwise would be.

The Duke principle is "attenuated" only in cases where the tax avoidance is abusive within the meaning of the General Anti-avoidance Rule (GAAR).[55]

---

[53] *Inland Revenue Commissioners v. Duke of Westminster* (1935), [1936] A.C. 1 (U.K. H.L.)

[54] As Justice Wilson stated in *Stubart Investments Ltd. v. R.*, [1984] C.T.C. 294, 84 D.T.C. 6305 (S.C.C.)318 [C.T.C.] 6325 ([D.T.C.]): "I think Lord Tomlin's principle is far too deeply entrenched in our tax law for the courts to reject it in the absence of clear statutory authority."

[55] *Canada Trustco Mortgage Co. v. R.*, [2005] 5 C.T.C. 215, (sub nom. *Canada Trustco Mortgage Co. v. Canada)* 2005 D.T.C. 5523 (Eng.), (sub nom. *Hypothèques Trustco Canada v. Canada)* 2005 D.T.C. 5547 (Fr.) (S.C.C.) and *Mathew v. R.*, 2005 SCC 55, [2005] 5 C.T.C. 244, (sub nom. *Mathew v. Canada)* 2005 D.T.C. 5538 (Eng., 2005 D.T.C. 5563 (Fr.) (S.C.C.)

2
HISTORY AND POLICY

2.1 — Introduction

Chapter 1 provides an overview of the role and structure of the income tax. This chapter briefly discusses the history of the Income Tax Act (the "Act") and fundamental tax policy issues. Subsequent chapters will further discuss the policy issues related to specific aspects of the income tax law.

A basic familiarity with tax policy and history is helpful to the understanding of the income tax law. The Act is laden with legislative judgments about social and economic policy. Tax policy debates often make the front page of newspapers and feature prominently in election campaigns. At the centre of the debate is the fundamental conflict between the society's demand for government provision of goods and services (such as health care and education) and each individual's desire to minimize his or her own tax burden. The outcome of the debate finds its way into the provisions of the Act, which inevitably reflects political compromises and balances competing interests.

2.2 — History

(a) — Confederation

At the time of confederation in 1867, the most important sources of governmental revenue were the "indirect" taxes of customs and excise, which accounted for 80 per cent of the revenues of the uniting provinces. By section 122 of the *British North America Act*, "the customs and excise laws of each province" were transferred to the new federal government. By subsection 91(3), the new federal government was given the power to raise money "by any mode or system of taxation", which authorized the imposition of any new taxes, direct or indirect. The provinces, by subsection 92(2), were confined to "direct" taxation and, by subsection 92(9), licence fees.

The courts have adopted, as their definition of direct and indirect taxes, the language of John Stuart Mill in 1848 as follows:[1]

> A direct tax is one which is demanded from the very person who it is intended or desired should pay it. Indirect taxes are those which are demanded from one person in the expectation and intention that he shall indemnify himself at the expense of another.

---

[1] *Bank of Toronto v. Lambe* (1887), 12 App. Cas. 575 582, [1917-1927] C.T.C. 82 87 (P.C.).

An income tax is an example of a direct tax, because the taxpayer is normally unable to pass on the burden of the tax to anyone else. A customs or excise tax, on the other hand, is indirect, because, although it is paid by the importer or manufacturer, the tax will normally be passed on as part of the price that the importer or manufacturer charges for the taxed goods.[2]

(b) — Provincial income taxes

Excluded from the historically lucrative indirect taxes, the provinces gradually developed various forms of direct taxation. Property taxes, corporation taxes (on the basis of place of business, paid-up capital, etc.), and inheritance taxes began to be levied by the turn of the century. Income taxes (being direct) were available, but the provinces initially shied away from income taxes because of their unpopularity. British Columbia and Prince Edward Island were the only provinces to levy income taxes in the half century after confederation. Between 1923 and 1939, five more provinces followed their example, and the remaining three waited until 1962. All provinces now levy income taxes.

(c) — Federal income tax

As discussed in chapter 1, the federal government first imposed an income tax in 1917, during World War I. The tax was supposed to be a temporary wartime measure because it was accepted that the field of direct taxation should be left to the provinces. This temporary tax became permanent after the war and, in 1948, the word "War" was dropped and the Act was renamed "The Income Tax Act".

(d) — Federal-provincial agreements

At the beginning of World War II, the federal government and seven provinces were each levying their own income taxes. In 1941, the provinces agreed to abandon their income taxes and leave the federal government alone in the field. The provinces were compensated for the lost revenue by grants from the federal government. This arrangement was intended to last only for the duration of the war, but after the war (in 1947) the federal government persuaded all provinces except Ontario and Quebec to enter into "tax rental agreements", under which the agreeing provinces would continue to refrain from enacting their own income taxes in return for grants ("rent") from the federal government. In 1952, on the renewal of the five-year agreements, Ontario joined the system, so that only Quebec was then levying a provincial income tax.

The tax rental agreements ended in 1962 and were replaced by the "tax collection agreements". Under these agreements, the provinces imposed their own income taxes at their own rates. However, it was agreed that, if a province levied its tax as

[2] On the distinction between direct and indirect taxes, and the constitutional position generally, see Hogg, *Constitutional Law of Canada* (5th ed., 2007), chs. 6 and 30. The most detailed account is La Forest, *The Allocation of Taxing Powers under the Canadian Constitution* (2nd ed., 1981).

a percentage of the federal tax (so that the federal Act became the basis of the provincial tax), the federal government would collect the provincial tax free of charge. In this way, taxpayers would only have to satisfy a single set of (federally-enacted) rules for the computation of their taxable income, and would only have to file a single return. In 1962, all provinces except Ontario and Quebec signed collection agreements covering both personal and corporate income taxes; Ontario signed a collection agreement for its personal income tax, but collected its own corporate income tax; Quebec collected its own personal and corporate income taxes. Alberta has since opted out of the corporate tax collection system, but remains within the personal tax collection system. The tax collection agreements have been renewed every five years. All provinces except Quebec have agreements with respect to personal income taxes, and all provinces except Quebec and Alberta have agreements with respect to corporate income taxes.[3] A province that has not entered into a tax collection agreement needs to provide for the collection of the provincial tax by the provincial government.

In 1997, the federal government agreed to enter into tax collection agreements allowing the provinces to compute personal tax directly on provincial taxable income rather than as a percentage of federal tax (which had been the previous system). All provinces now use this "tax on income" (TONI) approach which allows them to make adjustments in computing provincial taxable income and to choose their own tax rates and credits. Provincial taxes are still collected by the CRA (except in the case of Quebec).

(e) — Tax reform of 1971 and the Carter report

(i) — The Carter Report

The effect of the tax collection agreements is to make the federal Act extremely important, because it defines the tax base of not only the federal income taxes but most of the provincial income taxes as well. Since its genesis in 1917, the Act has been frequently amended, and it was substantially revised in 1945 and 1952. But in 1962, there was widespread agreement that a further revision was necessary. In that year, the federal government established a Royal Commission on Taxation under the chairmanship of Kenneth Carter, a chartered accountant who practised in Toronto. The Commission reported in 1966 with a six-volume document which constitutes perhaps the most thorough, lucid, and brilliant analysis of income tax policy that has ever been produced. The Carter Report provided a comprehensive study of Canada's income tax system, and a design for a radically different system of tax.[4]

---

[3]The agreement with Ontario is effective for taxation years ending after 2008.

[4]*Report of the Royal Commission on Taxation* (Carter Report) (1966), 6 volumes. The Report is admirably summarized in vol. 1, pp. 1–49. The Commission also published 30 studies on aspects of tax policy, which are listed in vol. 1, p. 131.

The Carter Report was acclaimed by tax experts all over the world, and will continue for a long time to be a major contribution to the literature of taxation.[5] The general philosophy of the report was that all gains in wealth should be taxed — "a buck is a buck is a buck" — and this led the Commission to recommend the inclusion in income of capital gains, gifts, inheritances, and windfalls. These and other proposals attracted strong opposition. The opposition came not only from those who would have had to pay more tax, but also from those who would have benefited from the general lowering of tax rates that would have been a consequence of the broadening of the tax base.

The federal government moved slowly in implementing the recommendations of the report. A government White Paper was issued in 1969 which accepted some of the report's recommendations, including the full taxation of capital gains.[6] A Senate Committee reported on the White Paper,[7] and so did a House of Commons committee.[8] Both committees thought that even the White Paper had reformed too much of the old system. In June 1971, the government introduced its final proposals for tax reform. These became the Act which was enacted in 1971 to take effect (for the most part) in 1972. That Act, revised by frequent amendments since 1972, continues in force today.

(ii) — Major changes

The end result of the process of tax reform was a far cry from the recommendations of the Carter Report. However, the 1971 legislation made three basic changes in the Act: (1) it broadened the tax base; (2) it restructured the rates of tax; and (3) it altered the taxation of corporations and shareholders so as to partially "integrate" the corporate and personal income taxes.

So far as the tax base was concerned, the principal reform was the inclusion of one-half of capital gains in income. Some other income which had previously not been taxable were also added to income; these included adult training allowances, research grants and scholarships and, most important in terms of revenue, employment insurance benefits.[9] At the same time there was some increase in deductions. Deductions from employment income were made more generous, including a general expense allowance of 3 per cent of employment income up to a maximum of

---

[5]Despite the importance of the Commission's report, it was not even published by the Canadian government, and exists in mimeograph form only.

[6]Benson, *Proposals for Tax Reform* (1969).

[7]*Report on the White Paper Proposals for Tax Reform presented to the Senate of Canada* (1970).

[8]*Eighteenth Report of the Standing Committee on Finance, Trade and Economic Affairs respecting the White Paper on Tax Reform* (1970).

[9]The rules for scholarships have changed over the years. At the present time, most scholarships are tax-exempt. See ch. 12, Other Income and Deductions, below.

$150.[10] The limits of deductibility of pension plan and savings plan contributions and of charitable donations were increased. New deductions were established for capital losses, unemployment insurance premiums, child care expenses and moving expenses.

The rate structure was altered by an increase in the personal and married exemptions (a tax-free bracket) and a reduction in tax rates at the top end of the scale. In other respects, tax rates rose slightly after reform. The increase in rates was required because the increases in exemptions and deductions more than offset the inclusion of one-half of capital gains and other increases in assessed income and had the effect of reducing the total amount of taxable income. Some increase in rates was therefore necessary to keep revenue constant. Only in the highest income bracket did taxable income rise after reform: in that bracket the inclusion of one-half of capital gains was the dominating factor.

In the corporate area, the 1971 Act allowed a low rate of tax (approximately 25 per cent)[11] on the investment income of private corporations and, within limits, on the active business income of Canadian-controlled private corporations. Dividends were to be taxed in the hands of shareholders by a gross-up-and-credit procedure which had the effect of giving the shareholder credit for at least some of the tax paid by the corporation, and in the case of income taxed at the low corporate rate, for all of the tax paid by the corporation.

(f) — Introduction of indexing

The years between the major tax reforms of 1971 and 1988 saw many alterations in the income tax structure. Perhaps the most important was the "indexing" of the system, which became effective in 1974. The effect of indexing is that the fixed-dollar deductions, credits, and tax brackets expand automatically by the rate of inflation, so that increases in a taxpayer's income that match the rate of inflation are taxed at the same average rate as the previous year's income. In the years of high inflation that followed, indexing caused a major expansion of the exemptions, credits, and brackets. From 1986 to 2000, the system was partially de-indexed. As a result of this change, only inflation above 3 per cent was taken into account by the indexing provisions, thus permitting an upward creep in government revenues without the need to enact an increase in rates. Full indexing was restored in 2000.

---

[10] This deduction was repealed in 1988 but its purpose is similar to the $1,000 employment tax credit introduced in 2006.

[11] In 1988, the rate was lowered to approximately 20 per cent. See ch. 15, Corporations and Shareholders, below.

(g) — Tax reform of 1988

In 1987, the government introduced a White Paper into Parliament, which proposed many amendments to the Act.[12] Most of these amendments were enacted in 1988,[13] the major changes being (1) the "flattening" of the rate structure, (2) the broadening of the tax base, (3) the conversion of many deductions from income into credits against tax, and (4) the introduction of the general anti-avoidance rule (GAAR). A second phase of tax reform, also contemplated by the 1987 white paper, resulted in more equitable and generous tax subsidies for retirement saving and the introduction of the Goods and Services Tax (GST) in 1991.

The most obvious change implemented by the tax reform of 1988 was the restructuring of the rates at which tax is levied on personal income. The number of tax brackets was reduced from ten to three, and the rates of federal tax were reduced. The rate structure following the 1988 reform was as follows: (a) 17 per cent on taxable income not exceeding $27,500; (b) 26 per cent on taxable income between $27,500 and $55,000; and (c) 29 per cent on taxable income exceeding $55,000.[14]

According to the white paper, the lower rates were designed to increase the incentives to work and save, and to bring Canada's rates of income tax into closer conformity with those of the United States.[15] As discussed below, the three bracket rate structure of 1988 continued in force until 2001, when the rates were reduced and a fourth bracket was added.[16]

Several changes in 1988 had the effect of broadening the base on which tax is levied. The major one was an increase in the inclusion rate of capital gains from its former level of one-half to two-thirds for 1988 and 1989, and to three-quarters for 1990 and subsequent years to 2000 (when it was moved back to one-half). Increasing the inclusion rate during this period saw the Canadian tax system move closer to Carter's recommendation of full inclusion and improved its equity. As well, the 1988 amendments included some restrictions on the deductibility of business expenses relating to travel (vehicle, meals, and entertainment), as well as the elimination of some deductions which continue today.

Before 1988, taxpayers were entitled to a number of personal deductions, for example, a basic personal exemption (to which everyone was entitled) and deductions for a dependent spouse and other dependants. There were also deductions for contributions to the Canada Pension Plan and Unemployment Insurance (now Employment Insurance), for charitable contributions, tuition fees and a number of other

---

[12] Wilson, *Tax Reform 1987: Income Tax Reform* (1987), 3.

[13] A second phase of tax reform, also contemplated by the 1987 White Paper, resulted in the introduction of the Goods and Services Tax (GST), which is a value-added sales tax. The GST was enacted in 1990, and came into force at the beginning of 1991.

[14] See s. 117 as it read at that time.

[15] Note 12, above, 69-70.

[16] There was a minor modification in 2000 when the rate applicable to the middle bracket was changed from 26% to 25%.

expenses not directly related to the earning of income. The trouble with these provisions was that they all took the form of deductions from income, and under progressive rates of tax a deduction from income is more valuable to a high-income taxpayer (whose income is being taxed at higher rates) than it is to a low-income taxpayer (whose income is being taxed at lower rates). The 1988 amendments converted these deductions into credits against tax.[17] The new credits yield the same reduction in tax to all taxpayers regardless of their level of income. This change from deductions to credits generally improved the equity of the system.[18]

The GAAR was one of the more controversial reforms of 1988. This provision denies taxpayers the tax benefits arising from any transactions that may reasonably be considered to have been undertaken primarily for the purpose of avoiding the payment of tax. The GAAR was introduced to catch avoidance behaviour that escaped the many specific anti-avoidance provisions of the Act. It was (and remains) controversial, because of the difficulty in applying it. The GAAR is discussed in greater detail in chapter 20.

(h) — 1988 to 2005

There were several significant amendments to the Act from 1989 to 2005. Many of these changes were designed to lower income taxes for individuals and corporations with the objective, at least in part, of making Canada more economically competitive with the United States. Other measures have had social policy objectives. Still others have been designed to better target tax preferences, encourage compliance and/or prevent tax avoidance.

2000 was an election year, and a number of tax reductions were introduced to enhance Canada's international competitiveness.[19] These measures included the reduction of the taxable portion of capital gains from three-quarters to one-half[20] as well as a number of changes to tax credits and tax rates in both personal income tax and corporate income tax. In the area of personal income tax, personal tax credits were increased, full indexation of personal tax rates and credits was reintroduced, a

[17] A few deductions, such as the $1,000 investment income deduction and the exemption for children under 18 were discontinued and not converted into credits.

[18] This conversion and the policy basis for tax credits generally is more fully explained under heading 14.7(a), "Nature of tax credits", below.

[19] These changes were proposed in Department of Finance, *February 28, 2000 Budget Plan and Notice of Ways and Means Motion* and the pre-election Department of Finance, *Economic Statement and Budget Update, Tax Measures: Supplementary Information and Notice of Ways and Means Motion, October 18, 2000*. Some of the changes were enacted in 2000; others were enacted in 2001.

[20] The fraction was first reduced from three-quarters to two-thirds (in the February 28, 2000 budget) for the period from February 28, 2000 to October 17, 2000 and then reduced to one-half (in the October 18, 2000 economic statement) for the period after October 17, 2000.

fourth tax bracket for taxable income over $100,000 (subject to indexing) was added,[21] and the 5 per cent surtax was eliminated.[22]

Corporate tax reductions were phased in starting in 2001, including a seven per cent general rate reduction[23] and an increase in the annual limit for claiming the 16 per cent small business rate reduction from $200,000 to $300,000.[24]

Several rules modelled on the U.S. tax system were also added during this period. These rules include a $100,000 deferral rule for employee stock options (repealed in 2010); a small business share capital gains deferral rule; reduction in the taxable portion of capital gains on charitable gifts of public company shares and employee stock options and ecologically-sensitive land to one-half of the normal fraction[25] an increase in tax depreciation rates for computer and data network equipment; an extension of the carry forward period for non-capital losses (from seven years to ten years), and the prohibition of a deduction for fines and penalties.

Some changes were aimed at meeting certain social policy objectives. These measures included: equal tax treatment of same-sex couples and heterosexual couples; introduction of the income-tested GST credit and child tax benefit payments to assist low-income families with children;[26] increased tax assistance for the cost of post-secondary education;[27] new tax relief for taxpayers who adopt a child[28] and

---

[21]This changed the graduate rate structure for individuals from three brackets in 2000 (with rates of 17%, 25% and 29%) to four brackets in 2001 (with rates of 16%, 22%, 26%, and 29%).

[22]For further discussion of personal tax credits, see heading 14.7, "Tax credits", below.

[23]The general rate reduction (available for income not subject to any preferential treatment) was cut by one per cent in 2001 with a schedule of further annual reductions to result in a seven per cent net rate reduction by 2004. Canadian controlled private corporations earnings were eligible for the seven percent reduction immediately on income earned between $200,000 and $300,000.

[24]The 2003 budget increased the $200,000 limit to $225,000 in 2003 with a schedule of further $25,000 increases to result in a $300,000 limit by 2006. (Income between this limit and $300,000 continued to be eligible for the seven per cent rate reduction.) The 2004 budget increased the limit to $300,000 in 2005 (a year earlier). Another 1.12% rate reduction took place in 2008, when the corporate surtax was be eliminated for small and medium sized businesses.

[25]That is one-quarter (one-half of one-half) in 2001. Gains were fully exempted in 2006.

[26]Heading 14.7, "Tax credits", below.

[27]*Ibid.*

[28]Effective 2005, a tax credit is available for eligible adoption expenses. The amount is $10,000 for each adoption and indexed annually.

taxpayers with disabilities and their families[29] and increased tax relief for charitable donations.[30]

Measures introduced to encourage tax compliance included the third-party penalty rules, the construction contractor reporting rules, the doubling of penalties for repeated failures to file tax returns or remit source deductions and an increase in the interest rate applicable to unpaid taxes.

A number of measures were also introduced to prevent tax avoidance: restrictions on the use of tax shelters; the deduction of interest expense on "weak currency loans"; the tax on split income "kiddie tax" (introduced to attack certain "income-splitting" arrangements with minor children); new transfer pricing rules to prevent cross-border tax avoidance; an increase in the collection period for unpaid taxes (from six to ten years); measures to counter abuses in connection with charitable giving; and retroactive amendments to ensure that GAAR will apply to income tax application rules, income tax regulations and tax treaties. New anti-avoidance measures to address the issue of tax havens,[31] interest deductibility, and the purchase of income trusts by pension funds were proposed but not enacted.

(i) — 2006 to present

Taxes were a major issue in the 2005-06 election and subsequent federal budgets have seen the Conservative government implement all but one of its election promises to lower taxes.[32] As a result, there was a great deal of tinkering with the tax system from 2006 onwards as a number of measures were introduced to reduce rates, increase credits and exemptions, and introduce new credits and exemptions.

Some measures focused on economic objectives. The GST rate was reduced from 7 per cent to 6 per cent effective July 1, 2006 to 5 per cent effective January 1, 2008.

---

[29]See heading 14.7, "Tax credits," below.

[30]The personal tax credit formula for charitable donations was changed to provide for an increased credit at 29%. The income limit for donations eligible for write off in a given year increased from 20% to 75%, for both corporations and individuals. As discussed above, an incentive was provided for taxpayers gifting of public company stock and public company employee stock options donated to a registered charity: the amount included in income was halved.

[31]Department of Finance, *Legislative Proposals and Draft Regulations Relating to Income Tax*, February 27, 2004.

[32]During the 2005-06 election, the Conservative party made a highly popular (but widely questioned) promise to introduce a general capital gains deferral rule (to apply, for example, on the sale of investments or cottages) if proceeds were reinvested within six months of the sale. No such rule has been introduced to date and the government is silent on the reason why. It seems likely that the reasons might include the logic of allowing such a general rule, the size of the tax expenditure involved and the complexities involved in designing a compliance system to ensure that the deferred capital gain was eventually reported. The Act currently allows a capital gains deferral if the proceeds are reinvested in very limited circumstances: see s. 44 and 44.1 of the Act.

Effective July 1, 2010 the provinces of Ontario and British Columbia will harmonize their provincial sales taxes with the GST. The harmonized system will be administered federally, as is the case with the HST for the maritime provinces (Newfoundland, New Brunswick and Nova Scotia) but not Quebec (which administers the GST/ HST in Quebec).

Personal tax cuts included staged reductions in the lowest tax bracket from 16% to 15%, increases in the basic and spouse (and spouse equivalent) tax credits and the re-introduction of a child tax credit for dependant children under 18.[33] The corporate tax reductions involved staged increases to the general rate reduction and the small business deduction and the repeal of the surtax and the large corporations tax.[34] Tax depreciation rates were increased for buildings and certain types of equipment in the 2007 budget and temporarily for computer equipment in the 2009 budget. The lifetime capital gains exemption for shares in small businesses and farming businesses was extended to fishing businesses in 2006 and increased from $750,000 in the 2007 budget. The rules were changed to fully exempt capital gains on charitable gifts of public company shares and employee stock options and ecologically-sensitive land in 2006. In 2008, tax-free savings accounts were introduced, effective 2009. The 2009 budget introduced a first time homebuyer's tax credit and a temporary home renovation tax credit.

A change made in 2006 moved the dividend gross-up and tax credit system closer to that originally envisaged by the Carter Commission. This was done by changing the gross-up and dividend tax credit rules to give individuals credit for more of the corporate tax paid.[35] As a result, the tax system has become more neutral for taxpayers investing in shares of a corporation (which pay corporate tax) and taxpayers investing in units of an income trust (which do not pay corporate tax). Ironically, these changes were not successful at stemming the popularity of income trusts as an investment vehicle because a greater number of the investors in income trusts were

---

[33]The lowest tax rate was reduced from 16% (in 2005) to 15.25 (in 2006) to 15.5 (in 2007) to 15% (in 2008). The rate of 15.25 in 2006 was due to the fact that a proposed 15% rate (announced by an earlier government) had been used for employer withholdings from January 1 to June 30, 2006. The 2006 budget announced increases to the basic and spouse credit to take place from 2006 to 2009. The 2007 budget brought the spouse (and spouse equivalent) credits up to the level of the basic credit and added a child tax credit. These measures are discussed in more detail in chapter 14.

[34]These measures, which are discussed in more detail in chapter 15, Corporations and Shareholders, include the following increasing the (general and manufacturing & processing) rate reduction to 13 per cent in 2011; increasing the rate of the small business deduction to 17 per cent in 2009 and increasing the annual limit for the small business deduction to $500,000 in 2009.

[35]As discussed in more detail in chapter 15, Corporations and Shareholders, there is now a higher 44% gross-up and tax credit (in 2010) for "eligible" dividends paid out of income subject to tax at the general corporate rate and a 25% gross-up and tax credit for ineligible dividends, paid out of corporate income taxed at lower rates.

tax-exempt entities, such as registered retirement savings plans (RRSPs). As a result, a further anti-avoidance measure was implemented: a distribution tax.[36]

Among the social-policy oriented measures are: (a) the tax reductions and deferrals for seniors (many of whom were expected to complain about the change in rules for income trusts), including increases to the age credit, a doubling of the pension credit (from $1,000 to $2,000 annually), an income splitting rule for income eligible for the pension credit and a delay in the time at which seniors must begin to receive income out of their RRSP savings from 69 and 71;[37] (b) more tax relief for one-earner families (especially those caring for children), including several of the items previously mentioned (increases to the spouse credit, the child tax credit and pension income splitting) as well as the introduction of a $100 monthly Universal Child Care Benefit (for all children under 6); (c) tax relief for low income earners[38] and employees in general;[39] (d) increased tax assistance for saving for post-secondary education[40] and for the cost of supporting taxpayers with disabilities.[41]

The federal government has chosen to subsidize a number of areas that are under provincial domain through the tax system rather than make additional transfers of funds to the provinces: these areas include public transit and fitness (new non-refundable credits), child care (the Universal Child Care Benefit and investment tax credits for day care construction) and post-secondary education (more generous registered education savings plan rules, a new textbook credit, and a tax exemption for scholarships).

Environmental issues also featured prominently. The government introduced measures to allow higher tax depreciation rates for environmentally-friendly energy generation and other equipment:

International measures were proposed to improve tax compliance, protect the Canadian tax base and keep Canadian rates competitive. The 2010 federal budget also proposed several other changes to improve fairness of the tax system. These include a "reportable transaction" system for tax avoidance transactions (similar to one recently introduced in Quebec), and closing loopholes for "cashed out" em-

---

[36]The distribution tax applies to amounts distributed by a "specified investment flow-through" (SIFT) trust or the income of a SIFT partnership. The tax is effective as of 2007 to new entities, but is deferred until 2011 for SIFTs that were publicly traded as of October 31, 2006.

[37]These measures are discussed under heading 12.4(b), "Tax assistance", and 12.4(d)(iv), "RRSP annuities", below.

[38]E.g., the Working Income Tax Benefit discussed under heading 14.7(c), "Refundable credits", below.

[39]E.g., the employment tax credit, discussed under heading 5.1(b)(v) "Balancing policy concerns", below.

[40]E.g. the textbook credit, discussed under heading 14.7(b), "Non-refundable credits", below.

[41]E.g., the disability savings plan discussed under heading 12.5(b) "Registered disability savings plans (RDSPs)", below.

ployee stock options and leasing property, and disallowing individual taxpayers from claiming cosmetic surgery as a medical expense.

2.3 — Policy objectives

(a) — Overview

The main purpose of any tax is to raise revenue. Why does Canada rely on the income tax as the main source of tax revenue? Is it "good" or "bad"? What are the criteria for evaluation? There is widespread agreement that the criteria are equity, neutrality, simplicity, and international competitiveness and that income tax is overall a "good" tax. However, there is less agreement as to the precise meaning of these criteria, the relative priorities that they should be given, and how they can be implemented. This is illustrated in the debates about "flat tax".

Table 2-1
Objectives of Income Tax

Equity	Equity (or fairness) requires a fair sharing of the tax burden based on ability to pay. This calls for vertical equity and horizontal equity.
Neutrality	Neutrality requires a tax system that does not affect people's behaviour. Business or personal opportunities, rather than tax planning, should drive business or personal decisions.
Simplicity	Compliance by taxpayers and administration by government are both easier and less costly in a system that is simple and understandable.
International competitiveness	The mobility of capital and skilled labour suggests that the Canadian tax system should be competitive with other countries, especially the United States.

(b) — Equity

(i) — Ability to pay principle

The Carter Commission took the view, which is still widely shared,[42] that equity (or fairness) should be the major objective of the income tax system. The Commission distinguished between "horizontal equity", which requires that persons "in similar circumstances" bear the same taxes, and "vertical equity", which requires that persons in different circumstances bear "appropriately different" taxes.[43]

Phrases such as horizontal equity and vertical equity do not help to decide the policy questions of what circumstances should be recognized by the tax system as relevant, and what differences in taxation should flow from differences in the cir-

[42] Fair Tax Commission (Ontario), *Fair Taxation in a Changing World* (1993), 44–68.

[43] Carter Report, note 4, above, vol. 1, 4-5.

cumstances. Carter held, and again his view is widely shared, that both dimensions of equity required that tax be levied in accordance with "ability to pay". How does one measure ability to pay? John Stuart Mill, the 19th century philosopher and economist, said that the idea of ability to pay was to achieve "equality of sacrifice".[44] By this he meant that contributions to the expenses of government should be so apportioned that each person "shall feel neither more nor less inconvenience from his share of the payment than any other person experiences from his". Mill acknowledged that this standard could not be completely realized", but he averred that "the first object in every political discussion should be to know what perfection is".

In practice, of course, it is very difficult to secure agreement on what counts as equality of sacrifice. The problem is not just that people differ greatly in wealth, but also that many other features of social and economic life arguably affect the amount of sacrifice that taxpayers must make. There is room for considerable difference of opinion as to how to design a tax system around the concept of equality of sacrifice (or ability to pay). For example, decisions have to be made about the rates of tax, about the tax base (what counts as "income"), about the tax unit (the individual or the family), and about the treatment of income received through intermediaries (such as corporations, partnerships, and trusts).

The Carter Commission took the view that the criterion of ability to pay required (1) that tax be levied at progressive rates; (2) that tax be levied on a "comprehensive tax base" as opposed to the relatively narrow concept of "income"; (3) that tax be levied on families as opposed to individuals; (4) that tax concessions to particular industries or activities be avoided; and (5) that corporate and personal income tax on corporate profits be "integrated" to avoid "double taxation". Each of these recommendations is examined in the appropriate place later in this book.

While the criterion of ability to pay is widely accepted as the measure of equity in a tax system, the opposition to Carter's recommendations showed that many people could not accept all the implications that Carter drew from that criterion. As explained above, the Act of 1971 accepted some of Carter's recommendations and rejected others, but the net effect of the reform was an improvement in the equity of the system. This pattern has continued with subsequent reforms seeking to improve the equity or fairness of the system. On the whole, however, recent changes indicate a major retreat from Carter's idea that equity should be the predominant objective in the design of tax system. If this trend continues, there may be more emphasis in the future on international competitiveness and lower taxes and consequently less emphasis on equity.

(ii) — Horizontal equity

The notion of horizontal equity underlies the movement towards a comprehensive tax base. Capital gains became taxable in 1972, albeit not fully. Many types of fringe benefits are taxable as they enhance the recipient's ability to pay just like

---

[44] Mill, *Principles of Political Economy* (1923), bk. 5, ch. 2, sec. 2.

wages and salaries. The introduction of many anti-avoidance rules is justified on ground of equity.

However, the Act falls short on horizontal equity in many respects. For example, the "source" theory of income excludes amounts that clearly add to a taxpayer's ability to pay from the tax base. All tax expenditure provisions violate the principle of horizontal equity, although other policy objectives provide legitimate justifications for them.

(iii) — Vertical equity

A person with a low income needs all or most of the income simply to survive. A person with a high income can provide for necessities and have a substantial amount left over. The taxpayer's ability to pay taxes is determined by the amount of income available for discretionary use. In general, the greater the total income, the higher is the fraction of that income which is available for discretionary use. The ability to pay principle dictates not merely that upper-income taxpayers should pay more dollars in tax than lower-income taxpayers, but that upper-income taxpayers should pay a greater proportion of their income in tax than lower-income taxpayers. This conclusion necessitates a progressive rate schedule.

The personal income tax is particularly adaptable to the graduated rates which make it progressive. That is because the taxpayer cannot usually shift the tax to others.[45] It can be designed to take account of the personal circumstances of each taxpayer, and in particular the total amount of the taxpayer's income, his or her family circumstances, and other factors which bear on the taxpayer's ability to pay.[46]

(c) — Neutrality

(i) — Definition

The Carter Commission argued, and many experts agree, that the tax system should be "neutral". What is meant by a neutral system is one that is "designed to bring about a minimum change in the allocation of resources within the private sector of the economy".[47] The reason that Carter gave for neutrality was that, "at least in the present state of knowledge, the allocation of resources in response to free market forces will in general give in the short run the best utilisation of resources, and in

---

[45]A personal income tax is called a "direct tax". This can be contrasted with an "indirect" tax. An indirect tax is levied on producers, importers or sellers in the expectation that they will pass it on to their customers in the form of higher prices for their products. An indirect tax cannot take account of the individual circumstances of the widely dispersed and unascertained class of people who will ultimately bear the tax, and so customs and excise duties and sales taxes tend to take the form of flat-rate charges on the value of each article or transaction which is taxed.

[46]See Carter Report, note 4, above, Vol. 3, p. 213.

[47]Carter Report, *ibid.*, vol. 2, 8.

the long run the most satisfactory rate of increase in the output of the economy".[48] In a neutral tax system, people's work practices and business and investment decisions would be no different than they would have been in a world without taxes. To the extent that behaviour is influenced by the tax system, there is tax-induced change in the allocation of society's resources; that is the effect of a tax system that is not neutral. Of course, a tax-induced change in behaviour may be a desirable change, but most tax-policy experts agree with Carter that the use of the tax system to accomplish social and economic goals is usually less effective and more expensive than the use of other policy instruments. This point is pursued in the later section of this chapter, under heading 2.4, "Tax expenditures", below.

(ii) — Distinguished from equity

Neutrality is not synonymous with equity. A poll tax levied in the same amount on every individual would be the most neutral tax; nothing could be done to avoid it, and therefore it would not change anyone's behaviour. But such a tax would not be an equitable tax because it would not be related to ability to pay.

However, in a system that is generally related to ability to pay, the provisions that violate neutrality (tax concessions) tend also to violate equity by abandoning the criterion of ability to pay in favour of other policy objectives. For example, take the case of the taxpayer who makes political contributions, charitable donations and contributions to a registered retirement savings plan, and who obtains the credits and the deductions that the tax system provides for these expenditures. That taxpayer will pay less tax than another taxpayer who has equal ability to pay but did not make the tax-favoured expenditures. The tax concessions violate equity, because they cause differences in the liability to pay tax that are unrelated to differences in the ability to pay tax.

(iii) — Deliberate policies

Despite all the arguments in favour of neutrality, it would certainly appear that the government continues to use the tax system to pursue various social and economic policies, often using deductions from income or credits against tax as the means of providing the desired incentive. The tax system has incentives for Canadian-owned small businesses, environmentally friendly equipment and vehicles (including public transit), capital gains, scientific research, post-secondary education, charitable donations, and for saving for retirement. It subsidizes families with children and dependants with disabilities. Many of these activities could be subsidized directly by government grants as opposed to subsidies delivered indirectly through the tax system.

It is fair to note that even the Carter Commission did not always remain true to its goal of neutrality. For example, the Commission favoured a tax deduction for per-

---

[48] *Ibid.*

sons who saved for their retirement[49] and a fast write-off of capital costs for new small businesses.[50] But these recommendations were considered compromises between the goal of neutrality and other considerations deemed of equal value in the circumstances. Concessions to help particular industries or activities were not, in Carter's system, to be a normal, recurring use of the income tax. The White Paper preceding the tax reform of 1971,[51] while agreeing that the tax system should not interfere seriously with economic growth and productivity, pointed out that the tax laws had long been used to provide incentives to certain kinds of valuable business activities, and stated that "the government believes they should continue to be so used in a number of specific ways that are clearly understood and justified". Those who make a practice of listening to budget speeches and of following the steady flow of amendments to the Act will appreciate that the goal of neutrality is in fact often compromised by the government in aid of other objectives.

(iv) — Unintended effects

The discussion to this point has assumed that the various violations of neutrality in the Act represent deliberate choices on the part of government. In most cases that is true, but in some cases the Act influences behaviour in ways that are not intended by government. For example, the fact that fewer deductions are available from income from employment than are available from income from business has led taxpayers to order their affairs so as to receive business income rather than employment income. The fact that capital gains are only one-half taxable has led taxpayers to order their affairs so as to receive capital gains rather than ordinary income. Similarly, the more generous tax treatment of incorporated businesses than unincorporated businesses has encouraged taxpayers to incorporate their businesses; and deductions for business-related automobile and entertainment expenses subsidized the automobile, restaurant, and entertainment industries until restrictions on these claims were introduced.

(d) — Simplicity

The policy objective of simplicity and administrative efficiency demands that compliance costs for taxpayers and administrative costs for the tax authorities be minimized as far as possible. If a tax is difficult to administer or if compliance burdens are excessive, no matter how perfect it may appear in theory or design, the tax will fail to serve its intended function as a reliable source of revenue. Therefore, this policy objective often requires some sacrifice of equity and neutrality concerns.

Simplicity has influenced the design of the rules in many key areas of income tax law. Examples are the taxation of employment income (which has very few deductions) and the timing of recognition of capital gains or losses (which are taxed on a realization rather than accrual basis). Simplicity is the reason for federal-provincial

---

[49] *Ibid.*, vol. 3, ch. 15.

[50] *Ibid.*, vol. 4, 276–282.

[51] *Proposals for Tax Reform* (1969), 7.

tax collection agreements that require taxpayers to only file on personal or corporate tax return based on federal and provincial rules that are fairly similar.[52]

(e) — International competitiveness

The growing globalization of the Canadian economy and the associated increasing mobility of capital inevitably impose some limits on Canadian sovereignty in determining its tax policy, especially in areas affecting cross-border trade and investment. Because capital is extremely mobile across international borders, national sovereignty over tax policy is severely threatened. For example, Canadians' view of equity and fairness may require high and steeply progressive rates on capital income, but Canada's ability to implement such a policy is thwarted by citizens shifting wealth into foreign corporations or trusts located in low-tax jurisdictions. The fact that the Canadian economy is highly integrated with the world economy, especially that of the United States means that Canadian tax policy decisions cannot be made in isolation.

Since 1987, one of the main impetuses for changes in the Canadian system has been international competitiveness, especially in the area of corporate income tax and taxation of investment income. For example, the corporate income tax rate is generally in line with that in other developed countries. Some tax reform measures, such as the deferral rule for employee stock options (repealed in 2010) were enacted to compete with the United States in retaining talented workers.[53]

2.4 — Tax expenditures

(a) — Concept

Each tax concession, whether in the form of a deduction or a credit or a rate-reduction or an omission from income, has a cost to government, namely, the amount of revenue foregone by the concession. Its effect on government revenue is the same as if the tax system lacked that particular concession, and the government made a direct expenditure of the cost of the concession to those persons who would have benefited from it. The effect of a tax concession is thus no different from that of an expenditure. The analogy to an expenditure was emphasized by Professor Stanley S. Surrey of Harvard Law School, who coined the term "tax expenditures" to describe tax preferences.[54]

---

[52]Simplicity is also the reason that a taxpayer no longer computes his or her entitlement to certain income-tested refundable credits and benefits, he simply ticks the box (in the case of the GST credit) or files a return (in the case of the Child Tax Benefit and the Guaranteed Income Supplement).

[53]See heading 5.9, "Employee stock options", below.

[54]Surrey, *Pathways to Tax Reform: The Concept of Tax Expenditures* (1973) and Surrey and McDaniel, *Tax Expenditures* (1985) are the seminal works on the topic.

(b) — Public scrutiny

What Surrey publicized was the absence of public scrutiny of tax expenditures in comparison with direct expenditures. The United States Treasury moved to correct this situation in 1969 by preparing a "tax expenditure budget", which listed and estimated the cost of various tax concessions in the United States' tax system. This became an annual practice which, under the *Congressional Budget Act* of 1974, is now required by law. Some American states have also begun to develop tax expenditure budgets.

In Canada, until 1979, tax expenditures were immune from the annual scrutiny which is applied to direct expenditures. The cost of a tax expenditure did not appear in any budget, and once established it did not need to win annual approval from the Treasury Board, Cabinet or Parliament. Indeed, the cost of a particular tax concession was only estimated officially upon its first introduction, and then only for the first year of its operation. If this estimate was wrong, or if the cost increased dramatically, there was no regular procedure for discovering the new facts, let alone debating them: no further figures were ever provided. And, despite the Carter Commission's widely-accepted warning of the inefficiency of tax concessions, there was rarely any examination of the degree to which a tax concession was accomplishing its stated objectives, or of who was benefiting from it. This situation attracted criticism, and various unofficial analyses of tax expenditures began to appear and to receive publicity.[55]

In 1979, the Department of Finance issued a document entitled "Government of Canada Tax Expenditure Account" (1979), in which an attempt was made to identify all of the tax concessions in the Canadian income tax system, and to estimate the cost in foregone revenue of each concession. The tax expenditure account was divided into the same categories as are used for direct expenditures in the public accounts of Canada. The figures were preceded by an analysis of the concept of a tax expenditure and the criteria for identifying it and estimating its cost. The document did not provide estimates for some of the concessions, no attempt was made to estimate the total cost, and no attempt was made to show the distribution of benefits by income classes. However, the document did show that there was a very large number of concessions, that many were very costly, and that they had been growing in both numbers and cost. The document, true to its scholarly approach, even speculated that the existence of budgetary restraint policies in the 1970s had led to an increase in tax expenditures as a means of avoiding the restraint policies.[56] The message implicit in this last comment was picked up by the federal government, which instituted a new budgetary management system (known as the

[55]National Council of Welfare, *The Hidden Welfare System* (1976); *The Hidden Welfare System Revisited* (Ottawa, 1979); Perry, "Fiscal Figures" (1976) 24 *Can. Tax J.* 528; Kesselman, "Non-Business Deductions and Tax Expenditures in Canada: Aggregates and Distributions" (1977) 25 *Can. Tax J.* 160; and Smith, *Tax Expenditures* (Can. Tax Foundation, 1979).

[56]Department of Finance, *Government of Canada Tax Expenditure Account* (1979), 30.

"envelope" system) under which tax expenditures as well as direct expenditures are taken into account in allocating spending limits ("expenditure envelopes") to each area of policy. In 1980, a second "Government of Canada Expenditure Account" reported this new system.

The budget introduced by Finance Minister MacEachen on November 12, 1981 was obviously influenced by the tax expenditure accounts of 1979 and 1980. That budget proposed to eliminate a number of tax preferences. This broadening of the tax base led to a parallel proposal to reduce rates of tax, so that the top marginal rate was to be reduced from approximately 62 per cent (including provincial tax) to approximately 50 per cent. This budget proved to be extremely controversial: the elimination of the tax preferences was vigorously attacked by various business groups. These attacks were so successful that many of the preferences were restored by the government. The lowering of rates, to which no one objected, but which made sense only as a complement to the elimination of the tax preferences, was not altered. The result was that the federal government endured much controversy, looked weak by backing down on many of its budget proposals, and, because of the lowering of rates, ended up with a system that raised less revenue. After this experience, the federal Liberal government lost interest in the removal of tax preferences. Later budgets did not touch any tax preferences and even introduced a few new ones. The government even stopped publishing the tax expenditure accounts: the publications of 1979 and 1980 were not repeated from 1981 to 1984.

In 1984, the Liberal government was defeated and a Progressive Conservative government took office. In 1985, the Department of Finance issued a document entitled "Account of the Cost of Selected Tax Measures", which was essentially an update of the accounts published in 1979 and 1980. Once again, tax expenditures, now described as "selective tax measures", were catalogued and costed. In 1988, in a different political climate, the Progressive Conservative government was able to do what had caused the Liberal government so much grief. The tax reform of 1988 eliminated a number of tax preferences and lowered rates.[57] However, the government did not resume issuing tax expenditure accounts until 1992. Since then, accounts have appeared annually, for the most part[58] and budgets with tax measures have included the related tax expenditures.

(c) — Measurement of tax expenditures

(i) — Difficulties of accounting

There are several difficulties in accounting for tax expenditures. The first is the difficulty of identifying them. How does one distinguish those deductions, credits, or other provisions which really are preferences to particular kinds of income from those provisions which are necessary in order to define net income? The latter class

---

[57]See heading 2.2(g), "Tax reform of 1988", above.

[58]E.g., Department of Finance, Tax Expenditures and Evaluations 2009 which provides tax expenditure estimates for 2004 through 2006 and projections for 2007 through 2009.

of deductions, which include, for example, routine business expenses, are not tax expenditures. But what about childcare expenses (about which there has been a great deal of debate)? As the first (1979) Canadian tax expenditure account pointed out,[59] it is "necessary to define a benchmark tax structure, deviations from which are to be classified as tax expenditures.": It is only after inventing a "benchmark tax structure" (which contains no tax preferences) that it is possible to determine whether a particular tax measure should be classified as a tax preference. The 1979 tax expenditure account[60] in cases of doubt decided to "err on the side of comprehensiveness" and reported doubtful items separately as "memorandum items".[61] This practice continues to this day and childcare expenses are included in this category. Needless to say, disagreement about the inclusion or exclusion of particular controversial items does not impair the usefulness of the bulk of a tax expenditure account.

A second problem concerns the treatment of tax provisions which seek to discourage an activity by taxing it more heavily, for example, the disallowance as a business expense of the cost of advertising in foreign media.[62] These "tax penalties" are departures from the "benchmark tax structure", and should probably be treated as "negative tax expenditures" since they offset some of the revenue lost through positive tax expenditures. The solution of the 1979 tax expenditure account,[63] which has been carried forward in later accounts, was to list such items ("memorandum items") separately from the tax expenditures, but to provide the same information about their revenue impact as was provided for the tax expenditures.

A third problem is estimating the amount of each tax expenditure. The amount consists of the revenue foregone by the tax concession, or, in other words, the extra revenue that would be raised if the tax concession were removed. The tax expenditure accounts estimate the cost "by simulating the change in federal revenues as if that provision alone were eliminated, keeping all other provisions in place",[64] so that the revenue impact is measured by reference to the existing rather than the benchmark tax structure. In fact, if a tax concession were removed, people would alter their behaviour, setting in train a series of changes with various effects on tax revenues. It is likely, therefore, that the full estimated cost of a tax expenditure would not actually be realized in additional tax revenue if the tax expenditure were

[59]Department of Finance, *Government of Canada Tax Expenditure Account* (1979), 4.

[60]*Ibid.*, 11.

[61]Department of Finance, *Government of Canada, Personal and Corporate Tax Expenditures* (1993), 5.

[62]S. 19.1 of the Act.

[63]Department of Finance, *Government of Canada Tax Expenditure Account* (1979), 11.

[64]*Ibid.*, 27.

to be eliminated.[65] In some cases, there is apparently insufficient information about a tax expenditure to enable any estimate to be calculated and this point is noted.[66]

(ii) — Tax expenditure estimates

Table 2-2 below contains the figures from Department of Finance's most recently published list of revenue losses for selected major personal income tax expenditures):[67]

Table 2-2

	2004	2005	2006	2007	2008	2009
				$ millions		
Charitable donation credit	2,000	2,260	2,480	2,495	2,380	2,380
Employment credit	-	-	470	1,785	1,860	1,880
Employee stock options	725	945	1,085	1,160	745	830
Basic credit	22,865	23,410	24,340	25,710	26,190	27,770
Spouse credit	1,195	1,205	1,205	1,285	1,305	1,420
Spouse equivalent credit[1]	665	665	675	730	740	765
Non-taxation of employer paid health benefits	2,155	2,170	2,310	2,490	2,620	2,710
Age Credit	1,490	1,400	1,810	1,735	1,850	2,185
Principal Residences	2,555	3,465	4,325	5,460	3,485	3,115

(d) — Different policy criteria

Tax expenditure analysis treats tax expenditures as if they were direct expenditures. Looking at provisions of the Act in this way, it is not appropriate to criticize them as violating tax equity or tax neutrality or eroding the tax base. These tax-policy criteria would not be used to criticize a direct expenditure, and they should not be used to criticize a tax expenditure either. Tax expenditure analysis assumes a benchmark tax structure that is equitable, neutral and comprehensive. The tax expenditure is then analyzed on its merits as if it were a separate assistance programme by asking three questions: How much does it cost? Does it fulfil its objectives? Who benefits from it?[68]

---

[65]This point is regularly acknowledged in the Department of Finance's tax expenditure accounts.

[66]For additional points, see Boadway, R, "Policy Forum: The Annual Tax Expenditure Accounts — A Critique," *2007 Can. Tax. J.*, Vol. 55 No. 1. and *Tax Expenditures and Public Policy in Comparative Perspective*, Can. Tax. Found., forthcoming.

[67]This table shows estimates and projections of tax expenditures by some of the major items. For a complete list of tax expenditures, see Department of Finance, Tax Expenditures and Evaluations 2009, Table 1. The spouse equivalent credit is also called the eligible dependant credit.

[68]The objectives of tax expenditures (taken from budget documents, speeches and other sources) were listed for the first time in Department of Finance, *Government of Canada Tax Expenditures* (1998).

The general thrust of tax expenditure analysis is to discourage policy-makers from using the tax system as the policy instrument for programmes of social assistance because of the following flaws: (1) the upside-down effect of tax deductions and the failure of either deductions or credits (except refundable credits) to help those without any taxable income; (2) the difficulty of estimating the cost and effects of a tax expenditure;[69] (3) the virtual impossibility of limiting the size of a tax expenditure by placing a "cap" on it; (4) the administrative problems caused by entrusting diverse social programmes to the tax administration instead of to more appropriate departments or agencies (whose budgets would reflect the cost); (5) the complexity which is introduced into the Act and to the tax returns which individuals must prepare; and (6) the erosion of public confidence in the fairness of the income tax when it is known that so many groups are allowed concessions or "loopholes".[70]

These flaws in the design of tax-expenditure programmes are serious, but a balanced view would have to concede that direct-expenditure programmes have their disadvantages as well. They too are often not easy to control effectively. They require a costly bureaucracy to administer them. In many cases, direct expenditures are discretionary, in the sense that officials must pass judgment on the qualifications of applicants or even choose between qualified applicants. Discretion has its merit, since in principle it enables assistance to be directed to where it is most needed. But discretion carries with it the danger that the administrators will succumb to pressures from members of Parliament and lobbyists of various kinds so that the administration will not be as fair as it ought to be. The provisions of the Act typically involve little discretion on the part of officials: the rules are set down in black and white and are administered with total indifference to political pressures.[71] The administration of social assistance programs through the tax system might actually be cost-effective compared to the direct expenditure alternative, especially if separate bureaucracies were set up to administer each program.

---

[69]Examples of failures in the design of tax expenditures are the deductions for Multiple Unit Residential Buildings (MURBs), which were discontinued in 1981, and the Scientific Research Tax Credits (SRTCs), which were discontinued in 1993. Both programmes were extremely costly. The former led to the subsidization of the builders of luxury apartment buildings. The latter were successfully claimed by companies who did not actually do any scientific research.

[70]In the *1994 Report of the Auditor General*, vol. 16, ch. 32, 22, the Auditor General pointed out that, despite the development of tax expenditure accounts, the monitoring, evaluation and reporting was still inferior to that applied to direct expenditures. He commented: "It is difficult, if not impossible, for Parliament to hold the government accountable for this spending through the tax system when it does not have proper information".

[71]Needless to say, tax expenditures can be designed to be conditional upon the exercise of some official discretion, and direct expenditures can be made non-discretionary.

2.5 — Tax policy-making

(a) — Politics versus principles

The process of making tax policy is inherently political. As the history of the tax system illustrates, the tax provisions in force today reflect yesterday's political compromises. According to the public choice theory, voters, politicians and political parties are primarily motivated out of self-interest and predicts that they will select taxes and other policies that maximize their utility.[72] Political parties favour policies that get them re-elected. Voters favour policies that maximize the benefits they get from government expenditures and minimize the taxes they have to pay. They may also favour some forms of taxes over others for psychological and ideological reasons. Overall, however, voters are "rationally ignorant" as it takes time and effort to understand issues (especially if they are complex) and the probability of an individual's vote actually affecting the election's outcome is negligible. Voters' psychological and ideological preferences are often more important than a complete understanding of the issues and the likely consequences of a party's policies unless the policies affect a voter's immediate interests.

Many tax reform proposals are made by political parties in connection with election campaigns. For example, the federal government's recent proposals to provide tax breaks to seniors (pension income credit and pension income splitting) are largely politically motivated. By targeting tax measures to voters who are relatively well-informed and organized (like senior citizens) is politically efficient. The political costs are less when they are dispersed widely among voters who don't organize because they don't have sufficiently common interests: "*a systematic tendency for 'exploitation' of the great by the small!*".[73] Levying taxes to protect the environment has also become accepted by the public. The "green levies" on automobiles introduced in the 2006 federal budget did not meet with much public outcry. Taxes on pollution have become a "sin" tax, like taxes on alcohol and tobacco and voters don't mind 'sin' taxes.

Political motivations also explain why all political parties like to provide tax subsidies and expenditures through the tax system. Even through the economic effect of the myriad of tax breaks is probably the same as lowering taxes in general, the government and voters much prefer tax breaks. For example, instead of keeping college and university tuition fees low by increasing the direct funding received by universities, the federal and provincial governments have chosen to direct the funding to students through student loan and low-income grant programs and through the tax system (though Registered Education Savings Plans, by not taxing scholar-

---

[72]See, for example, Gillespie, *Tax, Borrow and Spend: Financing Federal Spending in Canada*, 1867-1900 (Carleton University Press, 1991) and Hartle, "Some Analytical, Political and Normative Lessons from Carter" in Brooks, ed., *The Quest for Tax Reform* (Carswell, 1988) This is not to say that voters, politicians and political parties do not have altruistic, ethical or ideological motivations. It just means that their primary motivation is self-interest.

[73]Olson, *The Logic of Collective Action: Public Goods and the Theory of Groups*, (Harvard Univeristy Press, 1971) at 29.

ships and bursaries and by providing tuition, education, textbook and student loan interest credits). Voters prefer this: some may think that colleges and universities waste funds that are given to them, others may think that not everyone should go to college or university and that only the very best students and low-income students should be supported and that parents who save for this should be supported.

Despite the political nature of tax policymaking, principles remain fundamentally important. Major tax reforms have been based on adherence to fundamental principles of equity, neutrality and efficiency, although it is hard to adhere to all principles at the same time. For example, capital gains became taxable in 1972 for equity and neutrality reasons. In spite of the arguments that capital gains taxation adversely impacts entrepreneurship and savings and the proportion of taxable capital gains has changed over the years, capital gains remain taxable for the most part.[74] The perennial debate about the amount of personal income tax paid by high income Canadians also demonstrates that principles do matter in Canadian tax policy debates.

(b) — Progressive or flat tax rates

(i) — Progressive rates

As explained earlier, the reason for progressive tax rates is the idea of tax equity: a taxpayer's liability to tax should be based on his or her ability to pay. A person with a low income needs all or most of the income simply to survive. A person with a high income can provide for necessities and have a substantial amount left over. The taxpayer's ability to pay taxes is determined by the amount of income available for discretionary use. In general, the greater the total income, the higher is the fraction of that income which is available for discretionary use. The ability to pay principle dictates not merely that upper-income taxpayers should pay more dollars in tax than lower-income taxpayers, but that upper-income taxpayers should pay a greater proportion of their income in tax than lower-income taxpayers. This conclusion necessitates a progressive rate schedule. The personal income tax is particularly adaptable to the graduated rates which make it progressive. That is because the taxpayer cannot usually shift the tax to others.[75] It can be designed to take account of the personal circumstances of each taxpayer, and in particular the total amount of the taxpayer's income, his or her family circumstances, and other factors which bear on the taxpayer's ability to pay.

---

[74]Exceptions exist for principal residences and charitable gifts of public company stock and environmentally sensitive land.

[75]A personal income tax is called a "direct tax". This can be contrasted with an "indirect" tax. An indirect tax is levied on producers, importers or sellers in the expectation that they will pass it on to their customers in the form of higher prices for their products. An indirect tax cannot take account of the individual circumstances of the widely dispersed and unascertained class of people who will ultimately bear the tax, and so customs and excise duties and sales taxes tend to take the form of flat-rate charges on the value of each article or transaction which is taxed.

A subsidiary advantage of a progressive rate structure is that it has a stabilizing effect on the economy. In a time of economic decline, tax receipts are reduced disproportionately to the decline in taxable incomes, thereby helping to sustain disposable income and bolster consumer expenditures. In a time of economic expansion, tax receipts increase more than proportionately to the increase in taxable incomes, thereby acting as a brake on consumer expenditures. In this way, the tax system tends to restrain contractions or expansions of economic activity.[76]

There has been considerable debate of the question whether a progressive rate structure provides a disincentive to work. On the one hand, it is reasonable to expect that the incentive to work would decline as the after-tax return from work declines, creating a preference for leisure. On the other hand, it is also reasonable to expect that the reduction in disposable income which is caused by the income tax creates an incentive to work longer and harder to make up some of the lost income. It is hard to know what the net effect of these competing pulls will be on any given individual. Of course, most individuals have little choice as to their hours of work and cannot give effect to their preferences anyway. For those who do control their hours of work many influences other than after-tax monetary returns affect their decisions to work, for example, job satisfaction, power and prestige. Empirical studies suggest that the income tax has little effect on the total supply of labour in the economy.[77]

There is also room for debate about whether a progressive rate structure provides a disincentive to enterprise (risk-taking). On the one hand, it is reasonable to expect that the incentive to take risks would decline when any profits have to be shared with the government. On the other hand, since the tax system allows losses to be deducted, it is also reasonable to expect that the sharing of losses with the government would increase the incentive to take risks. As is the case with the propensity to work, the propensity to take risks seems to be pulled in opposite directions by a progressive tax structure. It seems likely that the income tax has little effect on the total amount of risk-taking in the economy.

Even if it can be said that a progressive income tax has little effect on the aggregate amount of work or risk-taking in the economy, it should not be assumed that it is entirely neutral. Individual taxpayers may well have reduced or increased their efforts as the result of the rising rates of tax. Even if the reductions are roughly balanced by the increases, so that the aggregate of effort is unchanged, there is still some distortion in the allocation of resources. As well, a progressive income tax diverts effort into attempts to avoid paying the higher rates of tax. Income splitting is the most obvious direct consequence of progressive rates.[78] Efforts to receive

---

[76]See Carter Report, note 4, above, vol. 3, p. 243.

[77]See generally; Rosen and others, *Public Finance in Canada*, (1999), ch. 21; Salyzyn, *Canadian Income Tax Policy* (4th ed., 1990), 221-224; Goode, The Individual Income Tax (1976), ch. 4; and Babey and others, "Effects of the personal income tax on work effort: a sample survey" (1978) 26 Can. Tax J. 582.

[78]See ch. 13, Income Splitting, below.

tax-free forms of income, for example, fringe benefits,[79] or less heavily taxed forms of income, for example, capital gains,[80] are also stimulated by high marginal rates. It is probably fair to conclude that many forms of tax avoidance would be abandoned if all income were taxed at a single, relatively low, flat rate. However, this consideration is not sufficient, in the view of most tax theorists, to outweigh the case for equity and progressive rates.

(ii) — Flat rate

Proponents of a flat rate usually rely on arguments based on neutrality, especially the disincentives to work and enterprise (discussed in the previous section) that are supposed to be created by progressive rates. The incentive to tax avoidance (also discussed in the previous section) is another argument against the progressive system. A flat-rate system would be somewhat simpler since complexities such as indexing, anti-income-splitting measures and the conversion of deductions to credits would not be needed in a flat-rate system. As for equity, the proponents of a flat-rate system would acknowledge the need for exemption of the lowest-income individuals, which of course makes the flat-rate system mildly progressive. Aside from this low-income exemption, the argument is that considerations based on ability to pay do not outweigh the advantages of a flat rate.

An argument for a flat rate can be framed in terms of fiscal accountability. According to this argument, the public (most of whom are not rich) accedes to increased governmental spending on the assumption that someone else (the rich) will pay for it. If taxes were levied at a single flat rate, it would be obvious to everyone (so the argument goes) that increases in spending would cause increases in everyone's taxes. Therefore, there would be a greater sense of shared responsibility for the expenses of government, and politicians would be required to be more prudent in their spending decisions.

Another argument for a flat rate proceeds from an assumption that taxes are really the purchase by taxpayers of governmental services. Since the most expensive governmental services, such as defence, criminal justice, education, medical care and highways are provided to all citizens, regardless of income, in roughly similar quantities, it follows that high-income individuals should not have to pay at a higher rate than low-income individuals. This is the most radical argument for a flat rate, because it rejects the proposition that equity favours a system based on the taxpayer's ability to pay. On the contrary, since the benefit of governmental services is not correlated to ability to pay, it is inequitable to base taxes on ability to pay. The difficulty with this argument is that there is no agreement on how the benefits of governmental services are distributed. At one extreme, it could be argued that the rich receive less than their fair share, because of their ability to purchase private alternatives to many governmental services such as public education, public transit, public parks and facilities; and of course they have no need for

---

[79]See ch. 5, Income from Employment, below.

[80]See ch. 10, Capital Gains, below.

the costly array of income-support programmes. At the other end of the political spectrum, it would be argued that the rich receive the enormous benefit of the protection of their wealth and power, and expenditures to the poor are really for the benefit of the rich — they are palliatives to forestall the revolution.

(iii) — Flattening the rates

Support for a flat rate has mostly been academic. Since the early 1980s, however, the ascendancy of conservative politics has revived interest in the idea. This has not yet led to the adoption of a flat rate in any of the English-speaking countries, but it did cause governments in the United States, the United Kingdom, Australia and New Zealand to move to flatter rate structures. Canada was not immune from these influences. The rates were significantly flattened since 1988.

From 1966 to 1971, the federal tax rates rose to a top marginal rate of 80 per cent, which was reached when taxable income exceeded $400,000. From 1972 to 1987, the top rate of federal tax became 47 per cent, which was reached at a taxable income of $60,000. In Ontario, when the federal rates were grossed-up by the provincial rate of tax, the top combined rate was 61 per cent; it was higher in most other provinces.[81] The tax reform of 1988 substantially altered the rate structure of the Act, reducing the total number of tax brackets from ten to three and reducing the top federal rate to 29 per cent. The reform in 2001 reduced the rates in these three brackets and added a fourth bracket. Taking into account Ontario's 2010 top rate of provincial tax plus surtaxes, the top rate of tax paid by taxpayers in Ontario is 46.41 per cent.

---

[81]There was a reduction in federal rates in 1977, but this was in part the consequence of new federal-provincial tax-sharing arrangements; provincial rates rose at the same time, and combined rates did not change much.

3
RESIDENCE

3.1 — Jurisdiction to tax

A country may wish to tax everyone in the world but it generally confines its taxes to people who have some connection with the country. It would be impossible for Canada to enforce a tax against people lacking any connection with Canada. Even if it were possible, there is no moral justification for forcing such people to help finance Canada's government. Canada, like every other country, has to employ some factor or factors to identify the class of people liable to pay Canadian income tax. Residence and source of income are the two most common factors, although residence is the dominant factor — the topic of this chapter.[1]

(a) — Residence

Residence is the principal connecting factor used for Canadian income tax purposes. It emphasizes the social and economic connections between a person and the taxing jurisdiction. The factor of residence, it would be argued, produces the largest class of taxpayers with strong social and economic ties with Canada. Canadian residents benefit from the public expenditures financed with tax revenues and thus have a moral obligation to finance the government; and they are all people against whom enforcement is practicable. It is probably the best of all the alternatives, although the taxation of a resident alien (who cannot vote) can be criticized as "taxation without representation", and the concept of residence (as we shall see) is far from precise.

Citizenship and domicile are two alternatives to residence that are used by other countries in determining tax jurisdiction. Citizenship (or nationality) is used by the United States (but not by Canada and most other countries). The factor of citizenship emphasizes the political connection between a person and the taxing jurisdiction. The argument for using this factor is that even citizens living outside the United States are entitled to protection by the U.S. government. Moreover, citizenship enables the taxing country to tax those of its citizens who have moved to tax havens such as the Bahamas or Bermuda (although such people could change their citizenship, and, even if they did not, enforcement would be difficult). The disadvantage of citizenship is that it would sweep in many people whose economic and social links with the taxing country had become very tenuous, and it would exclude many people living permanently in the taxing country. That is why the United States also taxes aliens who are residents in the United States.[2]

Domicile is used as a connecting factor in the United Kingdom. The concept of "domicile" is encrusted with archaic and often artificial rules. A person's "domicile of origin" (which is determined at birth, usually by the father's domicile) and a person's "domicile of dependence" (under which a married woman assumes the domicile of her husband) may bear little relationship to a person's actual permanent home. Even a person's "domicile of choice", which involves residing in a country with the intention of remaining there permanently, is not an entirely satisfactory criterion for taxation: the element of intention raises difficult questions of proof and excludes people who may be longstanding residents of the taxing country, even though they lack the intention to stay permanently.

---

[1]For further discussion of this issue, see Li, *International Taxation in the Age of Electronic Commerce: A Comparative Study* (2003), ch. 3; and Li, Cockfield and Wilkie, *International Taxation in Canada: Principles and Practices* (2007), ch. 4.

[2]For an overview of the United States international income tax system, see Doernberg, *International Taxation in a Nutshell* (5th ed.).

(b) — Source of income

Canada also uses source of income as a jurisdictional basis for taxation and imposes tax on non-residents having Canadian source income. A source-based tax is imposed by other countries as well. It is relatively easy to assess and enforce because non-residents generally have capital assets or physical presence in the host country. Because non-residents benefit from the public infrastructure provided by the host country in earning their income, they are expected to contribute to the public fisc through taxation.

However, source alone is not a satisfactory basis for an equitable income tax for other taxpayers, because taxing only Canadian source income does not take into consideration each taxpayer's total ability to pay. If source was the only basis of taxation in Canada, wealthy taxpayers would be able to arrange to earn their income from several different countries and thereby obtain all the advantages of splitting income. The "ability to pay" principle excludes source as the sole or primary basis of income tax liability because the ability to pay can only be measured on the basis of each taxpayer's entire world income.

(c) — Theoretical justifications

There are several theoretical and policy justifications for the taxation of international income on the basis of residence and the source of income. They include economic allegiance theory, benefit theory, the ability to pay principle, enforceability of tax collection.

The doctrine of economic allegiance was considered a starting point for modern international tax theory and administration.[3] The doctrine suggests that countries should be entitled to tax cross-border transactions if a taxpayer has a sufficient economic connection with the taxing country. To determine whether this connection exists, tax theorists have asked questions such as: (1) where is the value-added economic activity taking place? (2) where are the suppliers of capital located? and (3) where are consumers of goods and services located? The answer to the first question is relevant to source-based taxation, and the answer to the other two questions points to residence-based taxation.

The benefit theory is perhaps one of the most obvious arguments for exercising tax jurisdiction. Under this theory, those who benefit from the public services provided by a country should be charged for such services. In the context of corporate income tax, such benefits may be seen in the way of reducing the cost of production, or enhancing the profitability.[4] Income taxes could be viewed as "the prior claim of the state upon the private profits which public expenditures or the business environment maintained by the state have in part produced."[5] This theory justifies the taxa-

[3] Li, note 1 above, 60.

[4] Adams, "The Taxation of Business," *Proceedings of the Eleventh Annual Conference on Taxation*, National Tax Association, 1917, 185.

[5] *Ibid.*, at 192.

tion of residents as well as the taxation of domestic source income earned by non-residents.

The ability to pay principle is the foundation of progressive personal income taxation in Canada and other countries. Adam Smith has been credited with the earliest rendering of this theory. The first of his four famous canons regarding taxes is that "[t]he subjects of every state ought to contribute towards the support of the government, as nearly as possible, in proportion to their respective abilities."[6] As explained further in chapter 4, the ability to pay is measured by net income. This definition is the foundation of the "comprehensive income tax base" recommended by the Carter Report. The concept of ability to pay is inherently global — the income of a resident must include income earned from both domestic and foreign sources.[7] The taxation of Canadian residents on their worldwide income is consistent with this principle.

Both residence and source of income can be justified on grounds of enforceability, although source-based taxes are generally easier to collect. For example, Canadian tax on investment income (dividend, interest, rent or royalties) earned by non-residents is typically withheld by resident payers; Canadian tax on business income or employment income earned by non-residents can be collected because the taxpayer or the taxpayer's business assets are often in Canada. The collection of a residence-based tax is possible because the taxpayer has significant social and economic ties with Canada. However, it is more difficult to enforce than source-based taxation. Taxpayers may not accurately report their foreign income on their tax returns and it is very difficult for the tax administration to obtain and verify tax information in respect of offshore activities.

3.2 — Principles of worldwide taxation

(a) — Legal basis

Subsection 2(1) of the *Income Tax Act* (the "Act") provides that an income tax is payable on the taxable income of every person resident in Canada at any time of the year. The definition of "taxable income" in subsection 2(2) points to the definition of "income" in section 3. Income under section 3 is income "from a source inside or outside Canada" for the year. In other words, Canadian residents are liable for Canadian tax on their world income.

In contrast, a non-resident person is taxable in Canada only on income derived from Canadian sources, such as income from employment in Canada, carrying on business in Canada or the disposition of taxable Canadian property (under subsection 2(3) of Part I of the Act), and passive investment income-such as dividends, interest, rents or royalties-and other specified amounts — such as pension benefits and distributions from a trust (under Part XIII of the Act).

---

[6]Smith, *An Inquiry into the Nature and Causes of the Wealth of Nations* (Edwin Cannan ed., Methuen & Co. 1925) (1776), 310.

[7]*Report of the Royal Commission on Taxation* (Carter Report) (1966), 503.

In order to implement the principle of worldwide taxation, Canadian residents must report their foreign income accurately on their tax returns and the government must have the ability to verify taxpayers' information. Obtaining information on offshore income is particularly difficult if the foreign country has bank secrecy laws. Exchange of information between the Canadian government and foreign government is only possible if there is a tax treaty between Canada and the other country. The 2007 Federal Budget proposed that Canada will enter into Tax Information Exchange Agreements with some "tax haven" countries.

(b) — International double taxation

One important corollary of the worldwide income taxation principle is the potential double taxation of foreign income earned by Canadian residents. Foreign income is generally subject to tax in the foreign source country pursuant to that country's tax rules. The foreign tax thus constitutes an additional layer of tax imposed on the foreign income. Although taxpayers can often structure their foreign activities by minimizing foreign taxes or at least ensuring that foreign taxes are imposed instead, rather than on top, of Canadian tax, double taxation is a problem for taxpayers. Many taxpayers earn income in countries whose tax rates are comparable to or higher than Canadian tax rates.

The Act allows taxpayers to eliminate double taxation to the extent that foreign tax does not exceed Canadian tax otherwise payable. If foreign tax exceeds Canadian tax, the taxpayer is subject to additional tax on foreign income. Canadian tax treaties also provide relief from double taxation.

(c) — Avoiding Canadian tax through the use of foreign corporations and trusts

The principle of worldwide taxation of Canadian residents can be circumvented by Canadian residents through the use of foreign corporations or offshore trusts because a corporation or trust is taxed as a separate entity whose residence is determined separately (see below) and whose income is taxed separately from its legal owners. In the absence of anti-avoidance rules, Canadian taxation of foreign income can be deferred through the use of foreign corporations and other entities. The value of the tax deferral is tremendous if the foreign corporation or trust is located in a tax haven.

The anti-deferral rules in sections 91 to 95 are highly technical and extremely complex. It is beyond the scope of this book to fully discuss them. However, it is important to appreciate that these rules and the foreign reporting rules in sections 233.2 to 233.7 (which require taxpayers to identify foreign holdings) are designed to protect the Canadian tax base by ensuring that foreign investment income earned by Canadian residents is taxable in Canada, whether or not it is earned through an investment in a non-resident corporation or trust.

3.3 — Residence of individuals

(a) — Common law residence

Given the importance of the concept of residence, one might expect to find an exhaustive definition of this term in the Act. Such definition does not exist. The Act simply deems certain individuals to be residents in certain circumstances, leaving the meaning of residence to be defined in the common law. As Justice Rand of the Supreme Court of Canada stated in *Thomson v. M.N.R.* (1946):[8]

> It is quite impossible to give it a precise and inclusive definition. It is highly flexible, and its many shades of meaning vary not only in the contexts of different matters, but also in different aspects of the same matter.

Instead, there are a plethora of cases defining the meaning of residence. The Courts have held "residence" to be "a matter of the degree to which a person in mind and fact settles into or maintains or centralizes his ordinary mode of living with its accessories in social relations, interests and conveniences at or in the place in question."[9] Ultimately, the common law test is based on the facts and circumstances of the case.

The leading case on the residence of an individual is *Thomson*.[10] In this case, the taxpayer, a wealthy Canadian citizen who had gone to a lot of trouble to give up Canadian residence, was held nonetheless to be a resident of Canada. In 1923, he sold his home in New Brunswick, announced that Bermuda was now his residence, and went to Bermuda. In the following years, he actually spent very little time in Bermuda, mainly living in the United States, where he built a house which was kept permanently ready for occupancy and where he spent most of his time. Starting in 1932, he began to regularly return to New Brunswick for four or five of the warmer months every year, and he eventually built a house there which was kept available all year long. Every year, however, he kept his stay in New Brunswick to less than 183 days (to avoid the sojourning rule).[11] The taxpayer's wife and child accompanied him in these regular migrations. The Supreme Court of Canada, by a majority, held that the taxpayer was resident in Canada. Rand J., who wrote the principal opinion, said that the taxpayer's time in Canada was not a temporary "stay" or "visit":[12]

> His living in Canada is substantially as deep rooted and settled as in the United States. In terms of time [the United States] may take precedence but at best it is a case of *primus inter pares*. He is [in Canada] as at his "home"; and the mere limitation of time does not qualify that fact. ... That brings him within the most exacting of any reasonable interpretation of "resides" or "ordinarily resident.

---

[8][1946] S.C.R. 209 at 224, [1946] C.T.C. 51 63–4, 2 D.T.C. 812 815 (S.C.C.).

[9]Interpretation Bulletin IT-221R3, "Determination of an individual's residence status" (2002), para. 2.

[10]Note 8 above.

[11]See heading 3.4(c), "Sojourner", below.

[12]Note 8, above, 268, 64, and 817, respectively.

Taschereau J., who dissented, held that the taxpayer was "a resident of the United States, making occasional visits to Canada".[13]

Several points emerge from the *Thomson* case. First, the intention of the taxpayer, while obviously relevant in determining the "settled routine" of a taxpayer's life, is not determinative. In *Thomson* (as in many other cases), it was the external facts as to his customary mode of life which persuaded the Court that his home was in Canada, notwithstanding his intention not to be resident in Canada. Second, a person can be resident in more than one country at the same time. In *Thomson*, it was clear that the Court thought that the taxpayer was resident in the United States as well as in Canada (he was in fact being taxed in the United States as a resident).[14] Third, every person is presumed to be resident somewhere:[15]

> For the purposes of income tax legislation, it must be assumed that every person has at all times a residence. It is not necessary to this that he should have a home or a particular place of abode or even a shelter. He may sleep in the open. It is important only to ascertain the spatial bounds within which he spends his life or to which his ordered or customary living is related.

Although Rand J. points out in the above statement that a taxpayer may not have a home, the homeless rarely raise issues of income tax. It is "the peripatetic lifestyle of the leisurely wealthy"[16] that raises residence questions. Such people usually have at least one home. The country in which the taxpayer makes his or her home will be "the place where he, in the settled routine of his life, regularly, normally or customarily lives". The availability of a place where the taxpayer has the right to stay is usually the critical element in determining the country of residence, although the courts will look at other factors as well, such as the frequency and duration of visits, and the presence of social and business connections. The object of the exercise, though, is to identify the country in which the taxpayer is resident. If more than one country is indicated, the courts will not hesitate to find a person to be resident in more than one country. Nor is there anything surprising in the proposition that a person may be resident in more than one country — although it is rarely desirable from a tax standpoint.

As indicated in the discussion of *Thomson* above, the common law has established that several factors are important in determining whether an individual is resident in Canada but none are conclusive.

The maintenance of a *dwelling in Canada* available for occupation by the taxpayer, which is a key factor in the *Thomson* case. It is regarded by the CRA as the most

---

[13] *Ibid.*, 220, 60, and 822, respectively.

[14] The tax treaty between Canada and the United States now has rules for allocating to one country or the other a taxpayer who is resident in both countries.

[15] Note 8 above, 224-5, 64 and 815-6, respectively.

[16] *R. v. Reeder*, [1975] C.T.C. 256 260, 75 D.T.C. 5160 5162 (Fed. T.D.).

significant factor in determining whether a taxpayer has ceased to be a resident of Canada.[17]

Another factor is whether the taxpayer's spouse and children are residents of Canada. The relevance of having a spouse and children resident in Canada varies, depending on the other facts of the taxpayer's situation. One example is the *Allchin v. R.* case.[18] In this case, the taxpayer worked in the United States from 1992 to 1997. During this period she stayed with relatives and friends while her husband and two children lived in Canada. She also set up a U.S. bank account, arranged for her credit card bills to be sent to a U.S. address and attempted to move her family to the U.S. by retaining the services of an immigration lawyer. The Tax Court concluded that the taxpayer remained a Canadian resident during the years 1993 to 1995 because of the temporary nature of her accommodation and due to her continuing ties to Canada: her husband and children, her Ontario driver's license, her OHIP (Ontario health insurance) coverage, a club membership, and the fact that her husband swore in an affidavit when he purchased a house that his wife was a resident of Canada. Subsequently, however, the taxpayer was successful in arguing that she was a resident in the United States under the tie-breaker rules in the Canada-United States tax treaty.[19]

In contrast to *Allchin*, in *Shih v. R.*[20] and *Schujahn v. M.N.R.*,[21] the fact that the spouse and children stayed in Canada did not make the taxpayer who was living and working outside Canada a Canadian resident. In *Shih*, the primary reason for the spouse and children to stay in Canada was for the children to receive Canadian education and in *Schujahn*, the primary reason for the spouse and child to remain in Canada after the taxpayer had left Canada was to facilitate the sale of their house in Canada. One possible explanation is that, in these two cases, the taxpayers were originally non-Canadian residents and came to Canada temporarily, whereas the taxpayer in *Allchin* was trying to abandon Canadian residency.

---

[17]IT-221R3, note 9 above, para. 6.

[18][2003] 4 C.T.C. 2702, 2003 D.T.C. 935 (T.C.C.).

[19]See *Allchin v. R.*, [2005] 2 C.T.C. 2701, 2005 D.T.C. 603 (T.C.C.).

[20][2000] 2 C.T.C. 2921, 2000 D.T.C. 2072 (T.C.C.). In *Shih*, the taxpayer immigrated to Canada with his wife and three sons, purchased a home in Canada and returned to Taiwan to work in the same year. He visited Canada annually to see his family but his stays did not exceed 59 days in any given year. He had several residential ties to Taiwan: other family members; a job which he had held for 25 years; a house which he owned; various memberships; a driver's license and bank accounts. Based on these facts, the Court concluded that the taxpayer was a resident in Taiwan. The Court went on to inquire whether the taxpayer had a dual residence. The Court held that the taxpayer's connections with Canada (his house and wife and sons) were not strong enough to make him a resident of Canada. The taxpayer's primary reason for having a connection to Canada was to educate his children.

[21][1962] C.T.C. 364, 62 D.T.C. 1225 (Can. Ex. Ct.). This case is discussed in more detail in the text surrounding note 62 below.

For individuals attempting to abandon Canadian residence, the following factors are often relevant. First, the length of time during which the taxpayer is physically present in Canada.[22] Second, the taxpayer's ties to another country may be relevant factors. The assumption is that an individual must be resident somewhere at all times. If the taxpayer cannot establish to the satisfaction of the court that he or she is resident in a foreign country, the taxpayer may be considered a Canadian resident if he or she has ties to Canada.[23] However, the opposite is not true: the fact that an individual is a resident of another country does not mean that he or she cannot also be considered a resident of Canada (a dual resident).[24] Third, the taxpayer's social and economic ties with Canada. These ties include ownership of property (e.g., furniture, clothing, automobile, bank accounts, credit cards, etc.), club memberships, family, medical insurance coverage in Canada, and professional or other memberships in Canada (on a resident basis). Finally, the taxpayer's intention to return to Canada[25] and the failure to pay tax or file tax returns in a foreign country[26] could be relevant as well.

In cases where taxpayers are motivated to abandon their Canadian residence by moving to countries with lower taxes and warmer temperatures, the judge must determine if the taxpayer has sufficiently cut his or her ties with Canada to become a non-resident. In *Hauser v. R.*,[27] for example, an Air Canada pilot did not sufficiently "divorce" himself from Canada when moving to the Bahamas. Judge Rip of the Tax Court remarked:[28]

> Canada was a magnet that attracted the Hausers. After they set up residence in the Bahamas both of Mr. and Mrs. Hauser, and particularly Mr. Hauser, continued to have a presence in Canada. Mr. Hauser spent over a third of a year in Canada each year. Air Canada required Mr. Hauser to be in Canada to fly airplanes; he reported to work at Pearson Airport and other airports in Canada. Most of his flights left from and returned to Pearson; much of his training was at Pearson. Pearson Airport was part of the routine of life. Mr. Hauser's presence in Canada during the years in ap-

---

[22] *Thomson*, note 8 above, is an example.

[23] In *Ferguson v. Minister of National Revenue*, [1989] 2 C.T.C. 2387, 89 D.T.C. 634 (T.C.C.), the taxpayer was held to be a Canadian resident because the Court was not satisfied that he had established residence in Saudi Arabia.

[24] IT-221R3, note 9 above, para. 17.

[25] E.g., *Glow v. M.N.R.*, [1992] 2 C.T.C. 245, 92 D.T.C. 6467 (Fed. T.D.). The *Beament* decision emphasizes that intention is not the crucial factor in determining residence. In this case, the taxpayer always regarded his absence from Canada as temporary and intended to return. Nevertheless, he was held not to be a resident until his actual return. See also *Allchin* (in which the taxpayer was held to be a dual resident and the tie-breaker rules assigned her residency to the United States) note 18, above: the facts were similar and, in each case, the taxpayer did not intend to return to Canada.

[26] *R. v. Sherwood*, [1978] C.T.C. 713, 78 D.T.C. 6470 (Fed. T.D.).

[27] [2005] 4 C.T.C. 2260, 2005 D.T.C. 1151 (T.C.C. [General Procedure]); affirmed [2006] 4 C.T.C. 193, 2006 D.T.C. 6447 (Eng.) (F.C.A.).

[28] *Ibid.*, para. 58.

> peal was not occasional, casual, deviatory, intermittent or transitory. He was in Canada in great part because he had to be, to earn a living.

(b) — Ordinarily resident

Subsection 250(3) provides that: "a person resident in Canada includes a person who was at the relevant time ordinarily resident in Canada". This provision is often alluded to in the cases, but it is doubtful whether it adds anything to the common law. As Rand J. said in *Thomson*, if the common law concept of residence is given its full significance, "ordinarily resident" becomes "superfluous".[29]

However, subsection 250(3) can be relied upon together with the common law test to determine whether a person who has been absent from Canada for a significant period of time retains his or her Canadian residence. It reinforces the proposition that a temporary absence from Canada (even one lasting more than one or two years) does not necessarily involve a loss of Canadian residence.

Many people planning a temporary but lengthy period of absence from Canada, for example, on a transfer outside Canada, an exchange of jobs, a sabbatical leave or even an extended holiday, would like to establish non-resident status for Canadian tax purposes. However, unless an individual severs all significant residential ties with Canada (i.e., dwelling place, spouse or common-law partner and dependants) upon leaving the country, the CRA will generally consider the individual to remain a Canadian resident.[30] The CRA's position is supported by a number of cases, including a series of "sabbatical" cases decided by the Tax Review Board in 1980.[31] In each case, a university professor who had left Canada for up to one year on sabbatical leave was held to have retained his resident status. In each case, the professor had leased his home in Canada but had not severed all residential ties during his leave, and he had resumed teaching duties on returning to Canada.

Similar decisions were reached in some recent cases where the taxpayer left Canada for work in other countries. In *McFadyen v. R.*,[32] the taxpayer moved to Japan with his wife, who accepted a position at the Canadian embassy there. The taxpayer lived in Japan for three years and was employed there at various times. While in Japan, he obtained a certificate of residency of Japan. The Tax Court of Canada came to the conclusion that the taxpayer maintained ties with Canada that were

---

[29] Note 8, above, 226, 65, and 816, respectively.

[30] IT-221R3, note 9, above, paras. 4 and 6.

[31] *Saunders v. M.N.R.*, [1980] C.T.C. 2436, 80 D.T.C. 1392 (T.R.B.); *Mash v. M.N.R.*, [1980] C.T.C. 2443, 80 D.T.C. 1396 (T.R.B.); *Brinkerhoff v. M.N.R.*, [1980] C.T.C. 2441, 80 D.T.C. 1398 (T.R.B.); *Breskey v. M.N.R.*, [1980] C.T.C. 2445, 80 D.T.C. 1400 (T.R.B.); and *Magee v. M.N.R.*, [1980] C.T.C. 2450, 80 D.T.C. 1403 (T.R.B.).

[32] *McFadyen v. R.*, 2000 D.T.C. 2473, [2000] 4 C.T.C. 2573 (T.C.C. [General Procedure]); confirmed (2002), 2003 D.T.C. 5015, [2003] 2 C.T.C. 28 (Fed. C.A.); leave to appeal refused (2003), 2003 CarswellNat 999, 2003 CarswellNat 1000 (S.C.C.). Similar decisions were reached in *Gaudreau v. R.* (2004), 2005 D.T.C. 66, [2005] 1 C.T.C. 2701 (T.C.C. [General Procedure]); affirmed (2005), 2005 D.T.C. 5702 (Eng.), [2006] 1 C.T.C. 137 (F.C.A.).

largely economic but partly personal (family ties, real property, furniture and appliances, bank accounts, a safety deposit box, a registered retirement savings plan, credit cards, and a provincial driver's license), and thus considered him to be ordinarily resident in Canada during the period he was in Japan.[33]

In contrast, the taxpayer in *Nicholson v. R.*[34] was found to have severed his residential ties with Canada. The taxpayer was assigned by his employer to work in the United Kingdom for a year and half but maintained a matrimonial home in Canada and his provincial health program during that period. He was held not be a resident in Canada based on several factors, including: he had no intention to return to Canada when he accepted the position in the U.K.; he and his first wife were separated and divorced; and he lived with his new wife in the U.K. where her child attended school.

(c) — Sojourner

Paragraph 250(1)(a) provides that a person shall "be deemed to have been resident in Canada throughout a taxation year" if the person sojourned in Canada in the year for a period of, or periods the total of which is, 183 days or more."[35]

The term "sojourn" means something less than residence. A sojourner is a person who is physically present in Canada, but on a more transient basis than a resident. A sojourner lacks the settled home in Canada which would make him or her resident. A person who is a resident of another country and who comes to Canada on a vacation or business trip would be an example of a sojourner. In most cases, of course, a sojourner would stay in Canada for only a short period of time, but if the sojourner stays for a period of 183 days, or for several periods totaling 183 days, then the effect of paragraph 250(1)(a) is to tax the sojourner as if he or she were a resident for the whole year. The rationale is that a person spending so much time in Canada has a stake in the country which is not markedly different from that of a resident, and which entails a contribution to the financing of the government. There is also the administrative convenience that paragraph 250(1)(a) will eliminate some of the argumentation over whether a person is a resident or not.

---

[33]The T.C.C. decision was confirmed by the Federal Court of Appeal *McFadyen v. R.* (2002), 2003 D.T.C. 5015, [2003] 2 C.T.C. 28 (Fed. C.A.); leave to appeal refused (2003), 2003 CarswellNat 999, 2003 CarswellNat 1000 (S.C.C.). A similar decision was reached in *Gaudreau v. R.* (2004), 2005 D.T.C. 66, [2005] 1 C.T.C. 2701 (T.C.C. [General Procedure]); affirmed (2005), 2005 D.T.C. 5702 (Eng.), [2006] 1 C.T.C. 137 (F.C.A.).

[34](2003), 2004 D.T.C. 2013, [2004] 2 C.T.C. 2310 (T.C.C. [General Procedure]).

[35]S. 250(1)(b) also deems members of the armed forces and federal and provincial civil servants who are stationed outside Canada to have been resident in Canada. The most important and interesting provision is para. (a), quoted above, under which a person who "sojourned" in Canada for 183 days in a taxation year is deemed to have been resident for the entire year.

In the *Thomson* case,[36] the taxpayer contended that he was a mere sojourner in Canada, and that since he had never remained in Canada for 183 days in any year, he could not be deemed a resident. The Court held, however, that his visits to Canada did not have the transient character of sojourning: they were not unusual, casual or intermittent. On the contrary, they were part of the permanent, settled routine of his life. The taxpayer was therefore held to be resident in Canada for the year, although he had spent less than 183 days in the country. As we noticed earlier, the length of time spent physically present in Canada is not crucial in determining whether or not a person is a resident at common law. [37]It is, however, crucial in applying the 183-day-sojourning rule, because physical presence is essential to sojourning and sojourning has no taxation relevance unless it continues for 183 days.

(d) — Part-year resident

When an individual becomes a Canadian resident or ceases to be a Canadian resident, he or she is a resident for only part of a taxation year. Because subsection 2(1) taxes "every person resident in Canada at *any time* in the year" (emphasis added), part-year residents are taxable on their worldwide income earned during the entire year. Such a result is obviously very harsh and potentially discourages cross-border mobility of workers. Section 114 provides relief by allowing a part-year resident to exclude from taxable income all foreign income earned during the part of the year when the taxpayer was not resident in Canada.

The sojourning rule of paragraph 250(1)(a) does not interact very happily with section 114 because paragraph 250(1)(a) deems a sojourner to have been resident in Canada "throughout" the taxation year and section 114 applies only where a person was a resident for "part" of a taxation year. The word "sojourn" implies transient or short-term residence, so paragraph 250(1)(a) does not apply to a person who becomes or ceases to be resident in Canada during the year. Therefore a sojourner can never be a part-year resident for the purposes of section 114 and would have to pay tax as a resident for the entire year.[38]

3.4 — Residence of corporations

(a) — Common law residence

The primary taxing provisions of sections 2 and 3 apply to "persons" and "taxpayers", and both these terms include corporations. It is therefore as necessary for a corporation as it is for an individual to determine the place of residence in order to decide whether the corporation is liable to Canadian tax on its world income. In the

[36]Note 8, above.

[37]See *MacDonald v. M.N.R.* (1968), 68 D.T.C. 433 (T.A.B.) in which the taxpayer was held to be resident although he had spent only 166 days in Canada.

[38]If there is a treaty concluded between Canada and the taxpayer's regular residence country, the treaty tie-breaker rules (see heading 3.8, "Dual residency", below) will generally consider the sojourner to be a non-resident in Canada.

absence of any exhaustive definition of residence in the Act, the courts have developed a test of residence for corporations just as they have for individuals. The rule which developed in the United Kingdom and which has been adopted in Canada is that a corporation is resident in the country "where the central management and control actually abides".[39]

Corporate law confers on the board of directors of a corporation the legal power to manage the affairs of the corporation. In the ordinary case, therefore, the place where a corporation's board of directors meets will be the place where the central management and control actually abides. This was the result in *De Beers Consolidated Mines v. Howe* (1906),[40] in which the test was first enunciated. The corporation whose residence was in issue was incorporated in South Africa, had its head office in South Africa, and carried on its business of mining in South Africa. Because a majority of the board of directors lived in England, and the board always met in England and made all major policy decisions there, the House of Lords held that the corporation was resident in England.

Corporate law does not confer upon the shareholders of a corporation the power to manage its affairs. That is the task of the directors, who are not the servants or agents of the shareholders, and who are under no legal obligation to follow the wishes of the shareholders. Therefore, the residence of the shareholders is not normally relevant in determining the location of the central management and control of a corporation. However, the shareholders do own the corporation, and they do possess some important powers, in particular, the power to elect (or to remove) the directors. In a closely held corporation (or sometimes even in a widely held corporation), in which one shareholder or a group of shareholders wields effective voting power, the major shareholder will be able to influence the decisions of the directors, if he or she chooses to do so, and in some corporations the major shareholder will dictate the decisions of the directors.

In *Unit Construction Co. v. Bullock* (1959),[41] three corporations that were incorporated in Kenya, that carried on business in Kenya, and whose directors resided and met in Kenya, were held to be resident not in Kenya but in England. The three corporations were subsidiaries of an English corporation, and they were effectively controlled in fact from England by the directors of the parent corporation. The House of Lords held that the location of central management and control was a question of fact, and that in this case it actually resided in England.

It is usually difficult to determine whether the board of directors of a corporation is exercising an independent discretion, albeit influenced by a shareholder or other outsider, or whether the board has actually surrendered its discretion to the outsider. Even if the facts are known, the question is one of degree which is not easy to determine. In addition, however, there are often evidentiary problems in establish-

---

[39]*De Beers Consolidated Mines v. Howe*, [1906] A.C. 455 (H.L.), at 458.

[40]*Ibid.*

[41](1959), [1960] A.C. 351 (C.A.).

ing that a board of directors actually acts under the dictation of an outsider. It is significant that in *Unit Construction* it was to the advantage of the three Kenyan corporations and their parent for the corporations to be held resident in England, and the evidence of *de facto* control from England was therefore readily available.

There have been a number of Canadian cases in which the evidence appeared to establish *de facto* control by the major shareholder, and yet the courts refused to conclude that central management and control was exercised from outside the board of directors.[42] These cases reverted to a *de jure* control test, which was rejected by the House of Lords in *Unit Construction*. The results of these cases are admittedly hard to explain on any other basis. In general, however, there seems to be no reason to doubt that *Unit Construction* represents the law of Canada as well as the United Kingdom. Where it can be established that the board of directors of a corporation does not in fact exercise independent management and control, then the place of residence of the person who dictates the board's decisions is the place of residence of the corporation.

In a recent UK case, *Wood v. Holden*,[43] a holding company was incorporated in the Netherlands as part of a scheme designed to facilitate the sale of shares in an UK operating company owned by UK resident shareholders. Under UK tax law, the capital gain from the sale of the shares would be tax-free if the Dutch company is a non-resident. The Dutch company had one corporate director that signed all the documents in the Netherlands. The Dutch company was held by the Court of Appeal to be a resident in the Netherlands because its central management and control was located there. In reaching the decision, the Court stated that:[44]

> [I]t is essential to recognize the distinction between cases where management and control of the company was exercised through its own constitutional organs (the board of directors or the general meeting) and cases where the functions of those constitutional organs were 'usurped', in the sense that management and control was exercised independently of, or without regard to, those constitutional organs.

Unlike the facts-and-circumstances test for residence of individuals, the common law test for corporate residence is more formalistic. A corporation can reside virtually anywhere it chooses.

(b) — Statutory definition

Paragraph 250(4)(a) deems all corporations incorporated in Canada after April 26, 1965 to be resident in Canada. Corporations which were incorporated in Canada

---

[42] *Sifneos v. M.N.R.*, [1968] Tax A.B.C. 652, 68 D.T.C. 522 (T.A.B.); *Zehnder & Co. v. M.N.R.*, [1970] C.T.C. 85, 70 D.T.C. 6064 (Ex. Ct.); and *Bedford Overseas Freighters v. M.N.R.*, [1970] C.T.C. 69, 70 D.T.C. 6072 (Ex. Ct.).

[43] [2004] S.T.C. (S.C.D.) 416. The Special Commissioners' decision was reversed by Parker J. of the Chancery Division [2005] EWHC 547, [2005] All E.R. (D) 48 (Eng. Ch. Div.). Parker J.'s decision was upheld by the Court of Appeal: [2006] EWCA Civ 26, [2006] 2 B.C.L.C. 210 (Eng. C.A.).

[44] [2006] EWCA Civ 26, [2006] 2 B.C.L.C. 210 (Eng. C.A.), para. 27.

before April 27, 1965 are deemed to be resident in Canada if, at any time after April 26, 1965 they were resident in Canada under the common law test or carried on business in Canada (s. 250(4)(c)). Indeed, subsection 250(4) contains a type of "citizenship" test[45] for corporations and reduces the importance of the central management and control test in Canada.

3.5 — Residence of trusts

Subsection 104(2) provides that a trust shall be deemed to be "an individual". An individual is defined in subsection 248(1) as "a person other than a corporation". It follows that a trust is a "person" and a "taxpayer" so that sections 2 and 3 are applicable, and the question whether the trust is resident in Canada is as crucial as it is for genuine individuals and for corporations: if resident in Canada, the trust will be liable to Canadian tax on its world income; and if not resident in Canada, the trust will be liable to Canadian tax only on the Canadian-source income.

The Act does not supply any rules for determining the residence of a trust. It does not even include deemed residence rules comparable to those applicable to individuals and corporations. The CRA has adopted the position that the residence of a trust is a question of fact depending on the circumstances of each particular case. The CRA will generally consider a trust to reside where the managing or controlling trustee resides.[46] This position finds implicit support in subsection 104(1) of the Act, which provides that a reference to a trust shall be read as a reference to "the trustee . . . having ownership or control of the trust property". If a trust has a single trustee, and the trustee is resident in Canada, then it is clear that the trust is resident in Canada. The case is more troublesome where the trustee is not a resident of Canada, but the bulk of the trust's business or property interests are in Canada. It seems wrong that such a trust should be able to claim non-resident status. This was the situation in *Garron et al v. The Queen*,[47] a case which is under appeal at the time of writing.

In *Garron*, the Tax Court of Canada held that two trusts were resident in Canada because their "central management and control" was in Canada, even though the sole trustee of each trust was a corporation resident in Barbados. Because of this determination, the trusts were denied the exemption provided in Article XIV(4) of the Canada-Barbados Treaty and were taxable in Canada on a capital gain of approximately $500 million.

Garron involved a typical "offshore freeze". In an ordinary "estate freeze" (or "freeze"), shareholders exchange common shares of a corporation for fixed value preference shares ("freeze shares") and other family members buy new common

---

[45]See heading 3.1(a), "Residence", above, for a discussion of the citizen test for individuals.

[46]Interpretation Bulletin IT-447, "Residence of a trust or estate" (1980).

[47]2009 TCC 450, [2010] 2 C.T.C. 2346, 50 E.T.R. (3d) 241, (sub nom. *Garron Family Trust v. R.*) 2009 D.T.C. 1568 (Eng.) (T.C.C. [General Procedure]).

shares for a nominal amount.[48] No tax is owed at the time of the freeze because it takes place on a tax-deferred rollover basis.[49] As company grows in value, the common shares appreciate whereas the value of the freeze shares remains "frozen" or fixed. If the owners of the common shares are not resident in Canada, the freeze is called an "offshore freeze" and the goal of the exercise is to have capital gain on the sale of the common shares not subject to tax in Canada.

The facts in *Garron* were as follows:

(1) In 1998, the two shareholders (Mr. Dunin and a holding corporation owned by Mr. Garron, his wife and the Garron Family Trust) of PMPL Holdings Inc., a corporation resident in Canada worth $50 million, exchanged their common shares for freeze shares with a redemption amount of $50 million.

(2) A non-resident individual settled two trusts: the beneficiaries of one trust were Mr. Dunin and his family and the beneficiaries of the other trust were Mr. Garron and his family. The sole trustee of each trust was a corporation resident in Barbados. After they were settled, the two trusts subscribed for all the shares of newly incorporated Canadian holding corporations ("Holdcos") and these Holdcos then subscribed for common shares of PMPL for nominal consideration.

(3) In 2000, the two trusts disposed of most of the shares in the Holdcos realizing capital gains of some $450 million. The trusts claimed the exemption in Article XIV(4) of the Canada-Barbados treaty arguing that the trusts were resident in Barbados and therefore were not subject to tax on the gains in Canada (there was no tax on the gains in Barbados either).

In *Garron*, the Tax Court judge, Woods, J., concluded that the central management and control of each trust was in Canada and held that the trusts were resident in Canada. The trustee executed documents and provided incidental administrative services and did little else. Based on the evidence, Woods found that it was "more likely than not [that the trustee] had agreed from the outset that it would defer to the recommendations of Mr. Dunin and Mr. Garron. Further, I find that Mr. Dunin and Mr. Garron had understood this to be the arrangement from the outset." Among the many factors considered[50] was the fact that Mr. Dunin and Garron each had the power to replace the trust's "protector".[51]

Another difficult situation is a trust with several trustees, each resident in a different country. If we go back to the language of subsection 104(1), it is pertinent to ask: which trustee has the "ownership or control of the trust property"? The difficulty is that, under the general law of trusts, trustees own the trust property jointly, and, unless the trust instrument provides otherwise, trustees must act unanimously. Therefore, strictly speaking, no single trustee, and not even a majority of trustees,

---

[48]The value is nominal because the value of the corporation is equal to the value of the preference shares.

[49]See heading 17.9(d), "Estate Freeze", below.

[50]Note 47, above, para. 195 to 268.

[51]The protector is the person who has the power to replace the trustee.

has "ownership or control of the trust property". The factual situation may of course be quite different from what the law contemplates. One of several trustees may be the dominant figure in the administration of the trust with the others playing mainly a formal role.

There seems to be only one decided case on point, namely *Thibodeau Family Trust v. R.* (1978).[52] In that case, Gibson J. of the Federal Court Trial Division relied upon the cases dealing with the residence of corporations, and applied the central management and control test to determine the place of residence of a trust. There were three trustees, of whom two lived in Bermuda and a third lived in Canada. The Canadian resident trustee was not only a member of the family for whom the trust had been established, he was the chief executive officer of a corporation owned by the trust, and he seemed to have been active and influential in the investment program of the trust. The Court held that the central management and control of the trust was in Bermuda, and that the trust was not resident in Canada because:

- the trust instrument altered the general rule of unanimity by authorizing a majority of the trustees to make decisions binding on the trust;
- the day to day administration of the trust was in fact carried out in Bermuda by the Bermuda trustees;
- there was evidence that they did not always follow the wishes of the Canadian trustee; and
- the meetings of the trustees were held in Bermuda.

Until *Garron*, the following obiter by Gibson, J. in *Thibodeau* has been used as an argument to reject the central management and control test as a basis for determining the residence of a trust: that is, because of the fiduciary duties imposed upon trustees, they are not permitted to take direction from a third party:[53]

> The judicial formula for this respecting a corporation, in my view, cannot apply to trustees because trustees cannot delegate any of their authority to co-trustees. A trustee cannot adopt a "policy of masterly inactivity" as commented upon in *Underhill on the Law of Trusts and Trustees*, 12th Edition, page 284; and on the evidence, none of the trustees did adopt such a policy.

In *Garron*, Woods J., found the Thibodeau decision to be insufficient authority for rejecting the central management and control test since "adopting a similar test of residence for trusts and corporations promotes the important principles of consistency, predictability and fairness in the application of tax law."[54] At the time of writing (March 2010), *Garron* is under appeal.

---

[52] [1978] C.T.C. 539, 78 D.T.C. 6376 (Fed. T.D.).

[53] Note 52, above, para 6385.

[54] Note 47, above, para. 160.

3.6 — Provincial residence

The foregoing discussion has addressed the question of whether a particular taxpayer is resident in Canada. However, for resident taxpayers, it is also necessary to determine in which province the taxpayer is resident. This determines liability for provincial income tax, and since rates of provincial income tax vary considerably, it is a question of some importance.

For individuals, section 2601 of the *Income Tax Regulations* (the "Regulations") provides that the province in which the individual resided on the last day of the taxation year is entitled to tax the individual on his or her entire income for the year. It is immaterial that the individual may have resided in another province or provinces for most of the year, and (with one exception to be noted) it is immaterial that the individual's income may have been derived from sources outside the province.[55] Regulation 2601 makes an exception for an individual who has income from a business with a permanent establishment outside the province of last-day residence. In that case, the income attributable to the business is deemed to have been earned in the province or country where the permanent establishment is located.[56] Where an individual has permanent establishments in more than one province or country, regulation 2603 supplies rules for apportioning the income between the jurisdictions.

For corporations, regulation 402 allocates the income to the province in which the corporation had a permanent establishment in the taxation year. Where a corporation has permanent establishments in more than one province or country, rules similar to those for the business income of individuals enable the income to be apportioned between the jurisdictions.[57]

The regulations are silent on trusts, but since a trust is deemed by subsection 104(2) to be an individual, the rules for individuals would be applicable.

3.7 — Change in residence status

When a taxpayer changes residence during the year by either giving up or acquiring Canadian residence, there are two important tax consequences. One consequence is the part-year residence treatment under section 114 for individuals.[58] Another con-

---

[55]The constitutionality of a province taxing its residents in respect of income earned outside the province was upheld in *Kerr v. Supt. of Income Tax*, [1942] S.C.R. 435 (S.C.C.); and *Canadian Pacific Railway v. Manitoba (Treasurer)*, [1953] 4 D.L.R. 233 (Man. Q.B.).

[56]Income of an individual that escapes provincial tax (because it is income from a business with a permanent establishment outside Canada) is subject to a federal surtax of 52% of the appropriate proportion of the federal tax payable by the individual. In other words, the federal government takes up the tax room left open by the absence of provincial tax.

[57]Various special kinds of corporations are subjected to special rules by regs. 403–413.

[58]See heading 3.3(d), "Part-year resident", above.

sequence is the deemed disposition and reacquisition of property under section 128.1 for individuals and corporations.

Section 128.1 has the effect of imposing a "departure tax" on persons giving up Canadian residence.[59] The policy is to prevent Canadian residents from leaving the country without reporting capital gains which had accrued (but not been realized) while they were residents of Canada.[60] The technique employed by section 128.1 is to deem a taxpayer who has ceased to be a resident of Canada to have disposed of most property at fair market value immediately before ceasing to be a resident and to have re-acquired the same property at a cost equal to the deemed proceeds of disposition. This ensures that any accrued capital gains (or losses) are recognized for Canadian tax purposes. If adequate security is provided to the CRA, no tax is actually due until later when the property is actually sold (and no interest is charged until then). For people leaving Canada permanently, there is usually little doubt that residence has been lost. A difficulty can arise, however, in determining the date at which Canadian residence ceased. The date will usually be important as marking the end of the period when Canada taxes world income.[61] It is also important as marking the time at which the "departure tax" becomes applicable. In *Schujahn v. M.N.R.* (1962),[62] for example, the taxpayer was transferred by his employer to the United States on August 2, 1957. He departed Canada on that date and put his house up for sale. His wife and child remained in Canada in the house until it was sold, which was not until February 1958, and then they joined the taxpayer in the United States. Was he a resident of Canada for the whole of 1957 or only until August 2? The Exchequer Court held that he had given up residence on August 2. The continued occupation of the Canadian house by his family would normally indicate continued residence, but in this case "was explained in a satisfactory manner" as being solely for the purpose of facilitating the sale.

The deemed disposition and reacquisition rules also apply to taxpayers who become Canadian residents (i.e., immigrants) during the year. These rules ensure that capital gains accrued prior to becoming a Canadian resident are tax-free in Canada, but gains accrued after the date of immigration are taxable.

---

[59]Until 1994, these rules were contained in s. 48 of the Act, which was repealed and replaced by s. 128.1.

[60]As explained in ch. 10, Capital Gains, below, the general rule is that capital gains are taxed only when realized; that chapter also discusses in more detail the "deemed dispositions" of which the so-called departure tax is an example.

[61]See heading 3.3(d), "Part-year resident", above.

[62]Note 21, above.

3.8 — Dual residency

A person may be found to be a resident in both Canada and another country. Typical dual residence scenarios include that of

- an individual who is resident in a foreign country but who is deemed (under paragraph 250(1)(a)) to be a resident of Canada because he has sojourned 183 days or more in Canada
- a person, such as Mr. Thomson, who maintains strong residential ties with Canada and another country and
- a corporation that is incorporated in Canada after April 26, 1965 but has its place of central management and control in a foreign country (or vice versa).

In such cases, the person may be subject to worldwide taxation in both countries. This dual residency problem is dealt with under tax treaties. Tax treaties establish tie-breaker rules to identify only one country as being the one with the right to tax the person concerned. In the case of an individual, such factors as the place of permanent home, habitual abode and nationality are taken into account; where these factors do not supply an answer, the treaties allow "the competent authorities" of the two countries to determine the question "by mutual agreement". In the case of a corporation, the tie-breaker rules generally determine the corporation's residence on the basis of the place of management and control, the place of incorporation, or by mutual agreement.

3.9 — Deemed non-resident

Individuals and corporations that would otherwise be resident in Canada under Canadian law but are deemed to be resident in another country by virtue of a rule in a tax treaty are deemed not to be residents of Canada.[63] This rule ensures that a person is treated consistently under the Act and a treaty in order to prevent the taxpayer from taking advantage of the differences between domestic law and the tax treaty to avoid Canadian tax. For example, a corporation that was incorporated in the United States and has its place of central management and control in Canada is a Canadian resident under the common law, but a non-resident of Canada by virtue of the Canada-U.S. treaty. In the absence of subsection 250(5), this corporation would rely on its Canadian residence status to avoid Part XIII tax in respect of its Canadian-source investment income because Part XIII is applicable only to payments made to non-residents. In the meantime, this corporation could rely on its non-resident status under the treaty to avoid the withholding obligation under Part XIII when it pays investment income to its American investors because this withholding obligation is imposed on a Canadian resident.

---

[63]S. 250(5).

4
INCOME

4.1 — Section 3

What is income? For the purpose of the *Income Tax Act* (the "Act"), the short answer is: whatever section 3 is interpreted to say that it is. Paragraphs 3(a) and (b) determine the scope of "income" as follows:

> The income of a taxpayer for a taxation year for the purposes of this Part is the taxpayer's income for the year determined by the following rules:
>
> (a) determine the total of all amounts each of which is the taxpayer's income for the year (other than a taxable capital gain from the disposition of a property) from a source inside or outside Canada, including, without restricting the generality of the foregoing, the taxpayer's income for the year from each office, employment, business and property,
>
> (b) determine the amount, if any, by which
>
> (i) the total of
>
> (A) all of the taxpayer's taxable capital gains for the year from dispositions of property other than listed personal property, and
>
> (B) the taxpayer's taxable net gain for the year from dispositions of listed personal property, exceeds
>
> (ii) the amount, if any, by which the taxpayer's allowable capital losses for the year from dispositions of property other than listed personal property exceed the taxpayer's allowable business investment losses for the year,

There are several important points to consider in thinking about paragraphs 3(a) and (b):

(1) What is the ordinary meaning of "income"? How should income be defined from a theoretical and policy perspective?

(2) What is the notion of "source"? When and why might certain economic receipts that constitute income in a general sense not be taxable under section 3 for lacking a source?

(3) By using the phrase "including, without restricting the generality of the foregoing. . ." before the four enumerated sources in paragraph 3(a) and the phrase "without restricting the generality of section 3, there shall be included. . ." at the beginning of subsection 56(1) in subdivision d ("other income"), it is clear that Parliament did not intend to restrict "income from a

source" to income from the four enumerated sources (office, employment, business, property) and "other income". But, what other amounts should be taxed as income?

(4) The Act (in various places) specifically excludes certain amounts from being taxed as income. What is the policy rationale for each of these exclusions?

(5) How and why are capital gains taxed differently?

4.2 — The concept of income

Students of tax law may be surprised to find that there is no universally accepted definition of "income" for income tax purposes. Laypersons may find it hard to believe that there are major problems in defining income. They tend to think in terms of cash wages and salaries, and other items of money that "come in". Other items like interest and dividends are also easily identified as income. These items are all clearly income for tax purposes. However, there is a grey area, which is relatively small but has been the focus of judicial attention since the beginning of the income tax system.[1] The elusive nature of income makes it extremely difficult to formulate a definition that catches "the many shapes which income may assume and the illimitable variety of circumstances in which it may be derived".[2]

The concept of "income" is, on the other hand, fundamental to the scheme of the Act. Technically, it determines the tax base. Whether an item of receipt constitutes income determines whether it is subject to tax. If a receipt does not have the attributes of income, it is not taxable. In addition, since the Act is used as a policy instrument in the redistribution of income, the concept of income has significant policy implications. The manner in which income is defined makes a difference in designing tax expenditure provisions aimed at income redistribution. For example, all refundable tax credits which are designed to deliver (tax-free) social assistance through the tax system to low income earners are based on the income of the taxpayer and/or the taxpayer's spouse. Even several non-refundable credits are tested on the basis of the income of a taxpayer and/or his or her spouse and/or dependant.

Ideally, income should reflect a taxpayer's "ability to pay". Given that tax equity is one of the most important objectives of income taxation, the definition of income is inherently linked to tax equity. Therefore, the inquiry into the meaning of income goes well beyond technical issues and involves fundamental value judgments about tax equity.

---

[1] For example, ch. 11, Investing and Trading, below. There is a vast body of case law distinguishing between capital and income, capital gains and business income, and windfall gains and income gains.

[2] Hannan and Farnsworth, *The Principles of Income Taxation* (1952), 3.

(a) — Haig-Simons theory

When economists put their minds to the definition of income for tax purposes, they found the source theory underlying section 3 to be "narrow", "artificial", "eccentric", and "little less than absurd".[3] Why? Because the source theory of income was poorly adapted for tax purposes, where the object was to measure a taxpayer's ability to pay tax. Robert Murray Haig, an American economist writing in 1921, proposed a more comprehensive definition of income. Haig stated that, for tax purposes, the definition of income should be "the money value of the net accretion to one's economic power between two points of time".[4] Under this definition, any accretion to economic power in the course of a taxation year, regardless of its source, would count as income for the year.

In 1938, Henry C. Simons, another American economist, proposed a more elaborate version of Haig's definition. Simons stated: "Personal income may be defined as the algebraic sum of (1) the market value of rights exercised in consumption and (2) the change in the value of the store of property rights between the beginning and the end of the period in question".[5] This definition was fundamentally the same as Haig's, but Simons' definition explicitly took account of consumption, treating the value of the goods and services consumed by the taxpayer during the year as part of the taxpayer's accretion to wealth for that year.

According to Haig-Simons theory, income equals consumption plus gain in net worth over a taxation year. It does not matter whether the gain in net worth consists of periodic payments from a source (such as salary, wages, business income or property income), profits from the sale of property (capital gains), transfers from other people (such as gifts, inheritances or gambling winnings), the direct products of one's own labour (such as home-grown fruit and vegetables or home renovation), or the direct benefits of one's own property (such as the right to occupy one's own home). Nor does it matter whether the gain in net worth is expected or unexpected, regular or irregular, deliberate or accidental, realized or accrued, in cash or in kind. All gains should be taken into account in measuring a taxpayer's income for tax purposes.

The Haig-Simons definition of income has been used by analysts as a basis for testing the equity of the income tax. However, this definition has not been enacted into law in any country in the world. In defining income for tax purposes, the definition should provide not only a measure of an individual's ability to pay, but also be sufficiently practical to be administered by the government. The Haig-Simons definition is difficult to implement. It assumes that the accretion in wealth can be quantified in terms of market prices or at least objectively valued. In the case of unrealized gains and non-monetary benefits, this presents a huge valuation task, not to mention the problem of detection. It would be more convenient to tax gains on

---

[3]Haig in Haig (ed.), *The Federal Income Tax* (1921), 54.

[4]*Ibid.*, 59.

[5]Simons, *Personal Income Taxation* (1938), 50.

realization than on accrual. In addition, there is the liquidity issue. Taxpayers might have to sell the assets producing their income in order to pay their taxes, notwithstanding their increase in wealth. Finally, there may be overriding social and political reasons for not taxing certain economic gains, such as gifts, damages for pain and suffering, or the value of unpaid housework, even if they constitute gains.

(b) — Carter Commission's "comprehensive tax base"

(i) — Comprehensive tax base

The Carter Commission, which was much influenced by Haig and Simons, restated the Haig-Simons theory in these terms:[6]

> The comprehensive tax base has been defined as the sum of the market value of goods and services consumed or given away in the taxation year by the tax unit [the taxpayer], plus the annual change in the market value of the assets held by the unit.

The Carter Commission argued that the definition of income should be suited to the purpose for which the definition was to be used. If the definition was to be the basis of an equitable tax system, then it should be a reasonably comprehensive measure of the annual increase in a taxpayer's ability to pay tax. The traditional, source-based concept of income, however apt to other purposes (such as trust accounting), was not a satisfactory measure of the annual increase in a taxpayer's ability to pay tax, because it excluded from income so many accretions to wealth. In principle, income should include every accretion to wealth, regardless of its source, because every accretion to wealth increases the recipient's ability to pay tax. This theory, which became the Commission's guiding principle, was aptly described as "a buck is a buck is a buck".

The Carter Commission proposed that the traditional definition of income be replaced by a "comprehensive tax base", a concept that drew heavily on Haig-Simons theory but was not quite as comprehensive as the pure Haig-Simons definition. The Carter Commission recognized that many of the annual valuations require by the Haig-Simons theory were impractical. Accordingly, the Commission modified the definition so that, for the most, the additions to the tax base were confined to items that could readily be measured in dollars, such as realized capital gains, gifts, inheritances and windfalls.

(ii) — Taxation of capital gains

The most important (and perhaps the least radical) new element of Carter's comprehensive tax base, which was excluded from income under the traditional definition, was capital gains. The argument for the inclusion of capital gains as income is, of course, that they increase the wealth of the recipient, and hence the ability to pay, just as surely as income from employment, business or property does.

Moreover, the exclusion of capital gains seriously undermined the progressivity of the system. In both the United States, where capital gains have been taxed for a

---

[6] *Report of the Royal Commission on Taxation* (Carter Report) (1966), vol. 3, 39.

long time, and Canada, where capital gains have been taxed since 1972, capital gains comprise a very small proportion of the income reported by low-income individuals, and a very large proportion of the income reported by high-income individuals. The Carter Report displayed figures which showed that in the United States in 1963, when the percentage of capital gains to all other income reported by all individuals was 4 per cent, for individuals earning between $100,000 and $200,000 the relevant percentage was 48 per cent, and for individuals earning in excess of $200,000 the relevant percentage was 128 per cent.[7] The Carter Commission concluded that in Canada taxes were "probably a decreasing proportion of comprehensive income for upper income individuals and families", despite the fact that marginal rates at the time rose to 80 per cent.[8] The Commission concluded that the adoption of the comprehensive tax base (which of course would include gifts, inheritances and windfalls as well as capital gains) would allow a lowering of tax rates at all levels and a drastic lowering of rates at the upper levels. Its recommendation was to lower the top marginal rate from its level of 80 per cent all the way down to 50 per cent. It argued that after this drastic lowering of rates, the tax system would not only yield the same revenue as before, but would be *more* progressive than before.

The Carter Commission departed from the pure Haig-Simons theory in recommending against the inclusion of unrealized (or accrued) capital gains. The Commission recognized "that income arises where there is an increase in economic power, and that economic power increases when the market value of property increases".[9] The Commission also recognized that it was inequitable to tax gains only when realized "in that taxpayers who retain investments which have appreciated in value are, in effect, allowed a tax-free investment of the accumulated gains that are built up free of tax, while others, who turn over their investments, are denied this privilege".[10] Nevertheless, with some hesitation, the Commission concluded that the administrative problems involved in taxing accrued gains were too difficult, and accordingly recommended that capital gains be taxed only when realized. However, in order to limit the period for which recognition of gains could be postponed, the Commission recommended that there should be a "deemed disposition" of capital property on death, on the making of a gift and on giving up Canadian residence, even though no gain would actually be realized on those occasions.

The government was initially receptive to the Carter Commission's proposal that realized capital gains be included in full in income. The government's White Paper that followed the Carter Report mainly accepted the proposal,[11] but the government

---

[7] *Ibid.*, 332.

[8] *Ibid.*, vol. 2, 261.

[9] *Ibid.*, vol. 3, 378.

[10] *Ibid.*, 379.

[11] Benson, *Proposals for Tax Reform* (1969), 40. (An exception was to be made for publicly-traded Canadian corporate securities, the gains from which were to be only one-half included.)

altered its position during the period of debate on its White Paper. The final decision, embodied in the 1971 Act, was to tax gains only on a realization basis (except for Carter's Commission's deemed dispositions, which were accepted), and to include only one-half of realized gains in income. Thus the Carter Commission did succeed in adding capital gains to the tax base, albeit on a preferential basis.

(c) — Judicial interpretation

(i) — Ordinary meaning

Canadian courts recognize that "the notion of what receipts constitute income for purposes of taxation is central to the workings of the Act."[12] The word "income" "had to be given its ordinary meaning, bearing in mind the distinction between capital and income, and the ordinary concepts and usages of mankind."[13] Robertson J.A. states in *Bellingham v. R.* (1996):[14]

> Standing alone the term income is susceptible to widely diverging interpretations. Narrowly construed, income may be defined to include only those amounts received by taxpayers on a recurring basis. Broadly construed, income may be defined so as to capture all accretions to wealth. Canadian taxpayers are more likely to embrace the former definition. The latter approach reflects the economist's concern for achieving horizontal and vertical equity in a taxation system. Such a concern translates into a broad understanding of what receipt items should be included in income. This perspective is reflected in the Report of the Carter Commission.

The courts have generally adopted the narrower construction. As discussed below, capital receipts are not income, unrealized gains are not income, and income must have a source.

(ii) — Capital receipt distinguished

A receipt of money by a taxpayer for his or her own benefit is generally considered either as a receipt of a capital nature or as an income receipt. "Gifts may, perhaps, be in a separate category-a kind of no-man's land."[15] The distinction between income and capital can be analogized as the fruit and the tree. Income is fruit only and never the tree.[16]

---

[12] *Bellingham v. R.* (1995), [1996] 1 C.T.C. 187, 96 D.T.C. 6075 (Fed. C.A.), para. 24.

[13] *Curran v. Minister of National Revenue*, [1959] S.C.R. 850, [1959] C.T.C. 416, 59 D.T.C. 1247 (S.C.C.).

[14] Note 12, above, at 24.

[15] Strike pay was not income from a source.

[16] *Stratton's Independence v. Howbert*, 213 U.S. 399; and *Ryall v. Hoare*, [1923] K.B. 447, 8 T.C. 521 (K.B.). These cases have been accepted by Canadian courts. A recent Canadian case on this issue is *R. v. Fortino*, [2000] 1 C.T.C. 349, 2000 D.T.C. 6060 (Fed. C.A.) in which payments made under non-competition agreements were held to constitute capital receipts, and not taxable under s. 3. As discussed in note 54 below, there is draft legislation that contains a proposal to tax such payments.

The notion of "capital" is akin to a fund of "after-tax dollars". A taxpayer's savings out of after-tax salary, business profits, etc. are capital. So are his or her windfall gains, inheritances or other amounts received tax-free. Capital may be in the form of cash, personal assets, real property, or investments. There is a rich body of case law on the distinction between capital and income.[17] In making the distinction, the courts have held that payments for the surrender of a potential source of profit are capital receipts.[18] The tree is "capital" while the fruit is "income".

(iii) — Realization of income

The non-taxation of unrealized gains is one of the most fundamental aspects of Canadian income tax law. The Act provides for specific timing rules for the recognition of income from each of the enumerated sources and capital gains. For example, wages and salaries are taxable when received;[19] amounts in respect of property sold or services rendered in the course of business are recognized when they are receivable;[20] dividends are recognized as income when they are received;[21] and capital gains are recognized when a property is disposed of.[22] If a taxpayer buys a painting for $500 and it increases in value to $20,000, he or she has no income from capital gains until the painting is sold. However, the Act does not define the concept of "receipt" or "receivable". The courts have interpreted income for tax purposes as excluding unrealized appreciation.[23] This is different from the Haig-Simons definition of income, which includes accrued gains.

The realization requirement provides taxpayers with considerable flexibility in the timing of taxation of gains and losses. This ability to accelerate or postpone gains and losses is one of the major tools of tax planning. Over the past several decades, Parliament has made some inroads on the realization requirement where it is relatively easy to determine the value of some assets annually. For example, taxpayers holding certain "investment contracts"[24] must report interest on an annual basis even when the interest is not payable until the maturity date.[25] Financial institutions must recognize gains or losses on securities on an accrual basis under "mark-to-market" rules.[26]

---

[17]Ch. 11, Investing and Trading, below.

[18]*Fortino*, note 16, above.

[19]S. 5(1). See ch. 5, Income from Employment, below.

[20]S. 12(1)(b). See heading 7.3(b), "Accrual method of accounting", below.

[21]S. 12(1)(j). See heading 7.6, "Dividends", below.

[22]S. 40(1). See heading 10.3(c), "Realization", below.

[23]*Friedberg v. Canada*, [1993] 2 C.T.C. 306, 93 D.T.C. 5507 (S.C.C.).

[24]Defined under s. 12(11).

[25]S. 12(4).

[26]S. 142.5.

As discussed below, the courts have interpreted paragraph 3(a) very narrowly. If a receipt is not derived from a "source", it is generally not considered to constitute income for tax purposes.

4.3 — Income from a "source"

(a) — Source theory

The source theory has been influential in the drafting and interpreting of the Act. The theory is that income is a yield from a productive source. Section 3 codifies this theory by stating that only income from a source[27] is included in computing a taxpayer's income under paragraph 3(a) and that only a loss from a source is deductible under paragraph 3(d).

It has been suggested that the source theory of income arose in the United Kingdom at a time when the economy was primarily agricultural and it was natural to think of income in terms of the fruit and tree.[28] Another factor was probably the distinction between capital and income that the courts had developed for the law of trusts, where it was necessary to distinguish between the rights of a life tenant (or income beneficiary) and those of a remainderman (or capital beneficiary).[29] The idea that income was the yield from a productive source, and that the source itself was capital, became part of the Anglo-Canadian way of thinking about income. Accordingly, the *Income Tax Acts* of the United Kingdom and Canada, while taxing income from employment, business or property, did not at first attempt to tax capital gains, gifts, inheritances, or windfalls and many other miscellaneous receipts that were not considered to have a source.

(b) — Characteristics of an income source

For income tax purposes, the word "source" has been qualified by adjectives, such as "real", "productive", or "profitable". In *Nathan v. Federal Commissioner of Taxation (N.S. Wales)* (1918),[30] Isaacs J. stated that "source" means "something

[27]In addition to the "source concept of income" meaning, the word "source" is used to refer to the territorial source of income (e.g., income is earned from a source inside or outside Canada), or the type of income (e.g., when capital gains or s. 56 amounts are referred to as sources of income). For example, in *Schwartz v. R.*, [1996] 1 C.T.C. 303 313, 96 D.T.C. 6103 6108 (S.C.C.), La Forest J. writes: "Section 3 ... identifies, in para. (a), the five principal sources from which income can be generated: office, employment, business, property and capital gains". As it is well established in case law that capital gains are not from a productive source, but the disposition of a source of income, La Forest J. obviously used the word "source" to mean a category of income. "Source" is used in a similar sense in s. 56 where specified items are included in income.

[28]Carter Report, note 6, above, vol. 3, 64-65

[29]*Ibid.*, 65.

[30]25 C.L.R. 183 (Aust. H.C.).

which a practical man would regard as a real source of income".[31] In *R v. Cranswick* (1982),[32] LeDain J. stated that "income from a source will be that which is typically earned by it or which typically flows from it as the expected return". In *Bellingham*,[33] Robertson J.A. held that income from a source refers to a productive source (i.e., a source that is capable of producing income). In *Stewart v. R.* (2002),[34] Iacobucci and Bastarache JJ. held that "whether a taxpayer has a source of income from a particular activity is determined by considering whether the taxpayer intends to carry on the activity for profit, and whether there is evidence to support that intention".[35]

Based on the case law, an income source seems to have one or more of the following characteristics:

- It recurs on a periodic basis;[36]
- It involves organized effort, activity or pursuit on the part of the taxpayer;
- It involves a marketplace exchange;
- It gives rise to an enforceable claim to the payment by the taxpayer; and
- In the case of a business or property source, there is a pursuit of profit.[37]

Ultimately, the source of income is capital, labour, or a combination of both. Investment income, wages and salaries, and business income are thus typical categories of income. Personal goodwill, pain and suffering, good fortune, a hobby, or windfall does not generally constitute a source of income. Drawing the line between these two categories is difficult in many cases.[38]

(c) — Enumerated sources

Paragraph 3(a) identifies four traditional sources of income: office, employment, business, and property. The characterization of each of these sources is discussed in subsequent chapters of this book. It is worthwhile to note at this stage that these four sources are not exhaustive, leaving much room for judicial interpretation.

---

[31] *Ibid.*, 189, Isaacs J. (Australia). These words were quoted in *Robertson v. M.N.R.*, [1954] C.T.C. 110, 120-22, 54 D.T.C. 1062 1068 (Ex. Ct.); *James v. M.N.R.*, [1973] C.T.C. 457, 461-63, 73 D.T.C. 5333 5336 (Fed. T.D.).

[32] [1982] C.T.C. 69 73, 82 D.T.C. 6073 6076 (Fed. C.A.); leave to appeal refused (1982), 42 N.R. 335 (S.C.C.).

[33] [1996] 1 C.T.C. 187 198, 96 D.T.C. 6075 6081 (Fed. C.A.).

[34] 2002 SCC 46, 2002 D.T.C. 6969 (S.C.C.).

[35] *Ibid.*, para. 61.

[36] This factor has been considered an important factor in holding that personal gifts and windfalls are not income from a source.

[37] *Stewart*, note 34, above.

[38] See heading 4.3(c), "Enumerated sources" below.

In determining whether a receipt has a source, the courts tend to first fit the receipt into one of the enumerated sources before deciding that the receipt is a non-taxable gift or a windfall gain. Some examples include:

- The source of gains from gambling activities is the business of gambling in some cases.[39]
- The source of gifts received by a taxpayer in respect of employment is employment.[40]
- The source of payments "in consideration of the loss of pension rights, chances for advancement, and opportunities for re-employment" is employment.[41]
- The source of money stolen by a lawyer from his clients' trust accounts is business.[42]
- The source of fraudulently acquired funds from a company in which the taxpayer was an officer or employee is employment.[43]
- The source of damages and settlements may have a source from an enumerated source under the surrogatum principle.[44]

(d) — Unenumerated sources

Because "income from a source" is undefined in the Act, the concept must be given its ordinary meaning. Judicial interpretation of this concept has been very restrictive. The courts have been reluctant in finding that receipts with the characteristics of income are taxable where the source of the payment is not enumerated. For example, in *Canada v. Fries* (1990), the Supreme Court of Canada held that it was not satisfied that strike pay was "income ... from a source" within the meaning of section 3; and "the benefit of the doubt" should go to the taxpayers.[45] In a surprisingly brief judgment on an issue of fundamental importance, the Court did not analyze whether strike pay had the character of income and the fact that a union had an obligation to make payments to its members on strike.

---

[39]See *Graham v. Green (Inspector of Taxes)*, [1925] 2 K.B. 37, 9 Tax Cas. 309 (K.B.); and *M.N.R. v. Walker*, [1951] C.T.C. 334, 52 D.T.C. 1001 (Ex.Ct.).

[40]See heading 5.5, "Benefits — general scheme", below.

[41]*Curran v. M.N.R.*, [1959] S.C.R. 850, [1959] C.T.C. 416, 59 D.T.C. 1247 (S.C.C.).

[42]*Buckman v. M.N.R.*, [1991] 2 C.T.C. 2608, 91 D.T.C. 1249 (T.C.C.).

[43]*R. v. Poynton*, [1972] C.T.C. 411, 72 D.T.C. 6329 (Ont. C.A.).

[44]Under the *surrogatum* principle, the tax consequences of a damage or settlement payment depend on the tax treatment of the item for which the payment is intended to substitute. The *surrogatum* principle is discussed in detail under heading 4.7(a), below.

[45][1990] 2 S.C.R. 1322 1323, [1990] 2 C.T.C. 439, 90 D.T.C. 6662 (S.C.C.).

In *Schwartz v. Canada* (1996),[46] the Supreme Court of Canada held that a payment of damages for breach of contract was not taxable. The contract was a contract of employment, which the prospective employer had rescinded before the prospective employee had actually started work. The prospective employer paid the prospective employee $360,000 as damages for the breach of contract. The Court held that the payment was not income from the enumerated source of employment, because it was not possible to determine what portion of the damages related to foregone income under the contract of employment and what portion related to other factors. Following the line of cases that held that payments for wrongful dismissal were tax-free,[47] the Court refused to treat paragraph 3(a) as a general provision of the Act that captured the amount as income from an unenumerated source.

Although the payment in *Schwartz* was held to be a non-taxable windfall, La Forest J. for the majority affirmed the conventional view that the sources specifically mentioned in paragraph 3(a), namely, office, employment, business, and property, were not the only sources of income. He also referred with approval to the proposition that all accretions to wealth "regardless of source" should be included in the tax base in order to measure a taxpayer's ability to pay.[48] However, Major J., in a separate concurring opinion, took issue with this conventional view, stating that "a literal adoption of this position would arguably constitute a dramatic departure from established tax jurisprudence"[49] and should be limited to issues of "fundamental importance".[50] He even doubted whether there were any unenumerated sources of income, stating that: "In 1966, the Carter Commission recommended the extension of taxation to all source of income and all accretions to purchasing power, but its recommendations were not implemented by Parliament and it is hardly the role of the judiciary to do so."[51]

With respect, Major J.'s view is wrong as a matter of interpretation of section 3, which clearly leaves open the possibility of non-specified sources of income. It is also questionable in terms of the policy objectives of income tax. His approach permits some individuals to receive substantial additions to their economic power, repeatedly or occasionally, without paying tax as they would if the additions came from an enumerated source. Accordingly, the redistributive power of the income tax is perhaps reduced, and questions of its equity and neutrality are raised, and substantial revenue may be foregone. However, Major J. may be right as a matter

---

[46]Note 27, above.

[47]The Act was subsequently amended specifically to include such payments in income as retiring allowances. In *Schwartz, ibid.*, however, the Court found that the sum was not a "retiring allowance" within the meaning of subsection 56(1) because the statutory definition of a "retiring allowance" called for a "loss" of employment, and since the employment had never commenced it had not been lost.

[48]*Ibid.*, 327-8, 6115.

[49]*Ibid.*, 334, 6120.

[50]*Ibid.*, 336, 6121.

[51]*Ibid.*, 334–6, 6119–21.

of practical reality; based on past jurisprudence, the courts are very reluctant indeed to impose tax on receipts that are not specifically covered by the Act.

In reaction to the court's narrow interpretation of the source concept, Parliament often amends the Act by adding a specific rule. For example, in *Fortino* (1996)[52] the courts held that non-compete payments received under a restrictive covenant undertaken on the sale of a business did not constitute income from a source. In the past, when such payments were received by the vendor of the business, the payments were taxable as the proceeds from the disposition of property and thus resulting in capital gains. This position was reversed in *Manrell v. R.* (2003).[53] These decisions encouraged taxpayers to structure transactions and settlements to include non-compete payments. Draft section 56.4 was proposed in 2003 to tax non-compete payments as either income or capital gains.[54]

(e) — Illegal source

The source concept of income is not limited to income from lawful sources. The case law has clearly established the principle that earnings from illegal operations or illicit businesses, such as stealing from clients,[55] embezzlement,[56] or prostitution[57] is clearly taxable.

[52]Note 16 above.

[53][2003] 3 C.T.C. 50, 2003 D.T.C. 5225 (Fed. C.A.). In *Fortino*, note 16, above, the court did not address the issue of whether the payment could be characterized as the proceeds from the disposition of capital property (and a capital gain) and so this was the specific issue in *Manrell*. The unanimous decision in *Manrell* was that because the "right to compete" was not "property".

[54]Because these rules were first announced on October 7, 2003, they apply to amounts received or receivable by a taxpayer on or after that date. Proposed section 56.4 will include a non-competition payment in income (as "other income") except to the extent that all or part of the payment can reasonably be shown to represent proceeds of disposition. In other words, a payment received in connection with the sale of shares will not be taxed as a capital gain unless it is reasonable to consider it to be proceeds from the sale of shares; instead it will be fully included in income. Proposed amendments to section 68 will allow the CRA to reallocate amounts relating to restrictive covenants based on the fair market value of the shares sold. These amendments were contained in former Bill C-10 (2007), a technical amendments bill which, according to the 2010 federal budget papers, is to be reintroduced into Parliament.

[55]*Buckman*, note 42, above.

[56]*Poynton*, note 43, above, and *Taylor v. R.*, (sub nom. *Taylor v. Canada)* [1995] 2 C.T.C. 2133, 95 D.T.C. 591 (T.C.C.); affirmed (1997), [1997] 2 C.T.C. 201, 97 D.T.C. 5120 (Fed. C.A.); leave to appeal refused (1997), (sub nom. *Taylor v. Minister of National Revenue)* 223 N.R. 399 (note) (S.C.C.).

[57]*Minister of National Revenue v. Eldridge* (1964), [1964] C.T.C. 545, 64 D.T.C. 5338 (Can. Ex. Ct.).

Should the government seek to live on the avails of prostitution or other illegal activities? Is the State coming forward to take a share of unlawful gains? Rowlatt J. in *Mann v. Nash* (1932)[58] answered:

> It is mere rhetoric. The State is doing nothing of the kind; they are taxing the individual with reference to certain facts. They are not partners; they are not principals in the illegality, or sharers in the illegality; they are merely taxing a man in respect of those resources. I think it is only rhetoric to say that they are sharing in his profits, and a piece of rhetoric which is perfectly useless for the solution of the question which I have to decide.[59]

The taxation of illegal income removes the anomaly of having the income of an honest taxpayer taxed while the similar gains of a criminal are not. This overrides any concern about the double penalty of having a taxpayer prosecuted for the crime that resulted in his or her obtaining ill-gotten income and subsequently being required to pay taxes on the illegal income.[60]

4.4 — Statutory inclusions and exclusions

(a) — Capital gains

Paragraph 3(b) specifies that taxable capital gains are included in computing income. Until 1972, capital gains were excluded from income. Paragraph 3(b) was a legislative reaction to the Carter Commission's comprehensive tax base.

Although included in income under section 3, capital gains are not income from a source in a traditional sense — rather, capital gains are income from the disposition of a source. Subsection 9(3) also makes it clear that income from property does not include capital gains. The Act also "quarantines" capital losses from the traditional sources of income: capital losses (other than allowable business investment losses) can only be used to offset taxable capital gains. On the other hand, capital gains are only partially taxed (currently 50 per cent).

(b) — Other income

In addition to the enumerated sources, section 3 contemplates income from other sources. Subdivision d (sections 56 to 59.1) specifies items to be included in computing income. Amounts that are required to be included in income by subdivision d are clearly "income" in the sense that it increases the ability to pay but it is not clear whether the source is a "productive source". The inclusions are necessary to achieve certain policy objectives. For example, the inclusion in income of pension benefits and scholarships reflects the fundamental objective of equity based on the ability to pay principle. The inclusion in income of spousal support (in combination

---

[58](1932), 16 T.C. 523 530 (Eng. K.B.).

[59]This passage was quoted by Cattanach J. in *Eldridge*, note 57, above, para. 25.

[60]Expenses incurred by an illegal business are generally deductible. See heading 8.5(d), "Expenses of an illegal business", below.

with the deduction of the amounts to the payer under section 60) reflects a policy objective of providing tax subsidies to broken marriages.

As indicated earlier, in using the wording "without restricting the generality of section 3, there shall be included in computing the income of a taxpayer for a taxation year ..." at the beginning of subsection 56(1), Parliament made clear that the enumeration in section 56 was not to be interpreted as restricting the generality of section 3.[61] Therefore, it is possible that a receipt falling outside section 56 constitutes income from a source under section 3.

(c) — Exclusions

The Act specifically excludes a number of items from income. Examples include: amounts declared by any other federal statue, such as the *Indian Act*,[62] to be exempt from income tax (s. 81(1)(a)); income from property or capital gains from the disposition of property received as compensation for physical or mental injury (s. 81(1)(g.1), (g.2) and (5)); expense allowances paid to an elected member of assembly or elected officer (s. 81(2)(3)); and income from the office of the Governor-General of Canada (s. 81(1)(n)).

The Act also excludes amounts in computing income from a specific source (rather than from income in general). Examples are the benefit of an employer's contribution to a private health plan (s. 6(1)(a))[63] and one-half of all capital gains (s. 38(a)).[64] In a few instances, the exclusion is accomplished by deducting an amount (which may or may not be 100 per cent, depending on the circumstances) that would otherwise be included in income (typically called an "exemption"): examples are the principal residence exemption (s. 40(2)(b))[65] and the scholarship exemption (s. 56(3)).[66]

When the Act wants to include the amount in net income (which is used) but not to tax it, it achieves the same outcome as an exemption by including the amount in income under section 3, and then allowing a deduction in computing taxable in-

---

[61]In *Schwartz*, note 27, above, 328, 6116. Justice La Forest stated: "The phrasing adopted by Parliament, in s. 3(a) and in the introductory part of s. 56(1) is probably the strongest that could have been used to express the idea that income from *all* sources, enumerated or not, expressly provided for in subdivision d or not, was taxable under the Act".

[62]R.S.C. 1985, c. I-5. Indians on reserves are not subject to taxation in respect of the ownership or use of real or personal property situated on the reserve (s. 87). The courts have held that an Indian's employment income is personal property (*Nowegijick v. R.*, [1983] C.T.C. 20, 83 D.T.C. 5041 (S.C.C.); and *Williams v. R.*, [1992] 1 C.T.C. 225, 92 D.T.C. 6320 (S.C.C.). If the income is situated on a reserve, it is exempt from income tax. See CRA, Technical News No. 2, December 30, 1994.

[63]See ch. 5, Income from Employment, below.

[64]See ch. 10, Capital Gains, below.

[65]*Ibid.*

[66]See ch. 12, Other Income and Deductions, below.

come under Division e. One example is the taxable income deduction for taxable capital gains from the sale of qualified small business corporation shares (s. 110.6)[67] which effectively excludes these taxable capital gains from being taxed in the hands of individual. Another example is the deduction (s. 110(1)(f)) for welfare payments and workers' compensation payments which are initially included in the income of an individual (s. 56(1)).[68]

Tax credits also have the effect of excluding income from tax. For example the basic credit effectively exempts the first $8,929 earned by every taxpayer from income (s. 118(1)) and the pension credit effectively exempts the first $2,000 of pension income earned by every taxpayer from income (s. 118(3)).[69]

Finally, the income earned by certain taxpayers is exempt from tax under s. 149. These taxpayers include charities, non-profit organizations (hospitals and universities), pension plans and crown corporations. As explained in subsequent chapters, these exclusions are primarily tax expenditures, designed to fulfill social policy objectives.

4.5 — Gifts and inheritances

(a) — Personal gifts

The traditional concept of income did not include gifts and inheritances. Gifts are "voluntary and gratuitous transfer of property"[70] with no strings attached (i.e., there is no valuable consideration). Gifts can be made in cash or in kind. What should be the income tax consequences of receiving a gift?

(i) — Carter Commission recommendations

The Carter Commission's recommendation was to include gifts and inheritances in the comprehensive tax base. The argument was essentially the same as the argument for the inclusion of capital gains. Like capital gains, gifts and inheritances increase the economic power of those who receive them, and should therefore be included in a tax base that purports to measure ability to pay. As well, like capital gains, gifts and inheritances are received disproportionately by high-income individuals, so that their inclusion would steepen the progressivity of the income tax system.

However, the inclusion of gifts and inheritances in the income of the recipient, where they would be taxed at the graduated rates that applied to all of the recipient's ordinary income, would undoubtedly have increased the total burden of tax on gifts and inheritances. The severity of including a large gift or inheritance in the income of a single year (the problem is the same with capital gains and other non-

---

[67] See ch. 14, Taxable Income and Tax for Individuals.

[68] *Ibid.*

[69] *Ibid.*

[70] *Bellingham*, note 12 above, 198, 6081.

recurring receipts) was mitigated by recommendations for generous provisions for "forward averaging", which would have enabled taxpayers to smooth out their income by spreading the recognition (and enjoyment) of unusual income receipts over a period of years.[71] The problem of keeping track of numerous small gifts was addressed by a recommendation for the exemption of gifts up to an annual limit, so that only large gifts would need to be recorded and reported.

In 1966, when the Carter Commission reported, gifts and inheritances were subject to federal estate and gift taxes as well as provincial succession duties and gift taxes in Ontario, Quebec and British Columbia. However, these taxes were entirely independent of the income tax, and the rates and exemptions did not take account of the recipient's income. The Carter Commission recommended the repeal of these other taxes on gifts and inheritances.

The Carter Commission's proposal to tax gifts and inheritances as income was never accepted by the government and was not part of the 1971 Act. However, the federal government repealed its estate and gift taxes in 1971, giving as its reason the introduction of capital gains taxation with deemed dispositions on death and on gifts.[72] Over the next 14 years, all of the provinces withdrew from (or never entered) the field of death and gift taxation. Ironically, the indirect effect of the 1971 tax reform has been to substantially reduce the taxes exigible on gifts and inheritances. This is unfortunate because the taxation of wealth at the time of gift or inheritance has a place in a mix of taxes which seeks to reflect the ability to pay.

(ii) — Reasons for exclusion

An individual who works is taxed, but one who lives off the generosity of others is not. Why is it that gifts and inheritances are not income? The answer is probably that they are transfers of "capital" or that they are not from a productive source. As Robertson J. stated in *Bellingham*,[73]

> There is no need to cite authorities for the proposition that gifts and inheritances are immune from taxation. It is well accepted that these items represent non-recurring amounts and the transfer of old wealth. Underlying the source doctrine is the understanding that income involves the creation of new wealth. Gifts do not flow from a productive source of income.

From a policy perspective, there are perhaps three reasons for not taxing gifts and inheritances. First, the tax-free treatment of gifts may encourage, or at least not to discourage the redistribution of wealth which gifts often entail, as it is usually the richer taxpayers that give to the poorer ones, rather than vice versa. Second, it may make sense to keep tax auditors away from the Christmas tree and birthday cake —

---

[71]Averaging is briefly discussed under heading 1.5(c)(ii), "Income fluctuation", above. Since 1988, the Act has contained no averaging provisions.

[72]Capital gains arising on these deemed dispositions are discussed under heading 10.6, "Special events and deemed dispositions," below.

[73]Note 33, above, 198, 6081.

to relieve familial gifts from any tax cost or tax compliance requirements.[74] It may also be difficult for a recipient to pay an income tax on a gift, especially when the gift is in kind, not in cash. Third, the donor is taxed on any capital gains (as well as recaptured capital cost allowance) realized from making the gift.[75]

(b) — Commercial gifts

The tax-free treatment of gifts is limited to personal gifts. Gifts received in a business or employment context are treated differently. If an amount is given because of some relationship to an office or employment or a businesses, it is likely treated as income from an office, employment, or from a business. For example, subsection 5(1) specifically includes "gratuities" in computing income from an office or employment.[76] The value of a gold ring received by an employee for his long service to the company was a taxable benefit under section 6.[77] A sum of cash received by a professional swimmer from a newspaper was held to be a payment for services, despite the fact that the newspaper was not contractually liable to pay unless the taxpayer successfully swam Lake Ontario and the taxpayer did, in fact, fail by one-half mile (thus the payment was gratuitous).[78]

The same is generally true for gifts received in the course of a business if services are provided. For example, corporate gifts received by a self-employed unordained minister who conducted teaching sessions were held to be payment for services because the wife of one of the principal shareholders of the corporation regularly attended the sessions.[79] In comparison, a sum paid to the secretary of a company who had acted as liquidator in the voluntary winding-up without remuneration was not taxable, because the amount in question was paid by the shareholders after the winding-up as a tribute or testimonial and not as payment for services.[80] The distinction between a payment for services and a gift is easy to grasp but not always easy to apply.

---

[74]McNulty, *Federal Income Taxation of Individuals in a Nutshell* (6th edition) (1996), 62.

[75]Ss. 69(1)(b) and 70(5). There is no capital gain in the case of a spousal gift unless an election is made out of the spousal rollover rules in ss. 73(1) and 70(6).

[76]See ch. 5, Income from Employment, below, for a discussion of the inclusion for gifts under ss. 5 and 6.

[77]*Wisla v. R.* (1999), [2000] 1 C.T.C. 2823, 2000 D.T.C. 3563 (T.C.C. [Informal Procedure]). See also CRA Press Release, December 15, 2001, "Gifts and awards given by employers to their employees", which sets out the CRA's administrative $500 exemption for non-gifts and awards.

[78]*Campbell v. R.* (1958), 21 Tax A.B.C. 145, 59 D.T.C. 8 (Can. Tax App. Bd.).

[79]*Campbell v. R.*, (sub nom. *Campbell v. Canada)* [1992] 2 C.T.C. 2256, (sub nom. *Campbell v. Minister of National Revenue)* 92 D.T.C. 1855 (T.C.C.).

[80]*Cowan v. Seymour* (1919), [1920] 1 K.B. 500, 7 T.C. 372 (Eng. C.A.). In a Canadian case, *McMillan v. Minister of National Revenue*, [1982] C.T.C. 2345, 82 D.T.C. 1287 (T.R.B.), the taxpayer, who was an insurance broker, received gratuity payments from another broker when his major client switched to this broker on a tax-free basis.

(c) — Gift of property

While the value of gifts is tax-free to the donee, the donor may be liable to income tax on any capital gain realized at the time of gifting. As discussed further in Chapter 13 of this book, subsection 69(1) of the Act deems the donor to have sold the property for fair market value and the donor is forced to recognize any gain or loss for tax purposes. Gifting of property by one spouse to another or by a shareholder to his or her company can take place on a "rollover" basis, resulting in no immediate gain or loss to the donor.

4.6 — Windfalls

(a) — Tax exempt

Windfalls, such as a lottery prize or a valuable find, were not taxed when the Carter Commission reported. No doubt this reflected the "source" concept of income. Gambling activities are of a personal nature. Even compulsive gamblers who continually try their luck at a game of chance, winning is a matter of luck. "The "odds" of winning a game of chance such as Lotto 6/49 are a mathematically determined and unchanging ratio. The chances of one ticket winning the Lotto 6/49 jackpot are said to be one in 13.5 million."[81]

However, since windfalls increase taxable capacity no differently than dollars received in other ways, the Carter Commission recommended their inclusion in income.[82] Taxing gambling winnings[83] raised the question whether gambling losses should be deductible, to which the Carter Commission answered no (except against gambling winnings).

The government did not accept the Commission's recommendations with respect to windfalls.[84] When the House of Commons Standing Committee on Finance revisited this issue in 1994 and recommended that lottery and casino winnings over $500 be taxed, with losses deductible against winnings, these recommendations were also never implemented.[85] Windfalls accordingly remain untaxed.[86]

With the introduction of capital gains tax in Canada in 1972, it became necessary to deal with the possibility that lottery winnings which were not income might nonetheless attract tax as capital gains. To maintain the tax-free treatment, paragraph 40(2)(f) deems any gain or loss from the disposition of lottery tickets to be nil. As

---

[81] *Leblanc v. R.*, note 87, below, para 23.

[82] Carter Report, note 8, above, vol. 3, 70.

[83] *Ibid.*, 526-527.

[84] However, gambling winnings are taxable as income from a business if gambling activities were organized and carried out systematically. See heading 6.2(c)(iv), "Gambling", below.

[85] See Canada, House of Commons, *Confronting Canada's Deficit Crisis — Tenth Report of the Standing Committee on Finance* (1994), 32.

[86] In the United States, windfall gains are taxable under s. 61(a) of the *Internal Revenue Code*.

Bowman TCCJ succinctly stated in *Leblanc v. R.* (2006),[87] "the general perception that lottery winnings are not taxable is deeply embedded in the Canadian fiscal psyche." Whenever the idea is revisited (as it is from time to time), the issue is always whether to allow taxpayers a deduction for the cost of all their losing tickets (as the tax system does for one-half of capital losses).

(b) — Distinguished from Business

Gambling winnings are taxable as income from a business if gambling activities were organized and carried out systematically.[88] For example, gambling gains have been held to be taxable where the gambling was an adjunct or incident of a business carried on, for example, by a casino owner who gambles in his own casino or an owner of horses who trains and races horses and who bets on the races.[89] Similarly, gambling gains have been held taxable where a taxpayer uses his own expertise and skill to earn a livelihood in a gambling game in which skill is a significant component (for example the pool player who, in cold sobriety, challenges inebriated pool players to a game of pool).[90].

4.7 — Damages and settlements

(a) — The "surrogatum principle"

A person who suffers harm caused by another may seek compensation for (a) loss of income, (b) expenses incurred, (c) property destroyed, or (d) personal injury, as well as punitive damages. For tax purposes, damages or compensation received, either pursuant to a court judgment or an out-of-court settlement, may be considered as on account of income, capital, or windfall to the recipient. The nature of the injury or harm for which compensation is made generally determines the tax consequences of damages.

Under the *surrogatum* principle, the tax consequences of a damage or settlement payment depend on the tax treatment of the item for which the payment is intended to substitute:[91]

> Where, pursuant to a legal right, a trader receives from another person, compensation for the trader's failure to receive a sum of money which, if it had been received, would have been credited to the amount of profits (if any) arising in any year from the trade carried on by him at the time when the compensation is so received, the

[87] *Leblanc v. R.* (2006), 2007 D.T.C. 307 (Eng.), [2007] 2 C.T.C. 2248 (T.C.C. [General Procedure]), para. 38.

[88] See heading 6.2(c)(iv), "Gambling", below.

[89] *Badame v. Minister of National Revenue* (1951), 51 D.T.C. 29 (Can. Tax App. Bd.).

[90] *Luprypa v. R.*, 97 D.T.C. 1416, [1997] 3 C.T.C. 2363 (T.C.C.)

[91] This principle was articulated by Diplock L.J. in *London & Thames Haven Oil Wharves Ltd. v. Attwooll*, [1966] 3 All E.R. 145; reversed [1967] 2 All E.R. 124 134 (C.A.). It has been adopted and applied by the Federal Court of Appeal in *Manley*, note 92, below, and *Schwartz*, note 27.

compensation is to be treated for income tax purposes in the same way as that sum of money would have been treated if it had been received instead of the compensation.

Generally, compensation for a loss of income is taxed as income. For example, compensation for a finder's fee,[92] loss of profits,[93] or disability insurance benefits in arrears[94] have all been held to be taxable as income. The recovery of an expense is not income, unless the expense was deducted. A payment for damaged or destroyed property is treated as an amount received in a sale or exchange of the property.[95] A payment for the loss of capital is treated on account of capital. A capital receipt is generally not income. However, compensation on account of capital may be taxable if it is considered as "eligible capital amount",[96] or if there is a "disposition" of a "property" where the payment is made in exchange for the discharge of a legal right.[97] Damages for personal injuries and punitive damages are generally excluded from income.

Tsiaprailis v. R. (2005), was a Supreme Court of Canada case that dealt with the tax treatment of compensation for employer-provided disability insurance benefits

---

[92]*Manley v. R.*, [1985] 1 C.T.C. 186, 85 D.T.C. 5050 (Fed. C.A.); leave to appeal refused (1986), 67 N.R. 400 (note) (S.C.C.).

[93]For example, in *Charles R. Bell Ltd. v. R.*, [1992] 2 C.T.C. 260, 92 D.T.C. 6472 (Fed. C.A.); leave to appeal refused (1993), 156 N.R. 239 (note) (S.C.C.), the amount of the settlement received on termination of a distributorship agreement was held to be income since the payment was intended to replace the taxpayer's loss of profits. Similarly, in *Zygocki v. R,*, [1984] C.T.C. 280, 84 D.T.C. 6283 (Fed. T.D.), the amount received by the taxpayer, a trader in real estate, for termination of a contract was found to be income. In *Schofield Oil Ltd. v. Canada*, [1992] 1 C.T.C. 8, 92 D.T.C. 6022 (Fed. C.A.), a payment to release the taxpayer from remaining 20 months of contractual obligations was held to be compensation for future profits.

[94]In *Tsiaprailis v. R.*, [2005] 2 C.T.C. 1, 2005 D.T.C. 5119 (Eng.).

[95]Compensation for damages to depreciable property is included in the taxpayer's income (s. 12(1)(f)), but only to the extent that the compensation is not expended on repairing the damaged property. Repair costs are deducted in computing income. Compensation for the destruction or loss of a capital property is "proceeds of disposition" (s. 54), giving rise to either a capital gain or loss from the disposition of the property.

[96]Eligible capital amounts are proceeds received on the disposition of a business' intangible assets (e.g., goodwill). This topic is discussed in detail under heading 9.5, "Eligible capital expenditures", below. In *Pepsi Cola Canada Ltd. v. R.*, [1979] C.T.C. 454, 79 D.T.C. 5387 (Fed. C.A.), above, an amount received upon the termination of a bottling franchise was held to be payment for goodwill. A compensation for the loss of profits resulting from destruction or materially crippling of the whole structure of the taxpayer's profit-making apparatus was held to be on an account of capital: see *Pe Ben Industries Co. v. M.N.R.*, [1988] 2 C.T.C. 120, 88 D.T.C. 6347 (Fed. T.D.).

[97]According to *Mohawk Oil v M.N.R.*, [1992] 1 C.T.C. 195, 92 D.T.C. 6135 (F.C.A.), moneys paid in exchange for the discharge of even a questionable legal claim may constitute income in the hands of the taxpayer.

that would have been taxable under s. 6(1)(f) had they not been terminated. The taxpayer had sued the insurance company that had terminated the benefits and had received a lump sum settlement which released the insurance company from any obligation to pay any unpaid past or future benefits. Since paragraph 6(1)(f) requires amounts received "that were payable to the taxpayer on a periodic basis . . . pursuant . . . to a disability insurance plan" to be included in employment income, the Supreme Court, by a majority (of seven to three) found the payment for past benefits to be taxable, stating that:[98]

> "[t]o conclude that the payment for past benefits was not made "pursuant to" the insurance disability plan because it was paid to obtain a release from liability under the policy is to render the surrogatum principle meaningless."

Unfortunately, the Court, by majority did not apply the same logic to the portion of the settlement in respect of future benefits and upheld the Federal Court of Appeal decision that the future benefit portion was tax-free on the ground that it was not paid "pursuant to" the plan. With respect, this part of the decision does not make sense: the only difference between the past and future benefits was one of timing. The compensation for both portions of the payment can be traced to employment income and should be taxable under paragraph 6(1)(f).

(b) — Damages for personal injury

Damages for personal injuries are not income for tax purposes because they are not from a productive source. Justice Maloney stated in *Schwartz*: "In the case of the personal injury victim, the source of the right to damages is that person's right not to be injured by the tort of another. That is not a source of income within the contemplation of paragraph 3(a) of the *Income Tax Act*".[99]

Personal injuries include both physical injuries (the loss of a limb) and non-physical injuries (loss of dignity or reputation as a result of libel or defamation). Damages for personal injuries or death generally include amounts paid on account of compensation for pain and suffering, the loss of amenities of life, the loss of earning capacity, the shortened expectation of life, the loss of financial support caused by the death of the supporting individual, reimbursement of out-of-pocket expenses (such as medical and hospital expenses), or compensation for accrued or future loss of earnings.[100] Damages for personal injury may also include compensation for lost wages.

Several considerations may justify the exclusion of personal injury damages from taxation. It is offensive to tax a payment for pain and suffering, as the victim should be assisted rather than taxed. A recovery for out-of-pocket expenses should not be taxed, as there is no net accretion to wealth. A recovery of human capital (loss of

---

[98]Note 94 at para. 116.

[99]*R. v. Schwartz*, [1994] 2 C.T.C. 99, 94 D.T.C. 6249 (Fed. C.A.), para. 17. Although the Federal Court of Appeal decision was reversed by the Supreme Court of Canada (see note 27, above), this statement was not overruled.

[100]Interpretation Bulletin IT-365R2, "Damages, Settlements and Similar Receipts" (1987).

income earning capacity) should be tax-free. Similarly, a recovery for non-taxable items, such as personal reputation, good health, privacy, and the freedom from harassment, should not be taxable. Furthermore, the legal theory of personal injury damages (*restitutio in integrum*) is that the amount received is intended to put the plaintiff (the injured party) in the position that he or she would have been in if the tort had not been committed.[101] It follows that if the damage payments received were subject to tax, the after-tax amount received would be less than the actual damages incurred and the injured party would not be whole as before the injury.

(c) — Punitive damages

Punitive damages are amounts the person who caused the harm must pay to the victim as punishment for outrageous conduct. In *Bellingham*, the "additional interest" awarded to the taxpayer under the *Expropriation Act* was considered by the court to be a punitive damage award: the "true source of the award is the *Expropriation Act* which dictates as a matter of public policy, that expropriating authorities are obligated to pay a penal sum in circumstances where their behaviour falls below a prescribed standard".[102]

Because punitive damages are intended to punish the wrongdoer and not to compensate the victim, the victim may be considered an incidental beneficiary. Although a punitive award may actually put the victim in a better economic position than before the harm was experienced, it is not considered to be income from a source under section 3. Such an award was analogized with a gift in *Bellingham*, at least from the perspective of the recipient.[103] The absence of a market transaction or *quid pro quo* in relation to the punitive damages also led them to be characterized as windfalls.[104] Since both gifts and windfalls are excluded from income, punitive damages are similarly excluded.

4.8 — Imputed income

(a) — Non-taxation

Imputed income is a form of non-cash income. It consists of the flow of benefits derived from labour on one's own behalf or the benefits from the ownership of property. Economists generally consider imputed income as income that should be taxed because consumption is part of income under the Haig-Simons concept. The relevance of consumption to the measurement of income is that not all things which are used or consumed are purchased in ordinary market transactions. When a person uses (or consumes) his or her own personal services or his or her own property, this type of consumption increases the person's economic power and ability to pay.

---

[101] *Andrews v. Grand & Toy Alberta Ltd.*, [1978] 2 S.C.R. 229, 83 D.L.R. (3d) 452 (S.C.C.).

[102] *Bellingham*, note 33, above, 201.

[103] *Ibid.*

[104] Justice Robertson stated: "The critical factor is that the punitive damage award does not flow from either the performance or breach of a market transaction". *Ibid.*, 200, 6082.

It is clear, therefore, that a completely comprehensive definition of income must include the benefit of the personal services and personal property consumed by the taxpayer in the year. This benefit must be valued and "imputed" to the consumer as income.[105]

For the purposes of the Act, however, imputed income is not income from a source and, thus, is not taxable. The failure to tax imputed income creates inequities and inefficiencies. It also raises social issues, especially in respect of unpaid housework which is typically performed by women. However, the practical difficulties in subjecting imputed income to tax make taxation unlikely.

(b) — Owner-occupied home

The use of one's own property is a major source of imputed income. The imputed rent of an owner-occupied home provides the clearest example. The tenant has to pay rent out of his or her after-tax earnings in order to obtain the benefit of accommodation. The homeowner receives no taxable income from his or her investment in a home, which therefore provides the homeowner with a tax-free benefit of accommodation. If you doubt the great advantage enjoyed by the homeowner, consider the following example.

A taxpayer (the Homeowner in the chart below) with a marginal tax rate of 50 per cent owns a house, free and clear, which could be rented for $12,000 per year and he lives in the house. Assume that he moves to another city and becomes a renter (the Renter in the chart below). He leases his house in the old city for $12,000 per year and rents an equivalent house in the new city for $12,000 per year. See how this move leaves him worse off to the tune of $6,000 per year.

	Homeowner	**Renter**
Salary	$100,000	$100,000
Rental income (old city)	0	12,000
Taxable income	$100,000	$112,000
Tax (at 50 per cent)	(50,000)	(56,000)
Cost of rent (old city)	0	(12,000)
Discretionary income	$ 50,000	$ 44,000

Why does this happen? As a Homeowner, he paid no rent and received no rental income. But when he becomes a Renter, he pays rent of $12,000 and receives rental income of $12,000. If we disregard tax liability, his rental payment and his rental income cancel each other out perfectly. But the $12,000 the Renter pays is not deductible from taxable income, while the $12,000 he receives is subject to tax at 50 per cent. Therefore, the Renter becomes liable to pay an extra $6,000 in tax and the net result is that he is worse off by $6,000 each year. How would the position be changed if the imputed rent value of his home was brought into income for tax

[105]The Carter Commission recommended that imputed income continue to be exempt from tax.

purposes each year? When the taxpayer was a Homeowner, he would have had to include in his income a notional rent of $12,000 each year (just like the Renter), and this would increase his tax by $6,000. He would still pay no rent, and receive no rental income, but he would pay an additional amount of tax, namely $6,000.

The tax advantage which the homeowner enjoys by virtue of the non-taxation of imputed rent[106] could be corrected in one of two ways. The most obvious way is to bring imputed rent into income, and to allow the deduction for mortgage interest as an expense incurred to earn income. However, as noted by the Carter Commission, this raises the administrative problems of assessing the rental value of all owner-occupied dwellings in Canada, and it raises the policy problem of whether it is fair to tax imputed rent without also taxing other forms of imputed income. A second way of roughly equalizing the positions of owners and renters would be to allow renters to deduct for tax purposes some portion of the rent on their homes. This second approach was suggested by the Carter Commission as an alternative to taxing imputed income.[107] Rent is one of the most important types of personal consumption expenditures which are generally not deductible in computing net income. It is obviously administratively feasible but can only be justified as a tax expenditure.

(c) — Unpaid housework

The consumption of personal services is one element of imputed income. Most people buy clothes out of after-tax earnings. A person who makes his or her own clothes receives the same benefit tax-free (apart from the cost of materials). Home repairs or improvements, home-grown food and automobile maintenance by the owner are similar.

In a family where one spouse earns income and the other remains at home to care for children and keep house, the homemaker's duties are unpaid and consequently untaxed. Yet the unpaid household work confers a considerable benefit on the family, because the family is spared the cost of paying for child care and housework which the two-earner family would have to purchase.

The non-taxation of the value of unpaid household labour could be perceived as a tax benefit to the one-earner family[108] and a disincentive to seeking work outside the home. The reason for this perception is that the value of work performed by

---

[106]A complete analysis of the effect of the tax system on the relative costs of owning and renting a home would also have to take account of the exclusion from capital gains tax of the principal residence. This is another concession to the homeowner relative to the renter, because the renter must pay tax on any capital gains on all of his or her investments.

[107]Carter Report, note 6, above, vol. 3, 48.

[108]Although self-performed services are technically a form of tax avoidance, people do not resent this form of avoidance as it is achieved through personal initiative and effort rather than class privilege or expensive tax advice. Indeed, the largest amounts of imputed income from services would probably be concentrated in the lower-income groups, who cannot afford to pay for services such as house-cleaning, gardening or home repair.

women in the home is not taxed whereas the value of work performed outside the home is taxed. The non-taxation of housework also has implication in other areas involving the income tax treatment of families. For example, the child-care expense deduction is generally only available to the lower-earning parent and is generally only available for expenses incurred to earn income from employment or a business.[109] This means that a one-income family will not be able to claim a child care deduction because the stay-at-home parent (the lower earning parent) has no such qualifying income. Similarly, as discussed in Chapter 12, the contribution limits for government provided and tax-assisted retirement savings vehicles, such as the Canada Pension Plan (CPP) and registered retirement savings plans (RRSPs), are based on qualifying amounts of "income" for tax purposes.[110]

4.9 — Computation of income

(a) — Net concept

The notion that income is net of deductions is borne out by the history of section 3.[111] Section 3 of the 1917 *Income War Tax Act* stated that income "means the annual net profit or gain or gratuity . . ."[112] The word "net" in this provision stands out as affirming the ordinary meaning of profits and gains established by the English and Canadian courts.[113] When section 3 of the *Income War Tax Act* was replaced by section 3 of the 1948 *Income Tax Act*, the words "profit" and "gain" were dropped and the word "income" was used. This change in wording should not be interpreted as a change in Parliament's intention to overrule the common law principle[114] that income means net income, as other sections of the Act affirmed that

[109]See the definition of child care expenses in s. 63(3). There are some exceptions. For example, if the lower income spouse is attending a designated education institution or is infirm, child care expenses can be claimed by the higher income spouse (s. 63(2)). See headings 8.4(b), "Child care expenses", and 12.10 "Child care expenses", below.

[110]The Act allows the income-earning spouse to claim a credit for a dependent spouse who has very little income (s. 118(1)(a)). It also allows an income-earning spouse to use his or her own contribution limit to contribute to a spousal RRSP (s. 146(5.1) and to split his or her CPP retirement benefits with a spouse.

[111]*Ludco Enterprises Ltd. v. Canada* (2001), [2002] 1 C.T.C. 95, (sub nom. *Ludco Enterprises Ltd. v. R.)* 2001 D.T.C. 5505 (Eng.), 2001 D.T.C. 5518 (Fr.) (S.C.C.) para. 57 (per Iacobucci J.).

[112]The wording of s. 3 was changed into its present format in 1948. The reference to "annual profit or gain . . ." was replaced by "income from a source".

[113]LaBrie, *The Meaning of Income in the Law of Income Tax* (1953), 27.

[114]This principle is well entrenched in Canadian jurisprudence. See, for example, *Shaw v. Minister of National Revenue* (1939), [1938-39] C.T.C. 346 348 (S.C.C.); *Lumbers v. Minister of National Revenue*, [1944] C.T.C. 67 70 (S.C.C.); affirming [1943] C.T.C. 281, 2 D.T.C. 631 (Can. Ex. Ct.); affirmed [1944] S.C.R. 167 (S.C.C.); *Irwin v. Minister of National Revenue*, [1964] S.C.R. 662, [1964] C.T.C. 362, 64 D.T.C. 5227 (S.C.C.), 664 [S.C.R.], 364 [C.T.C.], 5228 [D.T.C.]; *Associated Investors of Canada Ltd. v. Minister of*

income is a net concept. For example, income from a business or property is the profit therefrom (section 9), and income from an office or employment is computed after deducting expenses listed in section 8 of the Act.

The net concept of income is also consistent with the economists' definition of income (net accretion in wealth) and the concept of comprehensive tax base. More importantly, the selection of income as the base implies that income should provide a measure of a taxpayer's ability to pay tax. The notion that income means net income serves to further that purpose, since only the amount of net income is subject to a taxpayer's control, representing a taxpayer's ability to pay.

(b) — Source by source

Income must be computed in accordance with the rules set forth in section 3. Paragraph 3(a) includes income from all sources inside and outside Canada, including, "without restricting the generality of the foregoing", the aggregate of income for a year from four enumerated sources: office, employment, business, and property. Detailed rules governing the calculation of net income from these four sources are provided in subdivision a (office or employment) and subdivision b (business or property) of Division B of Part I of the Act. Subdivision d requires the inclusion of a number of miscellaneous types of "other income".

Section 4 requires a source-by-source calculation. For the purpose of section 4, "source" means both the character of income (e.g., employment or business) and territorial source. If a business is carried on in two different locations, income or loss from each location must be determined separately.

(c) — Regular income v. taxable capital gains

Paragraph 3(b) requires the inclusion in income of net taxable capital gains (i.e. taxable capital gains net of allowable capital losses) from the disposition of a property. The detailed rules for computing taxable capital gains and allowable capital losses are contained in subdivision c of Division B of Part I of the Act.

As discussed further in Chapters 10 and 14, capital gains and losses are "quarantined". While capital gains are taxable in half, capital losses are recognized also in half. Furthermore, capital losses are generally limited to offset only capital gains, although taxable capital gains can be offset by regular losses. The "allowable business investment loss" is a hybrid to accord business loss treatment of certain capital losses. Chapter 11 discusses the motivations for taxpayers to characterize their profit or loss as either in the nature of a business or capital investment.

National Revenue, [1967] 2 Ex. C.R. 96, [1967] C.T.C. 138, 67 D.T.C. 5096 (Can. Ex. Ct.), 102 [Ex. C.R.]; *Symes v. R.* (1993), (sub nom. *Symes v. Canada*) [1994] 1 C.T.C. 40, 94 D.T.C. 6001 (S.C.C.); and *Canderel Ltd. v. R.*, [1998] 2 C.T.C. 35, 98 D.T.C. 6100 (S.C.C.).

(d) — Policy-based deductions

Paragraph 3(c) requires the taxpayer to add the amounts under paragraphs 3(a) and 3(b) and to subtract "other deductions" allowed by subdivision e.[115] These deductions are policy-based deductions, such as contributions to an RRSP under section 60, moving expense deduction under section 62, and child care expense under section 63. Because these expenses are not incurred for the purpose of earning income from a business, they are generally not deductible in computing business income. In order to encourage retirement savings and labour mobility, sections 60 and 62 specifically allow the deductions. Child care is an important social issue and section 63 is one of public policy instrument in this area.

(e) — Loss recognition

Paragraph 3(d) allows the deduction of current year losses from office or employment and business or property and the deduction of "allowable business investment losses." Finally, paragraphs 3(e) states that the amount determined under paragraph 3(d) is the taxpayer's income for the year. If the figure under paragraph 3(d) is negative, paragraph 3(f) deems the taxpayer's income to be nil.[116]

Finally, income under section 3 is a net concept: income from each of the enumerated sources is net of related deductions; taxable capital gains are net of allowable capital losses; and current year losses from the four enumerated sources are deductible.

---

[115] Because s. 4(2) specifically denies the deduction of items in subdivision e in determining income from a particular source, these items can only be claimed as subdivision e "other deductions".

[116] The computation of s. 3 income is further discussed in ch. 14, Taxable Income and Tax for Individuals, below.

5
INCOME FROM EMPLOYMENT

5.1 — Legislative scheme and policy

(a) — Legislative scheme

(i) — Statutory provisions

The subject of this chapter is income from an office or income from employment, are the first two sources of income listed in paragraph 3(a) of the *Income Tax Act* (the "Act"). The computation of income from an office or employment is provided for in subdivision B of Part I of the Act. The subdivision opens with subsection 5(1), which provides:

> Subject to this Part, a taxpayer's income for a taxation year from an office or employment is the salary, wages and other remuneration, including gratuities, received by the taxpayer in the year.

Sections 6 and 7 specifically include a large number of benefits and other forms of remuneration in computing income from an office or employment. Section 8 specifies the types of deductible expenses.

These rules address three general questions: 1) How is income characterized as income from office or income from employment? 2) What amounts are included or deducted in computing income from office or employment? 3) When is the amount included or deducted in computing income?

(ii) — Distinct regime

The regime for taxing income from an office or employment is different from that for income from other sources, mostly notably income from business. One major distinction is the scope of deductions. In computing business income, all expenses incurred for the purpose of earning income are deductible unless the deduction is specifically prohibited by the Act.[1] In contrast, in computing income from employment, no expenses are deductible unless section 8 specifically permits the deduction. As a result, income from employment is taxed more or less on a gross basis, whereas business income is taxed on a net basis after deductions.

Another major distinction is that the withholding tax system applies only to income from office or employment. Under this system, the payer of income (i.e., the employer) is legally required to withhold the income tax (as well as Canada Pension Plan contributions and Employment Insurance premiums) from the pay to the employee and submit the tax payment to the Minister of National Revenue.[2] The employee may receive a refund for the excessive amount of taxes withheld after filing a tax return.[3] The taxpayer loses the time value of money on the taxes withheld during the year.

Other distinctions exist with respect to timing and international employees. Income from employment is computed on a cash basis (amounts are included in the year received and expenses are deductible in the year paid), while business income is

---

[1]See heading 8.3, "Income earning purpose" below.

[2]Section 153 of the Act. Employers must also deduct payroll taxes, including the employer's share of Canada Pension Plan and Employment Insurance premiums as well as Worker's Safety Insurance Board (WSIB) premiums and provincial payroll taxes, such as the Ontario Employer Health tax.

[3]The excessive taxes are not automatically refunded in the absence of a tax return. For further discussion on the tax collection system, see chapter. 18.

recognized on an accrual-basis.[4] Individuals working in foreign countries or foreign individuals working in Canada are taxed more harshly in the host country if they earn income from employment as opposed to income from business.[5]

(b) — Policy

The distinct regime for taxing income from employment or office is justifiable on the policy grounds of tax base protection, equity and simplicity (or administrative efficiency). As discussed below, however, these policy objectives are sometimes conflicting and must be balanced in designing the tax rules.

(i) — Tax base protection

Employment income is a very important revenue base for taxation. Much of the income earned by Canadians is employment income and the personal income tax is the main source of revenue for the Canadian government.[6] Therefore, a tiny leakage in this tax base may cause a loss of tax revenue.

In order to minimize tax base erosion, the Act attempts to tax not only wages or salaries but also non-cash "fringe benefits" and other amounts that are in the nature of employee compensation. Non-taxation of fringe benefits would pose a threat to the tax base. The concern about tax base protection also helps explain the limited deductions available to employees.

(ii) — Equity

Equity is a key policy objective of the income tax. Vertical equity or progressive taxation is the hallmark of personal income tax. Because employment income accounts for the lion's share of the personal income tax base, the taxation of this type of income has serious equity implications.

With respect to the income inclusion rules under sections 6 and 7, the main policy concern is equity. If the Act taxed only an employee's salary or wages, employers and employees would become very fond of fringe benefits. Assuming that a fringe benefit is deductible by the employer as an expense of doing business, it is immaterial to the employer whether he or she pays an employee a full salary of $80,000 or a salary of $70,000 plus fringe benefits worth $10,000. But if the fringe benefits were not taxed as part of the employee's income, then (assuming that the employee's marginal rate is about 50 per cent) the fringe benefits would be worth nearly twice as much to the employee as they cost the employer, and the latter

---

[4]See heading 1.6(d), "Time value of money" and heading 6.5, "Methods of accounting", below.

[5]It is beyond the scope of this book to discuss international tax issues. For further reference, see Li, Cockfield and Wilkie, *International Taxation in Canada: Principles and Practices*.

[6]The shrinkage in the income tax base could also lead to the erosion of the base of payroll taxes. Employment income is also the base for payroll taxes which finance important parts of our social security system.

alternative would be equivalent to a fully-taxed salary of nearly $90,000. In effect, the government would be contributing to the employee's pay by foregoing tax on part of the pay.

Failure to tax fringe benefits violates the principle of equity. "A disparity in the tax treatment of an employee who receives all his compensation as salary and wages and one who receives the same amount of compensation but partly in the form of fringe benefits is not defensible".[7] Taxpayer inequity is most offensive in cases where highly paid executives receive tax-free economic benefits (e.g. items to assist them in their work such as a handheld electronic device, laptop and/or cell phone) that are denied to lower-paid employees, while the latter are compensated only in fully taxable cash. Furthermore, the non-taxation of non-cash compensation would increase inequities among employees in different types of business. In many industries, employees may receive (either free or purchased at a discount) goods and services which the employer sells to the general public. In other industries, employees receive relatively little non-cash compensation. In the absence of well-defined rules on the taxation of fringe benefits, taxpayers and their employers would devise tax-free compensation schemes by using a medium other than cash. These schemes would further shift a disproportionate tax burden to those individuals whose compensation is in the form of cash.

The fact that there are fewer deductions also allows for equity between employees: it means that higher-income employees who can afford to purchase additional items to assist them in their work (such as those listed above) cannot reduce their taxes by claiming the deductions for these items.

(iii) — Administrative efficiency

Administrative efficiency is a key policy concern in the taxation of employment income because of the sheer number of taxpayers affected. If millions of taxpayers had to spend time and resources figuring out their tax liability every year, the spring tax filing season would be a worse nightmare than what it already is. Many individuals do not keep proper accounting records for their income and expenses, and this would be a real problem because employment income is often a major source of income. Saving enough cash to pay taxes every year could also be a challenge to many taxpayers. Auditing and verifying the millions of individual tax returns would be costly to the government.

The policy goal of administrative efficiency justifies the use of withholding tax for employment income. Employers are called upon to assist the government in collecting taxes and to assist employees by providing accurate information at the end of the year.[8] It also helps explain the limited deductions available to employees. Employers are assumed to pay for work-related expenses. In addition, the Act relies

---

[7]*McNeill v. Minister of National Revenue* (1986), [1986] 2 C.T.C. 352, (sub nom. *McNeill v. R.*) 86 D.T.C. 6477 (Fed. T.D.), 363 [C.T.C.], 6485 [D.T.C.].

[8]Employers must provide employees with an information return (T5 slip), reporting the amount of employment income earned by each employee during the year.

heavily on employers to verify the types of deductions that can be claimed by employees (such as travel expenses and home office expenses).[9]

The administrative efficiency argument also helps explain the non-taxation of many fringe benefits that are of a minor nature and not readily susceptible to calculation. Although most fringe benefits would appear to be caught by the language of paragraph 6(1)(a), the CRA usually makes no attempt to assess some of them.[10] Examples include:[11] uniforms, employee discounts generally available to all employees if at least cost is charged, reimbursement of reasonable relocation expenses except for the loss on the sale of a house,[12] subsidized meals if at least the cost of the food and preparation is recovered; a maximum of $500 of non-cash gifts[13]; memberships in social clubs principally for the employer's advantage rather than the employee's; reasonable business trip expenses; and tuition paid for courses taken primarily for employer's benefit.

(iv) — Social policy

The fact that employment income is an important tax base makes it an useful instrument for the government to implement social policies. Many of these policies underlie the exclusions from taxing fringe benefits. Some examples are the statutory exclusions from taxation for employer contributions to a registered pension plan, group sickness/accident insurance plan (e.g., a group disability insurance

---

[9]E.g., subsection 8(10) requires an employer to sign a prescribed form T2200 to confirm that the requirements for the deductions claimed have been met (but not the amounts).

[10]For example, see Interpretation Bulletin IT-470R, "Employees' fringe benefits" (Consolidated to August 11, 1999), Part B. The CRA may attempt to assess where the value of the benefit is readily ascertainable or is seen as excessive. See *Monteith v. R.* (1997), [1998] 2 C.T.C. 2281, 98 D.T.C. 1306 (T.C.C.), where an employee received a taxable benefit in the form of a reserved parking space. See also *Dunlap v. R.*, [1998] 4 C.T.C. 2644, 98 D.T.C. 2053 (T.C.C.), where an employee was found to have received a taxable benefit from the company Christmas party. The CRA has indicated that it will not assess a taxable benefit with respect to Christmas parties as long as the amount spent per employee is within the tax-free gift amount (then $100 per person) plus ancillary costs, such as transportation home (CRA, *Technical News No.* 15, December 18, 1998). Given that the tax-free gift amount has since increased from $100 to $500, the CRA's assessing practice is likely to incorporate a $500 limit rather than a $100 limit.

[11]Most of these items are listed in IT-470R, *ibid.*

[12]As discussed under heading 5.7(c)(ii) "Statutory rules", below, the benefit relating to the reimbursement of a housing loss is determined based on the rules in ss. 6(20) to 6(22). Generally speaking, the first $15,000 of payment is tax-free and the benefit equals one-half of the excess amount.

[13]There is a separate $500 tax-free limit for a 5 year (or more) long service/anniversary award if at least 5 years since the last long service award. These rules are CRA administrative practice for 2010 and subsequent years according to see CRA, *Technical News No.* 40, June 2009. For prior years see CRA, *Press Release*, December 2001, and IT-470R, note 10 above.

plan), private health care services plan (e.g., a drug or dental plan), supplementary unemployment insurance plan, deferred profit sharing plan (paragraph 6(1)(a)(i)); counseling services relating to mental health and re-employment or retirement (paragraph 6(1)(a)(iv)). Other examples are the non-taxation of the value of board and lodging at a special work site or remote location (subsection 6(6)), and disability-related employment benefits (subsection 6(16)).

Some of the deductions allowed by section 8 are allowed for policy reasons. For example, a taxpayer who is a member of the clergy or a religious order can deduct expenses related to the residence (paragraph 8(1)(c)); musicians can deduct the cost of their instruments (paragraph 8(1)(p)); artists can deduct their employment costs (while ordinary employees cannot) (paragraph 8(1)(q)).

(v) — Balancing policy concerns

The current rules under sections 6, 7 and 8 represent an attempt to balance of the above policy concerns. However, inequity remains a major concern. This is most serious when a worker must pay for significant work-related expenses which are not deductible (such as books, tools, equipment, cell phones or electronic devices) given the limited deductions under section 8.[14] In *Gifford v. R.* (2004)[15] for example, a securities broker employed by an investment firm could not deduct the $100,000 cost relating to the purchase of a client list from another broker or the related interest expense (from borrowing to purchase the list). A self-employed securities broker, operating as an independent contractor, would be able to claim deductions from such expenses in computing his or her business income.

Needless to say, this discriminative treatment of employees violates the principles of both equity and neutrality and creates a tax incentive to earn (and pay) income in the form of business income rather than employment income. That was why the Carter Commission recommended that "all expenditures reasonably related to the gaining or producing of income" be deductible from income, regardless of the type of income involved.[16] This recommendation was not accepted by the government on ground of simplicity and administrative efficiency.[17] As a compromise, a stan-

---

[14]Paragraph 8(1)(j) only allows a deduction for capital cost allowance or interest expense in the case of an automobile or plane (and only in restricted circumstances). Recently introduced provisions allowing limited deductions for the employment costs of artists and the tool costs of apprentice mechanics are a limited acknowledgement of the need for additional deductions. Provisions of a more general nature would be far more equitable.

[15][2004] 2 C.T.C. 1, 2004 D.T.C. 6120 (Eng.), 2004 D.T.C. 6128 (Fr.) (S.C.C.).

[16]*Report of the Royal Commission on Taxation* (Carter Report), (1966), vol. 3, 76-87, 289-290.

[17]In the 1969 White Paper, which was issued after the Carter Report, the government criticized the recommendation on the grounds of administrative simplicity: that employees do not keep the kinds of detailed records that would be entailed, and that the administrative task of processing the claims would be too great. See Benson, *Proposals for Tax Reform* (1969), 10, 16.

dard deduction was allowed (initially $150, then raised to $1000) for all employment expenses from 1972 to 1987.[18] In 2006, this standard deduction was essentially re-introduced as a tax credit at the lowest tax rate.[19] This measure alleviates the unfairness of the prohibition against the deduction of employment-related expenses and, in some cases, it may actually be quite generous. To be fair, however, allowing an arbitrary standard amount results in only rough justice with a significant revenue loss: the tax expenditure related to this credit is projected to be $1.88 billion for 2009.[20]

5.2 — Characterization

(a) — Office and employment defined

(i) — Statutory definitions

Subsection 248(1) defines "office" and "employment" as follows:

> "office" means the position of an individual entitling the individual to a fixed or ascertainable stipend or remuneration and includes a judicial office, the office of a minister of the Crown, the office of a member of the Senate or House of Commons of Canada, a member of a legislative assembly or a member of a legislative or executive council and any other office, the incumbent of which is elected by popular vote or is elected or appointed in a representative capacity and also includes the position of a corporation director; and "officer" means a person holding such an office;
>
> "employment" means the position of an individual in the service of some other person (including Her Majesty or a foreign state or sovereign) and "servant" or "employee" means a person holding such a position;

Although subsection 5(1) uses the word "taxpayer", which is defined in subsection 248(1) to include a corporation as well as an individual, the definitions of "office" and "employment" both use the word "individual", which is defined in subsection 248(1) as not including a corporation. It follows that for tax purposes a corporation cannot receive income from an office or employment.

---

[18]The 1971 Act implemented the 1969 White Paper proposal, allowing all employees a deduction of 3 per cent of their income up to a ceiling of $150. The deduction was later raised to 20 per cent with a ceiling of $500 before it was eliminated in 1988 without any rationale, thus returning the tax system to the pre-1972 state of law from 1988 to 2005. (The 1987 White Paper simply made the point that the value of the basic personal tax credit available to all taxpayers, which was introduced at that time, would more than compensate for the elimination of both the employment expense deduction and the basic personal exemption for which the basic personal tax credit was a substitute. See Wilson, *Tax Reform 1987: Income Tax Reform* (1987), 88.)

[19]S. 118(10). In 2010, the value of the credit is $157.65 ($1,051 × 15%).

[20]Department of Finance, *Tax Expenditures and Evaluations 2009*, Table 1.

(ii) — Office or employment

Income from an office and income from employment are two separate sources of income under section 3. What is the difference between an "office" and "employment"? The definition of office says that an office entitles the holder to "a fixed or ascertainable stipend or remuneration", the contrast being with an entitlement to an uncertain figure such as the profit of an enterprise. But an employment nearly always has this characteristic as well, although it is not mentioned in the definition of employment.

The key to the difference is a phrase in the definition of employment that is missing from the definition of office, namely, "in the service of some other person". This requires a contract of service (or employment) between the taxpayer and an employer; where such a contract exists, the taxpayer is "employed" and his or her remuneration will be income from employment. However, where there is a fixed or ascertainable remuneration but no contract of service, the taxpayer will be an "officer" and his or her remuneration will be income from an office. The examples of offices (which are given in the definition of office) are judges, ministers of the Crown, members of legislative bodies and directors of corporations. These examples illustrate that an office, unlike employment, is not created by or dependent upon a contract of service between an employer and the particular holder. The position is created by statute or some other instrument, independently of the person who fills the position, and the position is filled in succession by successive holders.[21]

The distinction between an office and employment is not important for tax purposes. Income from an office and income from employment are lumped together under subdivision a and are computed in accordance with the same set of rules. The importance of the definitions is to enable a distinction to be drawn between income from an office or employment, on the one hand, and income from a business, on the other.

(b) — Business or office

The difference between income from an office and income from a business depends upon the requirement for an office of "a fixed or ascertainable stipend or remuneration". A business, by contrast, yields a profit which is not fixed or ascertainable in advance. A partner in a law firm derives business income, because he or she is not employed by anyone and his or her remuneration is calculated by reference to the profit of the firm. If the lawyer is appointed as a judge or ombudsman, or to a statutory board or commission, he or she is still not employed by anyone, but the fixed remuneration will make the taxpayer an officer, deriving income from an office.

---

[21] *MacKeen v. M.N.R.*, [1967] Tax A.B.C. 374 (T.A.B.).

(c) — Business or employment

(i) — "Contract of services" vs. "contract for services"

The difference between income from employment and income from a business depends upon the requirement for employment that the employee be "in the service" of an employer. In general, a person receiving income under a "contract of service" (or an employee) earns income from employment, whereas a person receiving income received under a "contract for services" (an independent contractor or a self-employed person) earns income from a business. In other words, the employee receives income under a contract of service. The self-employed person receives income under contracts for the supply of goods or services which his or her business produces.

In most cases, the distinction between the self-employed individual who receives income from a business and the employee who receives salary or wages is perfectly clear: the partner in the law firm and his or her assistant illustrate the two cases. The partner receives income from the business of practising law, and the assistant receives income from employment.

Where a taxpayer supplies services to one person (or to very few people), as opposed to many people, it is not always easy to determine whether the taxpayer is "in the service of" that other person. The answer depends upon the general law defining the employment relationship. The general law of all the provinces, including Quebec, draws a distinction between a "contract of service", which creates an employment relationship between the employer and the employee (or the master and the servant), and a "contract for services", which creates an independent contract relationship between the employer and the "independent contractor". The distinction arose first (and is still important) in the context of employment law and the law of torts: an employer (master) is vicariously liable for torts committed in the course of employment by an employee (servant) but an employer is not vicariously liable for torts committed by an independent contractor.

The leading cases on this issue are *Wiebe Door Services Ltd. v. Minister of National Revenue* (1986)[22] and *671122 Ontario Ltd. v. Sagaz Industries Canada Inc.* (2001).[23] In *Wiebe Door*, the Court cited the following statement as "perhaps the best synthesis found in the authorities" of the common law to date:

> . . .the fundamental test to be applied is this: "Is the person who has engaged himself to perform these services performing them as a person in business on his own account?" If the answer to that question is "yes," then the contract is a contract for services. If the answer is "no" then the contract is a contract of service. *No exhaustive list has been compiled and perhaps no exhaustive list can be compiled of considerations which are relevant in determining that question, nor can strict rules be laid down as to the relative weight which the various considerations should carry in*

---

[22][1986] 2 C.T.C. 200, 87 D.T.C. 5025 (Fed. C.A.).

[23]*671122 Ontario Ltd. v. Sagaz Industries Canada Inc.*, [2001] 4 C.T.C. 139, 204 D.L.R. (4th) 542 (S.C.C.); reconsideration refused (2001), 55 O.R. (3d) 782 (headnote only) (S.C.C.). This case dealt with matters of tort law, not tax law.

> *particular cases*.. . . The application of the general test may be easier in a case where the person who engages himself to perform the services does so in the course of an already established business of his own; but this factor is not decisive, and a person who engages himself to perform services for another may well be an independent contractor even though he has not entered into the contract in the course of an existing business carried on by him [emphasis added].[24]

In *Sagaz*, which followed *Wiebe Door*, Major J. of the Supreme Court summarized the *Wiebe Door's* non-exhaustive list of "considerations" as "factors":[25]

> The central question is whether the person who has been engaged to perform the services is performing them as a person in business on his own account. In making this determination, the level of control the employer has over the worker's activities will always be a factor. However, other factors to consider include whether the worker provides his or her own equipment, whether the worker hires his or her own helpers, the degree of financial risk taken by the worker, the degree of responsibility for investment and management held by the worker, and the worker's opportunity for profit in the performance of his or her tasks.
>
> *It bears repeating that the above factors constitute a non-exhaustive list, and there is no set formula as to their application. The relative weight of each will depend on the particular facts and circumstances of the case* [emphasis added].

(ii) — Control

The control test was originally the only test used to determine whether there was an employment relationship and is one of the several factors listed in *Sagaz*. This test looks at the degree of control that the entity has over the work that is to be performed by the worker and the manner of doing the work (for example, by specifying the hours of work, where the work will be done and/or by providing the place of work, any required equipment and any assistance). If the employer has a right or power to control the work and the manner of doing the work, this would indicate that the worker is an employee. If, on the other hand, the worker works independently, free of control and merely undertakes to produce a specified result, this would indicate that the worker is an independent contractor.

In a contract of service, the employer has a good deal of control: the employer has the power to specify not only the result to be accomplished by the employee, but also the manner of doing the work. In a contract for services, the employer will specify the result to be accomplished by the independent contractor with specialized knowledge (e.g., an architect will be hired to design a building, a lawyer will be hired to incorporate a company, and a courier will be hired to deliver a parcel) but it will be left to the independent contractor to determine the manner of achieving the result. The employer of an independent contractor will not tell the contractor what hours he or she should work or what equipment he or she should use or

---

[24]*Market Investigations v. Minister of Social Security*, [1968] 3 All E.R. 732 (Eng. Q.B.) at 738-39. The missing portion of text in the middle of the paragraph (after the italics) is very similar to the statement in *Sagaz* immediately below.

[25]Note 23 above, paras. 47 and 48. See also *ibid.*

what assistance he or she should retain. Those are matters to be left to the discretion of the contractor: the contractor fulfills his or her contract simply by accomplishing the promised result.

The shortcomings of control were acknowledged in *Wiebe Door* and were more recently reiterated in *Pletch v. R.* (2005):[26]

> I am faced with the frequently encountered problem of determining whether the independence in the performance of a role of a worker is attributable to the freedom that derives from the nature of the relationship, from the party in a position to control choosing not to exercise control or whether it is attributable to the nature of the tasks assigned and the worker's particular skills to perform such tasks without direction. In the case at bar the freedom of the worker derives primarily from the nature of the relationship which the worker imposed and from the worker's skills to perform the work.

In *Royal Winnipeg Ballet v. R.* (2006)[27] the Court found that the control test was not decisive because, even though the control exercised over dancers hired for the entire season was "extensive" it was the same as the control exercised over guest artists (hired to do similar work) who were regarded as independent contractors. In conclusion, although control is no longer regarded as a conclusive test on its own or even the most important test, it "will always be a factor" and it may be the only test valid in Quebec, which is governed by the Civil Code.[28]

(iii) — "Economic reality" test and other factors

In *Wiebe Door* the court actually applied an "economic reality" test which included the "combined force" of the factors of control, ownership of tools, chance of profit, and risk of loss[29] but the list of factors is non-exhaustive. Whether the worker hires his or her own helpers and the degree of responsibility for investment and management held by the worker is also relevant.[30] The fact whether the worker has other clients may also be a relevant factor in some cases.[31] The issue is whether a worker

---

[26] *W.B. Pletch Co. v. R.* (2005), 2005 TCC 400, 2006 D.T.C. 2065 (Eng.), [2006] 1 C.T.C. 2582 (T.C.C. [General Procedure]) at para. 9.

[27] *Royal Winnipeg Ballet v. R.* (2006), 2006 FCA 87, 2006 D.T.C. 6323 (Eng.) (F.C.A.).

[28] Article 2085 of the Civil Code of Quebec.

[29] This older "test" was originally stated in *Montreal (City) v. Montreal Locomotive Works Ltd.* (1946), [1947] 1 D.L.R. 161 (Quebec P.C.) at 169.

[30] Whether the services of the worker are an integral part of the employer's business was an older test, pre-*Wiebe Door*. See *Stevenson Jordan and Harrison, Ltd. v. MacDonald and Evans*, [1952] 1 T.L.R. 101 (Eng. C.A.) at 111.

[31] In *Pletch*, note 26 above, the court, after exhaustively listing the relevant factors, cited, as particularly relevant, the fact that neither the corporation nor the incorporated employee had other clients. In *Dynamic Industries Ltd. v. R.*, 2005 FCA 211, 2005 D.T.C. 5293, [2005] 3 C.T.C. 225 (F.C.A.), the Tax Court found that the taxpayer was a personal services largely on the basis of this factor because Dynamic only had one client during the three years under appeal although it had other clients in the taxation years before and after this period. On

is performing services as a person in business on his or her own account and that determination is made on the basis of the facts and circumstances of the case. In *Wolf v. R.* (2002),[32] for example, the Federal Court of Appeal held that a worker with specialized skills under a five-year contract with a Canadian company was self-employed on grounds that he had "financial risk" because the taxpayer had no job security or benefits, and the agreement entered into by the parties indicated their intent to have an independent contractor relationship.[33]

(iv) — Form of contract

In characterizing the relationship between a worker and his or her client, the form of the legal relationship is relevant unless the legal form does not reflect the true relationship between the parties or there is a sham.[34] In both *Wolf* and *Royal Winnipeg Ballet*, the Federal Court of Appeal was prepared to take into consideration the form of the contract between the two parties. In *Wolf*, Noël J.A. remarked:[35]

> I view their assessment of the control test, the integration test and the ownership of tool tests as not being conclusive either way. With respect to financial risk, I respectfully agree with my colleagues that the appellant in consideration for a higher pay gave up many of the benefits which usually accrue to an employee including job security. However, I also agree with the Tax Court Judge that the appellant was paid for hours worked regardless of the results achieved and that in that sense he bore no more risk than an ordinary employee. My assessment of the total relationship of the parties yields no clear result which is why I believe regard must be had to how the parties viewed their relationship.
>
> This is not a case where the parties labelled their relationship in a certain way with a view of achieving a tax benefit. No sham or window dressing of any sort is suggested. It follows that the manner in which the parties viewed their agreement must prevail unless they can be shown to have been mistaken as to the true nature of their relationship. In this respect, the evidence when assessed in the light of the relevant legal tests is at best neutral. As the parties considered that they were engaged in an independent contractor relationship and as they acted in a manner that was consistent with this relationship, I do not believe that it was open to the Tax Court Judge to disregard their understanding (compare *Montreal (City) v. Montreal Locomotive Works Ltd.* (1946), [1947] 1 D.L.R. 161 (Quebec P.C.), at page 170).

---

appeal, the Federal Court of Appeal reversed the Tax Court's judgment after taking into consideration that Dynamic had other clients in other years.

[32] *Wolf v. R.*, 2002 D.T.C. 6853, [2002] 3 C.T.C. 3 (Fed. C.A.).

[33] As a U.S. resident working in Canada as an independent contractor, Mr. Wolf was exempt from Canadian tax under Article XIV of the Canada-U.S. Income Tax Convention (1980). He would be taxable in Canada if he was an employee.

[34] See heading 20.2(c)(ii) below, "Form over substance".

[35] *Wolf*, note 32, above, paras. 123 and 124.

(d) — Incorporated employees

The distinct and discriminative regime for taxing employment income often motivates workers to use a corporate intermediary to render their services. For example, a software engineer can provide her services through a corporation by incorporating her personal services business. As the owner and manager of the company, she could enter into a service contract (on behalf of the company) with a former employer to provide the same services as she did previously. The relationship between the former employer and the company is a contract for services because the company cannot be an employee. In the absence of special anti-avoidance rules, the company would pay tax on the net profit from the business of providing services after deducting the business-related expenses (such as salary paid to employees, automobile expenses, and telephone expenses). The most obvious advantage of incorporating a personal services business would be more deductions.[36] A second tax advantage would be a lower rate of corporate tax (around 20%) because of the small business deduction for active business income. If the worker does not withdraw the profit from the corporation in the form of salary or dividends, the corporate tax (which is much lower than even the lowest personal tax rate) will be the only tax payable, resulting in a tax deferral (until the profit is withdrawn from the corporation). The corporation can also be used to split income among family members by having family members subscribe for shares of the company and by paying dividends on those shares.[37] More importantly, to the former employer, there is an advantage as well — no requirement for withholding income tax or paying the payroll taxes on amounts paid to the company.

The Act contains rules to more or less ignore the formal legal relationships in such circumstances and to treat the income from a personal service business in a similar manner to employment income. A personal services business is defined, in essence, as a business of providing services where the provider of the services (the "incorporated employee") or his spouse is also a specified shareholder of the corporation.[38] Income from a personal service business is not eligible for the small business deduction so that it is taxed at the regular corporate tax rate (which is still a bit lower than the top rate for individuals) so the deferral advantage is not as large. The company is denied deductions other than the salary paid to an incorporated employee and other expenses that are deductible in computing employment income and all deductions are computed on a cash basis.[39]

---

[36]This is due to the limitations under section 8.

[37]For further discussion, see chapter 13,"Income splitting", and chapter 15, "Corporations and Shareholders", below.

[38]S. 125(7) and 248(1) of the Act. A specified shareholder is generally a 10% shareholder.

[39]S. 18(1)(p) of the Act.

5.3 — Timing

(a) — Cash Method

Subsection 5(1) stipulates that a taxpayer's income from an office or employment for a taxation year must be "received by the taxpayer in the year". Similarly, a taxable benefit is generally included in income under section 6 or 7 when it is "received" or "enjoyed". Deductions are allowed under section 8 when they are paid. The effect of the word "received" and "paid" is to require employment income be reported for tax purposes on a "cash basis".[40]

Usually, there is not much doubt about the time for inclusion or deduction under the cash method. In order to prevent taxpayers from having complete freedom to decide when to report income, the receipt concept has been expanded to include the notion of "constructive receipt".

(b) — Receipt

Generally, when a taxpayer actually receives cash or property, there is no question about timing. Special issues arise when a taxpayer receives something other than cash, such as a cheque. A cheque is a mechanism for making payment and is generally treated as cash. When the payments of salary or wages are mailed to an employee, subsection 248(7) deems the payments to have been received on the day that they are mailed. Thus, a pay cheque mailed by the employer on December 31, 2007 and actually received by the employee in January 2008 would be deemed to have been received by the employee in 2007. The amount of the cheque would thus form part of the employee's income for 2007.

Whenever an employee is paid salary or wages in a different calendar year (the taxation year for individuals being the calendar year) than the year in which the pay was earned (normally when services are performed), the pay will be taxed in the year of receipt. This commonly occurs when an employee receives a late (retroactive) pay raise: the payment will be taxed in the year that the payment was received, not the year in which it was earned.[41] It will also occur when an employee

---

[40]The word "received" appears in other provisions as well, always calling for the "cash method" of accounting: see heading 6.5(a), "Cash method", below. Business income, on the other hand, is usually reported for tax purposes on an "accrual basis". See heading 6.5(b), "Accrual method", below.

[41]Because an employer will usually be reporting (business) income on an accrual basis, the employer will usually deduct an item of employee's salary in the year in which it was earned, even if it was not paid until a later year. The employee on the other hand will report the salary on a cash basis and will therefore not recognize an item of salary for tax purposes until it is received. This difference in the timing of the recognition of salary has been accepted by the courts. The early deduction of the salary expense and late inclusion of the salary in income results in a postponement of tax. If payment of the salary could be delayed for a long time, the postponement of tax would become exceedingly valuable. The Act has accordingly been amended to limit the availability of salary deferral. Subsection 78(4) re-

is paid in advance — in December 2007 for work to be done in January 2008 — the income will have to be recognized in 2007, not 2008.[42]

(c) — Constructive receipt

In order to constitute a "receipt" of money for tax law purposes, is it necessary for the taxpayer to "actually touch or feel it, or have it in his bank account?"[43] The Court answered in *Jean-Paul Morin v. The Queen* (1975):[44]

> We regret to say that this proposition seems to us absolutely inadmissible, because the word "receive" obviously means to get or to derive benefit from something, to enjoy its advantages without necessarily having it in one's hands.

When money is paid by an employer to a third party for the benefit of the taxpayer, the payment constituted constructive receipt in the hands of the taxpayer.[45] For example, in *Blenkarn v. Minister of National Revenue* (1963)[46] where the money to pay the taxpayer's salary in 1960 was available, but he voluntarily chose not to be paid until 1961, he was considered to have actually received the money. The payment was held to be "received" as soon as he had an unconditional right to be paid, which was in 1960.

5.4 — Salary, wages and other remuneration

(a) — Salary and wages

Subsection 5(1) brings into income from an office or employment "the salary, wages and other remuneration, including gratuities, received by the taxpayer in the year". The terms "salary" and "wages" are not defined for the purpose of section 5, although the phrase "salary or wages" is used elsewhere in the Act to mean income from an office or employment.[47] There is no distinction in principle, or in tax treatment, between "salary" and "wages". In common parlance, however, salary is usually computed by reference to a relatively long period, often a year, while wages

---

quires that any remuneration deducted by the employer that remains unpaid 180 days after the year-end must be added back into the employer's income.

[42]*Randall v. M.N.R.*, [1987] 2 C.T.C. 2265, 87 D.T.C. 553 (T.C.C.). The cases distinguish between an advance on account of future earnings, which is taxable in the year of receipt, and a loan from the employer to the employee, which is not: *Park v. M.N.R.* (1950), 1 Tax A.B.C. 391 (T.A.B.) (advance against future employment income held to be income); *Ferszt v. M.N.R.*, [1978] C.T.C. 2860, 78 D.T.C. 1648 (T.R.B.) (advance against future commissions held to be income).

[43]*Jean-Paul Morin v. The Queen* (1974), [1975] C.T.C. 106, 75 D.T.C. 5061 (Fed. T.D.), at page 110 (D.T.C. 5064).

[44]*Ibid.*

[45]*Markman v. Minister of National Revenue*, [1989] 1 C.T.C. 2381, 89 D.T.C. 253 (T.C.C.).

[46](1963), 32 Tax A.B.C. 321, 63 D.T.C. 581 (Can. Tax App. Bd.).

[47]S. 248(1): "salary or wages".

are usually computed by reference to a relatively short period, often an hour or a week.

(b) — Other remuneration

The phrase "other remuneration, including gratuities" typically includes tips, commissions, and other amounts that are similar in nature to wages or salaries. Other remuneration also includes directors fees (paragraph 6(1)(c)) and items listed in section 6. For example, under subsection 6(3), signing bonus and non-compete payments paid by an employer to an employee before or after the employment are taxable as employment income.

5.5 — Benefits — general scheme

(a) — Inclusion in income

Paragraph 6(1)(a) of the Act includes in a taxpayer's income from an office or employment:

> the value of board, lodging and other benefits of any kind whatever received or enjoyed by the taxpayer in the year in respect of, in the course of, or by virtue of an office or employment . . .

This paragraph goes on to list a number of benefits that are exempted from the general rule of taxability. Section 6 then continues on for some 12 pages, bringing into income other specific taxable benefits. Examples of specific benefits are discussed later under heading 5.7 below.

There are three essential issues in the application of paragraph 6(1)(a): (1) what is a "benefit"; (2) is there any relationship between the benefit and employment; and (3) what is the "value" of the benefit? Each of these is discussed below, following an examination of tax policy on the taxation of fringe benefits.

(b) — "Benefit" defined

(i) — Economic advantage or material acquisition

The Supreme Court of Canada in *R. v. Savage* (1983)[48] interpreted the word "benefit" in the context of subsection 6(1) to mean an economic advantage or material acquisition. Justice Dickson stated:[49]

> I do not believe the language to be restricted to benefits that are related to the office or employment in the sense that they represent a form of remuneration for services rendered. If it is a material acquisition which confers an economic benefit on the taxpayer and does not constitute an exemption, e.g., loan or gift, then it is within the all-embracing definition of s. 3.

[48][1983] C.T.C. 393, 83 D.T.C. 5409 (S.C.C.). The facts of this case are discussed later under heading 5.5(c), "Relationship to employment", below.

[49]*Ibid.*, at 399, 5414, approving the judgement of Evans, J.A. in *R. v. Poynton*, [1972] 3 O.R. 727 738, [1972] C.T.C. 411, 72 D.T.C. 6329 (Fed. C.A.).

The Court also found that the meaning of "benefit of any kind whatever" is clearly quite broad.[50] In light of the policy objectives of paragraph 6(1)(a), discussed earlier, any economic advantage or material acquisition received by an employee in respect of an employment should be taxable.

An economic advantage or benefit may be conferred upon an employee by an employer in various forms. Typical forms include: reimbursement of expenses incurred by the employee, free use of property owned by the employer, and allowances. In general, whether the benefit is taxable under paragraph 6(1)(a) depends on the underlying nature of the expense covered by the benefit: if it is in the nature of personal or living expenses, the benefit should be taxable; if it is in the nature of expenses incurred in the course of carrying out employment duties, the benefit should not be taxable. For example, if an employee purchases supplies for office use at the local stationery store and is reimbursed by the employer, the employee has received no benefit, thus is not, and should not be, taxable on the reimbursed expense. However, a reimbursement which covers a personal or living expense is taxable as a benefit under paragraph 6(1)(a). Examples include a reimbursement of the cost of purchasing a television for personal use, a reimbursement of legal fees incurred by an employee in defending criminal charges laid against him personally,[51] and the value of employer-provided free education of an employee's child.[52]

It is not always straightforward to determine whether the underlying nature of an expense is a personal expense or an employment-related outlay. For example, in *Huffman v. R.* (1989),[53] a plainclothes police officer was reimbursed by his employer for clothing expenses, despite the fact that the clothes he had to wear were regular suits and shirts. The Court accepted the taxpayer's evidence that he could not wear the clothes off duty because they were loose-fitting in order to accommodate the equipment carried by plainclothes officers and because of rapid wear-and-tear. Although clothes are generally a personal consumption expense, the Court was persuaded that this taxpayer had received no personal benefit from the clothes he had purchased for his employment. The reimbursement for his purchase of the clothes was therefore properly classified as the reimbursement of an employment-related outlay, and was accordingly not a taxable benefit.

---

[50] *Ibid.*

[51] *Clemiss v. M.N.R.*, [1992] 2 C.T.C. 232, 92 D.T.C. 6509 (Fed. T.D.). See also *Pellizzari v. M.N.R.*, [1987] 1 C.T.C. 2106, 87 D.T.C. 56 (T.C.C.).

[52] *E.g.*, *Detchon v. R.* (1995), [1996] 1 C.T.C. 2475 (T.C.C.). In contrast, however, in *Guay v. R.*, [1997] 3 C.T.C. 276, 97 D.T.C. 5267 (Fed. C.A.), reimbursement of an employee's children's private school tuition fees from the employer was not held to be a taxable benefit because the employee was required by his employer to work in different countries. In other words, the tuition fee expense was not considered to be a personal expense because it was imposed on the employee by the "permeability of his occupation".

[53] [1989] 1 C.T.C. 32, 89 D.T.C. 5006 (Fed. T.D.); affirmed [1990] 2 C.T.C. 132, 90 D.T.C. 6405 (Fed. C.A.).

Difficulty in identifying the underlying nature of the expense also arises in the case of travel expenses and housing costs. Employer-paid travel expenses may be categorized as personal expenses,[54] employment related outlay,[55] or mixed expenses,[56] depending on the purpose of the trip. If the primary purpose of the trip is the employer's business, not personal enjoyment, the travel expenses are regarded as employment related outlays giving rise to no personal benefit,[57] and are thus not taxable. The confusion in the case law in treating employer-provided housing benefits is discussed under heading 5.7(c) below.

(ii) — Convertible into money

The "convertible into money" doctrine was developed in *Tennant v. Smith* (1892):[58] if an in-kind benefit cannot be converted into money, it is not a taxable benefit to the employee. By including the phrase of "board, lodging and other benefits of any kind whatever", paragraph 6(1)(a) clearly contemplates the taxation of benefits that are not convertible into money and thus overrules *Tennant v. Smith.*

---

[54]*O'Brien v. M.N.R.*, [1967] Tax A.B.C. 250 (T.A.B.) (an employee posted abroad was held to receive a taxable benefit from periodic trips home made by his wife and children, paid for by his employer).

[55]*Romeril v. R.*, [1999] 1 C.T.C. 2535, 99 D.T.C. 221 (T.C.C.) (taxpayer attended a convention at request of the employer).

[56]In *Philp v. M.N.R.*, [1970] C.T.C. 330, 70 D.T.C. 6237 (Ex. Ct.), the Court found that the trip was of a combined holiday and business nature and that its value to the taxpayer as a holiday trip was one-half of the averaged cost of the trip.

[57]See, for example, *Lowe v. R.*, [1996] 2 C.T.C. 33, 96 D.T.C. 6226 (Fed. C.A.) where the taxpayer was sent by his employer to New Orleans to accompany the employer's successful brokers and their wives, who were expected to enjoy what was described as "four sun-filled days and fun-filled nights". The taxpayer was found to receive no personal benefit from the trip. While the taxpayer derived some personal pleasure from the trip, the Court found that he had little time left over for his own pleasure after looking after his employer's business, and any pleasure derived by the taxpayer was merely incidental to the trip's business purpose. The Court also found the taxpayer's wife's trip was for the purpose of the employer's business, as she attended the same meetings as her spouse. A similar conclusion was reached in *Arsens v. M.N.R.* (1969), 69 D.T.C. 81 (T.A.B.) where the cost of a trip to Disneyland in California which was undertaken primarily as a publicity promotion for the benefit of the employer's company was not considered to be personal benefits in the hands of the employees who attended on the trip.

[58][1892] A.C. 150 (H.L.). In *Tennant v. Smith* it was held that a bank employee, who was required to live in part of the bank premises, did not have to report the value of the accommodation as a benefit of his employment. Since the employee could not assign or sublet his right to occupy the premises, he had received no benefit that could be converted into money. Lord Macnaghten conceded that the employee had received a benefit in the sense of having been relieved of the expense of providing his own accommodation, but he asserted that a person is chargeable for income tax "not on what saves his pocket, but on what goes into his pocket".

This point was made clear in *Waffle v. M.N.R.* (1968).[59] The issue in this case was the taxability of the value of a Caribbean cruise supplied by the Ford Motor Company to the taxpayer, who was the employee of a Ford dealer. Justice Cattanach found as a fact that the taxpayer could not have assigned or otherwise converted his right to go on the cruise into cash; he either went on the cruise or he received nothing. To an argument founded on *Tennant v. Smith*, the judge replied that in his view the language of paragraph 6(1)(a) "overcomes the principle laid down in *Tennant v. Smith*".

(c) — Relationship to employment

Paragraph 6(1)(a) applies only to benefits received or enjoyed by the employee "in respect of, in the course of, or by virtue of an office or employment". The early jurisprudence interpreted this language to mean benefits received by a person in his or her capacity as an employee as remuneration for services.[60] However, in the *Savage* case,[61] the Supreme Court of Canada rejected the notion that paragraph 6(1)(a) required that benefits must be received in exchange for services performed by the employee.

In *Savage*, the taxpayer, who was employed by a life insurance company, had received a payment of $300 from her employer. The employer had offered its employees $100 per course as a "prize" for passing courses in life insurance, and the taxpayer had passed three courses. The employer did not require its employees to take the courses; they were taken voluntarily. Obviously, the $300 was a benefit, and the benefit had been provided by the taxpayer's employer; but was it received "in respect of, in the course of, or by virtue of" the taxpayer's employment? The Supreme Court of Canada answered yes. To be sure, the payment was not made for services rendered to the employer; it was made for passing courses. But paragraph 6(1)(a) did not require that a benefit represent a form of remuneration for services rendered; a looser connection to the employment was sufficient. In this case, the courses were taken by the taxpayer to improve her employment skills, not for any recreational motive; and this was enough to decide that the employer's payment to the taxpayer was "in respect of" her employment. The $300 was therefore held to be a taxable benefit under paragraph 6(1)(a). The Court held that benefits received in a person's capacity as an employee were covered by paragraph 6(1)(a), and indicated that the words "in respect of" are words of the "widest possible scope ... intended to convey some connection between two related subject matters".[62]

In effect, the Supreme Court of Canada's decision in *Savage* creates a presumption that any benefit received by an employee from his or her employer is derived from the employment relationship. For example, the value of free travel rewards received

---

[59] [1968] C.T.C. 572, 69 D.T.C. 5007 (Ex. Ct.).

[60] See, for example, *Estate of Phaneuf v. R.* (1977), [1978] C.T.C. 21, 78 D.T.C. 6001 (Fed. T.D.); and *Ransom v. M.N.R.*, [1967] C.T.C. 346, 67 D.T.C. 5235 (Ex. Ct.).

[61] *Savage*, note 48, above.

[62] *Ibid.*, 399, 5414.

out of a frequent flyer programme was considered a benefit received or enjoyed in respect of employment because the rewards were earned by the frequent travels of the employee in the course of his employment.[63] This presumption can be rebutted, but only if the employee can establish that the benefit is received in his or her personal capacity.[64] For example, a person might receive a wedding or birthday present from a friend who is also the recipient's employer; such a present would not be a benefit in respect of employment.[65]

When an employee receives a benefit from someone other than the employer, there is obviously no presumption that the benefit is received in respect of employment. However, there are cases in which third-party benefits have been held to be benefits in respect of employment. The *Waffle* case,[66] discussed earlier, is an example. In that case, the cruise was not provided by the employer, but by Ford Motor Company. There are other cases where a manufacturer or wholesaler has rewarded effort by an employee of a retailer with the result that the employee must report the reward as a taxable benefit from employment.[67]

(d) — Valuation

Paragraph 6(1)(a) calls for the inclusion in employment income of the "value" of benefits. The value is generally determined on the basis of the cost of providing the benefit by the employer and/or the fair market value of the benefit. In cases where taxable benefit and non-taxable benefit are mixed, a reasonable apportionment is necessary in order to determine the taxable portion of the benefit.

(i) — Cost to the employer

As discussed below, the value of a benefit is, strictly speaking, its fair market value. However, in certain cases, the cost to the employer has been used to value taxable benefits. Examples include benefits derived from Christmas parties,[68] the

---

[63] *Giffen v. R.*, [1995] 2 C.T.C. 2767, 96 D.T.C. 1011 (T.C.C.). This is no longer the case, according to CRA administrative practice, if a personal credit card is used: see note 72, below.

[64] In *Phillips v. M.N.R.*, [1994] 1 C.T.C. 383 387–88, 94 D.T.C. 6177 6180 (Fed. C.A.), although the Court did not reject outright the notion that an employee can receive a payment from an employer in his or her personal capacity, it indicated that such situations would be rare.

[65] *Cf. Busby v. R.*, [1986] 1 C.T.C. 147, 86 D.T.C. 6018 (Fed. T.D.) (stock option plan received by reason of taxpayer's personal relationship with his employer).

[66] *Waffle*, note 59, above.

[67] *Philp*, note 56, above, and *Ferguson v. M.N.R.* (1971), [1972] C.T.C. 2105, 72 D.T.C. 1097 (T.A.B.).

[68] *Dunlap*, note 10, above.

education of an employee's children,[69] and meals in an employer-subsidized cafeteria.[70]

Computing the value of the benefit using the employer's cost is generally easy because the employer typically claims a deduction for the same amount. As well as leading to symmetrical treatment of the employer and the employee, the cost to the employer also provides a figure which, in many situations, is reasonable to accept as being also the fair market value to the employee.[71]

In some cases, however, the cost to the employer does not necessarily measure the value to the employee and, in other cases, the benefit may cost the employer nothing. In these cases, the value of the benefit to the employee cannot be based on employer's cost and must instead be based on fair market value. One example is the use of an employer-provided home or vacation home if the cost to the employer (i.e., the monthly operating cost) is less than the rent that could be charged to a third party. Another is the benefit derived from an employee's frequent flyer points accumulated on business travels.[72]

(ii) — Fair market value

The "classic test" of fair market value assessment is "the price that would be willingly paid by a buyer who does not have to buy to a seller who does not have to sell".[73] This test does not require an actual market for the benefit. The test is based on a hypothetical market, and it requires an estimate to be made of the price upon which a willing seller and a willing buyer would agree for a similar benefit.

---

[69]*Detchon*, note 52, above.

[70]IT-470R, note 10, above, para. 28.

[71]Small differences between cost and fair market value would sometimes result from the employer's entitlement to some form of volume discount that would not be available to an individual purchaser of a single suit or vacation or other benefit. But this order of discrepancy could perhaps be overlooked or tolerated as a minor, through recognition of the lesser value to the employee because something was selected for him or her as opposed to being something that he or she selected.

[72]In *Giffen*, note 63, above, Bonner J. stated at 2777–8, and 1017 that "the value of a reward ticket in either business or first class was equal to that proportion of an unrestricted business or first class fare which the price of the most heavily discounted economy class fare on that flight is of the price of a full fare economy class ticket". For 2009 and subsequent years, the CRA will not require employment benefits to be computed where an employee's personal credit card is used as long as the points are not converted to cash, the plan or arrangement is not indicative of an alternate form of remuneration or the plan or arrangement is not for tax avoidance purposes. Company credit card points continue to be taxable. See CRA, Technical News No. 40, June 2009. The rationale for this change in CRA administrative practice appears to be simplicity and not equity: that is, because an employer has easy access to a company credit card statement (and therefore value of the reports redeemed), the employer can and must compute the benefit.

[73]*Steen v. Canada*, [1988] 1 C.T.C. 256 257, 88 D.T.C. 6171 6172 (Fed. C.A.).

The fair market value may be established on the basis of resale value of the property received from the employer. For example, the value of a gold ring given by an employer for long service was its scrap value because the ring was stamped with the employer's logo and the employee could not sell it as a piece of jewelry.[74] Another example is the case where the value of a new suit given as a Christmas bonus was the value of a second-hand suit (the value that can be realized if the employee sold the suit).[75] The fair market value may also be the cost of purchasing the item by the employee. An example would be the cost of a parking space paid for by the employer[76] or the cost of purchasing a ticket obtained with the frequent flyer points accumulated with business travels.[77]

The fair market value is generally an objective value. Should subjective value be taken into consideration as well? Assume a law professor would rather read the *Income Tax Act* than any other book, should an employer-provided copy of *Income Tax Act* be valued by including the value of additional enjoyment?[78] Should the tax system take seriously employee allegations that they would have said to their employers, "Please, don't give me that Mercedes!"?[79] These considerations would introduce a speculative and subjective element to the task of valuation that is probably not feasible.

(iii) — Apportionment

Sometimes a payment by an employer to or for the benefit of an employee has a dual character: it covers expenses incurred partly for the employer and partly for the personal benefit of the employee. It is difficult to ascertain the taxable value to the employee. A common cause of difficulty is the cost of transportation and accommodation for purposes which are partly employment-related and partly vacation. If the employer pays the entire bill, then the cost has to be apportioned between business and vacation, and the vacation element assessed to the employee as a benefit. Thus, a trip to the Bahamas supplied by a wholesaler to grocery store employees and their spouses, which involved a mixture of business and pleasure, was assessed as a taxable benefit to the extent of half of the cost of the trip.[80] A trip to Greece supplied by a wholesaler to the employee of a retailer to attend a business

---

[74] *Wisla v. R.*, [2000] 1 C.T.C. 2823 (T.C.C.).

[75] *Wilkins v. Rogerson*, [1960] Ch. 437 (Ch. Div.).

[76] *Richmond v. R.*, [1998] 3 C.T.C. 2552, 98 D.T.C. 1804 (T.C.C.); and *Monteith v. R.* (1997), [1998] 2 C.T.C. 2281, 98 D.T.C. 1306 (T.C.C.).

[77] See *Giffen*, notes 63 and 72, above.

[78] Economists describe this excess of satisfaction from property over its market price as consumer surplus. It is practically difficult to tax consumer surplus.

[79] Taxing the value of the Mercedes based on the market value may seem somewhat harsh in that benefits provided by an employer are rarely the free choice of the employee, and are undoubtedly less valuable to the employee than something which the employee freely purchased for him or herself.

[80] *Philp*, note 56, above.

convention which left time for several pleasure tours in Athens was assessed as a taxable benefit only to the extent of one-tenth.[81] A conference held by an insurance company in Phoenix, which included a full schedule of business activities for the company's employees, but which employees' spouses also attended at the employer's expense, was held not to include any element of benefit to the employees.[82] In other cases, however, the cost of the spouse's trip has been assessed as a benefit to the employee.[83]

Apportionment is also an issue where the employer's payment to or for the employee is for business purposes, but involves the provision of facilities that are unreasonably luxurious (and therefore expensive). In that situation, it is arguable that part of the cost should be attributed as a luxury element, which was unnecessary for the business purpose, and should be assessed as a benefit to the taxpayer. This line of argument was successful in *Zakoor v. M.N.R.* (1964),[84] where the employer supplied its president with a Cadillac. Although the proportion of personal use of the car was only one-fifth, it was held that the personal benefit from the provision of the car was enhanced by its luxurious character and should be assessed at one-third of the operating expenses. This principle still stands, although the result of this case for cars is now overruled by statutory rules discussed under heading 5.7(a), below.

5.6 — Allowances

(a) — Inclusion in income

Paragraph 6(1)(b) of the Act includes in a taxpayer's income from an office or employment:

> all amounts received by the taxpayer in the year as an allowance for personal or living expenses or as an allowance for any other purpose. ...

A number of allowances are exempted from the general rule of taxability by paragraph 6(1)(b) itself and by other provisions of the Act.[85] The most commonly encountered tax-free allowances are reasonable allowances for travel expenses and motor vehicle (or car) expenses.[86] If an allowance is included in income under par-

---

[81] *Ferguson*, note 67, above.

[82] *Hale v. M.N.R.*, [1968] C.T.C. 477, 68 D.T.C. 5326 (Ex. Ct.).

[83] *Shambrook v. M.N.R.* (1965), 40 Tax A.B.C. 28 (T.A.B.); and *Paton v. M.N.R.*, [1968] Tax A.B.C. 200 (T.A.B.).

[84] (1964), 35 Tax A.B.C. 338 (T.A.B.)

[85] *E.g.*, ss. 6(6), 81(2), 81(3), 81(3.1).

[86] S. 6(1)(b)(v) to (xi). Note that s. 6(1)(b)(vii) only excludes reasonable non-motor vehicle allowances for travel that is "away from" a municipality or metropolitan area where the employee normally reports. Effective 2009, the CRA will extend this treatment to reasonable allowances paid for travel "within" the municipality or metropolitan area if the allowance is paid primarily for the benefit of the employer (that is, to ensure that the employee's duties are undertaken in a more efficient manner during the course of a work shift, and where allowances paid are not indicative of an alternate form of remuneration). CRA, *Technical*

agraph 6(1)(b), the employee may sometimes be able to claim offsetting deductions discussed under heading 5.10(b), below.

(b) — "Allowance" defined

The term "allowance" is not defined in the Act. It has been defined by the CRA in these terms:[87]

> [T]he word "allowance" means any periodic or other payment that an employee receives from an employer, in addition to salary or wages, without having to account for its use.

The purpose of an allowance is to compensate the employee for expenses that he or she is likely to incur in the course of employment. Typical allowances include meal allowances (for meals while travelling on business, normally on a *per diem* basis)[88] and car allowances (for car expenses, normally on a mileage basis).[89]

(c) — Reimbursements distinguished

An "allowance" should be contrasted with a "reimbursement". Technically, an allowance for personal or living expenses is taxable under paragraph 6(1)(b), and a reimbursement for personal or living expenses is taxable under paragraph 6(1)(a). The distinction makes little difference in practice, as the amount is taxable in any event.[90] However, the distinction is relevant where paragraph 6(1)(b) specifically excludes an allowance from income. Such exclusions include: an allowance fixed by an Act of Parliament or by the Treasury Board; travel and separation allowances received by members of the Canadian Forces; allowances for travel expenses paid to an employee who is employed to sell property or negotiate contracts for the employer; allowances for travel expenses paid to an employees where the employee is required to travel away from the municipality where his or her employer's establishment is located; and allowances for the use of use of automobiles for travelling in the performance of the duties of an office or employment.

News No. 40, June 2009. The rationale appears to be fairness (because of the larger size of municipalities and cities today after the mergers that have taken place) as well as administrative simplicity.

[87]Interpretation Bulletin IT-522R, "Vehicle, travel and sales expenses of employees" (1996), para. 40.

[88]S. 6(1)(b)(v).

[89]S. 6(1)(b)(x) deems mileage allowances that are not "solely based on kilometres driven" to be unreasonable.

[90]Because the wording "personal or living expenses" is included in s. 6(1)(b), but not in s. 6(1)(a), in the past, the courts found it easier to find that an amount was taxable if it was characterized as an allowance. For example, in *Ransom*, note 60, the reimbursement of the loss from the sale of the house was considered a reimbursement and not taxable, whereas in *Canada v. MacDonald*, [1994] 2 C.T.C. 48, 94 D.T.C. 6262 (Fed. C.A.), monthly housing subsidy paid by employer to compensate for higher cost of accommodation was characterized as an allowance and taxable under s. 6(1)(b).

The main distinction between an allowance and reimbursement lies in the accountability of the expenses. An allowance does not require the recipient to account for the expenditure of the funds, whereas a reimbursement is a payment by an employer to an employee to repay the actual amount of expenses incurred by the employee. An "accountable advance" is not an allowance. An accountable advance is an amount given by an employer to an employee for expenses to be incurred by the employee on the employer's business, which advance is to be accounted for by the employee after expenses have been paid by the production of receipts and the return of any amount not so spent.[91]

5.7 — Benefits — Specific items

(a) — Automobiles

Automobiles are commonly used by employees who have to work in different places. Because of the personal benefit component of employer-provided cars and the luxury element of expensive cars, it is often difficult to determine the amount of taxable benefit. Therefore, the Act now contains detailed rules for computing taxable benefits in respect of employer-provided cars (the "standby charge").[92] For the same reasons, the Act also contains detailed rules restricting an employer's deduction in respect of tax-free mileage allowances[93] and car expenses.[94] The same restrictions on car expenses apply when an employee provides his or her own car for use in his or her employment.

The "standby charge" is the taxable benefit related to having the automobile available for use or on "standby".[95] Paragraph 6(1)(e) provides a "reasonable" standby charge formula that computes a maximum annual benefit of 24 per cent (2 per cent per month) of the original cost of an employer-owned car and two-thirds of the lease cost of an employer-leased car. The amount of the benefit is reduced if the employee's use of the car is primarily (more than 50 per cent) for employment purposes — that is, if the employee's personal use (including trips from home to the office and back) is less than 50 per cent or less of total mileage of the car.[96]

---

[91]See IT-522R, note 87, above, para. 50(b).

[92]Ss. 6(1)(e) and 6(2). The term "automobile", which is used in the employee taxable benefit rules in section 6, is defined in section 248(1) to exclude emergency response vehicles, taxis as well as vehicles that carry more than eight passengers and vans and pickup trucks that carry not more than two passengers.

[93]S. 18(1)(r).

[94]Ss. 67.2 and 67.3, reg. 7307 and Class 10.1, Sch. II of the Regulations.

[95]Ss. 6(1)(e), 6(2), 6(2.1).

[96]In these cases, the benefit is multiplied by the fraction of personal kilometres driven divided by 1,667 kilometres per month (s. 6(1)(e)). As a result, there will be no reduction at all if personal kilometres amount to at least 1,667 per month (on average), and a less than fair reduction if total kilometres driven each month are greater than 1,667 and a more than fair reduction if the total kilometres driven each month are less than 1,667.

As discussed earlier, there is a taxable benefit if an employee receives an unreasonable car mileage allowance[97] or if car expenses incurred for personal purposes are reimbursed by the employer.[98] For example, if an employer reimburses an employee for all of his or her car expenses (including the personal use component) it would be reasonable to compute the taxable benefit under paragraph 6(1)(a) by multiplying the total expenses reimbursed by the percentage of the kilometres driven that are personal in nature (including the trips from home to the office). This is exactly how the taxable benefit for operating costs is computed when an employee uses his or her own car and the employer reimburses the employee for all of the operating costs.[99]

However, if the employee uses an employer-provided car and the employer pays the car's operating costs, the benefit is computed quite differently according to some very arbitrary rules. In general, the benefit is based on a statutorily prescribed per kilometre amount (24 cents per kilometre in 2010) multiplied by the number of kilometres driven for personal purposes. For example, if an employee drives 10,000 kilometres for personal purposes, his or her benefit in 2010 will be $2,400. If the kilometres are driven primarily (more than 50 per cent of the kilometres) for employment purposes, the employee can elect to use one-half of the standby charge (the computation of which is discussed below) instead of the 24 cents per kilometre amount.

(b) — Loans

If an employer makes an interest-free loan to an employee, is there any taxable benefit to the employee? This question is answered by subsections 6(9) and 80.4(1). In essence, the transaction is recharacterized to reflect economic reality. The borrower/employee is deemed to owe a market rate of interest (established by the prescribed interest rate[100]) and the amount of interest payment waived by the lender/employer is a taxable benefit to the employee.

If the loan is received by virtue of employment and is used to buy a home, it may qualify as a home purchase loan.[101] If the employee moved at least 40 kilometres closer to a new work location, the loan may qualify for a special type of home

---

[97]Ss. 6(1)(b)(v), (vii.1), (x) and (xi).

[98]Ss. 6(1)(k) and (l).

[99]S. 6(1)(l). If the employer pays for all the operating expenses of the car (which is owned by the employee) and (for example) 40% of the kilometres driven are for personal use (including trips to and from the office), then 40% of the amount paid will be a taxable benefit. If the employer only pays for the 60% employment use component, there will be no taxable benefit.

[100]The "prescribed rate of interest" is set each quarter based on the average yield of 90 day treasury bills in the first month of the previous quarter: reg. 4301.

[101]S. 80.4(7).

purchase loan: a home relocation loan.[102] The prescribed rate used to compute the benefit for these two types of home purchase loans is the lesser of the prescribed rate at the time that the loan is made and the prescribed rate during the relevant period.[103] These loans are also deemed to be new loans every five years which means that the "prescribed rate at the time that the loan is made" changes every five years. This rule is an attempt to have the taxable benefit rules mirror commercial practice: that is, five-year fixed rate residential home mortgages.[104]

The borrower/employee may be eligible for an offsetting deduction for interest expense if the loan is used to purchase shares (or another investment) or to buy a car that is used for employment purposes. In these situations, the deemed "interest" benefit is deductible as interest expense.[105] This is a very sensible rule because it treats the deemed interest like real interest which would be deductible in the same circumstances. As a result, if the loan is used to purchase shares (or another investment) the deduction will equal the benefit and the net effect on the employee's income will be zero.[106] However, if the loan is used to buy a car that is used for employment purposes, it is unlikely that the deduction will completely offset the inclusion because it will only be a fraction of the deemed interest expense based on the employment use of the car.

(c) — Housing benefits

(i) — Confusion in the case law

The difficulty in drawing the line between taxable and non-taxable benefits is illustrated by a series of cases concerning the payment by an employer of an em-

---

[102]S. 248(1). The 40 kilometre test is borrowed from rules that allow a deduction for moving expenses in s. 62: see heading 12.9, "Moving Expenses", below. The home relocation loan deduction is described in s. 110(i)(j) and is available for the first five years of the loan.

[103]S. 80.4(4).

[104]S. 80.4(b)

[105]Ss. 80.5, 20(1)(c) and 8(1)(j).

[106]If the employee is also a shareholder of the employer corporation (or is connected to a shareholder) it is possible that instead of having a deemed interest benefit, the subsection 15(2) shareholder loan rules may apply to include the entire principal amount of the loan in income. This amount would be included as income from property in the year the loan is received. If the principal amount of the loan is included in income, the deemed interest benefit rules do not apply since this would result in double taxation (s. 80.4(3)(b)). These rules will not apply in cases where the loan is made in the ordinary course of business and employer's ordinary business is money lending, where it is reasonable to conclude that the loan is received because of the employee's employment (and not because of any person's shareholding), or where the loan is repaid within one year after end of the taxation year of the corporation in which the loan is made (ss. 15(2.3), (2.4) and (2.6)).

ployee's relocation expenses,[107] the most significant of which relates to housing. Housing costs and expenses typically include a loss from the sale of a house in the old location, an increase in the cost of purchasing a comparable house at the new location, and increased mortgage expenses (in the form of increased principal amount or higher interest rate). It was because of these cases that the statutory rules concerning relocation benefits were reformed in 1998.[108]

The first of these cases was *Ransom v. M.N.R.* (1967).[109] Ransom, who was an employee of Dupont of Canada, was transferred by Dupont from Sarnia to Montreal. The housing market in Sarnia was depressed at the time of the transfer with the result that Ransom incurred a loss on the sale of his house in Sarnia. The loss was reimbursed to him by Dupont. The Exchequer Court held that the reimbursement[110] was not taxable as a benefit because the loss had been incurred "by reason of" his employment. This decision seems open to criticism because, while it is true that the transfer was the reason for the sale of the house, the loss on sale is probably best regarded as one of the costs of Ransom's accommodation in Sarnia. The location of one's employment is ordinarily an important factor in choosing a house or apartment, but the costs associated with the house or apartment are consumption expenses nonetheless. It is arguable, therefore, that the payment to Ransom was a reimbursement of a personal expense, not an employment expense, and as such it should have been treated as a taxable benefit. Unfortunately, *Ransom* was followed in later cases.[111]

Where a taxpayer is relocated by his or her employer and does not incur a loss on the sale of the old home, but is required to pay more for a similar home in the new (more expensive) location, any payment made by the employer to offset the extra cost of the new home is a taxable benefit under paragraph 6(1)(a). This was decided by the Federal Court of Appeal in *R. v. Phillips* (1994).[112] In that case, the Canadian National Railway (CN) closed its New Brunswick facility and the taxpayer was transferred to CN's Winnipeg facility, and was provided with $10,000 as a relocation payment. The purpose of this payment was to offset the higher cost of housing in Winnipeg, as the taxpayer was required to sell his home in Moncton and purchase another house in the new location. The Court distinguished *Ransom* on the ground that the taxpayer in that case had been reimbursed for an actual loss on

---

[107]S. 62 permits the deduction from employment income (as well as business income) of moving expenses incurred on a change of work, provided that they have not been reimbursed by the employer; see heading 12.9, "Moving expenses", below.

[108]See heading 5.7(c)(ii), "Statutory rules", below.

[109]Note 60, above.

[110]See heading 5.6(c), "Reimbursements distinguished", above.

[111]*R. v. Splane*, [1990] 2 C.T.C. 199, 90 D.T.C. 6442 (Fed. T.D.); affirmed [1991] 2 C.T.C. 224, 91 D.T.C. 5549, 92 D.T.C. 6021 (Fed. C.A.); *Hoefele*, note 113, below; and *Siwik v. R.*, [1996] 2 C.T.C. 2417, 96 D.T.C. 1678 (T.C.C.)

[112][1994] 1 C.T.C. 383, 94 D.T.C. 6177 (Fed. C.A.); leave to appeal refused (1994), 5 C.C.P.B. 41 (note) (S.C.C.).

the sale of his home, while the taxpayer in *Phillips* had not. In *Phillips*, the taxpayer had been assisted by his employer in the purchase of a new and more valuable home: his net wealth had been increased by the employer's payment and was therefore taxable under paragraph 6(1)(a).

In *Canada v. Hoefele* (1995),[113] Petro-Canada assisted employees who were relocated from Calgary to Toronto by paying them a mortgage-interest subsidy, based on a finding that housing in Toronto cost 55 per cent more than housing in Calgary. The employee who moved to Toronto was reimbursed for the additional interest on his or her mortgage caused by the larger principal sum that had to be borrowed in order to buy a home in Toronto; the subsidy was capped at the average price differential for a comparable home in Calgary and Toronto. The Federal Court of Appeal held, by a majority, that the subsidy was not a taxable benefit, because the net worth of the employees had not been increased by the subsidy: they had comparable homes and no additional equity in those homes. The majority also rejected the application of subsection 80.4(1) on the basis that the loans taken out by the employees were incurred in order to own a home, not "because of or as a consequence of" their employment. As the dissenting opinion of Robertson J.A. pointed out, the majority's reasoning ignored the fact that the mortgage-interest subsidy, like the lump-sum payment in *Phillips*, helped the employee to purchase a more valuable home.[114] It is true that the lump-sum payment in *Phillips* had the effect of immediately increasing the net worth of the employee, whereas the interest subsidy in *Hoefele* had no immediate effect on the employee's net worth. But, in identifying an economic benefit, it is hard to see why the distinction between principal and interest should make any difference. The economic benefit to the employee of the interest subsidy does not disappear simply because the employer's payments are made over a period of time rather than once and for all. Indeed, a present value[115] can be placed on the future stream of payments made by the employer — and that is the value of the benefit to the employee.

In *R. v. Blanchard* (1995),[116] the taxpayer was employed by a mining company that required him to work in Fort McMurray, Alberta. In order to make the move to Fort

---

[113]Reported as *Krull v. Canada* as well as *Canada v. Hoefele* (1995), [1996] 1 C.T.C. 131, 95 D.T.C. 5062 (Fed. C.A.). The majority opinion was written by Linden J.A. with MacGuigan J. concurring; the dissenting opinion was written by Robertson J.A.

[114]Compare *Splane,* note 111, above, where a mortgage-interest subsidy on relocation compensated only for a rise in interest rates, covering the difference in interest payments between the old and the new mortgage on the same principal amount. Held, no taxable benefit to the employee. See also *Siwik*, note 111, above, where an interest-free loan was given to compensate for increased mortgage principal after a transfer to a higher-cost city. Held, no taxable benefit.

[115]The present value of a future payment is explained under heading 1.6(d), "Time value of money", above.

[116][1995] 2 C.T.C. 262, 95 D.T.C. 5479 (Fed. C.A.); leave to appeal refused (1996), 203 N.R. 320 (S.C.C.).

McMurray more attractive, the employer had a housing policy under which the employer agreed to buy back the homes of employees if they were relocated or if they left the company. The employer later terminated this housing policy, and paid $7,240 to the taxpayer (and the other employees who had the same right) as compensation for the rescission of the buy-back right. Was this payment taxable as a benefit of employment? The taxpayer argued that the payment had nothing to do with his past or future services to the employer; the payment was to compensate him for relinquishing a contractual right. The Federal Court of Appeal held that the payment was a benefit of employment. Following the *Savage* case, the Court concluded that "the smallest connection to employment" was required to trigger paragraph 6(1)(a) of the Act.[117] Since the taxpayer was eligible for the payment only by virtue of his employment, the payment should be treated as being "in respect of" the employment within the meaning of paragraph 6(1)(a).

(ii) — Statutory rules

The legislative response to *Ransom* was made in 1998 by introducing subsections 6(19) to (22). These provisions deal with payments made to employees who suffer losses on the sale of their homes as a result of work-related relocation. They apply where a taxpayer moves to a new residence that is at least 40 kilometres closer to a new work location. The first $15,000 of any payment received from his or her employer for an eligible housing loss is received tax free, and one-half of anything received above that amount is a taxable benefit to be included in income.[118] For example, if a relocating taxpayer lost $40,000 on the sale of his or her home, and was compensated for $30,000 of the loss by his or her employer, the taxpayer would have a taxable benefit of $7,500 (1/2 × ($30,000 - $15,000)).

The mortgage-interest subsidy cases, such as *Hoefele*, were addressed by the introduction of subsection 6(23).[119] Under this provision, the amount paid or the value of assistance provided by an employer to employees in respect of the cost of, the financing of, the use of, or the right to use, a residence is a taxable benefit.

Even with these statutory rules, the *Ransom* line of cases will likely remain important for distinguishing between reimbursements and taxable benefits in other contexts. See, for example, in *Guay v. R.* (1997),[120] the taxpayer was an employee whose job required periodic relocations outside Canada. He enrolled his children in a private French-language school that was compatible with an international system

---

[117] *Ibid.*, para 4.

[118] The total taxable benefit will be the same whether there is one payment to the taxpayer or several payments are made over a number of years.

[119] Another relevant provision is s. 80.4(1.1). A loan is deemed to have been received because of a taxpayer's office or employment and so is subject to subsection 80.4(1), if the loan would not have been made, or would have been made on different terms, but for the taxpayer's office or employment. This means that the intended use of the loan is irrelevant for determining whether a taxpayer has received a taxable benefit.

[120] *Guay*, note 52, above.

of French-language schooling, and was reimbursed for the schooling costs by his employer. The Federal Court of Appeal held that the decision to incur the schooling costs was imposed on the taxpayer by the nature of his employment. Therefore, the reimbursement did not fall within the scope of paragraph 6(1)(a). Applying *Hoefele*, the Court further stated that the reimbursement was not a benefit under paragraph 6(1)(a) because it only put the taxpayer in the same economic position he would have been in if he have not been forced by the nature of his employment to incur the schooling costs.[121]

5.8 — Compensation for loss of employment

Upon termination of employment, the departing employee may receive from the employer a lump-sum payment as compensation for the loss of employment.[122] The amount of the severance payment is normally calculated by reference to the salary that of the departing employee would have received during a legally-required period of notice. The period of notice may be stipulated by the contract of employment (or collective agreement) or by employment standards legislation or by a common law standard of reasonableness. Such payments are usually characterized as income from employment,[123] and are taxed accordingly.

In some cases, it will be arguable that the payment is a retiring allowance, which is fully taxed as "other income"[124] rather than income from employment. A retiring allowance is defined in subsection 248(1) to be

> an amount (other than a superannuation or pension benefit, an amount received as a consequence of the death of an employee or a benefit described in subparagraph 6(1)(a)(iv)) received
>
> > (a) on or after retirement of a taxpayer from an office or employment in recognition of the taxpayer's long service, or
> >
> > (b) in respect of a loss of an office or employment of a taxpayer, whether or not received as, on account or in lieu of payment of, damages or pursuant to an order or judgment of a competent tribunal, by the taxpayer or, after the tax-

---

[121]Compare to *Dionne v. R.* (1996), 97 D.T.C. 265 (T.C.C.); affirmed [1999] 2 C.T.C. 158, 98 D.T.C. 5282 (Fed. C.A.) (reimbursement of extra cost of food in a remote area denied).

[122]Sometimes the payment takes the form of a continuation of salary payments for an agreed period of time after the termination of employment.

[123]Interpretation Bulletin IT-365R2, "Damages, settlements and similar receipts" (1987), para. 15. S. 5 of the Act, which taxes "remuneration", is extended by s. 6(3) to include payments made under agreements entered into before or after the period of employment. A signing bonus, paid under an agreement made before employment starts, is caught, for example. A severance payment, even if made under an agreement entered into after employment ends, is also caught.

[124]For more discussion of retiring allowances, see heading 12.6, "Retiring Allowances", below.

payer's death, by a dependant or a relation of the taxpayer or by the legal representative of the taxpayer.

The definition of retiring allowance catches damages awards and out-of court settlements that otherwise would escape tax.

However, where a dismissed employee recovers damages for defamation[125] or for breach of a "pre-employment contract",[126] the damages are not considered income for purposes of the Act. Damages for breach of a contract of employment before the employment has actually commenced are also not considered to be income.[127]

5.9 — Employee stock options

(a) — "Employee stock option" defined

An employee stock option is a right conferred upon an employee to purchase a specified number of shares of the company at a fixed price during a certain period of time. The shares are issued from treasury by the employer and are not purchased on the open market. The option price is often the fair market value of the stock at the time that the option is granted, but it can be more or less than this amount. A stock option benefit arises if the employee exercises the option and buys the stock at a lower price than the current market value (or, alternatively, if the employee disposes of the option for a gain.)

(b) — Application of section 7

Section 7 governs the taxation of benefits arising from the issuance of stock options by a corporation to its employees. It is applicable where securities (typically shares of the capital stock of a corporation, subsection 7(7)) are to be acquired by an employee under an agreement whereby a "qualifying person" (defined under subsection 7(7) as a corporation or mutual fund trust) agrees to sell or issue to an employee. The securities can be the securities of the employer corporation or a corporation with which the employer corporation does not deal at arm's length, such as a parent, a subsidiary or sister corporation.

Section 7 applies to an "employee", which is defined in subsection 248(1) to include an officer. However, subsection 7(5) provides that section 7 does not apply "if the benefit conferred by the agreement was not received in respect of, in the course of, or by virtue of, the employment." This raises an interesting question — if a director (officer) of a corporation is granted the option to acquire shares of the corporation, does section 7 apply to tax the benefit arising from the option? The

---

[125] *Bedard v. M.N.R.* (1990), [1991] C.T.C. 2323, 91 D.T.C. 573 (T.C.C.).

[126] *Richardson v. M.N.R.*, [1988] 1 C.T.C. 2219, 88 D.T.C. 1134 (T.C.C.).

[127] *Schwartz v. Canada*, [1996] 1 S.C.R. 254, [1996] 1 C.T.C. 303, 96 D.T.C. 6103 (S.C.C.), discussed under heading 4.3(d), "Unenumerated Sources", above, and heading 12.6, "Retiring allowances", below.

courts answered "yes" in *Taylor v. M.N.R.* (1988).[128] Rip T.C.J. of the Tax Court of Canada stated:[129]

> The evidence leads me to infer the options were granted in consideration of the services Mr. Taylor was to perform as a director and he received the option *qua* director, an employee of each of the corporations. The benefits he received by the exercise of his rights under the option agreements are taxable pursuant to section 7(1) since he received the benefits by virtue of his employment with the corporations.

In *Scott v. R.* (1994),[130] the Federal Court of Appeal confirmed the reasoning in *Taylor*. These decisions make sense in terms of tax policy, as the Act generally treats income from an office and income from employment in the same manner. Tax equity would be violated if corporate directors could receive stock option benefits tax-free and, in practice, directors and senior management tend to receive the lion's share of stock option benefits.

Once it is determined that section 7 is applicable, four potential tax issues arise: (1) how to determine the amount of the taxable benefit? (2) When is the taxable benefit recognized for tax purposes? (3) How to reconcile the treatment of the benefit as employment income and the treatment of potential gain or loss to be accrued to the stock acquired under the option? (4) Should stock option benefit be treated preferably to ordinary wages or salaries, and if so, what type of preferential treatment?

(c) — Tax consequences

(i) — Taxable benefit

In general, a stock option, like any other property given to an employee as compensation, will be taxable when received by the employee. Under paragraph 7(1)(a), the employee is taxed on the difference between the option price (the amount the employee has paid for the stock) and the fair market value of the stock received when the option is exercised.

For example, if an employer provides an employee with an option to purchase shares worth $100,000 for a price of $20,000, if the option is exercised, the employee's taxable benefit will be the $80,000 difference between the $100,000 fair market value of the shares and the $20,000 paid. This treatment is similar to the situation where an employee who receives a bonus of $80,000 (obviously taxable under section 5) and buys the shares for $100,000.

(ii) — Timing of inclusion

Like other forms of employment income, the general timing rule applies to make the option taxable in the hands of the employee at the time when the benefit is

---

[128] [1988] 2 C.T.C. 2227, 88 D.T.C. 1571 (T.C.C.).

[129] *Ibid.*, 2234, 1576.

[130] [1994] 1 C.T.C. 330, 94 D.T.C. 6193 (Fed. C.A.) (stating at paragraph 16: "Pursuant to section 248(1) of the Act, an officer of a corporation is an employee of that corporation and necessarily has an employment relationship with the corporation").

received. Accordingly, there is no taxable benefit when the employee is given or "granted" an option to purchase shares or when this option right is vested. The taxable benefit is received only when the option is exercised and the shares are acquired or when the option is disposed of.[131] Deferral of recognition of the taxable benefit is available in the circumstances described under heading 5.9(d)(ii), below.

(iii) — Special deduction

When a stock option benefit is included in income under section 7, the employee is allowed a special deduction under paragraphs 110(1)(d) or (d.1) (a Division C deduction) in computing taxable income. The amount of the deduction is 50 per cent of the taxable benefit. Accordingly, the net inclusion in taxable income is comparable to a capital gain, which is only one-half taxable.[132]

The special deduction is only available under certain conditions. First, the employee must deal at arm's length with the employer. Second, he or she must generally receive shares (and not cash) on the exercise of the options and the shares must be "prescribed shares" (generally common shares).[133] If cash is received, the deduction may be claimed only if the employer elects not to take the deduction for the payment.[134] Third, the deduction is also generally available only if the stock option price is greater or equal to the fair market value of the shares on the date that the options are granted.[135] In the case of employee stock options in a company that was a Canadian-controlled private corporation (CCPC) at the time that the options were granted, this special deduction is also available if the shares are held for at least two years.[136]

Allowing the special deduction to an employee only if the employer elects not to take a deduction for the cash payment makes sense.

---

[131]Detailed rules in s. 7(1)(b) to (e) cover the tax consequences when options are disposed of prior to exercise.

[132]Ch. 10, Capital Gains, below.

[133]S. 7(1.1), 110(1)(d), 110(1)(d.1) Reg. 6204.

[134]The rules for cash payments are proposed rules effective for options exercised after 4 pm EST on March 4, 2010. See Department of Finance, 2010 *Federal Budget.* Although s. 7(3)(b) prevents the employer from claiming a deduction for the discount on the stock issued to employees, s. 7(3)(b) does not apply to deny the employer's deduction for a cash payment because no shares are issued. Before the 2010 federal budget, the fact that the employer can claim a deduction for the payment did not prevent the employee who received the cash payment from claiming the special deduction: see s.110(1)(d)(i)(B). In the CRA's view, the special deduction was allowed when the cash payment was considered a section 7 benefit and this was when it was received *only at the employee's option.* If the employer had the option to pay cash, the payment was considered a section 6 benefit. See Interpretation Bulletin IT-113R4, "Benefits to Employees — Stock Options", para 11.

[135]S. 110(1)(d).

[136]S. 110(1)(d.1)

(iv) — Adjusted cost base of the shares

A share purchased under an employee stock option plan is generally a capital property to the employee. When the share is sold, the employee will realize either a gain or loss, depending on the amount of proceeds of disposition (generally the sale price) and the adjusted cost base of the share.[137] The cost base of a share is generally the cost of purchasing the share.[138] In the above example, the cost of the share to the employee will be $20,000. If the share is sold for $140,000, the amount of capital gain would be $120,000. This result is incorrect because the employee's actual cost is $100,000, consisting of $20,000 paid for the stock option and $80,000 taxable benefit under section 7. In the absence of an increase in the cost base, the employee would be taxed twice on the $80,000: once as a taxable benefit under section 7, and again as a capital gain under section 39.

In order to prevent the potential double taxation, paragraph 53(1)(j) allows an adjustment to the cost base by adding the amount of the taxable benefit under section 7 to the cost of the shares. Therefore, the adjusted cost base of the shares purchased by the employee in the above example is $100,000. When the shares are sold for $140,000, only $40,000 capital gain will be realized; this gain represents the increase in value since the time that the shares were acquired. If the value of the shares decreases below $100,000, the employee will realize a capital loss.[139]

(d) — Preferential treatment

If employee stock option benefits were taxed like other benefits, the $80,000 benefit from the example above would be taxed in full in the hands of the employee in the year when the option is exercised. In fact, stock option benefits are taxed preferentially both in terms of the inclusion rate and, in the case of CCPC options, the timing of recognition

(i) — Capital gains-like taxation

As explained in chapters 4 and 10, capital gains are one-half taxable, whereas employment income is fully taxable. A stock option benefit is characterized as income from employment. However, because of the special deduction under paragraphs 110(1)(d) and (d.1) discussed above, only one-half of stock option benefit is actually taxed. In effect, a stock option benefit is taxed *like* a capital gain in terms of its

[137]Computation of capital gains or losses is discussed under heading 10.5, "Computation of gain or loss", below.

[138]See heading 10.4(e), "Adjusted cost base", below.

[139]A capital loss cannot offset the taxable stock option benefit because capital losses can only offset capital gains. See heading 14.4, "Losses", below.

inclusion rate,[140] but it is not characterized as a capital gain so it is not eligible for the capital gains exemption[141] and it cannot be offset by a capital loss.

(ii) — Deferral of recognition

Although stock option benefits are taxable when the option is exercised, an important exception exists for options acquired by arm's length[142] employees of CCPCs (the "CCPC deferral").[143] In this case, the year of recognition of the stock option benefit is automatically changed from the year of acquisition (the general rule) to the year of disposition.[144] The CCPC deferral helps employees of CCPCs (other than controlling shareholders and their family members) purchase shares issued by the employer.[145] This tax treatment is very beneficial since tax payment is postponed until the shares are sold.

A similar deferral (the "$100,000 deferral") was available for arm's length employees of public companies from February 29, 2000 to March 4, 2010.[146] The $100,000 deferral was borrowed from U.S. rules and was elective rather than automatic.[147]

---

[140]From March 31, 1977 to December 31, 1984, the employee stock option benefit relating to options in CCPCs was taxed as a capital gain. When the capital gains exemption under s. 110.6 was introduced in 1985, this tax treatment was changed in two ways: first, to extend it to the options in public companies and, second, to ensure a stock option benefit was not eligible for the capital gains exemption by characterizing it as employment income. The result of this change is still with us today: the net amount included in income is the same as for a capital gain (i.e., one-half) but is not characterized as a capital gain (and therefore cannot be eligible for the capital gains exemption or offset by a capital loss). This net amount consists of two parts: an employee benefit for the full amount and a Division C deduction equal to one-half of the benefit.

[141]See heading 10.2(f), "Tax subsidies for certain investments", below.

[142]The concept of "arm's length" is defined in s. 251(1). In this context, it would exclude an employee who is a controlling shareholder of the CCPC and his or her family members.

[143]S. 7(1.1). For the definition of CCPC, see heading 15.1(d), "Canadian-controlled private corporations", below.

[144]This could be an actual disposition or a deemed disposition when the taxpayer dies or becomes a non-resident.

[145]The company must be a CCPC at the date of grant but does not have to maintain this CCPC status after the options are granted. The company could, for example, be a public company when the options are exercised.

[146]The March 4, 2010 federal budget proposed to repeal the $100,000 deferral effective for options exercised after 4 pm EST March 4, 2010. See Department of Finance, 2010 *Federal Budget*.

[147]S. 7(9). A major difference between the now repealed Canadian $100,000 deferral and the U.S. rules from which they were drawn was that the U.S. rules treated the 1/2 income inclusion relating to the deferred stock option benefit as the equivalent of a taxable capital gain rather than regular income: see the "Incentive stock options" rules under s. 422 of the *Internal Revenue Code*. Another difference is that benefits relating to employee stock op-

Because the stock option benefit relating to shares qualifying for deferral will be taxed when the shares are sold, the Act provides ordering rules which deem these shares (called "deferral shares") to be sold last when a taxpayer owns other shares of the same corporation.[148] This rule will generally be beneficial to taxpayers since it gives the deferral shares the longest holding period possible.[149]

The tax benefit of deferral should always be balanced with other considerations such as investment risk. The tax rules add to this investment risk because allowable capital losses are only deductible against taxable capital gains and the one-half inclusion for the deferred stock option benefit is not a taxable capital gain. As a result, if the stock subsequently declines in value after acquisition, there may be adverse tax consequences.[150] Without a deferral, there is an incentive for employees to sell the shares acquired under the stock option plans as soon as they are purchased if he or she doesn't want to take on this investment risk.

---

tions that do not qualify for the U.S. $100,000 deferral rule are fully included in the employee's income and are deductible to the employer: s. 83(h) of the *Internal Revenue Code*.

[148]The general rule is that non-deferral shares of the same corporation are deemed to be sold first. Once all non-deferral shares are sold, the deferral shares that are acquired at the earliest date are deemed to be sold next: ss. 7(1.3) and 47(3).

[149]As an alternative, the employee can make a designation under s. 7(1.31) to deem the shares sold to be the shares acquired with the most recently exercised stock options. In order to make the designation, the shares must be sold within 30 days after they are acquired and there must be no other purchases or sales of stock during that 30-day period. This designation would be beneficial if the shares acquired with the most recently exercised stock options had a higher adjusted cost base than the shares that would otherwise be deemed to be sold (thus resulting in lower capital gains) and if the stock option benefit related to those shares was not eligible for deferral (and is therefore not triggered by the designation) effective for options exercised after February 27, 2000.

[150]The March 4, 2010 federal budget proposed a complicated set of rules to reduce these adverse tax consequences for a taxpayer who previously deferred his/her stock option benefit and sells the shares at a loss before 2015. If the election is made, a special tax will apply which will not exceed the proceeds received on the sale of the shares. The election: (a) eliminates the s. 7 benefit and s. 110(1)(d) deduction (which eliminates the tax on this benefit); (b) deems a taxable capital gain to be realized equal to the lesser of one-half of the s. 7 benefit and the allowable capital loss realized on the shares and (c) requires a special tax equal to the proceeds received on the sale of the shares. Individuals who sold their shares in previous years (before 2010) must elect by the filing due-date for their 2010 tax return. Individuals who have not sold their shares before 2010 must sell them before 2015 to take advantage of this election. Prior to 2010, the government provided similar leniency to employees of JDS Uniphase by way of a remission order. See "Tories forgive huge JDS tax bills," Ottawa Citizen, December 7, 2007 at http://www.canada.com/ottawacitizen/news/story.html?id=7e85020a-5522-460a-b6cb-526358eba111&k=58866.

(iii) — Policy justifications

Why should the benefit from stock compensation be taxed any differently than other forms of compensation? The answer is that it should not be — for reasons of equity and neutrality. The preferential treatment violates tax equity. Consider two employees working for the same company: Employee A receives a cash bonus of $80,000 and uses his bonus plus $20,000 in personal savings to purchase shares at a cost of $100,000; Employee B, who participates in the employee stock option plan, pays $20,000 to her employer to purchase shares with a fair market value of $100,000. Economically, both A and B receive from their employer compensation valued at $80,000. Employee B is taxed more favourably because only $40,000 is included in her taxable income, whereas Employee A must include the $80,000 bonus in his taxable income. The principle of neutrality is violated because employers are encouraged to remunerate employees in the form of stock option benefits rather than cash remuneration or other forms of taxable benefits.

The capital gains-like treatment of stock option benefits is justified mainly on grounds of tax expenditures, namely, to provide a tax subsidy to CCPCs as well other companies which might have difficulty in finding the cash to attract and pay highly skilled employees. When stock markets are rising, employee stock options are a popular component of compensation plans. Employee stock options have also been touted as a way to attract and retain employees and align their interests with those of shareholders. There is also the "brain-drain" argument: that is, in the absence of favourable taxation of stock options, highly skilled Canadian workers would move to the United States. As well, the capital gains-like treatment is now only available when the employer does not get a deduction.

The CCPC deferral treatment is also justified on pragmatic grounds: it is difficult for an employee to pay tax on a stock option benefit when he or she has not received any cash from the transaction. An employee may actually be short of cash because of the cost of exercising the option and purchasing the shares. The CCPC employee faces a greater hardship than the public company employee in this respect because CCPC shares are not as liquid. A public company employee can easily sell some of the shares acquired with the options in order to pay the tax but a CCPC employee may have great difficulty doing this.

5.10 — Non-taxable amounts

Section 6 excludes amounts from income for two main reasons. One is simplicity. An example is the administrative exemption for non-cash gifts totaling $500 or less. Another reason is to promote social policy goals. In other words, these are tax expenditures. Examples are the exclusions under paragraph 6(1)(a) for the value of employer contributions to private health plans and group accident or sickness plans (disability plans). It is good for society to have taxpayers covered by these employer-sponsored plans. If these benefits were taxed, healthier citizens would opt out of such plans, increasing the costs for those who really need them.

5.11 — Deductions

(a) — Deductions denied

The deductions that are allowed against employment income are confined to the specific expenses enumerated in section 8 of the Act and must be reasonable in the circumstances.[151] As noted earlier, this limitation is made explicit in subsection 8(2). There is no general deduction for of all expenses laid out to earn employment income. It has already been pointed out that this is a violation of equity and neutrality but justified on grounds of tax base protection and administrative simplicity.[152]

(b) — Deductions permitted

Section 8 permits the deduction for travel expenses,[153] legal expenses incurred to collect salary or wages,[154] union dues, professional membership dues, contributions to a registered pension plan,[155] and (when required by contract) supplies, the salaries of assistants, rent, and other specified amounts.[156] Sales personnel who receive commissions (or a bonus based on sales) are entitled to some extra deductions akin to those available against business income (such as meals and entertainment and promotion) but the total amount of these deductions (including the deduction for travel expenses) is limited by the commissions received.[157] As well, employees are only allowed to deduct interest expense and capital cost allowance (tax depreciation) in respect of automobiles and planes.[158] There are, however, no deductions for interest expense and capital cost allowance in respect of assets such as furniture and equipment, computers, or an office.

Travel expenses (including motor vehicle and meal expenses) are only allowed in closely defined circumstances. An employee who "was ordinarily required to carry on the duties of the office or employment away from the employer's place of business or in different places" may deduct his or her travel expenses under paragraphs 8(1)(h) and (h.1). However, the employee must be required to travel, must be required to pay the travel expenses incurred, and must not have received an allowance for travel expenses that was exempted from taxation under paragraph 6(1)(b) and a form T2200 must be signed by the employer regarding those requirements.[159]

---

[151] S. 67.

[152] See heading 5.1(b), "Policy", above.

[153] Ss. 8(1)(h), (h.1).

[154] S. 8(1)(b).

[155] S. 8(1)(m).

[156] Ss. 8(1)(i), 8(5).

[157] S. 8(1)(f). Only 50% of meals and entertainment costs are generally deductible (s. 67.1).

[158] S. 8(1)(j). See *Gifford*, note 15, above.

[159] S. 8(10).

Meal expenses are subject to additional restrictions[160] and are only one-half deductible.[161] Unless these conditions are met, the expenses are not deductible.

Travel expenses incurred in the course of employment, whether deductible or not, must be distinguished from the expenses of travel to or from the place of employment. Such commuting expenses are regarded as personal or living expenses. The journey from home to work is outside the scope of employment. It is true, of course, that the journey is made by reason of employment, but it is not made in the course of employment. This is well established in case law,[162] and also makes sense as a matter of tax policy. A line has to be drawn somewhere, and arrival at the place of work is a better point than departure from home. The nature of the journey from home to work is after all dictated primarily by a consumption decision as to the location of the home.[163]

In cases where an employee is required by the contract of employment to pay office rent, or to hire an assistant, or to purchase supplies, those expenses are deductible under paragraph 8(1)(i). The deduction for home office expenses is similar to that available to self-employed taxpayers but, as mentioned above, cannot include any claims for interest expense or capital cost allowance.[164] The deduction for supplies is confined to consumable supplies such as stationery. Items with longer lives such as books, tools, equipment, special clothing, and uniforms, are not deductible. Nor is there any provision for the deduction of entertainment expenses from employment income (except, as noted above, for sales personnel remunerated by commission or a bonus based on sales).

---

[160]S. 8(4).

[161]S. 67.1

[162]*Ricketts v. Colquhoun* (1925), [1926] A.C. 1 (H.L.); and *R. v. Diemert*, [1976] C.T.C. 301, 76 D.T.C. 6187 (Fed. T.D.).

[163]The classification of commuting expenses as personal expenses means, of course, that they are not only not deductible from employment income, they are not deductible from business income either. See heading 8.4(e), "Commuting expenses", below.

[164]The expense of a home office could be deductible under s. 8(1)(i) (as office rent and supplies), or under s. 8(1)(f) (for sales personnel remunerated by commission), or under s. 8(1)(q) (for artists' expenses not exceeding $1,000). The home-office deduction under s. 8(1)(i) and (f) is strictly regulated by s. 8(13), which imposes conditions virtually identical to those imposed by s. 18(12) on the home-office deduction from business income: heading 8.4(g), "Home-office expenses", below.

6
Income from Business or Property: Profit

6.1 — Legislative scheme

It will be recalled that paragraph 3(a) of the *Income Tax Act* (the "Act") includes in a taxpayer's income "the taxpayer's income for the year from each office, employment, business and property". In the previous chapter, we examined income from an office or employment. In this chapter and the next three chapters, we shall examine income from business or property, which is computed in accordance with the rules in sections 9 to 37. Because the computation rules are usually the same for income from business and income from property, it is generally unnecessary to distinguish between these two types of income.

Section 9 is the starting point for the calculation of a taxpayer's income from a business or property. Subsection 9(1) provides that "a taxpayer's income for a taxation year from a business or property is the taxpayer's profit from that business or property for the year." The concept of "profit" is thus central to section 9. It is computed in accordance with legal principles that incorporate accounting principles. Sections 10 to 37 modify (or in some cases reinforce) this calculation of profit by allowing, disallowing or otherwise regulating particular inclusions and deductions. Most of these rules are found in sections 12 (specific inclusions in computing profit), 18 and 20 (specific deductions in computing profit).

This chapter examines the concept of profit. Chapter 7 will examine specific inclusions in computing business or property income. Chapter 8 will examine specific deductions (not including deductions for capital expenditures); and chapter 9 will examine deductions for capital expenditures from business or property income.

6.2 — Characterization of "business" and "property" as a source

(a) — Importance of characterization

As already discussed in chapter 4, the characterization of income is of fundamental importance for the purposes of the Act. Because of the source concept of income under section 3, if an income or loss is not derived from a source (typically from a business or property) the income is not taxable under paragraph 3(a) and the loss is not deductible under paragraph 3(d). In other words, losses from personal pursuits are not deductible, whereas losses from failed commercial pursuits are. This point is highlighted by the discussion of tax shelter losses below.[1] The distinction between a business and employment determines the scope of deductions (see chapter 5, above) and the distinction between business or property income and capital gains determines whether the income is taxed in full or in half (see chapter 10, below). Finally, even though the computation rules are generally the same for income from

[1]See heading 6.2(b)(iii), "Policy concerns about potential abuse", below.

business and income from property, the Act regards them as separate sources and provides for differential treatment in many circumstances.

The Act provides a definition of "business" and "property", but these statutory definitions are often inconclusive. There is a rich body of case law that characterizes whether an activity constitutes a business or investment and distinguishes income from business or property from personal endeavors and other sources of income.

(b) — "Business" or "property" defined

(i) — Statutory definitions

Subsection 248(1) defines "business" and "property" as follows:

> "business" includes a profession, calling, trade, manufacture or undertaking of any kind whatever and ... an adventure or concern in the nature of trade but does not include an office or employment;
>
> "property" means property of any kind whatever whether real or personal or corporeal or incorporeal and, without restricting the generality of the foregoing, includes
>
> (a) a right of any kind whatever, a share or a chose in action,
>
> (b) unless a contrary intention is evident, money....

The statutory definition of "business" is merely inclusive: a profession, calling, trade or manufacture is included, as is an undertaking of any kind whatever if the activity is analogous to any of the listed activities. The listed activities are, in general, profit-motivated, organized, continuous or systematic operations. An "adventure or concern in the nature of trade" is generally an isolated, speculative transaction. In the absence of its specific inclusion in the definition of "business", the gain or loss from such a transaction would likely be characterized as a capital gain or loss, or a windfall. Overall, because the statutory definition of "business" is not exhaustive, the ordinary meaning of the word must be ascertained.

The statutory definition of "property" is extremely broad. It is generally clear whether something of value is property for tax purposes. However, because the statutory definition is tied to the ordinary meaning of "property" and "right", it is still important to refer to private law and case law for such meanings. For example, in *Manrell v. R.* (2003),[2] the Federal Court of Appeal held that the legal right to receive a non-competition payment is not a "right of any kind whatever", and thus not "property" as defined under the Act. According to the Court, "property" has consistently been interpreted as entailing an exclusive and legally enforceable claim and a shared right to carry on business did not meet this definition.

[2] 2003 D.T.C. 5225, [2003] 3 C.T.C. 50 (Fed. C.A.), discussed in ch. 4, above.

(ii) — Common law

The often-quoted common law definition of a "business" is "anything which occupies the time, attention and labour of a man for the purpose of profit."[3] Both income from a business and income from property are derived from activities undertaken in pursuit of profit, a test which was recently adopted by the Supreme Court in *Stewart*[4] and *Walls*.[5]

In *Stewart*, the taxpayer was engaged in property rental activities. He bought four condominium units from the same developer. The units were all rented to arm's length parties and there was no evidence that the taxpayer intended to make use of any of the properties for his personal benefit. The taxpayer incurred losses from the outset. The losses arose primarily from interest on money borrowed to acquire the units. Both the Tax Court and the Federal Court of Appeal found that there was no reasonable expectation of profit from property because the scheme "held out no expectation of profit from the rental income". The scheme was promoted by the vendor/developer as a tax shelter to "use rental losses to offset other income and realize a gain at the end of the day from the expected appreciation in the value of the property."[6] The Supreme Court reversed the lower courts' decisions and found that there was a source of property income because the investment was in pursuit of profit. The Court stated the "pursuit of profit" test as follows:[7]

> It is clear that in order to apply s. 9, the taxpayer must first determine whether he or she has a source of either business or property income. As has been pointed out, a commercial activity which falls short of being a business, may nevertheless be a source of property income. As well, it is clear that some taxpayer endeavours are neither businesses, nor sources of property income, but are mere personal activities. This is why, for example, barter transactions involving household labour are not taxed.[8] As such, the following two-stage approach with respect to the source question can be employed:
>
> > (i) Is the activity of the taxpayer undertaken in pursuit of profit, or is it a personal endeavour?
> >
> > (ii) If it is not a personal endeavour, is the source of the income a business or property?

---

[3]*Smith v. Anderson* (1880), 15 Ch. D. 247 (C.A.), most recently cited by the Supreme Court in *Stewart v. R.*, 2002 SCC 46, 2002 D.T.C. 6969 (S.C.C.), paras. 38 and 51. See also *Terminal Dock and Warehouse Co. Ltd. v. M.N.R.*, 68 D.T.C. 5060, [1968] C.T.C. 78 (Ex. Ct.); affirmed (1968), 68 D.T.C. 5316 (S.C.C.).

[4]*Stewart, ibid.*

[5]*Walls v. Canada*, 2002 SCC 47, [2002] 2 S.C.R. 684, [2002] 3 C.T.C. 421 (S.C.C.).

[6]*Stewart v. R.*, [2000] 2 C.T.C. 244, 2000 D.T.C. 6163 (Fed. C.A.), para. 10, citing the Tax Court Judge's finding.

[7]*Stewart*, note 3 above, paras. 50, 51, 53.

[8]Interpretation Bulletin IT-490, "Barter Transactions" (1982).

> . . .it is logical to conclude that an activity undertaken in pursuit of profit, regardless of the level of taxpayer activity, will be either a business or property source of income. . ..
>
> . . .Where the nature of an activity is clearly commercial, there is no need to analyze the taxpayer's business decisions. Such endeavours necessarily involve the pursuit of profit. As such, a source of income by definition exists, and there is no need to take the inquiry any further.

In *Walls*, the taxpayer incurred losses from a mini warehouse operated by a limited partnership, which was structured as a tax shelter. The losses were denied by the Tax Court for lack of a reasonable expectation of profit, but allowed by the Federal Court of Appeal because it was a commercial venture devoid of any personal elements. The Supreme Court applied the "pursuit of profit" test and held that the investment constituted an income source.[9] According to the Court, "it is self-evident that such an activity is commercial in nature, and there was no evidence of any element of personal use or benefit in the operation".[10]

The "pursuit of profit" test requires the taxpayer to have an intention to profit. The Court provided the following approach to applying this test where the nature of the activity is not clearly commercial:[11]

> "Does the taxpayer intend to carry on an activity for profit and is there evidence to support that intention?" This requires the taxpayer to establish that his or her predominant intention is to make a profit from the activity and that the activity has been carried out in accordance with objective standards of businesslike behaviour.

The determination that a taxpayer has an intention to make a profit does not depend upon the subjective view of the taxpayer, who is likely to be overly optimistic about the prospects of his or her activity. The subjective intention of the taxpayer must be supported by objective evidence. Moreover, to satisfy the subjective intention requirement, all that is needed is a "predominant" intention of profit. In other words, the taxpayer may have several intentions in undertaking an activity, but as long as the predominant intention is to make a profit, the test is met.

Objective factors, such as those listed by Dickson J. in *Moldowan* (1977)[12] must be relied upon to determine the taxpayer's intention to make a profit:[13] the profit and loss experience in past years; the taxpayer's training; the taxpayer's intended course of action to convert present losses into future profits; and the capability of the venture, as capitalized, to show a profit after capital cost allowance. The amount of time the taxpayer spends on the activity in question is also relevant.[14]

---

[9] The Court also found that there was a valid partnership relationship in *Walls*, note 5, above. See ch. 16, Partnerships, for a discussion of the taxation of partners of partnerships.

[10] *Walls*, *ibid.*, para. 20.

[11] *Stewart*, note 3, above, para. 54.

[12] [1977] C.T.C. 310 314, 77 D.T.C. 5213 5215 (S.C.C.).

[13] *Stewart*, note 3, above.

[14] *Sipley v. R.*, [1995] 2 C.T.C. 2073 2075 (T.C.C.).

There is no need to demonstrate that the taxpayer's expectation of profit is reasonable,[15] although a reasonable expectation of profit is a factor to be considered.

According to the Supreme Court, the word "profit" in the pursuit of profit test is not the "net profit" concept used for the purpose of section 9. Instead, the word means the layperson's notion of profit. Therefore, although capital gains are not considered to be profit from a business or property for the purposes of the Act, "the motivation of capital gains accords with the ordinary business person's understanding of "pursuit of profit", and may be taken into account [as one of several factors] in determining whether the taxpayer's activity is commercial in nature".[16] However, the motivation of capital gains cannot be the sole determinative factor, as the mere acquisition of property in anticipation of an eventual gain does not provide a source of income for the purposes of section 9, because subsection 9(3) stipulates that income from property excludes capital gains.

The Court provided no guidance as to what more is required in order to turn a passive ownership of property (the sale of which gives rise to a capital gain or loss) into a business or investment property. As discussed further below, such a broad interpretation of the "pursuit of profit" test means that as long as there is no personal use of the property, an investment qualifies as a source of income, even if there is no prospect of making any profit from the investment. This means that taxpayers, such as Mr. Stewart and Mr. Walls, can use such investment as tax shelters — investment vehicles that "shelter" taxes. A common feature of tax shelters is that the investment produces losses that can be used to offset income from other sources (typically employment or business income).

(iii) — Policy concerns about potential abuse

A business activity involves a degree of financial risk. Indeed, the taxation of business income softens the financial risk by allowing the deduction of business losses (and carryovers to other years if necessary). If a taxpayer engages in a business-like activity that consistently incurs losses (farming is the most common one), can the losses be deducted by the taxpayer (who may have other income, perhaps professional income, which would be sheltered by the losses)? Until the *Stewart* case, the courts had answered no to this question. For an activity to be a business, there had to be a "reasonable expectation of profit" (REOP).[17] The CRA had used the REOP test to deny the recognition of losses from personal hobbies and tax shelters on the

---

[15]See note 17, below.

[16]*Stewart*, note 3, above, para. 68. The Federal Court of Appeal decision in *Tonn v. R.*, [1996] 1 C.T.C. 205 226, 96 D.T.C. 6001 6011 also seemed to indicate that capital gains could be considered in determining whether the expectation of profit is reasonable.

[17]*Moldowan*, note 12, above, at 313, 5215. For a discussion of the "reasonable expectation of profit" test that was applied by the courts before *Stewart* to deny losses from hobby activities as well as unsuccessful commercial ventures, see headings 12.2(b) and 12.3(b) of Hogg, Magee and Cook, *Principles of Canadian Income Tax Law* (3rd ed.), at 220, 225.

grounds that these losses were not from a business or property source, and were thus not deductible under paragraph 3(d).

Many tax shelters involve investments in real estate or stocks. These investments offer the possibility of both earning rent or dividends (income from property) and of obtaining capital gains in the future. Because of the current deduction of interest expense and capital cost allowance in the case of rental property (see chapter 8), the income stream produces a loss, while the capital stream produces a profit. Until recently, the CRA typically challenged the deduction of losses on the grounds that: (1) interest was not deductible under paragraph 20(1)(c), as in *Ludco Enterprises Ltd. v. Canada* (2001),[18] and (2) there was no source of income for purposes of paragraph 3(d), as in *Stewart* and *Walls*. Now the CRA has lost on both grounds.

Based on the "pursuit of profit" test, as long as an investment is not personal in nature, it constitutes a business or property source. Because tax shelter investments are generally not personal pursuits, they are naturally commercial pursuits. For example, in *Ludco*,[19] the taxpayer deducted about $6 million in interest expenses during the period in which only $600,000 in dividends was received. The dividend stream was intended to generate losses as a result of the interest expense deduction. The investment was "profitable" to the taxpayer because of the favourable treatment of capital gains from the disposition of the shares. The Supreme Court allowed the interest deduction under paragraph 20(1)(c) without addressing the issue whether there is a source of income from property.

The *Stewart* and *Walls* cases have clearly terminated the use of the REOP test as a judicial stop-loss rule. The Court was in an unenviable position in these cases and in *Ludco*. If an investment activity was held not to constitute a business, then the taxpayer would be denied the losses on the income stream, while paying tax on the capital gains. In computing capital gains, no deduction is allowed for interest expenses incurred in respect of the investment property, as there is no mechanism under the Act that allows the taxpayer to capitalize interest expenses or the losses. This is contrary to the fundamental principle that income is a net concept (net of losses).

However, the Court's own "pursuit of profit" test is stretched when applied to an investment such as a tax shelter which, by design, produces losses. Tax shelter investments only produce "profit" if an "ordinary business person's" notion of "pursuit of profit" includes the "profit" that results from saving taxes. Many tax shelter investments *per se* would not produce any economic profit for the investor were it not for the immediate deductibility of losses on the income stream and the one-half taxation of the eventual capital gain. It is therefore highly questionable from a policy perspective whether tax shelter losses should be used to reduce or even eliminate the taxpayer's tax base.

---

[18](2001) (sub. nom. *Ludco Enterprises Ltd v. R.*) 2001 D.T.C. 5505 (Eng.) (sub. nom. *Ludco Enterprises Ltd. v. R.*) 2001 D.T.C. 5518 (Fr.), [2002] 1 C.T.C. 95 (S.C.C.).

[19]*Ibid.*

As the Supreme Court of Canada has repeatedly stated: "in matters of tax law, a court should always be reluctant to engage in judicial innovation and rule making".[20] It is clear that the solution to the tax shelter loss problem must come from the government. In October 2003, the Department of Finance released for public consultation draft legislation to restrict the deductibility of losses caused by the deduction of interest and other expenses based on an objective REOP test (draft section 3.1). This draft legislation attracted a great deal of controversy because of concerns about the potential effects on normal business and capital market activities. More modest legislative responses are under consideration.

(c) — Personal endeavours distinguished

(i) — Pursuit of personal pleasure

If an activity contains no personal element and is clearly commercial, it is (by definition) in the "pursuit of profit" and will be a source of income that is either a business or property, regardless of the level of activity.[21] If, however, an activity has a personal element, it will be necessary to consider first whether the activity is undertaken in "pursuit of profit" or is a personal endeavour. If an activity with a personal element is found to be in "pursuit of profit" (rather than a personal endeavour) it will be a source of income that is either business or property. Therefore, an activity undertaken predominantly for personal hobby, recreation, or other personal purposes is not a business. Of course, in the rare case where such an activity does yield a gain, as when a taxpayer's race horse unexpectedly produces net winnings in a particular year,[22] the gain is likely a tax-free windfall.

The fact that a commercial venture incurs losses year after year (as in *Stewart* and *Walls*) does not necessarily mean that no business or property source exists. Some money-losing activities that were found not to constitute a business source under the former "reasonable expectation of profit" test will now be characterized differently. This is true even "where a taxpayer does not organize his or her activities in a business-like manner" and "a reasonable expectation of profit has turned into an impossible dream".[23] For example, in *Landry v. R.* (1994),[24] the taxpayer was a 71-year-old lawyer who recommenced the practice of law after a hiatus of 23 years.

---

[20]For example, *Stewart*, note 3 above, para. 42.

[21]The Supreme Court was clear in *Stewart*, note 3, above, para. 52, that the pursuit of profit test is only relevant when the taxpayer's activity contains a personal element. "[W]here the nature of a taxpayer's venture contains elements which suggest that it could be considered a hobby or other personal pursuit, but the venture is undertaken in a sufficiently commercial manner, the venture will be considered a source of income for the purposes of the Act."

[22]*Hammond v. M.N.R.*, [1971] C.T.C. 663, 71 D.T.C. 5389 (Fed. T.D.).

[23]*Landry v. R.* (1994), [1995] 2 C.T.C. 3, 94 D.T.C. 6624 (Fed. C.A.), 6625, citing comments made by the Tax Court Judge Leave to appeal refused (1995), 187 N.R. 237 (S.C.C.) and reconsideration refused (February 8, 1996), Doc. 2437770 (S.C.C.).

[24]*Ibid.*

The case concerned the losses he claimed in respect of his legal practice. The Federal Court of Appeal found that the taxpayer had no reasonable expectation of profit, and thus no business income source: he had continued losses over 15 years, did not keep good records, did not have a budget, did not advertise other than through a listing in the telephone directory, did not always bill clients for services rendered, had not taken any professional development courses to update his skills, and had not changed his practices over the years in the face of these losses. The Supreme Court stated that the Federal Court of Appeal erred in this case because there existed no personal element.[25] With respect, it is arguable that Landry's law practice had personal elements — that is, the deductions relating to Landry's home office, as well as his personal satisfaction and standing in the community.[26]

(ii) — Hobbies

The "hobby farmer" has given rise to most of the cases regarding denial of loss deductions due to a finding of hobby rather than business,[27] but losses have been disallowed in other kinds of cases where a taxpayer could not show a reasonable expectation of profit: an author who had published six books;[28] a professional racing car driver who occasionally won prize money;[29] a restaurateur whose restaurant regularly attracted customers;[30] a producer of machine tools intended for sale;[31] a boat charter business where the owner was employed full time in other occupations and could not afford the 48-foot cruiser for his own use exclusively;[32] a horse-breeding and racing operator who spent the bulk of her time and energy on the operation;[33] a hobby dog breeder known as the best in the country;[34] and a lawyer with only two clients.[35] Under the new "pursuit of profit" test, the restaurant and law practice would be characterized as commercial ventures, constituting a business income source.[36]

---

[25]*Stewart*, note 3, above, para. 53.

[26]This point was mentioned by in *Tonn*, note 16, above, at 6011 (Fed. C.A.). However, this personal element argument was rejected by the Federal Court of Appeal in the subsequent decision in *Poetker v. M.N.R.*, [1996] 1 C.T.C. 202, 95 D.T.C. 5614 (Fed. C.A.).

[27]E.g., *Moldowan*, note 12, above.

[28]*Payette v. M.N.R.*, [1978] C.T.C. 2223, 78 D.T.C. 1811 (T.R.B.).

[29]*Cree v. M.N.R.*, [1978] C.T.C. 2472, 78 D.T.C. 1352 (T.R.B.).

[30]*Sirois v. M.N.R.* (1987), [1988] 1 C.T.C. 2147, 88 D.T.C. 1114 (T.C.C.).

[31]*Knight v. M.N.R.*, [1993] 2 C.T.C. 2975, 93 D.T.C. 1255 (T.C.C.).

[32]*Chequer v. R.*, [1988] 1 C.T.C. 257, 88 D.T.C. 6169 (Fed. T.D.).

[33]*Urquhart v. R.* (1996), 96 D.T.C. 3257 (T.C.C.).

[34]*Escudero v. M.N.R.*, [1981] C.T.C. 2340, 81 D.T.C. 301 (T.R.B.).

[35]*Landry*, note 23, above.

[36]*Stewart*, note 3, above, para. 53.

(iii) — Personal elements in rental properties

The element of personal benefit has also been present in many of the earlier cases in which rental losses have been denied for lack of a "reasonable expectation of profit" — for example, where the property is rented to friends[37] or relatives,[38] the rental property is part of the taxpayer's principal residence,[39] the rental property is in a resort area[40] or the property is intended to be a future retirement or vacation home.[41] In *Maloney v. M.N.R.* (1989),[42] for example, a taxpayer who let a house to his mother at a rent that was far below the mortgage interest, property taxes, and other maintenance expenses of the property was not allowed to deduct his annual losses. It was found that the taxpayer had no reasonable expectation of profit from the property. The annual losses were in the nature of gifts to his mother, and gifts are non-deductible consumption expenses. Under the new "pursuit of profit" test, it is likely that losses from such activities will continue to be denied since the activities will be characterized as personal endeavours not in the "pursuit of profit".

(iv) — Gambling

Gambling may be characterized as a personal hobby or a commercial activity. The line between the two is drawn on the basis of objective factors. On one end of the spectrum is bookmaking or operating a betting shop, which obviously constitutes a business activity. It makes no difference to the Act if the business is illegal: the profits from an illegal business are taxable on the same basis as those from a legal business. At the other end of the spectrum is the casual gambler whose activity is a hobby or recreation and whose winnings are therefore treated as windfalls (and whose losses are treated as consumption expenses).

When an individual devotes a great deal of time and effort to gambling, it is often difficult to determine whether the activity falls into the hobby category or the business category. In *M.N.R. v. Morden* (1961),[43] the taxpayer, a hotel proprietor, was an "inveterate gambler", who "was prepared to place a bet on the outcome of baseball, hockey and football matches, and on card games, whether he was a player or merely placed side bets". Despite the evidence of extensive gambling, the Court

---

[37] *Trojanowski v. M.N.R.*, [1984] C.T.C. 2841, 84 D.T.C. 1705 (T.C.C.).

[38] *Maloney v. M.N.R.*, [1989] 1 C.T.C. 2402, 89 D.T.C. 314 (T.C.C.); *Huot v. M.N.R.*, [1990] 2 C.T.C. 2364, 90 D.T.C. 1818 (T.C.C.); and *Carew v. R.*, [1994] 2 C.T.C. 2008, 94 D.T.C. 1415 (T.C.C.); affirmed [1999] 2 C.T.C. 269, 99 D.T.C. 5206 (Fed. C.A.).

[39] *Saleem v. M.N.R.*, [1984] C.T.C. 2660, 84 D.T.C. 1579 (T.C.C.); and *Cecato v. M.N.R.*, [1984] C.T.C. 2125, 84 D.T.C. 1110 (T.C.C.).

[40] *Perratt et al. v. M.N.R.*, [1985] 1 C.T.C. 2089, 85 D.T.C. 101 (T.C.C.); and *Meech v. M.N.R.*, [1987] 1 C.T.C. 421, 87 D.T.C. 5251 (Fed. T.D.).

[41] *Mason v. M.N.R.*, [1984] C.T.C. 2003, 84 D.T.C. 1001 (T.R.B.); and *Dallos v. M.N.R.*, [1985] 2 C.T.C. 2021, 85 D.T.C. 417 (T.C.C.).

[42] *Maloney*, note 38, above.

[43] [1961] C.T.C. 484, 61 D.T.C. 1266 (Ex. Ct.).

held that the evidence did not establish that the taxpayer "in relation to his betting activities conducted an enterprise of a commercial character or had so organized these activities as to make them a business calling or vocation". On the other hand, in *Walker v. M.N.R.* (1951),[44] the taxpayer, a farmer, was held to be engaged in the business of gambling and to be taxable on his winnings. In this case, the taxpayer regularly attended horse races in four cities and bet substantially and successfully at them; he was a part-owner of several horses and moved in a racing milieu which gave him access to inside information. The Court held that the gambling activity was not a mere amusement or hobby, but was sufficiently extensive and systematic to constitute a business. The facts in *Luprypa v. R.* (1997),[45] which followed *Walker*, were similar and the taxpayer was also held to carry on a business: he was a skilled gambler who gambled 5 days a week; gambling was his primary source of income; he had a system of minimizing the risk and he won most of the games played.

The volume of gambling and the size of winnings are relevant but not decisive factors in determining whether the taxpayer is a compulsive gambler in pursuit of the thrill of winning or an organized gambler in pursuit of livelihood. In *Leblanc v. R.* (2006)[46] the taxpayers were brothers. From 1996 to 1999, they played sport lotteries four to five times per week, purchasing thousands of tickets per week, paying friends to pick up tickets from stores, developing a computer program to help pick the games. During this period, they had gross winnings of approximately $55,500,000. The Minister included winnings in taxpayers' income from a business. The Court found that the taxpayers were compulsive gamblers on the basis of the facts that: they won in spite of having no system; they bet massively and recklessly; their chances of losing were far greater than their chances of winning; large number of bets in itself was not indicative of anything other than tendency to bet heavily; and they were not professional gamblers who assessed their risks, minimized them and relied on inside information and knowledge and skill. Bowman C.J.T.C. remarked:[47]

> They are not like the racehorse-owner, who has access to the trainers, the horses, the track conditions and other such insider information on which to base his wagers. Nor are they like seasoned card players or pool players who prey on unsuspecting, inexperienced opponents. Rather, they are more accurately described as compulsive gamblers, who are continually trying their luck at a game of chance.

---

[44][1951] C.T.C. 334, 52 D.T.C. 1001 (Ex. Ct.).

[45][1997] 3 C.T.C. 2363, 97 D.T.C. 1416 (T.C.C.). *Luprypa* was cited in *Epel v. R.*, 2003 D.T.C. 1361 (T.C.C.) with approval. The court in *Epel* concluded that the taxpayer was not engaged in a business because most of the facts present in *Luprypa* were not present in this case.

[46](2006), 2006 TCC 680, 2007 D.T.C. 307 (Eng.), [2007] 2 C.T.C. 2248 (T.C.C. [General Procedure]).

[47]*Ibid.*, para. 48.

(d) — Employment distinguished

Where a taxpayer provides services to a single person, or to a few people, it may be unclear whether the taxpayer's remuneration is income from a business or income from employment. (Although both types of income are taxed, income from a business is treated more favourably in several respects.) This distinction has been described in chapter 5, Income from Employment, above.

(e) — Capital gains distinguished

Where a property is sold at a profit, the taxation of this profit depends on the characterization of the profit as business income from trading or capital gains. This characterization is governed by case law principles that are discussed in chapter 11, Investing and Trading.

Where a property is held as an investment, it typically has two streams of gains: income from property and capital gains. Subsection 9(3) expressly provides that income from a property does not include any capital gain from the disposition of that property. Income from a property is the return that is obtained simply by owning the property, for example, rent on real estate, interest on bonds or dividends on shares. A capital gain arises only on the disposition of property; it is the return that is obtained when a property is disposed of for more than it cost. The main tax distinction between the two categories of income is that income from property is fully included in income, while capital gains are only 50 per cent included in income. There are also tax differences with respect to the deductibility of expenses and other matters.[48]

(f) — Business distinguished from property

(i) — Level of activity

As discussed earlier, both business income and property income are derived from activities undertaken in pursuit of profit. The difference between these two sources lies in the level of activity.[49] A business activity entails a certain level of "busyness". A commercial activity that falls short of being a business may constitute a source of property income. In other words, where the income is derived primarily from the ownership of property, it is income from property; where the income is derived primarily from the activity of the owner or the owner's employees, it is income from a business.

---

[48] See ch. 10, Capital Gains, below.

[49] In *Stewart*, note 3, above, para. 51, the Supreme Court noted that the difference between business and property sources was one of the level of activity: "Business income is generally distinguished from property income on the basis that a business requires an additional level of taxpayer activity... As such, it is logical to conclude that an activity undertaken in pursuit of profit, regardless of taxpayer activity will be either a business or property source of income."

The distinction has proved most difficult to draw in respect of the rental of real estate. It is obvious that the letting of property yields income from property. However, it is also obvious that a business will usually have a number of "capital assets", and yet the income yielded by those assets is simply part of the business income of the owner. *Prima facie*, of course, the rents derived from letting an apartment building, office building or shopping centre, are income from property. The rents are paid for the use of the property, not for services provided by the landlord. The difficulty arises from the fact that a landlord will often supply to the tenants, in addition to the right to occupy the rented premises, services of various kinds. Where the services supplied consist of only those services which are of a kind customarily included with rented premises, for example, maintenance of building, heating, air conditioning, water, electricity, and parking, the rent is still regarded as income from property. But if the services supplied go beyond those which are customary for an office building or apartment building or shopping centre (or whatever the property is), it becomes more plausible to characterize the owner's operation as a business rather than the mere letting of property. Services provided by an apartment building that would be indicative of a business classification would include services normally provided by a hotel, i.e., housekeeping, laundry service, restaurant and room service, etc. The extreme case is, of course, a hotel, where the extent of the services supplied to guests makes it obvious that it is a business. Where the range of services supplied by the landlord falls below hotel level, it becomes a question of degree whether the nature and extent of the services makes it appropriate to characterize the income as earned from a business.[50]

Another situation in which the distinction between income from a business and income from property needs to be made is where a landlord owns many apartment buildings (or other rental properties), and employs an extensive staff to manage them. In that case, where many people are occupied in the management of a landlord's properties, the level of activity will usually lead the courts to find that the landlord is engaged in a business, even if the level of activity involved in managing an individual property is low.[51]

The level-of-activity test applies to other kinds of property income as well. A bank, for example, earns its profits primarily from making loans to borrowers and charging them interest. Interest on a loan is normally income from property. But the level of activity that is involved in making many loans, with all the supervisory and ancillary services that are required, transforms income from property into income from a business. (In the banking example, it is also arguable that the provision of

---

[50]See generally Interpretation Bulletin IT-434R, "Rental of real property by individual" (1982); *Wertman v. M.N.R.*, [1964] C.T.C. 252, 64 D.T.C. 5158 (Ex. Ct.); and *Walsh and Micay v. M.N.R.*, [1965] C.T.C. 478, 65 D.T.C. 5293 (Ex. Ct.).

[51]For examples, see *Malenfant v. M.N.R.*, [1992] 2 C.T.C. 2431, 92 D.T.C. 2081 (T.C.C.); *Etoile Immobiliere S.A. v. M.N.R.*, [1992] 2 C.T.C. 2367, 92 D.T.C. 1984 (T.C.C.); and *Burri v. R.*, [1985] 2 C.T.C. 42, 85 D.T.C. 5287 (Fed. T.D.). The latter two cases also demonstrate the rebuttable presumption that income earned by a corporation pursuing the objects of its incorporation is income from a business.

banking services, such as cash withdrawals, chequing facilities, safety deposit boxes, foreign exchange transactions and the like, would in any case distinguish the banker from the mere lender of money.)

(ii) — Differential tax treatments

The Act draws some distinctions between business and property income in provisions that are scattered throughout the Act. The following is a partial list:

1. The attribution rules of sections 74.1 and 74.2 apply to income from "property", but not income from a business.

2. Prepaid amounts are included in income under paragraph 12(1)(a) if they are in respect of income from a business (sale of goods or services), but not income from property.

3. The capital cost allowance rules preclude the use of capital cost allowance deductions to create losses on income from "rental property",[52] but where the income is from a business the restrictions do not apply.

4. The deductions for cumulative eligible capital amounts (for the amortization of intangibles which have an indefinite life) are available "in respect of a business", but not property.

5. The rules regarding the taxation of Canadian controlled private corporations distinguish between income from an "active business", in respect of which the "small business deduction" is allowed under section 125, and a "specified investment business" (which excludes income from an active business), in respect of which a partial refund of tax is available under s. 129.

6. A non-resident is liable to Part I tax on income from carrying on business in Canada, but Part XIII tax on income from property (typically dividends, interest, rents and royalties).

6.3 — Concept of profit

(a) — Net concept

The concept of profit is not defined in the Act.[53] Therefore, the term "profit" has its ordinary meaning, which is generally found in the case law. Profit "is inherently a

[52]See heading 9.4(i)(ii), "Rental property", below.

[53]According to Iacobucci J. in *Canderel Ltd. v. R.*, [1998] 2 C.T.C. 35, 98 D.T.C. 6100 (S.C.C.), para. 29, this was a deliberative legislative choice and "reflects the reality that no single definition can adequately apply to the millions of different taxpayers bound by the Act . . . [because] each taxpayer must be able to compute his or her income in such a way as to constitute an accurate picture of his or her income situation, subject, of course, to express provisions in the Act which require specific treatment of certain types of expenses or receipts".

net concept which presupposes business expense deductions".[54] This means that costs and expenses incurred in earning income from a business or property are to be deducted against revenues in computing profit.[55] It is thus a matter of accounting.

(b) — Financial accounting versus tax

Taxpayers must compute profit for tax purposes as well as financial or commercial purposes. In many situations, the computation of profit for a taxation year is very simple and, if financial statements have already been prepared for an enterprise, the profit is likely to be the same as the income reported before income taxes on these statements. In other situations, different rules of computation are used in financial accounting and tax accounting. In such cases, the issue arises as to the relevance of financial accounting for income tax purposes.

The term "financial accounting rules" is used here to refer to accounting in accordance with "well-accepted business principles",[56] which include, but are not limited to, generally-accepted accounting principles (GAAP) (defined below). Businesses generally use GAAP to keep their books and records and prepare their financial statements, but some businesses do not have to use GAAP, if, for example, they are not required to have an audit or a review of their financial statements.

"GAAP" may be defined as the rules that are used by accountants in the preparation of financial statements, and are accepted by the accounting profession as producing useful information about the financial condition of the person or enterprise

---

[54]*Symes v. Canada*, [1993] 4 S.C.R. 695, [1994] 1 C.T.C. 40, 94 D.T.C. 6001 (S.C.C.) (per Iaccobucci J.), para. 40. The courts have stated that it is the reference to "profit" in s. 9(1) that provides the primary rule governing the deduction of expenses in the computation of income from business or property. See also *Daley v. M.N.R.*, [1950] C.T.C. 254, 4 D.T.C. 877 (Ex. Ct.); and *Royal Trust Co. v. M.N.R.*, [1957] C.T.C. 32, 57 D.T.C. 1055 (Ex. Ct.).

[55]The net concept is consistent with the logic of income tax. See headings 8.2(a), "Income tax logic", and 14.3, "Net income", below.

[56]Instead of relying directly on GAAP, the courts have said, at various times, that profit should be calculated in accordance with "well-accepted principles of commercial trading", "well-accepted principles of business (or accounting) practice", "ordinary commercial principles", and "well-accepted business principles". The problem was that the courts did not define what exactly these principles were or how they differed from GAAP. Some judgments seemed to indicate that they did not even include GAAP. While one might think that these terms have ordinary meanings, this was not so. All these terms were judicial inventions; they had no recognized meanings in the business, accounting or even legal communities as GAAP did. As a result, these terms have provided little or no guidance to taxpayers trying to determine their profit for tax purposes. In *Symes*, note 54, above, in which the question was whether child care expenses were deductible as a business expense, Iacobucci J. for the majority of the Supreme Court of Canada said (at para. 37) that it was not "appropriate" to rely on GAAP alone and that reliance should be placed on "well accepted principles of business (or accounting) practice" or "well accepted principles of commercial trading". In *Canderel*, note 53, above, Iacobucci J. specifically included GAAP as part of the well-accepted business principles.

that is the subject of the statements.[57] These "principles" become "generally accepted", not by legislation or other formal *imprimatur*, but simply by their acceptance and use by accountants. In court, GAAP rules are established by the expert evidence of accountants.[58]

An accounting principle will be regarded as "generally accepted" if it meets "at least one and usually more" of the following conditions:[59]

- the principle is actually followed in a significant number of cases;
- the method has support in pronouncements of professional bodies;
- the method finds support in the writings of academics and others.[60]

While GAAP is not definitive in determining profit for tax purposes, as a practical matter, GAAP represents well-accepted business principles in many cases. Many taxpayers carrying on business rely upon GAAP in preparing their financial statements. These taxpayers then use the same financial statement numbers for tax purposes, disclosed in a prescribed format using standardized coding[61] and accompanied by a form making only those adjustments that are specifically required by the Act or case law. Since the CRA accepts this practice, in most cases, profit will be determined for tax purposes according to GAAP unless the Act or case law modifies or prohibits the application of those principles.[62]

There are a number of situations where the tax law has specific rules that require a departure from GAAP. There are perhaps three major reasons for these differences.

---

[57]*Handbook of the Canadian Institute of Chartered Accountants (the CICA Handbook).*

[58]That is why a court that has to resolve a dispute about accounting principles will require the expert evidence of accountants as to the appropriate practice in that case. In *R. v. Moore*, [1987] 1 C.T.C. 377, 87 D.T.C. 5215 (Fed. C.A.), the Court noted that judges must be informed of GAAP by expert evidence, rather than by reference to textbooks or other reference materials, unless the texts are properly introduced in evidence or consented to by the parties.

[59]See Arnold, *Timing and Income Taxation* (Can. Tax Foundation, Toronto, 1983), 7.

[60]The latter two elements have their origin in the 1929 crash of the New York stock market. Before the crash, the accounting profession in North America had not established standard-setting bodies and there was little theoretical writing. After the crash, concerns about inadequate financial reporting, which received some of the blame for the market excesses that led to the crash, contributed to academic interest in accounting, and caused the accounting profession in the United States to establish standard-setting procedures. In Canada, standard setting did not occur until 1946, when the Canadian Institute of Chartered Accountants (CICA) formed a committee for that purpose.

[61]The standardized coding classifications are according to the CRA's General Index of Financial Information (referred to as the "GIFI"). The financial statement notes are also required to be attached to the tax return.

[62]In anticipation of the adoption of the CICA's adoption of International Financial Reporting Standards (IFRS) for public companies effective January 1, 2011, the government indicated in the March 4, 2010 federal budget that it would review the impact of IFRS on the Canadian income tax system and, where necessary, make changes. No changes have been announced at the time of writing (March 2010).

All of the reasons have to do with the fact that a tax system has objectives and concerns that are not relevant to financial accounting and vice versa. The income statement is one of three statements that financial accountants produce (the other two are the balance sheet and the cash flow statement) and the objectives of these three statements (along with the required note disclosures) are to assist users in predicting an entity's future earnings and cash flows. After the crash of 1929 (and in response to the crash), the focus in financial accounting was getting the income statement right. Accounting standards have evolved since then, and the focus is now on getting the balance sheet right. The measurement of income does not have the primacy in financial accounting that it once had.
The tax system, of course, only measures income and has different objectives : (1) it measures income to meet objectives of revenue generation, equity, simplicity and international competitiveness; (2) it is used as a tax expenditure tool to provide tax subsidies and concessions for certain types of activities and (3) it must always be concerned with a taxpayer's liquidity when it decides how to treat transactions that do not generate cash to pay tax.

One reason that is often cited as to why the Act and the case law depart from GAAP is the tax system's objective of raising revenues and GAAP's preoccupation with presenting a conservative picture of profit. Justice Iacobucci noted this problem in his judgment in *Symes v. Canada* (1993):[63]

> [W]hereas an accountant questioning the propriety of a deduction may be motivated by a desire to present an appropriately conservative picture of current profitability, the Income Tax Act is motivated by a different purpose: the raising of public revenues.

As noted above, the objectives of financial accounting are to assist financial statement users in predicting future earnings and cash flows. That is one of the reasons, for example, that conservatism (or prudence), the "matching" of revenue and expenses and the amortization of capital expenditures are accounting principles: it is important to put revenues and expenses in the right period. Estimates of a conservative nature are financial accounting's attempt to ensure that, when uncertainty exists, an entity's assets, revenues and gains are not overstated and, conversely, that its liabilities, expenses and losses are not understated.[64] For example:

- GAAP is conservative about revenues: it requires a receipt of income to be amortized over a number or years (rather than being recognized in the year of

---

[63]*Symes*, note 54, above, at para. 43. In *Symes* itself, acceptance of the taxpayer's argument that her child care expenses should be allowed as a business expense would have produced a lower figure for tax purposes than that yielded by generally accepted accounting principles.

[64]"Prudence" rather than "conservatism" is the new term used in CICA Handbook, Part I Framework for the Preparation and Presentation of Financial Statement (effective January 1, 2011), para. 37: "Prudence is the inclusion of a degree of caution in the exercise of the judgements needed in making the estimates required under conditions of uncertainty, such that assets or income are not overstated and liabilities or expenses are not understated. However, the exercise of prudence does not allow, for example, the creation of hidden reserves or excessive provisions, the deliberate understatement of assets or income, or the deliberate

receipt) if the services are to be provided over a number of years or the amount otherwise relates to a number of years. The Act sanctions this treatment in some cases but not in others.[65]

- GAAP is conservative about the value of assets: it requires an investment to initially be recorded at its historical cost and written down if the value becomes impaired. The Act only allows write-down in the case of inventory[66] and investments that have no value.[67] The Act generally does not allow unrealized gains to be recognized, however GAAP *requires*recognition of unrealized gains (and losses) for some items, and *allows*it for other items.[68]
- GAAP is conservative about recognizing liabilities: it requires a liability to be recognized when it can be reasonably estimated. The Act overrides this if the liabilities are reserves for contingencies and are not legal liabilities.[69]

However, the Act and the case law are often more conservative than GAAP when it comes to deductions for outlays and expenses: a full deduction or faster amortization rate is often available for tax purposes. Examples include the case law treatment of the tenant inducement payments, discussed below[70] and the Act's system

overstatement of liabilities or expenses, because the financial statements would not be neutral and, therefore, not have the quality of reliability."

[65]See heading 8.7(iv), "Unearned amounts reserve", below.

[66]S. 10.

[67]S. 50.

[68]As discussed under heading 8.8(d), "Valuation methods", below, the "fair market value" method under regulation 1801 allows unrealized gains to be recognized in the case of most types of inventory, although the method used by most taxpayers is the lower of cost or market (which is the only method allowed under GAAP) because it minimizes taxable income. GAAP does not allow the recognition of unrealized gains on inventory except for recoveries of previously recognized inventory write-downs. In the case of financial institutions, s. 142.5 of the Act makes the recognition of unrealized gains mandatory because it requires them to value the securities they own at fair market value. Under the CICA Handbook, Part I: International Financial Reporting Standards (IFRS), which are the CICA accounting standards for Canadian public companies effective January 1, 2011, the fair market value method can be used for many types of assets. Accounting Standards for Private Enterprises (ASPE or Private Enterprise GAAP), which comprise Part II of the CICA Handbook, are also effective January 1, 2011, and make use of the fair market value method as well, but to a lesser extent than that of IFRS. Note that effective January 1, 2011 we will be in a multiple GAAP environment in Canada as there will be one GAAP (IFRS) for public companies and another (ASPE) for private enterprises. (Private enterprises may use IFRS if they wish but the ASPE are less complex standards more suitable to the needs of the users of private enterprise statements.)

[69]S. 18(1)(e).

[70]The result of the "accurate picture" requirement is likely to be conservative because most taxpayers will choose a full deduction when give a choice (between claiming a full deduction in the year or amortizing the amount over a number of years) and the onus of proof is on the

for capital cost allowance which operates independently of GAAP's system for depreciation of the same assets.[71]

Another reason for the differences between financial accounting and tax accounting is the use of tax policy to provide subsidies or concessions for certain types of activities. Examples are the fast write-offs available for expenditures on research and development,[72] and disability related modifications and equipment,[73] and equipment that produces electricity or heat on an energy efficient basis.[74]

A third reason for departures from GAAP is the tax system's concern with a taxpayer having sufficient cash to pay the tax.[75] This liquidity concern explains why reserves for certain long-term receivables exist under the Act but not under GAAP[76] and why the case law and the provisions of the Act often support a full inclusion or deduction of a cash or near-cash item that is required to be amortized under GAAP.[77] This liquidity concern has also been suggested from time to time as the reason why unrealized gains should not be recognized for tax purposes even though they might be for accounting. In *Friedberg v. Canada* (1993),[78] for example, the Supreme Court of Canada held that the "mark-to-market" accounting method[79] was not appropriate for income tax purposes, even though the evidence indicated that it was the preferred method for financial accounting purposes in the particular circumstances.[80] Justice Iacobucci for a unanimous Court stated that:[81]

> [W]hile the "marked to market" accounting method proposed by the [Minister] may better describe the taxpayer's income position for some purposes, we are not satisfied that it can describe income for income tax purposes, nor are we satisfied that a margin account balance is the appropriate measure of realized income for tax purposes.

CRA to prove that the taxpayer's method is not appropriate: see heading 6.4,""Accurate picture" of profit requirement", below.

[71]See heading 9.4, "Capital cost allowance (CCA)", below.

[72]S. 37.

[73]S. 20(1)(qq) and 20(1)(rr).

[74]See Class 43.1 and 43.2, discussed under heading 9.4, "Capital cost allowance (CCA)", below.

[75]This is similar but not quite the same as the "ability to pay" principle, which is based on all economic resources, not just liquid resources, such as cash and near-cash.

[76]See S. 20(1)(n), discussed under heading 8.7(e)(iii), "Deferred payments reserve", and s. 40(1)(a)(iii), discussed under heading 10.5(b), "Proceeds due in a future year", below.

[77]See, for example *Canderel*, note 53, above.

[78][1993] 4 S.C.R. 285, [1993] 2 C.T.C. 306, 93 D.T.C. 5507 (S.C.C.).

[79]The marked to market method is another name for the fair market value method which recognizes unrealized gains and losses on futures contracts and other securities on an accrual basis

[80]See note 68 above regarding GAAP and the fair market value method

[81]Note 78, above, para. 3

As discussed in more detail in chapter 7,[82] the realization principle in income tax law is that a taxpayer must have the absolute right to the amount in order for it to be considered to be income. The rationale for this requirement would be the concern that taxes should not be imposed until income is certain and there is a reliable prospect of cash to pay the tax.

(c) — Question of law

Accounting principles and income tax law have evolved over the years from simple systems based on cash and the realization of profit to more sophisticated systems that reflect the complexity of business transactions today. Although income tax law has several objectives which financial accounting does not have, the objective of a meaningful measure of annual income is an objective common to both systems.

Over the years, however, the courts have been unwilling to rely directly on GAAP in calculating profit "to avoid delegating the criteria for the *legal* test of profit to the accounting profession".[83] If this was done and GAAP changed, so would profit for tax purposes.[84] The Supreme Court of Canada has made it very clear in its interpretative framework (discussed below) that the definition of profit in section 9 is a legal concept: it is determined based on the law and judicial interpretation and it is not based on accounting principles. This means that: (1) the court must determine the facts, hear the expert accounting evidence and decide what the relevant legal and accounting principles are; (2) accounting principles are not rules of law but only interpretative aids;[85] and (3) the computation of profit for tax purposes does not have to conform with the accounting method used in the financial statements. Accordingly, it is well established now that the determination of profit is a question of law and financial accounting principles are relevant to the determination of profit where the Act is silent or where statutory provisions require interpretation.

6.4 — Judicial guidelines

(a) — *Canderel*

The leading case on the determination of profit under section 9 of the Act is the Supreme Court of Canada's decision in *Canderel Ltd. v. R.* (1998).[86] In this deci-

---

[82]See heading 8.8(e), "Tracing inventories", below.

[83]*Canderel*, note 53, above, para. 3.

[84]GAAP changes occur slowly as its large base of standards evolve and many of the changes recently have been made with the goal of international harmonization of accounting standards where it makes sense. For example, effective January 2011, GAAP will change. The CICA will require International Financial Reporting Standards (IFRS) to be adopted by Canadian public companies and will allow private companies to choose a simpler GAAP (ASPE).

[85]See heading 6.4(d), "Financial accounting principles as interpretative aids", below.

[86]Note 53, above.

sion, the court provided a six-part interpretative framework for determining profit under section 9 of the Act. This framework is a useful summary of the current state of the law on this issue:[87]

> (1) The determination of profit is a question of law.
>
> (2) The profit of a business for a taxation year is to be determined by setting against the revenues from the business for that year the expense incurred in earning said income.
>
> . . . . .
>
> (3) In seeking to ascertain profit, the goal is to obtain an accurate picture of the taxpayer's profit for the given year.
>
> (4) In ascertaining profit, the taxpayer is free to adopt any method which is not inconsistent with
>
> (a) the provisions of the *Income Tax Act;*
>
> (b) established case law principles or "rules of law";
>
> (c) well-accepted business principles.
>
> (5) Well-accepted business principles, which include but are not limited to the formal codification found in G.A.A.P., and are not rules of law but interpretative aids. To the extent that they may influence the calculation of income, they will do so only on a case-by case basis depending on the facts of the taxpayers' financial situation.
>
> (6) On reassessment, once the taxpayer has shown that he has provided an accurate picture of income for the year, which is consistent with the Act, the case law, and well-accepted business principles, the onus shifts to the minister to show either that the figure provided does not represent an accurate picture or that another method of computation would provide a *more* accurate picture.

This framework was applied in two other Supreme Court cases decided on the same day as *Canderel*: *Toronto College Park Ltd. v. R.* (1998)[88] and *Ikea Ltd. v. R.* (1998).[89] The key elements of this framework are discussed below.

---

[87] *Canderel, ibid*., para. 53.

[88] [1998] 1 S.C.R. 183, [1998] 2 C.T.C. 78, 98 D.T.C. 6088 (S.C.C.).

[89] [1998] 1 S.C.R. 196, [1998] 2 C.T.C. 61, 98 D.T.C. 6092 (S.C.C.).

(b) — "Accurate picture" of profit requirement

(i) — The goal

According to the framework, the goal of determining profit is to provide an accurate picture of profit. Earlier cases have used both the phrase "accurate"[90] and the phrase "truer picture"[91] of income.

In each of *Canderel* and *Toronto College Park*, the taxpayers were landlords that had paid tenant inducement payments (TIPs) to tenants in order to induce them to enter into long-term lease contracts. The issue in these cases was not the deductibility of the TIPs, but the timing of deduction, that is, whether the TIPs should be deducted in full in the year of payment (current deduction) or deducted over the life of the leases to which they related (the so-called "amortization" method). Generally accepted accounting principles (GAAP)[92] allow TIPs to be recognized as either an operating expense, which is fully deductible in the year it was paid, or a capital expenditure amortized over the life of the relevant lease, depending on the circumstances. In both cases, the taxpayers' accountants had decided that the amortization method was the most appropriate financial statement method in the circumstances.[93] For tax purposes, the taxpayers claimed a full deduction in the year of payment which reduced the taxpayers' profit and resulted in a deferral of tax.The Minister reassessed the taxpayers, arguing that the TIPs should be amortized over the term of the lease in order for the deduct to be matched to the income from the lease contracts (the "matching" principle).

As to be explained in Chapters 8 and 9, the distinction between current expenses and capital expenses involves the issue of timing of deductions. The general principle is to determine whether an expense brings value to the business for the current year only, or to the current year as well as future years. If an expense has an "enduring benefit", it is a capital expense and should be amortized; if the value of an expense is totally used up in the current year, it is a current expense. The Supreme Court was unanimous in holding that the TIPs gave rise to significant immediate benefits to the general business of the taxpayer and that the matching principle was

---

[90]See, for example, *M.N.R. v. Publishers Guild of Canada Ltd.*, [1957] C.T.C. 1, 57 D.T.C. 1017 (Ex. Ct.) at 1026, "If the law does not prohibit the use of a particular system of accounting then the opinion of accountancy experts that it is an accepted system and is appropriate to the taxpayer's business and *most nearly accurately reflects his income position* should prevail with the Court if the reasons for the opinion commend themselves to it (italics added)".

[91]See *West Kootenay Power & Light Co. v. R.*, [1992] 1 C.T.C. 15, 92 D.T.C. 6023 (Fed. C.A.), cited with approval in *Canderel*, note 53, above, para. 43.

[92]The *Canada Business Corporations Act* and most provincial corporations and securities legislation require companies to prepare financial statements for their shareholders in accordance with generally accepted accounting principles as defined in the *CICA Handbook*.

[93]Amortization is the preferred GAAP method for tenant inducement payments.

not a rule of law.[94] Because there was no accurate way of apportioning the benefits, the Court allowed the taxpayers to deduct the TIPs in the year of payment because this resulted in an "accurate picture of profit." According to the Court, the Minister had not proved that the amortization method was more accurate.[95] The Court stated:[96]

> As I have already noted, I do not see how, under these circumstances, it is possible with any accuracy to amortize the payments over the term of the lease, in the absence of an established formula acceptable for tax purposes, which was not advanced by the Minister. It follows, then, that the TIPs were not referable to any particular items of income, i.e., they cannot be correlated directly, or at least not principally, with the rents generated by the leases which they induced. They therefore qualify as running expenses to which the matching principle does not apply: see *Oxford Shopping Centres. . .*

The notion of "running expenses"[97] will be further explained in Chapter 8.

In *Ikea*, the taxpayer was a tenant that received TIPs. The issue was whether the TIPs were received on account of income (thus taxable) as opposed to on account of capital (tax-free), and if the receipt was on account of income, whether the TIPs had to be included in income in the year of receipt.[98] The taxpayer had treated the amount as a non-taxable capital receipt for income tax purposes. On its financial statements, however, it had capitalized the amount used to make leasehold improvements and deferred and amortized the excess into income over the term of the lease. The Supreme Court held that the TIPs had to be included in Ikea's income in the year of the receipt.[99] Therefore, in effect, the TIPs are treated symmetrically for both the payer and the recipient: current inclusion in computing profit by the recipient, and current deduction by the payer.

---

[94]*Canderel*, note 53, above at para. 47.

[95]*Ibid.*, para. 64, and *Toronto College Park*, note 88, above, para.19. Presumably, if the taxpayers had wanted to amortize the payments over the term of the lease, they would have been able to do that as well since this method was just as accurate. However, if this had been the situation, the case would have never come to court.

[96]*Canderel*, note 53, above, para. 65, citing *Oxford Shopping Centres v. R.*, [1980] C.T.C. 7, 79 D.T.C. 5458 (Fed. T.D.).

[97]The term "running expense" is an invention of Anglo-Canadian income tax law and refers to an expense which is not "related to any particular item of revenue" but instead relates to "the running of the business as a whole." See discussion under heading 8.7(c), "Running expense", below.

[98]Had the payment been received after May 23, 1985, s. 12(1)(x) would have included it in income in the year received and there would have been no reason for this issue to have come to court.

[99]The Court considered TIPs to have the "quality of income" based on the case law (e.g. *Robertson v. M.N.R.*, [1944] C.T.C. 75, 2 D.T.C. 655 (Ex. Ct.)) and were not allowed to be amortized into income over the term of the lease. Whether an amount has the quality of income will be discussed in more detail under heading 7.3(a), "Timing-realization principle", below.

(ii) — Measurement of "accurate picture"

What is an "accurate picture" of profit? In *Canderel*, the Supreme Court of Canada stated that:[100]

> In the simplest cases, it will not even be necessary to resort formally to the various well-accepted business principles, as the simple formula by which revenues are set against expenditures incurred in earning them is always the basic determinant.

The Court did not define what it meant by an "accurate picture" of profit and it certainly did not apply the principle in any meaningful way.

All taxpayers must keep accurate records of transactions but how is an "accurate picture of profit" measured? With respect to the deduction of expenses, it is the CRA's view that "any method used should at least be capable of demonstrating why the expense in question is referable to revenues in that year rather than another year".[101] This seems reasonable and is good advice for taxpayers. However, the CRA's view may face two problems in practice. The first problem is that it requires "matching" and the matching principle has been held not to constitute a legal principle and need not be applied in all cases. A second problem is the "onus of proof" requirement under which a taxpayer's computation of profit is "presumed" to be accurate until the CRA proves that another method is more precise, based on the facts.

(iii) — Onus of proof

Normally the onus of proof is on the taxpayer in all tax matters other than penalties.[102] In *Canderel*, however, the Supreme Court made it clear that the onus is on the CRA to prove that the taxpayer's method of computing profit is not the most accurate or "truer picture". This means that the taxpayer's picture of profit is presumed to be "accurate" unless the CRA can prove otherwise. This was a new principle, established for the first time in *Canderel*. It is necessary to have the onus of proof on the CRA to allow taxpayers the freedom of choice to select accounting methods when both the Act and the case law are silent on the meaning of profit.

(c) — Freedom of choice of accounting methods within constraints

The framework established the principle that, within certain constraints, taxpayers have the freedom of choice in selecting accounting methods in computing profit.[103]

---

[100] See *Canderel*, note 53, above, para. 50.

[101] See CRA, "Deduction of Tenant Inducement Payments — July 21, 1999," *Canadian Window on Tax Document number 9913367*.

[102] See heading 18.4(c), "Burden of proof", below.

[103] This principle is helpful. In the past, the courts may have had difficulty resolving cases involving the determination of profit because, although the determination of profit is a question of law, the determination is essentially an accounting question based on the facts, the expert accounting evidence and the relevant legal and accounting principles. The courts did not hesitate to develop accounting policies for tax purposes in early cases (as in the case of

Explicitly providing taxpayers with the freedom of choice and putting the onus of proof on the CRA makes it easier for the courts and taxpayers. Treating well-accepted business principles as interpretative aids also restricts the impact that accounting principles may have on income tax law and avoids delegating the decision-making to the accounting profession (which may not want it).[104]

The "freedom of choice" is subject to constraints from three sources: (1) the provisions of the Act which are discussed in chapters 7 to 9, below; (2) case law principles and rules of law which dictate a particular result for a given transaction or "establish a clear set of criteria for determining whether an accounting method is acceptable for tax purposes";[105] and (3) well-accepted business principles. Consequently, the tax treatment of most items is straightforward. There are currently very few items of revenue or expense that are subject to any controversy. Only in the case of controversy is the "freedom of choice" principle relevant.

(d) — Financial accounting principles as interpretive aids

The framework in *Canderel* states that well-accepted business principles, (including GAAP), are not rules of law, but merely interpretative aids. Therefore, although the determination of profit is a question of law, GAAP is relevant to the determination of profit where the Act is silent or where statutory provisions require interpretation. More specifically, GAAP is very important as an interpretative aid with respect to the timing of recognition of revenue or a deduction or the method of profit computation.

---

the judicial invention of "running expenses"). However, in more recent years, the courts have been more hesitant to select accounting methods other than generally accepted accounting principles (GAAP) when the Act and the case law are silent. Examples of more recent cases are *West Kootenay*, note 91, above, and *R. v. Metropolitan Properties Co.*, [1985] 1 C.T.C. 169, 85 D.T.C. 5128 (Fed. T.D.).

[104]In the past, when the Act was being revised in the 1950's, the CICA was not supportive of the suggestion to explicitly require profit computation to be referenced to GAAP. According to a more recent informal discussion with a CICA staff member, many of the complaints that the CICA received about standards in the 1990's were related to the fact that the taxable capital calculation that the large corporations tax under Part I.3 of the Act was based on was explicitly based on GAAP balance sheet numbers for investments, liabilities and shareholder's equity. As discussed under heading 15.5(b)(iv), "Large corporations tax," below, although this tax was repealed for year ends commencing after December 31, 2007, the taxable capital computation is still relevant for determining whether the maximum limits for the small business deduction ($500,000) and the 35% scientific research and experimental development investment tax credit ($3 million) are available for an associated group of corporations.

[105]Walker, "Timing and Recognition of Income" [2000] *Can. Tax Foundation Conf. Rep* 29:1 to 54, 29:11. 29:16-17.

6.5 — Methods of accounting

As mentioned above, profit is computed in accordance with GAAP or well-accepted business principles. The rest of this chapter discusses the accounting methods that determine the time when receipts and expenditures are "recognized" (included in the income statement[106]) in computing profit. These methods will be revisited in subsequent chapters.

(a) — Cash method

The "cash method" of accounting is one way of determining which items of income and expense should be "recognized" (included in the income statement) for a particular year. Under the cash method, all items of income actually received in the accounting period are recognized for that period, and all expenses actually paid in the accounting period are recognized for that period. The income statement does not take account of amounts receivable or amounts payable.

The cash method of accounting has the advantage of simplicity, but has little else going for it. As a result, it is rarely used for business income and only farmers and fishermen[107] are allowed to use it for tax purposes.

The cash method will often fail to provide a realistic statement of the result of business operations for a particular period. For example, if revenue earned over two years was received in a lump sum in the second year, the cash method would make the first year (without the income) look unjustifiably bad, and the second year (with the income) look unjustifiably good. If a two-year supply of inventory was acquired in a single purchase, the cash method would make the first year (with its large inventory expense) look unjustifiably bad and the second year (with no inventory expense) look unjustifiably good. Under the cash method, even the cost of a capital asset, such as a building, machinery or vehicle, which would be useful to the business for many years, would be recognized as an expense in the year in which it was paid for. It should be noted that this method of accounting for capital assets has never been permitted for tax purposes, even for cash-method taxpayers, because of the Act's prohibition on the deduction of "capital" outlays.[108]

Generally speaking, income from property can be computed by either the cash method or the accrual method, provided that (1) either method would produce an appropriate statement of income, and (2) the method chosen is used consistently.[109]

---

[106]See the Appendix at the end of this book.

[107]S. 28 expressly permits income from a "farming or fishing business" to be computed by the cash method. The Act specifically requires amounts to be included in income when they become receivable in the case of the sale of goods and services which are sold in the course of a business other than farming or fishing (ss. 12(1)(b) and 28).

[108]S. 18(1)(b).

[109]Arnold, note 59, above, 84. This is not the position taken by the CRA in Interpretation Bulletin IT-261R, "Prepayment of rents" (1980), para. 5, which is as follows: "As a general

In the case of interest income, while the cash method is acceptable, the Act contains special rules that preclude the use of the cash method to postpone recognition of the income.[110] In the case of royalties and dividends from corporate shares, the Act requires the use of the cash method.[111] The Act contains no specific provisions for other kinds of property income, such as rents.

Capital gains, which can be reported in a business' financial statements, are taxed under a special code of rules in subdivision c.[112] It is not appropriate to describe those rules as either the cash method or the accrual method, but they are closer to the cash method, because they generally tax only realized gains.

(b) — Accrual method

For most businesses, the "accrual method" of accounting is the only one which is acceptable under general accounting principles. Under the accrual method, all items of revenue are recognized as income at the time when they are earned (even if they have not been received), and all expenditures are recognized as charges against income at the time when they are incurred (even if they have not been paid).[113] The general idea is that revenues should be matched to the period to which they relate and expenses should also be so matched. This is often described as the "matching" principle for financial accounting purposes.[114] Recognizing an item of revenue before it has been received or recognizing an expense before it has been paid, is known as making an "accrual", which leads to the description of the accrual method of accounting. The opposite process to accrual, namely, deferral, is, as we shall see, an equally important part of the so-called accrual method of accounting.

Revenue[115] is normally treated as "earned" for financial accounting purposes in the period in which the recipient substantially completes performance of everything he or she is required to do as long as the amount due is ascertainable and there is no

---

rule taxpayers must use the accrual method of accounting to calculate income from a business or property, unless the *Income Tax Act* provides otherwise in respect of specific items of income or expense."

[110]Ss. 12(3) and (4). See heading 7.8, "Interest", below.

[111]Ss. 12(1)(g) and (j), respectively.

[112]Ch. 10, Capital Gains, below.

[113]The following more technical definition of accrual accounting was provided by the U.S. Financial Accounting Standards Board in *Objectives of Financial Reporting by Business Enterprises, Statement of Financial Accounting Concepts No. 1* (Stamford: FASB, 1978) para. 44: "Accrual accounting attempts to record the financial effects on an enterprise of transactions and other events and circumstances that have cash consequences for an enterprise in the periods in which those transactions, events, and circumstances occur rather than only in the periods in which cash is received or paid by the enterprise".

[114]Similarly, profit for tax purposes is calculated by deducting from revenue the expenses incurred to earn that revenue, but treating the "matching principle" as a rule of law was rejected in *Canderel*, note 53, above, and *Toronto College Park*, note 88, above.

[115]See CICA Handbook, Part I, IAS 18, Revenue.

uncertainty about its collection. Thus a lawyer or other supplier of services will normally recognize a fee as revenue when he or she completes a client's work and is ready to render a bill. A seller of goods will normally recognize a sale as revenue when the goods are delivered. Of course, much of the lawyer's work may have been done in a year prior to the year of completion; and the seller of goods may have acquired and packaged the goods in a year prior to that of delivery. But revenue is not usually recognized prior to the point of completion, because until completion it is not clear how much (if any) revenue will be received.

An expense[116] is "incurred" when a cost is used up in the business to earn revenue. All of the costs which relate to the current period must be recognized in that period even if they have not yet been paid, and even if there is no immediate liability to pay them. For example, a telephone bill may not be received until several weeks after the calls have been made. Under the accrual system of accounting, the bill must be recognized as an expense of the period when the calls were made. This is also normally the case for tax purposes, unless the Act provides otherwise.[117]

Accrual is the process that occurs when no cash has moved, and yet an item of revenue or expense is recognized because it properly belongs in the current period. The reverse situation is when cash has moved but the amount received or paid is not recognized as revenue or expense of the current period. This is referred to as "deferral". Note that the term deferral in this context does not mean that receipt of the income or payment of the expense has been deferred or postponed. On the contrary, the income has been received or the expense has been paid, and it is only its recognition in the income statement of the business that has been deferred. If a business received a fee or price in the year before it had substantially completed performance of its side of the agreement, it would normally defer the item of income until it had substantially completed performance. The fee or price would increase the assets of the business by increasing cash. But it would not appear in the income statement for the year of receipt. Instead, it would be carried on the balance sheet as a liability. It is a liability in the loose accounting sense that if the recipient did not complete performance he or she would have to repay it. Then in the year of completion the receipt will be recognized as a revenue item in the income statement of that year, and the liability will disappear from the balance sheet. This is normally the case for tax purposes as well.[118]

(c) — Accounting for capital assets

We have already noticed that an expense is incurred when a cost is used up in the business to earn revenue. For example, the rent of the business premises and the

---

[116]See CICA Handbook, Part I, IAS Framework for the Preparation and Presentation of Financial Statements.

[117]E.g., s. 20(1)(aa) allows a deduction for landscaping expenses only if they have been paid in the year.

[118]For tax purposes, the deferral of an income receipt is regulated by ss. 12(1)(a) and 20(1)(m), discussed under heading 8.7(e)(iv), "Unearned amounts reserve", below.

salaries of employees may be regularly paid at the end of each month. These will be wholly recognized as expenses of the period to which they relate. They are costs that expire at the end of the period to which they relate. No question of deferral arises. But some costs have a continuing value to the business, meaning that they will benefit not only the current accounting period but future periods as well. For example, the purchase cost of buildings, machinery, vehicles and other things is not used up in the current accounting period, but will continue to benefit the business for as long as the things purchased continue to be useful. Such costs are not recognized as expenses of the current period. Instead of appearing in the income statement as expenses, they will appear in the balance sheet as assets. The process of holding back an expense from the current period, with the consequent creation of an asset, is another example of deferral; and an asset might equally be called a "deferred expense" or a "prepaid expense".

An asset other than land does not last forever, and the matching principle requires that the cost of the asset must be charged against income for the period in which the asset benefits the business. Land is deemed to be a permanent asset that never wears out. The accrual method of accounting requires that part of the cost of each capital asset except land should be treated as used up in each accounting period for which it is useful. The part of the cost which is deemed to be used up in an accounting period is usually called "depreciation" (or "amortization") and it is treated as an expense which is incurred in the period. The rate of depreciation should be calculated so that at the end of the asset's useful life its cost has been wholly amortized by the depreciation charges in the income statements for the period. For accounting purposes it is accurate to regard assets as simply prepaid expenses which eventually will be used up and disappear.

Depreciation (or amortization) is, as we have seen, the systematic allocation of costs which benefit more than one accounting period. The depreciation charge which is debited as an expense to the profit and loss account each year is simply a book entry; it requires no outlay of cash. The Act calls depreciation charges "capital cost allowances" and calls capital assets "depreciable property". Capital cost allowances are deductible for tax purposes against income from business or property. The deduction is explained in chapter 9, below.

(d) — Accounting for inventory

The cost of inventory is one of the most significant items of deduction in computing profit. Accounting for inventory is discussed in chapter 8, below.[119]

---

[119]Heading 8.8, "Inventory", below.

7
INCOME FROM BUSINESS OR PROPERTY: INCLUSIONS

7.1 — Inclusion rules

Sections 12 to 17 of the *Income Tax Act* (the "Act") contain the "inclusion" rules, which require certain amounts to be included in computing the income of a taxpayer for a taxation year as income from a business or property. Section 12 deals with revenue arising from common types of transactions (such as the sale of property, the rendering of a service and the receipt of interest, dividends, rent or royalties from an investment) as well as revenues arising from payments connected with the process of earning income from business or property (such as home insulation or energy conversion grants and tenant inducements). Sections 13 and 14, which are part of the scheme that keeps track of the annual write-offs taken for depreciable property and eligible capital property, require the taxpayer to "recapture" excessive depreciation where a depreciable property did not actually depreciate as much as estimated by the Act.[1] Sections 15 to 17 are anti-avoidance rules designed to tax shareholders and debt-holders on amounts and benefits that are similar to "dividends" or "interest". Section 15 includes in income the value of various benefits received by virtue of a shareholding, including shareholder loans received by individuals. Section 16 includes in income any "disguised" or "imputed" interest in blended payments, debt obligations issued at a discount or indexed debt obligations. Section 16.1 is an elective (optional) provision that is part of the legislative scheme designed to limit the tax advantages of leasing property.[2] Section 17 imputes interest to a Canadian corporation in respect of any amount owed to the corporation by a related foreign corporation (typically a parent or sister corporation) in certain circumstances.

This chapter discusses in detail the basic inclusion rules under section 12 and refers to other provisions to the extent that they help advance a basic understanding of these rules.

7.2 — Characterization

(a) — Income vs. capital receipt

Subsection 9(1) provides that a taxpayer's income[3] from a business is the profit therefrom. In computing profit, only amounts received on account of income are

---

[1]See headings 9.4, "Capital cost allowance" (CCA) and 9.5, "Eligible capital expenditures", below.

[2]Para. 20(1)(a) of the Act and subsections 1100(1.1) to (1.3) of the Regulation. For a brief discussion see heading 9.4(i)(iii), "Leasing property", below.

[3]It is sometimes overlooked that income from a business is reported by the owner of the business; the owner may be an individual or a corporation. A business owned by a corporation may once have been owned by the individual who "incorporated" the business. When an individual incorporates a business, the individual transfers all of the assets of the business to the corporation in return for shares in the corporation. After this has taken place, the corporation is the owner of the business, and therefore will report the income from the business. The former owner will no longer have business income to report. The former owner will continue to benefit from the success of the business, but the benefit will not take the form of business income. If the corporation distributes its profits to the individual as a shareholder, it will do so by paying dividends on the shares; dividends are a type of income from property (the property being the shares). If the individual has lent money to the corporation, the corporation may pay interest on the loan; interest is a type of income from property (the property

included. An amount received on account of capital is not income although the capital receipt may give rise to a capital gain, half of which is subject to tax. The distinction between income and capital needs to be made in the case of sale of property, damages, or other unusual receipts.

Where a taxpayer makes a profit from the sale of property, it may be unclear whether the profit is income from a business or a capital gain. As discussed in chapter 11, the answer usually turns on whether the property was purchased as an investment, in which case the profit will be a capital gain, or whether the property was purchased for resale, in which case the profit will be income from a business. Moreover, when a property is sold and the price is based on the production or use of the property sold, part of the sale price may be treated as royalty income under paragraph 12(1)(g) as opposed to a capital receipt.

Damages received by a taxpayer may be on account of income or capital. According to the surrogatum principle, the characterization damages is determined by the character of the item for which the compensation is intended to substitute.[4] For example, compensation received for loss of profit from non-performance of business contracts is characterized as a receipt of income. Compensation for loss of capital property, goodwill, or a source of business is generally on account of capital. The situation was the same for reimbursements under common law until paragraph 12(1)(x) was introduced in 1985. Paragraph 12(1)(x) requires that all reimbursements, inducements, grants and subsidies received in respect of the acquisition of an asset or the incurring of a deductible expense be included in income unless the amount has already reduced the cost of the property or the amount of the expense. Paragraph 12(1)(x) was introduced to clarify the tax treatment of tenant inducements which in some cases the courts had considered to be tax-free.[5]

(b) — Form and substance of transactions

The character of a transaction is important in terms of determining the source (as either a "business" or "property") as well as determining the timing of inclusion. As discussed below, the timing rule is different for income from a business and income from property. Furthermore, the timing rule is different for different types

---

being the loan, which is a chose in action). If the individual is a director of the corporation, the corporation may pay a director's fee; a director's fee is income from an office. If the individual is an employee of the corporation, the corporation may pay a salary or a bonus; a salary or bonus is income from employment. If the individual decides to sell his or her shares in the corporation, and does so at a profit, the profit will be a capital gain.

[4]See heading 4.7, "Damages and settlements", above.

[5]For a case which dealt with the uncertain situation that existed before the introduction of s. 12(1)(x) in 1985, see *Ikea Ltd. v. R.* (1998), [1998] 2 C.T.C. 61, 98 D.T.C. 6092 (S.C.C.), in which the tenant inducement payment received by the taxpayer lessee was characterized as an income receipt because it was received as either a reduction in rent or as reimbursement for assuming obligations under the lease, both of which were current expenses and on income account.

of business transactions (e.g., sale of property and services) and different types of income from property (e.g., dividends and interest).

The general principle of characterization for tax purposes is "form over substance". In the absence of a sham,[6] the legal form of the transaction adopted by the taxpayer is generally binding unless the Act provides otherwise. As noted at the beginning of this chapter, there are several anti-avoidance rules in sections 15 to 17 that adopt a "substance over form" approach. Under this approach, the legal form of the transaction is replaced by its economic or legal substance for the purpose of determining the tax treatment of the transaction. Another example of "substance over form" approach is the wording of paragraph 12(1)(g), which includes as income from property almost any amount based on the use of or production from property.[7]

7.3 — Timing

(a) — The realization principle

Profit is computed annually for income tax purposes. Thus, once a receipt is characterized as an income receipt, the next question is in which year the receipt should be included in income. This is a question of timing, which is generally governed by the realization principle.

According to the realization principle, an amount is not realized until it obtains the "quality of income".[8] The courts have enunciated the following test as to whether an amount received by a taxpayer has this quality: "Is his right to it absolute and under no restrictions, contractual or otherwise, as to its disposition, use or enjoyment?"[9] "[A]n amount may have the quality of income even though it is not actually received by the taxpayer, but only 'realized' in accordance with the accrual method of accounting."[10] The ultimate effect of the realization principle is that "amounts received or realized by a taxpayer, free of conditions or restrictions upon their use, are taxable in the year received, subject to any contrary provision of the Act or other rule of law".[11]

---

[6] The sham doctrine is discussed further in chapter 20.

[7] See heading 7.7, "Rent and royalties", below.

[8] *Ikea*, note 5, above, para. 37, citing *Robertson v. M.N.R.*, [1944] C.T.C. 75, 2 D.T.C. 655 (Ex. Ct.).

[9] *Robertson, ibid.*, 91, 661. Section 28 provides an exception for income from a farming and fishing business: such income can be reported using the "cash method" if the taxpayer so elects. The discussion in this chapter ignores this exception.

[10] *Ikea*, note 5, above, para. 37.

[11] *Ibid.*

(b) — Accrual method of accounting

(i) — Paragraph 12(1)(b)

Amounts receivable are generally included in computing income under the accrual method of accounting.[12] It does not matter that payment of the amount or some part of the amount might not be due until some future date.[13] This method is generally accepted for the purpose of computing profit under subsection 9(1).

In addition, paragraph 12(1)(b) includes in income:

> any amount receivable by the taxpayer in respect of property sold or services rendered in the course of a business in the year, notwithstanding that the amount or any part thereof is not due until a subsequent year, unless the method adopted by the taxpayer for computing income from the business and accepted for the purpose of this Part does not require the taxpayer to include any amount receivable in computing the taxpayer's income for a taxation year unless it has been received in the year, and for the purposes of this paragraph, an amount shall be deemed to have become receivable in respect of services rendered in the course of a business on the day that is the earlier of
>
> (i) the day on which the account in respect of the services was rendered, and
>
> (ii) the day on which the account in respect of those services would have been rendered had there been no undue delay in rendering the account in respect of the service;

This provision contains two important rules. First, it codifies the accrual method of accounting in respect of property sold or services rendered, the only exception being taxpayers permitted to utilize the cash method of accounting for tax purposes. Second, it contains a deeming rule in respect of services rendered: an amount for services rendered is deemed to become receivable on the earlier of the day on which the account was rendered (date of billing) and the day on which it would have been rendered had there been no undue delay (the "no undue delay" date).

Paragraph 12(1)(b) is not conclusive on the issue of the timing of recognition of income. Indeed, subsection 12(2) clearly states that paragraph 12(1)(b) is enacted "for greater certainty" and should not be interpreted to imply that any amount not referred to, such as amounts received or earned in the year, are not to be included in income from business. Therefore, an amount for services rendered but not yet billed, although not receivable under the deeming rules in paragraph 12(1)(b), may

---

[12] See heading 6.5(b), "Accrual method", above.

[13] Where the property sold is real property or all or part of the proceeds is outstanding at least two years, s. 20(1)(n) provides for an offsetting reserve deduction equal to a reasonable portion of the taxpayer's profit. This deduction recognizes the fact that the taxpayers need cash to pay tax and is available for a maximum of three years (s. 20(8)). See heading 8.7(e)(iii), "Deferred payments reserve", below.

still be considered "receivable" under the general meaning of the term "receivable" for purposes of subsection 9(1).[14]

(ii) — "Receivable"

There is no statutory definition of "receivable" in the Act. The long-accepted definition of the term derives from *M.N.R. v. J. Colford Contracting Co.* (1960),[15] in which Kearney J. stated:[16]

> In the absence of a statutory definition to the contrary, I think it is not enough that the so-called recipient has a precarious right to receive an amount in question, but he must have a clearly legal, though not necessarily immediate, right to receive it.

The time when a taxpayer obtains the legal right to receive an amount is determined by private law. In general, it is the time when the taxpayer has completed the performance of the services contracted for or when the taxpayer has delivered the property sold. In other words, an amount is receivable when all events have occurred that fix the right to receive it and the amount can be determined with reasonable accuracy.

The issue in *Colford* was the recognition of "holdbacks" for income tax purposes. In this case, the taxpayer was engaged in a construction business where the usual industry practice is for the client to make interim payments to the contractor from time to time based on formal progress reports. These progress payments are normally subject to a percentage "holdback" in order to ensure the satisfactory completion of the job. The holdbacks are normally not paid to the contractor until the client receives professional assurance that the work is acceptable. The Court in *Colford* held that holdbacks were not receivable because at private law the contractor had no legal right to the holdback until the certificates in question were issued by the architect or engineer.

Compensation for expropriated property, an arbitration award, or a court award is determined receivable by the coexistence of two conditions: a right to receive compensation and a binding agreement between the parties or a judgment fixing the amount. For example, in *M.N.R. v. Benaby Realties Ltd.* (1967),[17] the Court held that compensation for expropriated property became receivable when the amount was fixed by arbitration or agreement, notwithstanding that the right to receive

---

[14]This issue was examined in *Maritime Telegraph and Telephone*, note 33, below. Note, however, the section 34 exception for certain professionals, discussed under heading 7.5(c), "Professional services", below.

[15][1960] Ex. C.R. 433, [1960] C.T.C. 178, 60 D.T.C. 1131 (Ex. Ct.); affirmed [1962] C.T.C. 546, 62 D.T.C. 1338 (S.C.C.).

[16]*Ibid.*, at 441, 187, 1135. This test was adopted without question in *Maple Leaf Mills Ltd. v. M.N.R.*, [1977] 1 S.C.R. 558, [1976] C.T.C. 324, 76 D.T.C. 6182 (S.C.C.).

[17][1967] C.T.C. 418, 67 D.T.C. 5275 (S.C.C.).

compensation was acquired earlier, at the moment of expropriation.[18] The court held in other cases[19] that the possibility of a successful appeal did not derogate from the "quality of income" of the payments in issue at the time they were received. When paid to the taxpayer, the amounts were not subject to any specific or unfulfilled conditions, and the necessity of returning the moneys, in whole or in part, if the appeal was successful, was viewed as a condition subsequent which did not affect the unrestricted right of the taxpayer to use the funds when received.

(iii) — Advance payments for unearned items

Subparagraph 12(1)(a) requires an inclusion in income of any amount received in the year in the course of a business "that is on account of services not rendered or goods not delivered before the end of the year or that, for any other reason, may be regarded as not having been earned in the year or a previous year". Typical amounts contemplated by paragraph 12(1)(a)(i) include prepayments for work to be done under contract not yet begun or goods not yet delivered, and amounts received from the sales of transportation tickets, seasonal tickets, payments for the warranty of merchandise and container deposits.

Standing alone, paragraph 12(1)(a) represents a departure from the common law principle of realization. In general, an amount that has actually been received has the quality of income at the time of receipt, if the recipient has done what is required to earn it and thus has an immediate and unrestricted right to dispose of it.[20] By contrast, an amount received as a deposit against the fulfillment of a future obligation does not have the quality of income until the obligation is fulfilled.[21] However, subsection 20(1) allows a deduction for a reasonable reserve of unearned amounts that are included in income under paragraph 12(1)(a).[22] When the reserve deduction is combined with paragraph 12(1)(a), the net result is effectively the same as under the realization principle: unearned income is not included in comput-

---

[18]This decision was followed in *Vaughan Construction Co. Ltd. v. M.N.R.*, [1970] C.T.C. 350, 70 D.T.C. 6268 (S.C.C.).

[19]*The Cementation Co. (Canada) Ltd. v. M.N.R.*, [1977] C.T.C. 2360, 77 D.T.C. 249 (T.R.B.); *Commonwealth Construction Co. Ltd. v. R.*, [1982] C.T.C. 167, 82 D.T.C. 6152 (Fed. T.D.); and *R. v. Foothills Pipe Lines (Yukon) Ltd.*, [1990] 2 C.T.C. 448, 90 D.T.C. 6607 (Fed. C.A.) (application for leave to appeal to the Supreme Court dismissed).

[20]*Robertson*, note 8, above; *Ikea*, note 5, above.

[21]This is explained by Thorson J. in *Robertson, ibid.*, 92, 661: "Where an amount is paid as a deposit by way of security for the performance of a contract and held as such, it cannot be regarded as profit or gain to the holder until circumstances under which it may be retained by him to his own use have arisen and, until such time, it is not taxable income in his hands, for it lacks the essential quality of income, namely, that the recipient should have an absolute right to it and be under no restriction, contractual or otherwise, as to its disposition, use or enjoyment".

[22]Ss. 20(1)(m) and (m.2), which are discussed further under heading 8.7(e)(iv), "Unearned amounts reserve", below.

ing income until realized. This is consistent with the accounting treatment of prepaid income which is also based on the realization principle.

(c) — Cash method of accounting

Section 12 generally allows the use of cash method of accounting for amounts received outside paragraph 12(1)(b). These amounts are generally characterized as "income from property", which represent a passive return on investment as opposed to a reward for time, labour or attention expended in producing the return. Typical types of income from property include dividends, interest, rents, and royalties. If, however, sufficient time and effort are expended in the earning of these receipts, they may be characterized otherwise as income from a business.

7.4 — Sale of property

Where a property is sold in the course of a business, the amount receivable by the taxpayer must be recognized as income under paragraph 12(1)(b). The property sold in the course of a business is referred to as "inventory" in accounting. Paragraph 12(1)(b) does not apply to the sale of an investment property or capital property, which gives rise to capital gains or losses.[23] When does the sale price become receivable to the vendor? Is it the time when: (a) a purchase and sale contract is concluded; (b) title to the property passes to the purchaser; (c) the property is delivered; (d) the purchaser is billed; or (e) payment is received by the vendor?[24]

In a sale of goods, delivery of the property and passing of legal title to the property often occur simultaneously. In such a case, the sale price becomes receivable at the time of delivery.[25] For example, when you buy a book in a bookstore, all of the above mentioned events take place simultaneously. The timing of the recognition of the sale to the store is easily determined. However, if the book is to be delivered in a week, when does the sale price become receivable? According to the administrative policy of the CRA, the sale price becomes receivable on the date of exchange stipulated by the parties in the contract.[26] Where the date of exchange is not expressly stipulated, the time when attributes of ownership (primarily possession, use and risk) pass to the purchaser is presumed to be the date when the sale price is receivable.[27] Where property is sold or delivered, the rendering of an account (or

---

[23]See chapter 11, "Investing and trading", below.

[24]For an excellent discussion of the timing of recognition of the sale price, see Arnold, *Timing and Income Taxation* (Canadian Tax Paper No.71) (1983), 133–50.

[25]*Ibid.*, 136.

[26]CRA Interpretation Bulletin IT-170R, "Sale of Property — When Included in Income Computation" (1980), para. 7.

[27]IT-170R, *ibid.*, states in para. 8: "Factors that are strong indicators of the passing of ownership include: (a) physical or constructive possession, (b) entitlement to income from the property, (c) assumption of responsibility for insurance coverage, and (d) commencement of liability for interest on purchaser's debt that forms a part of the sale price".

invoice) is not a precondition to the right to payment.[28] Payments received before the delivery of the goods are included in income under paragraph 12(1)(a).

In the case of the sale of real property, many agreements provide a "closing date" for the completion of the sale. This is normally the date that beneficial ownership is intended to pass from the vendor to the purchaser and the time that the vendor is entitled to the sale price. Advance payments received by the vendor are not required to be included by paragraph 12(1)(a) which is applicable only to sale of goods (not real estate).

7.5 — Services

(a) — General timing rule

Payments for services generally become receivable when the performance of the services is completed. At such time, the taxpayer acquires the absolute and unconditional, although not necessarily immediate, legal right to demand payment, and the amount is reasonably ascertainable. Where under the terms of a contract, a taxpayer is to be paid for services rendered on an hourly or daily basis, the value of services rendered in a taxation year should be included in the taxpayer's income for that year.[29]

In *Maritime Telegraph and Telephone Company v. R.* (1992),[30] for example, revenues for unbilled telephone services rendered in the last month of the year were held to constitute receivables in law, and therefore income in the year. The Court found that the taxpayer's records indicated the exact times at which its services were rendered, making the amounts readily quantifiable at year-end. Therefore the timing of the recognition of the unbilled revenue is the same for supply of electricity (which is characterized as a sale of goods and was the issue in *West Kootenay Power and Light Company Ltd.* (1991))[31] as it is for the supply of telecommunications services in a business.

(b) — Modified accrual method

The timing of recognition of payments for services is also governed by paragraph 12(1)(b), which deems amounts for services rendered to become receivable on the earlier of the actual billing date or the "no undue delay" date.[32] Interpreted literally, paragraph 12(1)(b) applies to all types of services as it does not qualify the word

---

[28]*West Kootenay Power and Light Company Ltd. v. R.* (1991), [1992] 1 C.T.C. 15 25, 92 D.T.C. 6023 6030 (Fed. C.A.).

[29]This is the case even if the performance of services under the contract will not be completed until a subsequent year: Arnold, note 24, above, 175.

[30]Note 33, below

[31]Note 28, above.

[32]The definition of the "no undue delay" date is discussed under heading 7.3(b)(i), "Paragraph 12(1)(b)", above.

"services" by any adjective such as continuous or discrete, project by project, etc. However, the effect of the *Maritime Telegraph and Telephone Company* decision is that paragraph 12(1)(b) is "particularly applicable to businesses who deal in ... the sale of services when those services are performed at a discrete time or times".[33] This narrow interpretation makes sense as it treats taxpayers supplying telecommunication services and taxpayers supplying electricity services in the same way. However, one wonders why Parliament has not modified the words in the legislation or whether that was intended.

(c) — Professional services

Accountants, dentists, lawyers, doctors and chiropractors carrying on a professional practice (hereinafter referred to as the "listed professional practices") have an important tax advantage over taxpayers with respect to services that have not been billed because the work is incomplete. As discussed above, revenue from services provided by a professional are included in income under the general accrual method or the modified accrual method under paragraph 12(1)(b). However, an election is available under section 34 which allows the listed professional practices to exclude from business income any amount in respect of work in progress at the end of the year.[34]

Determining the "amount in respect of work in progress" is generally straightforward. Taxpayers keep track of their work in progress in their internal accounting system. For example, a law firm keeps track of its work in progress by recording the hours worked on a client by partners and staff members recorded at their various billing rates in their timesheets (often daily) as well as disbursements in respect of the client. Because work in progress in respect of professional services is defined as inventory, it is generally valued under subsection 10(1) by using the lower of cost and fair market value.[35]

The tax advantage conferred by section 34 can be seen from this example. Each of a law firm and an architect firm has one associate who earns a monthly salary of $20,000. The associate spends her entire month (200 hours at $300 per hour) in December 2010 working on one client's file. Assume the fair market value of the work in progress is $60,000 and the firm does not bill the client for the associate's time. The law firm may elect under section 34 not to include the $60,000 in income, thereby generating a loss of $20,000. The architect firm cannot make a section 34 election, and is required to capitalize the $20,000 as the cost of the work in progress inventory (because $20,000 is lower than the $60,000 market value under

---

[33]Reed T.C.J. in *Maritime Telegraph and Telephone Co. v. R.* (1990), [1991] 1 C.T.C. 28 31–32, 91 D.T.C. 5038 5041 (Fed. T.D.); affirmed [1992] 1 C.T.C. 264, 92 D.T.C. 6191 (Fed. C.A.).

[34]Where the election is made, it must be used in all subsequent taxation years unless the election is revoked with the permission of the CRA (s. 34(b)).

[35]See *CDSL Canada Ltd. v. Canada*, 2008 FCA 400, discussed under heading 8.8(d), Valuation methods, below.

subsection 10(1)).[36] Therefore, the architect firm has no income or loss for tax purposes. For financial reporting purposes, however, both the law firm and architect firm report a profit of $40,000 (accrued revenue of $60,000 less the payroll cost of $20,000). Both taxpayers had the same economic activity in the month and both report a profit of $40,000 on their financial statements. But the lawyer reports a $20,000 loss for tax purposes and the architect reports zero.

As a result, the section 34 election provides a significant timing benefit to the listed profession practices as compared to those carrying on other professional practices or providing other types of services.

7.6 — Dividends

The term "dividend" generally refers to a *pro rata* distribution from a corporation to its shareholders, unless the distribution is made on the liquidation of the corporation or on an authorized reduction of corporate capital.[37] Subsection 248(1) defines "dividend" to specifically include a "stock dividend", which is a dividend paid in shares of the corporation rather than cash.

Paragraphs 12(1)(j) and (k) require dividends be included in the income of a shareholder on a cash basis. The Act contains detailed rules regarding the taxation of dividends, which take into account the residence of the corporation, the nature of the underlying corporate income, and whether the shareholder is an individual or corporation. The main policy concern is the minimization of double taxation of income earned through corporations. These rules are discussed in further detail in chapter 15, below.

7.7 — Rent and royalties

(a) — "Payments based on production or use"

Paragraph 12(1)(g) requires a taxpayer to include in computing income any amount received that is dependent on the use of or production from property. Although this provision does not use the term "rent" or "royalties", rents and royalties are typical types of payments that are based on the use of or production from property.

A "rent" is generally a fixed payment (usually periodic) for the use of property (typically tangible property) for a given period of time, after which the right to use

---

[36]As discussed under heading 8.8(d), Valuation methods, below, the taxpayer in both cases could also elect to use market value (under regulation 1801) which would result in the same $40,000 profit as was reported for accounting purposes but this would not minimize his or her taxes.

[37]See, for example, *Hill v. Permanent Trustee Co. of New South Wales*, [1930] A.C. 720 (New South Wales P.C.); and *Commissioners of Inland Revenue v. Burrell*, [1924] 2 K.B. 52 (Eng. C.A.). This broad definition has been accepted by the CRA and Canadian courts. See, for example, *Cangro Resources Ltd. (in Liquidation) v. Minister of National Revenue*, [1967] Tax A.B.C. 852 (Can. Tax App. Bd.).

the property expires (that is, the right reverts back to the owner).[38] The word "royalty" connotes a payment calculated by reference to the use of intangible property, or to the production or revenue or profits from the use of the rights granted.[39]

(b) — Sales distinguished

Royalties or rents need to be distinguished from sales. In the absence of statutory rules, a distinction is made on the basis of the facts in each case. In general, if all the legal rights of a property are transferred, the transaction constitutes a sale; if less than all the rights are transferred, the transaction is a lease or licence and the payments are rents or royalties. Because intangible property rights are difficult to value, they are often transferred for consideration that depends on their productivity. An element of contingency in a payment for the use of a property is therefore the essence of a royalty payment.[40] Consequently, a payment may be characterized as a royalty even when the form of the transaction is a "sale", as long as the payment is based on the use or productivity of the property. It is irrelevant whether the amount of consideration is fixed or paid in instalments.[41]

Paragraph 12(1)(g) includes in income "any amount received by the taxpayer in the year that was dependent on the use of or production from property whether or not that amount was an instalment of the sale price of the property". It thus specifically includes payments that may be expressed as instalments of the sale price of property, but are actually payments depending on the use of or production from that property.[42] For example, proceeds from sales of gravel, sand, shale and topsoil were treated as rents or royalties when the purchase price was payable in fixed

---

[38]See comments by the Federal Court of Appeal in *R. v. Saint John Shipbuilding & Dry Dock Co.*, [1980] C.T.C. 352, 80 D.T.C. 6272 (Fed. C.A.); leave to appeal refused (1980), 34 N.R. 348n (S.C.C.).

[39]*M.N.R. v. Wain-Town Gas and Oil Co. Ltd.*, [1952] C.T.C. 147 151, 52 D.T.C. 1138 1140, per Kerwin J. The Courts have held, in *Vauban Productions v. R.*, [1975] C.T.C. 511, 75 D.T.C. 5371 (Fed. T.D.); affirmed [1979] C.T.C. 262, 79 D.T.C. 5186 (Fed. C.A.) that: "the term 'royalties' normally refers to a share in the profits or a share or percentage of a profit based on use or on the number of units, copies or articles sold, rented or used. When referring to a right, the amount of the royalty is related in some way to the degree of use of that right. ... Royalties, which are akin to rental payments ... are either based on the degree of use of the right or on the duration of use to be made of it...".

[40]*Grand Toys Ltd. v. M.N.R.*, [1990] 1 C.T.C. 2165, 90 D.T.C. 1059 (T.C.C.).

[41]For example, in *Vauban Productions*, note 39, above.

[42]Justice Dube stated in *Lackie v. R.*, [1978] C.T.C. 157, 78 D.T.C. 6128 (Fed. T.D.), para. 23 [D.T.C.]; ; affirmed [1979] C.T.C. 389, 79 D.T.C. 5309 (Fed. C.A.): "[I]f what is sold relates to the use of land, including excavation for gravel, that is a profit à prendre, thus taxable income. . .Profit à prendre implies a continuing licence, or continuous right to use land; a single final transaction transferring all the property (i.e. gravel) would not be a profit à prendre."

instalments (e.g., a fixed amount per cubic yard of shale removed).[43] Similarly, proceeds in the following situations were treated as royalties: the sale of a copyrighted sales manual for a fixed price, where payments were based on a percentage of the products sold by the purchaser;[44] and the sale of a franchise to supply natural gas, in return for an amount based on gross receipts from all the sales of natural gas under the franchise.[45] On the other hand, payments for the cutting of timber on farmland have been held to fall outside the scope of paragraph 12(1)(g) if the sale of timber is a one time sale of all the timber on the property.[46] The sale of agricultural land is excluded from the wording of paragraph 12(1)(g).

7.8 — Interest

(a) — Definition

The Act contains no definition of "interest". Interest is not a technical term, however, and may be broadly defined as any sum that must be paid by a borrower (debtor) to the lender (creditor) as the price for the loan.[47] Interest is usually expressed as a percentage per annum of the principal amount of the loan, although under the loan contract interest is usually payable more frequently than annually and can occasionally be paid less frequently. The borrower's obligation to pay interest ceases when the loan is repaid (redeemed), which normally occurs at a time (the maturity date) stipulated by the loan contract.

Interest rates are fixed by market forces. Some factors that bear on interest rates are particular to each loan, namely, the creditworthiness of the borrower, the value of any security provided by the borrower, and the terms of the loan. Other factors are of a more general application, the most important one being the expected rate of inflation over the term of the loan.

Every lender of money will want to be compensated for the expected decline in the purchasing power of the principal sum. For example, if inflation is expected at the rate of three per cent per annum over the life of the loan, it will be impossible to borrow money at rates that do not provide a return of several percentage points over three per cent. To the extent that interest simply compensates for the decline in the purchasing power of the principal of the loan, it ought not to be taxed at all. Only the real rate of interest (the actual rate minus the rate of inflation in a particu-

---

[43] *Pallett v. M.N.R.* (1959), 59 D.T.C. 230 (T.A.B.); *Irwin v. M.N.R.* (1963), 63 D.T.C. 251 (T.A.B.); *Flewelling v. M.N.R.* (1963), 63 D.T.C. 489 (T.A.B.); *Mouat v. M.N.R.* (1963), 63 D.T.C. 548 (T.A.B.); and *Lamon v. M.N.R.*, [1963] C.T.C. 68, 63 D.T.C. 1039 (Ex. Ct.).

[44] *Gingras v. M.N.R.*, [1963] C.T.C. 194, 63 D.T.C. 1142 (Ex. Ct.).

[45] See *Wain-Town Gas & Oil Company Ltd.*, note 39, above.

[46] See *Wright v. R.* (2002), [2003] 1 C.T.C. 2726, 2003 D.T.C. 763 (T.C.C. [General Procedure]).

[47] Some courts have called for narrower and more technical definitions of interest. See, for example, *A.G. Ont. v. Barfried Enterprises*, [1963] S.C.R. 570 (S.C.C.), which (in a non-tax context) required "daily accrual" for an amount to qualify as interest.

lar year) should have to be reported by the lender. The Act is remiss in not making any allowance for inflation in computing interest income. The full amount of the nominal interest, including the portion that merely compensates for inflation, must be included in the lender's income for tax purposes.[48]

Interest is generally income from property.[49] The property is the borrower's obligation to repay the loan (the details of which are found in the loan contract), which is commonly called a debt obligation. A debt obligation is a "chose in action", because what the lender has is a right to enforce the obligation against the borrower by legal action. A debt obligation may be a personal loan, a promissory note, a bank account, a term deposit, a guaranteed investment certificate, a mortgage, a treasury bill, a bond, a debenture, or a note. The nomenclature varies according to the personality of the borrower (issuer of security), the nature of the security, the term of the loan, and other characteristics of the obligation.

(b) — Special timing rules

Paragraph 12(1)(c) generally gives taxpayers the choice of reporting interest income by the "cash" method or by the "receivable" method. The choice of the method is dependent on the method regularly followed by the taxpayer in computing the taxpayer's income. For example, a bank whose business is lending money must use the accrual method, whereas a law professor who has a bank deposit can use the cash method.

These methods of reporting under paragraph 12(1)(c) make it possible for taxpayers to postpone the recognition of interest income in certain circumstances.[50] For example, government and corporate bonds often have interest coupons attached which may be clipped and cashed as they fall due. Taxpayers reporting bond interest by the cash method used to be able to postpone recognition of the interest on a corporate bond by not cashing the coupons as they fell due. Of course, if the uncashed coupons earned no interest, there would be no advantage in this practice, but some bond issues have a compounding feature under which uncashed coupons do earn interest. As another example, Canada Savings Bonds are available on a compound basis, under which no interest is payable during the term of the bond, and on the maturity date all of the interest, compounded, is paid to the bondholder (along with the principal sum). Taxpayers reporting bond interest by either the cash or the re-

---

[48]This same issue arises with respect to the taxation of capital gains: see heading 10.2(d), "Inflationary gains", below.

[49]Interest on money invested short-term for use in a business is income from the business: *R. v. Marsh & McLennan*, [1983] C.T.C. 231, 83 D.T.C. 5180 (Fed. T.D.); leave to appeal refused (1983), 52 N.R. 231 (S.C.C.); *R. v. Ensite*, [1983] C.T.C. 296, 83 D.T.C. 5319 (Fed. T.D.); affirmed [1986] 2 C.T.C. 459, 86 D.T.C. 6521 (S.C.C.); and *R. v. Brown Boveri Howden*, [1983] C.T.C. 301, 83 D.T.C. 5319 (Fed. C.A.); leave to appeal refused (1983), 52 N.R. 231 (S.C.C.).

[50]For the benefit of tax deferral, see heading 1.6(e), "Tax deferral", above.

ceivable method used to be able to postpone recognition of the interest on a compound bond until the maturity of the bond.

Subsections 12(3) and (4) were enacted to prevent such postponement.[51] Although these provisions do not directly amend paragraph 12(1)(c), for most debt obligations[52] the effect of these two provisions is to make the choices offered by paragraph 12(1)(c) illusory. Subsection 12(3) applies to corporations and partnerships, and it requires all interest "that accrues . . . to the end of the year" be reported annually, whether the interest is received, receivable or merely accrued. For example, if a corporation with a December 31 year-end held a bond upon which interest was payable on October 31 of each year, the corporation would be obliged to report not only the interest received or receivable on October 31 (after subtracting the two-month portion that would have been recognized in the previous year), but also the interest accrued from November 1 to December 31. In effect, subsection 12(3) requires corporations and partnerships to report interest income by the accrual method.

Subsection 12(4) applies to individuals, and requires that all interest on an "investment contract" that has accrued to each "anniversary day of the contract" be reported annually. An investment contract is broadly defined under subsection 12(11) to cover the standard forms of debt obligations, although there are some exclusions. The anniversary day is defined also under subsection 12(11) as the annual anniversary of "the day immediately preceding the date of issue of the contract". For example, the holder of a Canada Savings Bond that was issued on November 1, year 1 would have no interest income to report in year 1. He or she would have to report in year 2 the 12 months of interest accrued to October 31, year 2, even if the bond was a compound bond on which no interest was received or receivable in year 2. The same obligation to report the 12 months of interest accrued to October 31 would arise in year 3 and each succeeding year that the bond is retained.

Subsection 12(4) does not completely eliminate the choice of reporting methods offered in paragraph 12(1)(c). The cash or receivable method could be used if they would unfailingly recognize each year all of the interest accrued to the anniversary day of the investment contract. Subsection 12(4) allows this, because it requires the inclusion of interest accrued to the anniversary day only "to the extent that the interest was not otherwise included in computing the taxpayer's income for the taxation year or any preceding taxation year". However, subsection 12(4) does not allow the cash or receivable methods to be used if their effect would be to postpone

---

[51]All three provisions are subject to s. 12(4.1) for taxation years ending after September 1997. A financial institution or taxpayer in the business of lending money does not have to include interest in income under ss. 12(1)(c), 12(3) or 12(4), if the collection of the principal or interest of the underlying loan is uncertain. Other taxpayers must include the interest for doubtful debts in income and then can deduct a reserve under s. 20(1)(l)(i).

[52]Some debt obligations are exempted from ss. 12(3) and 12(4), for them, s. 12(1)(c) continues to govern.

the recognition of interest income that had accrued to the anniversary day of the investment contract.

(c) — Imputed interest in blended payments

Subsection 16(1) of the Act deals with "blended payments", that is, payments that combine income (typically interest) and capital. Many residential mortgages, for example, require the borrower to make regular payments that are partly interest and partly the repayment of the principal sum; the amount of the principal sum is steadily reduced over the life of the loan. Another example of a blended payment is when a treasury bill or commercial paper, which are sold at a discount because they do not pay interest, are redeemed on maturity for their face amount.

The legal form of blended payments may be a "sale" or "repayment of capital", but the true economic character of the transaction is, in part, interest. In such circumstances, paragraph 16(1)(a)[53] provides that, "the part of the amount that can reasonably be regarded as interest shall, irrespective of when the contract or arrangement was made or the form or legal effect thereof, be deemed to be interest on a debt obligation held by the person to whom the amount is paid or payable". This provision requires the recipient of the blended payments (the mortgagee in the case of a mortgage) to unblend the payments for tax purposes, so that the income component can be reported as income. (The repayment of the principal sum has no tax consequences.)[54]

Subsection 16(1) catches a concealed income element in a loan-repayment or instalment-purchase arrangement. In *M.N.R. v. Groulx* (1967),[55] for example, the taxpayer sold a farm to a purchaser for $395,000, of which $85,000 was payable immediately and $310,000 was payable in instalments over a period of six years; no interest was payable by the purchaser on the outstanding balance of the purchase price. The Supreme Court of Canada held that the payment of $310,000, which was received in instalments by the vendor-taxpayer, could reasonably be regarded as being, in part, a payment of interest by the purchaser. What the Court found, in effect, was that the purchaser had agreed to pay a price above the market value of the farm, in return for the vendor's agreement to forego interest on the unpaid balance of the purchase price. The Court therefore upheld the Minister's assessment

---

[53]S. 16(1)(b) deals with payments that blend capital and income other than interest. For example, where a sale transaction is caught by s. 12(1)(g) to give rise to royalty income.

[54]Where s. 16(1) is applied to payments made by a debtor to a creditor, the deemed interest element is added to the income of the creditor. Since s. 16(1) deems the interest portion of blended payments to be interest on a debt obligation, s. 20(1)(c) allows the debtor to deduct the deemed interest payments where the money borrowed or property purchased was used to earn income from a business or property. As a result, in cases where the debtor has borrowed to earn income from a business or property, there may be no net tax revenue to the government because of s. 16(1) unless the creditor (who includes the amount in income) is taxed at a lower rate than the debtor (who deducts the amount in computing income).

[55][1967] C.T.C. 422, 67 D.T.C. 5284 (S.C.C.).

under subsection 16(1) and treated a portion of the instalments of the purchase price as interest which was taxable to the taxpayer-vendor.[56]

Where property is sold for a price that is payable in instalments, as in *Groulx*, and the instalments are "genuinely" interest-free, the instalments have been held not to attract subsection 16(1).[57] This position has been accepted by the CRA.[58] While this position is understandable if the parties are not dealing at arm's length, for example, where a parent sells property to a child, it is difficult to see why subsection 16(1) should not always be applicable where the parties are at arm's length. Surely, the purchaser in every case must have paid more for the property than he or she would have had to pay with customary terms of financing.

In many cases, the borrower of money or the purchaser of property uses the money borrowed or property purchased to earn business or property income. If so, then any interest payable to the creditor (lender or vendor) will be deductible by the debtor (borrower or purchaser) as an expense of earning the business or property income under paragraph 20(1)(c). If the debts were interest-free, the debtor would not have an interest-expense deduction. In many cases, the debtor has little incentive to agree to pay a higher capital sum in lieu of interest since, although a higher price for property purchased could provide a stepped-up cost base for the purpose of computing subsequent capital gains or losses, this normally would not be as valuable as a current interest deduction. Where the debtor is in a much lower tax bracket than the creditor, or where the debtor is using the money or property for a personal use (such as to buy a house or a car), so that interest would not be deductible, there may well be an incentive to create an interest-free debt. It is immaterial to the debtor whether he or she makes payments of principal and interest, or simply larger principal payments, and yet the latter alternative would save the creditor tax. Here the parties' interests are not adverse with respect to tax, and subsection 16(1) is needed to protect the tax base.

(d) — Imputed interest in deferred payments

In commercial reality, any amount of deferred payment bears an element of interest. If taxpayer that sells a sofa for $1,100 payable one year after the date of sale should be economically indifferent to the two alternative arrangements: (1) sells the sofa for an immediate payment of $1,000 and lends the money to the purchaser at the market interest rate of 10% per year; and (2) sells the sofa for $1,100 payable one year later. The time value of $1000 for one year is $100. No rationale business person would forego this value. If there is no "free lunch" in business, there is certainly "no free money". However, this principle of time value of money is not

[56]See also *Club de Courses v. M.N.R.*, [1979] C.T.C. 3022, 79 D.T.C. 579 (T.R.B.), where the purchase price exceeded fair market value by $100,000.

[57]*Carter v. M.N.R.* (1964), 37 Tax A.B.C. 174, 65 D.T.C. 31 (T.A.B.); and *Martin v. M.N.R.* (1979), [1980] C.T.C. 2043, 80 D.T.C. 1052 (T.R.B.).

[58]Interpretation Bulletin IT-265R3, "Payments of income and capital combined" (1991), para. 8.

recognized by the Act, except in specific circumstances where subsection 16(1) is held applicable. The reason might be the administrative concerns of tracking the imputed interest in all deferred payment transactions.

(e) — Discounts

A bond or mortgage or other debt obligation may be issued at a discount, and may be traded at a discount. If a bond is issued by the borrower to the lender for a price (the loan) which is less than the face value or principal sum of the bond, then the bond is issued at a discount. For example, if a $1,000 bond was issued by the borrower (also called the debtor or issuer) for $900, which is all that the lender (also called the creditor or bondholder) would have to lend, then the bond would have been issued at a discount of $100. If a bond is sold by its owner for a price which is less than its face value or principal sum, then the bond is traded at a discount. For example, if the holder of a $1,000 bond sold the bond for $700, then the bond would have been traded at a discount of $300. Alternatively, a bond or mortgage or other debt obligation may be issued at a premium, and may be traded at a premium. A bond is issued at a premium if the issue price (the loan) is more than the face value or principal sum of the bond; and a bond is traded at a premium if it is sold by its owner for a price which is more than its face value or principal sum.

When a bond or mortgage or other debt obligation matures (reaches the due date for repayment), the debtor is obliged to pay the precise amount of the principal sum to the creditor (the holder of the obligation) regardless of the price for which the holder acquired the obligation. This means that if the holder acquired the bond (either on issue or by purchase) at a discount, on maturity, the holder will make a gain over and above the price that the holder paid to acquire the bond (by the amount of the discount). If, on the other hand, the holder acquired the bond at a premium, then on the maturity of the bond, the holder will receive less than the price that the holder paid for the bond (by the amount of the premium).

Interest rates in the financial markets vary in response to the supply of and demand for money, which are affected by a wide variety of factors, including the anticipated rate of inflation and the general economic outlook. There is no single current interest rate at any one time for all classes of debt obligations, because bonds, mortgages and other obligations differ in their maturity dates, in the security that they provide, and in the creditworthiness of the issuer. A discount or premium is the adjustment of the market to an interest rate that differs from the rate that is current at the time when a debt obligation is issued or traded. If a mortgage or bond or other debt obligation is issued with an interest rate that is less than the rate currently available for that class of obligation, the market value of the obligation will be "discounted" to a figure below its face value — a figure which will make the effective yield to the purchaser closer to the current interest rate. If a debt obligation is issued with an interest rate that is higher than the rate currently available for that class of obligation, the obligation will issue or trade at a premium — a figure higher than its face value which will make the effective yield to the purchaser closer to the current interest rate. (This is the reason for a phenomenon that some investors find puzzling: when interest rates rise, bond prices fall, and when interest rates fall, bond prices rise.)

(f) — Position of creditor

When a person acquires a bond, mortgage or other obligation, whether on its original issue or by purchase from an existing holder, the yield from the investment must be measured not merely by the rate of interest stipulated to be paid on the principal sum (or face value), but also by taking into account any discount or premium at which the holder acquired the obligation. A discount increases the yield to the holder above the rate of interest stipulated on the obligation. A premium reduces the yield to the holder below the rate of interest stipulated on the obligation.

Suppose P purchases from B (the creditor) a $10,000 bond at 5 per cent interest at a time when current interest rates are in excess of 10 per cent, and suppose P pays $6,000 for the bond. Until redemption, P (the new bondholder) will receive from the bond issuer $500 per annum ($10,000 at 5 per cent) for an effective yield to P of 8.33 per cent ($500 is 8.33 per cent of $6,000). Years later, on redemption, the bond issuer (B, who originally borrowed the $10,000 at 5 per cent) must repay the full $10,000, and will pay the full $10,000 to P. This represents a further gain to P of $4,000, because P only paid $6,000 for the bond. The prospect of this gain on redemption obviously influenced the market price of the bond. P has put up with a lower interest rate in the knowledge that the full face value of the bond will be received on redemption — and that the market value of the bond will rise as the redemption date approaches.

In the example given, when P purchased a debt obligation at a discount and then held it to maturity, the situation seems to call for the application of subsection 16(1). Surely, part of the redemption proceeds, namely, the discount, should "reasonably be regarded as being in part interest". If not, then P has a substantial tax saving in comparison with simply investing the $6,000 at the current interest rate. In fact, subsection 16(1) has generally been confined by the courts and the CRA to cases where an interest-free element in a transaction has been arranged by agreement between the parties. Accordingly, where an obligation is traded at a discount as the result of market forces outside the control of the parties, subsection 16(1) will not apply to the discount. This was decided by the Supreme Court of Canada in *Wood v. M.N.R.* (1969),[59] where it was held that an investor who purchased a mortgage at a substantial discount (from another investor) and then held the mortgage until maturity, did not have to report any part of the redemption proceeds as interest income.[60]

---

[59] [1969] C.T.C. 57, 69 D.T.C. 5073 (S.C.C.).

[60] This decision is somewhat weakened by the fact that in the Supreme Court of Canada the Minister abandoned the argument (which had succeeded before the Tax Appeal Board) that the discount should be treated as interest. The argument in the Supreme Court of Canada was accordingly addressed to the issue whether the taxpayer was an investor or a trader. He was

It is hard to support the result that a yield on debt which is taken in the form of a discount should be tax-free. Now that capital gains are taxed (they were not when *Wood* was decided), it is clear that the discount would be a capital gain, because section 54 expressly includes the redemption of a debt obligation in its definition of a "disposition" of property (which gives rise to capital gains). However, this redresses the anomaly only partially, because one-half of a capital gain is tax-free (section 38). By the same token, if the purchaser of a debt obligation paid a premium on purchase, and then held the obligation to maturity, the loss on redemption (of the amount of the premium) would be a capital and not an income loss, and only one-half of the loss would be deductible for tax purposes (and then only from taxable capital gains).[61]

The decision in the *Wood* case, that the discount there was not caught by subsection 16(1), is not necessarily a reliable guide to the tax treatment of a discount which arises on the original issue of a debt obligation (an "original-issue discount"). In *Wood*, the debt obligation had been purchased from an existing holder, and the discount had arisen because of a fall in the market value of the obligation. Where a discount arises on the original issue of the obligation, then it must have been deliberately created by the borrower-issuer, either of its own motion or at the insistence of the lender. In that situation, the case for applying subsection 16(1) and treating the discount as interest income is very strong. In *Satinder v. R.* (1995),[62] the Federal Court of Appeal held that an original-issue discount (OID) was indeed interest income.

The Act also contains a specific provision to cover debt obligations that pay no interest at all. Non-interest-bearing bonds are sometimes issued by a borrowing company, in which case they are called "zero coupon bonds". Sometimes they are created by a stockbroker who will strip the interest coupons off a conventional bond, which is then called a "stripped bond". The principal (residue) of the bond and the interest coupons are then sold separately as non-interest-bearing obligations. Zero coupon bonds and stripped bonds are issued or sold at a sufficient discount to make up for the lack of interest; the return to the bondholder consists solely of the discount at which the bond was purchased; nothing will be received until the maturity of the bond. When interest rates are high, zero coupon bonds and stripped bonds are attractive to investors who wish to lock-in a long-term rate of return, and who do not want to bother with reinvesting periodic income payments. If the Act made no specific provision for such interest-free obligations, then the discount would not be taxed under subsection 16(1) until it was "paid or payable"

---

held to be an investor; and his gain on redemption was accordingly tax-free, because capital gains were not then (before 1972) taxable.

[61]If the holder of a debt obligation is engaged in the business of trading in debt obligations, then any realized discount would be taxable in full as income from a business, and any realized premium loss would be deductible in full: see ch. 11, Investing and Trading, below. This was the issue in the *Wood* case, note 59 above.

[62]95 D.T.C. 5340 (Fed. C.A.).

on the maturity of the bond; in some cases, it would be arguable, following *Wood*, that the discount was only partially taxable as a capital gain. The Act, by subsection 12(9) and regulation 7000, deems the full amount of the discount on an interest-free debt obligation to accrue to the holder in annual instalments during the term of the bond; by virtue of subsections 12(3) and (4) the holder is required to report as interest income a prescribed amount of the discount in each taxation year that the obligation is held.[63]

[63] S. 12(9) applies to a "prescribed debt obligation", which is defined in Reg. 7000(1) to include several types of obligations that do not pay interest or have deferred interest payment terms. Reg. 7000(2) stipulates the rules for computing the prescribed amount of accrued interest to be included in income annually by holders of such obligations.

8
INCOME FROM BUSINESS OR PROPERTY: DEDUCTIONS

8.1 — Deduction rules

Deductions are amounts subtracted in computing income. They are important in income tax law because deductions are necessary to measure net income and a taxpayer's ability to pay. While the *Income Tax Act* (the "Act") recognizes the importance of financial accounting in the computation of profit for the purpose of section 9, sections 18 to 21 contain the general "deduction" rules that either codify, modify or supplement the accounting principles.[1] Section 18 is prohibitive: it denies a deduction of amounts that are not incurred for the purpose of earning income from business or property; it also prohibits deductions for specific types of items for various policy reasons. Section 19 addresses the deductibility of advertising expenses. Section 20 is "permissive", allowing the deduction for specified costs and expenses, such as the cost of depreciable property and interest expense. Section 21 gives the taxpayer an election to either deduct the interest expense or capitalize it when the borrowed money is used to acquire depreciable property or for exploration or development. In addition, sections 67 to 67.6 provide further limitations on deductions.

The two fundamental questions in deductions are: (1) deductibility, i.e., whether the amount is deductible, and (2) timing, i.e. when is the amount deductible. As discussed in this chapter, the answer to these questions is found in both the common law and the statutory provisions.

(a) — Deductibility

Whether an amount is deductible in computing income generally depends on whether the amount was incurred for the purpose of earning income from a business or property (the income-earning purpose test). In the absence of specific limitations, income-earning expenses are deductible, whereas expenses incurred for personal consumption or saving purposes which have nothing to do with the earning of income are not deductible. The line between income-earning expenses and personal or living expenses is a crucial one, and sometimes difficult to draw.

The deductibility question is governed by several statutory rules, as well as judicial interpretation of these rules. The most fundamental rule is subsection 9(1) of the Act, which brings into income a taxpayer's "profit" from a business or property. As discussed in chapter 6, profit is computed in accordance with "well-accepted business principles of accounting" (which include generally accepted accounting principles (GAAP)), unless this conflicts with the case law or the Act. Thus, it follows that in determining whether a particular expenditure or loss is deductible for tax purposes, the first enquiry must be whether the item would be deductible for accounting purposes. If an expense is deductible for accounting purposes, it will generally be deductible for tax purposes as well, unless it is disallowed by a provision of the Act or a principle established in the case law. Likewise, if an expense is not deductible for accounting purposes, then it will not be deductible for tax purposes either, unless it is permitted by a specific provision of the Act or a principle established in the case law. GAAP allows a deduction for expenses that are incurred for the purpose of producing income.

---

[1] E.g., s. 18(1)(l), disallowing certain club fees after their allowance in *Royal Trust Co. v. Minister of National Revenue*, [1957] C.T.C. 32, 57 D.T.C. 1055 (Can. Ex. Ct.); and s. 20(1)(cc), allowing certain lobbying expenses after their disallowance in *No. 237 v. Minister of National Revenue* (1955), 12 Tax A.B.C. 230, 55 D.T.C. 135 (Can. Tax App. Bd.).

There are numerous statutory provisions that specifically allow or disallow various deductions from business or property income. Most (but by no means all) of these provisions are to be found within sections 18 and 20 of the Act. For example, paragraphs 18(1)(a) and 18(1)(h) explicitly prohibit the deduction of expenses that are not incurred for the purpose of earning income. Moreover, as discussed below, the Act denies the deduction of certain income-earning purposes out of policy concerns.

(b) — Timing

Another major issue in connection with deductions is timing. Timing issues are extremely important both to tax policy and tax planning. Indeed, the acceleration of a deduction may be equivalent to a full or partial exclusion of the income generated by the deductible expense. An important tax planning objective is to achieve a tax deferral though the acceleration of a deduction or the mismatch of a deduction and income or taxable capital gains.

For the purposes of determining the timing of deductions, expenses are generally categorized for tax purposes as (1) current expenses which are fully deductible in the year in which they are incurred, or (2) capital expenses which are deductible over a period of time during which the expense has value to the business.[2]

Several provisions of the Act address the timing issue. For example, paragraph 18(1)(a) permits the deduction of current expenses when they are incurred but paragraph 18(1)(b) prohibits the deduction of an expenditure "on account of capital" (such as a deduction for the cost of a building or equipment). The distinction between capital and other expenditures is, as the Carter Commission commented, "one of timing and not of any inherent quality".[3] The timing of deduction of capital expenditures is controlled by paragraphs 20(1)(a) or (b) for most assets whose value decreases over time. Under these rules, the cost of the acquisition is recognized over the useful life of the assets. Each year, only a portion of the cost is deductible. Similarly, subsection 18(9) prohibits the deduction of prepaid expenses (such as prepaid insurance or prepaid advertising) in the year of outlay and allows the deduction of such expenses in the taxation year to which the expenses relate. Subsection 20(1) permits the deduction of reserves in some circumstances.

---

[2]This nomenclature sometimes confuses accountants because: (1) under GAAP, all items must "expensed" (i.e., deducted) over the period of time during which the asset has value to the business; (2) the term "expense" refers to the deduction claimed in the year; and (3) the term "capital asset" or "asset" refers to a cost that will have a value extending beyond one year and is therefore "capitalized" rather than "expensed" (i.e., deducted).

[3]*Report of the Royal Commission on Taxation* (Carter Report) (1966), vol. 4, 249. The Carter Commission would have dropped the use of the term capital altogether, but it is unfortunately still with us.

8.2 — Policy goals

(a) — Income tax logic

Income tax is a tax on income. The concept of income is used to measure a taxpayer's ability to pay, which is in turn measured by the taxpayer's personal consumption and savings. Consequently, the tax base should not be reduced by expenditures for personal enjoyment or for savings.

Income is a net concept. In the case of income from a business or property, income means profit, which is the amount of revenue net of deductions. The deduction of expenses incurred for income-earning purposes is logical in an income tax system because only the additional income produced by the expenses increases a taxpayer's ability to pay. Expenses incurred for personal purposes result in personal enjoyment. They should not be deductible because personal expenses do not generate additional income, and, more importantly, personal consumption is an important indicator of the ability to pay.[4] Allowing the deduction of a personal expense would result in inequity between taxpayers who have the same ability to pay. For example, allowing a taxpayer a $10,000 deduction is the same as allowing a taxpayer to receive $10,000 of his or her income on a tax-free basis.

The fact that savings should not reduce the tax base is reflected by the timing rules. The general timing rule is that expenses are only deductible in the year they are incurred if they bring to the business a value that is consumed in the year.[5] If the value of an expense is totally consumed in earning income, it does not increase the taxpayer's personal satisfaction or savings. Therefore, the total expense should be deductible and only the net income derived from the expense is taxable. On the other hand, if the value of an expenditure (e.g., the cost of purchasing a car used in the business) is not totally consumed in earning income within the year, the portion of the expense that is not consumed has a value that is no different than savings in any other form. In other words, the car still has a value at the end of the year, which is no different from the equivalent amount of cash in a bank account. Therefore, the portion of the expense underlying this value should not be deducted in the year.

(b) — Accurate measurement of profit

As stated by the Supreme Court of Canada in *Canderel Ltd. v. R.* (1998),[6] "the goal of the legal test of "profit" should be to determine which method of accounting best depicts the reality of the financial situation of the particular taxpayer." Obviously, personal expenses and other expenses incurred for non-income earning purposes

---

[4]See heading 4.2, "The concept of income" above.

[5]Brooks, "The Principles underlying the Deduction of Business Expenses" in Hansen, Krishna, Rendall (eds.), *Canadian Taxation* (1981), 206.

[6][1998] 2 C.T.C. 35, 98 D.T.C. 6100 (S.C.C.) where the Supreme Court of Canada stated at para. 53: "in seeking to ascertain profit, the goal is to obtain an accurate picture of the taxpayer's profit for the given year." This case is, discussed under heading 6.4, "Judicial guidelines", above and heading 8.7(c), "Running expenses", below.

are not deductible as they do not contribute to the production of profit. Allowing their deduction would distort the picture of profit. The Act also limits deductions for business expenses that have a strong "personal element" through provisions such as section 67 (unreasonable amounts) and subsection 18(12) (home office expense) and paragraphs 18(1)(a) and (h).

With respect to the timing of deductions, the goal of producing an accurate measurement of profit is accomplished by either applying the matching principle or some other appropriate methods. As discussed in chapter 6, the matching principle is an important accounting principle. This principle underlies some of the timing provisions of the Act, such as subsection 18(9) regarding prepaid expenses and paragraphs 20(1)(m) and 12(1)(a) regarding prepaid amounts for unearned income.

There have been many cases dealing with the timing of the deduction of expenses not addressed by statutory rules. Some of these cases have already been referred to in chapter 6 because they are cases that dealt with the meaning of "profit". The "accurate picture of profit" doctrine demands that an expense that is incurred in a year should be deductible in that year if its benefits are realized in that year. If the benefits will be realized over a period of years, the expense should be amortized if this produces a more accurate picture of profit. Amortization allows a "matching" of the benefit of the expense to the income derived from the expense. Where some benefits are immediate and others relate to future years, in the absence of statutory provisions, a taxpayer is allowed to choose between current deduction and amortization if the Minister does not prove that amortization results in a more accurate picture of profit. For example, in *Canderel*, a tenant inducement payment that benefited both the current year and future years was allowed to be deducted in the year in which it was incurred even through generally accepted accounting principles require such an amount to be amortized over the term of the lease.

(c) — Certainty and predictability

One of the goals of the Act is "to provide sufficient certainty and predictability to permit taxpayers to intelligently order their affairs."[7] In filing their tax returns, taxpayers must make various determinations as to the deductibility and timing of deductions of many types of expenses. It thus makes sense for tax law to provide as much certainty and predictability as possible. The detailed and sometimes highly technical rules under sections 18 to 21 certainly spell out the treatment of a large number of expenses, ranging from cost of capital property (s. 20(1)(a)) to kiwi loans (s. 20.3). The Act also contains general rules that apply to limit the deduction of certain expenses, such as entertainment expenses (s. 67.1) and fines and penalties (s. 67.6).

[7]The Supreme Court of Canada has reiterated this point in a number of its recent decisions, such as *Canada Trustco Mortgage Co. v. R.* (2005); *Mathew v. R.*; *65302 British Columbia Ltd. v. R.* (1999), [2000] 1 C.T.C. 57, 99 D.T.C. 5799 (Eng.), 99 D.T.C. 5814 (Fr.) (S.C.C.)

(d) — Controlling the abuse of business deductions

The Act contains a variety of specific rules to limit or deny particular types of deductions. For example, section 67 denies deductions for unreasonable amounts; section 67.1 limits deductions for entertainment expenses; and subsection 18(12) severely limits deductions for home office expenses by imposing a principle place of business test.[8] In the interest of simplicity and to prevent abuse, these rules establish arbitrary limits and arbitrary test. The result may be unfairness in individual cases. For example, a gift of a flower bouquet to a business client can be fully deducted whereas a gift of hockey ticket is only one-half deductible.

(e) — Tax policy as public policy

Is there any principle of public policy that would operate to deny the deduction of expenses that would otherwise be deductible under the Act? This question is commonly posed when a business proprietor attempts to deduct fines levied against him or her for illegal acts committed in the course of business. The same question is raised by attempts to deduct damages and similar payments, as well as bribes and other similar illegal expenditures. Traditionally, "the courts [would] not recognize a benefit accruing to a criminal from his crime".[9] In the case of the deductibility of fines, penalties, and damages, however, some cases allowed the deduction if the amounts were incurred for the purpose of earning income (e.g., *Imperial Oil Ltd. v. Minister of National Revenue* (1947)[10]), while other cases denied the deduction on the grounds that the deduction would reduce the sting of the law that imposed the fine, penalty or damages. The Supreme Court of Canada held in *65302 British Columbia Ltd. v. R.* (2000)[11] however, that fines and penalties will only be denied a deduction in the rare case that the breach is so "egregious or repulsive" that it cannot be justified as being incurred for the purpose of earning income. According to the Court, public policy determinations are best left to Parliament. In reaction to *65302 British Columbia Ltd.*, Parliament enacted section 67.6 to deny the deduction of most government fines and penalties imposed after March 22, 2004. The deductibility of damages, expenses of illegal businesses, and fines and penalties imposed under contracts etc. remain governed by case law principles.

In addition to section 67.6, the Act contains several provisions prohibiting the deduction of expenses on grounds of public policy.[12] Paragraph 18(1)(t) prohibits the

---

[8]As well as limiting the deduction to the income earned from the business.

[9]In *Day & Ross Ltd. v. R.*, [1976] C.T.C. 707, 76 D.T.C. 6433 (Fed. T.D.), at 716-7 [D.T.C.], Dubé J. citing Lord Atkin in *Beresford v. Royal Insurance Co.*, [1938] A.C. 586 (U.K. H.L.), 599.

[10]Note 16, below.

[11]Note 7, above. This case is discussed in detail under heading 8.5(b), "Fines and penalties", below.

[12]Somewhat related to this issue is paragraph 127(4.1)(b) which denies the deduction of a tax credit for federal political contributions if the taxpayer acquired a financial benefit from the contribution.

deduction of interest and penalties arising under the Act itself. Presumably this is to discourage taxpayers from violating the Act. Section 67.5 denies the deduction for illegal payments.

This chapter will now proceed to discuss the deductibility question under headings 8.3 to 8.6, and then the timing question under headings 8.7 to 8.8. Because paragraph 20(1)(c) is regarded as a complete code on the deduction of interest expenses in terms of both deductibility and timing, interest expense is discussed separately under heading 8.9 and other financing cost is discussed under heading 8.10. The chapter concludes with a note on mismatch and tax arbitrage.

8.3 — Income-earning purpose

The principle that only income-earning expenses are deductible is reflected in subsection 9(1), and paragraphs 18(1)(a) and (h). Paragraph 18(1)(a) prohibits the deduction of "an outlay or expense except to the extent that it was made or incurred by the taxpayer for the purposes of gaining or producing income from the business or property". Paragraph 18(1)(h) prohibits the deduction of "personal or living expenses of the taxpayer, other than travel expenses incurred by the taxpayer while away from home in the course of carrying on the taxpayer's business".[13]

These provisions may be viewed redundant in the sense of merely confirming what would be the result under section 9.[14] There are no examples of expenses that would be allowed for accounting principles but disallowed by paragraph 18(1)(a) or (b). However, in some cases the courts have found the statutory provisions useful additional hooks on which a decision can be hung. Thus, for example, a personal expense by a taxpayer would not be deductible for accounting purposes and therefore would not be deductible under section 9. This result is also confirmed by paragraph 18(1)(a) because a personal expense is not incurred for the purpose of gaining or producing income and by paragraph 18(1)(h) which prohibits yet again deductions for personal expenses. The statutory measures thus provide additional support for courts denying deductions for personal expenses.[15]

---

[13]However, for social and economic policy reasons, the deduction of some personal expenses is specifically allowed by the Act in computing income (e.g., child expenses under section 63, moving expenses under section 62) or in computing tax payable (e.g., tuition fees under section 118.5). See ch. 12, Other Income and Deductions, and ch. 14, Taxable Income and Tax for Individuals, below.

[14]Charitable donations are not deductible under s. 18(1)(a) if they are not incurred for the purpose of earning income. However, a deduction is available for corporations (s. 110.1, discussed under heading 15.5(a)(iii), "Charitable donations", below) and a personal tax credit is available for individuals (s. 118.1, discussed under heading 14.7(b), "Non-refundable credits", below).

[15]Iacobucci J. made this point very clear in *Symes v. Canada*, [1993] 4 S.C.R. 695, [1994] 1 C.T.C. 40, 94 D.T.C. 6001 (S.C.C.) at para. 44: "the well accepted principles of business practice encompassed by subsection 9(1) would generally operate to prohibit the deduction

The wording of paragraph 18(1)(a) makes it clear that the emphasis of the provision is purpose, not result; no causal nexus is required. An expense incurred for the purpose of earning income from a business or property is deductible even if it actually results in a loss.[16] It is also not necessary that the expense was "wholly, exclusively and necessarily laid out or expended for the purpose of earning the income".[17] Typical business expenses include wages paid to workers, rental of the business premise, interest on money borrowed to finance the business operations, and inventories.

Non-income earning expenses are typically those that are incurred for personal consumption or personal purposes (such as food, shelter, clothing, and personal entertainment) and those that are incurred for the purpose of earning capital gains or exempt income.[18] Some expenses are incurred for mixed purposes. Examples of mixed personal and business expenses are business entertainment, and travels. Examples of mixed income-earning purpose and capital gains-earning purpose are investment in stocks or real estate.

The Act is not very helpful in providing specific guidelines for drawing the line between income-earning purpose and non-income-earning purpose. Subsection 248(1) merely provides that "personal or living expenses" include

> the expenses of properties maintained by a person for the use or benefit of the taxpayer or any person connected with the taxpayer by blood relationship, marriage or common-law partnership or adoption, and not maintained in connection with a business carried on for profit or with a reasonable expectation of profit.

The usefulness of this statutory definition is limited since it is an inclusive definition that deals only with expenses related to properties maintained for the use or benefit of the taxpayer or a related person. It does not deal with other types of expenses that may be incurred for personal enjoyment (e.g., an entertainment or travel expense). Consequently, the distinction between an income-earning expense

---

of expenses which lack an income earning purpose, or which are personal expenses, just as much as paragraphs 18(1)(a) and (h) operate expressly to prohibit such deductions".

[16]See *Imperial Oil Ltd. v. M.N.R.*, [1947] C.T.C. 353, 3 D.T.C. 1090 (Ex. Ct.), discussed under heading 8.5(c), "Damages", below. However, an expense incurred for the purpose of earning exempt income is not deductible pursuant to certain provisions of the Act, such as ss. 18(1)(c) and 20(1)(c). Examples are ss. 18(1)(c) and 20(1)(c). Losses resulting from normal hazards of a business, such as fraud by employees or shoplifting, as well as losses caused by outside criminals, such as burglars, have been held to be deductible. The test is whether or not the money or property was taken in the course of business operations, and whether the risk of theft was inherent in those operations. See *Cassidy's Ltd. v. M.N.R.* (1989), [1990] 1 C.T.C. 2043, 89 D.T.C. 686 (T.C.C.); *Parkland Operations Ltd. v. R.* (1990), [1991] 1 C.T.C. 23, 90 D.T.C. 6676 (Fed. T.D.).

[17]This wording was found in the pre-1948 Act and is now replaced by the less restrictive wording of s. 18(1)(a). See *M.N.R. v. Premium Iron Ores Ltd.*, [1966] S.C.R. 685, [1966] C.T.C. 391, 66 D.T.C. 5280 (S.C.C.).

[18]See ss. 18(1)(c) and 20(1)(c). See also heading 4.4(c), "Exclusions".

and a personal or living expense must be made on a case-by-case basis in accordance with the common law.

8.4 — Personal and mixed expenses

The deduction of personal or living expenses is disallowed explicitly by paragraph 18(1)(h), and implicitly by paragraph 18(1)(a) and section 9. It is therefore crucial to distinguish between an income-earning expense and a personal or living expense. As mentioned above, some items are easy to categorize as income-earning expenses, some are easy to see as personal or living expenses, and others (such as travel and entertainment expenses) fall into an ambiguous or unclear category.

(a) — Common law tests

In determining whether an expense was incurred for an income-earning purpose or personal purpose, the following factors are considered by the court to be relevant, but none is conclusive on its own:[19]

1. Whether the expense is deductible according to accounting principles or practices such as GAAP. As mentioned earlier, this factor generally concludes the inquiry in many cases.
2. Whether the expense is normally incurred by other taxpayers carrying on similar businesses. If it is, there may be an increased likelihood that the expense is a business expense.
3. Whether a particular expense would have been incurred if the taxpayer were not engaged in the pursuit of business or property income or whether, in absence of the business activity, the need to incur an expense (such as food, clothing and shelter) would still be there.
4. Whether the taxpayer could have avoided the expense without affecting gross income.
5. Whether the expense is an expense "of the trader" or "of the trade". If the expense was an incident of the trade — part of the business operation itself, it is an income-earning expense.
6. Whether a particular expense was incurred in order to approach the income-producing circle (such as clothing, child care, housekeeping or commuting) or was incurred within the circle itself. Only the latter would be deductible as income-earning expenses.[20] This test may be of limited assistance in cases where the "personal circle" and "income-producing circle" overlap, such as in the case of home office expenses.

---

[19]These factors were summarized by Brooks, note 5, above, at 198–201 and were cited by Iacobucci J. in *Symes*, note 15, above, at para. 52.

[20]Iacobucci J. did not consider this test a helpful analytic tool in the *Symes* case, *ibid.*, para. 69, but said that it "may be of assistance in understanding generally accepted business expenses".

What if an expense is incurred for mixed or dual purposes? On its face, paragraph 18(1)(a) looks to be almost wholly otiose — clearly expenses not incurred for the purposes of gaining or producing income from business or property are not relevant for determining a taxpayer's net profit from business. However, the apportionment language — an expense is deductible *to the extent* that it was incurred for the purpose of gaining or producing income — suggests that taxpayers could have dual-purpose expenses that are only partially deductible; in fact, that is how the courts have sometimes interpreted it. For example, if a taxpayer made a trip to another city intending to spend half of the time in the other city for business and half for tourist and vacation purposes, under paragraph 18(1)(a) only half of the expenses would be deductible. Where apportionment on a case-by-case basis is difficult, the Act imposes arbitrary apportionment (such as the 50 per cent apportionment for meals and entertainment expenses in section 67.1).

In some cases involving entertainment or travel, the courts seem to have employed the "principal" purpose test: if the principal purpose of an expense was business, the expense is deductible, but if the principal purpose was personal, no deduction is allowed. For example, a medical professional-turned-educator was not allowed to deduct expenses incurred in travelling to Europe to study educational methods because the principal purpose of the expenses was held to be personal.[21] This "principal" purpose test is sometimes referred to as the "dominant" or "primary" purpose test.

The income-earning "purpose" test set out in paragraph 18(1)(a) forms the basis for judicial doctrines that limit opportunities for tax minimization by taxpayers who incur expenses for the dual purpose of deriving future income and achieving a tax benefit. In many cases, the test is supplemented by reliance on the "reasonable" requirement in section 67 of the Act and by limiting the amount of deductions to the amount of income (such as in the case of home-office expenses).

However, as demonstrated by the Supreme Court decision in *Ludco Enterprises Ltd. v. R.* (2001)[22] in the case of dual purpose interest expense incurred to earn property income as well as capital gains, the courts have taken a different approach — as long as there was an income purposes, the interest expense was deductible.

---

[21] *Cormack v. M.N.R.* (1965), 39 Tax A.B.C. 437 (T.A.B.). Brooks did an analysis of this issue in 1981 (note 5, above, 203) and found that in most cases, the whole cost of the trip was allowed as being incurred for a business purpose. In one case only 35 per cent of the cost was allowed (*A-1 Steel and Iron Foundry Ltd. v. M.N.R.* (1963), 31 Tax A.B.C. 338 (T.A.B.)), and in another only 15 per cent of the cost was allowed (*Kerr Farms Ltd. v. M.N.R.*, [1971] Tax A.B.C. 804 (T.A.B.)).

[22] (sub nom. *Ludco Enterprises Ltd. v. Canada*) [2001] 2 S.C.R. 1082, [2002] 1 C.T.C. 95, (sub nom. *Ludco Enterprises Ltd. v. R.*) 2001 D.T.C. 5505 (Eng.), 2001 D.T.C. 5518 (Fr.) (S.C.C.), discussed under heading 8.9(d), "Income-earning purpose test", below.

(b) — Child care expenses

The Act views child care expenses as personal or living expenses because they are dictated by personal consumption decisions such as whether to have children and how they should be cared for. Child care expenses are incurred to make a taxpayer available for work — they are not incurred in the course of business. Section 63 of the Act confers partial deductibility on child care expenses as an "other deduction" for social and economic policy reasons.[23] This statutory deduction is available to all taxpayers, including taxpayers carrying on business activities.

Beyond the deduction under section 63, can child care expenses be deducted as an expense of doing business? In *Symes v. Canada* (1993),[24] the Supreme Court of Canada answered no. The taxpayer in that case, a self-employed lawyer with two small children, paid a nanny to look after her children. The taxpayer testified that less expensive forms of child care were not satisfactory in light of the long and irregular hours of her litigation practice, and that she and her husband (who was employed) had made a "family decision" that she would pay for the nanny. In 1985, for example, she paid wages of $13,000 to the nanny, and claimed the full amount as a business expense.

A majority of the Supreme Court of Canada, in an opinion written by Iacobucci J., held that child care expenses would not be deductible as business expenses according to traditional tests of deductibility. Although child care expenses had to be borne in order to allow the taxpayer to go to the office, they were not incurred in the income-earning process, but merely to make the taxpayer available to the business. The deductibility of an expense was traditionally governed by the commercial needs of the business rather than by the personal circumstances of the proprietor. Iacobucci J. acknowledged that this rule respecting deductibility had developed at a time when businesspersons were mostly males with spouses who were at home during the day and looked after the family's children. In this situation, child care was a private matter, quite separate from a taxpayer's business activity. Now that businesspeople include women as well as men, and the care of their children is an inescapable part of their business arrangements, it might be appropriate for the courts to "reconceptualize" the nature of a business expense, and in particular to re-examine the rule that disallows expenses that are incurred to make the taxpayer available to the business. However, Iacobucci J. did not pursue this interesting suggestion, because he held that it was "unnecessary to determine whether reconceptualization is appropriate having regard to the presence of s. 63 in the Act".[25]

The Minister had denied the deduction as a business expense but allowed the taxpayer to deduct child care expenses under section 63. According to Iacobucci J., section 63 was an exhaustive provision for the deductibility of child care expenses,

---

[23]Section 63 is discussed further under heading 12.10, "Child care expenses", below.

[24]Note 15, above.

[25]*Ibid.*, 744, 62, 6017; he added (750-751, 66, 6020): "It is not necessary for me to decide whether, in the absence of s. 63, ss. 9, 18(1)(a) and 18(1)(h) are capable of comprehending a business expense deduction for child care".

leaving no room for their deductibility as business expenses. Section 63 explicitly applied to child care services purchased "to enable the taxpayer . . . to carry on a business", and the cap on the deduction was defined by reference to the taxpayer's "earned income", which explicitly included income from business. The cap on the section 63 deduction, as well as its limitation to the lower-earning parent, would be undermined if child care expenses were fully deductible from business income by whichever parent had actually paid the expenses.[26] In this case, for example, the "family decision" as to which parent should pay for child care placed the obligation on the wife, who earned business income, rather than the husband, who earned employment income. There was no suggestion that this decision had been driven by tax considerations, but the decision did make possible the argument that the expenses were business expenses. Iacobucci J. commented that "in many cases there would be more bookkeeping than reality about such a decision".[27] In the end, therefore, the majority of the Court[28] concluded that section 63 made clear that child care expenses were not deductible as business expenses. The Minister's assessment, which confined the taxpayer to the section 63 deduction, was accordingly upheld.

Symes is not only the leading case on the deductibility of child care expense — it is also the leading case on the application of section 15 of the *Charter of Rights and Freedoms*[29] (the "Charter") to the Act. The taxpayer argued that her section 15 Charter right was infringed by the Act. The Court split along gender lines on this issue. The majority (consisted of male judges) rejected an equality-based Charter challenge to the restrictions under section 63 on the deductibility of child care expenses. The majority rejected the argument that the restrictions had a disproportionate impact on women: although women were more likely to bear the social costs of child care, there was no evidence that women were more likely to bear the financial costs of child care; and the restrictions affected only the financial costs of child care.

(c) — Food and beverages

Like child care expenses, food and beverages have always been viewed as personal or living expenses because we all need food and water to survive regardless of income-earning activities. Acting upon Iacobucci J.'s suggestion in *Symes* that the

---

[26]The maximum available to Symes was $4,000 in respect of her two children and the amount has since been increased. Section 63 is discussed further under heading 12.10, "Child care expenses", below.

[27]*Symes*, note 15, above, 746, 63, 6018.

[28]L'Heureux-Dubé and McLachlin JJ. dissented, holding that the child care expenses were fully deductible as business expenses; that s. 63 did not preclude their deduction as business expenses, and that, if s. 63 had precluded the deduction, it would have contravened the equality guarantee of the Charter.

[29]Part I of the *Constitution Act, 1982*, being Schedule B to the *Canada Act 1982* (U.K.), 1982, c. 11.

courts might "reconceptualize" the nature of a business expense in light of changes in the work environment and society, the Federal Court of Appeal re-examined the deductibility of food and beverages in *Scott v. R.* (1998).[30] In this case, the taxpayer was a self-employed courier. He travelled approximately 150 kilometres per day on foot and the subway. His commission was based on the distance of the delivery and the weight of the package. Each day, he consumed an extra meal at the cost of $11 ($8 for food and $3 for bottled water and juice). He sought to deduct the $11 as business expenses. The deduction was allowed. The Court distinguished between the cost of regular food and beverages and the cost of extra food and beverages that Scott needed as a result of his business. The court analogized Scott's need for extra food and beverages to a courier who needed more gasoline for his car because of its business use.

Recall that Symes could not deduct her child care expenses as income-earning expenses even though they were incurred to enable her to earn business income. Scott could deduct the extra food needed to enable him to perform his job. In light of *Scott*, could Symes deduct the "extra" child care expenses required by the long hours of her law practice? Would *Scott* open the floodgates to a myriad of claims for deductions of what have traditionally been viewed as personal expenses? The Court rejected this argument because "the analogy between fuel for an automobile and fuel for the human body provides an appropriate line for the courts to draw".[31] For example, the Court said, a construction worker cannot deduct the cost of additional food, since there is no corresponding gasoline analogy. This may underestimate the creativity of taxpayers: how about an argument that the extra food consumed as a result of physically demanding work (using manual tools) is analogous to the energy cost of electronic tools?

(d) — Entertainment expenses

Entertainment expenses are amounts spent on entertaining customers and clients, including expenses for meals, parties, sporting events, theatres, and membership in social and recreational clubs. In *Royal Trust Co. v. M.N.R.* (1957),[32] the Exchequer Court held that a trust company could deduct for tax purposes fees paid by the company that were incurred by various of its officers in belonging to social and recreational clubs. The Court found that such payments were a normal business practice of trust companies, and produced business contacts and opportunities for the companies. The Court held that the payments were made for the purpose of gaining or producing income from the business and were deductible. Although the actual result in *Royal Trust* was reversed by the introduction of paragraph 18(1)(l) (which denies the deduction of membership fees in social and recreational clubs),[33]

---

[30][1998] 4 C.T.C. 103, 98 D.T.C. 6530 (Fed. C.A.).

[31]*Ibid.*, para. 11.

[32]Note 1, above.

[33]It would seem that the real point of the litigation in *Royal Trust* was to save the employees from having to pay tax on the benefits that they received from belonging to the clubs since, if

the principle remains intact — other entertainment expenses which have a dominant business purpose are deductible by the proprietor of the business[34] whereas expenses that are incurred primarily for personal purposes are not deductible.[35]

When entertainment expenses incurred for business purposes also provide personal pleasure to the individuals enjoying the entertainment (as in the case of a taxpayer taking her client to a professional baseball game) should the personal element be identified and denied a deduction? It is obvious that denying the full deduction (like paragraph 18(1)(l) does for club dues) is too heavy-handed — but the difficulty of isolating and valuing the element of personal enjoyment on a case-by-case basis is insurmountable. In order to overcome this problem, section 67.1 was introduced into the Act in 1988.

Section 67.1 limits the deductibility of expenses for "food or beverages or the enjoyment of entertainment" to 50 per cent of the amount actually paid, or 50 per cent of the "amount in respect thereof that would be reasonable in the circumstances".[36] This provision effectively deems 50 per cent of "reasonable" entertainment-style expenses to be personal expenditures, and allows the remainder to be deducted as business expenses. This rule applies even when a taxpayer can prove that he or she did not participate in the consumption or enjoyment.[37] If an expenditure for food or beverages or entertainment is unreasonable within the meaning of section 67.1, the section allows a deduction of 50 per cent of a "reasonable" portion of the expense.[38]

---

the expenses were sufficiently business-related to be deductible as business expenses (rather than salary and benefits), the amounts would not have reported as taxable benefits by the employees who belonged to the clubs. Paragraph 18(1)(l) now prohibits the deduction of membership fees in social and recreational clubs as well as the expenses for the use or maintenance of a yacht, a camp, a lodge, or a golf course in both cases. As discussed under heading 5.5(a), "Inclusion in income", above, the question of whether such an amount would be a taxable benefit to an employee would depend on the primary purpose of the expense: if the primary purpose is employment-related, there is no taxable benefit.

[34]*Riedle Brewery Ltd. v. M.N.R.*, [1939] S.C.R. 253, [1938-39] C.T.C. 312 (S.C.C.) (brewery could deduct cost of free beer to customers).

[35]*Roebuck v. M.N.R.* (1961), 26 Tax A.B.C. 11, 61 D.T.C. 72 (T.A.B.) (lawyer could not deduct cost of bar mitzvah, although many clients were invited).

[36]The allowable percentage was 80 per cent until it was reduced to 50 per cent in 1994.

[37]*Stapley v. R.*, [2006] 3 C.T.C. 188, 2006 D.T.C. 6075 (F.C.A.). In this case, a real estate broker gave vouchers for meals, drinks and entertainment to his clients and was denied the deduction for 50% of the cost of the gifts. Had he given other types of gifts (flowers or art work), he would have been able to deduct the full cost. See, for example, the cost of gifts of doughnuts to clients was fully deductible in *Caldwell v. R.*, [2003] 3 C.T.C. 2788 (T.C.C. [Informal Procedure]).

[38]S. 67.1(2) lists a number of situations where a taxpayer may deduct 100% of entertainment-style expenses: e.g., where the expense was incurred at a fund-raising event for a charity or where the expense relates to an event for all employees at a single work location (up to a maximum of six such events per year).

The rule that limits the deductibility of business expenses for food, beverages or entertainment to 50 per cent of the actual expense is arbitrary, but in many cases is probably a realistic apportionment. It is also desirable as a matter of tax policy. In the first place, the old rule of full deductibility was open to abuse by the incurring of excessively high or excessively frequent expenses which had only a tenuous relationship to business income but which the CRA could not in practice effectively police. In the second place, full deductibility may have violated neutrality by artificially stimulating the consumption of entertainment-type goods and services, thereby diverting to that sector of the economy resources that would in the absence of taxes be deployed elsewhere. In the third place, full deductibility may have violated equity since the element of untaxed personal benefit accrued mainly to taxpayers in business on their own account or employed in executive positions (the expense being paid and the deduction being taken by the employer), thus was not available to the majority of taxpayers. Moreover, the inequity was regressive (a breach of vertical as well as horizontal equity) since the advantage (like the advantage of social and recreational club memberships) accrued disproportionately to high-income people.

(e) — Commuting expenses

Expenses incurred to travel to and from the workplace are sometimes thought of as dual purpose expenses, but they are not. Commuting expenses are personal expenses. The journey to work is a precondition of earning income and the nature of the journey to work is dictated by personal consumption decisions such as to where to locate one's home and what mode of transportation to take. The courts have consistently treated commuting expenses to and from the workplace as personal expenses because they make a taxpayer available for work, but they are not incurred in the course of business. Once a taxpayer has travelled from home to the office, any business-related travel from the office, other than the journey home, is incurred in the course of the business and is a deductible business expense. Thus, the lawyer who travels from his or her office to the courthouse, and back again, does incur a deductible expense.

Using this logic, any business-related travel from a taxpayer's home office would be deductible since it is incurred in the course of business. In *Cumming v. M.N.R.* (1967),[39] the taxpayer was a doctor, an anaesthetist, who rendered all his professional services at a hospital near his home. However, he had no office at the hospital in which he could do the bookkeeping and paperwork of the practice, or read medical journals. He established an office at his home that was used exclusively for those purposes. The Exchequer Court held that the home office was the base from which the practice was operated. Therefore, the journeys to and from the hospital

[39] [1967] C.T.C. 462, 67 D.T.C. 5312 (Can. Ex. Ct.).

were not commutes, but were journeys made in the course of the practice. The expense of these journeys was accordingly deductible.[40]

(f) — Housekeeping expenses

The cost of housekeeping may play a role in the earning of business income, because it relieves the taxpayer of non-income-earning work and frees up time for income-earning purposes. It is however a personal or living expense which is non-deductible. Like commuting, housekeeping may make the taxpayer available for work, but it is not done in the course of the business or as part of the income-earning process. The concern here is that the tax base would be seriously eroded if all expenses that were preconditions to working were deductible. Food, clothing and housing, for example, are all necessary in order to maintain the ability to function at work.

Nevertheless, the disallowance of housekeeping expenses can lead to arbitrary results. In *Benton v. M.N.R.* (1952),[41] the Tax Appeal Board disallowed a farmer's cost of hiring a housekeeper. The farmer was in poor health and could not manage both the farm and housekeeping duties. Because housekeeping is a personal or living expense, the wages paid to the housekeeper were not deductible from the farmer's income. Had the farmer done the housework himself and hired a farm hand to work the farm, the farm hand's wages would have been deductible as an expense incurred to earn income from the farming business.[42]

(g) — Home-office expenses

The expenses of maintaining a home typically include utilities (heat, electricity and water), maintenance, property taxes and mortgage interest (or rent if the home is rented). If a businessperson does some business-related work at home, then the expenses of maintaining the home have a dual character. However, the courts have been unwilling to permit the deduction of any part of these expenses unless the businessperson maintained a separate room in the house as an office, and used the room exclusively for business purposes. In that case, the businessperson would be permitted to deduct a proportion of the expenses based on the proportion of floor space that the office bore to the total floor space of the home.[43]

---

[40]See *R. v. Cork*, [1990] 2 C.T.C. 116, 90 D.T.C. 6358 (Fed. C.A.), in which a mechanical draftsman's expenses of travelling from "home" to work were held deductible. As was the case in *Cumming*, the taxpayer in *Cork* used his home as the base of operations from which he carried on his business. The trips from his home-office to various job sites were therefore not commutes, but trips made in the course of doing business, and were accordingly deductible from income.

[41](1952), 6 Tax A.B.C. 230 (T.A.B.).

[42]Indeed, a portion of the wages paid to the housekeeper were held to be deductible, reflecting time spent by the housekeeper doing farm work.

[43]The business person could also deduct capital cost allowance on the portion of the home used for a home office but this is generally not advisable because it will result in that portion

In *Logan v. M.N.R.* (1967),[44] for example, a doctor was permitted to deduct the portion of home-office expenses that were attributable to a room in his home that was used as an office. The taxpayer was able to establish that the office was used exclusively for work-related activities, such as medical writing, bookkeeping, and meeting with other doctors. In *Mallouh v. M.N.R.* (1985),[45] by contrast, a doctor was denied a deduction for expense related to a home office that occupied half of the basement in the doctor's home. In that case, the office was more of a general study or den in which business-related work was not the exclusive activity.

In 1988, subsection 18(12) was added to the Act to establish more precise, and more restrictive, rules with respect to the deductibility of home office expenses.[46] When a home-office expense would satisfy the "exclusive use test" in the case law, so as to be "otherwise deductible", it must also satisfy one of the two tests in paragraph 18(12)(a): either the office must be the individual's "principal place of business" (subparagraph (i)),[47] or, if the office is not the principal place of business, it must be "used on a regular and continuous basis for meeting clients, customers or patients" or used exclusively for the purpose of earning business income (subparagraph (ii)). Where a home office fails to satisfy one of these two tests, no deduction will be allowed.

In essence, subsection 18(12) is a "stop-loss" rule, that is, to prevent taxpayers from generating loss by deducting the home-office expenses. In the absence of this rule, taxpayers can offset the loss against other income.[48] Technically, paragraph 18(12)(b) provides that the deduction for home office expenses is allowed only to the extent that the taxpayer has positive income from the business before that deduction. In other words, the home-office deduction cannot be used to create a loss or increase a loss. Paragraph (c) provides that expenses that are disallowed by paragraph (b) can be carried forward indefinitely so long as the home office continues to qualify for the deduction. Therefore, the portion of the home-office expenses that cannot be deducted in a particular year will be deductible in a future year if the income from the business is sufficient in that year. For example, suppose that in

---

of the home being ineligible for principal residence status. Principal residence status is important because s. 40(2)(b) allows gains from the disposition of a "principal residence" to be exempted from income tax. The effect of claiming capital cost allowance on the portion of a principal residence is discussed further under heading 10.8(b)(ii), "Ordinarily inhabited", below.

[44] 67 D.T.C. 189, [1967] Tax A.B.C. 276 (T.A.B.).

[45] [1985] 1 C.T.C. 2297, 85 D.T.C. 250 (T.C.C.).

[46] The rule permitting the deduction of home-office expenses by employees (s. 8(13)), which is discussed under heading 5.11(b), "Deductions permitted", above, contains the same restrictive language.

[47] The word "principal" is not defined. It is considered by CRA to have a meaning similar to "chief" or "main": Interpretation Bulletin IT-514, "Work space in home expenses", (1989), para. 2.

[48] For more discussion on losses, see chapter 14, below.

year one a taxpayer operating a home-based business has (in thousands) revenue of $10, home-office expenses of $3 and other expenses of $9: in year one, only $1 is deductible for the home office. In year two, if revenue has risen to $15 and expenses have remained the same, the full current home-office expenses of $3 will be deductible, as well as the $2 disallowed prior year's home-office expenses; this will leave a profit for tax purposes from the home-based business of $1.

8.5 — Cost of illegal or unethical activities

(a) — Kickbacks, Bribes and other illegal payments

Until the enactment of section 67.5, kickbacks, bribes and other illegal payments made or incurred by taxpayers for the purpose of earning or producing income were held deductible by the courts. For example, in *United Color & Chemicals Ltd. v. Minister of National Revenue* (1992)[49] the taxpayer paid "secret commissions" (kickbacks) to the purchasing agents of its customers in order to secure contracts. The Court allowed the deduction because the purpose of the payment was for the gaining or producing of income and "such arrangements were standard in the industry."[50]

The Act was amended after that because the deduction of illegal payments was considered to frustrate public policy. Section 67.5 currently prohibits the deduction of expenditures made in order to commit certain offences under the *Criminal Code* or the *Corruption of Foreign Public Officials Act* which include:

- Bribes to judges, public officials and law enforcement officers;[51]
- Payments made for the purpose of influencing municipal officers and payments made to buy an official appointment;
- Kickbacks and frauds on the government; and
- Bribes to foreign officials.

(b) — Fines and penalties

There are competing policy concerns with respect to the deductibility of fines and penalties. If the deduction of fines and penalties were allowed, the sting of fines is much reduced, or the objectives of the statute under which the fine is imposed may be frustrated. However, the real impact of a fine or penalty depends upon the wealth of the defendant because the sentencing court often has the discretion to consider the defendant's capacity to pay when fixing an appropriate fine. Moreo-

---

[49][1992] 1 C.T.C. 2321, 92 D.T.C. 1259 (T.C.C.).

[50]*Ibid.* para. 10.

[51]These include bribes to judges, public officials and law enforcement officers, payments made for the purpose of influencing municipal officers and payments made to buy an official appointment Until 1999, section 67.5 applied only to bribes to Canadian officials. Bribes to foreign officials are now included.

ver, the sentencing court may impose heavier fines to offset the advantage of tax deduction.

The denial of a deduction of a business expense that is contrary to public policy can be seen as a "tax penalty". These statutory provisions are the reverse of tax expenditure provisions.[52] They are departures from the net income concept, which requires that business expenses be deductible in computing income in an income tax. The overriding principle of tax policy is that tax should be levied in accordance with ability to pay; this entails the consequence that only net income should be subject to tax; and this leads to the conclusion that business-related fines should be deductible. To be sure, the ability to pay principle is occasionally departed from, but it should only be departed from in pursuit of a very strong competing policy. The question is whether the policy of giving full effect to the statutes under which the fines are imposed is sufficiently strong to outweigh the ability to pay principle.

In the absence of statutory rules, the courts must balance these competing policies. In the past, the court looked at whether the expense was avoidable or whether the unlawful act was incidental to the business being carried on (see *Imperial Oil*, above). In *Day and Ross v. R.* (1976),[53] for example, while allowing the deduction of the fines, the Court stressed that the unlawful acts (the violations of weight restrictions in the trucking industry) were not intentional or "avoidable", and were not "outrageous transgressions of public policy". Similarly, in *Rolland Paper Co. v. M.N.R.* (1960),[54] the Court, in allowing the deduction of the legal expenses of defending the anti-trust prosecution, was careful to repeat a statement made by the sentencing court that the directors of the company had not been "guilty of moral turpitude or wicked intention". The implication of these dicta was, of course, that a deliberate, outrageous or morally culpable illegality would require a tax court to deny the deductibility of a fine or associated legal expenses. This was confirmed in *65302 British Columbia Ltd.*[55]

In *65302 British Columbia Ltd.*, the taxpayer intentionally exceeded the production quota allotted to it by the British Columbia Egg Marketing Board rather than purchasing additional quota. When the over-production was discovered, the taxpayer was subjected to a levy of almost $270,000 and ordered to dispose of the

---

[52]See heading 2.4, "Tax expenditures", above.

[53]Note 9, above.

[54][1960] C.T.C. 158, 60 D.T.C. 1095 (Can. Ex. Ct.) para. 15. In this case, the issue did not involve a fine. A paper company was permitted to deduct the legal expenses of defending an anti-trust prosecution. The company was convicted and fined, but apparently did not attempt to deduct the fine. The Exchequer Court held that the company's illegal trade practices were "followed for the purpose of earning income from the business", and the legal expenses of defending the practices from prosecution were deductible.

[55]Note 7, above.

excess birds.[56] The taxpayer deducted the fine as a current business expense and the Minister reassessed, disallowing the deduction on existing case law. The Tax Court allowed the deduction. The Federal Court of Appeal reversed on the ground that the deduction would undermine the purpose of the B.C. egg marketing system. The Supreme Court unanimously allowed the taxpayer's appeal, but split (5-2) on the general question of the deductibility of fines and penalties. The majority held that all fines and penalties should be deductible if they were incurred for the purpose of earning income irrespective of public policy considerations. The minority reasoned that fines and penalties should be deductible only if the deduction did not frustrate or undermine the statutory scheme under which the fine or penalty is levied. The minority classified fines and penalties into two groups: those intended to have a deterrent effect and those intended to be compensatory. Public policy doctrine would deny the deduction of the former, but not the latter. The over-quota levy fell within the latter category and was thus deductible.

In determining whether the over-quota levy was incurred for the purpose of earning income, Iacobucci J. (writing the majority decision) rejected the three existing "public policy" tests on the basis that the language of paragraph 18(1)(a) did not support them. These tests were based on the statutory language contained in Canada's *Income War Tax Act*, R.S.C. 1927, c. 97, that prohibited the deduction of expenses which were not "wholly, exclusively and necessarily laid out or expended for the purpose of earning the income". This language was amended in 1948 to broaden the scope of deductible business expenses and the current language of paragraph 18(1)(a) did not support these tests.

Iacobucci J. stated that the question of public policy should be examined in light of the appropriate approach to statutory interpretation. He agreed with the modern rule of statutory interpretation,[57] namely, "the words of an Act are to be read in their entire context and in their grammatical and ordinary sense harmoniously with the scheme of the Act, the object of the Act, and the intention of Parliament." He also noted that the Court "has often been cautious in utilizing tools of statutory interpretation in order to stray from clear and unambiguous statutory language",[58] and "attention must be paid to the fact that the Act is one of the most detailed, complex, and comprehensive statutes in our legislature inventory and courts should be reluctant to embrace unexpressed notions of policy or principle under the guise of statutory interpretation".[59]

In rejecting the government's argument, Iacobucci, J. weighed the public policy argument against the deduction of the fines and carefully balanced it against the policy and other concerns discussed above. The policy concerns included equity

---

[56]Under the relevant provision legislation, an egg producer that failed to comply with the rules and orders of the Marketing Board could also be subject to more serious monetary fines and penalties, as well as imprisonment.

[57]*65302 British Columbia Ltd.*, note 7, above, para. 50.

[58]*Ibid.*, para. 51.

[59]*Ibid.*

(the ability to pay principle), neutrality (the accurate picture of profit principle) and the burden imposed on taxpayers and the courts because of the difficulty in distinguishing between the compensatory and deterrent portion of a fine or penalty. Iacobucci J. observed that expenses incurred to earn income from an illegal business were deductible even though it undermined the policy of the criminal law.[60] He also noted that Parliament had explicitly denied certain other expenses on what appeared to have been public policy grounds (e.g., section 67.5). In the end, Iacobucci J. fell back on the separation of powers between the courts and the legislature: "it is my view that such public policy determination are better left to Parliament".[61] He concluded by stating the following:[62]

> It is conceivable that a breach could be so egregious or repulsive that the fine subsequently imposed could not be justified as being incurred for the purpose of producing income. However, such situation would likely be rare and requires no further consideration in the context of this case, especially given that Parliament itself may choose to delineate such fines and penalties, as it has with fines imposed by the *Income Tax Act*. To repeat, Parliament may well be motivated to respond promptly and comprehensively to prohibit clearly and directly the deduction of all such fines and penalties, if Parliament so chooses.

Consequently, only fines paid in respect of committing "egregious or repulsive" acts are denied a deduction. Depending on meaning of "egregious" or "repulsive", the common law public policy exception is very narrow.

Parliament enacted section 67.6 to apply to fines and penalties imposed after March 22, 2004 under a law of a country or of a political subdivision of a country (including a state, province or territory) by any person or public body that has authority to impose the fine or penalty. The prohibition does not apply to "prescribed fines and penalties".

(c) — Damages

The courts have consistently held that damages and similar payments are deductible if they were incurred for the purpose of earning income. For example, in *Imperial Oil* (1947),[63] the taxpayer was allowed to deduct a damages settlement of $526,995 which it was obliged to pay as the result of a collision between one of its ships and another ship. The Exchequer Court held that the item was deductible. It was argued for the Minister that the expenditure had been made not for "the purpose of gaining or producing income" (as stipulated by paragraph 18(1)(a)), but to discharge a legal liability. Thorson P. pointed out that that was true of every expense. The language of paragraph 18(1)(a) could not be taken literally, because an expense by itself could never directly accomplish the purpose of gaining or producing income. The issue, his lordship said, was whether the liability that made the expense necessary

---

[60] See heading 8.5(d), "Expenses of illegal businesses", below.

[61] *65302 British Columbia Ltd.*, note 7, above, para. 62.

[62] *Ibid.*, para. 69

[63] Note 16, above.

arose "as part of the operations, transactions or services by which the taxpayer earned the income". If so, then it was part of the income-earning process, and it was deductible.[64] The Court reasoned that the transportation of petroleum products was one of Imperial Oil's business operations, and the risk of collision at sea (even when caused by the negligence of an employee) was a normal hazard of those operations. Therefore, any resulting liability for damages was one of the costs of Imperial Oil's operations and was therefore deductible.

In *McNeill v. R.* (2000),[65] the taxpayer was an accountant who deliberately breached a restrictive covenant which was a non-competition agreement on the sale of his practice. He was ordered to pay damages for this breach of contract. The Federal Court of Appeal applied *65302 British Columbia Ltd.* and allowed the taxpayer a deduction for the damages. There are no specific rules to deny such deductions.

(d) — Expenses of illegal businesses

There is no doubt that the income from an illegal business, such as bootlegging, bookmaking, or prostitution, is subject to tax.[66] This is an easier question than the deductibility of fines, because by taxing illegal income the tax policy (of taxing increases in ability to pay) and the public policy (of discouraging illegal activity) work in harmony. The only possible objection to taxing illegal income would be a feeling that the state should not live off the avails of prostitution or accept money which is otherwise tainted with illegality. But the Canadian tax system (in common with those of other countries) has not been troubled by such a scrupulous morality and has been happy to accept whatever money it can lay its hands on.[67]

Once it is accepted that the revenue of an illegal business is subject to tax, there is no plausible argument for disallowing the expenses of an illegal business. To disallow expenses would be to tax a gross income figure that is more than the "profit" from the business, and section 9 only purports to tax the "profit" — the revenue net of expenses. The courts surely have no mandate to use the tax system as a vehicle to impose extra penalties on illegal activity that is already penalized by other statutes. Most of the expenses of an illegal business will in any case be perfectly legitimate in themselves, for example, rent, utilities, supplies, and equipment. Those ex-

---

[64]Accord, *Premium Iron Ores* (1966), note 17, above (legal expenses incurred in contesting United States tax assessment deductible, although directed to saving money rather than making it).

[65][2000] 2 C.T.C. 304, 2000 D.T.C. 6211 (Fed. C.A.), para. 15.

[66]*Minister of Finance v. Smith* (1926), [1927] A.C. 193 (P.C.) (bootlegging); *cf. R. v. Poynton*, [1972] C.T.C. 411, 72 D.T.C. 6329 (Ont. C.A.) (proceeds of embezzlement taxable income, although not business income).

[67]In the debate about the deductibility of fines and penalties (under headings, 8.5(a) and (b), above), it has never been doubted that, when a legitimate business commits illegal acts that enhance its revenue (disregarding weight restrictions on truck loads, or price fixing, for example), the additional revenue is taxable.

penses that are illegitimate, for example, fines, penalties, bribes or kickbacks, surely do not raise any different issue than attempts by a legal business to deduct such expenses.

Decisions on this issue are not consistent. In *M.N.R. v. Eldridge* (1964),[68] the Exchequer Court held that the taxpayer, who carried on an illegal call girl business, could deduct business expenses such as rent, legal expenses, assistance for call girls, cost of bail bonds and casual wages.[69] In contrast, the cost of 15,000 pounds of marijuana seized by the authorities was not deductible to a drug dealer.[70]

8.6 — "Reasonable" requirement

(a) — Section 67

Section 67 of the Act provides as follows:

> In computing income, no deduction shall be made in respect of an outlay or expense in respect of which any amount is otherwise deductible under this Act, except to the extent that the outlay or expense was reasonable in the circumstances.

This provision prohibits the deduction of an expense except to the extent that the expense was "reasonable in the circumstances". This provision is in subdivision f of Part I, Division B (which is a miscellaneous collection of rules relating to the computation of income), rather than subdivision b, because section 67 is applicable to deductions from income from every source, not just business and property income. However, its main application is to deductions from business and property income because the deductions from other kinds of income are more closely regulated and less susceptible of abuse.

Like paragraph 18(1)(a), section 67, on its face, appears redundant — if an expense was unreasonably large, it presumably was not incurred for the purpose of deriving income. However, it is a convenient focus for courts, seeking to restrict deductions for dual-purpose expenses (that have personal elements) or payments between non-arm's length persons (that have the potential of income shifting and tax avoidance).

(b) — Unreasonable amount attributable to personal elements

There are a number of cases in which expenses have been wholly or partially disallowed on the ground that they purchased excessively luxurious facilities for the purpose sought to be achieved. The purchase of an expensive car has attracted suc-

---

[68] [1964] C.T.C. 545, 64 D.T.C. 5338 (Ex. Ct.).

[69] The difficulties in this case were not caused by the deductibility of expenses, but the poor record-keeping (apparently common in this line of business) and hence inadequate proof of expenses rather than any issue of principle. Those expenses that could be proved were allowed.

[70] *Neeb v. R.* (1997), 97 D.T.C. 895 (T.C.C.).

cessful challenge on this ground,[71] as have extravagant entertainment expenses[72] and travelling expenses.[73]

An unusual case is *No. 511 v. M.N.R.* (1958),[74] in which the taxpayer, a lumber company, sought to deduct the cost of sponsoring a baseball team. The Tax Appeal Board accepted that this was a legitimate and deductible form of advertising, but held that the actual expense of $22,500 was too high because it was more than half of the company's profits. The Board held that $5,000 would be the cost of a reasonable advertising campaign using newspaper and radio advertisements and the Board allowed a deduction of $5,000. Underlying this decision is probably an unexpressed factual judgment that the sponsorship of the baseball team was essentially a hobby for the principal shareholder of the taxpayer-corporation, so that the expense was only partially laid out for a business purpose. In this case, and in the luxury cases, section 67 is a vehicle by which an element of personal consumption is disallowed or stripped from an otherwise legitimate business expense. This could be done without recourse to section 67, since section 9, paragraphs 18(1)(a) and (h) all prohibit the deduction of non-business expenditures, but section 67 is a convenient tool.

(c) — Unreasonable amount in non-arm's length payments

Section 67 has been applied to payments of management fees, rents or salaries to non-arm's length parties.[75] A good example is *Mulder Bros. v. M.N.R.* (1967).[76] In that case, a corporation controlled by two brothers, A and B, paid salaries as follows: Brother A, $20,000; Brother B, $13,000; Brother B's wife, $13,000. All three persons genuinely worked as employees of the corporation, but the Minister took the view that the wife's services were only worth $6,000. In his opinion, the total salary of $26,000 paid to the B family had been divided between B and B's wife to produce the most favourable income-split rather than to reward their actual contributions of work. The Minister therefore used section 67 to reduce the company's tax deduction for the wife's salary to $6,000. The Tax Appeal Board raised the reasonable figure to $8,500, still disallowing the balance.[77]

---

[71]E.g., *Kent and Co. v. M.N.R.*, [1971] Tax A.B.C. 1158 (T.A.B.).

[72]E.g., *Chabot v. M.N.R.* (1961), 61 D.T.C. 193, 26 Tax A.B.C. 204 (T.A.B.).

[73]E.g., *No. 589 v. M.N.R.* (1958), 59 D.T.C. 41, 21 Tax A.B.C. 153 (T.A.B.).

[74]58 D.T.C. 307, 19 Tax A.B.C. 248 (T.A.B.).

[75]Related persons are deemed by s. 251(1) not to deal each other at arm's length, and thus are non-arm's length persons to each other. Individuals are related to each other by reason of blood, marriage, or adoption (s. 251(2)).

[76]67 D.T.C. 475, [1967] Tax A.B.C. 761 (T.A.B.).

[77]See also *Maduke Foods Ltd. v. R.*, [1989] 2 C.T.C. 284, 89 D.T.C. 5458 (Fed. T.D.), where the Court reduced a taxpayer's deduction for salaries paid to a shareholder's spouse and two children.

While corporate salaries have attracted the most frequent applications of section 67, other non-arm's-length payments are also vulnerable. For example, a dentist who sought to deduct $12,000 as rent for premises owned by his wife was limited to $5,000,[78] although a lawyer who sought to deduct $1,000 per month as a management fee to a corporation owned by himself and his wife successfully resisted an attack based on section 67.[79]

What constitutes "reasonable in the circumstances"? In *Costigane v. R.* (2003)[80] the Court held that the fees paid by a dentist to his family trust to do his bookkeeping were too high, and allowed a deduction for a lower amount based on a 15 percent mark-up on the cost of the services. In *Aessie v. R.* (2004),[81] on the other hand, an accountant with gross revenue of $55,000 was allowed to deduct management fees of $34,500 paid to his wife's management company for administrative services (including reception, typing, record keeping and other administrative activities). The Court found that the arrangement was "a common and reasonable business deal".

The only effect of section 67 is to disallow the deduction of an unreasonable expense to the extent that it is unreasonable. This has the effect of increasing the income of the payer. Section 67 says nothing however about the tax liability of the payee (recipient).[82]

8.7 — Timing of deductions

(a) — Current expenses vs. capital expenditures

The timing of the deduction for an expense is determined by the classification of the expense as current or capital. As explained above, the timing question is closely tied to the ability to pay principle and the "accurate picture" of profit doctrine which both require that expenses are deductible only if their value or benefits are realized or consumed in the year. This, in turn, requires a distinction between two major types of expenses: (a) expenses that bring to a business a value or benefit that is consumed in the year in which the expense is incurred (generally current ex-

[78] *Cohen v. M.N.R.* (1963), 63 D.T.C. 237, 31 Tax A.B.C. 216 (T.A.B.).

[79] *Shulman v. M.N.R.*, [1961] C.T.C. 385, 61 D.T.C. 1213 (Ex. Ct.); affirmed (1962), 62 D.T.C. 1166 (S.C.C.).

[80] [2003] 3 C.T.C. 2087, 2003 D.T.C. 254 (T.C.C. [General Procedure]).

[81] [2004] 4 C.T.C. 2159, 2004 TCC 421 (T.C.C. [Informal Procedure]).

[82] The payee must recognize the full amount of the payment received for tax purposes. In the *Mulder* case, note 76, above, the wife would have to report as income her full $13,000 salary, even though $4,500 of it had been denied to the employer as a deduction. The unreasonable portion of the salary would therefore be taxed twice. On the other hand, B would only have to report his salary of $13,000, even though it had in effect been found to be artificially low. Arguably, s. 56(2) could also be used to attribute the excess salary received by B's wife to B for tax purposes (see heading 13.9(a), "Indirect payment", below) but the courts have never been asked to rule on the issue. It is the CRA's view that both provisions could be applied to the same situation (see CRA, Technical Interpretation, No. 7-3861, July 1989).

penses); and (b) expenses that bring to the business an enduring value or benefit that is not consumed or realized in the year in which the expense is incurred (capital expenditures).[83] In between are expenses whose value or benefits last longer than a year, but are not as enduring in value as capital expenditures or are not attached to a particular item. These include the so-called running expenses and prepaid expenses.

Only current expenditures incurred for income-earning purposes are fully deductible. If an expenditure were characterized as a capital expenditure, paragraph 18(1)(b) would deny its deduction. As is explained in the next chapter, in the case of depreciable or wasting assets, capital expenditures incurred for income-earning purposes are deductible under paragraphs 20(1)(a) or (b), but only on an amortization basis. In effect, the deduction each year is limited to the portion of the cost in acquiring a "wasting" or "depreciable" asset that was "wasted away" during the year. In the case of non-wasting assets, the cost of acquisition is recognized as part of the cost base under the capital gains rules.

There are no statutory rules distinguishing between the different types of expenses. One significant factor affecting the development of the jurisprudence on the timing question is the fact that, unlike GAAP which provides rules for the recognition of all types of expenses, there are significant gaps in the statutory provisions dealing with current and capital expenditures. Some expenditures for long term benefits are not covered by the capital cost allowance rules under paragraph 20(1)(a) or the cumulative eligible capital amount deduction under paragraph 20(1)(b).[84] As a result, if the court applied judicial doctrines to find such an expense as a current expense, the taxpayer could claim an upfront deduction for a benefit with a lifetime of many years, clearly an inappropriate result. But if the court found the expense was a capital expenditure and it turned out *not* to be one that was deductible in accordance with paragraph 20(1)(a) or (b), the expense would *never* be recognized for tax purposes, clearly an equally inappropriate result. Faced with these options, a court had to choose between what it saw as the lesser of two evils, yielding considerable difficulty in reconciling the case law.

(b) — Current expenses

Current expenses are deductible when they are incurred: paragraph 18(1)(a) precludes a deduction if the amount cannot properly be described as an "expense in-

---

[83]There is, however, no statutory definition of what constitutes an expense on "capital account". Rather than use GAAP, the courts have relied on other sources, particularly trust law notions, to determine what is a capital expense and what is a current expense. Trust law notions were developed for very different purposes, namely to decide which of two competing classes of beneficiaries of a trust — the life or income beneficiaries or the remainder or capital beneficiaries — should bear the cost of expenses incurred by a trust and the use of trust law doctrines to characterize expenses for tax purposes has led to many problems.

[84]This is the deduction for the amortization of intangible assets, such as purchased goodwill or certain customer lists. It did not even exist before 1972.

curred". Neither the word "expense" nor the word "incurred" is defined in the Act. The case law principle is that an expense is incurred for tax purposes when the taxpayer has a clear legal obligation to pay the amount in question. In other words, the amount is payable even though payment may not be due until some time in the future.[85] Contingent liabilities often give rise to difficulties in determining whether an expense has incurred.

(i) — "Expense incurred"

In absence of a statutory definition, the term expense has been interpreted by the courts to be an obligation to pay a sum of money. For example, Pratte J. defined the term in *R. v. Burnco Industries Ltd. et al.* (1984)[86] as follows:

> . . . an expense, within the meaning of paragraph 18(1)(a) of the *Income Tax Act*, is an obligation to pay a sum of money. An expense cannot be said to be incurred by a taxpayer who is under no obligation to pay money to anyone. . . . [A]n obligation to do something which may in the future entail the necessity of paying money is not an expense.

The principle that a cost or expense is incurred only when the taxpayer has a clear legal, though not necessarily immediate, obligation to pay an amount is derived primarily from *J.L. Guay Ltée v. M.N.R.* (1971).[87] This case involved the deduction by a general contractor of construction holdbacks that were not payable until an architect's certificate was issued. The Court deferred the deduction of holdbacks until the year in which the architect's certificate was issued. The main reason cited by the Court was that there was an element of contingency as to the amount, if any, that would eventually be paid to the subcontractors. The Court indicated that the taxpayer was under no obligation to pay the amount of the holdbacks to the subcontractors until the architect's certificate was issued. Thus, it was possible that such amounts would never be paid. In other words, the liability itself, and not just its quantum, was contingent or conditional upon the issuance of the architect's certificate.

---

[85] This reflects the principle of realization: on the inclusion side, amounts are included in income when they become receivable; on the deduction side, amounts are deductible when they become payable.

[86] [1984] C.T.C. 337, 84 D.T.C. 6348 (Fed. C.A.). In this case, the taxpayer operated a gravel pit and was required to backfill areas excavated in the course of the year. The taxpayer sought to deduct an amount in computing its income for its 1974 taxation year as the estimated future cost of backfilling the gravel pit. The deduction was disallowed.

[87] [1971] C.T.C. 686, 71 D.T.C. 5423 (Fed. T.D.); affirmed [1973] C.T.C. 506, 73 D.T.C. 5373 (Fed. C.A.); affirmed [1975] C.T.C. 97, 75 D.T.C. 5094 (S.C.C.). The decision was affirmed without reasons by both the Federal Court of Appeal and the Supreme Court of Canada.

In general, the time when a payment becomes payable is the converse of when the payment becomes receivable to the payee.[88] The cost of services becomes payable when the services are rendered, and the cost of property becomes payable when the property is delivered. Thus, the time when the payment is actually made is largely irrelevant. For example, the salary for the month of December of year 1 is payable to the employee at the end of the month, even if the salary is not paid until January of year 2. Similarly, payroll taxes relating to salaries earned and vacation benefits relating to salaries earned but not paid in the year were held incurred in the year, and thus deductible.[89] However, as indicated in *Guay Ltee*, a contingent liability is not deductible. The deduction of contingent liabilities is also denied statutorily by paragraph 18(1)(e).

(ii) — Contingent liabilities

The often-quoted definition of "contingent liability" was articulated by Lord Guest in *Winter et al. v. IRC* (1961):[90]

> I should define a contingency as an event which may or may not occur and a contingent liability as a liability which depends for its existence upon an event which may or may not happen.

As Rothstein, J. stated in *Canada v. McLarty*:[91]

> The focus is therefore on two particular types of uncertainty: 1) whether an event may or may not occur; and 2) whether a liability depends for its existence upon whether that event may or may not happen.

In determining whether a legal obligation is contingent at a particular point in time, the correct question to ask is "whether the legal obligation has come into existence at that time, or whether no obligation will come into existence until the occurrence of an event that may not occur".[92] For example, an obligation to pay an amount equal to a percentage of earned revenues is a contingent obligation unless the reve-

---

[88]The result in *J.L. Guay Ltée, ibid.*, is the converse of the *M.N.R. v. Colford Contracting Co. Ltd.*, 60 D.T.C. 1131, [1960] C.T.C. 178 (Ex. Ct.); affirmed [1962] C.T.C. 546, 62 D.T.C. 1338 (S.C.C.). For a discussion of the latter case, see heading 7.3(b)(ii), "Receivable", above.

[89]In *Federation des caisses populaires Desjardins de Montreal et de l'Ouest du Quebec v. R.* (2001), [2002] 2 C.T.C. 1, 2001 D.T.C. 5173 (Fed. C.A.), the Court held an amount accrued for payroll taxes and benefits relating to vacation pay earned in the year was deductible in the year under s. 18(1)(a) since the legal obligation to pay the amount was incurred in the year. See also *Provigo Distributions Inc. v. R.* (2000), 2000 D.T.C. 2112, 33 C.C.L.I. (3d) 133 (T.C.C.); and *Wawang*, note 92, below.

[90](1961), [1963] A.C. 235 (H.L.).

[91]2008 SCC 26, para. 17

[92]*Wawang Forest Products Ltd. v. R.*, [1999] 2 C.T.C. 2966, 99 D.T.C. 759 (T.C.C.); reversed [2001] 2 C.T.C. 233, 2001 D.T.C. 5212 (Fed C.A.).

nues are earned.[93] Similarly, an obligation to pay a management bonus if the money is available is a contingent obligation unless the money is available.[94]

The *Canada v. McLarty* (2009) case[95] looks at whether a creditor's limited recourse can make an otherwise absolute liability contingent.[96] The taxpayer acquired a joint venture interest in seismic data from an oil and gas exploration and development corporation (Compton) for a cash payment of $15,000 and a non-recourse interest-bearing promissory note of $85,000. The terms of the note were as follows: (1) the principal and interest were initially to be paid from 60% of the cash flows from future sales or licensing of the data and from 20% of the production cash flow generated from petroleum rights from the drilling programs; and (2) if any principal or interest remained outstanding at the maturity date, the assets would be sold and 60% of the proceeds would be applied against the unpaid balance of the note, with the balance of the note forgiven. The taxpayer added $100,000 to his Canadian Exploration Expense (CEE) pool and deducted CEE of $81,655 in 1992 and $14,854 in 1994. The Minister reassessed the taxpayer on the basis that the seismic data had a fair market value of $32,182, not $100,000. Rothstein, J., writing for the majority of the Court and referring to *Mandel v. R.*,[97] found that if the cash flows had been the only recourse, the liability would have been contingent since these cash flows were events that may or may not happen. However, because the terms of the note also provided for additional security and made the result similar to what happens in a mortgage foreclosure, the debt was not contingent.[98] The

[93]*Mandel v. R.*, [1978] C.T.C. 780, 78 D.T.C. 6518 (Fed. C.A.); affirmed [1980] C.T.C. 130, 80 D.T.C. 6148 (S.C.C.).

[94]*R. v. Ken and Ray's Collins Bay Supermarket*, [1975] C.T.C. 504, 75 D.T.C. 5346 (Fed. T.D.); affirmed without written reasons (1977), [1978] C.T.C. xvi (Fed. C.A.); leave to appeal refused [1978] 1 S.C.R. ix (S.C.C.).

[95]Note 91, above.

[96]As the court explained, "In the context of debt, recourse means that the creditor has a right to repayment of a loan from the borrower, not just from the collateral that secured the loan. By contrast, non-recourse or limited recourse debt limits the creditor to recovery of specified security. The creditor is not entitled to seek repayment from the borrower should the proceeds from the disposition of the security be less than the total indebtedness." *McLarty*, note 91, above, para. 29.

[97]Note 93, above.

[98]In *Mandel*, *ibid*, the only conditions upon which the amount owing was to be repaid were the cash flows: there was no additional security as there was in *McLarty* note 91, above. In *Global Communications Ltd. v. The Queen*, 99 DTC 5377, the taxpayer had additional but the decision, which relied on *Mandel*, was short. According to Rothstein J. in *McLarty*, "it does not appear that in Global the court took account of the fact that on maturity of the note there was recourse to the asset pledged as security for repayment . . . and is not authoritative in circumstances such as in the case now before this Court."

minority found the liability to be contingent because both events (the cash flows and the sale) were events that may or may not happen.[99]

In *Canadian Pacific Limited v. M.N.R.* (1998)[100] the taxpayer was required by the *Workers' Compensation Act* (Ontario) to pay benefits to its workers and their dependents. At the time of each Workers' Compensation award, the taxpayer estimated the entire amounts payable based on the payee's life expectancy, added the entire amount to its Deferred Liabilities Account and deducted the entire amount for tax purposes in the year. As payments were made, they were deducted against the taxpayer's Deferred Liabilities Account and, if no further payment was required (because of the payee's death), the excess amount accrued would be included in the taxpayer's income in that year. On assessment, the Minister of Revenue (Ontario) denied the deduction for the addition to the Deferred Liabilities Account on the basis it was a contingent liability. The taxpayer appealed to Ontario Court (General Division), which dismissed the appeal. The taxpayer then appealed to the Court of Appeal for Ontario which allowed the appeal, concluding that the Deferred Liabilities Account was not a contingent account within the meaning of paragraph 18(1)(e) because of an existing statutory liability under the *Workers' Compensation Act* that was fixed and absolute. The Court stated:[101]

> [W]here a taxpayer has incurred a liability in a taxation year, and has placed money into an account to enable it to fulfill the liability, uncertainties surrounding the amount which will ultimately be paid will not per se result in the liabilities being classed as contingent, nor the account being classed as a contingent account.

The Court also found the deduction of the amounts was consistent with well-accepted business principles and reflected a "more accurate picture" of income.

Why is this a more accurate picture of income? There is no legal liability for this "amount". How can this amount be treated as an "expense" "incurred" or become "payable" for tax law purposes? Why does this reduce a taxpayer's ability to pay tax in the year? How can a current deduction provide a more accurate picture of

---

[99] Although the use of limited recourse debt (for purposes other than tax schemes) is not common in Canada, it is used by commercial real estate lenders if the valuation of the rental cash flows and the property are sufficient security. The problem in McLarty was not the legal obligation but the valuation. If the valuation of the CEE was truly $100,000, would a lender have accepted the security that Compton accepted (20% or 60% of certain cash flows and 60% of the proceeds on the sale of the property)? In absence of a legislative response, if the government wants to attack tax schemes using limited recourse debt in court, it must attack the valuation. As Rothstein J. said:

> What is at the root of the Minister's difficulty in this case is that the Minister believes the price of the asset McLarty acquired was overvalued and that the data, as the only collateral security, was insufficient to cover repayment of the note. . . .. There are remedies for the Minister where assets are overvalued solely to obtain a tax advantage. Trying to characterize the loan portion of the purchase price as contingent in this case was not one of them. (See note 91, above, para. 34.)

[100] [2000] 2 C.T.C. 331, 99 D.T.C. 5286 (Ont. C.A.).

[101] *Ibid.*, para. 43.

income than a deduction for the payment in the year when it is actually made to the worker?[102]

Even if the full amount of the contingent liability is eventually payable, the result of full current deduction of a future liability is that a taxpayer employer in a situation like the taxpayer in *Canadian Pacific* could be better off than if the accident never occurred because of the time of value arising from the tax savings that has resulted from the deduction. Let's use a simple illustration. Assume that the taxpayer is required to pay an injured worker $504,000 in 42 equal, annual instalments of $12,000. Further assume the rate of interest is 6 percent. The present value of the total liability is $182,694: i.e., the present value of 42 payments of $12,000 using a discount rate of 6%. If the taxpayer is taxed at the rate of 50% and is able to deduct the $504,000 currently, the present value of the reduction in taxes at the end of the year is $237,736; i.e., the present value of $252,000 received at the end of the year using a discount rate of 6%. Since the present value of the payments is less than the present value of the tax refund, the taxpayer is better off than if the accident never occurred by $55,041: i.e., $237,736 - $182,694.

In a more recent decision, *General Motors of Canada Ltd. v. R.* (2004),[103] the Federal Court of Appeal upheld an earlier Tax Court of Canada decision[104] denying the taxpayer's deduction for accruals relating to a special fund under its collective agreement on the basis that the accruals were in respect of a contingent liability. The facts are not that much different than *Canadian Pacific*. The accruals were pursuant to a formula in the collective agreement (based on $2 per hour of overtime in excess of a certain amount) and were to be used for specified programs "if needed" with excess was to be carried over into the next collective agreement. The court concluded that the amount was contingent because it depended on the occurrence of an event (the use of funds for specific programs) that might not occur.

(iii) — Contested or unincurred liabilities

In order to accurately compute income of a given year, the taxpayer's liability for items of indebtedness deducted cannot be contingent or contested. If a taxpayer is strenuously contesting liability in the courts, the taxpayer cannot deduct the contested amount. The taxpayer must await litigation or settlement and claim a deduction only for the taxation year in which the liability is finally adjudicated or settled.

---

[102]What is more amazing is that the CRA seemed to have accepted this decision and applied it to similar accruals such as unredeemed reward points. See the reference to *Canadian Pacific Limited v. M.N.R.*, note 100, above, in "Reward Points in Promo. Program, October 13, 2000," *Window On Canadian Tax Commentary Document Number 2000-0034027.*

[103][2005] 1 C.T.C. 56, 2004 D.T.C. 6716 (F.C.A.); leave to appeal refused (2005), 2005 CarswellNat 1376 (S.C.C.). Leave to appeal to the Supreme Court of Canada has been denied.

[104]*General Motors of Canada Ltd. v. R.* (2003), [2004] 1 C.T.C. 2999, 2003 D.T.C. 1533 (T.C.C. [General Procedure]); affirmed (2004), [2005] 1 C.T.C. 56, 2004 D.T.C. 6716 (F.C.A.); leave to appeal refused (2005), 2005 CarswellNat 1376 (S.C.C.).

This issue often arises in cases determining whether damages are deductible in the year in which the event occurred or in the year in which the damages payment is finally determined. The courts have held that it is the latter because the taxpayer's liability to pay damages is ascertained and becomes an absolute and unconditional obligation only when the taxpayer's liability for damages and the quantum of damages are finally ascertained by the court or binding settlement between the parties.[105]

Similarly, estimated liabilities are not deductible. The taxpayer in *Northwood Pulp and Timber Ltd. v. R.* (1998)[106] had a statutory obligation to do reforestation work after logging. The taxpayer sought to deduct the estimated costs of reforestation before the work was done. The deduction was denied for the reason that the expenses had not been incurred.

(c) — Running expenses

The term "running expense" is not an accounting term: it is an invention of Anglo-Canadian income tax law. On the basis of the case law, "running expenses" can be defined as expenses which are not "related to any particular item of revenue"[107] but relate to "the running of the business as a whole".[108] The benefits of running expenses generally extend beyond the current year. In *Vallambrosa Rubber Co. v. Farmer* (1910),[109] the Court used a milk and cow analogy to describe running expenses and explain why they should be fully deductible in the year in which they are incurred:[110]

> Supposing a man conducted a milk business, it really comes to the limits of absurdity to suppose that he would not be allowed to charge for the keep of one of his cows because at a particular time of the year, towards the end of the year of assessment, that cow was not in milk, and therefore the profit which he was going to get from the cow would be outside the year of assessment. . . .

The courts have said that the matching principle does not apply to running expenses "even though the deduction of a particularly heavy item of running expense in the year in which it is paid will distort the income for that particular year".[111] For

---

[105] *McNeill*, note 65 above, para. 19.

[106] [1999] 2 C.T.C. 53, 98 D.T.C. 6640 (Fed. C.A.); leave to appeal refused (1999), 242 N.R. 400 (note) (S.C.C.).

[107] In *Oxford Shopping Centres v. R.* (1979), [1980] C.T.C. 7 18, 79 D.T.C. 5458 5466 (Fed. T.D.); affirmed [1981] C.T.C. 128, 81 D.T.C. 5065 (Fed. C.A.), Thurlow A.C.J. referred to a running expense as an "expense that is not referable or related to any particular item of revenue".

[108] In *Naval Colliery Co. v. Commissioners of Inland Revenue* (1928), 12 T.C. 1017 1027 (H.L.), Rowlatt J. defined a "running expense" as an "expenditure incurred on the running of the business as a whole in each year".

[109] 5 T.C. 529 (Sess. Ct.).

[110] *Ibid.*, at 535.

[111] *Oxford Shopping Centres*, note 107, above, at para. 40.

example, in *Oxford Shopping Centres v. R.* (1979),[112] the taxpayer-developer paid a municipality $490,050 for improvements to roadways near one of the taxpayer's shopping centres. The taxpayer deducted that amount in full in computing its income for tax purposes for 1973, but deferred the amount and amortized it over 15 years for accounting purposes. The first line of argument of the Minister was that the expenditure was on account of capital. The second line of argument was that the expenditure, if current, had to be deferred and amortized. In deciding in favour of the taxpayer, the Federal Court of Appeal held that the expenditure was not on account of capital and that, because the amount was a running expense that "is not referable or related to any particular item of revenue", it could be deducted in full in 1973.

In *Canderel*,[113] as noted earlier, tenant inducement payments were held to be running expenses. The taxpayer was in the business of managing and developing commercial real estate properties and, in 1986, had paid tenants amounts totalling $1,208,369 as inducements to enter into leases. The taxpayer deducted the full amount of these payments in computing its income for tax purposes for 1986. The Minister disallowed the amount and recomputed the deduction as $69,274 by amortizing the payments over the initial term of the related leases. In allowing the taxpayer's appeal, the Supreme Court of Canada held that the tenant inducement payments were running expenses because they "were not referable to any particular items of income, i.e., they cannot be correlated directly, or at least not principally, with the rents generated by the leases which they induced".[114] Therefore *Canderel* could deduct the payments for tax purposes in the year that they were made, even though the payments were amortized for accounting purposes.

The decision in *Canderel* reaffirms the legal principle that running expenses are fully deductible in the year incurred. It also illustrates how difficult it is to determine whether an expenditure is a running expense. The question is whether the expenditure relates to the taxpayer's business as a whole or to a particular revenue stream. If it is principally related to a specific source of revenue, then it must be amortized over the period during which the revenue is received. At first blush, it may seem clear cut that a tenant inducement payment is principally related to a specific stream of income because each payment is for a specific lease. However, the Supreme Court of Canada in *Canderel* found that the inducement payments were made primarily to achieve other benefits: by getting tenants to enter into leases, *Canderel* was able to generate income in the current year, to satisfy the conditions of its financing arrangements and obtain further financing, and to maintain its reputation and market position.

---

[112] *Ibid.*

[113] Note 6, above. See *Toronto College Park v. R.*, [1998] 1 S.C.R. 183, [1998] 2 C.T.C. 78, 98 D.T.C. 6088 (S.C.C.) which followed *Canderel*.

[114] *Canderel*, *ibid.*, para. 65.

(d) — Prepaid expenses

A "prepaid expense" is generally an expense paid in respect of services or goods to be received in a future year. Examples are rent or municipal taxes paid in advance of the period to which they relate, insurance premiums on multi-year policies, and expenditures on promotional material (catalogues, brochures, etc.) to be used in a future year.

Prima facie, prepaid expenses appear to be a type of capital expense, at least where the benefit has a life extending into the following taxation year.[115] But the consequence of this definition would be that paragraph 18(1)(b) would prohibit the deduction of every prepaid expense, except in accordance with the amortization rules governing depreciable property and eligible capital expenditures. On the other hand, prepaid expenses are not current expenses as they generate a benefit in future years. Therefore, in principle, these expenses should be recognized over the period of years in which their benefit is realized.

Under the accrual method of accounting, prepaid expenses are not fully deductible from income in the year of payment. The portion of the expense that applies to the current accounting year is recognized as an expense of that year. The unused balance of the payment is recognized as an expense of the following year.[116]

The accounting treatment of prepaid expense is generally accepted for tax purposes. Subsection 18(9) expressly stipulates that certain categories of prepaid expenses must not be deducted in full in the year of payment, and must be deducted in the years to which they relate. The stipulated categories of prepaid expenses are payments for future services, interest, taxes, rent, royalties, and insurance. It is not clear why subsection 18(9) is limited to those categories of prepayments. The CRA takes the view that this provision was "enacted for greater certainty", and, although it does not cover all categories of prepaid expenses, there is a general requirement that "the accounting for these expenses for income tax purposes should be in accordance with generally accepted accounting principles which would, in most cases, require that the expenses be matched to the year in which the benefit is to be derived".[117]

---

[115]Most "capital expenditures" are "assets" for accounting purposes. A "prepaid expense" creates an asset for accounting purposes, although the asset may be short-lived. For example, if a tenant (who is a business proprietor) pays one month's rent in advance for business premises, the tenant acquires an asset, namely, the right to occupy the rented premises for one month. Yet the rent is obviously an expense that is fully deductible from income under the accrual method of accounting and for tax purposes under section 9. If the tenant pays two years' rent in advance, then the tenant acquires a similar asset, namely, the right to occupy the rented premises for two years.

[116]This is accomplished by the accounting procedure of deferral. At the end of the first year, the unused part of the prepaid rent will be deferred (held back) and will appear on the tenant's balance sheet as an asset.

[117]Interpretation Bulletin IT-417R2, "Prepaid expenses and deferred charges", (1997), summary.

Where subsection 18(9) does not apply to an expenditure because it is not for future services, the courts appear to allow the taxpayer the flexibility of deducting the expense either in the year in which it is incurred or over the period of years to which it reasonably relates in accordance with the matching principle and the accurate picture of profit principle. In *M.N.R. v. Tower Investment* (1972),[118] the taxpayer sought to defer and deduct over a three-year period the cost of an advertising campaign incurred in the current year. The purpose of the advertising campaign was to find tenants for 24 apartment buildings built by the taxpayer. The taxpayer in its own accounts only deducted a small portion of the advertising expenditure in year one when rental income was low and wrote off the rest of the expenditure in years two and three when the apartments were fully rented. The taxpayer sought to treat the expenditure in the same way for tax purposes. The Minister took the position that expenditure had to be deducted from income for tax purposes in year one — the year in which it was actually incurred. The Federal Court agreed with the taxpayer that the advertising expenditures "were not current expenditures in the normal sense. They were laid out to bring in income not only for the year they were made but for future years."[119]

In *Tower Investment*, the Minister argued that the advertising expenditures had to be deducted in the year in which they were made, and the taxpayer argued that they should be spread over several years. In most cases, of course, the taxpayer will prefer an immediate deduction for tax purposes of costs which have been deferred for accounting purposes. The taxpayer did this, for example, in *Canderel,* and won.[120]

(e) — Reserves

(i) — Special rules

The terms "reserve" and "contingency" are very similar. The ordinary meaning of "reserve" is to "set aside" an amount for the future. The most commonly encountered accounting reserve is for deferred taxes.[121] This expense sets aside an addi-

---

[118][1972] C.T.C. 182, 72 D.T.C. 6161 (Fed. T.D.).

[119]*Ibid.*, para. 23.

[120]In contrast, the taxpayer in *Neonex International v. R.*, [1978] C.T.C. 485, 78 D.T.C. 6339 (Fed. C.A.). claimed for tax purposes the immediate deduction of expenditures incurred in the manufacture of signs that were sold in a future accounting period. The taxpayer deferred the expenditures for accounting purposes. The Minister disallowed the deduction. The disallowance of the deduction was upheld by the Federal Court of Appeal, with Urie J. commenting that the taxpayer's profit "would not be portrayed fairly or accurately if it were permitted to adopt this method [immediate deduction] for tax purposes" (para. 41).

[121]Accountants consider this reserve to be a "liability". A corporation's deferred tax "liability" is the additional tax that would be payable if all assets were sold and all liabilities were settled at the amounts recorded on its financial statements. In other words, if the tax cost of a corporation's net assets is less than that accounting cost, there will be a deferred tax liability equal to that amount multiplied by the current tax rate. Each year, this liability is adjusted for

tional amount of income tax expense when accounting income is greater than taxable income. The purpose of the reserve is to better match the tax expense to the accounting income. Because a reserve is a not a legal liability, an increase in a reserve is not an "expense incurred" within the meaning of paragraph 18(1)(a). The Act generally prohibits the deduction of liabilities that are merely contingent, or of "reserves" to provide for expected future liabilities (paragraph 18(1)(e)). A number of reserves are, however, specifically authorized by the Act. They include:

- Reserve for doubtful debts (paragraph 20(1)(l));
- Reserve for unearned amounts (paragraph 20(1)(m));
- Reserve for deferred payments (paragraph 20(1)(n)).[122]

Technically, these reserve deductions deviate from the general principle on timing of deductions. However, they do reflect the ability to pay principle and "accurate picture" of income principle by taxing income when it is economically realized. For example, under the realization principle encompassed in subsection 9(1) or paragraph 12(1)(b), amounts receivable from goods sold or services rendered must be included in computing income, irrespective of whether the amounts are due or paid. When an account receivable becomes doubtful, the amount included may be less than the amount actually realized by the taxpayer. The reserve for doubtful debts represents attempts to reduce the value of an account receivable to the amount likely to be realized. Similarly, when the amounts receivable become due over a period of years (i.e., in instalment sales), the reserve for deferred payments under paragraph 20(1)(n) apportions the income realized over the period during which the proceeds of sale are received. As discussed in the previous chapter, paragraph 12(1)(a) includes unearned income (amounts for goods not yet delivered and services not yet rendered). The reserve for unearned income defers the recognition of income to the year in which the income is realized from the delivery of goods or rendering services. The combination of paragraphs 12(1)(a) and 20(1)(m) reflects the realization principle.

(ii) — Doubtful debts reserve and bad debt writeoffs

Paragraph 20(1)(l) permits a deduction in computing income from a business or property of "a reasonable amount as a reserve for . . . doubtful debts" that have

---

differences arising in the year: e.g., because the rates used to determine the capital cost deduction under s. 20(1)(a) are greater than the accounting depreciation rates or because the tax rate changes. See *CICA Handbook*, section 3465 and CICA Handbook, Part I International Accounting Standard (IAS) 12.

[122]Other reserves allowed for tax include: (a) reserve for loan guarantees of a financial institution (s. 20(1)(l.1)); (b) manufacturer's warranty reserve for amounts paid or payable to an insurer to insure liability under warranty agreement (s. 20(1)(m.1)); and (c) reserve for quadrennial survey with respect to ships (s. 20(1)(o)). Taxpayers may record an uninsured warranty reserve as a liability on their financial statements but no deduction is not allowed for tax purposes under s. 20.

been previously included in computing income or that have arisen from loans made in the ordinary course of a money-lending business.

The term "doubtful debt" is undefined in the Act. It "can mean only what it says — the debt is owing and possible of collection, but that possibility is not sufficiently certain in the mind of the taxpayer that he wishes to be placed in the disadvantageous position of having to pay income tax thereon before that possibility has become more of a certainty".[123] If there is a reasonable doubt that an account receivable is not collectible, it is a doubtful debt.[124]

Only a "reasonable amount" of the doubtful debt is deductible under paragraph 20(1)(l). The reasonable amount is generally calculated on an estimate as to what percentage of a doubtful debt will probably not be collected.[125] The reserve under paragraph 20(1)(l) must be added back to income under paragraph 12(1)(d) in the following year. If the debt remains doubtful, another reserve can be deducted. Eventually, when the debt becomes "bad", a deduction is permitted by paragraph 20(1)(p).[126]

---

[123] *Highfield Corporation Ltd. v. M.N.R.*, [1982] C.T.C. 2812 2828, 82 D.T.C. 1835 1847 (T.A.B.). See also *Copley Noyes & Randall Ltd. v. R.*, [1991] 1 C.T.C. 541, 91 D.T.C. 5291 (Fed. T.D.), para. 30.

[124] The case law with respect to the doubtful debt reserve seems to leave with the taxpayer a great degree of flexibility in using business judgement with regard to the inclusion amounts in such a reserve. However, there are some objective factors that the courts have looked at in determining whether a debt is reasonably doubtful: the age of the overdue account, although delay in payment alone is not a sufficient factor; the history of the account; the financial position of the debtor; any increase or decrease in the debtor's total sales; the taxpayer's past bad debt experience; and the general business condition in the country and the business condition in the particularly locality. See *No. 81 v. M.N.R.* (1953), 8 Tax A.B.C. 82, 53 D.T.C. 98 104 (T.A.B.).

[125] Interpretation Bulletin, IT-442R, "Bad Debts and Reserve for Doubtful Debts," (1991), para. 24, stated: "This calculation should preferably be based on the taxpayer's past history of bad debts, the experience in the industry if that information is available, general and local economic conditions, costs of collection, etc. This procedure may result in a reserve being calculated as a percentage of the total amount of the doubtful debts or a series of percentages relating to an age-analysis of those debts. However, a reserve that is merely based on a percentage of all debts, whether doubtful or not, a percentage of gross sales or some similar calculation is not considered to be a reserve determined on a reasonable basis as required by s. 20(1)(l)(i). However, a reserve for doubtful debts that is less than the amount that could have been claimed in accordance with a determination such as that described above will be viewed as a reasonable amount".

[126] There is no requirement that a s. 20(1)(p) amount be added back in the following year. However, if the "bad" debt is actually collected, the amount is included in income under s. 12(1)(i).

If the taxpayer's business is not in the business of lending money, a bad debt on a loan or advance[127] to another corporation is normally a capital loss or business investment loss recognized under section 50 of the Act.[128] The loss on the payment of a loan guarantee is also normally a capital loss.[129] However, if the payment under the guarantee[130] or the advance[131] or loan is made for income producing purposes related to the taxpayer's own business, the loss will be on account of income and fully deductible.

(iii) — Deferred payments reserve

Paragraph 20(1)(n) effectively postpones the realization of income when the payment of the purchase price for a property sold is deferred to a future year. It provides:

> Where an amount included in computing a taxpayer's income from the business for the year or a preceding taxation year in respect of property sold in the course of the business is payable to the taxpayer after the end of the year and, except where the property is real property, all or part of the amount was, at the time of the sale, not due until at least 2 years after that time, [a taxpayer may deduct] a reasonable amount as a reserve in respect of such part of the amount as can reasonably be regarded as a portion of the profit from the sale;

Technically, three conditions must be met for a deferred payment reserve deduction: (a) the amount from the sale of the property must be included in income; (b) the property must be an inventory property; and (c) except where the property is

---

[127]See *Stewart & Morrison Ltd. v. M.N.R.*, [1972] CTC 73, 72 DTC 6049 (S.C.C.), in which the loss from the non-repayment of cash advances made for the purpose of providing working capital to a related corporation was held to be a capital loss.

[128]One half of a capital loss is deductible as an allowable capital loss (s. 38(b)) and one half of a business investment loss is deductible as an allowable business investment loss (s. 38(c)). These concepts are discussed in more detail in chapter 14, Taxable Income and Tax for Individuals.

[129]See *M.N.R. v. Steer*, [1967] S.C.R. 34, in which the taxpayer's guarantee of another corporation's indebtedness was held to be the equivalent of a loan and monies paid to discharge that indebtedness were held to be a capital loss. See also *Shaw-Almex Industries Ltd. vs. the Queen*, 2009 TCC 538.

[130]See *Easton v. Canada*, [1998] 2 FC 44, [1997] F.C.J. No 1282 (QL), in which the payment under a guarantee made for income producing purposes related to the taxpayer's own business (and not that of the corporation for which the loan was repaid) was held to be on income account.

[131]See *Valiant Cleaning Technology Inc. v. The Queen*, 2008 TCC 637, is which a loss from non-repayment of cash advances made to a non-resident subsidiary were held to be made with the view of expansion and made for the purpose of protecting the revenue stream of the Canadian operation. See also *L. Berman & Co. Ltd. v. M.N.R.*, [1961] CTC 237 (Ex. Court), in which the loss from voluntary payments to the suppliers of its subsidiary were held to be deductible because the taxpayer wished to continue to do business with those suppliers in the future and these payments protected the taxpayer's goodwill.

real property, all or part of the purchase price must not be due until at least two years after the time of the sale.[132] The amount of the reserve is the amount that "can reasonably be regarded as a portion of the profit from the sale". This requires the computation of the "profit" from the sale, and then a reasonable apportionment of such profit. The apportionment is considered reasonable if it is based on the ratio of the amount not due until after the end of the year to the total sale price.[133] Expressed as a formula, the amount of reserve is determined as follows:

$$\text{Profit} \times \frac{\text{Amount not due until after the end of the year}}{\text{Total sale price}} = \text{reserve}$$

The amount of reserve deduction in year one under paragraph 20(1)(n) must be included in computing income in year two under subparagraph 12(1)(e)(ii). If the conditions for the reserve are met in year two, the taxpayer may deduct a reserve in that year, in which case this amount must be included in income in year three.

For example, in year one, a taxpayer sells inventory property with a cost of $60,000 for a price of $100,000, of which $50,000 is payable immediately and $25,000 in each of year two and three. The taxpayer's profit from the sale is $40,000 (the $100,000 sale price *less* the $60,000 cost of the property sold), but he or she will receive only half of the sale price, and thus, half of the profit in the year of sale. By virtue of paragraph 20(1)(n), the taxpayer may deduct a reserve in year one of $20,000, computed as follows:

Year 1

$$\$40{,}000 \times \frac{\text{Amount not due until after the end of year 1 (\$50,000)}}{\text{Total sale price (\$100,000)}} = \$20{,}000$$

Consequently, the taxpayer's profit from the sale for year one will be $20,000 ($40,000 total profit from the sale less the reserve of $20,000). For each of year two and three, the taxpayer's net income from the sale will be $10,000, computed as follows:

Year 2

Income inclusion (s. 12(1)(e) re: reserve in year 1)	$20,000
Less:	
Reserve = $40,000 × 25,000 / $100,000	($10,000)
Net income	$10,000

Year 3

Income inclusion (s. 12(1)(e) re: reserve in year 2)	$10,000

[132] S. 20(8)(b) prohibits a deduction under s. 20(1)(n) if the sale occurred more than 36 months before the end of the year. Therefore, the deferred payment reserve is available only for a maximum of four years.

[133] CRA, Interpretation Bulletin, IT-154R2 "Income Tax Special Reserves", (1988). This formula is the same as that for a deferred payment reserve in respect of capital gains (para. 40(1)(a)).

Less:	
Reserve	
= $40,000 × 0 (no amount due after year 3) / $100,000	0
Net income	$10,000

The $40,000 profit from the sale is thus recognized over the period of three years in which the sale price is received.

(iv) — Unearned amounts reserve

Under paragraph 20(1)(m), a taxpayer may deduct a reasonable amount in respect of goods that will be delivered, or services that will be rendered, in a subsequent year. The reserve is available only in respect of amounts included in the taxpayer's income from a business under paragraph 12(1)(a), which includes in income amounts received by a taxpayer that have not yet been earned (or realized). In effect, paragraph 20(1)(m) allows a better "matching" of the cost and revenue. In the absence of this reserve, a taxpayer would include an amount in income that is received but not earned in one year, and recognize the cost of earning that income in a future year, resulting in an inaccurate picture of income in both relevant years.

Like the two other reserves, the amount of reserve must be "reasonable". What is "reasonable" is a question of fact depending upon the circumstances. The CRA's administrative policy is to allow the full amount included under paragraph 12(1)(a) as a reasonable amount for the reserve "in respect of those goods or services which past experience or other things indicate will have to be delivered or provided after the end of the year".[134] Therefore, the reserve completely offsets the inclusion under paragraph 12(1)(a), and no profit will be taxable until the future year in which the income is earned.[135]

The reserve is not available for an obligation to deliver land in the future. By virtue of subsection 20(6), reserves in respect of articles of food and drink or transportation that must be provided after the end of the taxation year are in effect limited to one year. Revenue from unredeemed food or drink coupons or transportation tickets must be recognized in the year following the sale of the coupons or tickets.

The paragraph 20(1)(m) reserve is also not available for an obligation in respect of warranty, indemnity or guarantee (paragraph 20(7)(a)).[136] This applies to service or

[134] *Ibid.*, para. 4.

[135] The reserve under s. 20(1)(m) must be included in income in the subsequent year under s. 12(1)(a). If goods are not delivered in that year or services not rendered in that year, another reserve is available, in which case the reserve in year two must be included in income in year three, and so on.

[136] See *Sears Canada Inc. v. R.*, [1986] 2 C.T.C. 80, 86 D.T.C. 6304 (Fed. T.D.); upheld (1988), [1989] 1 C.T.C. 127, 89 D.T.C. 5039 (Fed. C.A.); leave to appeal refused (1989), 100 N.R. 160 (note) (S.C.C.), in which the Court found that the taxpayer's maintenance agreement for appliances should be characterized as indemnities.

maintenance agreements including computer hardware and software maintenance agreements provided by the vendor.[137]

8.8 — Inventory

(a) — What is inventory?

In a merchandising or manufacturing business, there will be assets that have been purchased either for immediate resale or for resale after they have been assembled or used in the manufacture of some product. Such assets are called "inventory"[138] or "stock-in-trade". What assets constitute inventory depends upon the nature of the business. Motor vehicles, which would be capital assets for most businesses, will be inventory for an automobile dealer. Stocks and bonds, which would normally be investments, will be inventory for a security dealer. Even a business which supplies services, such as a law firm, will have an inventory of work in progress, meaning those tasks upon which work has been done but which have not yet been completed and billed.

(b) — A matter of timing

The cost of inventory is clearly deductible in computing profit under subsection 9(1). The only major issue is the timing of the deduction. Should the cost of inventory be deducted at the time when the cost was incurred (i.e., purchased) like other expenses, or when the goods were sold? In the absence of any statutory provisions, this issue is governed by accounting principles.[139]

Under the cash method of accounting, the cost of all inventory purchased in one year would have to be treated as an expense for that year even if only some of the inventory was sold in that year. This would probably result in poor profits or a loss for that year. Next year when the rest of the inventory was sold, the cost of those goods sold would not be reflected as an expense and the year's profit would be high. This is a mismatch of revenue and expenses which does not fairly present the actual operation of the business.[140] Therefore, the cash method of accounting can-

---

[137]See CRA Document No. 2001-0110895 (E), Technical Interpretation, "Provision of Services (TEI): 12(1)(a), 18(1)(e), 20(1)(m), 20(7)", Dec. 4, 2001.

[138]S. 248(1) contains a broad definition of "inventory".

[139]The Act assumes the use of inventory accounting for tax purposes because it contains several provisions dealing with detailed aspects of inventory accounting.

[140]As discussed under heading 7.5(c), Professional Services, above, the s. 34 election effectively allows accountants, dentists, lawyers, doctors and chiropractors to value their work in progress inventory at zero. S. 10(6) allows a similar election to an individual engaged in business that is an "artistic endeavour": the artist can elect nil as the value of his or her closing inventory. The effect of the election in each case is to allow the individuals to write off the costs involved in the year that they were incurred rather than the year that the work is billed or sold.

not be used by a merchandising or manufacturing business with substantial inventories.

The accrual method of accounting recognizes as an expense for an accounting period only the cost of those goods sold during the period, and carries the goods still on hand at the end of the period as an asset on the balance sheet. Actually, the cost of inventory is treated in exactly the same way as other costs incurred by a business. To the extent that inventory has been sold (goods sold), its cost has been used up in the current period and is accordingly recognized as an expense. To the extent that inventory has not been sold (closing inventory), its cost has a continuing value to the business and is accordingly carried on the balance sheet as an asset of the business. The treatment of closing inventory is of course just another example of the deferral of an expense.

Accordingly, inventory accounting is aimed at accurately reflecting income by matching inventory cost against related revenues. It also prevents inventory manipulation to defer the recognition of profit. If inventory costs were deductible at the time when they were incurred, a taxpayer could charge off and deduct the costs of buying or producing *all* property during the year against his receipts from selling *some* of them. By building up the supply of property in inventory over the years, the taxpayer could indefinitely postpone recognition of any profit, or the taxpayer could manipulate the recognition to suit his or her purposes, apart from the real gains from the business activities. Inventory accounting prevents this opportunity by limiting the deduction for the cost of goods sold to the cost of those goods that were *actually* sold during the taxation year in question.

(c) — Cost of goods sold

The most obvious way of calculating the cost of goods sold is to keep a record of the actual cost of each item in stock, and to keep a record of the sale of each item sold. At the end of the year all of the costs of the items sold can be totalled and recognized as an expense (cost of goods sold), and all of the costs of the items unsold can be totalled and included as an asset in the closing inventory. This method of determining inventory cost is called "specific identification", and it is acceptable for accounting purposes. It is however normally used only by businesses with a relatively small volume of high-cost, heterogeneous inventory and a relatively low turnover, such as dealers in automobiles, antiques or arts. For businesses that manufacture or sell a high volume of homogeneous goods, such as bread or shoes or nuts and bolts, it is not feasible to keep the kinds of records entailed by the method of specific identification.

For most businesses, the best that can be done is to keep records of the cost of (a) inventory on hand at the beginning of the accounting year ("opening inventory"), (b) inventory purchased during the year ("purchases"), and (c) inventory on hand at the end of the year ("closing inventory" — generally ascertained by a physical count of the business's stock). These three figures enable the business to calculate the cost of goods sold in that year. The formula is as follows:[141]

Cost of goods sold = opening inventory + purchases – closing inventory.

The computation of the cost of goods sold involves two steps. The first is valuation: to choose a method by which an overall cost/value is assigned to the goods in inventory at the beginning and at the end of the year. Because subsection 10(2) requires that the value attributed to the opening inventory be the same as that attributed to the closing inventory of the previous year,[142] the key is to determine the cost or value of the "closing inventory". The second step is tracing: to choose a way by which to determine the goods in the closing inventory and how much they cost. This is necessary because the cost of those goods unsold at the year end must not be treated as part of the cost of goods sold (since they are still on hand).

(d) — Valuation methods

By a process of counting or measuring or weighing, it is ordinarily fairly easy to determine the number of units in the inventory at any given time. But tax computations must be made in dollars, and to put the inventory into dollars requires assigning a value in dollars or cents to each unit in the inventory. What value should be used: cost or fair market value? If the fair market value of a closing inventory item is lower than its cost, GAAP requires the inventory item to be written down to its market value. This results in the fair market value of the item being reported on the balance sheet and the amount of the write-down being recognized as an expense of the period. As a result, the write-down will reduce the income of the year by the unrealized loss in market value of the goods still on hand. On the other hand, if the market price has been going up, an inventory item valued at market price would include in income the unrealized increase in market value of the goods still on hand.

The main method for valuing inventory in the Act is the "lower of cost or fair market value" method under subsection 10(1). It is clear from the "Subject to this Part" wording in subsection 9(1) that subsection 10(1) overrides the common law rules for computing profit under section 9. Taxpayers can use the method under subsection 10(1) even when a different method of valuation under the accounting rules produces a more accurate picture of profit.[143]

---

[141]This formula has been accepted for tax purposes. See, for example, *Friesen v. R.*, (sub nom. *Friesen v. Canada*) [1995] 2 C.T.C. 369, 95 D.T.C. 5551 (S.C.C.).

[142]This is to ensure that a business calculates its cost of goods sold properly and no profits would escape tax by a break in the continuity of the inventory figures between the end of one year and the beginning of the next.

[143]*CDSL Canada Ltd. v. Canada*, 2008 FCA 400. The taxpayers in CDSL were a group of companies carrying on a computer technology consulting business. For accounting purposes, the taxpayers accounted for their work in progress using the "percentage of completion" method which includes in inventory the profit related to work completed but not billed. However, for tax purposes, they valued the work in progress at the lower of cost or market,

Neither the term "cost" nor "fair market value" is defined in the Act. Generally speaking, cost is the actual laid down cost,[144] and fair market value of inventories is determined in accordance with accounting principles.[145]

There are two exceptions to the lower of cost or fair market value method. The first exception is the "fair market value" method under regulation 1801. The write-up (or write-down) required under the fair market value method is added or deducted in computing the profit for the period. For financial institutions, however, this method is mandatory; section 142.5 requires them to value the securities they own at fair market value. The second exception is the cost method under subsection 10(1.01), which is mandatory for inventories of a business that is an adventure in the nature of trade.[146]

Taxpayers are allowed to choose between the lower of cost or fair market value method and the fair market value method. Once a method is chosen, the taxpayer is generally required to use it consistently. A change from the first to the second method, or vice versa, cannot be made without the Minister's permission.[147]

---

in accordance with the method set out in subsection 10(1). The Court held that the taxpayers could do this even though this practice did not produce an accurate picture of the income under section 9.

[144]In the case of inventories of merchandise purchased for resale or of raw materials, the cost is the laid-down cost, which includes the invoice cost plus customs and excise duties, freight and insurance charges. In the case of goods in process or finished goods in the inventory of a manufacturer, the cost includes the cost of direct labour and in some cases the applicable share of overhead expenses (such as heat, light, power, and maintenance, property taxes, and insurance). In the case of professional services, "work in progress" is inventory (s. 10(5)(a)) but accountants, dentists, lawyers, doctors and chiropractors can make a s. 34 election to effectively value it at nil: see heading 7.5(c), Professional Services, above. In the case of other professionals providing services (e.g., engineers, architects, consultants, etc.), the cost is the salary of staff members plus disbursements.

[145]Pursuant to generally accepted accounting principles, the fair market value of an inventory item may be based on one of the following three prices: (1) the prevailing purchase price (useful for raw materials); (2) the selling price (useful for finished goods); or (3) the cost of replacement (useful for semi-finished goods where it is usually not possible to obtain a purchase price and it is not possible to sell the article). Paragraph 10(4)(b) requires the use of the third method in respect of an inventory item that is advertising or packaging material, parts, supplies or other property of this nature. Paragraph 10(4)(a) provides that the fair market value of work in progress of a professional business is the amount that can reasonably be expected to become receivable after the end of the year.

[146]This rule was introduced to override the situation in Friesen, note 141, above, in which the taxpayer owned only one asset in inventory (as a single parcel of land inventory) and his business was an adventure in the nature of trade. The definition of an adventure in the nature of trade is discussed under heading 11.3, "Adventure in the nature of trade", below.

[147]S. 10(2.1).

(e) — Tracing inventories

The identification of the cost of a closing inventory presents difficulty when (as is usual) inventory has been purchased at different prices. Where this is the case, there are a number of methods of placing a value on the cost of goods sold. One is the "average cost" method, which assumes that the cost of each unit of closing inventory and of goods sold was the average of the cost of all units held at the beginning of the year (opening inventory) and purchased during the year (purchases). A second method is FIFO (first in, first out), which assumes that the goods sold were the first goods purchased, and allocates the most recent costs to closing inventory and the oldest costs to the goods sold. The LIFO method (last in, first out) makes the opposite assumption, allocating the oldest costs to closing inventory and the most recent costs to the goods sold. Each of these methods is generally accepted for accounting purposes. Each method has advantages and disadvantages from an accounting standpoint, the details of which are beyond the scope of this work.

The LIFO method is generally acceptable for accounting purposes, although in Canada it is not as widely used as FIFO. However, in *M.N.R. v. Anaconda American Brass* (1955),[148] the Privy Council held that the LIFO method was not acceptable for tax purposes. Since the Act was then (and still is) entirely silent as to the mode of determining the cost of inventory, and since it was clear from the expert evidence of accountants that the LIFO method produced the fairest picture of Anaconda's operations, this was an unfortunate result. Their lordships could not accept that a proper matching of expenses against related revenue could involve disregard of the physical flow of goods. Of course, the FIFO method which Anaconda had to substitute for tax purposes is not necessarily consistent with the physical flow of goods where they are non-perishable as in Anaconda's case. But the fundamental objection to their lordships' reasoning is that the accrual basis of accounting often requires that items of revenue and expense be recognized in an accounting period in disregard of the actual movement of goods or cash. The only questions are whether the recognition involves a matching of related outgo and income, and whether it otherwise presents a fair picture of the year's operations. Once competent accountants have given affirmative responses to these questions, as they did in Anaconda's case, it is very difficult to see why their lordships should be worrying about whether the metals used by the brass mill were taken off the top or the bottom of the pile. In the Exchequer Court,[149] Thorson P. wrote a long judgment which clearly set out the rationale of the LIFO method of determining inventory cost, showed why it was especially appropriate to Anaconda's operations, and concluded that it should be accepted for tax purposes. After reading this judgment, which was affirmed by a majority of the Supreme Court of Canada,[150] it is difficult to take seriously the unsophisticated opinion of the Privy Council. However, the

---

[148] [1955] C.T.C. 311, 55 D.T.C. 1220, [1956] A.C. 85 (P.C.).

[149] [1952] Ex. C.R. 297, [1952] C.T.C. 116, 52 D.T.C. 111 (Ex. Ct.).

[150] [1954] S.C.R. 737, [1954] C.T.C. 335, 54 D.T.C. 1179 (S.C.C.).

Privy Council's decision still remains the law. The LIFO method is therefore unacceptable for tax purposes.

8.9 — Interest expense

(a) — Paragraph 20(1)(c)

Paragraph 20(1)(c) provides that interest on money borrowed by the taxpayer to earn income from a business or property is deductible. This provision deals with both of the two fundamental questions:

- On the question of deductibility, paragraph 20(1)(c) imposes a purpose test: interest is deductible only if the borrowed money is used for the purpose of earning income from a business or property.
- On the question of timing, paragraph 20(1)(c) provides that an interest expense is deductible when the interest is paid or payable following the method (cash or accrual) regularly followed by the taxpayer.[151]

In addition, paragraph 20(1)(c) imposes the "reasonable" requirement — interest is deductible only to the extent that it is a reasonable amount. It is the deductibility[152] issue that has generated most of the litigation involving paragraph 20(1)(c) and is discussed in more detail below.

(b) — "Interest" defined

The term "interest" is not defined under the Act. The courts have interpreted "interest" to refer to "the return or consideration or compensation for the use or retention by one person of a sum of money, belonging to, in a colloquial sense, or owed to, another".[153] In other words, the cost of using someone else's money or "borrowed money"[154] is interest. Interest is generally computed by reference to a principal amount at a specified rate. Interest rates are fixed by market forces. Some factors that bear on the interest rate are particular to each loan, namely, the creditworthi-

[151]The law on this point is summarized in Interpretation Bulletin IT-533, *Interest Deductibility and Related Issues*, dated October 31, 2003, paras. 5 and 6. S. 20(1)(d) provides that interest on interest (compound interest) must be deducted for tax purposes on a paid basis.

[152]There are some other specific provisions relating to interest that override the deductiblitily rule in s. 20(1)(c), e.g., ss. 18(2), 18(3.1), and 67.2.

[153]*References as to the Validity of Section 6 of the Farm Security Act, 1944 of Saskatchewan*, [1947] S.C.R. 394; affirmed (1948), [1949] A.C. 110 (P.C.). This definition was quoted by McLachlin, J. in *Shell*, note 156, below, para. 30.

[154]For an example of interest on a legal obligation which is not "borrowed money", see *Parthenon Investments v. R.*, [1997] 3 C.T.C. 152, 97 D.T.C. 5343 (Fed. C.A.), in which the Court found that interest paid on a note issued as payment of a dividend was not deductible since the note was not "borrowed money". This appears to be the correct result according to a strict reading of s. 20(1)(c) but it seems rather harsh since, if the dividend had been paid in cash and the cash had been loaned back to the company, the interest on the loan would then have been deductible (since the loan would constitute "borrowed money").

ness of the borrower, the value of any security provided by the borrower and the term of the loan. Other factors are of general application, and the most important one is the expected rate of inflation over the term of the loan. For purpose of the Act, interest is the nominal interest, including the portion that merely compensates for inflation or currency or other financial risk.

The characterization of a payment as interest is based on the contract between the lender and the borrower. According to the jurisprudence, unless there is a sham, there is no need to examine the economic realities of the borrowing transactions.[155] For example, in *Shell Canada Ltd. v. R.* (1999),[156] a "weak-currency hedge loan" was used to create the financial equivalent of a nine per cent US dollar loan. Rather than borrowing in US dollars and paying interest of nine per cent, Shell borrowed 150 million in NZ dollars and paid interest of 15 per cent. Upon receiving the loan in NZ dollars, Shell immediately converted the funds into US dollars and entered into a forward contract with a bank to convert US dollars into NZ dollars at predetermined exchange rates on the interest payment dates and the principal repayment due date. When the loan was due, the taxpayer repaid about US $21 million less than it originally received when it had converted the loan proceeds from NZ dollars into US dollars in the first place. This foreign currency exchange gain was reported by Shell as a capital gain which was, accordingly, only partially taxable (and Shell used it to offset capital loss carryovers).

The Minister allowed Shell to deduct only interest payable at the rate it would have paid had it borrowed US dollars (i.e., nine per cent). Based on the economic realities of the transactions, the excess interest payment was converted into exchange gains and should not be deductible under paragraph 20(1)(c). The Supreme Court of Canada rejected that argument and permitted the taxpayer to deduct the full amount of interest paid. McLachlin J. (as she then was) found that, as between Shell and the foreign lenders, there was no indication that the payments made by Shell were "anything but consideration for the use . . . of the NZ$150 million that Shell had borrowed".[157] She further stated:[158]

> This Court has repeatedly held that courts must be sensitive to the economic realities of a particular transaction, rather than being bound to what first appears to be its legal form. . . . But there are at least two caveats to this rule. First, this Court has never held that the economic realities of a situation can be used to recharacterize a taxpayer's bona fide legal relationships. To the contrary, we have held that, absent a specific provision of the Act to the contrary or a finding that they are a sham, the taxpayer's legal relationships must be respected in tax cases.

Consequently, the legal form of a transaction governs its characterization. Where a *bona fide* lending agreement refers to a payment as interest, that payment is interest

---

[155]The form and substance doctrine is discussed in more detail under heading 20.2(c)(ii), "Form over substance", below.

[156][1999] 3 S.C.R. 622, [1999] 4 C.T.C. 313, 99 D.T.C. 5669 (S.C.C.).

[157]*Ibid.*, para. 30.

[158]*Ibid.*, para. 39.

for tax purposes. Although the specific result of *Shell Canada* has been reversed by section 20.3,[159] the approach to characterization of transactions remains the law.

(c) — Legislative purpose

The Supreme Court of Canada seems to have committed itself to the proposition that, if there were no statutory allowance for the deduction of interest, an interest expense would not be deductible because it is an outlay "on account of capital", which is not deductible according to paragraph 18(1)(b).[160] The only possible exception appears to be interest expense incurred by money lenders: it is considered to be a current expense.[161] According to the Court, paragraph 20(1)(c) is an incentive provision designed to encourage the accumulation of capital that produces taxable income.[162]

This approach is contrary to general principles on the timing of deductions. Ordinary interest is not a "capital expenditure" as there is no enduring benefit which arises from ordinary interest payments. Ordinary interest is paid in arrears as the price for the use of borrowed funds in the period prior to payment. The minute interest is paid, the borrower starts accruing a new liability to pay more interest for the continued use of borrowed funds. Thus, GAAP treats interest as an ordinary and necessary expense of earning income that is deductible, just like other business expenses, to arrive at a taxpayer's net income. However, until the Supreme Court of Canada reverses its position, taxpayers (other than money lenders) must comply with paragraph 20(1)(c) in order for an interest expense to be deductible.

(d) — Income-earning purpose test

To be deductible under paragraph 20(1)(c), an interest expense must be paid or payable on the borrowed money used for the purpose of earning income from a business or property. If money is borrowed to purchase a home, a cottage, a personal car or a vacation, the interest is not deductible, because these are consumption expenditures that yield no taxable income from a business or property.[163] Similarly, if the borrowed funds are used to earn exempt income, the interest is not deductible. Subsection 9(3) explicitly provides that a capital gain is not income

---

[159]S. 20.3 limits the deduction for interest expense in respect of a weak currency debt for taxation years ending after February 27, 2000, to the amount that would have been deductible if the taxpayer had instead incurred or assumed an equivalent amount of debt in the final currency.

[160]*Canada Safeway v. M.N.R.*, [1957] S.C.R. 717 722-723, 727, [1957] C.T.C. 335 340-341, 344, 57 D.T.C. 1239 1241-1242, 1244 (S.C.C.); *Bronfman Trust v. R.*, [1987] 1 S.C.R. 32 45, [1987] 1 C.T.C. 117 124, 87 D.T.C. 5059 5064 (S.C.C.); and *Ludco*, note 22, above.

[161]*Gifford v. R.*, 2004 SCC 15, [2004] 2 C.T.C. 1, 2004 D.T.C. 6120 (Eng.) (S.C.C.).

[162]For example, *Shell*, note 156, above, para. 28; *Ludco*, note 22, para. 63.

[163]If the tax system recognized the recurring benefits from taxpayer-owned property as imputed income, then of course interest expenses related to the purchase of a home, cottage or car would become deductible: see heading 4.8, "Imputed income", above.

from property. Therefore, if the borrowed funds are used to earn capital gains, the interest is not deductible. Borrowed funds are often used to acquire property that has the potential to produce both income and a capital gain. This is frequently the case with common shares traded on public stock exchanges and rental properties. Ideally, the amount of the interest should be apportioned and only the portion relating to the earning of income should be deductible. In practice however, the entire expenses is considered deductible by the courts and by the CRA.[164]

In the case of other dual-purpose (income-earning and personal) expenses, the courts have generally looked at the primary or dominant purpose of the expense.[165] The CRA has argued the same approach be taken when interpreting paragraph 20(1)(c). The Supreme Court of Canada rejected this argument in a unanimous decision in *Ludco Enterprises Ltd.* (2001).[166]

The taxpayers in the *Ludco* case (a private Canadian company, the major shareholder, and his children) borrowed a total of approximately $6.5 million in the years 1978-1979 and used the funds to acquire shares in two companies incorporated in Panama with headquarters in the Bahamas (well-known tax havens). The offshore companies invested in interest-bearing Canadian and United States government bonds. The interest earned on these bonds was significantly less than the interest expense incurred on the borrowing. Why would the taxpayers invest in a money-losing scheme? The answer lies in the tax savings. The interest income earned by the offshore companies was not subject to Canadian income tax or foreign income taxes. The taxpayers' Canadian tax exposure was limited to dividends received and the capital gains realized on the ultimate disposition of the shares. The tax savings arise for two reasons:

- The first is timing. While interest expenses are currently deductible in computing income, dividends are taxable only when received and capital gains are taxable only when realized through a disposition of the shares. The annual deduction of interest results in a loss from property and the loss is used to offset the taxpayers' income from other sources.
- The second reason is the preferential treatment of capital gains. While interest expense is deducted in full, capital gains are taxable in half.

To secure these tax savings, the taxpayers' investment in the offshore companies was designed to generate minimal dividends and to maximize capital gains through the accumulation of profit for reinvestment. Over the eight years during which the taxpayers held the shares, dividends totalling $600,000 were received. Over the same period, interest expenses totalling approximately $6 million were incurred and deducted in computing the taxpayers' income. In 1985, as a result of the introduction of the anti-avoidance rule (section 94.1), the scheme ceased to work effec-

164 IT-533, note 151, above.

165 See heading 8.4, "Personal and mixed expenses", above.

166 Note 22, above.

tively and the taxpayers disposed of their shares, realizing a capital gain of $9.2 million.

The issue in *Ludco* was simple: Was the $6.5 million in borrowed funds used by the taxpayers for the purpose of earning income when the investments cannot (by design) make an overall profit (net profit) from the investment?

All three lower courts held that the interest was not deductible because the taxpayers had used the borrowed money to realize a capital gain on the disposition of the shares of the offshore companies, not to earn income from property (i.e., dividends). The Supreme Court of Canada reversed the lower courts' decisions. The Court set aside any notion that the tax-avoidance nature of the use of the borrowed funds had a role to play in the interpretation of paragraph 20(1)(c). Iacobucci J. writing for a unanimous court, first reiterated the Court's approach to statutory interpretation: "courts should not be quick to embellish the provisions of the Act in response to concerns about tax avoidance when it is open to Parliament to be precise and specific with respect to any mischief to be prevented".[167] He then examined the meaning of "purpose" and "income" in the context of paragraph 20(1)(c) and held that the proper test is whether the taxpayer had a reasonable expectation of earning gross income.

(i) — "Any" not "the" purpose

Iacobucci J. rejected the argument put forward by the government that the text of paragraph 20(1)(c) requires a primary, dominant or *bona fide* income-earning purpose. He stated:[168]

> Apart from the use of the definite article "the," which on closer analysis is hardly conclusive of the issue before us, nothing in the text of the provision indicates that the requisite purpose must be the exclusive, primary, or dominant purpose or that multiple purposes are to be somehow ranked in importance in order to determine the taxpayer's "real" purpose. Therefore, it is perfectly consistent with the language of section 20(1)(c)(i) that a taxpayer who uses borrowed money to make an investment for more than one purpose may be entitled to deduct interest charged, provided that one of those purposes is to earn income.

He did not mention that there is nothing in the wording of paragraph 20(1)(c) to suggest that "any" purpose, no matter how ancillary or remote, is sufficient to satisfy the purpose requirement.

Apart from the wording of paragraph 20(1)(c), Iacobucci J. gave three other reasons for rejecting the *bona fide* and dominant purpose tests.[169] First, the Court has found that an ancillary intention to make a profit is sufficient to establish the existence of a valid partnership (by showing an intention to carry on business in common with a view to profit). Second, "reading the tests into subparagraph 20(1)(c)(i) would re-

---

[167] *Ibid.*, para. 39.

[168] *Ibid.*, para. 50.

[169] *Ibid.*, para. 53.

quire a rewriting of the provision to introduce a concept of degree, exclusivity, or primacy in the taxpayer's purposes"; and "this Court has repeatedly stated that in matters of tax law, a court should always be reluctant to engage in judicial innovation and rule-making".[170] Finally, the application of the tests is impractical in the context of investments in securities, as it would "open the door to many reassessments and in each case impose on taxpayers a tremendous burden to justify that their real or dominant purpose was to earn income".[171]

After rejecting a *bona fide* or dominant purpose test, Iacobucci J. concluded that the appropriate test is a reasonable expectation of income test. Considering all the circumstances, a taxpayer must have a reasonable expectation of income from the property acquired with borrowed money at the time that the investment was made. What does "income" mean?

(ii) — "Gross" not "net" income

Iacobucci J. held that "income" in the context of paragraph 20(1)(c) does not mean "net" income, but rather "gross" income. He rejected the argument that "income", although undefined in the Act, has the ordinary meaning of "net income" or "profit":[172]

> Nowhere in the language of the provision is a quantitative test suggested. Nor is there any support in the text of the Act for an interpretation of "income" that involves a judicial assessment of sufficiency of income. Such an approach would be too subjective and certainty is to be preferred in the area of tax law.

He also noted that in paragraph 20(1)(c), the term "income" is used in contrast to the concept of exempt income. He presumed, without explaining why, that this was a "gross income" concept rather than a "net income" concept. He did not refer to subsection 9(1) which provides that income from a business or property is the profit therefrom.[173]

---

[170] *Ibid.*

[171] According to Arnold, Iacobucci J.'s comment that a real or dominant purpose test is impractical regarding securities is simply wrong. The long-standing practice has shown that taxpayers have been entitled to deduct interest on borrowed money used to acquire common shares as a result of the CRA's administrative policy. The CRA has taken the position that, in general, interest on borrowed funds used to acquire common shares is deductible; when, however, there is no possibility for the dividends to exceed the interest, the CRA's position is that the interest is deductible only to the extent of the dividends actually received. See Arnold, "Supreme Court of Canada Issues Two Controversial Decisions on Interest Deductibility", *Tax Notes Int'l* (Dec.17, 2001) 1219.

[172] *Ludco*, note 22, above, para. 59.

[173] In *Mark Resources Inc. v. R.*, [1993] 2 C.T.C. 2259, 93 D.T.C. 1004 (T.C.C.), Bowman T.C.J. of the Tax Court of Canada did not consider s. 9 to be a definitional provision, but rather a provision that allows the use of ordinary principles of commercial accounting in computing income from a business or property. This reasoning was accepted by Letourneau, J.A. (dissenting) in the Federal Court of Appeal's decision in *Ludco*: [1999] 3 C.T.C. 601, 99 D.T.C. 5153.

Further, Iacobucci J. suggested that he was bolstered in his conclusion by the fact that if Parliament had intended interest to be deductible only if the borrowed funds were used to earn net income, it could have expressly said so. He noted that, in both 1981 and 1991, Parliament had proposed amendments that would have restricted interest deduction to the amount of net income received from the application of the borrowed funds.[174] These amendments might not have been necessary if "income" in paragraph 20(1)(c) had been understood to mean net income.[175] This reasoning is unconvincing. The counter argument is that: if Parliament had intended interest to be deductible when borrowed funds were used to produce gross revenue, it could equally have expressly said so. Moreover, the amendments might be considered unnecessary because Parliament thought that the courts would interpret paragraph 20(1)(c) to require a "net income" test.[176] Finally, according to Iacobucci J., a gross income test for paragraph 20(1)(c) would better serve the purpose of this provision (i.e., to encourage the accumulation of capital that would produce income).

The Court's conclusion that income is a gross concept is controversial. As explained in chapter 4, income has generally been understood to be a net concept. The conclusion is also inconsistent with an earlier Supreme Court of Canada's decision in *Deputy Minister of Revenue (Quebec) v. Lipson* (1979)[177] in which the words construed by the Court are substantially the same as the words in paragraph 20(1)(c). In *Lipson*, the Court stated that "in order for an expense to be admissible as a deduction from a taxpayer's income, it must have been incurred in order to make a profit. It is not enough that the expense was incurred in order to obtain gross revenue."[178]

(iii) — "Reasonable" expectation of gross income

Given that the new purpose test in paragraph 20(1)(c) requires the taxpayer to have reasonable expectation of gross income, what are the factors to be considered in establishing "reasonableness"? Iacobucci J. found that the objective documentary evidence indicated that the taxpayers in *Ludco* had a reasonable expectation of income. He stated:[179]

> Although earning income was not the principal factor that motivated Mr. Ludmer to invest in the Companies, upon reading the relevant documents he did anticipate the receipt of dividend income. In my view, Mr. Ludmer's expectation of dividend income was reasonable.

---

[174] S. 20(1)(qq) was proposed as part of the 1991 draft legislation dealing with, *inter alia*, interest deductibility on money borrowed to pay a dividend. It would permit interest to be deductible up to the amount included in the taxpayer's income regarding the shares purchased with the borrowed money. This provision was not enacted.

[175] *Ibid.*

[176] Arnold, note 171, above.

[177] [1979] C.T.C. 247, [1979] 1 S.C.R. 833 (S.C.C.).

[178] *Ibid.*, para. 12.

[179] *Ludco*, note 22, above, para. 68.

There is no sufficiency-of-income requirement in applying the test, short of "sham, window dressing or other vitiating circumstance".[180] The Court found no sham in *Ludco*. It appears that gross income that amounts to one-tenth or more of the interest cost of the borrowed money does not amount to window dressing.[181]

(iv) — Different purpose tests for interest and other expenses

In light of the Supreme Court of Canada's decision in *Ludco*, there appear to be different tests for the deduction of interest under paragraph 20(1)(c) and the deduction of other income-earning expenses under subsection 9(1) and paragraph 18(1)(a). The purpose test for interest is reasonable expectation of earning gross income (even when the income-earning purpose is ancillary), whereas the purpose test for other expenses is more restrictive. For example, in the case of dual-purpose personal and business expenses, the courts have applied the primary or dominant purpose test or apportioned the mixed expenses to effectively allow the portion of the expense incurred in respect of earning income. In contrast, interest expense, which has a mixed income-earning and capital gains-earning purpose, is fully deductible, even though the primary purpose may be the earning of capital gains.

It is questionable whether such differences are warranted by either the wording of the relevant statutory provisions or the intention of Parliament.[182] While the Supreme Court of Canada has said on several occasions that courts should always be reluctant to engage in judicial innovation and rulemaking,[183] some of the Court's decisions are actually prime examples of judicial innovation and rulemaking.[184] The decision in *Ludco* introduced a new purpose test; "it upsets a long-standing and well-established rule that whenever the phrase "for the purpose of earning income" is used in the Act, it means for the purpose of earning net income or profit".[185] If the *Ludco* test were applied to replace the primary purpose test in the case of mixed personal and business expenses, self-employed taxpayers could argue that their "commuting expenses" and other dual-purpose expenses were deductible on this basis.

---

[180]*Ibid.*, para. 68.

[181]This "reasonable expectation of gross income" test for determining interest deductibility should be distinguished from the "pursuit of profit" test in for determining the existence of a business income or property income source. Under the latter test, "reasonable expectation of profit" is one of several factors to be examined in determining whether an activity undertaken by the taxpayer was in "pursuit of profit". See heading 6.2(b)(ii), "Common law", above.

[182]The CRA has accepted this interpretation in Interpretation Bulletin IT-533, "Interest Deductibility and Related Issues", (2003).

[183]See, for example, *Ludco*, note 22, above, para. 38; *Shell*, note 156, above, para. 43; and *65302 British Columbia Ltd. v. R.*, note 7, para. 62.

[184]For example, the *65302 British Columbia Ltd. v. R.* decision, *ibid.*, radically changed the law on disallowance of deduction on grounds of public policy.

[185]Arnold, note 171 above, 1227.

(e) — Tracing the use of borrowed money

(i) — Money is fungible

Since only interest on money borrowed for the purpose of earning income is deductible under paragraph 20(1)(c), it is necessary to determine the purpose of the borrowed money. Because money is fungible, there is no "correct" way to determine, with any degree of certainty, the purpose for which funds were borrowed. For purposes of paragraph 20(1)(c), the courts have held that the proper test is whether "a direct link can be drawn between the borrowed money and an eligible use".[186] This requires that the use of the borrowed funds be determined by factually tracing the use of the funds. It is the current use of the borrowed funds that governs.

Under the tracing approach, the ordering of a taxpayer's transactions is crucial, especially where borrowed funds are commingled with other funds (e.g., by being deposited to a bank account that contains other funds of the taxpayer). Assume that a taxpayer has $1,000 cash in a bank and borrows $1,000. If the taxpayer uses the borrowed funds to buy shares, the interest on the loan is deductible. The fact that the taxpayer may subsequently use the $1,000 cash as a down payment for a car (for personal use) will not affect the interest deductibility. However, if the taxpayer had used the cash to buy the shares and then borrowed the loan to buy his car, the interest would not be deductible. The taxpayer has the burden of ordering the use of the funds. Because income-earning interest expense is deductible and personal interest is not, a taxpayer generally would arrange his or her affairs so as to use the borrowed funds to finance income-earning expenditures and to use savings to finance personal expenditures.

Needless to say, the tracing approach presents tax savings opportunities for those who plan their transactions carefully and creates "traps" for tax increases or random tax consequences for the unknowing or unwary and people with better ways to spend their time.

(ii) — Current use

The general rule is that it is "the current use rather than the original use of borrowed funds" that determines eligibility for a deduction.[187] If funds were originally borrowed for an ineligible use (to buy a cottage, for example), and the ineligible use was changed to an eligible use (by the sale of the cottage and the use of the proceeds to purchase income-earning investments, for example), then the interest expense on the loan, which had been non-deductible, would become deductible as from the commencement of the eligible use. Conversely, if funds were originally borrowed for an eligible use (to buy a rental property, for example), and the eligible use was changed to an ineligible one (by the taxpayer occupying the property as a personal residence, for example), then the interest expense on the loan, which had

---

[186] *Shell*, note 156, above; and *Singleton*, note 199 below.

[187] *Bronfman Trust*, note 160, above.

been deductible, would cease to be deductible as from the commencement of the ineligible use.

The current-use rule was applied relentlessly by the courts to deny the deductibility of interest expenses where the income source that funds were borrowed to acquire had disappeared. For example, a taxpayer who borrowed to purchase shares in a company that subsequently went bankrupt was denied a deduction for the continuing interest expense on the loan once the shares had ceased to be a source of income.[188] And a taxpayer who borrowed money to buy shares that he sold at a loss, leaving the loan outstanding, was denied a deduction for the continuing interest expense after the shares had been sold and had ceased to be a source of income.[189] In these cases, although the unfortunate taxpayer was under a continuing obligation to make interest payments to a creditor, the borrowed money no longer had an income-earning use to the taxpayer because the income source had disappeared. Therefore, the current-use rule required a denial of deductibility for the interest payments.

The denial of the deduction of a continuing interest expense after the loss of the source of income that was acquired with the borrowed money was a harsh rule. In 1994, the Act was amended to abrogate this rule. Section 20.1, the so-called "disappearing source" rule, creates an exception to the current-use rule by allowing the deduction of the continuing interest expense after the loss of the income source. When a property[190] purchased with borrowed money ceases to earn income (or a business purchased with borrowed money ceases to be carried on), and there is still a portion of the loan outstanding, section 20.1 deems the unpaid balance of the loan to continue to be used for the purpose of earning income from a business or property.[191] Because of this deeming rule, the related interest expense continues to be deductible under paragraph 20(1)(c).

The Supreme Court decision in *Tennant v. M.N.R.* (1996)[192] (which occurred after the introduction of section 20.1) indicated that subsection 20.1(1) (which applies to capital property) was unnecessary. In *Tennant v. M.N.R.*, the taxpayer borrowed $1 million to purchase one million common shares at $1 per share. The shares were an income-earning property, and so the interest on the loan was deductible. The taxpayer later used one of the rollover provisions under the Act to exchange the shares

---

[188] *Lyons v. M.N.R.*, [1984] C.T.C. 2690, 84 D.T.C. 1633 (T.C.C.).

[189] *Emerson v. R.*, [1986] 1 C.T.C. 422, 86 D.T.C. 6184 (Fed. C.A.); leave to appeal refused (1986), 70 N.R. 160n (S.C.C.).

[190] The section does not apply to real estate or depreciable property, which is used to provide rental or leasing income. The property most commonly covered by this section will be stocks and bonds.

[191] In order to preclude abuse, s. 20.1 contains detailed rules to determine the portion of the borrowed money that is truly applicable to the lost source of income.

[192] [1996] 1 S.C.R. 305, [1996] 1 C.T.C. 290, 96 D.T.C. 6121 (S.C.C.).

for some other shares with a declared fair market value of $1,000.[193] The full amount of the loan remained outstanding and the question was whether the taxpayer could continue to deduct the interest on the entire principal sum of $1 million. The Minister took the position that only $1,000 of the loan could now be traced to an eligible use and the only interest that was deductible was interest on $1,000 of the principal sum. The Supreme Court of Canada held that the full amount of the interest continued to be deductible. When the taxpayer exchanged the original shares for the replacement shares, he was continuing to invest the entire proceeds of the loan in an eligible income-earning use. The ability to deduct the full amount of the interest depended on the use to which the proceeds of the loan, or any property substituted for the proceeds, were put. It did not matter whether the property had declined in value, just as it would not have mattered if the property had increased in value. The interest deduction was based on the amount of the loan, not on the value or cost of the replacement property.

(iii) — Direct use

In classifying the use to which borrowed funds have been put, it is the direct use that is determinative. For example, a taxpayer who borrows money for the purpose of purchasing a personal residence is denied a deduction for the interest payments on the loan even if the loan enabled the taxpayer to retain income-earning investments.[194] In that case, the ineligibility of the direct use of the borrowed funds (to purchase the home) disqualifies the interest payments from deductibility, despite the fact that the indirect use (to preserve investments) did yield income from property.

The direct-use rule was confirmed in *Bronfman Trust v. R.* (1987),[195] where a trust made a payment of capital to a beneficiary. Judging that the time was not right to sell any of the trust's investments, the trustees borrowed the money to make the capital payment. Three years later, the trustees did sell off some of the trust's investments and repaid the loan. The trust (which is deemed to be an individual for tax purposes) sought to deduct the interest payments in each of the three years that the loan was outstanding. In this case, the direct use of the borrowed funds was ineligible for the deduction, because the payment to the beneficiary yielded no income from business or property. The trust argued, however, that the indirect use of the borrowed funds had yielded income from property, because the trust had retained investments that without the loan would have been sold, and those investments had produced income. The Supreme Court of Canada held that it was the direct use that was determinative, and denied the deduction. Dickson C.J.C., who wrote for the Court, pointed out that, if the preservation of income-producing assets counted as an eligible use, then any loan for any purpose (a vacation, for example)

---

[193] *Ibid.*, 308, 292, 6122. This principle was confirmed in *Ludco* in the case of a rollover under s. 85.

[194] *Toolsie v. R.*, [1986] 1 C.T.C. 216, 86 D.T.C. 6117 (Fed. T.D.).

[195] Note 160, above.

would give rise to deductible interest, provided the borrower owned income-producing assets. This would be unfair as between rich and poor (the rich would always qualify for the deduction), and "would make a mockery of the statutory requirement that, for interest payments to be deductible, borrowed money must be used for circumscribed income-earning purposes".[196]

It is not always easy to determine what is a direct use of borrowed money, and what is an indirect use. If a company borrows money in order to honour a guarantee that it gave for its parent company to enable the parent company to obtain a bank loan, is that a borrowing for the purpose of earning income from the business? The Federal Court of Appeal has suggested, in *obiter*, that the answer is no, even if the guarantor-company received consideration for the guarantee.[197] Superficially, it is easy to say that the direct use of the funds is to pay the parent company's debt, which is not an income-producing use. But, at least if consideration were given for the guarantee, the payment could as easily be analyzed as satisfying an obligation of the guarantor-company, which (assuming the obligation was incurred for business purposes) would seem to satisfy the direct-use rule.[198]

In spite of the difficulties in tracing, the *Singleton v. R.* (2001)[199] decision reaffirms the importance of tracing and the taxpayer's right to order his affairs to achieve tax savings. In this case, Mr. Singleton was a partner in a small law firm. On October 27, 1988, he had at least $300,000 in his capital account with the firm. On that day, he withdrew the $300,000 from his capital account and used the money to buy a personal residence. Later that day, he borrowed approximately $300,000 from a bank and deposited it into his capital account in the law firm. There was some disagreement as to the exact sequence of the transactions that occurred on that day, but all relevant cheques were deposited and honoured. The taxpayer paid interest on the loan and deducted interest under paragraph 20(1)(c) in computing his income from the partnership. The Minister denied the deduction. The Tax Court of Canada took a realistic and practical view of the transactions (i.e., the "shuffle of cheques" as described by Judge Bowman) and held that the taxpayer borrowed $300,000 for the purpose of buying a house, and the interest was thus not deductible. The Federal Court of Appeal disagreed on the basis that each of the transactions must be considered separately and independently. Under this approach, it was clear that the taxpayer used the borrowed funds to refinance his capital account, and the interest was thus deductible. This approach was upheld by the Supreme Court of Canada. In a 5-2 decision, the majority of the Court held that the interest was deductible. The Court reiterated the standard refrains that economic realities

---

[196] *Ibid.*, 49, 126, 5065.

[197] *74712 Alberta Ltd. v. R.*, [1997] 2 C.T.C. 30, 97 D.T.C. 5126 (Fed. C.A.).

[198] This is the CRA's position in IT-533, note 151, above, para. 33. Other examples are also provided.

[199] [2002] 1 C.T.C. 121, 2001 D.T.C. 5533 (S.C.C.).

are irrelevant and that taxpayers are entitled to structure their affairs to reduce tax.[200]

The general anti-avoidance rule (GAAR) under section 245 was not argued in the *Singleton* case. In *Lipson v. R.* (2008),[201] the court applied the GAAR to deny the tax benefit arising from a series of transactions characterized as "*Singleton* with a spousal twist" case. The court found the "twist", not the *Singleton* type of transactions, offensive under the GAAR.

(f) — Timing of deduction

Interest expense is deductible when it is paid or payable. An issue about when interest is payable may arise when the obligation to pay interest may be deferred under the loan agreement. For example, in *Collins et al v The Queen* (2008),[202] the taxpayer had an obligation to pay interest on a $1.5 million loan at a 10% simple interest rate per year with a minimum interest payments of $20,000 per year for the first 15 years and any accrued and unpaid interest payable at the end of 16th year (July 31, 2008). In addition, the taxpayer had a "settlement option" under which the taxpayer could opt to make a lump sum payment with a portion of the debt forgiven by the creditor. During the years in question (1994 to 1996), the taxpayer paid the minimum of $20,000 per year but, following the accrual method of computing income, claimed a deduction for the amount of accrued interest computed at 10% of the principal amount (that is, $150,000). The CRA denied the deductions for the accrued interest on the basis that the taxpayer had no legal obligation to pay such accrued interest in the year because it was payable on July 31, 2008 and only if the taxpayers failed to exercise the option. In finding that the taxpayers' obligation to pay the accrued interest was a legal obligation, even though the taxpayers had a right to exercise the settlement option, the Federal Court of Appeal found that: "It is not the appellants' obligation to pay the interest that is contingent, but the appellants' right to exercise the settlement option."[203]

The principal established in *Collins* was that, since "payable" is determined by the "legal obligation to pay", having the option of paying a minimum amount or a "settlement option" does not change the legal obligation. In *Collins*, the annual deduction for the accrued interest and inclusion of debt forgiven was better for the taxpayer than deducting the actual interest payment without debt forgiven inclu-

---

[200] LeBel J., in dissent, was of the view that the economic realities of a situation are relevant in determining whether the legal relations are *bona fide*. The majority of the Supreme Court does not agree: see heading 20.2(c)(ii), "Form over substance", below.

[201] For further discussion, see heading 20.4(f)(c), "*Lipson*".

[202] 2010 FCA 12. At the time of writing (March 2010), it is not known yet whether the Crown will seek leave to appeal to the Supreme Court of Canada. In *Barbican Properties Inc. v. The Queen*, 97 D.T.C. 5008, the Federal Court of Appeal dismissed the taxpayer's appeal from a Tax Court judgment that denied the deduction of deferred interest because it was a contingent liability.

[203] *Ibid.* Para. 18.

sion. At the time that the Tax Court heard the case in April 2008, the taxpayers had made all of the $20,000 annual interest payments to date and intended to exercise the settlement option at July 31, 2008 so that the lender would be obligated to forgive a large part of the principal and interest. Deducting the accrued interest currently and suffering the consequences of the section 80 forgiveness of debt rules later was advantageous both in terms of timing and the amount of the income inclusion.

8.10 — Other costs of financing

(a) — Debt distinguished from equity

A fundamental principle of tax law is that dividends paid by a corporation to its shareholders are not deductible in computing the corporation's income. Dividends are paid out of after-tax profits and are thus not incurred for the purpose of earning income.

As mentioned already, the Act does not define either "interest" or "dividend". As such, the characterization issue is determined in accordance with the "form over substance" doctrine at common law. In certain cases, however, where tax avoidance is the main reason for choosing the form of financing, the Act provides rules for treating the cost of financing in accordance with its true or economic nature. Examples are the "preferred shares" rules,[204] a discussion of which is beyond the scope of this book.

(b) — Borrowing cost

In addition to the interest expense on borrowed money, the raising of capital (whether by issuing shares or partnership units or by borrowing) involves many other costs, for example, the fees that must be paid to lawyers, accountants, banks, underwriters and appraisers. Unlike interest, these costs do not recur: they are incurred once and for all, and they provide an enduring benefit to the business, because the business will make use of the capital for a long time. We shall see in the next chapter, which deals with capital expenditures, that expenditures to provide an enduring benefit to a business are classified as capital expenditures and (subject to important exceptions) their deductibility is denied by paragraph 18(1)(b). In order to encourage new capital investment, prior to 1988, paragraph 20(1)(e) allowed a full deduction for financing expenses[205] in the year that they were incurred. In

---

[204]These include the taxable preferred share rules (sections 191–191.4; s. 187.2) and the term preferred share rules (s. 112(2.1), and s. 84(4.2).

[205]The eligible costs are defined in s. 20(1)(e), which requires that they be "not otherwise deductible". Costs which are otherwise deductible include annual financing fees on debt (s. 20(e.1)), premiums on life insurance required as collateral (s. 20(1)(e.2)), interest on debt (s. 20(1)(c)) and discounts on debt (s. 20(1)(f)). "Participating interest" paid on company bonds, which was computed as 15% of the company's operating surplus, was held to be deductible under either s. 20(1)(c) as interest or under s. 20(1)(e)(ii) as a financing expense: *Sherway Centre Ltd. v. R.*, [1998] 2 C.T.C. 343, 98 D.T.C. 6121 (Fed. C.A.).

1988, this provision was amended to spread the deduction over a five-year period on a straight-line basis: one-fifth of the expenses is deductible in each year. The purpose of spreading the deduction was "to achieve a better matching of expenses and revenues".[206]

Another cost of debt financing is incurred when there is a discount given on the issuance of debt. Suppose a company wishes to borrow money through the issue of bonds (or other debt instruments). Even when tax considerations are neutral, a company may wish to issue its bonds at a discount, because "that is the easiest way of honing the effective interest rate".[207] In order to make its bonds saleable at the time of issue, the company has to fix an interest rate at which they will be attractive to investors, but of course the company does not want to pay any more than it has to. The precise adjustment between supply and demand might involve an interest rate going as far as four decimal places. In order to avoid this, the company will often fix the rate of interest on its bonds at an even figure which is slightly below what it judges the market will require, and it will achieve the final adjustment between supply and demand by varying the purchase price of the bonds, for example, by issuing $1,000 bonds at $995. The discount has the effect of increasing the yield to the investors who purchase the bonds. If the company's judgment as to the market proves wrong, or if the market later falls before the issue has been fully sold, then the discount can be increased.

There does not seem to be any good reason why a discount should not be fully deductible by the borrower, just as interest is fully deductible when the borrowed money is acquired for the purpose of earning income from a business or property. This is the treatment that the Act accords to a "shallow" discount,[208] which is a discount of less than three per cent of the principal amount of the bond;[209] shallow discount is fully deductible (subparagraph 20(1)(f)(i)). But a "deep" discount, that is, a discount of more than three per cent, is only one-half deductible (subparagraph 20(1)(f)(ii)).[210] A deep discount is thus treated as comparable to a capital loss,

---

[206]Department of Finance, *Technical Notes* (Carswell), s. 20(1)(e).

[207]Grover and Iacobucci, *Materials on Canadian Income Tax* (3rd. ed., 1976), 193. (The statement is not in the current edition of this casebook, now edited by Edgar, Li and Sandler.)

[208]S. 20(1)(f)(i) does not permit the deduction until the discount is "paid", that is, on the maturity of the bond. The correct accounting treatment would be to amortize the discount over the life of the loan. On the other hand, the holder of the bond does not have to report the discount as income under s. 16(1) until it is "paid or payable".

[209]S. 20(1)(f)(i) imposes a second condition as well, namely, that the actual yield on the sum paid for the bond must not exceed 4/3 of the interest payable on the face value of the bond. This condition will always be satisfied when the discount is 3% or less, except in the case of short-term obligations (when the discount has a larger impact on the yield).

[210]In the case of a tax-exempt entity, such as a municipality, the restriction on the deductibility of deep discounts is of no significance. S. 16(3) discourages the issue of deep discount bonds (defined by reference to the 4/3 rule, *ibid.*) by requiring that deep discounts on bonds

which is also only one-half deductible. This would make sense if the discount were treated as a capital gain in the hands of the bondholder, but, as noted in chapter 7,[211] an original issue discount is normally taxed in full as interest under subsection 16(1) when it is paid to the bondholder on the maturity of the bond.

(c) — Foreign exchange losses

When Canadian taxpayers borrow money from foreign lenders, they may incur exchange losses if the Canadian dollar has depreciated against the foreign currency during the period of the borrowing. For example, in *Imperial Oil Ltd. v. R.* (2006),[212] the taxpayer had issued debentures denominated in U.S. dollars. Between the date of issue and the date of redemption of the debentures the U.S. dollar had appreciated against the Canadian dollar. The taxpayer suffered C$27.8 million of foreign exchange loss on redemption. The issue is whether the taxpayer can deduct this loss from its income under s. 20(1)(f) of the Act.

As discussed above, paragraph 20(1)(f) permits the taxpayer to deduct the amount by which the original issue proceeds of the debt are exceeded by the amount paid in satisfaction of the principal amount of the debt. The question is whether the deduction is limited to "discount" arising from the original issuance of the debt? After examining the wording, structure and scheme of s. 20(1)(f), other provisions of the Act (such as s. 39(2) which allows a deduction for foreign exchange losses on capital account), as well as the intention of Parliament in enacting s. 20(1)(f), the Majority of the Court held that this provision does not allow deductions for foreign exchange losses. This decision makes sense in terms of the approach to statutory interpretation. It also makes sense in terms of preventing a "mismatch" of the tax treatment of exchange gains and losses because taxpayers will inevitably argue that exchange gains are on capital account, and half-taxable.

The characterization of foreign exchange gains and losses is generally based on the character of the underlying transaction.[213] In the case of *Imperial Oil*, the borrowing transaction was on capital account, and so is the exchange loss. In the case of exchange loss incurred in relation to foreign trade (e.g., amounts payable to purchase foreign goods or services) would be on current account as the underlying transaction is on income account. In such a case, the foreign exchange loss is an intrinsic element of the price paid for a goods or services. Exchange losses are

---

issued by tax-exempt entities must be included in the income of the lender for the year in which he or she acquired the bond. This is a harsh rule because the discount will not be received until the maturity of the bond. Therefore, tax-exempt entities do not issue deep-discount bonds.

[211] See heading 7.8(e), "Discounts", above.

[212] *Imperial Oil Ltd. v. R.* (2006), 2006 SCC 46, (sub nom. *Imperial Oil Ltd. v. Canada)* 2006 D.T.C. 6639 (Eng.), 2006 D.T.C. 6660 (Fr.) (S.C.C) and (2006), [2007] 1 C.T.C. 41 (S.C.C.) per Binnie, J., para. 73. This case is also discussed under heading 19.4(c), The *Imperial Oil* (2006) case, below.

[213] *Ibid.*, para. 45.

deductible if the goods or services are purchased for the purpose of earning income.[214]

8.11 — Mismatch and tax arbitrage

Taxpayers often make business and investment decisions that are motivated by, and result in, substantial tax savings. For example, taxpayers may take advantage of the mismatch between fully deductible expenses and preferably taxed capital gains. A common example is interest incurred to purchase rental properties[215] (as in the case of *Stewart v. R.* (2002)[216]) or shares (as in the case of *Ludco*). Often, an investor's interest expenses will exceed the current income from rent or dividend. The loss will shelter income from other sources. Overall, the taxpayer will derive a profit if the investment property appreciates in value each year. However, while interest expenses are deductible when paid, recognition of the offsetting gains can be deferred until the property is sold and the gain is "realized". What's more, while interest is normally deductible in full, capital gains are partially tax-free.

The mismatch also occurs with respect to the timing of the interest deduction and the dividend inclusion for an investment in common shares. Because dividends are taxed on a cash basis and there is no legal requirement that dividends on common shares are paid periodically, even when the amount of dividend received is equal to the amount of interest expenses, the time value of money resulted from the current interest deduction and deferred recognition of dividends is significant. Where dividends are excluded from income[217] or treated more favourably to other income,[218] and interest expense is entirely deductible, taxpayers often will find that their total tax liability is negative — less than zero — on a fully leveraged investment.

From a policy perspective, the issue of mismatch can be addressed by eliminating the differential treatments that cause the mismatch. For example, capital gains could be taxed the same as ordinary income; dividends could be taxed the same as other income; or the imputed rental value of housing could be taxable. It is unlikely, however, that these tax preferences will be repealed. So the only feasible

---

[214]See also, *Tembec Inc. v. The Queen*, 2009 DTC 5089 (FCA), which followed *Imperial Oil, ibid.*

[215]In the case of rental properties, the other major deduction is capital cost allowance, but it is limited by regulation 1100(11) to the amount of rental income.

[216]2002 D.T.C. 6969, 2002 SCC 46 (discussed under heading 6.2(b)(ii), "Common law", above.

[217]For example, inter-corporate dividends are received tax-free under s. 112(1) and dividends received by a corporation from a foreign affiliate out of the affiliate's exempt surplus are effectively exempt from Canadian tax by virtue of s. 113(1).

[218]E.g., because of the gross-up and dividend tax credit available to an individual receiving a dividend from a taxable Canadian corporation (s. 82(1)(b)).

means of preventing mismatch is the disallowance of interest and other deductions in appropriate circumstances.[219]

The government proposed section 3.1 in October 2003[220] in reaction to the Supreme Court of Canada decision in *Ludco*,[221] *Stewart*[222] and *Walls*.[223] Draft section 3.1 proposed to restrict the deduction of losses, including those resulting from interest deductions, based on a reasonable expectation of profit test. This legislation has since been withdrawn because of almost universal concerns about its effect on normal business and capital market activities.

[219]With respect to capital cost allowance and rental/leasing income, subsections 1100(11) and (15) of the *Income Tax Regulations* require matching in the case of rental properties and leasing properties. See heading 9.4(i), "Limitations on CCA deductions".

[220]Proposed s. 3.1 read as follows applicable to taxation years beginning after 2004: "(1) A taxpayer has a loss for a taxation year from a source that is a business or property only if, in the year, it is reasonable to expect that the taxpayer will realize a cumulative profit from that business or property for the period in which the taxpayer has carried on, and can reasonably be expected to carry on, that business or has held, and can reasonably be expected to hold, that property. (2) For the purpose of subsection (1), profit is determined without reference to capital gains or capital losses."

[221]Note 22, above.

[222]Note 216, above.

[223]*Walls v. Canada*, [2002] 2 S.C.R. 684, [2002] 3 C.T.C. 421, 2002 D.T.C. 6960 (S.C.C.).

9
INCOME FROM BUSINESS OR PROPERTY: CAPITAL EXPENDITURES

9.1 — A timing issue

(a) — Capital versus current expenditures

While current expenses incurred for the purpose of earning income from a business or property are immediately deductible, paragraph 18(1)(b) of the *Income Tax Act* (the "Act") prohibits the deduction of "an outlay, loss or replacement of capital, a payment on account of capital or an allowance in respect of depreciation, obsolescence or depletion except as expressly permitted by this Part". This does not mean that capital expenditures are not recognized for tax purposes. Most are eventually deductible, but just not fully in the current year. A capital expenditure is generally capitalized — that is, added to the taxpayer's cost of the asset with respect to which the expenditure is incurred. This amount either will be recovered when the asset is sold or over some period of time during which the asset is held, through a series of deductions for depreciation or amortization.

Distinguishing deductible current expenses from non-deductible capital expenses can be as difficult as distinguishing income-earning expenses from personal expenses. The distinction is nevertheless essential to an income tax. As mentioned in chapter 8, there are two fundamental issues in the deductibility of expenses: (1) whether an expense was incurred for the purpose of earning income from a business or property, and (2) the timing of deduction. The distinction between income-earning expenses and personal expenses lies in the purpose test, whereas the distinction between current and capital expenditures is purely a timing question. The question of whether an expenditure is on account of capital must not be confused with the question of whether an expenditure has been made for the purpose of earning income from a business or property. The latter question is logically prior to the former. An expenditure which lacks an income earning purpose (such as a personal consumption expenditure) is not deductible for that reason, and it is never necessary to decide whether it is capital or current. A capital expenditure in the present context is therefore invariably an expenditure which is made for an income producing purpose.

The timing issue is closely tied to the timing of the benefits of an expenditure: the benefits of the capital expenditure will continue for a substantial period of time, whereas the benefits of the current expense will not last beyond the current accounting period. Both accounting principles and tax policy are in agreement on the point that expenditures that produce an enduring benefit to a business should not be immediately deductible in full. The corollary of this proposition is that such expenditures should be amortized over the period for which they do confer a benefit on a business.

The non-deduction of capital expenditures is consistent with income tax logic.[1] When the value of an expenditure is not totally consumed within the year, the portion that is not consumed has value in the future. This value represents an asset, not a cost incurred in earning income, and thus, should not be deducted in computing profit. Another way of explaining the timing issue is to compare the cost of purchasing a capital asset with pre-payment of rent (prepaid rent). If one considers the example of a taxpayer paying ten years' rent in advance in one lump sum, it is obvious that only one tenth of that sum should be recognized as having been used up each year, and that the unused balance should be regarded as an asset.[2] More commonly, of course, a long lived asset is acquired by way of a purchase than by prepaying rent, but the same basic analysis holds. The cost of buying a building with a life of ten years is like paying ten years' rent in advance. The total cost must be amortized over the period of the life of the building. The idea is to match the cost of the asset against the revenues which it helps to produce in order to provide an accurate picture of profit for each year.

(b) — Tax deferral and the impact of capitalizing expenses

The question of when an expense can be deducted in computing profit is important to both taxpayers and the government. If an expenditure that should be capitalized is permitted to be deducted immediately, at a minimum, the taxpayer will postpone tax liability on the income offset by the deduction. The ability to accelerate deductions, and thereby defer tax, is a major advantage to taxpayers.

Tax deferral is valuable even if the tax on the income in a later year is identical in amount to the tax saved from a deduction in an earlier year. The deferral advantage is well understood. It is clear that a taxpayer would be wealthier if she were allowed to wait until 2010 to pay $100,000 of taxes owed for 2007. She could put the $100,000 in the bank and earn interest, or invest it in other productive assets, or pay

[1]See heading 8.2(a), "Income tax logic", above.

[2]See heading 8.7(d), "Prepaid expenses", above.

off a loan and avoid interest expenses. As explained in chapter 1, the particular value of postponing tax by deferring income or accelerating deductions depends upon tax rates, interest rates (or the time value of money), and the length of deferral.

One easy way to think of the value of tax deferral is by analogy to an interest-free loan. The actual amount of the loan depends upon the taxpayer's tax bracket and the duration of the loan depends upon the length of the deferral. Assume a taxpayer has revenue of $100 each year. In year one, she incurs a $100 expense. If the expense is a capital expenditure, $50 of which is deductible immediately and $50 deductible in year two, the taxpayer's profit will be $50 in each of year one and year two. If she pays tax at the rate of 40 percent, her tax liability will be $20 each year (40% × [$100 - $50]). But if the expense is a current expense, it is fully deductible in year one. The taxpayer's profit for year one will be zero ($100 - $100) and she will owe no income tax. Her profit for year two will be $100, and her tax liability in year 2 will be $40. In other words, although the total tax liability is $40, a current expense deduction in year one defers the payment of $20 of the tax until year 2. The $20 deferred is (in effect) a one-year interest-free loan of $20 from the government.

9.2 — "Capital expenditure" defined

(a) — Common law tests

The Act does not define the term "capital expenditure". The meaning of this term is thus determined on the basis of case law principles. There are many cases in which the courts have had to determine whether or not a particular expenditure is on account of capital. A number of tests have been developed, but none is conclusive. As Sir Wilfred Greene noted in 1938:[3]

> . . . there have been . . . many cases where this matter of capital or income has been debated. There have been many cases which fall upon the borderline: indeed, in many cases it is almost true to say that the spin of a coin would decide the matter almost as satisfactorily as an attempt to find reasons.

The leading Canadian case is *Johns-Manville Canada Inc. v. R* (1985).[4] In this case, the taxpayer operated an open-pit asbestos mine and purchased land on a regular basis in order to extend the perimeter of the mine to maintain a gradual slope and prevent landslides. The taxpayer deducted the cost of land as a current business expense. The Minister disallowed the deduction on the ground that the cost was a capital expenditure. After considering the existing Canadian and foreign jurisprudence,[5] the Supreme Court of Canada held that the cost was a current expense.

---

[3] *British Salmson Aero Engines Ltd. v. CIR* (1938), 22 TC 29 43 (K.B.).

[4] [1985] 2 S.C.R. 46, [1985] 2 C.T.C. 111, 85 D.T.C. 5373 (S.C.C.).

[5] These tests have also been followed in *Gifford v. Canada*, 2004 SCC 15, [2004] 2 C.T.C. 1, 2004 D.T.C. 6120 (Eng.) (S.C.C.); affirming the decision of the Fed. C.A. [2002] 4 C.T.C. 64, 2002 D.T.C. 7197 which outlines and follows the tests in *Johns-Manville*, note 4 above.

The tests that are often referred to include the so-called "enduring benefit" test, the "recurring expenditures" test, and a residual test. The meaning and application of these tests are discussed below, followed by a discussion of the characterization of certain specific items — expenditures incurred in respect of the acquisition of assets, the repair of tangible assets, the protection of intangible assets, websites and domain names, corporate takeovers, goodwill, advertising, client lists, and expenditures incurred with respect to a new business.

(i) — Enduring benefit test

While a variety of definitions of "capital expenditures" have been offered, most of the cases have used the "enduring benefit" test. The test was formulated by Viscount Cave L.C. in *British Insulated and Helsby Cables v. Atherton* (1926):[6]

> But, when an expenditure is made, not only once and for all, but with a view to bringing into existence an asset or an advantage for the enduring benefit of a trade, I think there is very good reason (in the absence of special circumstances leading to an opposite conclusion) for treating such an expenditure as properly attributable not to revenue but to capital.

The expenditure in issue in *British Insulated* was a large lump sum paid by a company to provide the initial funding to establish a new pension scheme for its employees. The House of Lords held that this payment could not be deducted in full from current revenue as the company claimed. The benefit of the payment would last for many years beyond the current year, because it would "obtain for the company the substantial and lasting advantage of being in a position throughout its business life to secure and retain the services of a contented and efficient staff". It followed that the expenditure had brought into existence "an asset or an advantage for the enduring benefit of a trade". The expenditure was therefore a capital one.

The "enduring benefit" test asks the right question. If an expenditure is made to produce a benefit to the business that will last beyond the current taxation year, then it should not be deducted in full in the current year. That would understate the income for the current year. However, if one really takes seriously the concept of capital expenditure as anything that benefits the business beyond the current period in which the expenditure is made, it would require capitalizing every salesperson's salary, since his or her selling activities create goodwill for the company and goodwill is an asset yielding income beyond the year in which the salary expense is incurred. It is a result that naturally makes little sense. Overall, though, the enduring benefit test is helpful and is often used together with other tests.

The business structure vs. earning process test, which is derived from the enduring benefit test, is sometimes considered to be a separate test on its own by the court.[7] This test makes the distinction between capital and current expenditures by asking this question: is the payment made for the establishment or expansion of the busi-

---

[6][1926] A.C. 205 213–4 (H.L.).

[7]This test was cited in *Johns-Manville*, note 4 above, and *Canada Starch Co. v. M.N.R*, note 29, below.

ness structure that has an enduring benefit (the payment is on account of capital) or is the payment made as "part of the money-earning process" (the payment is a current expense)? As Lord Radcliffe stated in *Commissioner of Taxes v. Nchanga Consolidated Copper Mines Ltd.* (1964):[8]

> [The] courts have stressed the importance of observing a demarcation between the cost of creating, acquiring or enlarging the permanent (which does not mean perpetual) structure of which the income is to be the produce or fruit and the cost of earning that income itself or performing the income-earning operations.

In *B.P. Australia Ltd. v. Commissioner of Taxation of Commonwealth of Australia* (1966),[9] for example, an inducement payment to a service station operator that entered into an exclusive agency agreement to distribute the taxpayer's products was characterized as a current expense on the basis that the expenditure was made as part of the money-earning process in the continuous and recurrent struggle to get orders and sell petrol. Applying a similar test, the court in *Sun Newspapers* (1938)[10] reached an opposite conclusion: a lump-sum non-competition payment made to a competitor was characterized as a capital expenditure on the ground that the expenditure was a large non-recurrent unusual expenditure made for the purpose of obtaining an advantage for the enduring benefit of the taxpayer's trade, namely, the exclusion of what might have been serious competition.

(ii) — Recurring expenditures

It has been suggested, although not as a conclusive test, that a "capital expenditure is a thing that is going to be spent once and for all, and an income expenditure is a thing that is going to recur every year".[11] If a payment is a one-time expenditure, it is generally a capital expenditure and if it is part of an ongoing periodic number of payments, it is generally a current expenditure. This can be seen, for example, in the facts of the two cases discussed above: the current expense in *B.P. Australia Ltd.* was a recurring expenditure whereas the capital expenditure in *Sun Newspapers* was not.

However, the recurring expenditure test simply does not ask the right question.[12] The idea that a capital expenditure is made "once and for all" is not always true because many businesses purchase new capital assets every year. Annual expenditures to purchase new machines, trucks, etc., for example, are recurring, but they are capital expenditures because each provides an enduring benefit to the business. On the other hand, a current expenditure, which provides a benefit to the business

---

[8][1964] A.C. 948 960, cited in *B.P. Australia Ltd.*, note 9 below, 262 which was cited in *Rona*, note 22, below, 987.

[9][1966] A.C. 224 (P.C.).

[10]*Sun Newspapers Ltd. v. Federal Commissioner of Taxation* (1938), 61 C.L.R. 337 (Australia H.C.), at 363, cited with approval by the F.C.A. in *Gifford v. Canada*, [2002] 4 C.T.C. 64, 2002 D.T.C. 7197, para.19.

[11]*Ounsworth v. Vickers*, [1915] 3 K.B. 267 273.

[12]See the discussion in *Rona*, note 22, below.

which is exhausted in the current year, could be of an unusual or non recurring kind. An example is a severance payment made when a senior employee is dismissed. Despite its weaknesses as a test, the distinction between recurring and non-recurring expenses is still useful as it provides a very crude, but perhaps workable, demarcation between those capital expenditures that can feasibly capitalized and those that cannot be.[13]

(iii) — Residual test in favour of the taxpayer

If the two above tests fail to characterize an expense, a "residual test" has been applied to characterize an expense in favour of the taxpayer. The fact that a business expense would otherwise be treated as a "nothing" for income tax purposes and not deductible in computing profit has influenced the court's decision in a number of cases.[14] For example, the Supreme Court of Canada relied on this test in reaching its decision in *Johns-Manville* that the cost of land, although generally a capital expenditure, was a current expense to *Johns-Manville*:[15]

> [If] the interpretation of a taxation statute is unclear, and one reasonable interpretation leads to a deduction to the credit of a taxpayer and the other leaves the taxpayer with no relief from clearly bona fide expenditures in the course of his business activities, the general rules of interpretation of taxing statutes would direct the tribunal to the former interpretation.

If the cost of land were capitalized, the cost would not be deductible at all in computing profit. This is because, as discussed below, land is not depreciable property and therefore no capital cost allowance can be claimed.[16]

(b) — Acquisition of assets

Under the enduring benefit test, if a payment is made with a view to bringing into existence an asset for the enduring benefit of a trade or business, it is a capital

---

[13]In businesses where a particular kind of expenditure regularly recurs and there is no risk of serious income distortion, the regular recurrence will usually justify treating the expenditures as current. Many businesses treat the purchase of books or small tools as current expenses, even though the books or tools provide a value to the business which lasts for several years. For accounting purposes this is justified, since the recurring expenditures are not large in relation to the size of the business, are similar each year, and are not markedly different from the depreciation charges which would be available if the books and tools were treated as capital assets and depreciated. There is no reason why relatively small recurring expenditures which are currently deductible for accounting purposes should not also be currently deductible for tax purposes and this appears to be accepted by the CRA. In the case of small tools costing less than $500, this is also accomplished by their inclusion in Class 12, a capital cost allowance class which has a rate of 100%: see heading 9.4(b)(ii), "Rate of CCA", below.

[14]See heading 9.2(d), "Protection of intangible assets", below.

[15]Note 4 above, at 67, 123, 5382.

[16]See heading 9.4,"Capital cost allowance (CCA)", below.

expenditure. Thus, capital expenditures typically include the acquisition of business or investment assets that will last longer than the current taxation year.

Depending on the manner of recognizing the cost, capital assets are categorized as:

- depreciable properties (such as a computer, building, machine, or other tangible asset the value of which wastes away during a period of time), the cost of which is recognized or recovered under the capital cost allowance system;
- intangible properties (such as patents, trademarks, and goodwill) used in earning income from a business (not property), the cost of which is recognized either under the capital cost allowance system or the "cumulative eligible capital amount" system;[17]
- non-depreciable capital property (typically land,[18] shares and bonds), the cost of which is recovered only when the property is sold;
- natural resources, such as oil or gas well, mine or timber limit, the cost of which is recognized under the depletion system;[19]
- "nothings", the cost of which are never deductible in computing income or capital gains. Examples are expenditures that did not result in acquisition of any assets mentioned above, intangible property acquired to earn income from property (which are not eligible capital expenditures), and expenditures that cannot be deducted because of statutory prohibitions.[20]

The acquisition cost of an asset typically includes the full cost to the taxpayer of acquiring the asset. It includes legal, accounting, engineering and other fees incurred to acquire the property. If a capital asset is constructed by the taxpayer, the cost of construction is a capital expenditure. Therefore, costs that otherwise would be deductible, such as wages paid to construction workers, must be capitalized and included in the asset's basis when they are paid in connection with the construction of a capital asset.[21] In the case of acquisition of shares, the acquisition cost includes

---

[17]See heading 9.5, "Eligible capital expenditures", below.

[18]Subsection 18(2) requires the capitalization of interest and property taxes incurred in connection with vacant land unless the land is held primarily for the purpose of producing income therefrom for the year or is used in the course of a business. The capitalized interest and properties are not deductible as current expenses, but added to the cost of land. The purpose of these provisions is to prevent the taxpayer from generating losses by deducting the interest or property taxes.

[19]A discussion of the allowance for oil or gas well, mine or timber limit under s. 65 is beyond the scope of this book.

[20]Examples of such expenditures include expenses of recreational facilities or clubs (s. 18(1)(l)) and the non deductible portion of meals and entertainment (s. 67.1).

[21]In *Wharf Properties Ltd. v. Commissioner of Inland Revenue*, [1997] 2 W.L.R. 334 (P.C.), Lord Hoffmann stated at 338: "But whether such payments are of a capital or revenue nature depends on their purpose. The wages of an electrician employed in the construction of a building by an owner who intends to retain the building as a capital investment are part of its capital cost. The wages of the same electrician employed by a construction company, or by

the amount paid to the vendor, as well as legal, accounting and appraisal costs incurred by the taxpayer in negotiating a purchase of shares. If the project is abandoned, the costs relating to the proposed acquisitions are considered to be eligible capital expenditures, three quarters of which are "eligible capital property" which may be amortized under rules similar to the capital cost allowance rules.[22]

(c) — Repair of tangible assets

Every business has to expend money regularly to repair or maintain damaged or worn out equipment and other tangible assets. Often the repair or maintenance will involve the purchase and installation of new parts, for example, a new window for a building or a new muffler for an automobile, and those parts have a life that is expected to last long beyond the current accounting period. Yet no one would doubt that the cost of the window or the muffler should be treated as a currently deductible expense. The cost is small in relation to the asset being repaired, the cost is of a kind that will regularly recur, and its purpose is simply to restore the original asset to its normal operating capacity. However, where the cost is large in relation to the asset being repaired (or improved), where it is not of a kind that will regularly recur, and where the purpose is to improve the quality of the asset substantially beyond its original condition, then the cost will be treated as a capital expenditure.

In *Earl v. M.N.R.* (1993),[23] the taxpayer spent $33,039 on the purchase of a new roof for a commercial rental property. In reporting her income for tax purposes for the year, the taxpayer claimed the entire amount as a current expense. The Minister disagreed, arguing that the amount was a capital expenditure. The Tax Court of Canada agreed with the Minister's assessment, and found that "the new pitched roof created an improvement to the building of an enduring nature and was different in kind from the old flat roof".[24]

The difficulty in drawing the line when the various considerations do not all point in the same direction is illustrated by a comparison between *Canada Steamship Lines v. M.N.R.* (1966)[25] and *Shabro Investments v. R.* (1979).[26] In the *Canada*

---

the building owner in maintaining the building when it is completed and let, are a revenue expense."

[22]*Graham Construction and Engineering (1985) Ltd. v. R.*, 97 D.T.C. 342 (T.C.C.), in which expenses paid to lawyers and accountants related to proposed acquisitions were held to be eligible capital expenditures. See also *Rona Inc. v. R.*, [2003] 4 C.T.C. 2974, 2003 D.T.C. 979, 2003 D.T.C. 264 (T.C.C.), in which recurring costs relating to an expansion plan were held to be capital expenditures. Costs relating to some fifty abandoned projects, including an unsuccessful takeover bid were held to be eligible capital expenditures which are discussed under heading 9.5, below

[23][1993] 1 C.T.C. 2081, 93 D.T.C. 65 (T.C.C.).

[24]*Ibid.*, 2087; 68.

[25][1966] C.T.C. 255, 66 D.T.C. 5205 (Ex. Ct.).

[26][1979] C.T.C. 125, 79 D.T.C. 5104 (Fed. C.A.).

Steamship case, the taxpayer had replaced the floors and walls of the cargo carrying holds in its ships. The expenditures involved were substantial in relation to the value of the ships and in relation to the repair experience of previous years. On the other hand, the work was necessitated by normal wear and tear (so that it was recurrent in one sense), and the new floors and walls did no more than restore the holds of the ships to full operating capacity (so that there was no substantial improvement or addition to the ships). The Exchequer Court held that the expenditures were current expenses.[27]

In the *Shabro Investments* case, the issue concerned the replacement of a concrete floor in a commercial building. The original floor had consisted of concrete slabs reinforced by wire mesh laid directly on land fill; the floor broke when the underlying ground subsided. The taxpayer spent $95,000 in 1973 in removing the broken floor, in driving new piles to properly support the new floor, and in pouring a new reinforced concrete floor supported by the new piles. The result of all this effort was simply to provide a ground floor that was suitable for its intended use, and to restore the building to normal operating condition. On the other hand, the expense was substantial and unlikely to recur, and the new floor was an improvement in quality over its inadequate predecessor. The Federal Court of Appeal held that the expenditure was capital.

(d) — Protection of intangible assets

The "enduring benefit" test requires the costs of asset acquisition to be capitalized. What about expenses incurred in the defence or protection of title or property? Should they be capitalized as well? Because any lawsuit might affect a taxpayer's title to property, the issue of capitalization has been considered by Canadian courts, but not consistently.

In *M.N.R. v. Dominion Natural Gas Co.* (1940),[28] the legal costs of defending a challenge to Dominion Natural Gas's licence to supply gas to a particular locality were held to confer an enduring benefit and therefore to be capital expenditures. The Supreme Court found that there was no distinction between the expenses incurred to obtain the right to carry on a business and those incurred for the purpose of preserving that right. There was an enduring benefit in the sense that after the litigation, the taxpayer had a less vulnerable and more valuable licence than it had ever had before.

In contrast, the *Canada Starch Co. v. M.N.R.* (1968)[29] case involved a payment made by the taxpayer to a competitor to settle a dispute about Canada Starch's right to use a particular trade mark. The Court held that the settlement payment was a current expense because it related to "process" of earning income rather than the

---

[27]However, on another issue, the cost of replacing boilers on one of the steamships, the Court treated the expenditure as capital: the new boilers were of a different and superior kind than those they were purchased to replace.

[28][1940-41] C.T.C. 155, [1920–1940] 1 D.T.C. 499–133 (S.C.C.).

[29][1968] C.T.C. 466, 68 D.T.C. 5320 (Ex. Ct.).

"business entity, structure, or organization".[30] The Court also applied the "enduring benefit" test to reinforce its conclusion. A similar decision was reached in *Kellogg Co. of Canada v. M.N.R.* (1943),[31] where the cost of litigating a dispute about Kellogg's right to use the name "Shredded Wheat" was held not to be a capital expenditure.

The decision in *Canada Starch* and *Kellogg* are hard to reconcile with *Dominion Natural Gas*. These two cases have been defended on the basis that "expenses made to preserve capital assets should be deductible as current expenses".[32] There is an implicit analogy to the repair of a tangible asset. While the litigation in *Canada Starch* and *Kellogg* did have the effect of protecting an asset (an intangible asset), it did not simply restore the situation as it existed before the litigation. Arguably, the effect of the litigation was to remove a cloud on the taxpayer's title to use a particular business mark or name. The removal of that cloud improved the quality of the taxpayer's title, thereby conferring an enduring benefit on the business. On the other hand, however, the title might be challenged by other parties and Canada Starch or Kellogg would need to defend the title whenever that happened. In this sense, the expenditures in *Canada Starch* and *Kellogg* were like the repair of tangible assets and were likely to recur.

The effect of the decisions in *Canada Starch* and *Kellogg* was to permit the expenditures in question to be wholly deducted in the year in which they were incurred. It is possible that the Courts' reluctance to hold that these expenditures were capital in nature was related to the fact that if the expenditures were capital they could not be deducted at all. This was the position before 1972, because at that time most capital expenditures for intangibles were "nothings". The harshness of this result may well have influenced courts to lean in favour of treating expenditures for intangibles as current expenses.[33] The 1971 Act eliminated most of the former nothings by treating most capital expenditures for intangibles as "eligible capital expenditures", three quarters of which are "eligible capital property" which may be amortized under rules similar to the capital cost allowance rules.[34]

---

[30]The business structure vs. earning process test, which is derived from the enduring benefit test and is sometimes considered to be a separate test on its own, is also discussed briefly under heading 9.2(a)(i), "Enduring benefit test", above.

[31][1943] C.T.C. 1, 2 D.T.C. 601 (S.C.C.).

[32]Brooks, "The Principles Underlying the Deduction of Business Expenses," in Hansen, Krishna, Randall (eds.) *Canadian Taxation* (1981), 206-222, at 221.

[33]See also *Algoma Central Railway v. M.N.R.*, [1968] C.T.C. 161, 68 D.T.C. 5096 (S.C.C.), where the cost of a survey designed to encourage the future development of the area served by the Algoma Central Railway was held to be currently deductible.

[34]The expenditures in *Canada Starch* and *Kellogg*, if classified as capital expenditures, would now be deductible as eligible capital expenditures. Admittedly, eligible capital expenditures are only three quarters deductible, and then only at the rate of 7 per cent (of the declining balance), but it is submitted that the present Act's explicit recognition of capital expenditures for intangibles makes any pre 1972 judicial propensity in favour of classifying

(e) — Websites and domain names

Corporations and other entities often incur significant costs to develop internet websites to promote and sell their products and/or services. Not surprisingly, many of these costs are deducted as current expenses for accounting purposes because of their short economic life. Examples of costs that would be capitalized include the costs of hardware, software and original graphics.

In order to characterize expenditures incurred in acquiring domain names for tax purposes, one must simply ask the question: "Does it have an enduring benefit?" In situations where the domain name is well-known and is equivalent to a trademark, trade name or service mark and would have an enduring benefit, the cost is likely a capital expenditure. On the other hand, if the domain name has a limited life, the cost of its acquisition is likely a current expenditure.

(f) — Corporate takeovers

While expenditures that help create or enhance a separate and distinct asset are capital expenditures, it by no means follows, that capital expenditures are limited to such expenditures. The enduring benefit test clearly refers to an expenditure that can bring into existence an "advantage" or an asset for these enduring benefit of the trade or business. The cost of corporate takeovers and goodwill are such expenditures.

As indicated in *Canada Starch*, above, the courts have recognized that expenses incurred in connection with the corporation's structure that benefit future operations are capital expenditures. In the case of takeover bids, the courts seem to have considered the cost incurred in the course of fighting a hostile takeover bids to be capital expenditures, whereas the expenses incurred to facilitate friendly takeovers are current expenses (presumably the target business will continue to operate after the takeover).[35] On the other hand, expenses incurred by a taxpayer (the acquirer) for a proposed takeover are generally characterized as capital expenses. In *Neonex International Ltd. v. M.N.R.* (1978),[36] for example, the Court stated that "legal ex-

---

intangibles as current expenses no longer appropriate. See heading 9.5, "Eligible capital expenditures", below.

[35]In *Goulangerie St-Augustin Inc. v. Canada*, [1995] 2 C.T.C. 2149, 95 D.T.C. 56 (T.C.C.); affirmed 97 D.T.C. 5012 (F.C.A.), the taxpayer incurred the cost of preparing information circulars in connection with three friendly takeover bids. The expenses were held to be current expenses. The Tax Court of Canada noted, however, that if the corporation had incurred expenses to fight the takeover bids, "in particular by hiring a business appraiser to show that those bids were not reasonable or other advisors to assist it in putting defence mechanisms into place, the expenses would have been characterized as payments on account of capital within the meaning of s. 18(1)(b) of the Act."

[36][1978] C.T.C. 485, 78 D.T.C. 6339 (F.C.A.).

penses . . . incurred in an effort to complete the takeover . . . were outlays associated with an investment transaction and thus were made on capital account."[37]

(g) — Goodwill

Goodwill consists of all the intangible advantages possessed by an established business: its name and reputation, its location, the nature of its competition, its connections with suppliers, the expertise of its employees, the loyalty of its customers, and other hard to define characteristics which spell the difference between business success and business failure. It is essentially "the capitalized value of the earning power of a going concern business over and above a reasonable return on the value of its other assets".[38]

Goodwill can be created by the taxpayer through advertising and other promotional efforts, or be purchased together with a going-concern business. The case law clearly establishes that "advertising expenses paid out while a business is operating, and directed to attract customers to a business, are current expenses,"[39] and that "expenses of other measures taken by a businessman with a view to introducing particular products to the market — such as market surveys and industrial design studies — are also current expenses."[40] These expenses are incurred in the process of carrying on a business.

The cost of purchasing goodwill is, however, a capital expenditure. Goodwill is an important type of intangible assets, the cost of which is treated as eligible capital expenditures. When a person buys a business, he or she is concerned primarily with the earning capacity of the business as a going concern. The value of particular tangible capital assets in the business such as land, buildings, machinery, and so on, is not particularly significant since the purchaser does not plan to sell the assets but to use them in the business. The price of the business will normally exceed the value of all the tangible assets; otherwise the vendor would "break up" the business and sell each individual asset rather than selling the business as a going concern. A common method of valuing a business is to multiply the last year's earnings (or the average earnings of several prior years) by a figure called an "earnings multiple". The appropriate multiple would be obtained by negotiation between vendor and purchaser, but would depend primarily on the price at which similar businesses are

---

[37]*Ibid.*, at 496–7; 6346. See also *Graham Construction and Engineering* and *Rona*, note 22, above.

[38]Harris, *Canadian Income Taxation* (4th ed., 1986), 171.

[39]*Algoma Central Railway v. M.N.R.*, [1967] C.T.C. 130 136–7, 67 D.T.C. 5091 5095 (S.C.C.); affirmed [1968] C.T.C. 161, 68 D.T.C. 5096 (Ex. Ct.). Justice Mogan also stated this succinctly in *Graham Construction and Engineering*, note 22, above at 345: "There is no doubt that certain costs (e.g. advertising) incurred for the purpose of expanding an existing business are deductible as current expenses in computing income. Similarly, certain other costs incurred to expand a business (e.g. the purchase of shares to acquire a new subsidiary carrying on a similar business) are an outlay of capital and not deductible."

[40]*Canada Starch Co.*, note 29, above, [1968] C.T.C. 466 474, 68 D.T.C. 5320 5324–5.

being traded. Thus, if a business earns $40,000 after tax, and its earnings multiple is 10, the value of the business is $400,000. Suppose that a purchaser acquires a business for $400,000, and the tangible assets acquired are worth a total of $150,000. What did the purchaser acquire for the remaining $250,000? The answer is goodwill. Goodwill is like other business assets that contribute to the earning capacity of the business.

One way of acquiring goodwill is to purchase a client list. In *Gifford*,[41] the taxpayer, a securities broker, paid $100,000 to "purchase" a client list from another broker. They entered into agreement, under which the other broker would agree to provide a written endorsement of Gifford to his clients, not to provide brokerage services to the clients on the list, and not to provide material information about these clients to anyone without Gifford's consent. In characterizing the $100,000 payment as a capital expenditure, the Supreme Court made the following statement:[42]

> Under the tests outlined in *Johns-Manville*, supra, the client list was a capital asset for a number of reasons. It significantly expanded Mr. Gifford's client network, the structure within which he earned his employment income. The purchase of someone else's accumulated goodwill is not the same as the recurring marketing expenses the appellant would have had to incur to create his own goodwill. As well this payment secured the discontinuance of competition. Finally, it was a payment made with the intention of securing an asset of enduring benefit that would provide Mr. Gifford with a lasting advantage.

(h) — Expenses with respect to a new business

Expenses incurred in entering a new business may be characterized as capital expenditures or current expenditures. In general, start-up costs or expenditures incurred prior to entering a new business are capitalized and costs of earning the income or performing the income-earning operations are current expenses. If the expense was incurred to change or expand to a new business, it usually is capitalized.[43]

In *Firestone v. R.*[44] the taxpayer set out to create a venture capital business by purchasing financially distressed businesses and making them profitable. For this purpose, he incurred expenses in order to investigate the prospect of acquiring a number of businesses as well as expenses to supervise the operation of the business once it was acquired. The investigation expenses were characterized as capital ex-

---

[41]Note 5, above. Although the taxpayer in this case was an employee, the characterization of the payment was relevant because paragraph 8(1)(f) stated that he was not entitled to deduct capital expenditures incurred to earning employment income other than a few specific items allowed under paragraph 8(1)(j).

[42]*Gifford*, *ibid.*, para. 21.

[43]See *Hallstrom's Property Ltd. v. Federal Commissioner of Taxation* (1946), 72 C.L.R. 634 (Aus. H.C.), followed in *Johns-Manville*, note 4, above.

[44][1987] 2 C.T.C. 1, 87 D.T.C. 5237 (Fed. C.A.).

penses, but the supervision expenses were characterized as current expenses. The distinction between going into business and being in business was made in other cases.[45] The distinction is sometimes unclear, especially where a taxpayer is expanding a business. In *Bowater Power Co. v. M.N.R.*,[46] for example, the taxpayer was in the business of generating and selling electric power and energy and incurred engineering costs with respect to the feasibility of increasing the capacity and capability of its plants. The costs were characterized as current expenses because they were incurred while the business was operating and were part of the cost of this business.

9.3 — Recovery of capital expenditures

The discussion in this chapter so far has focused primarily on the distinction between immediate deduction and capitalization. We will now consider the principal mechanism for recovering capital expenditures over a number of years.

(a) — Statutory guesswork

Ideally, the portion of the cost recovered through a deduction each year represents the annual loss in value of the depreciable assets that results from their use in the taxpayer's business. The question to be answered is: how much less are such assets worth at the end of the year than they were at the beginning? The "loss" or "waste" in value is treated as a business expense and deductible in computing profit. Such deduction would reflect a taxpayer's accurate picture of profit. However, the Act has never attempted to measure the economic loss in value directly. Such measurement would be impossible as a practical matter because of the need to measure annually the changes in value of an untold number of business and investment assets. For administrative reasons, the statutory rules governing the deduction of capital expenditures merely "estimate" the amount of decline in value and arbitrarily determine the amount of deduction each year.

The Act and extensive provisions in the *Income Tax Regulations* (the "Regulations") provide for the following mechanisms for the recovery of capital expenditures:

- capital cost allowance (paragraph 20(1)(a)) in respect of cost of acquiring tangible property,

---

[45]E.g., *M.N.R. v. M.P. Drilling Ltd.*, [1976] C.T.C. 58, 76 D.T.C. 6028 (Fed. C.A.). See also *Graham Construction and Engineering* and *Rona*, note 22, above, and *Pantorama Industries v. R.*, [2005] 2 C.T.C. 336, 2005 D.T.C. 5230 (Eng.) (F.C.A.). In *Pantorama*, which was heard after *Rona*, professional fees incurred to find new store locations and to negotiate leases and renewals were held to be a current expense because the taxpayer was not engaged in an expansion of the business but rather in a consolidation of the business (with more stores being closed than opened). This was so even though the fees were computed based on the surface area leased (in the case of new leases) and the duration of renewals.

[46][1971] C.T.C. 818, 71 D.T.C. 5469 (Fed. C.A.).

- cumulative eligible capital amount (paragraph 20(1)(b)) in respect of the cost of acquiring intangible assets used in earning business income; and
- depletion (section 65) in respect of the cost of certain natural resource properties.[47]

If a capital expenditure does not qualify for any of these rules, its deduction is prohibited by paragraph 18(1)(b). There are only a few such prohibited expenditures. Because the above deductions are allowed for an asset whose value is presumed to be wasted away in the processing of earning income, land does not have a determinable useful life and its cost is not deductible under any of the above systems. Similarly, the cost of investment assets, such as shares and bonds, is not recovered under any of the mechanisms. We shall see that some capital expenditures, those which are outside the capital cost allowance provisions, were not deductible at all before 1972 (even if an accountant would have amortized them over a period of years); they were tax "nothings". The 1971 Act introduced the concept of eligible capital expenditures, which includes most of the former "nothings", and the Act makes provision for their amortization.

(b) — Accounting methods

Accounting principles allow the use of two alternative methods of estimating the decline in value each year (the so-called "depreciation"): the straight-line method and declining-balance method.

(i) — Straight-line method

The "straight line" method is the simplest to understand conceptually. Under this method, the cost of the asset is allocated evenly over the useful life of the asset. Thus, if a machine with a useful life of five years is acquired for $1,000, the amount of depreciation (or cost recovered through deduction) is $200 each year for five years. The unused balance of the cost (waiting for use in future years) is recorded as the "net book value" of the machine. For example:

Year	Unrecovered Cost (net book value)	Rate (% of cost)	Depreciation Expense
1	$1,000	20%	$200
2	$800	20%	$200
3	$600	20%	$200
4	$400	20%	$200
5	$200	20%	$200

At the end of year 5, the asset has been completely written off ($200 - $200 = $0), and it will disappear from the balance sheet.

[47] A discussion of s. 65 is beyond the scope of this book. The capital cost allowance system is discussed under heading 9.4, below, and the cumulative eligible capital amount system is discussed under heading 9.5, below.

The straight line method is most commonly used by public companies in Canada to calculate depreciation for accounting purposes,[48] but not for general income tax purposes.[49] The statutory schemes mentioned earlier are based on the declining-balance method.

(ii) — Declining-balance method

The declining balance method involves applying a uniform rate of depreciation to the unrecovered cost of the asset. Because the amount of unrecovered cost decreases each year, the amount of depreciation decreases accordingly, hence the name of "declining-balance method". This method calls for a higher rate of depreciation in order to recover the cost. Normally about twice the straight line rate would be used (see below: a 40% "declining- balance" rate is necessary to do the job that a 20% "straight-line" rate would do). Under the declining balance method, the book value of an asset never reaches zero, reflecting perhaps the reality that there is usually some salvage value at the end of the asset's useful life.

Assume again that in year one a business acquires a machine with a useful life of five years for a cost of $1,000, and now assume that the declining balance method at a rate of 40 per cent is employed.

Year	Unrecovered Cost (net book value)	Rate (% of unrecovered cost)	Depreciation Expense
1	$1,000	40%	$400
2	$600	40%	$240
3	$360	40%	$144
4	$216	40%	$86.40
5	$129.60	40%	$51.84

At the end of year 5, the asset has been written down to $77.76 ($129.60 - $51.84 = $77.76). The figure of $77.76 is the net book value which will appear in the balance sheet.

Under the declining balance method, the amount of depreciation is greatest in the first year of the asset's life and declines progressively each year thereafter. It recognizes the fact that assets are normally acquired in expectation of fairly early advantage, and it therefore seems prudent to write off their cost more rapidly in the early years when the anticipated economic benefits are more certain. This method also recognizes the fact that a fall in value is likely to be greater in the early rather than the later years, and therefore more of the cost should be charged as an expense in

---

[48]Private companies often use the capital cost allowance rates, which follow a declining balance method (as discussed above).

[49]The straight-line method can be used for specified classes of depreciable property (e.g., regs. 1100(1)(b), (c), (p), (q), (t), (v)) as well as depreciable property owned by fishermen and farmers (Regs. 1700-1704).

the early years. Despite these apparent advantages, the declining balance method is less widely used for accounting purposes by public companies than the straight line method. For tax purposes, however, it is the method underlying the design of the capital cost allowance system.

9.4 — Capital cost allowance (CCA)

(a) — Overview

The capital cost allowance (CCA) system is designed to make a set of uniform and necessarily arbitrary rules as acceptable as possible. Without uniform rules for all taxpayers, the system would be difficult to administer, and it would give rise to the possibility of taxpayers in similar situations paying different amounts of tax.[50] "Capital cost allowance" is a term used in the Act. Its equivalence in accounting is "depreciation".

It will be recalled that paragraph 18(1)(b) prohibits the deduction from business or property income of "capital" expenditures "except as expressly permitted by this Part". Paragraph 20(1)(a) goes on to expressly permit the deduction of:

> such part of the capital cost to the taxpayer of property, or such amount in respect of the capital cost to the taxpayer of property, if any, as is allowed by regulation;

Paragraph 20(1)(a) authorizes regulations to provide details for the calculation of the amount of CCA deductible each year. The property in respect of which CCA may be claimed is called "depreciable property".

Regulation 1100(1) stipulates the rate of CCA which may be deducted in respect of each class of depreciable property. The rate is applied to the "undepreciated capital cost" (UCC) to the taxpayer "as of the end of the taxation year (before making any deduction under this subsection for the taxation year) of property of the class". Expressed as a formula,

$$\text{CCA} = \text{CCA rate} \times \text{UCC at end of year}$$

Key to this regime are the definition of UCC and the notion of "class" of property. It is the UCC of the class at "the end of the taxation year" that provides the base from which the CCA deduction is calculated (subject to the half year rule, explained below).[51] Thus the general rule is that if the class has no UCC at the end of the year, then no CCA can be claimed for the class. Special rules apply to certain

---

[50]This was the situation before 1948, when the Act gave the Minister discretion as to whether to allow a taxpayer's depreciation charges, and the Minister normally accepted the taxpayer's book depreciation. Since various different methods and rates were acceptable under generally accepted accounting principles, the same variety was accepted by the tax system. Uniform rules for income tax purposes were introduced into the Act in 1948, but with the restriction that taxpayers could not claim a CCA deduction for tax purposes that was greater than their book depreciation. In 1954, the restriction was lifted, so that the tax rules operated independently of a taxpayer's accounting practices.

[51]Under heading 9.4(f), "Half year rule", below.

properties, such as rental properties, leasing properties and "expensive" automobiles.[52]

When a depreciable property is disposed of by the taxpayer, adjustments are made to the UCC of the class. Depending on the proceeds of disposition and the UCC prior to the disposition, the taxpayer may realize a "terminal loss" (which is a deduction) or "recapture" (which is an inclusion in income).

(b) — Depreciable property and CCA rates

(i) — Meaning

"Depreciable property" is defined in subsection 248(1), which refers to subsection 13(21). Subsection 13(21) provides that "depreciable property" means any property of the taxpayer in respect of which a CCA deduction is allowed. Regulation 1100(1) permits a taxpayer to deduct a CCA in respect of property comprised in any of 46 prescribed classes listed in Schedule II,[53] each of which is allocated a particular CCA rate. It is the property listed in Schedule II that comprises "depreciable property". In order to provide more certainty, the regulations specifically exclude the following types of property from any of the classes:

- Property that was not acquired for the purpose of gaining or producing income.[54] The cost of such property has nothing to do with earning income from either business or property and should, therefore, not be recognized in computing profit.
- Inventory. The cost of inventory is deductible as a current expense, not capital expenditure.[55]
- Land.[56] Land does not wear out and it is not appropriate to make any deduction for its depreciation. Since buildings are depreciable properties, when a single cost is paid for both the building and the land, the cost must be apportioned between the land and the building, with only the building portion eligible for the CCA.

---

[52]The special rules for rental properties and leasing property are discussed under headings 9.4(i)(ii), "Rental property" and 9.4(i)(iii), "Leasing property", below. There is also an exception for "expensive" automobiles costing more than a threshold amount ($30,000, if acquired after 2000). A separate pool is set up for each automobile and the original capital cost is deemed to be $30,000 (plus applicable sales taxes) rather than the actual cost. In the year of disposal, one half of the CCA that would have been allowed in respect of the automobile (had it not been disposed of) may be claimed: reg. 1100(2.5). Class 10.1 automobiles are also exempt from the recapture (s. 13(2)) and terminal loss (s. 20(16.1)) rules. These exemptions from the normal rules which apply on the disposition of depreciable property are somewhat logical, given that the CCA for these "expensive" automobiles has been restricted.

[53]That is, Class 1 to Class 52, including Class 10.1, Class 43.1 and Class 43.2.

[54]Reg. 1102(1)(c).

[55]Reg. 1102(1)(b). See heading 8.8, "Inventory", above.

[56]Reg. 1102(2).

- Most intangible property.[57] Expenditures for intangible property are amortized under the "eligible capital expenditures" system, which is described later.[58]

Depreciable properties are generally tangible assets that have a limited useful life and tend to decline in value over time. They are used by the taxpayer in earning income from a business or property.

(ii) — Rate of CCA

The rate of CCA for each class is prescribed by the Regulations. Schedule II of the Regulations lists the contents of each class. The classes for some of the more common types of depreciable property are as follows:

Class 1: (4%) buildings[59] acquired after 1987;

Class 1 (10%) previously unused buildings acquired after March 17, 2007 and used 90% or more for manufacturing or processing in Canada;

Class 1 (6%) previously unused buildings acquired after March 17, 2007 used 90% or more for a non-residential purpose other than manufacturing;

Class 8: (20%) tangible capital property that is not included in another class (e.g., furniture);

Class 10: (30%) automotive equipment (including automobiles costing $30,000 or less) and films;[60]

Class 10.1: (30%) automobiles costing more than $30,000 (if acquired after 2000);[61]

---

[57]Intangible properties which do qualify as depreciable properties are listed in Class 14 ("patent, franchise, concession or licence for a limited period in respect of property") and Class 44 ("a patent, or a right to use patented information for a limited or unlimited period"). A Class 44 asset can be treated as a Class 14 asset (if it has a limited life) or as an eligible capital expenditure (if it has an unlimited life), if the taxpayer so elects. Since the Class 44 capital cost allowance rate is 25% (declining balance), which allows for a relatively fast write off, it is usually advantageous to treat the asset as a Class 44 asset.

[58]Under heading 9.5, "Eligible capital expenditures", below.

[59]The cost of buildings in Class 1 includes component parts, such as air conditioning equipment, heating equipment and elevators, whether the rate is 4%, 6% or 10%.

[60]Class 10 also includes computer equipment and systems software acquired before March 23, 2004. Purchases after March 22, 2004 are included in class 45 which has a higher rate than Class 10 (45% as compared to 30%). Transitional rules allowed 2004 purchases after March 23, 2004 to be treated as a Class 10 asset (rather than a Class 45 asset) if a separate class election was made under Regulation 1101(5p).

[61]Amounts for automobiles acquired prior to that date are set out in paragraph 13(7)(g) and Regulation 7307. Class 10.1 refers to passenger vehicles costing more than $20,000 because this was the initial dollar threshold when Class 10.1 and the term "passenger vehicle" were introduced in 1987. (Section 248(1) defines the term "passenger vehicle" to be an automobile acquired after June 18, 1987.)

Class 12: (100%) computer application software, videos, and tools costing less than $200;

Class 13 (straight line)[62] leasehold interests;

Class 14 (straight line)[63] patents, franchise or license for a limited period not included in Class 44;

Class 29: (50% straight line)[64] previously unused machinery and equipment used in manufacturing or processing acquired after March 18, 2007 and before 2012;

Class 43: (30%) manufacturing and processing equipment;

Class 44: (25%) patent or license to use a patent;

Class 45: (45%) computer equipment and related systems software acquired after March 22, 2004;[65]

Class 46: (30%) data network infrastructure equipment and related systems software acquired after March 22, 2004;

Class 50: (55%) computer and related systems software purchased after March 18, 2007 and before January 28, 2009 and after January 2011; and

Class 52 (100%): computer and related systems software purchased after January 27, 2009 and before February, 2011.

Class 8 (20 per cent) is a catch all category that includes "a tangible capital property that is not included in another class". The classes of Schedule II therefore include the costs of nearly all tangible property acquired "for the purpose of gaining or producing income",[66] but not deductible in the year it was paid because it was a capital expenditure.[67]

(iii) — Accelerated cost recovery

On the whole, the rates of CCA are fairly generous so that it happens quite often that the CCA deduction is more favourable to the taxpayer than the depreciation expense which the taxpayer deducts for accounting purposes. The declining balance

---

[62]Reg. 1100(1)(b) and Schedule III.

[63]Reg. 1100(1)(c): over the legal life of the property. A taxpayer can choose to use either Class 14 or Class 44 in the case of patents or licenses to use a patent.

[64]There is a half-year rule which makes the rate 25% in the year of acquisition, 50% in the following year and 25% in the second following year.

[65]The March 19, 2007 federal budget proposed to increase the rates for property that would otherwise be included in class 43 and 45 for purchases on or after March 19, 2007. The rate for manufacturing and processing equipment is to be temporarily increased from 30% to 50% for purchases before 2009. The rate of compute equipment is to be increased from 45% to 55%.

[66]Reg. 1102(1)(c).

[67]Reg.1102(1)(a).

method produces high CCA deductions in the early years of an asset's life and thereby reduces profit and the tax thereon in those years. No tax is actually avoided, because the high deductions of the earlier years will be offset by lower deductions in the later years. But some tax is deferred to later years, and such tax deferral is advantageous, leaving money which would otherwise have been paid in taxes available for use in the business. In addition, the Act (or regulations) permits especially accelerated cost recovery (or fast write offs) of some assets in order to provide tax to encourage certain kinds of investment or activity. Examples include fast write-offs for pollution abatement equipment, equipment used in scientific research and development, and information technology.[68]

(c) — Undepreciated capital cost (UCC)

(i) — Meaning

Subsection 13(21) defines "undepreciated capital cost" as follows:

> "undepreciated capital cost" to a taxpayer of depreciable property of a prescribed class as of any time means the amount determined by the formula
>
> $$(A + B + C + D + D.1) - (E + E.1 + F + G + H + I + J + K)$$
>
> where
>
> A is the total of all amounts each of which is the capital cost to the taxpayer of a depreciable property of the class acquired before that time,
>
> B is the total of all amounts included in the taxpayer's income under this section for a taxation year ending before that time, to the extent that those amounts relate to depreciable property of the class . . .
>
> [C, D and D.1 are special cases.]
>
> E is the total depreciation allowed to the taxpayer for property of the class before that time,
>
> [E.1 is a special case.]
>
> F is the total of all amounts each of which is an amount in respect of a disposition before that time of property . . . of the taxpayer of the class, and is the lesser of
>
> (a) the proceeds of disposition of the property minus any outlays and expenses to the extent that they were made or incurred by the taxpayer for the purpose of making the disposition, and
>
> (b) the capital cost to the taxpayer of the property,
>
> [G, H, I, J and K are special cases.]

The above definition includes positive elements (namely, items A, B, C, D and D.1 representing amounts to be added to the UCC) and negative elements (namely,

[68]Equipment used for scientific research and development in Canada is not only fully deductible (s. 37(1)), it is eligible for an investment tax credit (s. 127(5)). Related expenses (e.g., salaries) receive the same treatment.

items E, E.1, F, G, H, I, J and K, representing amounts to be subtracted from the UCC).

The two key positive elements are items A and B:[69]

- Item A requires that when a depreciable property of a prescribed class is acquired the capital cost of the property must be added to the UCC.
- Item B brings the UCC back to zero after there has been a recapture.[70]

The two key negative elements are items E and F:[71]

- Item E requires the subtraction of "total depreciation" previously allowed to the taxpayer. "Total depreciation" is defined in subsection 13(21) as the sum of all deductions claimed for that class for CCA and terminal losses.[72]
- Item F requires that, when depreciable property of a prescribed class is disposed of, the proceeds of disposition up to the capital cost of the property must be subtracted from the UCC. If the property is disposed of for more than its capital cost, only the capital cost is subtracted. The gain over capital cost is a capital gain and is thus left out of the UCC account.

(ii) — Cumulative account

The concept of UCC is the basis for the computation of the CCA. It is essentially the unrecovered cost of the assets in a prescribed class. It is a cumulative tax account that tracks the acquisitions, dispositions, and the CCA deductions in respect of the class throughout the history of the class. In computing the UCC of a class, the original capital cost of each property in the class is added, the proceeds of disposition of each property (capped by the capital cost) are subtracted, and the CCA previously claimed is also subtracted.

(iii) — Class concept

UCC is computed for each class of property. Assets are grouped in a class on the basis of their estimated useful life. One advantage of the class method is its simplicity. Another advantage is that some assets may last longer than their estimated life while others may have to be retired prematurely. In a group of related assets, any under depreciation on some assets will probably be balanced by over depreciation on others. It is not even necessary that all assets in the class have the same estimated useful life, so long as a single rate can be established for the whole class which is about the average of the various estimated useful lives. Nor is it necessary

---

[69]Items C, D and D.1 are also positive elements added into UCC, but they deal with special cases outside the scope of this book.

[70]This will be clearer after the recapture rule, explained below, has been understood.

[71]The definition of UCC also includes four more negative elements, items G through K, which deal with special cases outside the scope of this book.

[72]See heading 9.4(h)(iii), "Terminal loss", below.

that the assets in the class be purchased at the same time or for the same price. On the purchase of a new asset, its cost is added to the UCC of the class.

On the sale or retirement of an existing asset, the proceeds of its disposition (or its original capital cost, if that is less than the proceeds of disposition) are subtracted from the UCC of the class. At any given time, the UCC of the class will not necessarily be the sum of the unrecovered cost of all the assets in the group, because the UCC will also reflect any gains and losses on the disposition of former assets of the group. This discrepancy between the UCC of the class and the sum of the individual assets' unrecovered cost is not a real concern, because the whole theory of the class method is that gains and losses will roughly cancel each other out in the long run.

In certain circumstances, similar properties may be placed in separate classes. For example, each rental building that costs $50,000 or more is required to be put in a separate class.[73] The rationale for this rule is to prevent taxpayers from avoiding the recapture (see below) of CCA upon the disposition of a rental property by acquiring another similar property of the same class. Similar properties used for earning income from different sources must be placed in separate classes as well because profit for each source must be computed separately and the CCA in respect of each source must be determined.[74] For example, where a taxpayer owns a building for business use and another similar building to earn rental income, each of the buildings must be placed into a separate class.

(d) — Capital cost

(i) — Meaning

The capital cost of each depreciable property is added under Item A to the UCC of the class to which the property belongs. It is the base from which the CCA deduction is determined. In the absence of a statutory definition, the term "capital cost" or "cost" takes its ordinary meaning. Cost generally means the laid-down cost when acquiring an asset. For the purposes of determining the CCA, capital cost refers to the "the actual, factual, or historical cost to the [taxpayer] of the depreciable property when acquired."[75] It is the full cost to the taxpayer of acquiring the property, which includes not only the purchase price, but also legal, accounting, engineering and other fees incurred upon acquisition. In the case of a property a taxpayer manufactures for the taxpayer's own use, it includes material, labour and overhead costs reasonably attributable to the property.

---

[73]Reg. 1101(1ac).

[74]For an earlier discussion of the concept of source, see heading 4.3, "Income from a source", above.

[75]See *Cockshutt Farm Equipment of Canada Ltd. v. M.N.R.* (1966), 41 Tax A.B.C. 386, 66 D.T.C. 544 (Can. Tax. App. Bd.) (an unexpected increase in the taxpayer's outlay for depreciable property purchased abroad, caused by an adverse fluctuation in the rate of foreign exchange, was held not to form part of the capital cost of the property acquired).

Because CCA is allowed only if the taxpayer has ownership of an asset, a distinction should be made between a purchase and a lease in cases where a lease has the economic substance of a purchase. But the Supreme Court has made it clear that the economic substance of a transaction is irrelevant to the characterization of the transaction for tax purposes:[76] as long as the legal relationship created by the terms of the agreement is a purchase and there is no sham, it is a purchase. This is the case in *Canada Trustco Mortgage Co. v. R.*[77] The taxpayer purchased a fleet of trailers from an American company and immediately leased back the same fleet to that company. The trailers never physically left the American company, although a complex set of legal agreements were entered into and offshore companies were used to arrange the transactions. The primary motivation for the transactions was to generate CCA deductions. All three levels of the court found that the taxpayer was entitled to claim CCA in respect of the trailers and that the general anti-avoidance rules did not apply.

The Act contains a number of special rules for determining the cost of acquisition of property. With respect to building, subsection 18(3.1) requires the capitalization of certain soft costs that are attributable to the period of, and relating to, the construction, renovation or alteration of the building so that such costs are added to the cost of the building.[78] Soft costs include amounts such as interest and other financing expenses, property taxes, mortgage insurance fees, legal and accounting expenses, site investigation fees, which would otherwise be deductible as current expenses.

Where a taxpayer acquires a property by way of a gift, the cost of the property is deemed to be its fair market value at the time of the gift.[79] In certain cases, the Act allows a property to "rollover" from one taxpayer (the transferor) to another taxpayer (the transferee) on a cost-basis;[80] that is, the cost to the transferee is deemed to be the original cost to the transferor, irrespective of the fair market value at the time of the transfer. Such rollovers are available to inter-spouse transfers of property, and the gift of farm property to a child.[81]

---

[76]See heading 20.2(c), "Interpretive principles", below.

[77]*Canada Trustco Mortgage Co. v. R.* (2005), [2005] 5 C.T.C. 215, (sub nom. *Canada Trustco Mortgage Co. v. Canada)* 2005 D.T.C. 5523 (Eng.), (sub nom. *Hypothèques Trustco Canada v. Canada)* 2005 D.T.C. 5547 (Fr.) (S.C.C.). This case is discussed in more detail under heading 20.4, "General anti-avoidance rule (GAAR)", below.

[78]S. 18(3.1) to (8.7).

[79]S. 69(1)(c).

[80]Examples are the corporate reorganization rules under ss. 85, 87 and 88(1). A discussion of these rules is beyond the scope of this book.

[81]Rollovers are discussed in more detail under heading 13.4(b), "Rollovers for transfers to spouse or common-law partner" (intra-family rollovers). In cases where a depreciable property is acquired from a non-arm's length person and the transferor has claimed CCA in respect of the property, there are special rules for determining the cost of the property (e.g., s.13(7)(e), 73(3), 70(6)).

Where a taxpayer acquires a property from a non-arm's length person (typically a person related to the taxpayer)[82] and the purchase price is higher than the fair market value, the cost of the property is deemed under paragraph 69(1)(a) to be the fair market value.[83] The capital cost of luxury passenger vehicles is deemed under paragraph 13(7)(g) to be $30,000 for CCA purposes, even if the actual cost exceeds this amount. This reflects the policy concern that the use of luxury cars has an element of personal consumption that should not deductible in computing profit.[84]

(ii) — Apportionment

Section 68 requires a single purchase price to be allocated between different categories of property where relevant for tax purposes. The most common case is land and building, since these are normally sold together.[85] Section 68 imposes a test of reasonableness on the allocation of values. The parties to a sale and purchase agreement normally have adverse interests with respect to the allocation. The vendor would prefer a higher allocation to the land since any gain on the land is only 50 percent taxable as a capital gain, and a lower allocation to the building to minimize recapture of CCA (as discussed below, a recapture is included in income). The purchaser would prefer a higher allocation to the building so as to maximize future CCA, and a lower allocation to the land so that future appreciation will be taxed as a capital gain.[86] When the parties' interests are adverse, if they reach an agreement on the allocation of value, the apportionment in the agreement is generally considered reasonable.[87]

(iii) — Timing of acquisition

When should the cost of acquiring a depreciable property be added to the UCC calculation? The wording of item A in the UCC definition suggests that the cost of a depreciable property may be added only when the property is "acquired" by the

---

[82]S. 251.

[83]For further discussion of s. 69(1), see heading 13.4, "Non-arm's length transfer of property", below.

[84]This issue is similar to the reasonableness standard discussed under heading 8.6, "Reasonable requirement", above.

[85]Another common case is the allocation of the purchase price of a business among the various categories of tangible property that are eligible for different rates of capital cost allowance, and goodwill, which is an eligible capital expenditure (discussed under heading 9.5 below).

[86]Paragraph 13(21.1)(a) will adjust this allocation if the proceeds of disposition allocated to the building is less than the UCC of the building, where, at the same time, the vendor is claiming a capital gain on the subjacent land. The purpose of this rule is to prevent the vendor from having a terminal loss on the building (which is deductible) while at the same time having a capital gain on the land (which is three quarters taxable). Accordingly, the purchaser of the property is not affected.

[87]See, for example, *Canada v. Golden*, [1986] 1 S.C.R. 209.

taxpayer. According to the jurisprudence, "the proper test as to when property is acquired must relate to the title to the property in question or to the normal incidents of title, either actual or constructive, such as possession, use and risk."[88] In other words, "the purchaser must have a current ownership right in the asset itself and not merely rights under a contract, of which the asset is the subject, to acquire it in the future."[89] In determining whether or not ownership is acquired by the taxpayer, the legal relationship between the taxpayer and the vendor must be reviewed and general laws on contract, property, as well as provincial Sale of Goods Act need to be considered. In addition to the general principles, subsection 13(26) provides that the cost of property purchased by a taxpayer may not be added to the UCC of a class until the property purchased becomes "available for use" or until 24 months after the actual acquisition of the property. Subsection 13(27) provides that property becomes available for use when it is "first used by the taxpayer for the purpose of earning income".[90] The purpose of this rule is to prevent a taxpayer from claiming CCA on depreciable property that is not being used in the business, for example, machinery that had been bought but was still sitting in its packing case at the end of the taxation year or a newly constructed building is not yet occupied by the taxpayer. This deeming rule ensures that a depreciable asset is actually used in the income-earning process so that its depreciation is matched with the income that it helps to generate.

(e) — Proceeds of disposition

(i) — Meaning

This term is relevant to the computation of the UCC when a depreciable property is disposed of (Item F of the UCC definition). As discussed below, it is also relevant to the determination of terminal loss or recapture, as well as capital gains when a depreciable property is disposed of for proceeds in excess of the capital cost of the property.

Subsection 248(1) defines "disposition" to include "any transaction or event entitling a taxpayer to proceeds of disposition of the property". For the purposes of CCA calculation, "proceeds of disposition" is defined in subsection 13(21) to include:

(a) the sale price of property that has been sold;

(b) compensation for property unlawfully taken;

(c) compensation for property destroyed and any amount payable under a policy of insurance in respect of loss or destruction of property;

---

[88] *Warden Drilling Ltd. v. M.N.R.*, [1969] C.T.C. 265, 69 D.T.C. 5194 (Ex. Ct.), para. 24.

[89] Interpretation Bulletin IT-285R2, "Capital cost allowance — general comments" (1994), para. 17.

[90] This is the straightforward case. The definition of "available for use" in ss. 13(27), 13(28) and 13(29) is long and complicated and includes special rules for special kinds of property.

(d) compensation for property taken under statutory authority or the sale price of property sold to a person by whom notice of an intention to take it under statutory authority was given;

(e) compensation for property injuriously affected, whether lawfully or unlawfully or under statutory authority or otherwise; and

(f) compensation for property damaged and any amount payable under a policy of insurance in respect of damage to property, except to the extent that the compensation or amount, as the case may be, has within a reasonable time after the damage been expended on repairing the damage.

Because the above definitions are merely extensive, one still needs to apply the ordinary meaning of these terms. In *R. v. Compagnie Immobiliere BCN Ltée*,[91] the Supreme Court of Canada held that the term "disposition of property" should be given the broadest possible meaning, including the destruction of tangible property or the extinction of an item of intangible property. Therefore, a property is "disposed of" for tax purposes when it is sold or abandoned by the owner (for example when a building is demolished or a car is given away for free), or when it is destroyed or stolen without any insurance coverage. In the case of a gift, the disposition is deemed to have been made at fair market value.[92] The proceeds of disposition are zero when a property is destroyed or stolen without insurance coverage.

(ii) — Timing

The time to account for proceeds of disposition is when the proceeds become receivable. Under the general principles of realization, proceeds of disposition become receivable when the taxpayer has acquired the legal, not necessarily immediate, right to payment.[93] In the case of a sale of property, a disposition generally occurs when title to the property has passed to the purchaser. However, the normal incidence of title, namely, possession, use and risk, have to be examined in order to determine whether ownership has transferred and the taxpayer is legally entitled to be compensated.[94] The provincial legislation, governing the sale of good is also important in determining when property is disposed of for tax purposes because the

---

[91][1979] C.T.C. 71, 79 D.T.C. 5068 (S.C.C.).

[92]S.69(1)(b). If the donee is the spouse of the donor, the gift may take place at a cost-basis: the proceeds of disposition are deemed to be equal to the UCC of the asset (s.73(1)).

[93]See heading 7.3, "Timing principles", above.

[94]*Browning Harvey Ltd. v. M.N.R.*, [1990] 1 C.T.C. 161, 90 D.T.C. 6105 (Fed. T.D.) (The normal incidence of title — namely possession, use and risk — must be examined: there is no disposition of property when only the right to use the property is transferred while other incidence of ownership, such as the right to dispose of it or to use it as security remained with the transferor).

disposition of property takes place when ownership is passed under provincial law.[95]

In some cases, taxpayers are able to take advantage of the timing rule. For example, in *Hewlett Packard (Canada) Ltd. v. R.* (2004),[96] the taxpayer had an October 31 year end and, every October, it purchased a new fleet of automobiles to replace the fleet it had purchased in the previous year. Although the cars were exchanged in October, the agreement (and the relevant provincial legislation) provided that title to the old fleet remained with the taxpayer in October and did not transfer to the other party (Ford) until November. Accordingly, the taxpayer recorded the purchase as an addition to its Class 10 asset pool in October but did not record the disposition as a reduction to the same pool until November, with the result being that CCA was able to be claimed on both the old fleet and the new fleet each year. The Federal Court of Appeal held that the provincial law was determinative even though exchanges were effectively completed in October and the taxpayer had an "absolute enforceable entitlement to be paid" for the old fleet in October. The economic reality that the taxpayer used only one fleet of cars at any point in time was not considered relevant.

In the case of involuntary dispositions (i.e. expropriation, loss, theft, or destruction), subsection 44(2) deems a property to be disposed of at the earliest of the following times: (a) the date of an agreement fixing the full amount of compensation; (b) the date on which a board, tribunal or court finally determines the amount of compensation; and (c) if the taxpayer does not commence some kind of legal proceeding within two years of the loss, destruction, or expropriation, the date that is two years after the loss, destruction, or expropriation.

(f) — Half year rule

We noticed earlier in this chapter that the CCA for each year is calculated as a percentage of the UCC "as of the end of the taxation year". Before 1981, when a depreciable property was acquired during the year — even close to the end of the year — the taxpayer was able to add the full cost of the newly acquired property to the UCC, and thereby claiming the full amount of CCA in respect of the property, even though it had not been owned for the full year. In that case, of course, the taxpayer had not in fact suffered a full year of depreciation. In 1981, regulation 1100(2) introduced the "half year rule", the effect of which is to deny to the taxpayer 50 per cent of the CCA that would otherwise be available in respect of a depreciable property acquired during the taxation year.[97]

---

[95] This was confirmed in a unanimous decision in *Hewlett Packard (Canada) Ltd. v. R.*, [2004] 4 C.T.C. 230, 2004 D.T.C. 6498 (F.C.A.); reversing (2003), [2004] 1 C.T.C. 2683, 2003 D.T.C. 1324 (T.C.C. [Informal Procedure]).

[96] *Ibid.*

[97] Certain assets in Class 12 are exempted from the half year rule. Other classes of depreciable property are exempted from the application of the half year rule, either because they have

The half year rule still provides some tax advantage for the taxpayer who acquires a depreciable property after the half way point of the year. The more accurate method would be to prorate the CCA according to the number of days in the year that the property was owned (and available for use).[98] This would present no special difficulty if each depreciable property were depreciated individually. As we have noticed, however, the Act and regulations require that CCA be calculated by the class method, and it would be quite complicated to arrange a system of prorating for the portion of the CCA attributable to those assets in the class that were acquired during the last taxation year. The half year rule is easier to apply than a more refined rule would be.

Regulation 1100(2) applies only when a taxpayer acquired a depreciable property in the taxation year. In that case, the CCA for the year of acquisition is calculated on the basis of a notional UCC defined by regulation 1100(2), rather than the actual UCC. The notional UCC is derived by first calculating the actual UCC as of the end of the year (including the full capital cost of acquisitions), and then subtracting 50 per cent of the capital cost of acquisitions during the year. If depreciable property of the same class was disposed of in the year, then 50 per cent of the net figure (cost of acquisitions minus proceeds of dispositions up to capital cost) is subtracted from the UCC. The notional UCC is used only to calculate CCA for the year of acquisition. Note that if the proceeds of dispositions exceeded the cost of acquisitions, then regulation 1100(2) does not apply; there must be a net increase in the UCC account for regulation 1100(2) to apply.

(g) — Example of CCA computation

Suppose in year 1 the taxpayer purchases four Class 8 assets at a unit cost of $100. There is no disposition of any assets during the year. The actual UCC (without taking into account of the half-year rule) is $400, which is the amount in "A" in the UCC definition. The notional UCC under the half-year rule is $200, which is $400 (actual UCC) - 50% of [$400 (cost of newly acquired assets) - 0 (proceeds of disposition)]. Thus, the amount of CCA is $40, which is $200 (UCC) × 20% (Class 8 rate).

Suppose in year 2 the taxpayer purchases another Class 8 asset at a cost of $100, and sells a Class 8 asset for proceeds of disposition of $80. The elements of the UCC are as follows:

A is $500, which is the total capital cost of Class 8 assets ($400 + $100);

---

their own version of the half year rule, namely, Classes 13, 24, 27, 29 and 34, or because they have other special features, namely, Classes 14 and 15 (reg. 1100(2)(a)(iii) and (iv)).

[98] This is what the regulations require when a taxpayer has a short taxation year (less than 365 days) (reg. 1100(3)). A short taxation year will occur in a variety of situations, for example, if a business is started or ended during a taxation year, or if an individual carrying on business dies, or if a corporation carrying on business is wound up, undergoes a change of control, or amalgamates with another company, or if a change of fiscal period is approved by the Minister.

E is $40, which is depreciation allowed for year 1;

F is $80, which is the lesser of the proceeds of disposition ($80) and the capital cost of the property ($100)

UCC = A - (E + F) = $500 - ($40 + $80) = $380

The actual UCC at the end of year 2 is thus $380. Under the half-year rule, the notional UCC is $370, that is $380 (actual UCC) - 50% of [$100 (cost of newly acquired property) - $80 (proceeds of disposition of asset purchased in year 1)]. The amount of CCA is thus $74 ($370 × 20%).

In year 3, there are no new acquisitions or dispositions. The elements of the UCC are as follows:

A is $500

E is $114 ($40 + $74)

F is $80

UCC = A - (E +F) = 500 - (114 +80) = 306

CCA for year 3 is $61.20.

The above calculations illustrate the application of the statutory definition of UCC and the half-year rule. In accounting practice, a simpler method is followed. An opening UCC is computed for each year. The opening UCC is increased by the cost of acquisitions and subtracted by the proceeds of dispositions during the year to arrive at the year-end UCC. The year-end UCC is multiplied by the depreciation rate to calculate the amount of CCA. The year-end UCC less the CCA is the closing UCC. The closing UCC of the previous year is the opening UCC of the following year.

When the half-year rule applies, the notional UCC is used only to calculate CCA for the year of acquisition. The opening balance of the UCC for the next year is the actual UCC, that is, the UCC calculated with the total cost of acquisitions and proceeds of dispositions taken into account. Of course, the opening balance will be higher than it would have been if regulation 1100(2) did not exist, because the CCA for the previous year (which will have been subtracted from the UCC) was artificially reduced by the operation of regulation 1100(2).

Using the same facts as in the example above, the opening UCC for year 1 is nil. The actual UCC at the end of year 1 is $400. The notional UCC is $200 ($400 - 50% of $400). The CCA for year 1 is calculated on the basis of the notional UCC, yielding a CCA deduction of $40. The closing UCC at the end of year 1 is $360 ($400 - $40).

For year 2, the opening UCC is $360. The actual year-end UCC is $380, which is $360 (opening UCC) + $100 (new acquisition) - $80 (disposition during the year). The notional UCC under the half-year rule is $370, which is $380 (actual UCC) - 50% of ($100 - $80). CCA is $74. The closing UCC is $306 ($380 - $74).

For year 3, the opening UCC is $306. Since there is no acquisition or disposition during the year, the year end UCC is $306. CCA is $61.20. The closing UCC is $244.80. The calculation of the CCA for year 2 exhausts the usefulness of the notional UCC. The opening balance of the UCC account for year 3 will be the actual UCC, namely, $306.

(h) — Retirement of depreciable property

(i) — No more guesswork

As explained earlier, the CCA regime is based on estimations about the extent of depreciation each year during the useful life of depreciable property. The amount of CCA deduction is arbitrary and may not reflect the actual amount of decrease in value. The exact amount of depreciation is known only when a depreciable property is disposed of. It might be that the CCA estimation is perfect, too generous, or too restrictive. This is measured by comparing the proceeds of disposition and the UCC of the property.

Assume a prescribed class has only one asset. The capital cost of the asset is $100, CCA deducted is $60, and the UCC immediately before the disposition is $40. The final reconciliation of the CCA and actual depreciation can be summarized as follows:

- If the proceeds of disposition are equal to the UCC ($40), the actual depreciation is $60 and the estimated CCA is also $60. The guesswork is perfect. After the disposition, the UCC is zero: $100 (Item A) - [$60 (Item E) and $40 (Item F)] = nil. The result is that taxpayer paid $100 to acquire a property used in earning profit and $60 was consumed in the income-earning process and deducted in computing profit. $40 residual value is recovered when the property is sold. The total capital cost of $100 is thus fully recovered.
- If the proceeds of disposition are $50, and thus exceed the UCC of the asset, then it is evident that too much CCA has been claimed in prior years: the estimated depreciation under the CCA system is $60, while the actual depreciation is only $50. In order to correct the over-deduction of CCA and understatement of profit in prior years, the proceeds of disposition in excess of the UCC (i.e., $10) should be added back to income. This is what subsection 13(1) does: it requires the amount of excess be added to income, which is known as the "recapture" of CCA.
- If the proceeds of disposition are $20 and less than the UCC, then it is evident that too little CCA has been claimed in prior years (actual depreciation is $80 while CCA deduction is $60). Because the total depreciation ($80) was used in earning profit and should thus be deducted in computing profit. Subsection 20(16) accordingly allows the deduction, which is known as a "terminal loss" deduction.

To make things more complex, the depreciable property may actually appreciate in value and fetch a price of $115 when it is sold. In such case, the CCA system estimate is completely incorrect. The full amount of CCA deducted should be "recaptured" in the year when the property is disposed of. What about the appreciation (i.e., $15, which the proceeds of disposition exceed the original capital cost)? There is no justification for including this amount of gain in computing profit, because it has never been deducted in prior years. It is treated as a capital gain and subject to a separate system of taxation (see ch. 10, below). The gain is not recaptured under section 13. Section 13 makes it clear that the maximum sum that can be recaptured is the amount of the CCA that has been claimed in prior years. It accomplishes this result by providing that the amount of the recapture is calculated by subtracting from the UCC the lesser of the proceeds of disposition and the original capital cost.

The following example provides an overview of four depreciable properties, each acquired in year 1 for $100, each depreciated at different rates for tax purposes (because each was in a different class with no other assets in the class), and each disposed of in year 6 for various proceeds of disposition.

	Asset 1	**Asset 2**	**Asset 3**	**Asset 4**
1. Cost in year 1	100	100	100	100
2. UCC before sale	40	50	60	70
3. Proceeds of disposition	40	70	110	30
4. Recapture	Nil	20	40	Nil
5. Capital gain	Nil	Nil	10	Nil
6. Terminal loss	Nil	Nil	Nil	40

Asset 1 yielded proceeds of disposition equal to its UCC, which showed that CCA had exactly matched the actual decline in value and that no recapture or terminal loss was required. Asset 2 yielded proceeds of disposition which exceeded its UCC by $20, requiring recognition of a recapture of that amount in income for year 6. Asset 3 yielded proceeds of disposition which exceeded the original capital cost of the asset by $10, requiring recognition of a capital gain of that amount (one half taxable) and a recapture of $40 (all the CCA claimed) in income for year 6. Asset 4 yielded proceeds of disposition which were $40 less than UCC, showing that actual depreciation had exceeded the CCA claimed and requiring recognition of a terminal loss of $40.

The above example assumes that there is a single asset in each class. If there is more than one asset in the class, the UCC of the class is used in determining recapture or terminal loss. On the sale or retirement of an existing asset, the proceeds of its disposition (or its original capital cost, if that is less than the proceeds of disposition) are subtracted from the UCC of the class.

(ii) — Recapture

Subsection 13(1) provides as follows:

> Where, at the end of a taxation year, the total of the amounts determined for E to J in the definition "undepreciated capital cost" in subsection (21) in respect of a taxpayer's depreciable property of a particular prescribed class exceeds the total of the amounts determined for A to D in that definition in respect thereof, the excess shall be included in computing the taxpayer's income for the year.

When the negative elements of the definition of UCC exceed the positive elements, so that for a prescribed class of depreciable property there is a negative balance in the UCC account at the end of the taxation year, that negative balance must be included in income. A negative balance could only arise by dispositions of property in the class for proceeds which exceed the positive balance of the UCC of the class immediately before the dispositions.[99] As we noted earlier, when this occurs it means that the CCA that has been deducted in previous years has been greater than the actual decline in value of the property in the class. The recapture puts back into income the difference between the CCA that was previously claimed and the actual decline in the value of the property.

Subsection 13(1) only affects a recapture if the UCC account has a negative balance "at the end of a taxation year". This means that when a depreciable property is sold for more than the UCC of its class, the recapture will be avoided if another depreciable property of the same class costing more than the amount of recapture is acquired before the end of the taxation year. The new property will shelter the tax liability arising on the disposition of the old property, because, at the end of the taxation year, the UCC will show a positive balance and subsection 13(1) will be inapplicable. In the case of "rental property" (buildings used to earn rental income), the deferral of tax by this means has been deemed sufficiently important to warrant an exception to the normal class basis of CCA.[100] After a recapture has been recognized under subsection 13(1), the negative balance in the UCC account rises to nil for the following year. This occurs because item B of the UCC definition adds the amount of the recapture to the UCC.

Because a recapture is included in income, it is fully taxable. If the taxpayer has to replace the former property with new property in order to carry on the business, it would be beneficial to taxpayers to defer the recognition of the recapture and use the total proceeds of disposition to acquire the replacement property. Subsection 13(4) provides the taxpayer with an election to defer all or part of the recapture if the disposition of property is involuntary (stolen or lost) or the property disposed of is a "former business property" and the taxpayer acquires a replacement property by the deadline specified in the Act. The mechanism for the deferral is to effectively transfer part of the proceeds of disposition of the former property from the year of the disposition to the year in which the replacement property is acquired so that there is no negative balance in the UCC account.

(iii) — Terminal loss

Subsection 20(16) provides as follows:

> Notwithstanding paragraphs 18(1)(a), (b) and (h), where at the end of a taxation year,
>
> the total of all amounts used to determine A to D in the definition "undepreciated capital cost" in subsection 13(21) in respect of a taxpayer's depreciable property of a

---

[99]Note that the amount deducted from the UCC of the class is the lesser of the proceeds of disposition and the capital cost of the property disposed (item F in the UCC definition). As discussed earlier, where the proceeds of disposition of a depreciable property exceed the capital cost of the property, the excess must be recognized as a capital gain (one-half taxable): see heading 9.4(c)(i), "Meaning", above.

[100]Under heading 9.4(i)(ii), "Rental property", below.

particular class exceeds the total of all amounts used to determine E to J in that definition in respect of that property, and

(b) the taxpayer no longer owns any property of that class, in computing the taxpayer's income for the year

(c) there shall be deducted the amount of the excess determined under paragraph (a), and

(d) no amount shall be deducted for the year under paragraph (1)(a) in respect of property of that class.

A terminal loss arises only if the taxpayer no longer owns any property in the class and the balance in the UCC of the class is positive. If there are still assets in the class, the taxpayer can only claim a CCA deduction on the basis of the positive UCC at the end of the year. A terminal loss occurs when the proceeds of disposition of all the property in the class fail to recover the UCC of the class. As noted earlier, this means that the CCA taken in previous years is less than the actual depreciation of the property of the class. The amount of the terminal loss is the difference between the CCA that was previously claimed and actual depreciation.

The time for the determination of a terminal loss is "at the end of a taxation year". Therefore, if dispositions trigger a negative UCC balance during the year, but assets of the same class are acquired before the end of the year, there is no terminal loss.

(iv) — Review example

	UCC — *Class 16 (40%)*
Year 1	
T purchases two trucks (his only Class 16 assets) for hauling freight in his transport business at a cost of $100,000 each (Item A of UCC definition)	
UCC otherwise determined at year end	$200,000
Notional UCC under the half-year rule	
= UCC - 50% of [new A - new F of UCC definition]	
$200,000 - 50% × (200,000 - 0) = $100,000	
CCA = 40% × $100,000[a]	($40,000)
Closing UCC at the end of year 1	$160,000
Year 2	
T purchases truck #3 for $20,000 (added to item A in UCC definition)	$20,000
T sells truck #1 for $90,000 (item F in UCC definition)	(90,000)
T sells truck #2 for $130,000 (i.e., $30,000 more than capital cost[b]) (item F of UCC definition is capped by cost amount)	(100,000)
UCC at year-end (negative balance)[c]	(10,000)

	UCC — *Class 16 (40%)*
A = capital cost of truck # 1, 2 and 3	
= \$200,000 + \$20,000 = \$220,000	
B = nil	
E = CCA in year 1 = \$40,000	
F = POD for truck #1 and cost of truck #2	
= \$90,000 + \$100,000	
UCC = \$220,000 - (\$40,000 + \$190,000)	
= (\$10,000)	
Recapture under s. 13(1) = \$10,000	
Notes: 1) Half-year rule does not apply because there is no net addition to UCC	
2) No CCA for year 2	
Year 3	
Recapture for year 2 (Item B of UCC definition)	\$10,000
T purchases truck #4 for \$60,000[d]	\$60,000
UCC otherwise determined at year-end	\$60,000
A = capital cost of all 4 trucks purchased	
\$200,000 + \$20,000 + \$60,000 = \$280,000	
B = recapture = \$10,000	
E = total CCA allowed = \$40,000	
F = POD of truck #1 and POD up to cost of truck #2	
= \$190,000	
UCC = [\$280,000 + \$10,000] - [\$40,000+ \$190,000]	
= \$60,000	
Notional UCC under half-year rule	
= UCC - 50% of [\$60,000 - 0] = \$30,000[e]	
CCA for year 3 = 40% × notional UCC	(\$12,000)
Closing UCC at end of year 3	\$48,000
Year 4	
T sells truck #3 and #4 for a total of \$30,000	(\$30,000)
UCC at year-end	\$18,000
A = \$280,000	
B = \$10,000	
E = \$40,000 (year 1 CCA) + \$12,000 (year 3 CCA) = \$52,000	
F = POD of Truck #1, 3 and 4, and POD of truck #2 capped by capital cost = \$190,000 + \$30,000	

	UCC — *Class 16 (40%)*
UCC = [$280,000 + $10,000] - [$52,000 + $220,000] = $290,000 - $272,000 = $18,000	
Terminal loss (no longer owns any Class 16 assets)	($18,000)
UCC at year-end	NIL

Notes:

a T may claim less than full capital cost allowance if he chooses (reg. 1100(1) "not exceeding"), and this choice might be made to minimize current losses or to utilize loss carryovers from earlier years.

b A capital gain of $30,000 will have to be recognized on the sale of truck #2.

c The half year rule (reg. 1100(2)) has no application if no capital cost allowance can be claimed. Even if there were a positive balance in the UCC account for year 2, so that capital cost allowance could have been claimed, the half year rule would still not apply because in year 2 the proceeds of dispositions exceeded the cost of acquisitions.

d If this truck had been purchased in the previous year, it would have avoided the recapture in year 2.

e UCC - 50% of [new A - new F of UCC definition].

(i) — Limitations on CCA deductions

(i) — Tax shelter losses

CCA deductions may give rise to a loss from a business or property. Such losses are generally deductible against income from other sources. In some cases, when the losses are "created" by the taxpayer to shelter other income, the recognition of such losses is inappropriate in terms of policy. The Act contains numerous stop-loss rules;[101] including the two below.

(ii) — Rental property

Taxpayers invest in buildings and other rental properties for dual purposes: to earn income from rent, which is typically characterized as income from property, as well as to realize capital gains from the increase in value of the properties. It is not uncommon that the rental income is modest, while the potential of a capital gain is significant. Some investment vehicles are structured to generate losses from the income stream while the property appreciates in value and generate a capital gain when sold.

For the purposes of the CCA regime, the total capital cost of the rental property is added to the UCC and subject to the CCA deduction. As explained earlier, the de-

[101]These rules are discussed under heading 10.7, "Stop-loss rules" and heading 14.4(c), "Limitations on deductions for losses" below.

clining-balance method of depreciation that underlies the design of the CCA system results in greater deductions in early years. For example, the CCA on an apartment building or office building, in particular, will provide substantial annual deductions to the owner, especially in the early years of the life of the building, although the building may not be declining in value at all. If the CCA exceeded the net rental income from the property (before CCA), then a loss would be generated for tax purposes. Not only would the owner report no income from that property, the loss would be available to offset the owner's income from other sources as well.[102] The losses from rental properties are "artificial" in that no economic loss has really been suffered.

Regulation 1100(11) was adopted in 1972 to restrict the CCA that may be claimed on a "rental property".[103] A rental property is defined in regulation 1100(14) as a building used "principally for the purpose of gaining or producing gross revenue that is rent".[104] The effect of regulation 1100(11) is to limit the CCA which may be claimed on a rental property to a maximum of the rental income less all deductions other than CCA. This provision means that CCA on a rental property can be deducted only to the point where the income from the property for tax purposes is reduced to zero. CCA deductions may not be used to create or increase losses which would shelter the owner's income from other sources. If the taxpayer owns more than one rental property, capital cost allowance on one rental property can be used to offset rental income on another rental property. This is because the income and losses for all rental properties (after deducting expenses but before claiming capital cost allowance) are added together in order to determine the limit for the overall capital cost allowance claim. For example, consider a taxpayer with two Class 1 buildings with an UCC of $40,000 each, the first with a rental profit of $1,000 before capital cost allowance and the second with a rental profit of $5,000 before capital cost allowance. The total capital cost allowance claim on the buildings is $3,200 - the lesser of $3,200 (4% capital cost allowance rate on 2 assets at $40,000 each) and $6,000. The capital cost allowance on the first building is not restricted to $1,000 because the taxpayer's overall rental profit is $6,000. However, if there were a rental loss of $5,000 on the second building (rather than a $5,000 profit), no capital cost allowance could be claimed on either building because there is a net rental loss of $4,000 on the two buildings.

---

[102]See headings 14.4 and 14.5, below.

[103]There is also a requirement that each rental property acquired for more than $50,000 be placed in a separate class (reg. 1101(1ac)). This prevents the sheltering of recapture of capital cost allowance on the disposition of the property: see the discussion under heading 9.4(h)(ii), "Recapture", above.

[104]The word "principally" is considered to mean more than 50%, generally based on floor space: *Mother's Pizza Parlour v. R.*, [1988] 2 C.T.C. 197, 88 D.T.C. 6397 (Fed. C.A.). If the "principally" test is met, the entire building is classified as a rental property: *Canada Trust Co. v. M.N.R.*, [1985] 1 C.T.C. 2367, 85 D.T.C. 322 (T.C.C.).

(iii) — Leasing property

Similar restrictions under regulations 1100(15) apply to "leasing property", which is moveable depreciable property used "principally for the purpose of gaining or producing gross revenue that is rent, royalty or leasing revenue".[105] Examples would be construction equipment, boats or aircraft, which are rented out to users.

A subset of leasing property is "specified leasing property", which is leasing property worth more than $25,000 and is subject to additional restrictions.[106] These restrictions were introduced in 1989 in response to a proliferation of sale leaseback transactions by non taxable entities, such as government agencies, municipal bodies, charities and corporations with large losses or loss carryforwards. For example, a transit authority might own a fleet of buses upon which it would not be able to claim CCA, because the authority was tax exempt. The transit authority would sell the buses to a taxable entity (the lessor), which could claim CCA on the buses, and which would lease the buses back to the transit authority. The transit authority would receive not only the purchase price of the buses, but also favourable rental rates as the lessor would pass on part of the tax savings generated by the lessor's CCA deduction on the buses. Both the lessor and the lessee (the transit authority) would be better off — at the expense of the tax system. This practice has now been blocked by deeming the sale leaseback of "specified leasing property" to be a loan of the purchase price by the lessor to the lessee at the government's prescribed interest rate,[107] so that the rent received by the lessor is deemed to be a blended payment of interest and principal on the loan. The lessor's claim to CCA[108] is restricted to the amount of principal notionally repaid on the loan each year.[109]

These statutory rules are necessary in order to ensure that CCA deductions are not used as tax shelters. A similar effect would be achieved by deeming a financing lease to be a sale or a loan. This is the approach taken under generally accepted accounting principles which deem a lease to be a sale or a loan for accounting purposes on the basis of the economic substance of the situation.[110] Such an approach has not been adopted for tax law purposes: as long as the legal relationship

---

[105]Reg. 1100(17). Corporations are exempt from the rental and leasing property restrictions if their "principal business" (accounting for 90% of gross revenues) is the leasing, rental, development or sale of real property (reg. 1100(12), in the case of the rental property restriction) or the renting or leasing of leasing property (reg. 1100(16), in the case of the leasing property restriction).

[106]Regs. 1100(1.1) to (1.3).

[107]Adjusted quarterly under reg. 4302.

[108]There is also a requirement that each specified leasing property be placed in a separate class (reg. 1100(1.1)), as is the requirement for rental properties acquired for more than $50,000 (note 103, above).

[109]The rules discussed above apply to the lessor. Section 16.1 gives lessees the opportunity to elect to be under similar rules in certain circumstances.

[110]These types of leases are called "capital leases" for accounting purposes.

created by the terms of the agreement is a lease and there is no sham, a lease is a lease for tax purposes.[111]

Moreover, a number of properties are exempted under Regulations 1100(1.3) from the "specified lease property" definition. Trailers, office furniture, etc. are among such exempt properties. It is because of these exemptions that purchase and lease-back transactions, such as those in the *Canada Trustco Mortgage Co. v. R.*,[112] continue to provide significant tax savings.

9.5 — Eligible capital expenditures

(a) — Amortization of intangibles

Intangibles typically include purchased goodwill, trade marks, quotas, franchises and licences for an unlimited period, customer lists, "know how", stock exchange seats, and organization costs.[113] Most intangibles, and, notably, goodwill, are not listed in Schedule II and are therefore not "depreciable property".[114] Therefore, in the absence of the statutory amortization rules under paragraph 20(1)(b), the cost of acquiring intangibles is denied of a deduction by paragraph 18(1)(b).

Historically, when a taxpayer purchased a business, the portion of the purchase price allocated to goodwill was not deductible. Goodwill and some other expenditures came to be called "nothings". The Carter Commission proposed that the cost of purchased goodwill (and other intangible assets of more or less permanent life) should continue to be non deductible for tax purposes, on the basis that goodwill, like land, generally does not depreciate.[115] Other classes of expenditures for intangibles which have a long run but not permanent value to the business were to be listed and pooled in a new capital cost allowance class with a rate of 20 per cent. Any other costs of intangibles were to be deductible in full when incurred.

The government did not accept Carter's recommendations in detail, but it did ameliorate the treatment of "nothings". The 1971 Act provided for the amortization of most of the former nothings (including purchased goodwill) by the creation of a category of capital expenditures called "eligible capital expenditures". One half of eligible capital expenditures were to be placed in a pool called "cumulative eligible capital" (CEC) and amortized (by way of a CECA deduction) at a maximum rate of

---

[111]Until *Shell Canada Limited v. R.*, 99 D.T.C. 5669, [1999] 4 C.T.C. 313 (S.C.C.), the CRA took the position was there was a "capital lease" rule for tax purposes based on the economic substance of the transaction: see Interpretation Bulletin IT 233R, "Lease option agreements; Sale leaseback agreements" (1983), withdrawn on June 14, 2001.

[112]Note 77, above.

[113]For example, legal fees for incorporation of a company. Costs of financing are not eligible capital expenditures, because they are specifically deductible under s. 20(1)(e) over a five year period: see heading 8.10, "Other costs of financing", above.

[114]See heading, 9.4(b)(ii), "Rate of CCA", above, for the restricted list of intangible properties that qualify as Class 14 and Class 44 assets.

[115]*Report of the Royal Commission on Taxation* (Carter report) (1966), vol. 4, 245.

10 per cent per annum by the declining balance method. In 1988, the Act was amended to increase the portion of an eligible capital expenditure that is added to the pool of cumulative eligible capital from one half to three quarters. At the same time, the rate at which the cumulative eligible capital could be written off each year was reduced from 10 per cent to 7 per cent, still on a declining balance basis.[116]

(b) — "Eligible capital expenditure" defined

The term "eligible capital expenditure" is defined in subsection 14(5) as an expenditure "on account of capital for the purpose of gaining or producing income from the business", subject to a number of exclusions. The definition excludes capital expenditures for tangible property (whether land or depreciable property) and for those types of intangible property that are depreciable property. This leaves within the definition a residuary class of capital expenditures that includes most capital expenditures for intangibles. The intangible property that is purchased with an eligible capital expenditure is described in section 54 as "eligible capital property". The most important of these expenditures is the cost of goodwill.[117]

(c) — Deduction

Paragraph 20(1)(b) allows a deduction not exceeding 7 per cent of the "cumulative eligible capital" (CEC) at the end of each year.[118] The deduction, which is called "CECA" is taken on a declining balance basis.

The CEC account, which is defined in subsection 14(5), is operated in much the same way as the UCC account of a class of depreciable property. The CEC account is increased by three quarters of each eligible capital expenditure (purchase of eligible capital property), and it is reduced by three quarters of the proceeds of disposition of eligible capital property. A recapture and a terminal allowance (similar to "terminal loss") each causes the account to be reset to zero. A recapture is included

---

[116]The rate reduction nearly offsets the effect of the increase in the size of the CEC pool, so that since 1988 annual CECA deductions from cumulative eligible capital have become only slightly higher than they were before 1988 (e.g., for an eligible capital expenditure of $200, 10 per cent of $100 = $10; 7 per cent of $150 = $10.50). The reason for the change was to mirror the increase in the inclusion rate of capital gains from one-half to three-quarters, which was effective in 1990. The idea at that time was that any "economic gain" on the sale of cumulative eligible capital should be taxed at roughly the same preferential basis as capital gains. The CECA system that exists today is essentially the 1988 system except for two rules governing dispositions: (1) the rule which adjusts the inclusion rate for any economic gain to one-half (which is the current capital gains inclusion rate) and (2) the rule that allows an individual to elect to treat the economic gain as a capital gain rather than business income (except in the case of the sale of goodwill). The details of these rules are discussed in note 127, below.

[117]See heading 9.2(g), "Goodwill", above.

[118]There is no half year rule to reduce the deduction that can be taken in the year that an eligible capital expenditure is made. The half year rule of reg. 1100(2) with respect to depreciable property is described under heading 9.4(f), "Half year rule", above.

in income under subsection 14(1); it occurs if the account falls to a negative figure as the result of a disposition of eligible capital property.[119] A terminal allowance is deductible under subsection 24(1); it occurs if the account has a positive balance when the taxpayer ceases to carry on the business.

Example

	Cumulative eligible capital
Year 1	
T purchases goodwill for $100,000	
CEC at end of year 1 (before CECA)	$75,000
CECA deduction for year 1 under s. 20(1)(b) (7%)[a]	(5,250)
CEC at end of year 1	69,750
Year 2	
T sells goodwill for $140,000[b]	(105,000)
T purchases new "customer lists" for $80,000[c]	60,000
CEC at end of year 2 before CECA	24,750
CECA deduction for year 2 under s. 20(1)(b) (7%)	(1,733)
CEC at end of year 2	23,017
Year 3	
T ceases to carry on business.	

[119]Three-quarters of the proceeds of disposition is deducted from the CEC account, even if three-quarters of the cost was never added to the CEC account. If the balance is negative, the rules are as follows for taxation years ending after October 17, 2000. Include in income two amounts: (1) the lesser of (a) the negative CEC balance and (b) the CECA amounts claimed in respect of the asset in prior years and (2) 2/3 of the negative CEC balance minus the amount in (1). For example, if the original eligible capital expenditure is $1,000, the sale price is $10,000, the CEC balance before the sale is zero and past CECA claims in respect of the asset are $750, then amount 1 is $750 (the lesser of $7,500 [3/4 × $10,000] and $750) and amount 2 is $4,500 ([$7,500 - $750] × 2/3). The effect of this is to include in income the recapture of CECA (amount 1 = $750) plus 1/2 of any economic gain over cost (amount 2 = $4,500 = 1/2 [$10,000 - $1,000]). The use of the 2/3's fraction converts the inclusion rate of the gain over cost (the economic gain) from 3/4 to 1/2, which is the capital gains inclusion rate. The sum of (1) and (2) is included in business income under section 14. However, an individual (but not a corporation) can elect to treat any gain over original cost on eligible capital property (other than goodwill) to be a capital gain rather than business income (s. 14(1.01)). This election is helpful if the taxpayer has undeducted allowable capital losses (which can only be deducted against taxable capital gains). The gain over original cost is also relevant for determining the capital dividend account of a private corporation, because one half of this gain (i.e., the non taxable portion) is added to the corporation's capital dividend account (see paragraph (c) of the definition of capital dividend account in s. 89(1)). As discussed in chapter 15, below, a private corporation can elect to pay tax free dividends to its shareholders out of its capital dividend account.

	Cumulative eligible capital
CEC at end of year 3 before terminal allowance	
Terminal allowance (s. 24(1))[d]	(23,017)
CEC at end of year 3	NIL

Notes:

a T may claim less than the full deduction if he chooses (s. 20(1)(b) "not exceeding 7%"), and this choice may be sensible in a situation of current losses or available loss carryovers.

b The full three-quarters of proceeds is subtracted from CEC despite the fact that part of the proceeds represents a gain over original cost of $100,000.

c This purchase restores the CEC account to a positive balance and shelters the inclusion in income under s. 14(1) of $35,250 which would otherwise have been caused by the sale of goodwill.

d No deduction can be taken under s. 20(1)(b) for year 3, and the CEC is reduced to nil by s. 24(1)(c).

10
Capital Gains

10.1 — History

The history of the tax treatment of capital gains has already been discussed.[1] Capital gains were initially excluded from the tax base by virtue of the "source theory" which dominated the Anglo-Canadian conception of income. Under the Haig-Simons conception of income,[2] capital gains (along with all other accretions to net worth) had to be taxed. The "comprehensive tax base" urged by the Carter Commission also included capital gains, although the Commission conceded that it was impracticable to assess capital gains which had accrued but had not been realized, hence the Commission recommended that (with some exceptions) only realized gains should be included.[3] The ultimate compromise, which was enacted in 1971, was to include only one-half of realized capital gains in income, and to allow the deduction of one-half of capital losses against those gains. In this way, capital gains became taxable for the first time in 1972,[4] but on a basis more favourable than other types of income. The tax reform of 1988 increased the inclusion rate from

[1]See heading 4.2(b), "Carter Commission's "comprehensive tax base"", above.

[2]See heading 4.2(a), "Haig-Simons theory", above.

[3]Note 1, above.

[4]This raised the transitional problem of how to exempt from tax those capital gains accrued on property owned on January 1, 1972, the date of commencement of the new system. The solution turned out to be quite complicated: Income Tax Application Rules, s. 26(3) (tax-free zone rule), and s. 26(7) (election of valuation day value). The significance of these provisions has not yet disappeared, because some taxpayers continue to own capital properties that they owned on January 1, 1972. However, the transitional provisions are outside the scope of this book.

one-half to three-quarters, thereby reducing but not eliminating the tax preference for capital gains. In 2000, the inclusion rate was changed back to 50 per cent.

While it is common to refer to the "capital gains tax", the description is not really accurate. There is no separate tax on capital gains. Capital gains are simply another type of income, one-half of which are included in a taxpayer's income under paragraph 3(b) of the *Income Tax Act* (the "Act"), along with the taxpayer's income from other sources, such as employment, business or property, which are included in full under paragraph 3(a).

10.2 — Policy

The issues of policy to be addressed in this chapter are: (1) Should capital gains be taxed at all and (2) if so, should they be taxed on a preferential basis?

(a) — Equity

Should capital gains be taxed at all? This raises for reconsideration the arguments in favour of a reasonably comprehensive tax base. If tax is to be levied in accordance with ability to pay, then every increase in a taxpayer's ability to pay should be included in income, subject only to considerations of administrative feasibility. Since a capital gain represents an increase in the taxpayer's ability to pay tax, the capital gain should be included in income (and a capital loss should be deducted from income). This argument is of course grounded in the idea of tax equity: in comparing the taxable capacity of different taxpayers, "a buck is a buck is a buck". The taxpayer who makes a dollar in the form of a capital gain should be treated no differently than the taxpayer who makes a dollar in the form of income from employment or business or property.

The equity argument is reinforced in the case of capital gains by the fact that capital gains are derived disproportionately by high-income individuals. The Carter Commission used statistics from the United States, where capital gains had been taxed for a long time, to show that capital gains tend to form a small proportion of the income reported by low-income individuals, and a large proportion of the income reported by high-income individuals. Indeed, the Commission concluded that the inclusion of capital gains in income would permit a drastic lowering of tax rates at the upper levels of income while actually improving the true progressivity of the system. In fact, as Carter predicted, the capital gains reported in Canada since tax reform in 1971 have been disproportionately concentrated in the upper-income classes. The inclusion of capital gains, even on a preferential basis, has therefore contributed to the progressivity (vertical equity) of the system.

(b) — Neutrality

The case for taxation of capital gains may also be based on the ground of neutrality. When capital gains are untaxed or preferentially taxed, taxpayers will go to great lengths to arrange their affairs so that the profit is obtained in the form of a capital gain instead of ordinary income. If a tax system was neutral in its treatment of capital gains and other forms of income, there would be no tax incentive to take profits in the form of capital gains, and no need for complicated anti-avoidance measures. The Carter Commission recognized this[5] and it is still true today.

It is because of the current preferential tax treatment of capital gains that one of the most significant problem areas in the tax system today arises: the mismatch that results when a taxpayer holding an investment that generates income as well as a capital gain. As discussed in chapter 8,[6] the most common types of investment are rental property or shares. The taxpayer is able to currently deduct related expenses (e.g., interest) in full in computing income from business or property while the capital gain accrued to the investment is not taxable until the investment is sold and is taxed only in half. Because the current deductions often exceed the rental or dividend income, a loss will be created and the taxpayer can use the loss to shelter income from other sources. The problem of mismatch would not exist if capital gains were not subject to differential tax treatment.

(c) — Certainty

The certainty of the law would be increased by eliminating the difficult task of distinguishing between capital gains and ordinary income. No issue has generated more litigation than the question of whether a profit realized on the sale of property is business income or a capital gain. A glance at every volume of reported tax cases will demonstrate this point.[7] As explained in chapter 11, if the sale of the property is held to be a trade or an "adventure or concern in the nature of trade", then the profit is business income. If, on the other hand, the sale is held to be the realization of an investment, the profit is a capital gain. It is often difficult to formulate satisfactory legal tests to distinguish between these kinds of transactions, and the evidentiary problems involved are significant.[8]

(d) — Inflationary gains

Tax policy objectives of equity, neutrality and certainty generally support the taxation of capital gains. As discussed below, however, capital gains are taxed only in part, leaving a portion of capital gains exempt from income. Why the compromise? One explanation is the effect of inflation. In a world without inflation, the arguments for full taxation of capital gains which were canvassed earlier are overwhelming. But, as long as many capital gains are caused mainly by inflation, it would be inequitable to move to full taxation of capital gains without at the same time adjusting the system for inflation. The one-half inclusion of capital gains could conceivably be defended as a crude adjustment for inflation. As shown in the

---

[5]*Report of the Royal Commission on Taxation* (Carter Report) (1966), vol. 3, 334-335.

[6]See heading 8.11, "Mismatch and tax arbitrage", above.

[7]Chapter 11, Investing and Trading, below.

[8]*Carter Report*, note 5, above, 335-336

following example, however, this approach results in arbitrary treatment of taxpayers. Compare the following three taxpayers:

> Taxpayer A earns $20 of income from employment in 2005.
>
> Taxpayer B sells in 2007 an asset for $40 which he had bought for $20 just a few weeks earlier.
>
> Taxpayer C sells in 2007 an asset for $40 which she had bought for $20 ten years earlier. In that ten years the consumer price index has advanced by 100 per cent, or in other words, the dollar has depreciated by 50 per cent.

A's capacity to pay tax has increased by $20 and he should be taxed on that figure. B's capacity to pay has also increased by $20 and he should be taxed on that figure. C's capacity to pay has increased not one iota, because the increase in the nominal dollar value of her property simply reflects the decline in the value of the dollar; C's gain should not be taxed at all.[9] The present system will impose full taxation on A's gain, as it should; but only one-half taxation on B's gain, which should be fully taxed; and one-half taxation on C's gain, which should not be taxed at all. Only A is appropriately taxed. The taxation of B and C do not reflect the increases in the taxpayers' ability to pay, and are therefore inequitable.

As long as capital gains are only partially taxed, the system is inequitable (and not neutral) as between the taxpayer who makes ordinary income (A, above) and the taxpayer who makes a real (not inflation-caused) capital gain (B, above). But, as long as the system is not adjusted for inflation, even partial taxation is too severe for the taxpayer whose gain has simply matched the rate of inflation (C, above). Because the Act allows no adjustments for inflation in computing capital gains, this results in the taxation of inflation-induced capital gains. The effect of inflation on the gain cannot be cancelled out by adjusting the *rate* of tax payable by the taxpayer on the gain. The only way in which the effect of inflation can be cancelled out is by eliminating the *gain itself*. The gain is totally illusory and should not be taxed at all.

The required reforms are therefore twofold: (1) capital gains should be fully taxed, but (2) the system should be adjusted to cancel out the effect of inflation. If the system were changed in these two ways, A and B would be taxed equally, reflecting their equal increases in their ability to pay, and C would not be taxed at all, reflecting the illusory character of her gain. There is no technical difficulty in implementing full taxation of capital gains. Indeed, it would greatly simplify the tax system, as Carter pointed out.[10] Nor is it technically difficult to adjust capital gains

---

[9]In *MacDonald v. M.N.R.*, [1984] C.T.C. 2624, 84 D.T.C. 1602 (T.C.C.), a taxpayer argued that his inflation-induced capital gains on real property should not be subject to tax. The Tax Court of Canada held that in the absence of statutory provisions exempting inflationary gains from taxation, the inflation-induced component of capital gains cannot be deducted in computing the amount of a taxable capital gain.

[10]Notes 5 and 8, above.

for inflation, although any adjustment will increase the complexity of the tax system.

One way in which capital gains could be adjusted for inflation is by indexing the cost base of capital property, in a manner similar to the way that the Act indexes personal income tax brackets and personal tax credits.[11] In the example above, C's actual cost was $20, but over a period of 100 per cent inflation the cost should be notionally increased by 100 per cent (the rate of inflation) to $40. Selling the asset for $40 would not then involve the recognition of any gain, because the proceeds of disposition would not exceed the indexed cost base. Selling the asset for $45 would involve the recognition of a gain of $5 because that would be a real gain in purchasing power — a gain over and above the rate of inflation. Selling the asset for $35 would involve the recognition of a loss of $5 since the nominal gain of $15 would represent a loss in real purchasing power of $5.[12]

Another way in which capital gains could be adjusted for inflation is by "tapering". This consists of including in income a smaller portion of a capital gain the longer a capital property is held. For example, a gain realized during the first year of ownership might be fully taxable, with the inclusion rate declining by (say) 10 percentage points for each year of ownership. A gain realized during the third year of ownership would be 70 per cent taxable. After a period of ownership of ten years, the gain would be exempt.

(e) — Risk taking and investment disincentives

Capital gains are, in essence, profits from selling investments. A capital gains tax may be perceived as discouraging risk taking and investment because of the "lock-in" effect and the "bunching effect".

For administrative reasons, capital gains are taxed when they are realized, not when the gains are accrued during the ownership of the investment assets. A disadvantage for the taxpayer of the realization basis of capital gains taxation is the "bunching" of several years' gains into a single year, the year of realization. This may cause the gains to be taxed at a higher marginal rate than if they had been recognized annually over the period of accrual. The Act used to offer relief from "bunching" by allowing persons with "lumpy incomes" to take advantage of averaging provisions. These averaging provisions have now been repealed. Of course, a large proportion of capital gains is derived by taxpayers in the top rate bracket, who cannot be pushed into a higher bracket by gains realized in a particular year.

Another effect of the realization basis of capital gains taxation is to discourage an owner from selling an asset that has appreciated substantially in value. As long as

---

[11]This is discussed in more detail under heading 14.6(d), "Indexing for inflation", below.

[12]Indexing the cost base would apply even where capital property has been acquired with borrowed money. Although borrowed money provides the leverage to increase the owner's equity by far more than the rate of inflation, the interest payable to the lender will reflect the anticipated rate of inflation at the time of the loan, so that much of the owner's apparent gain has been paid to the lender in the form of higher interest rates.

the asset is retained, no tax has to be paid; as soon as the asset is sold, tax must be paid on the capital gain realized. The owner feels "locked in" by the potential tax liability. Of course, an owner will still sell the asset if he or she needs the money or if the asset is expected to fall in value. But the owner will be reluctant to sell the asset merely to put the money to another use because there would be less money available for the other use. This lock-in effect is a disincentive for the owner to put his or her property to its most profitable (efficient) use. While economists are not agreed on the seriousness of this problem, it seems intuitively obvious that it must have an adverse effect on the nation's productivity.[13] The present system places limits on the lock-in effect by providing that on the death of a taxpayer there is a "deemed disposition" of all of the deceased's capital property at fair market value.[14]

(f) — Tax subsidies for certain investments

Recognizing the potential adverse impact on investments and policy reasons for promoting investment in home ownership, small businesses, farm properties and fishing properties, the Act provides "exemptions" for gains from the sale of such properties. The lifetime exemption is provided under section 110.6 of the Act in the form of a Division C deduction in computing taxable income. All capital gains derived by an individual (corporations were not eligible) from the disposition of qualified properties are exempt from tax up to a lifetime limit of $750,000.[15] Qualified properties are "qualified small business corporation shares" (shares in a Canadian-controlled private corporation engaged in active business in Canada),[16] "quali-

---

[13]It is for this reason that the Act currently allows taxpayers to defer capital gains if proceeds are reinvested in very limited circumstances (see, for example, sections 44, 44.1) but no general rule exists. The current federal government made an election promise in 2006 to introduce a more general capital gains deferral rule (to apply, for example, on the sale of investments or cottages) if proceeds were reinvested within six months. No such rule has been introduced in the 2006 or 2007 federal budgets and the government is silent on the reason why. It seems likely that the reasons might include the logic of allowing such a general rule, the size of the tax expenditure involved and the complexities involved in ensuring that the deferred capital gain was eventually reported.

[14]S. 70(5).

[15]The history of the lifetime exemption is as follows. It was first introduced in 1985 for all capital gains. The limit was initially $100,000, and was scheduled to be raised to $500,000 in 1990. The tax reform of 1988 capped the general exemption at its 1987 level of $100,000 but an additional $400,000 exemption remained available for qualified properties. The general $100,000 lifetime exemption remained in the Act until 1994 when it was repealed. The $500,000 lifetime limit for qualified properties remained until March 19, 2007, when it was increased to $750,000 for dispositions on or after March 19, 2007. Taxpayers who had used their $500,000 limit before March 19, 2007 were given an extra $250,000.

[16]Several tests must be met, one of which is that the corporation must be a "small business corporation" at the date of sale.

fied farm property" (real property used in the business of farming),[17] and "qualified fishing property" (real property, fishing vessels and eligible capital property used principally in a fishing business).[18]

The "principal residence exemption" under paragraph 40(2)(b) excludes all capital gains from the disposition of a qualified principal residence (essentially the family home). The policy justifications and technical rules for this exemption are discussed later in this chapter.

10.3 — Statutory framework

(a) — Inclusion in income

Paragraph 3(b) of the Act includes in income "taxable capital gains" less "allowable capital losses". Sections 38 to 55 then supply the rules for the computation of taxable capital gains and allowable capital losses. Among these provisions, sections 38, 39, 40 and 54 are the basic rules. Section 38 provides that taxable capital gains are 50 per cent of capital gains and allowable capital losses are 50 per cent of capital losses. Section 39 stipulates that a gain from the disposition of a property is a capital gain if that gain is not taxed as income from a source under paragraph 3(a). Section 40 contains the rules for the computation of a gain or loss. Section 54 provides a definition for the key concepts, including "capital property", "proceeds of disposition", "disposition", and "adjusted cost base".

A "taxable capital gain" is defined in paragraph 38(a) as 50 per cent of a "capital gain", and an "allowable capital loss" is defined in paragraph 38(b) as 50 per cent of a "capital loss". Since it is "taxable capital gains" rather than "capital gains" which are brought into income, and "allowable capital losses" rather than "capital losses" which are deductible, it is the definitions of taxable capital gains and allowable capital losses which implement the policy of including only one-half of capital gains in income.

A gain or loss is computed in accordance with section 40, a provision that is considered later in more detail. A gain or loss, which is derived from a "disposition" of "property", is measured by calculating the difference between the "proceeds of disposition" of the property and the "adjusted cost base" of the property. If the proceeds of disposition are more than the adjusted cost base of the property, the excess is a capital gain. If the proceeds of disposition are less than the adjusted cost base of the property, the deficiency is a capital loss.

(b) — Characterization of capital gains

Any gain is a capital gain unless the gain is otherwise taxed as income under paragraph 3(a). This is derived from the words in brackets in paragraph 39(1)(a). These

---

[17]As well as real property, an interest in a family farm partnership and shares in a family farm corporation are eligible for the exemption. The same is true for fishing property, discussed below.

[18]This category was added for dispositions after May 1, 2006.

words have the effect of excluding from capital gains treatment any property the disposition of which gives rise to ordinary income — ordinary income being income from employment, business, property or any other source except taxable capital gains. Similarly, paragraph 39(1)(b) excludes losses from a disposition of property from capital losses if the losses are otherwise treated as losses from a regular source.

The most important example of property excluded by the bracketed words of paragraph 39(1)(a) and (b) is the inventory of a business. For example, if an automobile dealer sells a car at a profit, he or she has made a gain from the disposition of property; but the gain is not a capital gain, because the profit of a trader on the sale of his or her inventory is ordinary income — income from a business. Another example is property bought on speculation as an "adventure or concern in the nature of trade". For example, if a person sells a parcel of real estate which he or she acquired with the intention of making a profit by early resale, this person too has made a gain from the disposition of property; but again it is not a capital gain because the profit of an adventure or concern in the nature of trade is ordinary income — income from a business. It is often difficult to determine whether a taxpayer who has profited (or lost) from transactions in property is (1) a trader, in which case the property is inventory and the profit is business income, or (2) a speculator, in which case the property is speculative property and the profit is also business income, or (3) simply an investor who has realized an investment, in which case the profit is a capital gain. These distinctions have produced more case law than any other issue under the Act, and are discussed in chapter 11, "Investing and Trading", below.

The important point for present purposes is that the capital gains category is a residuary category, including only those gains from the disposition of property which would not otherwise be taxed. Not only does this exclude profits from trading or from an adventure in the nature of trade, it also excludes any other gain which is taxed elsewhere in the Act. For example, gains on stock options granted to employees are included in employment income by section 7.[19]

(c) — Realization

The general rule is that a capital gain or loss is not recognized for tax purposes until it has been realized by the disposition of the property. A gain that has accrued through the appreciation in value of a property, but has not been realized, is not recognized for tax purposes. This rule is complemented by subsection 9(3), which

[19]S. 39(1)(a) reinforces the general exclusion of gains taxed elsewhere with a number of specific exemptions of property that receives distinctive tax treatment elsewhere: eligible capital property, cultural property, Canadian resource property, foreign resource property, timber resource property and insurance policies. S. 39(1)(b), dealing with capital losses, contains the same set of exclusions, but with the important addition of depreciable property. The special case of depreciable property, giving rise to capital gains but not capital losses, is considered in the next section.

provides that income (or loss) from a property, which is computed under subdivision b, does not include any capital gain (or loss) from the disposition of that property. It is the disposition which distinguishes capital gains from property income, such as rent, interest or dividends, to which the property-owner is entitled by virtue of merely holding the property.

There are two main reasons why capital gains are not taxed until they have been realized: (1) the administrative problem of annually evaluating all capital property so as to assess accrued capital gains; and (2) the liquidity problem for taxpayers in finding the cash to pay tax on gains that have not yielded any cash. The realization basis gives taxpayers control over the timing of the recognition of capital gains. This is itself an important tax advantage. To be sure, sometimes circumstances outside the taxpayer's control will require a sale of capital property at a time which is inopportune for tax purposes. For the most part, however, the sale of property is a voluntary act, and the taxpayer will not do it without regard for tax considerations. An example of an opportune time to sell an asset sheltering a capital gain would be when a loss has accrued on another asset. On selling both assets, the gain on one would be absorbed by the loss on the other. Disadvantages of the realization basis of capital gains taxation are the "bunching" and "lock-in" effect mentioned above.

10.4 — Basic concepts

(a) — Capital property

A capital gain or loss is a gain or loss from a disposition of "property". If there is no disposition of property, there is no capital gain or loss. However, there are some exceptional classes of property the disposition of which does not give rise to a capital gain or loss. "Capital property" is a convenient term to describe property the disposition of which will give rise to capital gains or losses.[20]

Capital property of a taxpayer is defined in section 54 as:

> (a) any depreciable property of the taxpayer, and
>
> (b) any property (other than depreciable property), any gain or loss from the disposition of which would, if the property were disposed of, be a capital gain or a capital loss, as the case may be, of the taxpayer;

In order to determine what property is capital property it is necessary to turn to section 39 of the Act, which specifies which kinds of property do not give rise to capital gains or losses. The excluded property is not capital property. All property not excluded is capital property.

[20] The special case of depreciable property, giving rise to capital gains but not capital losses, is considered under heading 10.4(b), "Depreciable property", below.

(b) — Depreciable property

Depreciable property is anomalous in that its disposition may give rise to capital gains, but not to capital losses. Nevertheless, section 54 includes depreciable property in the definition of capital property.

"Depreciable property" is defined by subsection 13(21) as property in respect of which capital cost allowance may be claimed under paragraph 20(1)(a); that means, of course, property which has been acquired "for the purpose of gaining or producing income". The reason why depreciable property is excluded from *capital loss* treatment is that losses on depreciable property are fully deductible from business or property income as either capital cost allowance under paragraph 20(1)(a) or terminal loss under subsection 20(16).[21] The reason why depreciable property is not excluded from *capital gains* treatment is because any gain over capital cost on the disposition of depreciable property is not taxed under business or property income under subdivision b and must therefore be included in the capital gains category. Of course, any recapture of capital cost allowance on the disposition of depreciable property is taxed under subdivision b under subsection 13(1).

(c) — Disposition

(i) — Meaning

"Disposition" is defined in subsection 248(1) as including "any transaction or event entitling a taxpayer to proceeds of disposition of property".[22] This definition points to the definition of "proceeds of disposition". [23]When the two definitions are read together, it is clear that a disposition includes a sale of property, an expropriation of property for compensation, an insured loss or injury to property, and the redemption or cancellation of a loan.[24] By far the most common form of disposition would be a sale of property. But a disposition need not be a voluntary act by the owner of property: expropriation, loss and redemption would normally be involuntary.[25] A disposition need not involve the continued existence of the property or the acquisition of the property by someone else: destruction of property by fire or the redemption of a debt would lead to the disappearance of the property, yet those events are dispositions.

Can there be a "disposition" without "proceeds of disposition"? The definition of a disposition as "any transaction or event entitling a taxpayer to proceeds of disposi-

[21]See heading 9.4(b), "Depreciable property and CCA rates", above.

[22]The definition goes on to list a number of specific transactions that are included or excluded.

[23]See heading 10.4(d), "Proceeds of disposition", below .

[24]The redemption or cancellation of a loan is expressly mentioned in the definition of disposition.

[25]In the case of involuntary dispositions, where the taxpayer uses the proceeds of disposition to purchase a replacement property, s. 44(1) enables the taxpayer to elect to defer recognition of any capital gain until the replacement property is disposed of.

tion" would suggest that the existence of proceeds of disposition is essential. But the definition of disposition is not exhaustive: it uses the word "includes" rather than the word "means"; and there is no policy reason why a total loss, such as an uninsured casualty loss, should be excluded when a partial loss, such as an underinsured casualty loss, is included. In general, a disposition occurs "where possession, control and all other aspects of property ownership are relinquished", even if "there is no consideration flowing to the person disposing of the property".[26] Thus, there would be a disposition if a capital property were stolen, destroyed, lost, abandoned or confiscated without any right to compensation or insurance. In such a case, the proceeds of disposition would be zero for the purpose of computing the capital loss from the disposition.

An *inter vivos* gift also gives rise to a disposition. This conclusion is reinforced by the terms of paragraph 69(1)(b), which provides that, where a taxpayer has "disposed of" anything "by way of gift", he or she shall be deemed to have received proceeds of disposition therefore equal to its fair market value. This paragraph provides that the proceeds of disposition are deemed to be the fair market value of the gift rather than the actual proceeds of zero. Similarly, the effect of the passing of property on death is not left to the operation of the general capital gains provisions. Subsection 70(5) provides that, where a taxpayer has died, the taxpayer shall be deemed to have disposed, immediately before his or her death, of all of his or her capital property and to have received proceeds of disposition equal to the property's fair market value. These deemed dispositions on a gift and on death, as well as the Act's other deemed dispositions, are discussed later in this chapter.[27]

(ii) — Timing

The timing of a disposition determines the timing of taxing capital gains. So, when does a disposition occur? A typical situation would be where a contract of sale is entered into in one taxation year, and the closing date (when, normally, legal title and possession is given and the bulk of the consideration is received) occurs in the next taxation year. In which year must any gain or loss on the sale be recognized? This depends upon whether the disposition takes place for tax purposes on the contract date or on the closing date.

It will be recalled that the definition of a disposition is "a transaction or event entitling the taxpayer to proceeds of disposition of property". The time of a disposition therefore depends upon the question when the taxpayer becomes "entitled" to the proceeds of disposition. Is that the contract date or the closing date? In support of the contract date, it could be said that on the making of a contract of sale, the vendor becomes entitled to the proceeds of disposition in that the vendor has legally enforceable rights against the purchaser. As well, at that point the price is fixed so any future change in the value of the property will affect the tax position of the purchaser and not the vendor. On the other hand, in support of the closing date,

---

[26]Interpretation Bulletin IT-460, "Dispositions — absence of consideration" (1980), para. 1.

[27]See heading 10.6, "Special events and deemed dispositions", below.

it could be said that the vendor's right to be paid is normally subject to the fulfilment of conditions by the vendor, and in particular the delivery of clear title and vacant possession on the closing date. If the definition of disposition were read as calling for an unconditional entitlement to proceeds of disposition, the closing date would normally be indicated. As well, it could be added that the owner should not become liable to pay tax until he or she has actually received or obtained the indefeasible right to receive the gain upon which he or she is taxed.

The timing of a disposition is also relevant to the right of the vendor or purchaser to claim capital cost allowance on depreciable property. The definition of "disposition" in subsection 248(1) applies for both capital cost allowance purposes and capital gains purposes. Where a sale of depreciable property straddles the end of the taxation year, the question will arise whether it is the vendor or purchaser who can claim capital cost allowance on the property for that year. For capital cost allowance purposes, the closing date would seem more appropriate than the contract date, because the vendor normally has the continued use of the property until the closing date, and the purchaser has not normally obtained the use of the property until then.[28] Arguably, the date of disposition for capital gains purposes and the dates of disposition and acquisition for capital cost allowance purposes should be the same, and the relevant date should be the closing date.[29]

In the case of involuntary dispositions, subsection 44(2) deems the time at which the proceeds of disposition become receivable (i.e., the time of disposition) to be the earliest of: (1) the day the taxpayer agreed to an amount as full compensation for the property lost, destroyed, taken or sold; (2) the day the amount of compensation is finally determined by a court or tribunal; or (3) where a claim, suit, appeal or other proceeding is not taken before a tribunal or court, the day that is two years following the day of the loss, destruction or taking of the property.

(d) — Proceeds of disposition

On a disposition of capital property, any gain or loss is measured by the difference between the "proceeds of disposition" of the property and the "adjusted cost base" of the property. As defined in section 54, "proceeds of disposition" essentially consist of the gross proceeds realized by the disposition: the price received on sale, the compensation received on expropriation, the insurance proceeds received on loss, and so on.

---

[28]In the case of the purchaser, the "available for use" rule would normally postpone any right to claim capital cost allowance until after the closing date: see heading 9.4(d)(iii), "Timing of acquisition", above.

[29]Interpretation Bulletin IT-133, "Stock exchange transactions — date of disposition of shares" (1973), para. 3. For a discussion of the acquisition date for capital cost allowance purposes, see Interpretation Bulletin IT-285R2, "Capital cost allowance — General Comments" (1994), paras. 16–19.

(e) — Adjusted cost base

The other essential element to be brought into account in computing a capital gain or loss is the "adjusted cost base" of the property. This term is defined in section 54, which reads (in part) as follows:

> "adjusted cost base" to a taxpayer of any property at any time means, except as otherwise provided,
>
> (a) where the property is depreciable property of the taxpayer, the capital cost to the taxpayer of the property as of that time, and
>
> (b) in any other case, the cost to the taxpayer of the property adjusted, as of that time, in accordance with section 53. ...

With respect to depreciable property, the "adjusted cost base" is the "capital cost" of the property, the figure upon which capital cost allowance under paragraph 20(1)(a) is computed. It is essential that those two figures be the same so that the capital gain provisions work in harmony with the capital cost allowance provisions. The term "capital cost" is not defined in the Act; it is simply the actual cost of the property, including with the purchase price any expenses or fees required to complete the acquisition.[30]

With respect to non-depreciable capital property, the adjusted cost base is the "cost" of the property "adjusted" in accordance with section 53. "Cost" is not defined in the Act, and it simply means the actual cost of the property, including expenses of acquisition.[31] Thus the "cost" of non-depreciable property is no different from the "capital cost" of depreciable property. Non-depreciable property differs from depreciable property in that the cost of non-depreciable property is subject to adjustment under section 53, whereas the capital cost of depreciable property is not subject to adjustment. It is the possibility of actual cost being adjusted under section 53 which, although only applicable to non-depreciable property, gives rise to the term *adjusted* cost base. Section 53 provides for either upward (subsection 53(1)) or downward (subsection 53(2)) adjustments to actual cost which are basically designed to make the taxation of capital gains compatible with the other parts of the Act. For example, property taxes and interest charges on non income-producing land are not deductible by the owner (subsection 18(2)), but they can be added to the adjusted cost base of the land under paragraph 53(1)(h) (an upward adjustment). Many of the section 53 adjustments are technical in nature and have no application to the majority of capital transactions.

Property owned in 1972, when the taxation of capital gains was introduced, is subject to special deemed cost provisions which are designed to ensure that gains accrued prior to 1972 are not subject to tax. Property owned in 1994, when the lifetime capital gains exemption was abolished, may also have an artificial cost base,

---

[30] IT-285R2, *ibid.*, paras. 8-9.

[31] In *R. v. Sterling*, [1985] 1 C.T.C. 275, 85 D.T.C. 5199 (Fed. C.A.), it was held that interest on money borrowed to purchase gold (which was not tax deductible) was not part of the gold's adjusted cost base. The interest payments related to the source of the funds used to make the purchase, and not directly to the cost of acquiring the property purchased.

namely, its elected value on February 22, 1994; the election that produces that result was explained earlier in this chapter.[32] In addition, the various "deemed dispositions" give rise to deemed cost as well as deemed proceeds of disposition. Finally, the "rollovers" give rise to deemed cost as well as deemed proceeds of disposition; the rollovers are discussed in chapter 13.[33]

10.5 — Computation of gain or loss

(a) — Proceeds due within the year

The computation of a gain or loss is governed by subsection 40(1) of the Act. The straightforward case is where the taxpayer who has disposed of capital property is entitled to be paid in full in the year of the disposition. In that case, if the proceeds of disposition exceed the adjusted cost base of the property plus the expenses of the disposition, the excess is the amount of the gain. If the adjusted cost base plus the expenses of the disposition exceed the proceeds of disposition, the excess is the amount of the loss. For example, if T sells a capital property with an adjusted cost base of $80 for proceeds of disposition of $100, incurring selling expenses of $5, T has to recognize a capital gain of $15 ($100 - ($80 + $5) = $15). If the proceeds of disposition were $60, T would have to recognize a capital loss of $25 ($80 + $5 - $60 = $25). Of course, only one-half of these figures would constitute the "taxable capital gain" and the "allowable capital loss", respectively.

Subsection 40(1) refers specifically to the expenses of dispositions ("any outlays and expenses to the extent that they were made or incurred by the taxpayer for the purpose of making the disposition"), but makes no reference to the expenses incurred on the acquisition of the property. In practice, however, the expenses of acquisition may be treated as part of the cost of capital property, so that the expenses of acquisition also reduce the capital gain or increase the capital loss.

(b) — Proceeds due in a future year

Subsection 40(1) permits the establishment of a "reserve for future proceeds" where the taxpayer who has disposed of capital property is not entitled to full payment of the proceeds of disposition in the year of disposition. The common case is a sale where part of the price is payable at the time of the disposition and the balance is payable by instalments over a period of years.

The general idea, consistent with the realization basis of the system, is that as long as the taxpayer has not become entitled to receive the full proceeds of disposition, then the taxpayer should not have to recognize the full gain for tax purposes. This idea is implemented by permitting the taxpayer to deduct from his or her gain in the year of disposition a "reasonable" reserve to reflect that a portion of the proceeds of disposition are not due in the year of disposition. A reasonable reserve would consist of the proportion of the gain that equals the proportion of the proceeds of dispo-

[32]See heading 10.2(f), "Tax subsidies for certain investments", above.

[33]See heading 13.4, "Non-arm's length transfer of property", below.

sition that are "not due to the taxpayer until after the end of the year". For example, if Vendor sold a capital property to Purchaser on the terms that only one-third of the purchase price was payable in the year of disposition, this would leave two-thirds of the purchase price due after the end of the year of disposition, which would enable Vendor to claim a reserve of two-thirds of the gain. In later years, as instalments of the price are paid, portions of the reserve are recognized. In this way, recognition of the capital gain is spread over the years in which the proceeds of disposition are payable (subject to the five-year limitation discussed below).

The reserve established by subparagraph 40(1)(a)(iii) must not exceed the lesser of (1) the proportion of the gain which equals the proportion of the proceeds of disposition that are not payable until after the end of the taxation year (clause 40(1)(a)(iii)(C)), and (2) one-fifth of the gain multiplied by an amount equal to four minus "the number of preceding taxation years of the taxpayer ending after the disposition of the property" (clause 40(1)(a)(iii)(D)). It is the second limitation, established by clause 40(1)(a)(iii)(D), that limits the life of the reserve to five years, and requires the taxpayer to recognize at least one-fifth of the capital gain over each year in which the reserve is claimed.[34]

In the year of disposition of a capital property for future proceeds, subparagraph 40(1)(a)(i) requires the full capital gain to be reported, but subparagraph 40(1)(a)(iii) then permits the taxpayer to reduce the gain by the amount of a reasonable reserve, up to a maximum of four-fifths of the gain (clause 40(1)(a)(iii)(D)). In the second year, subparagraph 40(1)(a)(ii) becomes applicable, requiring the previous year's reserve to be reported, but, if some portion of the proceeds are still not due until after the end of the second year, subparagraph 40(1)(a)(iii) will again permit the taxpayer to claim a reasonable reserve, up to a maximum of three-fifths of the gain (clause 40(1)(a)(iii)(D)). In the third year, the second year's reserve will have to be reported, but, if some portion of the proceeds are still not due until after the third year, subparagraph 40(1)(a)(iii) will again permit the taxpayer to claim a reasonable reserve, this time up to a maximum of two-fifths of the gain (clause 40(1)(a)(iii)(D)). This process will continue until the earliest of (1) the year in which the taxpayer has received the entire proceeds of disposition, and (2) the fifth taxation year after the disposition of the property, at which point clause 40(1)(a)(iii)(D) establishes a maximum reserve of zero-fifths of the proceeds of disposition, which of course equals $0, requiring the taxpayer to recognize the remainder of the gain, whether or not any proceeds of disposition remain outstanding.[35]

---

[34] The life of the reserve is extended to ten years in respect of dispositions of farming property to a child: s. 40(1.1).

[35] There are two further limitations on the life of the reserve: a reserve cannot be claimed by a person who becomes non-resident (s. 40(2)(a)(i)) or in the year of death (s. 72(1)(c)), but there is an exception for a spouse or spouse trust: (s. 72(2)(b)).

The operation of paragraph 40(1)(a) may be illustrated by the following example:

> T in year one disposes of a capital property with an adjusted cost base (ACB) of \$100 for proceeds of disposition (POD) of \$300, payable as to \$75 in year one, a further \$75 in year two, and as to the remaining \$150 in year ten (with interest).

In this example, T has made a capital gain of \$200 (\$300 - \$100 = \$200) in year one, the year of disposition. However, since the proceeds of disposition are payable over ten years, T may claim a reserve under subsection 40(1), thereby spreading the gain over five years (the maximum life of the reserve under clause 40(1)(a)(iii)(D), even though the last of the proceeds will not become payable for ten years). T's gain for the five taxation years ending after the disposition would be as follows:

Year 1 (year of disposition)

Gain otherwise determined (s. 40(1)(a)(i)):		
POD	\$300	
ACB	100	
	\$200	\$200
Less: reserve for future proceeds		
Lesser of:		
s. 40(1)(a)(iii)(C) reasonable reserve:		
\$200 × 225 (POD not due) =	150	
\$300 (total POD)		
(the gain multiplied by the proportion of the proceeds that is not yet due)		
s. 40(1)(a)(iii)(D) formula reserve:		
\$200 × 1/5 × (4 - 0) =	160	(150)
(1/5 of the gain multiplied by an amount equal to 4 minus the number of taxation years ending after the disposition)		
Gain for year 1:		\$50

Year 2

Reserve claimed in preceding year (s. 40(1)(a)(ii))		\$150
Less: reserve for future proceeds		
Lesser of:		
s. 40(1)(a)(iii)(C) reasonable reserve:		
\$200 × \$150/\$300 =	\$100	
s. 40(1)(a)(iii)(D) formula reserve:		
200/5 × (4 - 1) =	120	(100)
Gain for year 2:		\$50

Year 3

Reserve claimed in preceding year (s. 40(1)(a)(ii))		$100
Less: reserve for future proceeds		
Lesser of:		
s. 40(1)(a)(iii)(C) reasonable reserve:		
$200 × $150/$300 =	$100	
s. 40(1)(a)(iii)(D) formula reserve:		
$200/5 × (4 - 2) =	80	(80)
Gain for year 3		$20

Year 4

Reserve claimed in preceding year (s. 40(1)(a)(ii))		$80
Less: reserve for future proceeds		
Lesser of		
s. 40(1)(a)(iii)(C) reasonable reserve:		
$200 × $150/$300 =	$100	
s. 40(1)(a)(iii)(D) formula reserve:		
$200/5 × (4 - 3)	40	(40)
Gain for year 4		$40

Year 5

Reserve claimed in preceding year (s. 40(1)(a)(ii))		$40
Less: reserve for future proceeds		
Lesser of		
s. 40(1)(a)(iii)(C) reasonable reserve:		
$200 × $150/$300 =	$100	
s. 40(1)(a)(iii)(D) formula reserve:		
$200/5 × (4 - 4)	0	0
Gain for year 5		$40

In year 6 nothing will be reported — no reserve was claimed in the preceding year. The capital gain of $200 has now been fully recognized.

The reserve for future proceeds is expressed in subparagraph 40(1)(a)(iii) as "such amount as the taxpayer may claim ...". These words make the reserve optional. The taxpayer is not required to claim the reserve, nor, if the taxpayer does claim the reserve, to claim the full "reasonable amount". Ordinarily, of course, the taxpayer will want to claim the maximum reserve possible, since the claim enables the taxpayer to postpone payment of some tax. But special circumstances could make it desirable not to claim the reserve, for example, a year of exceptionally low income, or the availability of capital losses to offset the gain.

(c) — Loss

The computation of a loss is provided for in paragraph 40(1)(b), which makes no provision for a reserve for future proceeds. Thus, if a capital loss is suffered on a disposition for future proceeds, the full loss must be recognized in the year of disposition. The taxpayer will be happy to recognize the full loss as soon as possible. If the loss cannot be fully deducted in the year of disposition (allowable capital losses can only be deducted against taxable capital gains), the loss carryover rules would be applicable, permitting (at the discretion of the taxpayer) a carryback for three years and an indefinite carryforward.

10.6 — Special events and deemed dispositions

(a) — Purpose

The realization basis of capital gains taxation, if adhered to without exceptions, would enable the owners of capital property to postpone paying tax on accrued gains for as long as the gains were not realized. This would not be tolerable as a matter of tax policy, because of the loss of revenue to the government, the inequity of according such a valuable preference to owners of capital property, and the lock-in effect of unrealized capital gains. The Act provides for a number of "deemed dispositions", whereby a taxpayer is deemed to have received proceeds of disposition equal to the fair market value of the capital property, although that capital property has not in fact been converted into cash or otherwise realized. The purpose of deemed dispositions is to place limits on the period for which capital gains taxation can be postponed.

On the death of a taxpayer, for example, all of his or her capital property is deemed to have been disposed of at its fair market value, thereby forcing recognition of any accrued gains or losses. On a gift of capital property, the donor is deemed to have disposed of the property at its fair market value, and must therefore recognize any accrued gain or loss on the property. In the case of death or a gift, there is in fact a disposition since property passes from the taxpayer to a successor or donee, but there are no proceeds of disposition. The provisions for the so-called deemed dispositions on death or a gift really supply only deemed proceeds of disposition. However, there are also deemed dispositions on the 21st anniversary of a trust, on the change of use of capital property, and on becoming non-resident. In these cases, the taxpayer continues to own the property; there has been no relinquishment of ownership and therefore no actual disposition. The deemed disposition provisions supply both a deemed disposition and deemed proceeds of disposition.

The deemed dispositions raise the twin problems associated with accrual-basis capital gains taxation. First, there is the administrative problem for the government of using valuations for the calculation of tax on a gain that has not been realized. Secondly, there is the liquidity problem for the taxpayer of finding cash to pay tax on a gain that has not been realized. However, most jurisdictions seize upon death or a gift as an occasion for the payment of a tax of some kind. It is certainly administratively feasible, and it is probably not normally especially harsh to taxpayers, considering that a major liquidity problem can be foreseen and provided for by life insurance, for example.

(b) — Death

The most important of the deemed dispositions occurs on the death of an owner of capital property. There is an actual disposition on death in the sense that the deceased's property passes immediately by operation of law to the personal representative (called the "legal representative" in the Act), and ultimately to the deceased's successors designated by will or, if there is no will, provincial intestacy law. However, neither the legal representative nor the successors provide any proceeds of disposition and so the tax consequences of death have to be treated specifically by the Act. The objective is to require the capital gains accrued during the deceased's lifetime to be recognized for tax purposes in the deceased's last taxation year (the terminal year). This is accomplished by subsection 70(5), which provides that, on the death of a taxpayer, the deceased taxpayer is deemed to have disposed of all of his or her capital property for proceeds of disposition equal to the fair market value of the property.

The deemed disposition of a deceased taxpayer's capital property is deemed to have occurred "immediately before the taxpayer's death". This brings any taxable capital gains (or recapture of capital cost allowance) into the income of the deceased's terminal year, rather than into the income of the deceased's estate (which becomes a new taxpayer). Thus, recognition of capital gains cannot be postponed beyond the lifetime of the owner of the appreciated property. The lock-in effect caused by unrealized capital gains is therefore also limited to the lifetime of the owner. The successor to the capital property (the person inheriting the property) is deemed to acquire the property at its fair market value (paragraph 70(5)(b)). The successor is not locked-in, because the inherited property is no longer sheltering any untaxed capital gains, and until fresh gains have accrued the successor has no tax incentive not to sell the property.

The deemed disposition of capital property on death can be avoided by the owner giving the property away before death. But there is also a deemed disposition at fair market value on the making of an *inter vivos* gift of capital property (paragraph 69(1)(b)), so that an *inter vivos* gift has the same effect as death in forcing the recognition of accrued capital gains or losses. Where a deceased taxpayer's property is inherited by a spouse or spouse trust, or (in the case of farming property) a child of the taxpayer, recognition of accrued gains can be postponed through rollover provisions which are applicable to those dispositions, as well as to *inter vivos* gifts to a spouse or spouse trust or (in the case of farming property) a child.[36]

The general rule, therefore, is that all accrued capital gains have to be recognized on death. As well, property cannot be passed from generation to generation by *inter vivos* gift without recognizing accrued capital gains, because on a gift of capital property, the general rule is also that there is a deemed disposition at fair market

[36]See heading 13.4, "Non-arm's length transfer of property", below.

value.[37] The new owner by inheritance or by gift takes the property fully tax-paid, and is not locked-in until new gains have accrued.

(c) — Gift

As noted earlier, a deemed disposition on a gift of capital property is necessary to complement the deemed disposition on death. The deemed disposition on death can be avoided by an *inter vivos* gift to the next generation, but the Act exacts the price of immediate recognition by the donor of any unrealized gains accrued up to the time of the gift. Under paragraph 69(1)(b), where a person has made an *inter vivos* gift of property (or has made a non-arm's-length sale for inadequate consideration), the donor is deemed to have received proceeds of disposition equal to the fair market value of the property. Thus any accrued gains (or losses) must be recognized by the donor at the time of the gift.[38] Under paragraph 69(1)(c), the donee of the gift is deemed to acquire the property at its fair market value, the intent being to step up the donee's cost base so that the donee never has to pay tax on the gain that was taxed at the time of the gift.[39]

(d) — Trust

Subsection 104(4) imposes, at 21-year intervals, a deemed disposition at fair market value on all capital property held by a trust. Generally, this deemed disposition occurs on the 21st anniversary of the creation of the trust, and again on the 42nd

---

[37]S. 69(1).

[38]When a donor makes a gift of property to a registered charity, the donor can claim a tax credit or deduction for the fair market value of the donation (see heading 14.7, "Tax credits", below), but, because of the deemed disposition, the donor must generally report a taxable capital gain equal to 50 per cent of the accrued capital gain on the donated property. However, for gifts of publicly-traded securities and ecologically sensitive land made to a registered charity after May 1, 2006, none of the accrued capital gain is included in income: see 38(a.1) and (a.2). This rule was originally introduced in 1997 as a temporary reduced 25% inclusion rate for gifts of publicly traded securities (to expire at the end of 2001). The stated purpose of this rule at that time was is to provide a level of tax assistance for donations of "eligible appreciated capital property which is comparable to that in the U.S." This tax expenditure violates the Canadian income tax system's fundamental principles of equity and neutrality. For individuals alone, the cost is projected to be $34 million for 2009: See Canada, *Tax Expenditures and Evaluations 2009*, Table 1. The cost of the non-taxation of these gains has grown dramatically from 2004 when it was estimated as only $8 million. If one includes the cost of the donation credit, the tax expenditure increases to $2,008 million in 2003 and approximately $2,414 million in 2009.

[39]The language of s. 69(1)(c) does not precisely match that of s. 69(1)(b) in that s. 69(1)(c) makes no reference to a non-arms-length sale for inadequate consideration. Accordingly, s. 69(1)(c) would not step up the cost base in that situation, leading to double taxation of the deemed gain.

anniversary, and again on the 63rd anniversary, and so on every 21 years until the trust is terminated.[40] Why is it necessary?

A gift of property to a trust, whether on death or *inter vivos*, gives rise to a deemed disposition under subsection 70(5) or paragraph 69(1)(b), just like a gift to an individual. A sale of property to a trust gives rise to the normal rules requiring recognition of any realized gain or loss, again just like a sale to an individual. Indeed, a trust is deemed to be an individual by the Act.[41] However, once capital property has been acquired by a trust, it is sheltered for a long time from the deemed disposition on death. A trust never dies, and it can be made to last as long as a hundred years despite the rule against perpetuities (which requires that all interests be vested within a life in being plus 21 years). Even on the termination of a trust, the distribution of capital property to the capital beneficiaries does not involve recognition of accrued capital gains.[42] The Act therefore had to make special provision to preclude the use of a trust to postpone for excessive periods of time the recognition of capital gains.

The 21-year deemed disposition of capital property in a trust differs from the deemed dispositions on death or gift in that the 21-year deemed disposition is not triggered by any event akin to a disposition, but simply by a passage of 21 years. Its purposes are the same as those of the deemed disposition on death, that is to say, to limit the period for which tax on accrued capital gains can be postponed, and to reduce the lock-in effect of a realization-based capital gains tax.

(e) — Change of use

Subsection 45(1) provides for a deemed disposition at fair market value where property which was acquired for a non-income-producing use is converted to an income-producing use (subparagraph 45(1)(a)(i)), and vice versa (subparagraph 45(1)(a)(ii)). For example, if an automobile acquired for the personal use of the owner was later used for business purposes, on the change of use there would be a deemed disposition. If a cottage acquired to earn rental income was later used for recreational purposes by the owner, on the change of use there would be a deemed disposition. Where a property is used for both non-income-producing and income-producing purposes a change in the proportion of use for each purpose gives rise to a partial deemed disposition (paragraph 45(1)(c)).

One reason for the deemed disposition on the change of use of property is the distinctive capital gains treatment of "personal-use property": while gains on personal-use property are taxable, losses are not allowable.[43] One consequence of the dis-

---

[40]This is the general rule to which there are a variety of exceptions and qualifications. The taxation of trusts is the topic of chapter 17, below; and the 21-year deemed disposition is more fully discussed under heading 17.5(b), "Deemed disposition of trust property", below.

[41]S. 104(2)

[42]S. 107(2).

[43]See heading 10.7(c), "Personal-use property losses", below.

tinctive treatment of personal-use property is that on a change of use of a capital property it is necessary to segregate a period of personal use (non-income-producing), when losses are not allowable, from a period of income-producing use, when losses are allowable. Another reason for segregating a period of non-income-producing use from a period of income-producing use is that capital cost allowance may not be claimed against non-income-producing property, but may be claimed against some kinds of income-producing property (those that qualify as depreciable property). The deemed disposition on the change of use thus draws a line that marks the end or the beginning of the allowability of capital losses and the deductibility of capital cost allowance.

The distinction between non-income-producing and income-producing uses is critical for the recognition of both capital losses and capital cost allowance. Other changes of use will usually make no difference. Hence, there is no deemed disposition under subsection 45(1) if a capital property change of use does not move that property from the income-producing category to the non-income-producing category, or vice versa. For example, there would be no deemed disposition under subsection 45(1) if a building acquired to earn rental income were converted into an office for the owner's business. This is because there would have been a change of use from an investment to a capital asset in a business. Since both uses are income-producing, subsection 45(1) would not apply.

Subsections 45(2) and (3) offer elections that allow a taxpayer to postpone the deemed disposition on a change of use from non-income-producing to income-producing, and (in the case of a principal residence only) vice versa. The elections are discussed in the later section of this chapter on principal residence.

(f) — Departure from Canada

Subsection 128.1(4) of the Act provides that when a taxpayer ceases to be a resident of Canada there is a deemed disposition at fair market value of all of the departing taxpayer's property, with certain exceptions. The purpose is to tax the gains accrued while the taxpayer was resident in Canada; otherwise the gains would escape Canadian tax altogether after the taxpayer became a non-resident of Canada. This deemed disposition is often called a "departure tax". Similar rules apply to taxpayers who become a Canadian resident during the year.

10.7 — Stop-loss rules

(a) — Capital losses "quarantined"

We have already noted that a capital loss is calculated the same way as a capital gain; it is the difference between the adjusted cost base of the property disposed of and its proceeds of disposition. And, just as the Act recognizes only one-half of a capital gain, calling the taxable portion a "taxable capital gain", so too the Act recognizes only one-half of a capital loss, calling it an "allowable capital loss".

Under section 3, allowable capital losses are deductible only against taxable capital gains. This restriction on deductibility and other aspects of the treatment of capital losses are best understood in the context of the tax treatment of other losses. More detailed consideration of the current deductibility of allowable capital losses, and of the carryover to other years of unused capital losses, including the concept of an "allowable business investment loss", is discussed in chapter 14, Taxable Income and Tax for Individuals.

Because capital gains are one-half taxable and capital losses are one-half deductible, it is to a taxpayer's advantage to characterize a gain from the disposition of property as a capital gain and a loss from the disposition of property as a fully-deductible business loss (mostly on the basis of that the purchase and sale of the property is an adventure in the nature of trade). For the CRA, on the other hand, the motivation is typically reversed. As discussed in detail in chapter 11, this is the practical context for the cases involving the distinction between investing and trading.

The Act contains a number of "stop-loss" rules that deny a deduction for a capital loss in circumstances where, based on policy grounds, no deduction should be permitted. Several of the rules are based on the policy premise that no loss should be allowed where a disposition results in little or no change in the beneficial ownership of the disposed property.[44] An example of this type of stop loss rule is the superficial loss rule which is discussed immediately below.

A second type of stop-loss rule denies or restricts a loss on the disposition of personal-use property and is based on the policy premise that losses on personal use property are generally consumption expenses. There is a rule that denies the deduction for losses on the disposition of personal-use properties other than listed personal properties. There is also a rule that restricts the deduction for losses on the disposition of listed personal properties to gains on the disposition of listed personal properties (a list of collectibles such as art and jewelry). These two rules are discussed under headings (c) and (d), respectively, below.

(b) — Superficial losses

Subparagraph 40(2)(g)(i) deems a "superficial loss" to be nil. A superficial loss is defined in section 54 as a taxpayer's loss from the disposition of a property in any case where:

> (a) during the period that begins 30 days before and ends 30 days after the disposition, the taxpayer or a person affiliated with the taxpayer acquires a property (in this definition referred to as the "substituted property") that is, or is identical to, the particular property, and
>
> (b) at the end of that period, the taxpayer or a person affiliated with the taxpayer owns or had a right to acquire the substituted property ...

The definition of affiliated persons and persons affiliated with each other is contained in subsection 251.1(1). The list of persons affiliated with a taxpayer includes the taxpayer, his or her spouse, and any corporation controlled by the taxpayer or

---

[44]For example, losses are denied on a disposition of property to a registered retirement savings plan trust (s. 40(2)(g)(iv)(B)) and to a controlled corporation (ss. 40(2)(g)(i), 13(21.2), and 40(3.3)).

his or her spouse.[45] The list does not include the parents, siblings or children of the taxpayer or corporations controlled by those persons.

Consider the example of T, who in 2007 holds 100 shares in XYZ Ltd. The shares have declined in value by $600, but T does not want to get rid of them because she believes that the value of the shares will eventually rise again. However, she would like to claim an allowable capital loss of $300 (one-half of $600), because she has a taxable capital gain of about that amount which could be sheltered by the allowable capital loss. If it were not for the superficial loss rule, T could sell the shares for their current price, which would result in a $600 loss, and immediately buy another 100 XYZ shares for the same price. That way, she would still have the same investment,[46] but she would have crystallized the accrued loss on the shares. The effect of the superficial loss rule of subparagraph 40(2)(g)(i) is to block this practice by deeming T's loss to be nil if she purchased the replacement shares[47] within 30 days of (before or after) selling the original shares.[48] If T waited more than 30 days to purchase the replacement shares (or if she bought them more than 30 days before selling the original shares), then the superficial loss rule would not apply and the loss would be allowable.

The definition of superficial loss includes the case where the taxpayer's property has been acquired (within the 30-day period) by the taxpayer's spouse.[49] This element of the definition precludes T from crystallizing the loss by giving her shares to her spouse and electing out of the section 73 rollover. The gift coupled with the election causes a deemed disposition at fair market value (paragraph 69(1)(b)), but the superficial loss rule deems the resulting loss to be nil. However, the superficial loss rule does not apply to a testamentary gift (i.e., a gift as a consequence of death, such as a gift by will) from one spouse to another.[50] This is because a testamentary gift is unlikely to be motivated by tax avoidance. As a result, there is no reason to disallow the loss.

---

[45]For a more complete listing, see s. 251.1.

[46]The sale and purchase of the shares would normally involve transaction costs in the form of brokerage fees. These costs have been ignored in the example in the text, but T would obviously be attracted to the sale and purchase only if the tax benefit of the loss (if it were allowed) was worth more than the transaction costs.

[47]If T had purchased only 50 shares, instead of the full 100, then only half the loss would be a superficial loss.

[48]The lower adjusted cost base of the substituted property is adjusted upward by the amount of the superficial loss: s. 53(1)(f).

[49]The list of affiliated persons in s. 251.1 does not include a spousal trust.

[50]The definition of "superficial loss" in s. 54 excludes a deemed disposition under s. 70. Therefore, if property is left by will to a spouse, and the legal representative elects against the s. 70(6) rollover, there is a deemed disposition at fair market value (s. 70(5)), and any resulting capital loss is allowable to the deceased.

(c) — Personal-use property losses

"Personal-use property" is defined in section 54 as property owned by a taxpayer "that is used primarily for the personal use or enjoyment of the taxpayer" or of "a person related to the taxpayer". It thus includes such things as cottages, cars, bicycles, boats, sporting or recreational equipment, household appliances, furniture and clothing. It also includes principal residences, but the unique tax treatment of the principal residence is explained separately later in section 10.8 "Principal residence exemption".

Subparagraph 40(2)(g)(iii) provides that a loss from the disposition of personal-use property (other than "listed personal property", discussed below) is deemed to be nil. The reason for the no-loss rule is that the depreciation of personal-use property is normally the result of its having been used for the personal enjoyment of the taxpayer. The decline in value is therefore treated as an expense of consumption which, like other expenses of consumption, should not be recognized for tax purposes. The same argument does not apply to *gains* on personal-use property: they are real additions to the owner's wealth and are accordingly taxed as capital gains (subject to the $1,000 rule, discussed below). For example, Taxpayer A purchases a car for his personal use for $7,000, and sells it three years later for $4,000. Subparagraph 40(2)(g)(iii) deems the loss to be nil. The actual loss of $3,000 is treated as the cost of using a car for personal use. However, if the car were sold for $8,000, the $1,000 gain must be recognized as a capital gain, one-half taxable.

Another peculiarity of the tax treatment of personal-use property is the $1,000 rule. Subsection 46(1) deems the adjusted cost base and the proceeds of disposition of personal-use property to be the higher of the actual figures or $1,000. The effect of this deeming rule is to exempt small transactions in personal-use property from the capital gains rules. Subsection 46(1) ensures that, where personal-use property with an adjusted cost base of less than $1,000 is sold for proceeds of disposition of less than $1,000, no capital gain is recognized. This is because both the adjusted cost base and the proceeds of disposition are deemed to be the same figure, namely, $1,000. For example, Taxpayer C disposes of a bike with an adjusted cost base of $700 for proceeds of disposition of $900. By subsection 46(1), the adjusted cost base is deemed to be $1,000 and the proceeds of disposition are deemed to be $1,000, yielding a capital gain of zero.

Where the adjusted cost base is less than $1,000, but the proceeds of disposition exceed $1,000, a capital gain will have to be recognized, but subsection 46(1) will still bump the adjusted cost base up to $1,000, reducing the capital gain. In the previous example, if C's proceeds of disposition of the bike were $1,200, her actual gain would be $500 ($1,200-$700 = $500), but her deemed gain would be only $200 ($1,200-$1,000 = $200). Where the adjusted cost base and the proceeds of disposition are each more than $1,000, subsection 46(1) will have no application, and any capital gain will be computed on the basis of the actual figures. (In order to preclude abuse of the $1,000 rule, there are special rules for the disposition of part of a personal-use property or part of a set of personal-use properties which require the $1,000 limit to be prorated: subsections 46(2), (3).)

Subsection 46(1) can have the effect of eliminating or reducing capital losses as well as capital gains. The elimination or reduction of losses on the disposition of personal-use property is relevant only for listed personal property, since by virtue of subparagraph 40(2)(g)(iii) losses on the disposition of other kinds of personal-use property are deemed to be nil. For example, Taxpayer D disposes of a painting with an adjusted cost base of $2,500 for proceeds of disposition of $400. Since a painting is listed personal property (discussed below), subparagraph 40(2)(g)(iii) does not deem the loss to be nil. However, subsection 46(1) deems the proceeds of disposition to be $1,000, thereby reducing the capital loss from its actual figure of $2,100 ($2,500-$400 = $2,100) to a deemed figure of $1,500 ($2,500-$1,000 = $1,500).

(d) — Listed personal property losses

There is an exception to the rule that there can be no capital losses on personal-use property, and that relates to "listed personal property". Listed personal property is defined in section 54 to include: print, etching, drawing, painting, sculpture, or other similar work of art, jewellery, rare folio, rare manuscript, or rare book, stamp, or coin.

Although listed personal property is personal-use property (as the definition states), capital losses on listed personal property are deductible, but only against capital gains from listed personal property. The reason for this special treatment is that art, jewellery, rare books, stamps and coins, while they are used for the personal use or enjoyment of the owner, also have the characteristics of investments. Declines in their value would not normally be attributable to use, but to changing market conditions similar to those which affect other forms of investment. Since a decline in the value of listed personal property is not likely to be a consumption expense, there is no reason to treat it any differently than the decline in the value of capital property generally. However, the Act strikes a compromise between treating it as personal-use property, in which case losses would be disallowed, and treating it as non-personal-use property, in which case losses would be allowed in accordance with the general capital loss rules. The compromise is provided by paragraph 3(b) and subsections 41(2) and (3). Clause 3(b)(i)(B) brings into income a taxpayer's "taxable net gain for the year from dispositions of listed personal property". The "net gain" is a figure which is derived by deducting losses from gains on personal-use property in accordance with the rules established by subsection 41(2) and the "taxable net gain" is one-half of the net gain (subsection 41(1)). If losses on dispositions of listed personal property exceed gains in a taxation year, the net loss is not deductible under subparagraph 3(b)(ii) or paragraph 3(e). The net loss is called the taxpayer's "listed-personal-property loss" for the year (subsection 41(3)), and it may be carried back three years and forward seven years and deducted against gains on listed personal property in those years in accordance with the rules in subsection 41(2).

10.8 — Principal residence exemption

(a) — Tax expenditure

By virtue of paragraph 40(2)(b), capital gains from the disposition of a "principal residence" are exempted from income tax. Projections indicate that the cost of this exemption to the federal government will be over $3.115 billion in 2009.[51] Why is such an exemption necessary?

In Canada, it is widely accepted that a capital gain on the sale of a home should not attract tax.[52] Where a home is sold, and a new home is to be purchased, any capital gain on the disposition of the old home is an illusory gain in the sense that the new home will have to be purchased in the same inflated market as the old home was sold. On the other hand, a similar comment could be made about many other capital gains, especially where they are solely the result of inflation. Certainly, the gain on a home would not seem to warrant special treatment in cases where the taxpayer buys the new home in a town where prices are lower (or buys a cheaper home), or if the taxpayer moves into rented accommodation, or if the taxpayer dies and the family assets are being realized. In these cases, however, there still seems to be an emotional objection to levying tax on any gain on the home.

The principal residence exemption is best perceived as a tax expenditure. The exemption provides an incentive for home ownership. More houses bought lead to more business activities generated for builders, landscapers, interior decorators, furniture makers, home appliance makers, real estate agents, bankers, insurers, lawyers, and so forth. Home ownership is also socially desirable and provides for an important means of savings for retirement.

Assuming that the principal residence exemption is justified, the next question is how to design the rules to ensure that the exemption is appropriately targeted by providing the right incentive to the "right" people while avoiding unnecessary loopholes. The design questions include: (1) What type of property should be treated as a "residence"? (2) What conditions are necessary to turn a "residence" into a "principal" residence? (3) Does the principal residence have to be situated in Canada? (4) Should a family be allowed to claim the exemption for more than one principal residence? (5) Should there be a cap on the amount of exemption? (6) Should the exemption be limited to Canadian resident taxpayers? (7) Can the exemption be designed to allow flexibility for taxpayers who buy and sell a house in the same year, rent out part of the house, or use part of the house as a home office? How the Act deals with these questions is discussed below.

---

[51] Canada, *Tax Expenditures and Evaluations* (2009), Table 1.

[52] Even the Carter Commission was willing to allow an exemption for at least part of the capital gain on a taxpayer's home. The Commission recommended that there be an exemption of $1,000 gain per year, plus the value of improvements. The government's White Paper accepted the Carter recommendations, but the final governmental decision was to exempt altogether (in most situations) any gain on the disposition of a taxpayer's "principal residence".

(b) — "Principal residence"

"Principal residence" is defined in section 54 of the Act. For a property to qualify as a principal residence in a particular taxation year it must satisfy three basic requirements: (1) the property must be "owned, whether jointly with another person or otherwise ... by the taxpayer"; (2) the property must be "ordinarily inhabited" in the year by the taxpayer or the taxpayer's spouse (or former spouse) or child; and (3) the property must be "designated" by the taxpayer to be his or her principal residence for the year.[53]

(i) — Ownership

Ownership is an obvious element of the definition of principal residence, because only the owner is entitled to receive, and is liable to pay tax on, any capital gain on the disposition of a property. Section 54 does not require that the taxpayer be the sole owner of a principal residence. A co-ownership is also possible.[54]

(ii) — "Ordinarily inhabited"

Paragraph (a) of the definition of "principal residence" stipulates that, in order to qualify as a principal residence for a particular year, the property must have been "ordinarily inhabited" in the year by the taxpayer, the taxpayer's spouse or former spouse or the taxpayer's child.

The term "ordinarily inhabited" is not defined in the Act. Whether a housing unit is "ordinarily inhabited" is determined on the basis of the facts in each case.[55] A

---

[53]A principal residence may also be owned by a trust, provided similar requirements are satisfied: see the references to "personal trust" in s. 54 definition of "principal residence".

[54]In the case of a co-ownership, each co-owner would determine his or her ability to designate his or her share of the property as a principal residence for the period of ownership independently. For example, if A and B jointly own a house (a capital property) and A (but not B) has "ordinarily inhabited" the house for the period of their joint ownership, only A will be able to designate the property as a principal residence. As a result, if the gain on the property is $20,000, A will be able to shelter his or her 50% share of the gain with a principle residence exemption — B will have to report his or her 50% share as a $10,000 capital gain. However, if A and B were spouses or common-law partners (or formerly spouses or partners but separated), the fact that B did not ordinarily inhabit the house would not matter. B (as well as A) would be entitled to designate the house as a principal residence for the period of ownership (because s. 54 permits occupation by the taxpayer's "spouse or former spouse", etc.).

[55]The CRA's position is found in Interpretation Bulletin IT-120R6, "Principal residence" (2003), para. 12:

> The question of whether a housing unit is ordinarily inhabited in the year by a person must be resolved on the basis of the facts in each particular case. Even if a person inhabits a housing unit only for a short period of time in the year, this is sufficient for the housing unit to be considered "ordinarily inhabited in the year" by that person. For example, even if a person disposes of his or her residence early in the year or acquires it late in the year, the housing unit can be considered to be

short-time occupancy seems to suffice.[56] A principal residence can be outside Canada, such as a condominium in Florida, a ski lodge in Austria or a villa in the south of France.[57] While this appears implausible, the Act does not stipulate that the principal residence be in Canada, and since a person can be resident in more than one country at a time, it can hardly be doubted that a person could be resident in Canada and still "ordinarily inhabit" a property outside Canada. Under the CRA's interpretation of ordinarily inhabited, a taxpayer may own more than one property that is "ordinarily inhabited" by the taxpayer in a taxation year. The word "principal" in "principal residence" is not regarded as excluding a cottage in the country (for example) even if the taxpayer also owns a house in the city.[58]

Sometimes a taxpayer will use a house property partly to earn business or property income. For example, a homeowner may use one room as a home office; or the homeowner may operate a day care business in the home; or the homeowner may rent a room to a tenant; or the owner of a cottage (or other seasonal residence) may rent it for part of the year. The CRA takes the position[59] that the whole of the property still qualifies as ordinarily inhabited by the owner so long as (a) the income-producing use "is ancillary to the main use of the property as a residence";[60] (b) the taxpayer did not make structural changes to the property to accommodate the income-producing use; and (c) the taxpayer does not claim capital cost allowance on the property. If these conditions are not satisfied, then the portion of the house used for the income-producing purpose would be ineligible for principal resi-

---

ordinarily inhabited in the year by that person by virtue of his or her living in it in the year before such sale or after such acquisition, as the case may be. Or, for example, a seasonal residence can be considered to be ordinarily inhabited in the year by a person who occupies it only during his or her vacation, provided that the main reason for owning the property is not to gain or produce income. With regard to the latter stipulation, a person receiving only incidental rental income from a seasonal residence is not considered to own the property mainly for the purpose of gaining or producing income.

[56]But see *Ennist v. M.N.R.*, [1985] 2 C.T.C. 2398, 85 D.T.C. 669 (T.C.C.) (where a taxpayer occupied a newly-purchased condominium for only 24 hours because he was transferred to another city; held the condominium was not ordinarily inhabited, and the principal residence designation was denied).

[57]IT-120R6, note 55, above, para. 40.

[58]However, a taxpayer is precluded from having more than one principal residence in any given year by the restrictions on designation, which are explained in the next section of this chapter. The taxpayer is permitted to designate either the city house or the country cottage (in our example), but he or she cannot designate both in the same year.

[59]IT-120R6, note 55, above, para. 32.

[60]In *Saccamono v. M.N.R.*, [1986] 2 C.T.C. 2269, 86 D.T.C. 1699 (T.C.C.), it was held that the taxpayer ordinarily inhabited the whole of a property that was 70% rented to existing tenants when the taxpayer acquired it; the taxpayer, although occupying only 30% of the property, intended to occupy the entire property.

dence status. The rest of the property, which is used as a residence, would be ordinarily inhabited by the owner and therefore eligible for principal residence status.

(iii) — Surrounding land

The definition of principal residence deems the property to include "the land subjacent to the housing unit and such portion of any immediately contiguous land as can reasonably be regarded as contributing to the use and enjoyment of the housing unit as a residence". If the total area of land under and around the principal residence exceeds half a hectare (which is approximately one acre), then the definition stipulates that "the excess shall be deemed not to have contributed to the use and enjoyment of the housing unit as a residence unless the taxpayer establishes that it was necessary to such use and enjoyment".

In rural municipalities, there are often zoning restrictions that impose on residential land minimum lot sizes in excess of half a hectare. The Courts have held that the existence of such a restriction is one way to establish whether the land in excess of half a hectare was "necessary" to the "use and enjoyment" of the housing unit as a residence. For example, in *R. v. Yates*,[61] the taxpayer's property was 10 acres and the minimum lot size was 10 acres at the date of purchase and 25 acres at the date of sale. The entire lot was considered part of the principal residence. In *Carlile v. R.*[62] the taxpayer owned a 33 acre property which was in excess of the 25 acre minimum lot size in effect from valuation day until the time of disposition. The majority of the Court found that the entire lot qualified as a principal residence because the local authority would not have authorized a partition resulting in one lot being less than 25 acres.[63]

(iv) — Designation

In order to qualify as a principal residence for a particular year the property must be "designated" by the taxpayer to be his or her principal residence for that year. The designation is made in the income tax return for the year in which the property is

---

[61][1986] 2 C.T.C. 48, 86 D.T.C. 6296 (Fed. C.A.); affirming [1983] C.T.C. 105, 106, 83 D.T.C. 5158, 5159 (Fed. C.A.).

[62][1995] 2 C.T.C. 273, 95 D.T.C. 5483 (Fed. C.A.). The minority opinion was that, on the balance of probabilities, the partition would have been allowed and that the property accordingly failed to qualify for the principal residence exemption.

[63]The CRA's view is "that the mere existence of such a municipal law or regulation on the date the taxpayer acquired the property does not immediately qualify the excess land for purposes of the principal residence exemption. For example, if the taxpayer could have made an application for severance of the excess land and it is likely that such a request would have been approved, the taxpayer would generally not be considered to have been required to acquire the excess land. Furthermore, regardless of the above, where any portion of the land in excess of one-half hectare is not used for residential purposes but rather for income-producing purposes, such portion is usually not considered to be necessary for the use and enjoyment of the housing unit as a residence.": IT-120R6, note 55, above, para. 16.

disposed of; at that time, the taxpayer designates the property as his or her principal residence for all the years for which he or she claims the property as a principal residence.[64] In each year, a taxpayer may designate only one property as a principal residence, even if the taxpayer owned and ordinarily inhabited more than one property.[65] A taxpayer may designate a property to be his or her principal residence for a particular year only if no other property has been designated for that year by the taxpayer *or by the taxpayer's spouse* (or by the taxpayer's unmarried children under 18). The reference to the spouse (and child) restricts the designation to one principal residence per family per year.

(c) — Residence requirement

In order to become entitled to the principal residence exemption for a particular year, paragraph 40(2)(b) stipulates not only that the property must be designated as the taxpayer's principal residence for that year, but also that the taxpayer must be resident in Canada during that year. A taxpayer who leaves his or her principal residence in Canada, rents it (making an election under subsection 45(2)), and who becomes non-resident for a period, cannot count the period of non-residence in reduction of the gain on a subsequent disposition of the house. The "one plus" formula in paragraph 40(2)(b) (discussed below), and the rule that part of a year equals a taxation year, may suffice to overcome one or two years of non-residence, but more than that will result in a portion of the gain being recognized for tax purposes.

(d) — Mechanism of exemption

The exemption of the gain on the disposition of a principal residence is contained in paragraph 40(2)(b),[66] which provides as follows:

> where the taxpayer is an individual, the taxpayer's gain for a taxation year from the disposition of a property that was the taxpayer's principal residence at any time after the date (in this section referred to as the "acquisition date") that is the later of December 31, 1971 and the day on which the taxpayer last acquired or reacquired it, as the case may be, is the amount determined by the formula

---

[64] Regulation 2301. CRA's administrative position is more lenient. Form T2091, upon which the designation is made, need not be filed unless there is some remaining taxable capital gain on the residence after making the designation: IT-120R6, note 55, above, para. 17.

[65] Before 1982, it was possible for two spouses to each designate a property as his or her principal residence. In 1982, the definition of principal residence was amended to limit the designation to one property per family unit.

[66] The tax-exempt status of the principal residence is referable only to capital gains. If the gain from the disposition of a principle residence is characterized as income from a business, the exemption does not apply. This is the case where the acquisition and disposition of a principal residence, or more likely a series of principal residences, is held to be trading in the properties (i.e., the carrying on of a business). E.g., *May v. M.N.R.*, [1980] C.T.C. 2457, 80 D.T.C. 1413 (T.R.B.); affirmed (1981), [1982] C.T.C. 66, 82 D.T.C. 6072 (Fed. T.D.).

$$A - \frac{(A \times B)}{C - D}$$

where

A is the amount that would .... be the taxpayer's gain therefrom for the year,

B is one plus the number of taxation years that end after the acquisition date for which the property was the taxpayer's principal residence and during which the taxpayer was resident in Canada,

C is the number of taxation years that end after the acquisition date during which the taxpayer owned the property whether jointly with another person or otherwise, and

D is[67] ....

Paragraph 40(2)(b) does not simply exempt the capital gain on the disposition of a principal residence from tax. Instead, it provides a formula for the calculation of the capital gain. The formula results in a zero capital gain for a property which has been designated as the taxpayer's principal residence for the entire period of the taxpayer's ownership and a proportionately reduced capital gain for a property which has been designated as the taxpayer's principal residence for only part of that period.[68] For most purposes, the formula may be stated as follows:

$$\text{Capital Gain} = \text{Gain} - \frac{\text{Gain} \times (1 + \text{Number of years designated as principal residence})}{\text{Number of years owned}}$$

Under the paragraph 40(2)(b) formula, one first calculates the gain on the disposition of the principal residence in the usual way, namely, by subtracting the adjusted cost base from the proceeds of disposition. The capital gain is computed by subtracting a fraction of the gain from the gain. The numerator (top) of the fraction is one plus the number of taxation years ending after 1971 for which the property has been designated as the taxpayer's principal residence and the taxpayer was resident in Canada. The denominator (bottom) of the fraction is the number of taxation years ending after 1971 during which the taxpayer owned the property. The term "taxation year" includes the whole or any part of a taxation year.

Where the numerator and denominator of the fraction are equal, then the amount to be deducted from the gain will be equal to the gain. As a result, the capital gain on the property will be zero. Because this formula includes "one plus" in the numerator, it will sometimes yield a numerator which is one more than the denominator. This produces the clumsy result that the amount to be deducted from the gain will

---

[67]D is relevant only if the property was owned on February 22, 1994 and an election in respect of the lifetime capital gains exemption election was made on the property. Otherwise D is zero (s. 40(2)(b)(ii)). For a brief discussion of this special election, see note 15, above.

[68]Note that a taxpayer's principal residence for a taxation year is the residence he or she has designated as his or her principal residence for that taxation year (paragraph (c) of the definition in section 54 discussed under heading 10.8(b), "Principal residence", above). Therefore, in order to qualify for the formula under s. 40(2)(b), the residence must be designated as a principal residence for at least one taxation year during the period of ownership.

be larger than the gain. This will give a negative figure. The Act provides by section 257 that the negative figure is to be treated as nil.

The reason for including "one plus" in the formula for the numerator is to deal with the situation where the taxpayer is unable to designate the property as a principal residence for one of the years in which he or she owned it. This will arise where the property was purchased in the same year that a previous principal residence was sold. Only one property can be designated as a principal residence in any one taxation year, and in the year of sale and purchase the taxpayer probably will have designated the property sold as his or her principal residence. On the sale of the second residence, the taxpayer is only able to designate it as his or her principal residence for one less than the actual number of years that he or she owned it. The addition of one year to the numerator corrects this problem by bringing the fraction up to one, thereby cancelling out all of the gain.

Example

A house was purchased by T in 2008 for $200,000, was ordinarily inhabited by T, and was sold by T in 2010 for $230,000.

The sale of the house in 2010 has yielded a gain of $30,000. If T, in the taxation return for 2010 were to designate the house as his or her principal residence for 2009 and 2010, a total of two years, his or her gain under paragraph 40(2)(b) would be zero, calculated as follows:

Gain (G):	$30,000
Less Exemption (E): 30,000 × (1 + 2)/3	30,000
Capital Gain [(G) - (E)]	0

In this example, T did not designate the house as her principal residence for 2008. The designation would not have been available for 2008 if it had been used to exempt the gain on a previous residence disposed of in 2008. However, the "one plus" rule of paragraph 40(2)(b) makes up for the missing year and enables the gain to be reduced to zero. If T had been able to designate the house as her principal residence for 2008, then she would only need to use 2008 and 2009 to reduce her gain to zero. She could then save 2010 for her next principal residence.

If a taxpayer owns more than one property that she ordinarily inhabits (within the meaning of the principal residence definition in section 54), things become more complicated. Now she must calculate the gain per year on each property, and factor in the "one plus" rule, to determine how best to allocate each year of principal residence designation.

Example

A house was purchased by T in 2006 for $100,000, was ordinarily inhabited by T, and was sold in 2010 for $150,000.

A cottage was purchased by T in 2007 for $80,000, was ordinarily inhabited by T, and was sold in 2010 for $140,000.

A ski chalet was purchased by T in 2008 for $120,000, was ordinarily inhabited by T, and was sold in 2010 for $140,000.

In this example, T has sold three properties in 2010, and each of them is eligible for the principal residence designation. Only one can be designated each year. Which should be selected? Naturally, the principal residence designation should be used to minimize the capital gain that has to be reported by the taxpayer. This is achieved by maximizing the principal residence designation on the residence(s) with the biggest gain per year while taking advantage of the "one plus" rule (which requires that you must designate a year to get the "one plus").

There is room for some variation in the actual calendar years designated for each property (although the property must be owned in the year of designation). One possible allocation would look like this:

	House	**Cottage**	**Ski chalet**
Gain (G)	$50,000	$60,000	$20,000
Years owned (Y)	5 (2006–2010)	4 (2007–2010)	3 (2008–2010)
Gain per year (G/Y)	$10,000	$15,000[a]	$6,667
Years designated	1 (2006)	3 (2007–2009)	1 (2010)
Exemption (E)	$50,000 × (1 + 1)/5	$60,000 × (3 + 1)/4	$20,000 × (1 + 1)/3
	= $20,000	= $60,000	= $13,334
Capital Gain = (G) - (E)	$30,000	0	$6,666

Notes:

a A maximum designation of 3 years is made in respect to this residence because it has the highest gain per year.

In this example, we assumed that the three principal residences were sold in the same year, which would not often happen in practice. If, for example, the ski chalet was not sold in 2010 and T had no intention of selling it in the near future, then the eventual gain on the property would be uncertain (it might even fall in value). Even if the property were likely to increase in value, the time value of money[69] would diminish the value of any tax savings to be derived many years hence from the designation of the ski chalet, which has the lowest gain per year. On these facts, it might be better not to save a year of designation for the ski chalet, and to obtain the immediate tax saving that would be derived by designating the house for a second year.

Paragraph 40(2)(b) will result in an apportionment of the gain in some situations where the property disposed of was used as a principal residence for some of the period of the taxpayer's ownership, and as an income-producing property for the rest of the taxpayer's ownership. However, in order to identify the situations where this occurs, we must first consider the provisions of the Act that deal with a change of use of capital property.

---

[69] See heading 1.6(d), "Time value of money", above.

(e) — Change of use rules

(i) — Deemed disposition

Paragraph 45(1)(a) provides for a deemed disposition at fair market value when property is converted from a non-income-producing use to an income-producing use, and vice versa. This deemed disposition has already been briefly discussed.[70] It is of general application within subdivision c of the Act, but our present concern is with its application to a house acquired as a principal residence and subsequently used to earn rent. In that case, the conversion to rental use would result in a deemed disposition at fair market value. There would be no taxable capital gain, even if the property had increased in value, because the property had been used exclusively as the taxpayer's principal residence. Nor would there be an allowable capital loss, even if the property had declined in value, because the property would be personal-use property where capital losses are not allowable. However, there would be three indirect tax consequences: (1) the property could no longer be designated as a principal residence; (2) the capital cost of the property (from which capital cost allowance could be claimed) would be adjusted upwards or downwards based on the fair market value of the building;[71] and (3) the fair market value of the property (land and building) at the time of the change of use would become the adjusted cost base of the property for capital gains purposes.[72]

If the former principal residence, now used to earn rent, were sold, then any gain (or loss) over fair market value at the time of the change of use would have to be recognized for tax purposes. There would be no apportionment of the gain under paragraph 40(2)(b), because the tax-free status of the principal residence was recognized at the time of the change of use; the deemed disposition at that time marked a fresh break with a new cost base.

(ii) — Election

The deemed disposition on a change from a non-income-producing use to an income-producing use can be avoided by making an election under subsection 45(2). Subsection 45(2) permits a taxpayer who has changed property from a non-income-producing use to an income-producing use to elect to "be deemed not to have begun to use the property for the purpose of gaining or producing income"; in that case, no deemed disposition occurs until "the taxpayer rescinds the election". An election under subsection 45(2), thereby avoiding the deemed disposition, will postpone the recognition of any accrued capital gain or loss: the property will retain its existing adjusted cost base. The election will also prevent the taxpayer from claiming capital cost allowance in respect of the property, because regulation 1102(1)(c) excludes from the classes of depreciable property any property "that

---

[70] See heading 10.6(e), "Change of use", above.

[71] The adjustment upwards is only for one-half of the gain (s. 13(7)(b)).

[72] S. 45(1)(a)(iv).

was not acquired by the taxpayer for the purpose of gaining or producing income".[73]

When a principal residence is converted to an income-producing use, paragraph (b) of the definition of "principal residence" in section 54 makes clear that a subsection 45(2) election will enable the property to continue to be designated as a principal residence, notwithstanding the fact that the property is no longer "ordinarily inhabited by the taxpayer". However, paragraph (d) of the definition provides that the designation as a principal residence can continue for only four years;[74] at the end of four years, the designation is no longer available.[75] Paragraph (d) is designed to meet the case of the taxpayer who moves out of his or her principal residence with the intention of returning to it within four years. A disposition of a principal residence which has been rented for four years or less, and in respect of which a subsection 45(2) election has been made, will accordingly attract no taxable capital gain.

The election under subsection 45(2) to avoid the deemed disposition is available only where property is converted from a non-income-producing use to an income-producing use. It does not apply to the opposite case, where property is converted from an income-producing use to a non-income-producing use, despite the fact that this change of use also causes a deemed disposition under paragraph 45(1)(a). However, subsection 45(3) provides an election in this case, so long as the property "becomes the principal residence of the taxpayer". This covers the case where a taxpayer acquires a house for the purpose of earning income, rents it to a tenant, and later on, after the tenant leaves, the taxpayer moves into the house himself and occupies it as a personal residence. Subsection 45(3) allows the taxpayer to elect against the deemed disposition that would otherwise be caused by the change of use that occurred when he began to occupy the property. This election enables the taxpayer to postpone the recognition of any capital gain on the property that had accrued up to the time of the change of use.[76] When the property is eventually disposed of, the principal residence designation will be available for four of the years

[73]Needless to say, the income yielded by the property will be subject to tax as business or property income under subdivision b, and all applicable expenses except capital cost allowance will be deductible.

[74]The four-year period in which a principal residence designation continues to be available in respect of income-producing property is indefinitely extended by s. 54.1. S. 54.1 applies where a taxpayer has moved out of his or her home as the result of the relocation of the taxpayer's place of employment by his or her employer, and where the taxpayer subsequently moves back into the house while still employed by the same employer or immediately following the termination of his or her employment by that employer.

[75]The expiry of the four-year designation window does not cause a deemed disposition of the property. That will not occur until the s. 45(2) election is actually rescinded.

[76]S. 45(4) provides that the s. 45(3) election is not available if the taxpayer has been deducting capital cost allowance in respect of the property. The restriction means that s. 45(3) cannot be used to postpone the recapture of capital cost allowance.

that the house was rented[77] as well as the later years when the house was actually occupied by the taxpayer.

(iii) — Partial change of use

Where a property, including a principal residence, has a partial change of use, paragraph 45(1)(c) provides for a partial deemed disposition. There is no provision in the Act allowing this deemed disposition to be avoided by election.

With respect to a principal residence, a common situation is where the owner, who used to use the property exclusively as a residence, takes in a boarder or uses one room as an office. In this kind of case, where the business or rental use of the property is ancillary to the main use of the residence, the CRA takes the position that a change of use is not deemed to have occurred and that the entire property continues to qualify as a principal residence.[78] Moreover, provided that the taxpayer has set aside and used a certain area of the residence solely for the purpose of producing income, the taxpayer "may claim the expenses (other than CCA) pertaining to the portion of the property used for income-producing purposes". However, the taxpayer may not claim capital cost allowance on any portion of the residence; if the taxpayer does so, the CRA's position is that a change of use has occurred.[79] If a partial change of use in a principal residence is deemed to have occurred, whether because the new income-producing use is more than merely ancillary to the residential use, or because the owner wishes to claim capital cost allowance on the portion of the building used for the income-producing purpose, then a deemed disposition under paragraph 45(1)(c) occurs. Under paragraph 45(1)(c), the taxpayer is deemed to have disposed of the income-producing portion of the property for proceeds equal to the proportion of the fair market value of the property which the new income-producing use of the property bears to the total use of the property. Any gain will, of course, be tax-free because of the principal residence exemption of paragraph 40(2)(b), but on a subsequent disposition of the property any gain which is attributable to the income-producing portion of the property will be subject to tax as a capital gain. Any recaptured capital cost allowance will also come back into income.

The apportionment between residential and income-producing uses is made on the basis of the area of the home used for each purpose[80] and the expenses claimed

---

[77]Paragraphs (b) and (d) of the definition of principal residence (s. 54) allow the four-year window to a property that is subject to a s. 45(3) election as well as a s. 45(2) election. In addition, the "one plus" formula in s. 40(2)(b)(i) and the rule that part of a year equals a taxation year may have the effect of subtracting one or two years from the income-producing period and adding them to the principal residence period.

[78]IT-120R6, note 55, above, para. 32.

[79]*Ibid.*

[80]*Ibid.*, para. 30.

against the income pertaining to the income-producing portion must be "a reasonable portion of the expenses relating to the whole property".[81]

[81] *Ibid.*, para. 31.

11
INVESTING AND TRADING

11.1 — Capital or income

(a) — Importance of characterization

When a profit is made on the sale of property, the profit may be either a capital gain or income from a business; it cannot be income from property.[1] The characterization is important because the *Income Tax Act* (the "Act") treats capital gains or losses differently from business income or losses.

---

[1] S. 9(3).

Most of the vast quantity of litigation concerning the proper classification of transactions with property is generated by the preferential treatment of capital gains (which are only one-half taxable) over income from a business (which is fully taxable).[2] Where a transaction with property yields a profit, it is the taxpayer who argues that the transaction was an investment to be taxed on capital account, and it is the Minister who argues that the transaction was a trade or speculation to be taxed on income account. But a transaction with property does not always yield a profit.

When it yields a loss, the same problem of classification arises, because the Act accords dissimilar treatment to capital losses and business (or other income) losses. Capital losses are one-half deductible, and are only deductible against taxable capital gains. Business losses are deductible in full, and are deductible against income from all sources. Therefore, a loss on a capital transaction is generally accorded worse tax treatment than a loss on an income transaction. Accordingly, when a loss is in issue we find the normal roles of taxpayer and Minister reversed. Now it is the taxpayer who argues that he or she was a trader or speculator, and it is the Minister who argues that the taxpayer was an investor. One example (of many) is *Bossin v. R.* (1976),[3] in which the taxpayer had lost money on the stock market, and in which Collier J. could not resist commenting that, if the taxpayer had made a profit, "the Minister would then, I suspect, have been making diametrically opposite arguments in this Court"![4]

Taxpayers sometime attempt to get the best of both worlds by treating gains on capital account and losses on revenue account in respect of similar transactions. The courts are not very sympathetic. For example, the taxpayer in *Rajchgot v. R.* (2005)[5] was an astute businessperson with a history of investing in the stock market. He had always treated his gains and losses on account of capital until 1997 when he suffered large losses from his investments in Tee-Comm Electronics Inc. (Tee-Comm). The taxpayer attempted to convince the court that the Tee-Comm investment was different from all of his other investments because he conducted himself as "trader" as opposed to "investor": because he had detailed knowledge of the company, spent time monitoring the company's operations, and held the stock

---

[2]The stakes were not as high between January 1, 1988 and October 17, 2000, when capital gains were two-thirds or three-quarters taxable. But the stakes were very high before 1972, when capital gains were not taxed at all.

[3][1976] C.T.C. 358, 76 D.T.C. 6196 (Fed. T.D.).

[4]*Ibid.*, at 371, 6205.

[5]*Rajchgot v. R.*, [2005] 5 C.T.C. 1, 2005 D.T.C. 5607 (Eng.) (F.C.A.) affirming; *Rajchgot v. R.* (2004), [2005] 2 C.T.C. 2262, 2004 D.T.C. 3090 (T.C.C. [General Procedure]). Similarly, in *Corvalan v. R.*, [2006] 3 C.T.C. 2198, 2006 D.T.C. 2907 (Eng.) (T.C.C. [General Procedure]), the taxpayer exercised employee stock options to purchase shares of his employer. Until 1997, he had been reporting the sale of such shares as dispositions of capital property. Although the court noted that treatment of earlier dispositions is not be determinative of present dispositions, it can be indicative of the taxpayer's intention. The court found nothing in evidence to distinguish 1997 transactions from prior transactions except that, in 1997, there were losses instead of gains.

for only a limited period of time. The taxpayer did not prevail at either the Tax Court or the Federal Court of Appeal.

(b) — Investing and trading distinguished

Cases in which the distinction between a capital gain/loss and business income/loss must be made generally fall into the following categories:

1. *Investment.* A dentist sells her Bell Canada stock, which she acquired as an income-producing investment. Any profit is a capital gain.

2. *Personal-use property.* A bank employee sells his cottage, which he acquired for recreation. Any profit is a capital gain.

3. *Capital asset.* A shoe manufacturer intending to move the location of her business, sells the factory for more than she paid for it. Any profit is a capital gain.[6]

4. *Inventory.* An automobile dealer sells a car in the course of his business. Any profit is income from a business.

5. *Speculation.* A lawyer sells gold, which she acquired with a view to resale at a profit. Any profit is income from a business.

The Act is not particularly helpful in distinguishing between these categories. The definition of a "capital gain" in paragraph 39(1)(a) says in effect that a capital gain is a gain from the disposition of property which would not be taxed as ordinary income. The definition of a "capital loss" in paragraph 39(1)(b) is similar. This sends us to the definitions of various kinds of ordinary income, and specifically for present purposes to the definition of income from a business. "Business" is defined in subsection 248(1) to include a "trade", or "an adventure or concern in the nature of trade". There are no definitions of "trade" or "adventure or concern in the nature of trade". Therefore, the characterization is left to the courts.

The case law characterization depends on the traditional Anglo-Canadian assumption that income must be a yield from a productive source.[7] In most cases, however, the characterization is straight forward: where property is purchased for some purpose other than resale, any gain realized when the property is eventually sold is a capital gain. Therefore, the profit on the sale of an investment (case 1, above), or of a property used for personal consumption (case 2, above), or of an income-producing business asset (case 3, above) is characterized as a capital gain. The profit on the sale of inventory property (case 4, above) or the speculative property (case 5, above) is characterized as business income. The key is to distinguish between "trading" and "investing". As discussed below, trading can be "systematic" or "speculative".

---

[6]There may also be included in income a recapture of capital cost allowance. See heading 9.4(h)(ii), "Recapture", above.

[7]See heading 4.3(a), "Source theory", above.

11.2 — Trade

(a) — Frequency of transactions

As the case of the automobile dealer (case 4, above) shows, the profit from trading in property is income from a business. Anyone who buys and sells property in a systematic manner in pursuit of profit is a trader. This is so even if trading in property is not the person's main line of business.

In *Scott v. M.N.R.* (1963),[8] the Supreme Court of Canada held that a lawyer who over a period of eight years had purchased 149 agreements and mortgages at a discount, using both his own and borrowed money, and who had then realized a profit by holding the obligations to maturity, was a trader whose gains were income from a business. In *Forest Lane Holdings Ltd. v. M.N.R.* (1990),[9] the Federal Court — Trial Division held that a corporation carried on a business of securities trading over the two year period in question based on the volume of transactions, the holding period of the securities and the fact that the principal shareholder was an investment dealer. The taxpayer corporation's conduct was the same as an investment dealer trading on his own account. By contrast, in *Wood v. M.N.R.* (1969),[10] the Supreme Court of Canada held that a lawyer who over a period of seven years purchased 13 mortgages at a discount, using only his own money, and then realized a profit by holding the mortgages to maturity, was an investor whose gains were capital gains (which were then untaxed). The Court in *Wood* emphasized that small factual differences could change the result in these cases, and held that the smaller volume of transactions and the exclusive use of savings (as opposed to borrowings) "was consistent with the making of personal investments out of his savings and not with the carrying on of a business".[11]

(b) — Relationship to taxpayer's other work

Where a series of transactions are related to the taxpayer's ordinary work, this will strengthen the inference that he or she is engaged in trading rather than personal investment. In *Cooper v. Stubbs* (1925),[12] for example, a member of a firm of cotton brokers, who also purchased and sold cotton futures on his own account, carrying out about 50 transactions per year, was held to be in the business of trading in cotton futures. Similarly, in *Morrison v. M.N.R.* (1927),[13] a member of a firm of grain commission merchants, who also bought and sold grain on his own account, carrying out 260 transactions in the taxation year in issue, was held to be a trader.

---

[8] [1963] S.C.R. 223, [1963] C.T.C. 176, 63 D.T.C. 1121 (S.C.C.).

[9] [1987] 1 C.T.C. 2051, 87 D.T.C. 1 (T.C.C.); affirmed [1990] 2 C.T.C. 305, 90 D.T.C. 6495 (Fed. T.D.).

[10] [1969] S.C.R. 330, [1969] C.T.C. 57, 69 D.T.C. 5073 (S.C.C.).

[11] *Ibid.*, at 334, 60, 5075.

[12] [1925] 2 K.B. 753 (C.A.).

[13] (1927), [1928] Ex. C.R. 75 (Ex. Ct.).

In *Whittall v. M.N.R.* (1967),[14] a member of a firm of stockbrokers who bought and sold corporate shares and oil and gas rights on his own account was held to be a trader. In all these cases, the skill and experience of the taxpayer, coupled with the frequency of the transactions, led the courts to conclude that the profits were the product of an organized business activity, namely, trading.

(c) — Inventory

Property that has been purchased for resale as part of a business is of course inventory or stock-in-trade,[15] whereas property that is used in a business to produce income over a period of time (buildings, machinery, vehicles, etc.) is depreciable property.[16] A profit on the sale of inventory is income from a business, but a profit on the sale of depreciable property is a capital gain[17] as is the profit on the sale of land used in a business.[18]

Within a business, a capital property may be converted into inventory in certain circumstances. For example, in *Canadian Kodak Sales v. M.N.R.* (1954),[19] machines known as "recordaks" were rented by Kodak to customers; the recordaks were treated in Kodak's financial accounts as capital (fixed) assets and capital cost allowance was claimed for tax purposes. However, in 1951 there was a change of marketing policy and in that year and the following year half of all the leased recordaks were sold to the customers who had been renting them. Were the profits on these sales on account of capital or income? The Exchequer Court held that the profits were income. In effect, the Court decided that the change in corporate policy in 1951 and 1952, which had made the recordaks available for sale, had converted those recordaks that were sold from capital assets (the sale of which would have been on account of capital) to inventory (the sale of which gave rise to business income).[20]

---

[14][1967] C.T.C. 377 394, 67 D.T.C. 5264 5274 (S.C.C.).

[15]See heading 8.8, "Inventory", above.

[16]See heading 9.4(b), "Depreciable property and CCA rates", above.

[17]In the case of depreciable property, the portion of the proceeds of disposition in excess of capital cost is a capital gain. If the proceeds are less than the capital cost, there is no capital loss; the tax consequences are governed by the rules respecting capital cost allowance, recapture and terminal loss: heading 9.4(h), "Retirement of depreciable property", above.

[18]Land is generally classified as non-depreciable property: see heading 9.2, ""Capital expenditure" defined", above.

[19][1954] C.T.C. 375, 54 D.T.C. 1194 (Ex. Ct.).

[20]In *Edmund Peachey v. R.*, [1979] C.T.C. 51, 79 D.T.C. 5064 (Fed. C.A.); leave to appeal refused (1979), 28 N.R. 85n (S.C.C.), land that had been acquired for subdivision and sale was rezoned so that this plan became impossible. When the land eventually was sold, the corporate taxpayer argued that it had been converted from inventory to a capital asset so that the profit on sale was a capital gain. The Federal Court of Appeal rejected this argument on the facts, but the Court accepted that land (or other property) acquired as inventory could be converted to another purpose. What was required, however, and was lacking in this case, was

11.3 — Adventure in the nature of trade

(a) — Isolated transaction

"An adventure or concern in the nature of trade" is included in the definition of "business" under subsection 248(1). The word "adventure" indicates that the dealing is isolated (or involves very few transactions) and speculative in nature. The essence of "trade" is systematic buying and selling with a view to profit. An adventure or concern *in the nature of trade* is an isolated transaction (which lacks the frequency or system of a trade) in which the taxpayer buys property with the intention of selling it at a profit, and then sells it (normally at a profit, but sometimes at a loss). Accordingly, when a taxpayer enters into an isolated transaction (or only a few transactions), he or she is not a trader. But, if the transaction was a speculative one, intended to yield a profit, it is in the nature of a business.[21]

The courts have used a number of factors to determine whether a taxpayer was engaged in an adventure in the nature of trade or in a capital transaction. The overriding requirement is a scheme for profit making. The most important factor is the taxpayer's intention at the time of purchase of the property.[22]

(b) — Intention to trade

(i) — Intention on acquisition

The intention of the taxpayer at the time of the acquisition of the property is the critical factor considered by the courts in distinguishing between an adventure or concern in the nature of trade and an investment. If the taxpayer's intention was to resell the property at a profit, then the transaction is an adventure in the nature of trade and any profit will be taxed as business income. If, on the other hand, the taxpayer's intention was to hold the property as a source of regular income (or any purpose other than resale), then the transaction is an investment and any profit will be taxed as a capital gain.

How to establish a taxpayer's intention? In the nature of things, the taxpayer's oral evidence of his or her intention is self-serving and is bound to be suspect, so the courts have tended to rely primarily on the objective facts surrounding the purchase of the property, the subsequent course of dealing and the circumstances of the sale

---

an "unequivocal positive act implementing a change of intention". Presumably, constructing on the land a building for use by the taxpayer would have been an example of such an act.

[21]See *M.N.R. v. Taylor*, note 24, below and *Regal Heights v. M.N.R.* note 32, below. Property that is the subject of an adventure in the nature of trade is inventory: *Friesen v. R.*, [1995] 3 S.C.R. 103, [1995] 2 C.T.C. 369, 95 D.T.C. 5551 (S.C.C.). The inventory of an adventure in the nature of trade must be valued at cost (s. 10(1.01)) rather than at the lower of cost or fair market value. See heading 8.8, "Inventory", above.

[22]These factors were reviewed in *Friesen*, *ibid.*, and were cited in *Hayes*, note 72, below at para. 102.

in order to determine whether the taxpayer acquired the property as an investment or as a speculation. These objective factors include:

- whether the taxpayer acquired the property with borrowed funds;
- the period of ownership of the property;
- efforts made to attract purchasers or to make the property more marketable;
- the skill and experience of the taxpayer;
- the relationship of the transaction to the taxpayer's ordinary business;
- the nature of the property, especially whether it yields regular income;
- and the circumstances of the eventual sale, especially whether it arose from something unanticipated at the time of purchase.[23]

Take the nature of property as an example. When a taxpayer buys and sells property which is not for personal use and which will not yield income there is a presumption that the taxpayer purchased the property with the intention of reselling it at a profit. In *M.N.R. v. Taylor* (1956),[24] the taxpayer purchased 1,500 tons of lead occupying 22 railway cars which he sold at a profit. This was an isolated transaction: the taxpayer had never made a similar purchase before. The Court held that the transaction was an adventure in the nature of trade, pointing out that the taxpayer could do nothing with such an asset except sell it; he could not have acquired it for any other purpose. The same conclusion has been reached with respect to the purchase and sale of commercial quantities of toilet paper,[25] whisky,[26] sugar,[27] and sulphuric acid.[28] These assets could be turned to account only by resale. They could not by their very nature be regarded as investments.

The taxpayer's skill and experience, as well as the period of ownership and the frequency of the transactions, were relevant factors in assessing the taxpayer's intention in *Dubé v. R.* (2005).[29] Dube was a building inspector and self-employed for several years in the field of architecture. In March 2001, he purchased a building and sold it within six months to someone he had met inspecting another building. He used the profit on this sale to purchase a second building which he again sold within six months for a profit (in March 2002) to a contractor he had met in connection with his ownership of this building. In 2002, he purchased a third building and used it as his residence and office. The court held that the sales in 2001 and

[23]See e.g., Interpretation Bulletin IT-459, "Adventure or concern in the nature of trade" (1980).

[24][1956] C.T.C. 189, 56 D.T.C. 1125 (Ex. Ct.).

[25]*Rutledge v. C.I.R.* (1929), 14 T.C. 490 (Scotland Ct. Sess.).

[26]*C.I.R. v. Fraser* (1942), 24 T.C. 498 (Scotland Ct. Sess.).

[27]*Atlantic Sugar Refineries v. M.N.R.*, [1948] C.T.C. 326 (Ex. Ct.); affirmed [1949] S.C.R. 706, [1949] C.T.C. 196, 49 D.T.C. 602 (S.C.C.).

[28]*Honeyman v. M.N.R.*, [1955] C.T.C. 151, 55 D.T.C. 1094 (Ex. Ct.).

[29]*Dubé v. R.* (2005), 2005 TCC 779, [2007] 2 C.T.C. 2437, 2007 D.T.C. 468 (Eng.) (T.C.C. [Informal Procedure]).

2002 gave rise to business income because the taxpayer's primary intention was to sell the buildings rather than to keep them for rental purposes. The taxpayer testified that it became necessary to sell the buildings because the estimated repairs and renovations required to turn them into rental properties were too expensive and this was only determined *after* he purchased the building. The court reasoned that if the taxpayer had truly intended to retain the two buildings at issue (as opposed to selling them for a profit with view to obtaining funds to purchase the third building), there was no doubt that the taxpayer would have inspected them himself (and determined the cost of renovations) *before* buying them, given that he had the skills and experience to do so.

On the basis of the jurisprudence,[30] the issue of whether an isolated transaction is in the nature of trade turns on the intention of the taxpayer at the time when he or she acquired the property. If that intention was something else, for example, to hold the property as an income-earning investment, or to use the property as a capital (fixed) asset in a business, or to use the property for personal purposes, then the subsequent sale of the property will be treated as a capital transaction. As it was pithily commented: "One of the first rules relating to true capital gains is that if one is to be had it should not be deliberately sought"![31]

(ii) — Secondary intention

One of the difficulties with relying on intention as a key factor in the classification of transactions is that a taxpayer may have more than one intention at the time when he or she purchases property. This fact has given rise to the "secondary intention" doctrine. If property is purchased with the primary intention of using it in some non-speculative way, but with a secondary (alternative) intention of selling it at a profit if the primary purpose proves impracticable, then if the secondary intention is carried out the transaction will be held to be on account of income rather than capital. For example, in the leading case of *Regal Heights v. M.N.R.* (1960),[32] the taxpayer acquired undeveloped land with the primary intention of building a shopping centre on the site. After some development work had been done, the plan was abandoned when it was discovered that another shopping centre was to be built only two miles from the taxpayer's property. The taxpayer then sold the land at a profit. In the Supreme Court of Canada, it was held that the profit was income from a business. The trial judge had found that the corporate taxpayer's primary intention was to develop the land into a shopping centre, but the judge had also found that there was a good chance that the shopping centre plan might not come off and that the taxpayer was aware of this and had a secondary intention to sell the land at a profit if the primary intention became impracticable. The Supreme Court of Canada accepted these findings and held that the existence of the secondary intention made the enterprise an adventure in the nature of trade.

---

[30] *Irrigation Industries*, note 54, below, being an exception.

[31] Stikeman, *Canada Tax Service* (Carswell, looseleaf), vol. 2, commentary to s. 9.

[32] [1960] S.C.R. 902, [1960] C.T.C. 384, 60 D.T.C. 1270 (S.C.C.).

Since *Regal Heights* was decided, there has been a flood of cases on the secondary intention doctrine. While the cases have not been entirely consistent, two decisions of the Federal Court of Appeal (none of the cases have gone to the Supreme Court of Canada) have helped to define the state of mind that will qualify as a secondary intention. In *Reicher v. R.* (1975),[33] the taxpayer, who was a professional engineer, acquired land to construct an office building. The building was constructed, the taxpayer moved his offices into it, and excess space was rented to third parties. However, about a year later, the taxpayer sold the property at a profit, taking back a lease from the purchaser. The taxpayer testified that the sale-and-lease-back had been caused by financial difficulties which had arisen unexpectedly after the project was well under way. The Federal Court of Appeal accepted this explanation for the early sale and held that resale was not a motivating reason for the acquisition of the property; the transaction was therefore not an adventure in the nature of trade. A similar decision was reached in *Hiwako Investments v. R.* (1978),[34] where the taxpayer purchased a group of apartment buildings, and then sold them at a profit less than a year later. The sale had been made after it was discovered that the buildings were less profitable than anticipated, and in response to an unsolicited offer. The Federal Court of Appeal recognized that the taxpayer purchased the property for capital appreciation as well as the rental income. But this alone did not amount to a secondary intention to sell. The Court held that resale was not a motivating reason for the purchase. Therefore, the secondary intention doctrine did not apply, and the transaction was not an adventure in the nature of trade.

What *Reicher* and *Hiwako* establish is that the secondary intention to sell must have existed at the time when the property was acquired, and that it must have been "an operating motivation" or a "motivating reason" for the acquisition of the property. This language is intended to emphasize that a secondary intention does not exist merely because the taxpayer contemplates the possibility of resale of the property. That would be too strict a test, because any prudent investor would have that possibility in mind when purchasing an investment. In other words, it is not necessary for the taxpayer who claims to be an investor to show that his or her exclusive purpose was to acquire an investment. One commentator suggests that the prospect of resale at a profit is a motivating reason only if the taxpayer would still have acquired the property as a speculation in the absence of the primary intention to build a shopping centre (or whatever).[35] This may pitch the test too high, but certainly the secondary intention doctrine will not be satisfied unless the prospect of resale at a profit was an important factor in the decision to acquire the property.

---

[33] [1975] C.T.C. 659, 76 D.T.C. 6001 (Fed. C.A.).

[34] [1978] C.T.C. 378, 78 D.T.C. 6281 (Fed. C.A.).

[35] McDonnell, (1977) 25 *Can. Tax J.* 618, 620; see also case comments (1976) 24 *Can. Tax J.* 120; (1978) 26 *Can. Tax J.* 412.

(iii) — Differing intentions

Since the intention of the taxpayer is the key, it follows that two parties to the same transaction may receive different tax treatment. When a farmer sells the farm to a developer, the farmer's gain is capital, because the property was acquired as a farm. But when the developer subdivides the property and sells off the lots, the developer's gain is income from a business, because the property was acquired for resale.

(iv) — Change of intention

What is the legal position when a taxpayer's intention changes between the time of acquisition of the property and the time of sale? We have already noticed that assets in a business may be converted from inventory to fixed assets or vice versa.[36] Can a change of intention have a similar effect on an isolated transaction?

It is necessary to draw a distinction between property acquired as an investment (or for some other purpose not including resale) and property acquired for resale. In the former case (the investment), it is difficult to contend that a change of intention could convert the transaction into an adventure in the nature of trade. After all, the sale of an investment is inevitably preceded by a decision and efforts to sell the asset. If this change in the intention of the taxpayer converted the transaction into an adventure in the nature of trade, then a capital gain could never be generated by a voluntary disposition, but only by an involuntary disposition such as an expropriation. That is, of course, ridiculous in light of the numerous cases which have held that the sale of an asset which was acquired to hold as an investment was on capital account. However, there are very few cases in which a court explicitly considered the effect of a taxpayer's decision to stop holding property as a source of income (or other purpose) and to turn it to account by sale.

One case in which the taxpayer's change of intention was considered is *McGuire v. M.N.R.* (1956).[37] In that case, the taxpayer had bought a small farm with the intention of living on it and working it as a farm, which was what he did for nine years. Then he subdivided the property into 52 lots, and sold the lots. This activity was relied upon by the Minister as showing that the taxpayer had embarked on a speculative venture. The Exchequer Court rejected the Minister's argument, holding that, since the property was not purchased for resale, the subsequent efforts to sell the property did not turn it into a speculative venture. The taxpayer's profit was held to be a capital gain. The English Court of Appeal reached the same result on similar facts in *Taylor v. Good* (1974).[38] These cases reflect the common-sense proposition that the decision to sell a property acquired for some purpose other than resale, and

---

[36] Under heading 11.2(c), "Inventory", above.

[37] [1956] C.T.C. 98, 56 D.T.C. 1042 (Ex. Ct.).

[38] (1974), 49 T.C. 277 (C.A.).

efforts to make the sale as advantageous as possible, do not convert the transaction into an adventure in the nature of trade.[39]

With respect to property acquired for resale, a change of intention evidenced by objective facts might well convert a speculative purchase into a capital transaction. If, for example, we reversed the chronology of *McGuire* and supposed that land purchased for subdivision and sale was converted by the owner into a farm upon which he lived and worked for a substantial period of time. When the property was eventually sold it would be arguable, on the analogy of the change of use of business assets,[40] that the property had lost its speculative character and the sale was on capital account. Less clear, perhaps, is the case where property purchased for resale is simply held for a very long time before resale. Here it would be arguable that some time in the long period of ownership the property must have ceased to be an object of trade and became an investment.[41]

(v) — Corporate intention

In many of the foregoing cases, the taxpayer was a corporation. In determining the intention of the corporation, the courts have invariably lifted the corporate veil and attributed to the corporation the intention of those individuals who control the corporation. In particular, it is clear that statements of purpose in the corporation's memorandum of association or other constituting instrument are of little relevance to the present enquiry, which turns on actual and not fictional intention.[42] The rule which is applied in these tax cases seems to be no different from the "directing mind" principle, which is used to determine corporate intention in other branches of the law, such as tort[43] or criminal.[44]

---

[39]*Contra*, *Dawd v. M.N.R.*, [1981] C.T.C. 2999, 81 D.T.C. 888 (T.R.B.); and *Turnbull v. M.N.R.*, [1984] C.T.C. 2800, 84 D.T.C. 1720 (T.C.C.). In both cases, the courts held that land originally purchased for reasons other than resale was converted to inventory by the owners' efforts to sell the land. The courts took the view that the amount of preparation for sale was more consistent with a business venture than with the steps an ordinary owner would take in preparing to sell a capital asset. As a result, the courts held that the properties were "converted" from capital assets to inventory when the owners committed themselves to subdividing and selling the properties. This required the courts to determine the dates at which the properties were converted to inventory: any gain in the value of the properties before the "conversion dates" would be on account of capital, while gains after the commitment to subdivide and sell would be on account of income.

[40]Under heading 10.6(e), "Change of use", above.

[41]*Cf. M.N.R. v. Thibeault*, [1964] C.T.C. 232, 64 D.T.C. 5151 (Ex. Ct.).

[42]*Sutton Lumber and Trading Co. v. M.N.R.*, [1953] 2 S.C.R. 77, [1953] C.T.C. 237, 53 D.T.C. 1158 (S.C.C.); *C.W. Logging Co. v. M.N.R.*, [1956] C.T.C. 15, 56 D.T.C. 1007 (Ex. Ct.); and *Regal Heights*, note 32, above.

[43]*Lennard's Carrying Co. v. Asiatic Petroleum* (1914), [1915] A.C. 705 (H.L.).

[44]*Tesco Supermarkets v. Nattrass* (1971), [1972] A.C. 153 (H.L.).

11.4 — Typical transactions

(a) — Real estate

Developed land that produces income representing a reasonable rate of return on its capital cost may obviously be either an investment or a speculation, depending upon the intention with which it was acquired. If the intention was to hold the land as a source of income, then it is an investment and any profit (or loss) on sale will receive capital treatment. If the intention was to take a profit by reselling the land, then any profit (or loss) on sale will receive income treatment. In many cases, of course, the acquisition of land will be motivated by both the intention to hold it as an investment as well as the intention of selling the property at a profit.[45]

In *H. Fine and Sons v. M.N.R.* (1984),[46] the taxpayer corporation purchased land and erected a warehouse on the site. The taxpayer began carrying on business at the site, but experienced financial difficulties several years later, forcing it to sell off some of the land. In reporting its income for the taxation year in question, the taxpayer reported the gain from the sale of the land as a capital gain. The Federal Court-Trial Division agreed with the taxpayer. The taxpayer had purchased the land not for a speculative purpose but with the intention of using it as a capital (fixed) asset of the business. Therefore, the transaction was not an adventure in the nature of trade, and the gain was on account of capital. In *Paquet v. M.N.R.* (1981),[47] the taxpayer had purchased a farm with the intention of working the land, and had only sold for a profit after receiving unsolicited offers from family and friends. As was the case in *H. Fine and Sons*, the taxpayer in *Paquet* was found not to have purchased the property with a speculative intention, and the profit from the sale was accordingly held to be a capital gain.

What about undeveloped land which yields little or no income and which has not been purchased for recreation or development? On the one hand, undeveloped land is like a commodity (such as lead) in that it can produce a return to the owner only by being sold. On the other hand, undeveloped land is unlike most commodities in that it is sometimes purchased and held for a long time as a store of value.[48] In two cases, taxpayers have been able to establish that non-income-producing land was held as an investment. In both *M.N.R. v. Lawee* (1972)[49] and *Montfort Lakes Estates v. R.* (1979),[50] the Federal Court-Trial Division found that the land had been acquired to provide security against inflation over a long term without any

---

[45] An attempt is made to analyze that situation under heading 11.3(b)(ii), "Secondary intention", above.

[46] [1984] C.T.C. 500, 84 D.T.C. 6520 (Fed. T.D.).

[47] (1981), [1982] C.T.C. 2144, 82 D.T.C. 1148 (T.R.B.).

[48] Gold and silver are sometimes purchased for this reason too. See the discussion under heading 11.4(c), "Commodities", below.

[49] [1972] C.T.C. 359, 72 D.T.C. 6342 (Fed. T.D.).

[50] [1980] C.T.C. 27, 79 D.T.C. 5467 (Fed. T.D.).

intention of sale at an early opportunity. When resale did occur (after nine years in *Lawee* and 18 years in *Montfort*), the profit was held to be a capital gain.

The CRA has issued an interpretation bulletin which describes some of the factors that have been used by the courts to assess a taxpayer's intention.[51] The list includes the feasibility of the taxpayer's intention and the extent to which it was carried out, the geographical location and zoned use of the real estate, evidence of change in the taxpayer's intention, the extent to which borrowed money was used and the terms of financing, the length of time throughout which the real estate was held, the factors that motivated the sale of the real estate (e.g., financial difficulty or an unsolicited offer) and evidence that the taxpayer had dealt extensively in real estate in the past.[52]

Unlike Canadian securities (discussed below), there is no statutory election to treat real estate as capital property. As a result, the classification of transactions in real estate continues to be a major field of battle in the courts. A recent example is the *Friesen* case[53] in which the purchase of a tract of vacant land was held by the Supreme Court of Canada to constitute an adventure in the nature of trade.

(b) — Securities

"Securities" typically include corporate shares and debt obligations. The classification of gains or losses from the sale of securities is generally governed by common law principles. With respect to "Canadian securities", however, taxpayers are allowed to elect under subsection 39(4) to treat the securities as capital property.

(i) — Common law principles

When a taxpayer buys and sells property that is a traditional kind of investment, in the absence of a pattern of trading, the normal inference would be that the transaction was an investment and that any profit was a capital gain. In *Irrigation Industries v. M.N.R.* (1962),[54] the Supreme Court of Canada held that the purchase of shares in a company, made with borrowed money, and followed by sale only a month later (when the loan was called), was not an adventure in the nature of trade, but merely an investment. It seemed clear on the facts, and did not seem to be denied by the Court, that the taxpayer's purchase of the shares was speculative, not designed to yield income in the form of dividends, but rather to yield a quick profit on resale. If this is so, then the decision is wrong. Justice Martland for the Court said that corporate shares were intrinsically an investment in contrast to articles of commerce; and it did not matter that the shares were purchased "with the intention

---

[51] Interpretation Bulletin IT-218R, "Profit, capital gains and losses from the sale of real estate" (1986).

[52] *Ibid.*, para. 3.

[53] Note 21, above. The characterization of the transaction as a business transaction was favourable to the taxpayer because the taxpayer wanted to recognize business losses.

[54] [1962] S.C.R. 346, [1962] C.T.C. 215, 62 D.T.C. 1131 (S.C.C.).

of disposing of the shares at a profit as soon as reasonably possible". But, with respect, the nature of the property is relevant only as casting light on the intention of the taxpayer. Once it is established that the taxpayer's intention was to speculate, the Court should have held that the transaction was an adventure in the nature of trade.

The general thrust of Justice Martland's opinion in *Irrigation Industries* was to deny that an isolated transaction in corporate shares could ever be treated as an adventure in the nature of trade. Later decisions of the Supreme Court of Canada, however, have made clear that this implausible proposition is not good law. In *M.N.R. v. Foreign Power Securities Corp.* (1967),[55] for example, the taxpayer (an investment company) sold at a profit a number of shares from its portfolio. The Supreme Court of Canada held that the profit was a capital gain and not income. This decision was based not on any inherent quality of corporate shares, but on the intention of the taxpayer. The Court held that the taxpayer had acquired the shares "as investments to be held as a source of income". The taxpayer had not acquired the shares for the purpose of resale, and had sold them only because its officers had concluded that "the shares had reached a price that was unreasonably high". In *M.N.R. v. Sissons* (1969),[56] the Supreme Court of Canada held that a purchase of corporate debentures at a discount was an adventure in the nature of trade, so that the profit obtained on maturity was income from a business. This was an isolated transaction by an individual who was a dealer in postage stamps. Yet Justice Pigeon said that it was an adventure in the nature of trade, because "the purpose of the operation was not to earn income from the securities but to make a profit on prompt realization".

Foreign Power and *Sissons* confirm that the classification of transactions in corporate securities (whether shares or debt) does not depend upon any inherent characteristics of such securities, but on the intention with which they are acquired. If that intention is to hold the securities as a source of income (as in *Foreign Power*), then any profit on sale will be capital; if that intention is to make a profit by prompt realization (as in *Sissons*), then any profit on sale will be income. In other words, the intention test has survived the dicta of *Irrigation Industries*.[57]

While the foregoing cases all concerned corporate securities, the same principles apply to other income-producing assets, such as mortgages and other debt obligations and developed real estate. The income-producing character of the property (in

---

[55] [1967] S.C.R. 295, [1967] C.T.C. 116, 67 D.T.C. 5084 (S.C.C.).

[56] [1969] S.C.R. 507, [1969] C.T.C. 184, 69 D.T.C. 5152 (S.C.C.).

[57] *Accord, Bossin v. R.*, [1976] C.T.C. 358, 76 D.T.C. 6196 (Fed. T.D.); *Tamas v. R.*, [1981] C.T.C. 220, 81 D.T.C. 5150 (Fed. T.D.); *Becker v. M.N.R.* (1982), [1983] C.T.C. 11, 83 D.T.C. 5032 (Fed. C.A.); *Placements Bourget v. M.N.R.*, [1988] 2 C.T.C. 8, 88 D.T.C. 5427 (Fed. T.D.); *Karben Holding v. M.N.R.*, [1989] 2 C.T.C. 145, 89 D.T.C. 5413 (Fed. T.D.); *McGroarty v. M.N.R.*, [1989] 1 C.T.C. 2280, 89 D.T.C. 185 (T.C.C.); affirmed [1994] 2 C.T.C. 52, 94 D.T.C. 6276 (Fed. T.D.); and *Pollock v. M.N.R.* (1993), [1994] 1 C.T.C. 3, 94 D.T.C. 6050 (Fed. C.A.).

contrast to commodities) will give rise to a presumption that the property is held as an investment, but that presumption will be rebutted if the facts clearly indicate that the property was acquired not to yield income but to yield a profit on early sale.

(ii) — Canadian securities election

The question of whether transactions in corporate securities are on account of capital or income is also affected by subsections (4), (5) and (6) of section 39, which were added to the Act in 1977. Subsection 39(4) permits a taxpayer to elect capital treatment for all dispositions of "Canadian securities" made by the taxpayer in the year of election and in any future year. "Canadian security" is defined in subsection 39(6) as meaning shares or debt of a corporation resident in Canada.[58] This election is permanent: the taxpayer is bound to accept capital treatment of dispositions of Canadian securities in future years. Capital treatment is, of course, the most favourable treatment of gains, but it may be unwelcome if losses are incurred in future years.

The election is available to both individuals and corporations, provided that they are Canadian residents. Subsection 39(5) excludes "a trader or dealer in securities" and other classes of persons from the election. The terms "trader" and "dealer" are not defined in the Act. In the context of subsection 39(5), the terms clearly include persons who hold themselves out to the public as dealers in shares, bonds or other securities. On the basis of Federal Court of Appeal in *R. v. Vancouver Art Metal Works* (1993),[59] a private trader is also excluded from the statutory election. This means that a purported election under subsection 39(4) does not preclude litigation on the vexed question of whether a person is or is not a trader, which greatly reduces the usefulness of the subsection 39(4) election. As we have seen, a person held not to be a trader would be entitled to capital gains treatment anyway, except in respect of a particular transaction held to be an adventure in the nature of trade. By virtue of the decision in *Vancouver Art Metal Works*, the only purpose served by a subsection 39(4) election is to preclude the question of whether a particular transaction by a non-trader is an adventure in the nature of trade.

(c) — Commodities

As discussed above,[60] there is a presumption that a commodities transaction is an adventure in the nature of trade. This presumption will be rebutted where the facts clearly point to an intention to invest. A commodity such as gold may be purchased without any intention of early resale. Being non-income-producing, gold can only be turned to account by resale, but there is a class of gold purchasers who do in fact have no intention of resale in the foreseeable future. They see gold as a "store of value", providing security against inflation, or against the volatility of paper curren-

---

[58]There is an exception for "prescribed" securities, which are defined in Reg. 6200.

[59][1993] 1 C.T.C. 346, 93 D.T.C. 5116 (Fed. C.A.); leave to appeal refused (1993), 160 N.R. 314n (S.C.C.).

[60]Under heading 11.4(a), "Real estate", above.

cies, or against the instability of governments; and notwithstanding the absence of regular income they buy gold with the intention of holding it for as long as possible. While there are no reported cases in which gold has been held to be an investment, there are cases in which undeveloped land has been held to be an investment on the ground that it was purchased as a long-term store of value.[61] These cases would apply to gold (or silver or other commodities) acquired for the same reason.[62]

(d) — Foreign exchange

Gains or losses on foreign exchange are often incidental to other transactions. Property or services may be bought or sold by a Canadian resident in terms of a foreign currency, and the foreign exchange rate may change between the time when the obligation to pay is created and the time when payment is made. In this situation, the primary transaction is the sale or purchase of the property or services. If that transaction is on income account, for example, a purchase of inventory or a sale of professional services, then the foreign exchange gain or loss will also be on account of income. If the primary transaction is on capital account, for example, the purchase or sale of an investment, then any foreign exchange or loss will also be on capital account. Gains or losses experienced through buying and selling foreign currency are subject to the same tax treatment as commodities,[63] including the administratively-established election that has been described.[64]

---

[61] *Ibid.*

[62] In Interpretation Bulletin IT-346R, "Commodity futures and certain commodities" (1978), paras. 7 and 8, the CRA states that "as a general rule" it is "acceptable" for "speculators" to report all their gains (or losses) from transactions in commodity futures or in commodities either as capital gains (or losses) or as business income (or loss), provided the same reporting is followed consistently from year to year. This position allows a "speculator" to elect the tax treatment that he or she prefers. However, if business income treatment is used in 1976 or a subsequent year, the CRA has stated that it will not permit a change to capital gains treatment. The term "speculator" is defined in para. 6 as a person who does not come within the following three categories: (1) a person whose transactions are part of business operations that use commodities (e.g., a distillery); (2) a person whose transactions are based on special insider information; and (3) a corporation whose prime or only activity is trading in commodities. The CRA insists on income treatment for persons in the three categories. Since this election is not expressly authorized by the Act (unlike, for example, the election with respect to Canadian securities under s. 39(4), it is technically not binding on either the taxpayer or the Minister. Further, if a taxpayer changes from capital gains treatment to business income treatment, the CRA may reassess the taxpayer's returns, treating the gains and losses for those years on a consistent basis. See CRA, Technical Interpretation, Document no. 9829965 (1998).

[63] See heading 11.4(c), "Commodities", above.

[64] See generally, Interpretation Bulletin IT-95R, "Foreign exchange gains and losses" (1980), para. 6. A difference is created by s. 39(2), which provides that only an amount in excess of $200 of an individual's gain or loss on the disposition of foreign currency is taxable or allowable as a capital gain or loss.

The characterization of exchange gains as on account of capital or income was also an issue in *Shell Canada Ltd. v. R.* (1999)[65] and *Canadian Pacific Ltd. v. R.* (2002).[66] In these cases, the taxpayer borrowed in a weak currency at an interest rate higher than a hard currency, such as United States dollar. To protect against currency risks, the taxpayer entered into forward contracts and realized an exchange gain. The exchange gain was reported as a capital gain, while the nominal interest (which included a portion intended to compensate the lender for potential currency risks) was deducted in full. The taxpayer's characterization was upheld by the courts. The Supreme Court of Canada stated in *Shell* that "the characterization of a foreign exchange gain or loss generally follows the characterization of the underlying transaction."[67] Thus, "if the underlying transaction was entered into for the purpose of acquiring funds to be used for capital purposes, any foreign exchange gain or loss in respect of that transaction will also be on capital account."[68] In these cases, because the debt obligations were on account of capital, the foreign exchange gain arising from the devaluation of the weak currency loans was also received on account of capital.[69]

(e) — Hedging

Hedging is an important tool used by businesses to manage their financial risk. Corporations often have exposure to fluctuations in all kinds of financial prices in the course of carrying on their regular business operations. Financial prices include foreign exchange rates, interest rates, commodity prices and equity prices. The effect of changes in these prices on corporate profit can be overwhelming: a corporation's profit may be reduced significantly by falling commodity prices or increased as a result of a windfall gain attributable to the decline of the Canadian dollar. Like

---

[65][1999] 4 C.T.C. 313, 99 D.T.C. 5669 (Eng.) (S.C.C.).

[66][2002] 2 C.T.C. 197, 2002 D.T.C. 6742 (Fed. C.A.) The Federal Court of Appeal in *Canadian Pacific* also naturally followed the Supreme Court of Canada's decision in *Shell Canada*, but also went further in concluding that the transactions are free from the general anti-avoidance rule. GAAR and the *Canadian Pacific* case are discussed briefly under heading 20.5, "Application of the GAAR", below.

[67]*Shell Canada*, note 65, above, para. 68.

[68]*Ibid.*

[69]As is often the case when the result of a court decision is unacceptable to the government, the result of the *Shell Canada* case has now been reversed by statute — in this case, by the weak currency loan rules in section 20.3. A "weak currency loan" is defined to exist if the loan proceeds are in currency other than the final currency (the currency that the funds are to be put to use in), the debt exceeds $500,000, and the interest rate of the debt is more than two points (2%) higher than the rate in the final currency. If a "weak currency loan" exists, then the tax consequences are: (1) the deduction for the interest expense on the loan is limited to the interest that would have been paid on a final currency loan (i.e., excess interest of 2% or more denied), (2) all foreign exchange gains or losses are on income account (even if the loan is capital property), and (3) any interest denied in (1) can be used to reduce any foreign exchange gain (or increase any foreign exchange loss on the settlement of the debt).

buying insurance against the risks of theft or fire, businesses enter into hedging contracts to minimize the risk caused by price changes.

For tax purposes, the gain or loss from a hedging transaction must be characterized either as a capital gain or capital loss or as business income or loss. The characterization is generally determined by the nature of the transaction to which the hedge relates. For example, in *Shell*[70] the gain from the foreign exchange contract entered into to hedge a weak-currency loan was held to be on account of capital because the loan agreement was characterized as on account of capital and Shell Canada would not have entered into the loan agreement in the absence of the foreign exchange contract. On the other hand, if a hedge relates to the purchase of inventory property, the gain would be on account of income.

In addition to the insurance-type hedging transactions, there are the so-called "convertible hedges" that are used as "win-win" investment products. A "win-win" situation means that an investor would win from the cash flow generated by the investment, from the appreciation in value of the investment, and from tax refunds if they incurred losses. In simple terms, a convertible hedge consists of two positions, a short position and a long position. One taxpayer takes the short position by selling common stock of a security that the seller does not own (the shorted stock). For the sale to be completed, the stock must be borrowed (generally from the securities dealer). The result of a short position is that the seller receives the cash price of the shorted stock and is liable to return the borrowed securities at a future date. At the same time, a second taxpayer takes the long position and purchases a security that is convertible into the stock that has been sold short. The conversion feature means that the second taxpayer has a source for the stock that the first taxpayer must eventually return to the lender that supported the short sale. In an economic sense, the two taxpayer's investments are integrated. In technical terms, their brokerage accounts are cross-guaranteed for margin requirements, which allows the second taxpayer to use the credit position of the first taxpayer's short sale to purchase the long position in the convertible security.[71]

---

[70]Note 65, above. In *Shell Canada*, a "weak-currency hedge loan" was used to create the financial equivalent of a nine per cent US dollar loan. Rather than borrowing in US dollars and paying interest of nine per cent, Shell borrowed 150 million in NZ dollars and paid interest of 15 per cent. Upon receiving the loan in NZ dollars, Shell immediately converted the funds into US dollars and entered into a forward contract with a bank to convert US dollars into NZ dollars at predetermined exchange rates on the interest payment dates and the principal repayment due date. When the loan was due, Shell repaid about US $21 million less than it originally received when it had converted the loan proceeds from NZ dollars into US dollars in the first place. This $21 million foreign currency exchange gain was reported by Shell as a capital gain. The court held that the interest of 15 per cent was deductible under s. 20(1)(c) because the characterization of a payment as interest is based on the contract between the lender and the borrower and, unless there is a sham, there is no need to examine the economic realities of the borrowing transactions.

[71]When an investor borrows money to pay in part for the purchase of securities, she can borrow from her securities broker by opening a "margin account" with the broker. The por-

The exposure to the price fluctuation of the shorted common stock is hedged once the two taxpayers have established their long and short positions. In the meantime, the convertible security held in the long position produces an income stream of dividends or interest. A convertible security may be a convertible preferred share, a convertible debenture or a warrant. If the stock price rises, there will be a gain on long position (because the price of the convertible security will increase) but there will be a loss on the short position. If the stock price falls, the opposite is true: there will be a gain on the short position, and a loss on the long position.

An example of convertible hedge is found in *Hayes v. R.* (2003)[72] which involves several taxpayers, including Gordon Rezek. On April 27, 1988, Mr. Rezek sold short 30,704 Laidlaw common shares and coincidently bought 10,100 Laidlaw preferred shares. On May 20, 1988, Mr. Rezek sold the 10,100 convertible preferred shares for $477,075 and Ms. Fahrngruber (who subsequently married Mr. Rezek) bought 10,100 Laidlaw convertible preferred shares. The result was that Mr. Rezek held a short position in Laidlaw common shares and Ms. Fahrngruber held a long position in Laidlaw convertible preferred shares (which were convertible into 37,709 common shares). Viewing the components separately, Mr. Rezek's sale created a $138,431 loss in his account, which he claimed on his 1988 tax return, resulting in a tax refund of approximately $80,000. In August 1988, Ms. Fahrngruber then converted the convertible preferred shares into 30,709 Laidlaw common shares.[73] This left Mr. Rezek and Ms. Fahrngruber in what was referred to as a common-common position. The experts agreed that taken together there was absolutely no economic benefit to this position. It was clear that a common-long/common-short position cannot be held in one account, as they would simply cancel each other out.

The main tax benefit of a convertible hedge is to deduct the losses in computing income. Of course, the effectiveness of this strategy depends on the characterization of the losses as capital losses or business losses, because business losses are fully deductible and capital losses are deductible in half and only against capital gains. The taxpayers in *Hayes* characterized their losses as business losses.

---

tion of the purchase price that the investor must deposit is called margin and is the investor's initial equity in the account. The loan from the broker is secured by the securities that are purchased by the investor.

[72][2004] 1 C.T.C. 2605, 2003 D.T.C. 1205 (T.C.C. [General Procedure]); reversed by the FCA: see note 77, below. There are several earlier cases dealing with similar transactions: *Schultz v. R.*, [1993] 2 C.T.C. 2409, 93 D.T.C. 953 (T.C.C.); affirmed [1996] 2 C.T.C. 127, 95 D.T.C. 5657 (Fed. C.A.); *Carter v. R.*, [1999] 2 C.T.C. 2553, 99 D.T.C. 585 (T.C.C.); upheld [2001] 4 C.T.C. 79, 2001 D.T.C. 5560 (Fed. C.A.).

[73]Note that there was a five share discrepancy from what Mr. Rezek held: Ms. Fahrngruber simply sold the five shares.

At the outset of his decision, Miller T.C.J. stated:[74]

> [T]he conundrum in applying tax principles to the financially innovative strategy of convertible hedging is that tax laws have not necessarily kept apace with the ingenuity of the financial community. It is therefore appropriate, when viewing the transactions through the tax looking glass, that the focus not be so finely adjusted as to preclude a broad, common sense, but equally innovative, approach to the application of our tax laws. A square peg does fit in a round hole if the round hole is big enough.

On the issue of characterization of the gains or losses, Miller T.C.J. concluded that the gains or losses were from business because the taxpayers were engaged in an adventure (investing in convertible hedging) in the nature of trade. In reaching this decision, he examined: the fact that the taxpayers collapsed some of the convertible hedges in less than a year (conduct indicative of an intent to trade rather than long-term investment); intentions of the taxpayers at the time they acquired the convertible hedges; the method of financing through margin accounts; and the very nature of the convertible hedge itself.

However, Miller T.C.J. did not stop there. He also considered whether the two legs of a convertible hedge (i.e., the short position and the long position) should be considered together as being one property that satisfies the broad definition of "property" in the Act, and whether taxpayers who entered into transactions with a relative should be considered to be in a partnership or agency relation.

Miller T.C.J. held that each convertible hedge (as opposed to each leg of the hedge) was a stand-alone investment constituting a business by virtue of being an adventure in the nature of trade. He relied on the broad definition of "property" in the Act, under which the rights implicit in a convertible hedge justified its characterization as property. In addition, he relied on the fact that the broker through which these transactions occurred allowed the taxpayer to rely on one leg of the transaction to satisfy margin requirements relating to the other leg. The taxpayers understood the cash flow was a net determination and not one-sided determination of each component. The common view of the taxpayers was that the convertible hedge itself was the investment and not its components. Furthermore, he held that a right can only be characterized as property if it is property of a "source" of income contemplated by Section 3 of the Act. The separate legs of the convertible hedge must be viewed together, since only as a whole do they constitute the source to be taxed. It is the net result of each convertible hedge (i.e., the gain or loss from each of the short and long position must be offset first) that is the business profit or loss, which must then be split by the "co-adventurers".[75]

---

[74] *Hayes*, note 72, above, para. 2.

[75] Miller T.C.J. did not find the two parties to a convertible hedge were partners of a partnership for tax purposes. This conclusion must be contrasted with the decision in *Schultz*, note 72, above, in which the Federal Court Appeal found a partnership existed between the two parties.

As a result, the source of the loss for tax purposes is the investment in each convertible hedge, and the amount of loss is not the amount derived from the disposition of a particular component of the convertible hedge. Using Mr. Rezek's Laidlaw convertible hedge as an example, Miller T.C.J. determined that the loss in the convertible hedge was $2,880:[76]

> [T]hat is, the income and outlays of both co-adventurers in convertible hedging up to the date of disposition of the convertible hedge being August 12, 1988. On May 20, 1988, Mr. Rezek claimed a loss on the sale of the long component of the convertible hedge. But the convertible hedge has not actually collapsed. It continues in two accounts. In the life of the convertible hedge there has been no disposition. In tax terms this can perhaps be described as a rollover of the convertible hedge from a single account to a dual account convertible hedge. The co-adventurer, Gloria Rezek, has now joined Mr. Rezek in his convertible hedge adventure. The property forming the substance of the adventure, the convertible hedge itself, has not changed; it has not been disposed of. There is simply no disposition for tax purposes until the subject matter of the adventure has been disposed of. This does not ignore the legal realities as Mr. Shaw might proclaim. Indeed, it is the legal reality.

Miller T.C.J.'s reasoning is innovative in order to fit the peg in a big round hole. However, the Federal Court of Appeal held that his reasoning was legally wrong. First, it was not his role to be innovative in this manner. Rothstein J.A. (now at the Supreme Court) stated that:[77]

> The Tax Court judge's approach implies that the role of the Court is to interpret the Act so as to restrict innovative tax avoidance measures. I think that approach is wrong in law. In Canada, it is not the role of the Court to act as the protector of the public revenue. It is for Parliament to enact measures for doing so.

Secondly, Miller T.C.J.'s interpretation of "property" was incorrect. According to Rothstein J.A., the limited convertible hedge margin arrangements were not enforceable against the brokers, were not rights accruing to the appellants, and thus not a separate property. Third, synthesizing the acquisition of convertible securities with the short sale of common shares constitutes a re-characterization of the effect of transactions, which violates the principle against re-characterization in the absence of sham.[78] "It may be that the separate transactions were part of the convertible hedge strategy with its risks and benefits, but that does not permit the re-characterization of ordinary market transactions for tax purposes."[79]

---

[76]*Hayes*, note 72, above, para. 181.

[77]*Hayes et al v The Queen et al*, (sub nom. *Rezek et al)* 2005 FCA 227, (sub nom. *Rezek v. R.)* 2005 D.T.C. 5373, [2005] 3 C.T.C. 241; leave to appeal refused (2005), 2005 CarswellNat 4210, 2005 CarswellNat 4211 (S.C.C.); leave to appeal refused (2005), 2005 CarswellNat 4212, 2005 CarswellNat 4213 (S.C.C.); leave to appeal refused (2005), 2005 CarswellNat 4204, 2005 CarswellNat 4205 (S.C.C.); leave to appeal refused (2005), 2005 CarswellNat 4214, 2005 CarswellNat 4215 (S.C.C.); leave to appeal refused (2005), 2005 CarswellNat 4206, 2005 CarswellNat 4207 (S.C.C.).

[78]For more discussion on this principle, see chapter 19.

[79]Note 77 above, para. 57.

(f) — Derivative financial instruments

Hedging contracts are just one type of derivative financial instruments (or "derivatives"). A derivative is a financial contract that gets (or "derives") its value from fluctuations in the value of other assets or property: the payments required under the contract may be linked to the price of a stock, a commodity, an interest rate or a foreign exchange rate. An option is another type of derivative. An option is a contract that gives its owner the right to buy or sell a particular asset at a fixed price within a specified period of time. The person who sells the option has an obligation to make good on his or her end of the contract.

Derivatives challenge the tax system in two ways: tax deferral and tax arbitrage. Derivatives can be used so that tax deductible expenses and losses can be incurred today but income and capital gains can be postponed until they are realized. One example of tax deferral is the *Friedberg v. Canada* (1993) case (discussed in Chapter 6).[80] Because the taxpayer was able to report his income from trading in futures contracts on a realization basis, he was able to defer tax by choosing to realize losses (but not gains). The Supreme Court ruled unanimously in the taxpayer's favour, stating that the mark to market accounting method (which recognizes unrealized gains and losses) was not "an appropriate measure of realized income for tax purposes".[81]

Derivatives can also be used to create tax arbitrage. When derivatives are used with traditional types of debt and equity securities to create transactions (or "synthetic securities") that have the same financial and economic results but very different legal characteristics, because of this unbundling of financial/economic "substance" and legal "form", derivatives provide opportunities to change the character of income as well as to provide tax deferral opportunities.

The extent to which the financial/economic "substance" of a security can be replicated by using derivatives is illustrated by the following example of how a "synthetic" share can be created using debt and options. Using the theory underlying derivatives, it can be proven mathematically that the financial and economic results of buying (or issuing) a share can be replicated by buying (or issuing) debt and simultaneously selling and buying options on the share. While the proof of this is beyond the scope of this book, it is easy to see that the legal characteristics of the share and the "synthetic" share are very different, as can be the tax consequences of owning or issuing them. Interest and dividend payments result in very different tax consequences to both the payor and the recipient since dividends on shares of taxable Canadian corporations are favourably taxed in the hands of the recipient but are not deductible to the payor corporation.[82] As well, if the gain or loss on the options

---

[80] [1993] 4 S.C.R. 285, [1993] 2 C.T.C. 306, 93 D.T.C. 5507 (S.C.C.), discussed under heading 6.3(b) "Financial accounting versus tax", above.

[81] *Ibid.* Financial institutions are now not able to do this since they are required to use the mark to market method, effective for taxation years after ending after October 31, 1994 (s. 142.5).

[82] See ch. 15, Corporations and Shareholders, below.

is taxed on a realization basis, the taxation of any gain can be deferred until the options are exercised. The courts have not yet had an opportunity to look at this type of transaction.

12
OTHER INCOME AND DEDUCTIONS

12.1 — Legislative scheme

(a) — Income from other sources

The concept of income for tax purposes has been discussed in chapter 4. One important feature of income is that it must have a source. Therefore, even if an amount increases a taxpayer's ability to pay, the amount is not income under paragraph 3(a) of the *Income Tax Act* (the "Act") unless it has a source.[1]

As discussed in chapter 4, the wording in paragraph 3(a) contemplates that income from "other sources" may be taxable, and some of these "other sources" are specified by sections 56 to 59.1 in subdivision d of Division B of Part I of the Act. In theory, amounts that are not specifically included in subdivision a (employment income), subdivision b (income from business or property), subdivision c (capital gains), or subdivision d (other income) are not necessarily free of tax. An amount could still be characterized as income "from a source" within the meaning of paragraph 3(a), in which case it would be taxable. However, the courts have shown no disposition to add new sources of income to those covered by subdivisions a, b, c, or d.[2] Therefore, for practical purposes, if an amount is not caught by these subdivisions, it is very likely that it is not taxable. For greater certainty, section 81 contains a list of items that are definitely not taxable.

---

[1]Because capital gains have not traditionally been considered to have a "source", paragraph 3(b) specifically includes taxable capital gains in computing income.

[2]*Canada v. Fries*, [1990] 2 S.C.R. 1322, [1990] 2 C.T.C. 439, 90 D.T.C. 6662 (S.C.C.); and *Schwartz v. Canada*, [1996] 1 S.C.R. 254, [1996] 1 C.T.C. 303, 96 D.T.C. 6103 (S.C.C.). See also heading 4.3, "Income from a source", above.

Subdivision d includes in income certain amounts which are collectively known as "other income". They generally fall into one of the following categories, some of which are explained in more detail later in this chapter:

(1) Tax-deferred income, including pension income, income from registered retirement savings plans (RRSPs), and income from other deferred income plans;

(2) Workers' compensation, social assistance payments, employment insurance benefits and Universal Child Care Benefit (UCCB) payments;

(3) Spousal and child support;

(4) Retiring allowances;

(5) Annuity payments;[3]

(6) Death benefits (in excess of $10,000);[4]

(7) Research grants (net of expenses);

(8) Scholarships, bursaries and prizes for achievement (net of the exemption); and

---

[3]An annuity is a contract to receive a periodic payment and is usually purchased from a life insurance company. (The owner of the annuity contract is called the "annuitant".) There are two basic types of annuities: "life annuities" and "term annuities". A "life annuity" is an annuity that is paid for the remainder of the annuitant's life or his or her spouse's life. A "term annuity", on the other hand, has a fixed term, that is, the annuity will be paid for a fixed number of years only. A life annuity can also have a "guaranteed term", that is, payments will be guaranteed for a fixed number of years even if the annuitant dies before the end of that period. A life annuity can also have "joint and last survivor benefits", in which case the amount will be paid until the later of the dates of death of the annuitant or his spouse (i.e., the "last survivor's" date of death). The amount of the annuity that can be purchased for a certain dollar amount (e.g., $100,000) varies, depending upon interest rates and, if it is a life annuity, the age of the taxpayer (and his or her spouse, if the annuity has joint and last survivor benefits). The income portion of an annuity payment is included in income in the following manner: first, the entire amount of the annuity payment is included in income (s. 56(1)(d)) and then the capital element of the annuity payment is deducted (s. 60(a)) since the capital element is a return of the annuitant's invested after-tax capital. These rules apply only to annuities purchased with after-tax funds. Pension annuities and RRSP annuities, on the other hand, are fully taxed. There is no capital amount to deduct because they are purchased with tax-sheltered retirement savings: see the discussion under heading 12.4, "Tax-assisted private pension plans", below.

[4]Death benefits, which are included in income under s. 56(1)(a)(iii), are defined in s. 248(1) as amounts received "on or after the death of an employee in recognition of the employee's service in an office or employmen. . ..". The definition goes on to exclude the first $10,000 received and to allocate the $10,000 tax-free limit first to the employee's spouse. If any of the $10,000 limit remains, and payments are received by other taxpayers (e.g., the employee's children), the limit is allocated to others in proportion to the payments received by them. (The first $10,000 tax-free amount is technically not a death benefit.)

(9) Non-competition payments.[5]

(b) — Subdivision e deductions

Another important feature of the concept of income under section 3 is that income is net of deductions. Income from each source (office, employment, business or property) under paragraph 3(a) is net of deductible expenses. Taxable capital gains under paragraph 3(b) are net of adjusted cost base and selling expenses. These deductions are inherently connected to the earning of income or capital gains. In addition, paragraph 3(c) recognizes additional expenses that are not otherwise deductible. Just like "other income" sources mentioned above, these "other deductions" are statutorily defined in sections 60 to 66.8 in subdivision e. Subdivision e amounts can be deducted from any of the income sources under paragraph 3(a) or taxable capital gains under paragraph 3(b).

Items deductible under subdivision e include contributions to registered retirement savings plans (RRSPs); payments for spousal support;[6] the capital element of annuity payments;[7] and the proposed deduction for pension income splitting.[8] They also include child care expenses and moving expenses that are not deductible in computing income from a business. As explained below, subdivision e deductions are mostly policy-based deductions. As such, eligibility for each deduction is restricted based on defined criteria. Furthermore, in many cases, the maximum claim is limited to amounts determined based on underlying policies.

12.2 — Policy objectives

There are several policy justifications for the inclusions and deductions in subdivisions d and e. One is the ability to pay. In the absence of the subdivision d, amounts such as retiring allowances[9] and non-competition payments[10] which clearly increase the taxpayer's ability to pay, would be received tax-free under case law. Another main justification is the use of the Act to achieve social and economic policy goals.[11] These goals typically include: the stimulation or stabilization of the economy; income support for the retired, the poor and the disabled; assistance to families; mobility of Canadians; and equitable taxation of taxpayers. The use of the

---

[5] S. 56.4, discussed under heading 4.3(d), "Unenumerated sources", above.

[6] See heading 12.7, "Spousal and child support", below.

[7] S. 60(a).

[8] Proposed s. 60.03(1), discussed under heading 12.4, "Tax-assisted private pension plans", below.

[9] See *Atkins*, note 85 below.

[10] See *Fortino v. R.* (1999), [2000] 1 C.T.C. 349, (sub nom. *R. v. Fortino)* 2000 D.T.C. 6060 (Fed. C.A.), and *Manrell v. R.*, [2003] 3 C.T.C. 50, 2003 D.T.C. 5225 (Fed. C.A.), discussed under heading 4.3(d), Unenumerated sources, above.

[11] See heading 2.4, "Tax expenditures", above.

Act as a policy instrument generally leads to a refinement of the "income" calculation by either allowing limited deductions that are otherwise denied under general principles of tax law, excluding amounts that are otherwise taxable,[12] or allowing the amounts to be taxed in the hands of a lower income spouse or common-law partner.

For example, the moving expense deduction in section 62 helps increase the mobility of taxpayers. The exemption of scholarships in paragraph 56(1)(n) reduces barriers to a university or college education. The child care expense deduction in section 63 helps reduce barriers to joining the workforce and to a university or college education. The tax preferences for retirement savings are designed to encourage Canadians to save for their retirement as well as to accumulate capital for investment. Through the deduction of payment by the payer and inclusion by the payee, the Act provides a subsidy to divorced couples if the tax savings from the payer's deduction exceeds the tax cost to the payee.

12.3 — Public pensions

Paragraph 56(1)(a) includes in income receipts from two types of public pension program: the federal *Old Age Security Act* and similar provincial laws; and the Canada Pension Plan (CPP) and provincial pension plans.

The Old Age Security program pays pensions, supplements and spouse's (or common-law partner's) allowances to persons who have reached the age of 65.[13] The basic pension is paid to all longstanding Canadian residents, but since 1989 it has been "clawed back" through the income tax system, so that pensioners with incomes in excess of $66,733 (2010) have to repay, in accordance with a statutory formula, all or part of the payments that they receive.[14]

The CPP (and its only provincial equivalent, the Quebec Pension Plan) also pays retirement benefits, generally to persons who have reached the age of 65.[15] The CPP differs from the Old Age Security program in two important respects. First,

---

[12]In addition, some policy goals are achieved through Division C deductions in computing taxable income or through the use of tax credits. Division C deductions and tax credits are covered in chapter 14, Taxable Income and Tax for Individuals.

[13]In its 1995 budget, the federal government proposed introducing an income-tested benefit for seniors, which would be tax-free. The "senior's benefit" was to come into effect in 2001 but this proposal was withdrawn in 1998.

[14]The amount that must be repaid (or "clawed back") is the lesser of the Old Age Security payments received and 15% of the taxpayer's Division B income in excess of $66,733 for 2010 (s. 180.2). The amount of Old Age Security so repaid is deductible in computing the taxpayer's income (s. 60(w)).

[15]The CPP also pays disability pensions, death benefits, survivor benefits and reduced pensions to those under 65 years of age.

the CPP is contributory,[16] and benefits are paid only in respect of persons who have contributed to the CPP during their working years. Secondly, the CPP is not income-tested, and benefits are paid (and not clawed back) in accordance with the entitlement built up through contributions, regardless of the amount of other income received by the pensioner.

12.4 — Tax-assisted private pension plans

(a) — Types of plans

Section 56 specifically includes payments out of the following plans in income: registered pension plans (RPPs);[17] deferred profit sharing plans (DPSPs);[18] registered retirement savings plans (RRSPs);[19] and registered retirement income funds (RRIFs).[20] RPPs and DPSPs are employer sponsored plans whereas RRSPs are established by individuals (and an RRIF is a continuation of an RRSP). They are all privately funded and privately organized plans, but receive public subsidy through tax assistance.

(b) — Tax assistance

The major form of tax assistance provided by these plans is tax deferral. Deferral occurs because contributions to the plan are presently deductible by the contributor and the amount contributed is not taxable until it is paid out to the taxpayer.[21] This deferral is "sweetened" by the tax exemption of investment earnings accumulated within the plan. As a result, the funds in the plans (both contributions and accumulated income) are not subject to tax until they are withdrawn. Because recognition of the income for tax purposes is deferred until the benefits are withdrawn from the plans (normally at retirement), the plans are often called "deferred income plans".

In addition to tax deferral, taxpayers receive tax savings if they are taxed at a lower marginal rate when funds are withdrawn from the plan, as is often the case after

---

[16]Employee CPP contributions are matched by their employers. Self-employed taxpayers pay twice the amount paid by employees because their contributions are not so matched. An employee's CPP contributions are eligible for a tax credit (s. 118.7) and an employer's CPP contributions are deductible (s. 9). The regime for self-employed taxpayers mirrors this: one-half of their contributions are eligible for credit (s. 118.7) and the other half is eligible for a deduction (s. 60(e)).

[17]S. 56(1)(a)(i).

[18]S. 56(1)(i).

[19]S. 56(1)(h).

[20]S. 56(1)(t).

[21]As discussed in Chapter 5, s. 6(1)(a) exempts employer RPP and DPSP contributions from inclusion in employment income and s. 8(1)(m) provides a deduction in computing employment income for employee RPP contributions. Subdivision b of the Act allows an employee to deduct RPP and DPSP contributions unless they exceed the limits specified in s. 20(1)(q) and (y) respectively.

retirement. The first \$2,000 of pension income is effectively tax-free because of the \$2,000 pension credit.[22] Further tax savings are available if pensioners split their pension income with a spouse or common-law partner who is taxed at a lower rate and is not otherwise able to use his or her pension credit. It is possible to do this at the contribution stage under the spousal RRSP program. Under this program, a taxpayer can contribute to the RRSP of his or her spouse or common-law partner.[23] When withdrawals are made, the withdrawals are taxed in the hands of the spouse or common-law partner, except to the extent of contributions made to the plan in the year of withdrawal or previous two years. Income splitting is also possible when pension payments are received. Under subsection 60.03(1), a pensioner can split up to 50 per cent of his or her pension income with a spouse or common law partner for tax purposes.[24]

(i) — Benefit of tax deferral

The benefit of tax deferral occurs because of the time value of money. By deferring taxes, tax-assisted retirement savings plans allow taxpayers to invest before-tax dollars and reinvest a before-tax return, which enables them to accumulate more retirement savings than under regular methods. The amount of income that can be accumulated under such plans is therefore far greater than could be earned by investing after-tax dollars in an investment vehicle that was not sheltered from tax.

Compare the situation of two taxpayers: Taxpayer A, who saves for retirement using an RRSP or RPP and Taxpayer B, who saves for retirement outside an RRSP or RPP. Assume that they are both subject to tax at a combined federal provincial rate of 40 per cent, they can both save only \$10,000 of their pre tax income each year and they can earn an annual pre tax return of 10 per cent on their investments. At the end of ten years, Taxpayer A would accumulate \$159,370 before taxes (\$10,000 × a future value factor of 15.937) whereas Taxpayer B could save and invest only \$79,086 (\$6,000 × 13.181). Taxpayer B's accumulation is much lower for two reasons: first, because only the after tax amount of \$6,000 (\$10,000 × (1 - 40%)) could be saved each year and, second, because the annual income earned on the investment would be only 6 per cent after taxes (10% × (1 - 40%)). Even if Taxpayer A is subject to tax at 40 per cent when she withdraws the funds from her RRSP or RPP

---

[22]See heading 14.7(b), "Non-refundable credits", below. The pension credit under s. 118(3) is equal to 15.5% of the first \$2,000 of "pension income" (for persons aged 65 or over) or "qualified pension income" (for persons under 65). The term "qualified pension income" refers to RPP income only unless the amount (e.g., a RRSP annuity or RRIF payment) is received as a result of the death of the individual's spouse or common-law partner. Starting at age 65, periodic payments out of funds accumulated in all types of private pension plans qualify for the credit.

[23]The term "common-law partner" is defined in s. 248(1) to include both common-law spouses and same-sex partners.

[24]The amount elected is included in the pension transferee's income under s. 56(1)(a.2) and deducted from the pensioner's income under s. 60(c).

at the end of the tenth year, she will have $95,622 ($159,370 × 60%) rather than $79,046, an increase of over $16,000 in ten years.

The above analysis assumes that the income earned by Taxpayer B outside the RPP or RRSP is ordinary income (e.g., interest) which is taxed at full rates. The income could also be a dividend or a capital gain, both of which are taxed at preferential rates. (In reality, the income might be a mixture of the three.) Let's compare the situations of Taxpayer A and B, assuming that the amount invested earns capital gains rather than ordinary income. In this case, Taxpayer B's annual after tax income is $8,000 ($10,000 (1 - 20%)) rather than $6,000 because the effective rate on the capital gain is 20% (1/2 × 40%). At the end of ten years, Taxpayer B would have accumulated $105,448 ($8,000 × 13.181), which is approximately $10,000 greater than the $95,622 ($159,370 × 60%) that Taxpayer A will have when she withdraws the funds out of her RRSP or RPP and pays the tax. Note that this analysis assumes that the capital gain is realized each year. If the capital gain is not realized until the end of ten years, Taxpayer B's accumulation is even higher: $127,512 ($159, 370 × 80%), because the $10,000 capital gain accruing annually is not taxed until the end of ten years. As can be seen, the tax deferral advantage is not so great with respect to income that receives preferential treatment under the Act. Capital gains earned outside an RRSP are taxed at the one-half inclusion rate. Similarly, dividends from taxable Canadian corporations earned outside an RRSP are taxed at a reduced rate because of the dividend "gross up" and "dividend tax credit."[25]

(ii) — Policy implications

Regarded as tax expenditures,[26] one might well question the distributional effects of the measures providing tax assistance to retirement savings vehicles. Like all deductions, these measures deliver a larger benefit to those with high incomes than to those with low incomes. Indeed, private saving for retirement is simply beyond the capacity of those whose incomes barely provide the necessities of life. A case can be made for the proposition that tax assistance for private saving should be reduced or eliminated, and the revenue saved should be directed to the enrichment

---

[25]See ch.15, Corporations and Shareholders, below. All income earned inside an RPP or RRSP, however, is fully taxed when it is eventually withdrawn from the plan.

[26]Ontario Fair Tax Commission, *Fair Taxation in a Changing World* (1993), 327, described tax assistance for private retirement savings as "the biggest tax expenditure in the personal income tax system and, arguably, the most important social program delivered through the tax system". The tax expenditure looks much smaller when the net effect of contributions, withdrawals and the non taxation of investment income is present valued and the data has also been reported this way in recent tax expenditure accounts. The net tax expenditure for retirement savings plans in 2009 was recently estimated to be $11,330 million for RPPs and $8,520 million for RRSPs. See Department of Finance, *Tax Expenditures and Evaluations — 2009*, Table 1. Data is also separately reported for the individual tax expenditures associated with RRSP and RPP contributions and withdrawals and the non taxation of investment income earned in those plans. Data for DPSPs is not available.

of the public pensions provided by the (underfunded) CPP[27] and the (unfunded) Old Age Security program.[28] However, in view of the current desire for tax cuts (rather than increases), the steadily aging population of Canada and other government priorities (like health care and reducing the deficit), it is obvious that private saving will continue to be the major source of retirement income for most people.[29] Measures to encourage taxpayers and their employers to make private provision for retirement during their working years, and thereby relieve the public purse from full responsibility, are easy to justify on these pragmatic grounds.

It is also possible to contest the view that tax assistance for private saving for retirement is a tax expenditure, that is, a "social program delivered through the tax system".[30] It could be argued that, in calculating the amount of income earned each year by an individual for tax purposes, it is appropriate to set aside a portion of the income to provide for the individual's retirement. The analogy is that of the business proprietor, who sets aside a portion of the business income (depreciation charges or capital cost allowance) to allow for the wearing out of the capital assets employed in the business. It is arguable that an individual whose income is derived from his or her own effort should be permitted to make provision for the wearing out of his or her human capital — the decline in ability and energy that will inevitably come with old age. On this basis, the provisions in the Act for retirement saving are not so much a social program as tax measures to spread individual earned income over a longer period and thereby better measure income for tax purposes on an annual basis.[31]

(iii) — Design objectives

The ultimate purpose of the tax-assisted pension regimes is obviously to encourage savings for retirement. Related to this are three design objectives. The first objective is to permit individuals to have an equal amount of tax assistance irrespective

---

[27]Legislation to reform the Canada Pension Plan was introduced in 1997. Among the changes have been annual increases in CPP premiums. Without these changes, actuaries estimated that the Canada Pension Plan would have been exhausted by 2015: Godfrey, *Your Voice in Ottawa*, May 1997, 2 (mimeo).

[28]The Ontario Fair Tax Commission, note 26, above, 327-333, recommended that the upper limits for the deductions for contributions to RPPs and RRSPs be reduced, and that the deductions be converted to credits. This has not happened.

[29]For a recent discussion of alternatives being discussed to enhance private saving, see Department of Finance, *Ensuring the Ongoing Strength of Canada's Retirement Income System* (March 24, 2010) at http://www.fin.gc.ca/activty/consult/retirement-eng.asp#background.

[30]The Ontario Fair Tax Commission, note 26, above, 323-333.

[31]Another way of looking at it is to view the retirement savings provisions as a way of converting the income tax system into "a modified form of expenditure tax" or a "consumption tax". The provisions do this by exempting savings from tax and taxing them only on withdrawal. This was how the Carter Commission viewed these provisions: *Report of the Royal Commission on Taxation* (Carter Report) (1966), vol. 3, 411-412.

of the form of retirement plan utilized. The second objective is to provide taxpayers with flexibility as to the timing of contributions to retirement plans. The third design objective (and arguably the most mechanical of the three) is to design a system that will allow taxpayers to achieve a targeted level of retirement income on a tax assisted basis by setting appropriate contribution limits.

The first objective was met by integrating the contribution limits for the various types of tax-assisted retirement savings plans. Prior to 1991,[32] taxpayers who were members of the most generous defined benefit RPPs had a considerable advantage over other taxpayers. Pension reform attempted to put all types of tax-assisted retirement savings plans on equal footing. Contribution limits were adjusted so that the amounts that a member of defined benefit RPPs could save on a tax-assisted basis was no more than a taxpayer could save using a combination of a defined contribution RPP, DPSP and/or RRSP. All these measures resulted in increases in the tax-deductible contribution limits for defined contribution RPPs, RRSPs, and DPSPs in 1991.

The second objective (flexibility) is met by allowing taxpayers to carry forward their unused RRSP contributions and allowing them temporary tax-free RRSP withdrawals to purchase a home or invest in higher education.

The third design objective (tax assistance for a targeted level of retirement income) is met as follows. The current system is based on the premise that the maximum tax-assisted pension benefit should be 2 per cent per year of the average Canadian's best three years of earnings multiplied by his or her number of years of service (to a maximum of 35 years). To fund this maximum pension benefit, the maximum benefit to be accrued each year is based on the average industrial wage and in 2010 is set at $2,494.44.[33]

The system also assumes that it takes $9 today to buy a $1 pension benefit and this assumption creates the link between defined benefit pension plans and money purchase plans. Because of this assumption, the maximum limit for contributions to a money purchase RPP is always set at 9 times the maximum benefit accrual for the year. For 2010, for example, the maximum limit for contributions to a money

---

[32] The tax reform of 1988, which made a number of fundamental changes to the tax system, also included proposals for reform of the tax-assisted pension regime: Department of Finance, *Improved Pensions for Canadians* (1985). The pension reform proposals were originally to be enacted in 1986 at the same time as the rest of the measures of the Tax Reform of 1986 (which were actually enacted in 1988). However, because of various implementation issues, the pension reform proposals did not become law until January 1, 1991.

[33] The maximum benefit accruals are indexed by the average industrial wage starting in 2010. Before 2010, they were legislated: $1,833.33 in 2004, $2,000 in 2005, $2,111 in 2006, $2,222 in 2007, $2,333 in 2008, $2,444 in 2009 respectively. For over a decade before 2004, the maximum benefit accrual was fixed at $1,722.22. ($1,722.22 × 35 equals $60,278, which was two and one-half times the average industrial wage in the year that the amounts were originally determined.)

purchase RPP is set at $22,450 for 2010 (9 × $2,494.44).[34] Only employers contribute to deferred profit sharing plans (DPSPs), so the maximum contribution limit for a DPSP contribution is one-half of the RPP money purchase limit for the year: that is, $11,225 in 2010 (1/2 × $22,450). Since the maximum pension to be accrued annually is 2 per cent of earnings, it follows that another limit for RPPs and DPSPs is 18% of the employee's earnings.

As mentioned earlier, RPP, DPSP and RRSP contribution limits are integrated: contributions made to one plan will reduce contributions that can be made to another plan. To make things easier for taxpayers, the system is designed so that the CRA calculates RRSP contributions limits for taxpayers based on contributions made to RPPs and DPSPs for the immediately preceding year (as reflected in the taxpayer's "pension adjustment") and the taxpayer's earned income in that previous year. The reason for the one year lag is to allow the employer time to report the information to the CRA and to allow the CRA time to report the calculation to the taxpayer.[35] Because of this one-year lag, it follows, therefore, that the maximum RRSP limit is always equal to the money purchase RPP limit for the immediately preceding year. In other words, the maximum RRSP limit is $22,000 for 2010 and $22,450 for 2011.[36] It also follows that another RRSP limit is 18% of the previous year's "earned income".[37]

The above discussion tells us where the numbers that the system uses for RRSPs come from. Here is how the system works for 2010. (1) Employers report a taxpayer's "pension adjustment" (defined below) for the 2009 year (the previous year) in respect of RPP and DPSP plans on the taxpayer's 2009 T4 slip in February 2010. (2) The 2009 pension adjustment is reported (but not included in income) on the taxpayer's 2009 tax return which is due on April 30 or June 15, 2010. (3) The CRA uses the 2009 "pension adjustment" and other information reported in the taxpayer's return to calculate the taxpayer's maximum deductible RRSP contribution for 2009 and reports the amount to the taxpayer on a 2009 notice of assessment (which would normally be received within a few weeks or months of filing the 2009 return).

The terms "earned income" and "pension adjustment" (PA) are defined in the following section of this chapter, but it is important, at this point, to note that the purpose of the PA is to integrate tax-assisted retirement savings through the various

---

[34]The limit is indexed by the industrial wage, starting in 2010. Before 2010, the limit was set by legislation: in each of the years 2004 to 2009, the limit was 9 times the maximum benefit accruals in *ibid* for the year (e.g., 9 × $2,444 = $22,000 for 2009).

[35]The CRA also has an automated Tax Information Phone Service (called "TIPS") that a taxpayer can phone to find out his or her RRSP contribution limit. The taxpayer's social insurance number, birthday, and the total income reported on his or her prior year's return must be entered to obtain this information.

[36]The limit for 2011 is known at the time of writing (March 2010) because it is the 2010 RPP limit.

[37]S. 60(i).

plans. The contribution limits for RPPs, DPSPs and RRSPs are set (based on the numbers above) so that the amount that an individual who is a member of an RPP and/or DPSP can save on a tax-assisted basis is (theoretically) no greater or less than if he or she was not a member of a DPSP or RPP and could only save using an RRSP. It is the PA that ties these three systems together: the PA reflects an estimate of a taxpayer's tax-assisted retirement savings for the year using an RPP or DPSP and is deducted from the taxpayer's RRSP contribution limit for the following year. For example, if a taxpayer's 2010 RRSP contribution limit before PA was $22,000 (the maximum limit) and his or her 2009 PA (in respect of contributions to an RPP and a DPSP in that year) was $10,000, he or she could only contribute $12,000 to an RRSP in 2010.

(c) — Employer-sponsored plans

(i) — Registered pension plans (RPPs)

Registered pension plans (RPPs) are private employer-sponsored retirement savings plans that are regulated by the CRA and by provincial pension benefit legislation and were first introduced into the income tax legislation in 1919. Normally, both the employer and the employee contribute to an RPP, although "non-contributory" plans (to which only the employer contributes) also exist.

An RPP enjoys special status under the Act: contributions to an RPP by employers and employees are tax deductible,[38] contributions by employers are not taxed to the employees as benefits from employment (subparagraph 6(1)(a)(i)) and the investment income earned by the plan is not subject to tax (paragraph 149(1)(o)). The funds accumulated and invested in an RPP on a tax-free basis only begin to be taxed when a taxpayer withdraws amounts from the plan (subparagraph 56(1)(a)(i)). In most cases, this occurs on retirement, when the taxpayer receives his or her pension income in the form of a monthly life annuity.[39] The first $2,000 of pension annuity income received from an RPP is eligible for the 15 per cent pension income credit.[40]

There are two types of RPPs: "defined benefit" plans and "defined contribution" plans (sometimes called "money purchase" plans). Some plans are a combination of these two types. In a defined benefit plan, the employer agrees to provide a "defined benefit" at retirement; the defined benefit is usually expressed as a percentage of the employee's earnings for each year of service. The earnings figure used is usually an average of earnings in the last years of service, such as the aver-

---

[38]S. 8(1)(m) allows an employee a deduction for his contribution (within limits) and s. 20(1)(q) allows an employer a deduction for his or her contribution in respect of an employee.

[39]Under most provincial pension benefit legislation, an RPP becomes vested after two years of service. Once an RPP is vested, benefits cannot be received except in the form of a life annuity on retirement. See note 4, above, for the various types of annuities.

[40]S. 118(3).

age earnings in the last three years of service. For example, if the employer agreed to provide a defined benefit of 2 per cent of earnings per year of service, and an employee had average annual earnings of $50,000 and 20 years of service, the employee's pension benefit would be $20,000. The amount required to be contributed to the plan to fund this defined benefit would be determined by an actuary, who would take into consideration such factors as the income expected to be earned on plan investments as well as employee turnover and mortality rates. The plan document would specify how the amount required to fund the defined benefit would be split between the employer and the employee. In a defined contribution (or money purchase) plan, the employer agrees to make "defined contributions" to the plan on behalf of each employee. For example, the employer might agree to contribute a certain percentage of an employee's wages or a fixed dollar amount (the employee would usually also contribute a defined amount). In a defined contribution plan, there is no agreement or guarantee as to the amount of pension benefit that the employee will eventually receive (as is the case in a defined benefit plan); the amount of pension benefit is simply the pension annuity that can be purchased with the employee's share of the fund that has accumulated by the time of the employee's retirement. This will depend on the level of employer and employee contributions, the investment income earned on those contributions over the years to retirement and the interest rates at the time of purchase of the pension annuity.

If an employee changes jobs, the funds to which the employee is entitled in the former employer's pension plan can be transferred directly to the new employer's pension plan (or a RRSP) on a tax-free basis.[41]

(ii) — Deferred profit sharing plans (DPSPs)

Deferred profit sharing plans (DPSPs) are private employer-sponsored profit-sharing plans. They were first introduced into the Act in 1961. The Act sets maximum limits on contributions by an employer and does not allow an employee to contribute. The contributions by an employer to a DPSP are not fixed like contributions to a defined contribution RPP, but fluctuate according to the employer's profitability. However, a DPSP is similar to a defined contribution (or money purchase) RPP in that the pension benefit consists simply of what can be purchased with the accumulated fund at the time of retirement or withdrawal of benefits.

The tax regime for DPSP contributions is similar to the regime for RPP contributions. Contributions by an employer to a DPSP within the limits of the Act are tax deductible to the employer (subsection 147(8)) and are not included in the employee's income as a benefit from employment. As well, the investment income earned by the plan is not subject to tax. Withdrawals from a DPSP may be made at any time (subject to any restrictions set out in the plan agreement), and when they are made, they are included in income (paragraph 56(1)(i)).

---

[41]These and other direct transfers of tax-assisted retirement savings are discussed later, under heading 12.4(e), "Contributions vs. direct transfers to RPPs, RRSPs and DPSPs", below.

(d) — Registered retirement savings plans (RRSPs)

(i) — Definition of RRSP

Registered retirement savings plans (RRSPs) are private retirement savings plans that can be established by individuals for their own retirement. They were first introduced into the Act in 1957 to help those individuals who were not members of company pension plans. As will be explained in more detail, the Act sets limits on contributions, and allows a deduction for contributions. The investment income earned by the plan is not subject to tax.

An RRSP is like a defined contribution (money purchase) RPP in that the amount of the pension annuity is not defined, but depends upon what can be purchased at the time of retirement.[42] Unlike a defined contribution RPP, however, no minimum annual contributions need be made to an RRSP. Withdrawals from an RRSP may be made at any time, and, when they are made, they are included in income.[43] The RRSP differs from the RPP and the DPSP in that only the RRSP can be established by an individual, and only that individual (or his or her spouse or common-law partner) can make contributions to the RRSP. RPPs and DPSPs, on the other hand, must be sponsored by an employer, and the employer must make contributions for the employees who are members of the plan.

As mentioned already, RRSPs are more flexible than RPPs. While the funds in a RPP are generally locked-in, as discussed below, a taxpayer is able to make temporary use of RRSP funds to buy a home or go to college or university under the rules for the RRSP Home Buyer's Plan or the RRSP Lifelong Learning Plan, respectively.

(ii) — Contributions based on earned income

If a taxpayer is not a member of an RPP or DPSP and has always contributed the maximum tax-deductible RRSP contributions[44] in previous years, his or her RRSP contribution limit is the lesser of 18 per cent of the previous year's earned income

---

[42]RRSPs are purchased from banks and other financial institutions. The investment can take the form of a special savings account, a term deposit or a mutual fund, or the RRSP can be self-administered, in which case it can invest in a variety of items. Investments in an RRSP are subject to restrictions: there are restrictions on the amount of foreign investments and on investments in real estate and shares of private corporations. Financial institutions offering self-administered RRSPs often impose annual service charges which are not tax deductible (s. 18(1)(u)).

[43]S. 56(1)(h).

[44]S. 146(5) allows an individual a deduction for contributions to an RRSP (within limits). Ss. 20(1)(q) and 20(1)(y), respectively, allow an employer a deduction for contributions to an RPP and DPSP (within limits). S. 8(1)(m) allows an employee a deduction for his contribution to an RPP (within limits). Contributions in excess of these limits may deregister the plan (which will cause the funds accumulated in the plan to be immediately taxable). Subparagraph 6(1)(a)(i) states that an employer's contribution to an RPP or DPSP is not a taxable benefit.

and the maximum contribution limit for the year (e.g., $22,000 in 2010).[45] In order to claim a deduction, the amount must be contributed in the year or within 60 days of the following year[46] to either the taxpayer's RRSP and/or the RRSP of the taxpayer's spouse or common-law partner.[47] (However, there is no doubling up of the taxpayer's contribution limit: the taxpayer can use this limit for his/her own RRSP or a spousal RRSP).

Earned income is defined in subsection 146(1).[48] Its principal components are employment income, CPP disability payments, and spousal and taxable child support payments received. Property income is not included, except for real estate rental income and certain royalty income. Losses from business and spousal and tax deductible child support payments made are deducted in arriving at the net figure of earned income.[49]

These rules are best illustrated by way of an example. Assume that a taxpayer who is not a member of an RPP or DPSP earned a $50,000 salary in 2010 and paid $20,000 of deductible spousal support in that year. His 2010 RRSP contribution limit would be $5,400, which is the lesser of 18 per cent of his $30,000 of earned income ($50,000 - $20,000) and $19,000. If he contributed only $4,000 to his RRSP (or his spouse's RRSP) by the March 1, 2011 deadline, he would be able to carry forward his undeducted RRSP contribution room of $1,400 ($5,400 - $4,000). If, in this example, the taxpayer had not made his maximum tax deductible RRSP contributions in a previous year, the amount of his maximum deductible 2010 RRSP contribution would be increased by the amount of the deficiency.[50]

---

[45]See discussion in text around note 37.

[46]In the case of a year which is a leap year, 60 days after the end of the year is February 29; otherwise it falls on March 1. If any deadline occurs on a weekend, the deadline is extended to the next business day: *Interpretation Act*, R.S.C. 1985, c. I-21, s. 26.

[47]Ss. 146(5) and (5.1).

[48]The definition of "earned income" in s. 146(1) is different from the definition of "earned income" for child care expense purposes (s. 63(3)).

[49]Child support payments paid under agreements made or varied after April 30, 1997 (or elected upon) are not taxable to the recipient or deductible to the payor. The tax treatment of spousal and child support payments is discussed under heading 12.7, "Spousal and child support", below.

[50]Using the above example, but assuming that the taxpayer had undeducted RRSP contribution room from 2009 of $2,000, results in a maximum tax deductible 2010 RRSP contribution limit of $7,400 ($5,400 from above plus $2,000). If the taxpayer still only contributes $4,000 to his RRSP for 2010, he will have a $3,400 undeducted contribution room to carry forward to future years. See definition of unused contribution room in s. 146(1). Individuals who terminate employment after 1996 will also have added to their unused contribution room a Pension Adjustment Reversal (PAR), equal to the excess of the PAs reported over the years (from their former employer's RPP or DPSP) over the termination benefit actually received.

If a taxpayer is a member of an RPP or DPSP, the formula becomes more complicated. In that case, the concept of the "pension adjustment" (PA) is used to reduce the taxpayer's RRSP contribution limits for a particular year. Omitting complications, a taxpayer's PA consists of (1) the amount of the contributions (by the employer as well as the employee) to a defined contribution RPP, plus (2) a figure derived from the benefit accrued under a defined benefit RPP, plus (3) the amount of the contributions (by the employer) to a DPSP. As explained earlier, the PA will prevent a taxpayer from achieving extra tax assistance through membership of an RPP or DPSP as well as an RRSP.

The rules we have discussed so far are in respect of the regular RRSP contributions based on earned income. In addition to making RRSP contributions based on "earned income", a taxpayer can also make contributions in respect of a retiring allowance[51] received on the termination of employment or a "refund of premiums"[52] received on the death of a spouse or parent. RRSP contributions are commonly made in cash but can be made using investments if a taxpayer has a self-administered RRSP. If an investment is transferred to an RRSP, the amount of the contribution is the fair market value of the investment and there is a deemed disposition under section 69 at the fair market value of the investment. Accordingly, if the investment is a Canada Savings Bond or other interest-bearing security, accrued interest to the date of transfer (which has not been previously included in the taxpayer's income) must be recognized in the year of the transfer. If the investment consists of stocks or bonds that have appreciated in value, a capital gain will have to be recognized on the transfer. If the investment has gone down in value, however, the capital loss is denied.[53]

(iii) — Withdrawals

Withdrawals from a taxpayer's RRSP are generally included in the taxpayer's income in the year of withdrawal. Tax is withheld on the withdrawal[54] and additional tax may be owing when the taxpayer's return is filed.

If a taxpayer makes a withdrawal from his or her RRSP (or receives RRSP annuity payments), and his or her spouse or common-law partner has made a contribution to the RRSP in the year of the withdrawal or the previous two years, the withdrawal will be included in the income of the spouse or common-law partner to the extent of the contributions made by this person within this period of time. For example, if a husband made a $5,000 withdrawal from his RRSP in 2010 and his wife had made contributions of $1,000 to any of her husband's RRSPs in each of the years 2008, 2009 and 2010, $3,000 would be taxed in the wife's hands (that is, the $1,000 contributed in the year of withdrawal and the previous two years) and

---

[51] S. 60(j.1), discussed under heading 12.6, "Retiring allowances", below.

[52] S. 60(l), discussed under heading 12.4(d)(vi), "Tax consequences on death", below.

[53] S. 40(2)(g)(iv).

[54] Reg. 103. The withholding tax is lowest (10%) if amounts of $5,000 or less are withdrawn at a time.

$2,000 ($5,000 - $3,000) would be taxed in the husband's hands. This "attribution" rule limits the amount of income splitting that can be done with spousal RRSPs.[55] In order to avoid this attribution rule, the contributing spouse must stop contributing to the RRSP for three years before any withdrawal is made.

There are two exceptions to the general rule that withdrawals are included in income: the Home Buyer's Plan and the Lifelong Learning Plan. The Home Buyer's Plan assists a taxpayer to buy a home by allowing the taxpayer to withdraw up to $20,000 from his or her RRSP for this purpose without any tax.[56] Any money so withdrawn must be repaid to the RRSP in stipulated annual instalments over 15 years. In order to be considered a home buyer, neither the taxpayer nor the taxpayer's spouse or common-law partner must have owned a home in any of the five years before the year of withdrawal and must have repaid any previously withdrawn amounts.[57] Contributions to an RRSP that are withdrawn under the Home Buyer's Plan within 90 days are not deductible.

The Lifelong Learning Plan operates in a manner very similar to the Home Buyer's Plan. It allows tax-free withdrawals from the RRSP of an individual, or his or her spouse's or common-law partner's in order to finance the individual's education. Up to $20,000 can be withdrawn from RRSPs over a period of up to four years, with a maximum withdrawal in any particular year of $10,000.[58] The amounts withdrawn must be repaid to the RRSP over a ten year period starting no later than five years after the first RRSP withdrawal. The repayment period begins earlier where the student has been out of a qualifying educational program for two consecutive years.

(iv) — RRSP annuities

If a taxpayer owns an RRSP at the end of the year in which he or she turns 71,[59] then the total value of the RRSP is included in his or her income for the year. In order to prevent this, a taxpayer must purchase either an RRSP annuity or a registered retirement income fund (RRIF) (or a combination of the two) with the funds

---

[55] If a taxpayer's RRSP is converted to a registered retirement income fund (RRIF) (discussed under heading 12.4(d)(v), below) any RRIF payment in excess of the minimum payment amount will be included in his or her spouse's income to the extent of spousal contributions made in the year of payment or the previous two years (s. 146.3(5.1)).

[56] S. 146.01.

[57] Withdrawals from an RRSP made in order to purchase more suitable housing for an individual entitled to the disability tax credit available under s. 118.3(1) are not subject to the requirement that a home has not been owned with the last five years and the withdrawals can be made by individuals related to the disabled person (s. 146.01(1)).

[58] S. 146.02(1).

[59] The age at which an individual's RPP, RRSP or DPSP is required to mature was increased from 69 to 71 effective 2007.

in the RRSP before the end of the year the taxpayer turns 71. The funds in the RRSP are transferred directly to the RRSP annuity or RRIF on a tax-free basis.[60]

RRSP annuities can be life annuities or term annuities. Life annuities may have a guaranteed term and may have joint and last survivor benefits.[61] Term annuities must provide benefits up to age 90. If the taxpayer's spouse is younger than the taxpayer, the taxpayer may elect to have the term annuity pay benefits until the spouse reaches age 90.

(v) — Registered retirement income funds (RRIFs)

A registered retirement income fund (RRIF) is, as has just been explained, an alternative to the RRSP annuity as the vehicle by which the RRSP pension is delivered. A RRIF is basically an extension of an RRSP and can be self-administered.[62] RRIFs pay out a minimum amount which increases each year based on a formula, but the taxpayer may withdraw any amount in excess of this minimum amount. The major differences between an RRSP annuity and RRIF are as follows: (1) the RRIF provides greater tax deferral because (under the statutory formula) the RRIF payments increase over time; (2) the RRIF provides more flexibility as to investments and may be self-administered; (3) the payout under a RRIF does not depend on interest rates at the time of purchase; (4) the payout under a RRIF is more flexible since any amount in excess of the minimum amount can be withdrawn; and (5) the payout under an RRSP annuity is guaranteed whereas the payout under a RRIF is not.

(vi) — Tax consequences on death

The general rule is that the value of a taxpayer's RRSP, RRSP annuity or RRIF is included in the taxpayer's income in the year of death under subsection 146(8.8)[63]. But if the beneficiary of the RRSP is the deceased taxpayer's spouse, the spouse will pay tax on the amounts received.[64] A rollover is available under paragraph 60(l). Any lump-sum payment received by a spouse out of a deceased taxpayer's

---

[60] S. 146(16).

[61] See note 3, above, for an explanation of these terms.

[62] Financial institutions offering self-administered RRIFs often charge annual administration fees which are not tax deductible (s. 18(1)(u)).

[63] If the fair market value of the RRSP on liquidation is less than the amount included in income in year of death, s.146(8.92) allows the loss to be carried back to the deceased's final return. This is similar to the rule in s. 164(6) that allows a net capital loss incurred in the first taxation year of estate to be carried back to the deceased's final return.

[64] If the spouse is not named as the beneficiary under the RRSP or RRSP annuity document, the legal representative of the deceased and the spouse can jointly elect to treat the amount as a "refund of premiums" and have the amounts taxed in the spouse's hands, so long as the spouse is entitled to at least that amount under the will (s. 146(8.1)). (It is, however, preferable to name the spouse as beneficiary under the plan in order to avoid probate fees.) In the case of a RRIF, there is no such election.

RRSP is called a "refund of premiums" and the spouse can claim an offsetting deduction under paragraph 60(l) if the amount of the refund of premiums is contributed by the spouse to an RRSP or is used by the spouse to purchase an RRSP annuity or RRIF annuity within the year of death or within 60 days of that year. Often, because of the amount of tax that would have to be withheld on the payment of the refund of premiums to the spouse, these contributions are made by arranging for the trustee of the deceased's plan to make the transfer directly to the spouse's plan.

A similar, but more restrictive, rollover is available if the beneficiary of the deceased's RRSP is a child or grandchild who was "financially dependent"on the deceased.[65] As in the case of a refund of premiums received by a spouse, the amount included in the financially dependent child or grandchild's hands as a refund of premiums can be offset with a deduction under paragraph 60(l) in certain circumstances. In the case of financially dependent child or grandchild who is mentally or physically infirm, the deduction may be used for a contribution to an RRSP or a Registered Disability Savings Plan (RDSP)[66] for the child; in the case of a financially dependent child or grandchild who is not mentally or physically infirm, the deduction is available only for the cost of the purchase of a term annuity to age 18. In the case of a child or grandchild who is 18 years of age or older and not infirm, no deduction is available.

Because a deceased's RRSP can yield a significant amount, the rules respecting a refund of premiums on death are important in estate planning. Consideration should always be given to leaving an RRSP by will to a spouse or qualifying child or grandchild so as to take advantage of the rollover. Leaving an RRSP to a qualifying child or grandchild rather than a spouse may result in future tax savings if the child is taxed at a lower rate than the spouse on payments out of the plan.

(e) — Contributions vs. direct transfers to RPPs, RRSPs and DPSPs

As discussed already, contributions to RPPs are made by both employees and employers and an employee's contributions are typically made through payroll deductions. Taxpayers can make RRSP contributions in respect of: (a) regular earned income to his/her own RRSP as well as a spousal RRSP, (b) the qualifying portion

[65]According to the definition of "refund of premiums" in s. 146(1), "financially dependent" means that the child earned less than the basic personal credit amount under s. 118(1)(c) in the previous year. If the child was financially dependent because of a mental or physical infirmity, the income limit is increased (see definition of refund of premiums in subsections 146(1) and 146(1.1)).

[66]The March 4, 2010 federal budget contains the proposal to allow a transfer of a refund of premiums to an RDSP. The amount transferred cannot exceed the beneficiary's RDSP contribution room (lifetime maximum of $200,000). For deaths occurring after 2007 and before 2011, the RDSP contribution must be made before January 1, 2012 to qualify for the rollover. See heading 12.5(c), "Registered Disability Savings Plans (RDSP)", below, for a further discussion of RDSPs.

of a retiring allowance, and (c) a refund of premiums received on the death of a spouse or parent.

While an individual normally contributes to an RPP through payroll deductions, RRSP contributions are usually made directly by the contributor. There are, however, employee "group RRSP" plans,[67] which are funded by monthly payroll deductions and qualify as deductible RRSP contributions to the employee. In many cases, RRSP contributions in respect of retiring allowances and refunds of premiums are made directly to the taxpayer's RRSP by the payer of the amount on the taxpayer's behalf.[68] In all these cases, the section 60 deduction is available to the taxpayer for the RRSP contribution, regardless of whether the contribution is made by the taxpayer or by someone else. In contrast, employer contributions to RPPs and DPSPs must be transferred directly to the plan — they cannot first be given to the taxpayer and then contributed by the taxpayer.

In addition to contributions, tax-free "direct transfers" to RRSPs, RPPs and DPSPs are allowed by the Act. These "direct transfers" include:

(1) transfers from an RPP to an RPP or RRSP (subsection 147.3);

(2) transfers from a DPSP to an RPP, RRSP or DPSP (subsection 147(19)); and

(3) transfers from an RRSP to an RPP, RRSP or RRIF (subsection 147(16)).

The first two transfers allow a taxpayer who is terminating employment, and who is entitled to funds or benefits under the employer's RPP or DPSP, to have the funds transferred on a tax-free basis directly by the plan trustee to a new employer's plan or an RRSP.[69] The third transfer allows taxpayers with RRSPs to move their RRSPs to different financial institutions and to purchase RRSP annuities and RRIFs, all on a tax-free basis.

---

[67]The advantage of "group RRSP" plans and payroll deductions is that the employer can make an adjustment to tax withheld at source for the RRSP contribution (as the employer does for RPP contributions). Because an adjustment is made to tax withheld at source, there is no waiting for a tax refund.

[68]This is done in order to avoid the tax that would have to be withheld if the amounts were first paid to the taxpayer and then contributed by the taxpayer to his or her RRSP. Since these amounts are usually quite large, the tax withheld would be significant.

[69]Provincial pension benefit legislation generally restricts the transfer of RPP benefits to "locked-in" RRSPs and life income funds (LIFs, which are essentially "locked-in" RRIFs). Unlike normal RRSPs, no withdrawals can be made from a "locked-in" RRSP and accumulated funds in a "locked in" RRSP can only be used to purchase a life annuity (not a term annuity or RRIF). Unlike normal RRIFs, which continue to pay out benefits after age 80 (according to a formula), the funds remaining in a LIF at age 80 must be used to purchase a life annuity.

12.5 — Other Tax-assisted savings plans

(a) — Tax-free savings accounts (TFSAs)

A tax-free savings account (TFSA) is designed to enable a taxpayer to save on a tax-free basis. TFSAs were introduced effective 2009 for Canadian residents age 18 or over and the maximum annual contribution for each of the years 2009 and 2010 is $5,000. Contribution limits are to be indexed for inflation (rounded to the nearest $500) and there is an indefinite carry forward of unused TFSA contribution limit.[70] Contributions are not deductible but income accumulates tax-free in plan and will not be taxed when withdrawn.[71]

If a taxpayer's marginal rate is the same in the year of contribution and withdrawal, he or she will be indifferent to saving in a RRSP and TFSA. This can be illustrated by using an example similar to the one in heading 12.4(b)(i), "Benefit of tax deferral." Assume, for example, that two taxpayers are subject to tax at a combined federal provincial rate of 40 per cent, they can both save only $8,000 of their pre tax income each year and they can earn an annual pre tax return of 10 per cent on their investments. The RRSP Saver saves in a RRSP and the TFSA Saver saves in a TFSA. At the end of ten years, the RRSP Saver would accumulate $127,496 before taxes ($8,000 × a future value factor of 15.937) whereas the TFSA Saver could save and invest only $76,498 ($4,800 × 15.937). The TFSA Saver's accumulation is lower because only the after tax amount of $4,800 ($8,000 × (1 - 40%)) can be saved each year. However if the RRSP Saver is subject to tax at 40 per cent when he or she withdraws the funds at the end of the tenth year, the two taxpayers will have the same amount after taxes: $76,498 ($127,496 × 60%).

If a taxpayer's marginal rate in the year of withdrawal is projected to be higher than in the years of contribution (e.g., an individual who has just joined the workforce and expects future increases in annual earnings to push him or her into a higher tax bracket), he or she will prefer a TFSA. For example, if the taxpayers' marginal rate had been 25% in the years of contribution and 40% in the year of withdrawal, the TSFA Saver would have had a higher accumulation: this is because the RRSP Saver would still have $76,498 after the taxes (at 40%) are paid on the withdrawal ($8,000 × a present value factor of 15.937 × 60%) but the TFSA Saver would have $95,622 on withdrawal ($8,000 × 15.937 × 75%), because a higher amount of $6,000 (75 per cent of $8,000: or $8,000 × (1 - 25%) could be contributed and saved each year.

Conversely, if a taxpayer's marginal rate in the years of contribution is expected to be higher than in the year of withdrawal (e.g., on retirement), the RRSP Saver will have a higher after-tax accumulation. For example, if the taxpayers' marginal rate is 40% in the years of contribution but only 25% in the year of withdrawal, the RRSP Saver will have $95,622 ($8,000 × a present value factor of 15.937 × 75%)

[70]S. 207.01. Like RRSPs, there is a 1 per cent per month penalty tax on overcontributions: s.207.02.

[71]S. 146.2.

after taxes but the TFSA Saver will only have $76,498 ($8,000 × a present value factor of 15.937 × 60%).

As the previous example illustrates, the after-tax accumulations of the TFSA Saver and the RRSP Saver will only be equal when the marginal rates in the year of contribution and withdrawal are equal: TFSAs offer a tax advantage to those who expect their marginal tax rate to increase in the future because of rising incomes. TFSAs offer other advantages as well. Unlike RRSPs, amounts withdrawn can be contributed back to the plan after the end of the year of withdrawal. As well, there is no spousal attribution.[72]

The tax expenditure associated with TFSA is estimated at $45 million for 2009.[73] While low income taxpayers will enjoy some of this tax expenditure because TFSA withdrawals will not reduce any income-tested tax benefits or social assistance payments, it is likely that this measure will primarily benefit higher income taxpayers.

Like RRSPs, there is continued tax deferral if a TFSA is left to a spouse on death. If a spouse or common-law partner is not named as the successor on death, the TFSA will lose exempt status and any income and capital gains accrued after death will be subject to tax.[74]

(b) — Registered education savings plans (RESPs)

A registered education savings plan (RESP) is designed to enable a taxpayer (the "subscriber") to save for the post-secondary education of a "beneficiary", who is normally, but not necessarily, the child or grandchild of the subscriber. If the beneficiary of an RESP does not attend a post-secondary institution, a substitute beneficiary can usually be named. There are two main types of RESPs: "scholarship trust" plans (which pool contributions from any subscribers) and self-administered plans (which are set up by a single subscriber). As well, "family plan" RESPs can be set up for more than one beneficiary and "joint plans" can be set up to accept contributions from more than one subscriber.

Unlike the private retirement plans discussed above, contributions to an RESP are not tax deductible. However, like the private retirement plans, an RESP is an income-deferred plan because it offers three important advantages: (1) the federal government provides an annual grant (maximum: $500 per year, lifetime limit: $7,200) equal to 20 per cent of RESP contributions made per beneficiary;[75] (2) the income from investments earned within the plan is not taxed until it is distributed; and (3) when money is withdrawn from the plan and distributed to the beneficiary (who must by then be a student at a post-secondary institution), the income earned in the plan plus the amount of federal contributions are taxed as income of the

---

[72]S. 74.5(12). Like RRSPs, there is no deduction for interest on money borrowed to invest in a TFSA: s. 18(11). Unlike RRSPs, TFSAs can be used as collateral for a loan.

[73]*Tax Expenditures and Evaluations 2009*, note 26, above, Table 1.

[74]S. 207.02(2).

[75]Before 2007, the maximum grant was $400 per year.

beneficiary, not the subscriber. The original contributions are not taxed when they are distributed to the student because income tax has already been paid on those amounts by the contributor to the RESP.

The rules for RESPs are contained in section 146.1. There are no annual contribution limits[76] but the maximum federal grant is paid when annual contributions are $2,500. If annual contributions of $2,500 are made, the $7,200 lifetime grant limit would be reached after 14 years (since 14 × $500 = $7,000). At that point total contributions would be $36,000 (14 × $2,500) and further contributions could be made (until the annuitant is 21 years of age or $50,000 lifetime contribution limit per beneficiary is reached, whichever is the earliest).[77] The RESP is no longer eligible for federal grants once the beneficiary is 18. Excess contributions are subject to a penalty tax of one per cent per month (12 per cent per year). Income earned within an RESP can accumulate on a tax-free basis for up to 25 years but after that time, the plan is deregistered.

For many years, the major disadvantage of an RESP was that the income earned inside the plan was forfeited if a beneficiary (or substitute beneficiary) did not attend a post-secondary institution. In order to make them more attractive, the Act now permits a subscriber to withdraw any accumulated income under such circumstances if the RESP has been running for ten years and each living beneficiary is at least 21 years old.[78] If the subscriber has enough contribution room, up to $50,000 of RESP income can be transferred on a tax-free basis to the RRSP of the subscriber or the subscriber's spouse.[79] Otherwise, any RESP income so withdrawn is subject to a special 20 per cent tax under the Act, as well as regular income tax. In either event, the contributions made by a subscriber are returned to him or her tax-free and any federal grants received by the RESP have to be repaid.

Enhanced rules are in place to help low income families save for their children's post-secondary education using RESPs. These include an enhanced federal grant and an additional RESP grant, called the Canada Learning Bond (CLB), for each year that a child's family is eligible for the child tax benefit supplement.[80]

---

[76]Before 2007, there was a $4,000 annual contribution limit.

[77]Before 2007, the lifetime limit was $42,000. The system that existed before 2007, was based on a $2,000 annual contribution (a pre-1997 annual maximum) with an expected contribution period of 21 years (21 years × $2,000 = $42,000). The 1997 federal budget, which introduced the 20% grant, increased the annual contribution to $4,000 in 1997 in light of increases in tuition fees and to help parents who had not made maximum use of RESPs make up for missed contributions. The 2007 budget removed the annual contribution limit and increased the lifetime limit to $50,000.

[78]These two requirements are waived if the beneficiary is eligible for the disability tax credit.

[79]The $50,000 is a lifetime limit and it is effective for 1999 and later years. Before 1999, the lifetime limit was $40,000 (s. 204.94).

[80]The child tax benefit is discussed briefly under heading 14.7(c), "Refundable credits", below.

(c) — Registered Disability Savings Plans (RDSPs)

Effective 2008, a new tax-assisted program, called the Registered Disability Savings Plan (RDSP), is proposed to enable parents and others to save specifically for this purpose if the child is eligible for the disability tax credit.[81] The RDSP is similar in concept to the RESP: contributions are non-tax deductible but the income from investments earned within the plan is not taxed until it is distributed. Like RESPs, contributions to an RDSP are eligible for a grant and an enhanced grant rate and an additional grant (called the Canada Disability Savings Bond) is provided for low-income families.[82] The March 4, 2010 federal budget has increased the usefulness of the RDSP as a tax-deferred savings device because it contains the proposal to allow a tax-deferred rollover of a parent or grandparent's RRSP on death to a RDSP of a child or grandchild.[83]

12.6 — Retiring allowances

(a) — Meaning of "retiring allowance"

Retiring allowances are included in income.[84] However, unlike other types of income, retiring allowance enjoy a special tax advantage — the "eligible" portion may be contributed to an RRSP and qualify for tax deductions.

Subsection 248(1) defines a "retiring allowance" as:

> an amount ... received....
>
> > (a) on or after retirement of a taxpayer from an office or employment in recognition of the taxpayer's long service, or

---

[81]S. 118.3, discussed under heading 14.7(b), "Non-refundable tax credits", below.

[82]Contributions are limited to a lifetime maximum of $200,000 per child and can be made until the end of the year in which the child attains 59 years of age.The Canada Disability Savings Grant (CDSG) is equal to 100% to 300% of RDSP contributions, (maximum: $3,500) depending on family net income. For low-income families, the Canada Disability Savings Bonds (CDSB) provides up to an additional $1,000. The March 4, 2010 Budget contains a proposal to allow a carry forward of the CDSG and CDSB room, retroactive to the introduction of RDSPs in 2008. (There is a similar carryforward for RESPs.) The carry forward can be used in 2011 and subsequent years.

[83]The amount transferred cannot exceed the beneficiary's RDSP contribution room (lifetime maximum of $200,000). For deaths occurring after 2007 and before 2011, the RDSP contribution must be made before January 1, 2012 to qualify for the rollover. See heading 12.4(d)(vi), "Tax consequences on death", above, for a further discussion of this rollover.

[84]Retiring allowances are taxed in the year received and may be paid in installments, although any interest element included in the installment payment would not be a retiring allowance.

(b) in respect of a loss of an office or employment of a taxpayer, whether or not received as, on account or in lieu of payment of, damages[85] or pursuant to an order or judgment of a competent tribunal,

by the taxpayer or, after the taxpayer's death, by a dependant or a relation of the taxpayer or by the legal representative of the taxpayer.

In order to receive a retiring allowance, there must be either a "retirement" or a "loss" of office or employment. The definition of "retiring allowance" captures both the traditional "retirement" payment — a payment made "on or after retirement" in recognition of "long service"[86] — as well as compensation "in respect of a loss of an office or employment."[87] Payments made under early retirement arrangements are generally considered to be payments in respect of loss of office because early retirement arrangements are generally put in place to eliminate jobs.[88] All compensation for loss of employment, voluntary or involuntary, is treated as a retiring allowance. For example, most damages awards and out-of-court settlements in respect of a loss of office or employment are taxed as retiring al-

---

[85]Before 1978, the definition of retiring allowance did not include damages and if the departing employee sued the employer for wrongful dismissal and recovered damages, then the damages would be received free of tax. This was because an award of damages for breach of contract (or for a tort or other cause of action) is not income for tax purposes. This was so, even though the amount of a damages award for wrongful dismissal would be computed by reference to exactly the same considerations (that is, the amount of salary that would have been paid during a required period of notice) as would be applied to the computation of a consensual severance payment. Since court-awarded damages were free of tax, it was also held that an out-of-court settlement of a wrongful dismissal action also escaped tax. See *The Queen v. Atkins*, 76 D.T.C. 6258, [1976] C.T.C. 497 (Fed. C.A.); affirming 75 D.T.C. 5263, [1975] C.T.C. 377 (Fed. T.D.).

[86]Payments in respect of "long service" would be determined by reference to the total number of years in an employee's career with a particular employer or affiliated employers and would include accumulated sick leave. Based on *Harel v. Quebec (Deputy Minister of Revenue)*, [1977] C.T.C. 441, 77 D.T.C. 5438 (S.C.C.), the CRA takes the view that the payment of "accumulated sick leave credits" qualifies as a retiring allowance (Interpretation Bulletin IT-337R4, "Retiring allowances", (2003), para. 3) but not the payment of accrued vacation pay.

[87]*Ibid.*, at paras. 14 and 15 contains a list of payments which the CRA considers to be employment income rather than a retiring allowance. The list includes accrued vacation pay, a retention bonus for reporting to work until the termination date and amounts that represent deferred compensation. Because of the reference to "damages" in the definition of retiring allowance, a payment in lieu of earnings for a period of reasonable notice of termination is considered to be a retiring allowance when it is included in a payment of damages but employment income, when it is not.

[88]Interpretation Bulletin IT-337R4, note 86, above, para. 6. The distinction between traditional retirement and payment in respect of loss of employment or office is important only if the payment is received before the date of termination. This is because s. 248(1) requires a payment in recognition of long service to be received "on or after retirement" but contains no similar restriction for a payment "in respect of a loss of an office."

lowances. This would include payment for general damages related to the loss of employment (e.g., for loss of self-respect, humiliation, mental anguish, hurt feelings etc.) but not for personal injuries sustained before or after the loss of employment that are separate and unrelated to the loss of employment (e.g. for human rights violations, harassment during employment, or defamation after dismissal).[89]

In order to qualify a payment as a retiring allowance, there must exist an employment or office first. In *Schwartz v. Canada* (1996),[90] for example, the taxpayer entered into a contract of employment with a prospective employer, but the employer rescinded the contract before the taxpayer had actually started working for the employer. Following negotiations, the prospective employer paid the taxpayer $360,000 as damages for breach of contract. The Supreme Court of Canada held that the amount paid to the taxpayer was not a retiring allowance. The Court reasoned that, since the taxpayer was not in fact employed by the prospective employer at the time when the contract was rescinded, there had been no loss of employment.[91]

In *Schwartz*, there was no loss of employment because employment had not started. The more common source of doubt concerns the employee who is undoubtedly employed before the date of the "retirement" and continues to maintain a relationship with the employer after that time. In *Serafini v. M.N.R.* (1989),[92] for example, the taxpayer continued to receive full salary and benefits and to accrue pension benefits for a 12 month period after his so-called "retirement". It was only after the 12 month period elapsed that the employee began to receive his pension benefits. The Tax Court of Canada decided that the payments during the 12 month period constituted employment income even though the employee did not perform any duties of employment. Stating that the taxpayer's situation was similar "to a pre-retirement leave with full pay and benefits",[93] the court found that the date of retirement was after the end of the 12 month period.[94]

---

[89]*Ibid.*, para. 12.

[90]Note 2, above. This case is also discussed in detail under heading 4.3(d), "Unenumerated sources", above.

[91]To assist in determining the meaning of the term "employment", the Supreme Court compared the definition of "retiring allowance" to the wording of s. 80.4(1). S. 80.4(1) requires an income inclusion in certain circumstances when an individual has received a loan by virtue of his or her "office or employment or intended office or employment". As a consequence of the distinction between "employment" and "intended employment" in s. 80.4(1), the Supreme Court drew the inference that the meaning of "employment" for purposes of the Act did not include amounts related to prospective employment.

[92][1989] 2 C.T.C. 2437, 89 D.T.C. 653 (T.C.C.).

[93]*Ibid.*, 2442, 657.

[94]The CRA's position with respect to the timing of retirement and loss of office is in line with this case: continued participation in a company health plan providing medical, dental and long term disability coverage "would not, in itself, indicate that employment has not terminated, particularly if the employer's plan specifically permits former employees to be

Payments received by a taxpayer from the previous owner of the business where the taxpayer worked may qualify as retiring allowances even if the taxpayer continues to work in the same business after the change of ownership. In *Henderson v. M.N.R.* (1991),[95] for example, the taxpayer was the controlling shareholder and manager of a corporation that sold its drugstore business to Shopper's Drug Mart. The taxpayer continued to work on a part-time basis as a pharmacist for Shopper's Drug Mart, in the same location that his corporation had previously operated, as well as another location. Notwithstanding his employment by the new owner of the business, the Tax Court of Canada held that amounts paid to him by his corporation in the year of sale and the following year qualified as retiring allowances, since the payments were in recognition of long service and he had in fact retired from his employment with his corporation.[96]

(b) — Tax treatment

A retiring allowance is included in income in the year of receipt under subparagraph 56(1)(a)(ii). However, the "qualifying" portion of the retiring allowance may be contributed to an RRSP and qualify for the deduction under paragraph 60(j.1).[97] The "qualifying" portion is $2,000 per year of service before 1996[98] plus an addi-

---

covered under the plan. However, if pension benefits continue to accrue, the accrual indicates that there is an existing employment relationship, since such benefits only accrue to employees. The fact that the employer does not require an individual to report to work is not, by itself, determinative of whether the individual has retired. For example, an individual who has been given a leave of absence for educational purposes is still an employee." See IT-337R4, note 86, above, para. 4.

[95][1991] 2 C.T.C. 2048, 91 D.T.C. 1116 (T.C.C.).

[96]IT-337R4, note 86, above, at para. 8, also provides three other examples of when retirement or loss of office might occur in similar situations. These include the situations of (1) a government employee who retires from a full-time position but accepts a part-time position with no pension benefits, (2) a former employee who continues on as a corporate director (other than a director of a public company) at nominal compensation and (3) a former employee who carries on certain administrative duties for no remuneration after the sale of the employer's business.

[97]The rules respecting withholding of tax are also different for a retiring allowance than for income from employment: s. 153(1)(c), reg. 103(4). The CRA has stated that there is no withholding requirement if the retiring allowance (or a part thereof) is paid directly to an RRSP if the payer has reasonable grounds to believe the transfer is within the deduction limits under s. 60(j.1) or ss. 146(5) or (5.1): *ibid.*, para. 25.

[98]Before 1982, there was no limit on the amount of the retiring allowance that could be rolled tax-free into an RRSP or RPP. According to the Minister of Finance in his budget speech in 1981 (when s. 60(j.1) was introduced), "senior executives ... typically arrange to receive a large lump-sum payment upon retirement which they may then contribute tax-free to their RRSP.... The amount of these retiring allowances has increased dramatically in recent years and in some instances amounts to several hundreds of thousands of dollars". In 1982, s. 60(j.1) was enacted to restrict the tax-free rollover of retiring allowances. The amount of RRSP and RPP contribution that was deductible under s. 60(j.1) was initially

tional $1,500 for each year before 1989 for which no RPP or DPSP benefits were earned.

For example, an employee ceases employment on October 1, 2007 after working for the same employer since March 1, 1985. The employee receives a retiring allowance of $50,000. All his pension benefits have vested. However, because of a one year waiting period before he could join the company pension plan, he earned no pension benefits for 1985. In this example, the "qualifying" portion is $23,500 ($2,000 × 11 years before 1996 plus $1,500 × 1 non-vested year before 1989).

This preferential tax treatment is available to both traditional retirement payments and early retirement payments. Because early retirement programs have become a popular way for public and private sector employers to "downsize" and reduce their employee costs, this tax deduction has become increasingly well-used and important.

12.7 — Spousal and child support

(a) — Definitions

Subsection 56.1(4) contains the following definitions of support amount and child support amount:

> "support amount" means an amount payable or receivable as an allowance on a periodic basis for the maintenance of the recipient, children of the recipient or both the recipient and children of the recipient, if the recipient has discretion as to the use of the amount, and
>
> (a) the recipient is the spouse or common-law partner or former spouse or common-law partner of the payer, the recipient and payer are living separate and apart because of the breakdown of their marriage or common-law partnership and the amount is receivable under an order of a competent tribunal or under a written agreement; or
>
> (b) the payer is a natural parent of a child of the recipient and the amount is receivable under an order made by a competent tribunal in accordance with the laws of a province.
>
> "child support amount" means any support amount that is not identified in the agreement or order under which it is receivable as being solely for the support of a recipient who is a spouse or common-law partner or former spouse or common-law partner of the payer or who is a parent of a child of whom the payer is a natural parent.

To constitute a "support amount" in case of breakdown of marriage or common-law partnership, a payment must satisfy the following requirements: (1) the pay-

---

limited to $3,500 per year of service, which was the limit for employer contributions to RPPs at the time. In 1989, the limit was reduced to $2,000 per year of service, with the $3,500 limit still applying for pre-1989 years where RPP or DPSP pension benefits had not been earned. Because of the measures implemented with pension reform in 1991, increasing RRSP limits and enabling taxpayers to carry forward their unused contribution limits, the s. 60(j.1) deduction was eliminated for years of service after 1995. Persons retiring after 1995 are still able to use the deduction, but only for years of service before 1996.

ments must be an "allowance" (discussed below); (2) the payments must be made "on a periodic basis" (a lump-sum payment is not deductible);[99] (3) the payer and recipient must be "living separate and apart" from each other; and (4) the payment must be made under the terms of either a court order or a "written agreement". In the case where there has been no marriage or common-law partnership between the payer and the recipient, but the payer is the parent of a child of the recipient, a "support amount" must also be an "allowance", made "on a periodic basis", and the payer must have been living "separate and apart" from the recipient. However, the definition is more restrictive than that for a marriage or partnership breakdown: the payment must have been made under a court order; a written agreement will not suffice for such payments, let alone anything less formal.

In order for a payment to constitute an "allowance", the recipient must have "discretion as to the use of the amount". As a result, payments made directly to third parties for the benefit of the spouse (or former spouse) or children are excluded from the definition of support amount, because in that case the recipient would have no "discretion as to the use of the amount". Common examples of third-party payments include payment of rent, mortgage payments,[100] tuition fees, dental, and counseling expenses. Subsections 56.1(2) and 60.1(2) create an exception to the general rule by deeming a third-party payment to be an "allowance payable on a periodic basis" and deeming the recipient to "have discretion as to the use of that amount" if the order or written agreement provides that these subsections "shall apply". These provisions allow third-party payments to be treated as "support amounts" if the payer and the recipient so agree and the payments are paid pursuant to a court order or written agreement (if applicable) which refers to subsections 56.1(2) and 60.1(2).

---

[99]See *McKimmon v. R.* (1989), [1990] 1 C.T.C. 109, 89 D.T.C. 6088 (Fed. C.A.) in which the Court distinguished between a periodic payment which is an allowance and a payment made as an instalment of a capital amount. Some of the criteria listed by the Court in *McKimmon* are summarized in Interpretation Bulletin IT-530R, "Support Payments", (2003), para. 22: a lump-sum payment covering periodic payments which are in arrears will be considered to be a periodic payment; it will therefore be deductible to the payer and taxable to the recipient in the year of payment. Because of our graduated system of tax, a single lump sum received on account of periodic payments in arrears may be taxed at a higher rate than the periodic payments would have been. To ameliorate this result, the Act now contains averaging rules that adjust the tax rate on retroactive lump-sum payments to the amount that would have been owed if the periodic payments had been received when they were due. To this amount is added the interest at the prescribed rate for the late payment of the taxes: ss. 110.2 and 120.3.1.

[100]*Gagnon v. R.*, [1986] 1 S.C.R. 264, [1986] 1 C.T.C. 410, 86 D.T.C. 6179 (S.C.C.) allowed such an amount to be deducted as an allowance; the result was reversed by the enactment of former s. 56(12), which required that the recipient have "discretion as to the use of the amount" in order for the amount to be a deductible. This requirement is now contained in the definition of support amount in s. 56.1(4).

Payments made before a written agreement or court order has come into existence are deemed to have been "paid and received thereunder" if the agreement or order so provides and the payments are made in the year that the agreement or order is made or in the previous year.[101] This allows taxpayers to make payments that qualify for the deduction-inclusion treatment and still have some time to negotiate a written agreement or obtain a court order.[102]

(b) — Deduction-inclusion system

Payments for the support of a spouse or former spouse are deductible by the payer under paragraph 60(b), and must be included in the income of the recipient under paragraph 56(1)(b).[103] These rules do not apply to child support payments required to be made under agreements or orders made or varied after April 30, 1997 (or orders in place before May 1, 1997 if the payer and the recipient so elect). Payments made pursuant to such orders will not be taxable in the hands of the recipient and will not be deductible in the hands of the payer.[104]

(c) — Policy objectives

The full deductibility of payments for spousal and child support is an anomaly, because the payments have no connection to the earning of income. In an intact family, they are consumption expenses that are not deductible against any source of income. It is therefore odd that the payments should be deductible when a family has broken up. Once deductibility is allowed, however, it is sound tax policy to require the recipient to report the payments and pay income tax on them. Otherwise, the income represented by the payments would escape tax altogether.

---

[101] Ss. 56.1(3) and 60.1(3).

[102] Legal expenses paid to establish the right to support are treated as payments on account of capital and are therefore not deductible; however, legal fees paid to enforce the payments after the right has been established are deductible. *Sembinelli v. M.N.R.*, [1994] 2 C.T.C. 378, 94 D.T.C. 6636 (Fed. C.A.).

[103] Earned income for RRSP purposes is reduced by support amounts paid and deducted from income under s. 60(b) and increased by support amounts received and included in income under s. 56(1)(b). See paras. (b) and (f) of the definition of earned income in s. 146(1).

[104] Ss. 60(b) (deduction) and 56(1)(b) (inclusion) contain the formula "A — (B + C)" to describe the payments that they cover. Amount "A" in the formula is the total of "support amounts" (i.e., spousal and child support payments) paid and received during the year when the payer and recipient were living separate and apart. Amount "B" in the formula is the total of "child support amounts" that became receivable during the year under an agreement or order made or varied after April 30, 1997 (or orders in place before May 1, 1997 if the payer and the recipient so elect). (See definition of "commencement day" in s. 56.1(4).) Amount "C" in the formula is the total of all "support amounts" included or deducted in a previous year. The net result of the formula is that all support amounts are deductible by the payer and included in the income of the recipient, except for child support payments (described in B) and support amounts received in the year but included in income in a prior year.

So why was the deduction-inclusion introduced in the first place and why was it modified in 1997?

The deduction-inclusion system was introduced into the Act in 1942 with the avowed purpose of providing a subsidy to split families to assist with the additional expenses of maintaining two households.[105] The system was based on the premise that the payer is usually in a higher tax bracket than the recipient; when that is the case, the diversion of some income from the payer to the recipient creates an income-split which reduces the total amount of tax that is payable.[106] The subsidy provided by the deduction-inclusion system is the difference between the cost in foregone revenue caused by the payer's deduction and the amount of revenue raised by the recipient's inclusion. The Government of Canada treats the subsidy as a tax expenditure with a projected value of $100 million for 2009.[107] Since this figure excludes provincial taxes, which in the aggregate amount to about 50 per cent of federal tax, the combined federal-provincial tax expenditure was about $150 million in 2009 ($100 million × 1.5).

If the universe unfolded as it should, this subsidy would be reflected in a higher level of support payments: the deductibility of the payments for the higher-income payer should enable the lower-income payee to negotiate, or obtain in court, a higher level of support than could be provided if the payments were not deductible, and that higher level of support should more than offset the tax that the recipient would become liable to pay. The tax benefit will not, however, be shifted forward to the recipient if the amount of support is fixed without regard for the tax consequences to payer and recipient. And, in those cases where the recipient is in the same (or a higher) tax bracket as the payer, the deduction-inclusion system produces no tax benefit.[108]

In *Thibaudeau v. Canada* (1995),[109] a recipient of child-support payments challenged the validity of former paragraph 56(1)(b), the provision that required her to include the payments in her income. She argued that paragraph 56(1)(b) was a violation of the equality guarantee in section 15 of the *Charter of Rights and Freedoms* (the "Charter"), because paragraph 56(1)(b) discriminated against separated custodial parents by forcing them to pay the tax on support payments. The Supreme Court of Canada, by a majority, rejected the argument and upheld paragraph

[105]The legislative history is related in *Thibaudeau v. Canada*, [1995] 1 C.T.C. 382 at 390, 95 D.T.C. 5273 at 5281 (S.C.C.).

[106]See ch. 13, Income Splitting, below.

[107]*Tax Expenditures and Evaluations — 2009*, note 26, above, Table 1.

[108]If the recipient's child tax benefit and GST credit are being reduced by the inclusion, the recipient's marginal tax rate would include the rates at which these payments are phased out. The child tax benefit (s. 122.6) and GST credit (s. 122.5) are discussed in ch. 14, under heading 14.7(c), "Refundable credits", below.

[109]Note 105, above. The principal majority opinion was written by Gonthier J. Short concurring opinions were written by Sopinka J., with whom La Forest J. agreed, and by Cory J. and Iacobucci JJ. Dissenting opinions were written by McLachlin J. and L'Heureux-Dubé J.

56(1)(b). The Court held that the provision should not be assessed in isolation from paragraph 60(b) (which is the matching deduction for the payer spouse) and the family law system, under which support orders and agreements are made. The deduction-inclusion system resulted in a reduction of tax for the majority of separated couples. While it was the payer who received the benefit of the deduction, the deduction increased the payer's ability to pay support. While it was the recipient who suffered the tax burden, the family law system required that the tax burden be taken into account in fixing the amount of support, so that the amount should be grossed-up to fully compensate the recipient for the additional tax liability. In Thibaudeau's case, the family court had taken her additional tax liability into account, but it appeared that the liability had been underestimated and that the gross-up for tax was, therefore, insufficient.[110] In deciding against Thibaudeau, the Court held that this deficiency should be remedied by a review of the support order by the family court. Although some separated custodial parents did not benefit from the deduction-inclusion system, as a group custodial parents did benefit.[111] Therefore the Act did not discriminate against them, and there was no breach of equality rights under section 15 of the Charter.

Although Thibaudeau lost the court battle, she won the war against the deduction-inclusion system for child support. The Government of Canada, in consultation with the provinces, announced its intention to reform the child support system within months of the *Thibaudeau* decision. These reforms are now law: they include the introduction of a no deduction-no inclusion system for child support agreements or orders made or varied after April 30, 1997 (discussed above), guidelines for calculating the child support to be paid (to reduce legal costs and improve the fairness and consistency of amounts awarded), and improvements in the enforcement of court-ordered child support.

---

[110]The Court did not consider the question, upon which no evidence seemed to have been led, as to how much lower the support order would have been if the deduction in s. 60(b) did not exist. Without some estimate of this, it is not apparent, merely from the inadequacy of the tax gross-up, that Thibaudeau was worse off than she would have been in a world without the deduction-inclusion system.

[111]Justices McLachlin and L'Heureux-Dubé dissented primarily on the grounds that the family law system could not be relied upon to shift the tax benefit forward to the custodial spouse. By conferring the benefit of the deduction on the non-custodial spouse and imposing the burden of the tax on the custodial spouse, the Act was discriminatory. A subsequent study of 708 cases of court-ordered child support contained in a Department of Justice data base, found that 77% of the recipients would be better off under the new child support family law and tax rules (and 23% of the them would be worse off): Feltham and Macnaughton, "The New Child Support Rules and Existing Awards: Choosing the Best Tax and Family Law Regime" (1996) 44 *Can. Tax J.* 1265, 1285.

12.8 — Other amounts

(a) — Scholarships, bursaries and awards

Paragraph 56(1)(n) includes scholarships, bursaries and awards in income net of the exemption available under subsection 56(3). Starting in 2006, a full exemption is available for most scholarships and bursaries received in connection with a post-secondary program which is eligible for the education credit.[112] The increased exemption is intended to assist students in an era when tuition costs are rising, which is ironically caused, in part, by the lack of public funding of post-secondary education.[113] Starting in 2007, scholarships and bursaries received in connection with enrolment in an elementary or secondary school program are also eligible for a full exemption.[114] By doing this, the federal government has made another tax policy choice: to use the tax system to reduce the barriers to private school for those who are eligible for scholarships and bursaries rather than increasing provincial transfer payments to provide more direct funding to the public school system.

Awards are exempt from tax if they are received in connection with the production of a literary, dramatic, musical or artistic work.[115] In any other case, the exemption is $500.

---

[112]Before 2006, the exemption was capped at $3,000. The March 4, 2010 budget contains three proposals in connection with this exemption and post-secondary education. The first proposal is to limit the tax exempt portion of a scholarship or bursary to the total of the tuition fees and the cost of program-related materials if the taxpayer is enrolled in a part-time program (except for students qualifying for the disability credit). The second proposal is to exclude scholarships or bursaries for post-doctorate study from the scholarship income exemption: programs consisting principally of research must lead to a degree or diploma (e.g. Masters, PhD) to qualify. Post-doctorate study will also not qualify for the education or tuition credit. The third proposal is intended to clarify that the scholarship income exemption applies only to awards that can reasonably be regarded as being received in connection with enrolment in the eligible institution for the duration of the period that relates to the award. All three proposals are effective 2010.

[113]As discussed under heading 14.7(b), "Non-refundable credits", below, the tuition, education and textbook credits are provided under s. 118.6(2). Most college and university programs qualify unless the tuition is reimbursed by an employer as a tax-free benefit: see 118.6(1) in the case of the education credit. Students receiving scholarships and bursaries may claim these non-refundable credits whereas employees whose tuition fees are paid for by their employers (as a tax-free benefit) cannot. Employer-paid tuition fees are a tax-free benefit when the courses are taken primarily for employment: see chapter 5, above.

[114]This is effective 2007. Before 2007, such scholarships were only eligible for a $500 exemption.

[115]Awards that reimburse personal or living expenses, and expenses that are otherwise deductible in computing income and expenses do not qualify: s. 56(3).

(b) — Employment insurance

Benefits provided under the federal Employment Insurance Act are included in income under 56(1)(a)(iv). The benefits are paid to all Canadians who are eligible because of unemployment but are "clawed back" through the income tax system, so that recipients with incomes in excess of $50,000 (2007) have to repay some of the benefits that they receive.[116] Paragraph 60(n) provides a deduction for this repayment.

(c) — Worker's compensation and social assistance

Workers' compensation and social assistance[117] payments are included in income under paragraphs 56(1)(v) and (u). The amounts are not taxed, however, because they are deducted in computing taxable income under paragraph 110(1)(f). The section 56 inclusion serves an important purpose because, as we shall see in chapter 14, income under section 3 (rather than taxable income) is used as a "means test" for various income-tested tax refundable credits (the refundable GST credit,[118] the Canada child tax benefit,[119] the Working Income Tax Benefit,[120] and the refundable medical expense credit,[121]) as well as claims for dependants by others[122] and the age credit.[123] As discussed earlier, income (rather than taxable income) is also used to determine how much of a taxpayer's Old Age Security[124] and EI payments must be "clawed back" and repaid. Section 56 includes the payments for this purpose but paragraph 110(1)(f) (a deduction after the net income) excludes the payments from taxable income, which is the basis for computing tax. Therefore, these payments are not subject to tax.

What is the rationale for excluding these payments from taxable income? There is a good argument for taxing these payments because they increase the recipient's abil-

---

[116]When the income of recipient exceeds 1.25 times the maximum yearly insurable earnings (1.25 × $43,200 in 2010), the general rule is that the lesser of 30% of the excess income or 30% of the benefits must be repaid.

[117]Social assistance payments are payments made by the federal, provincial and municipal governments to assist low-income taxpayers. The federal "guaranteed income supplement" and "spouse's allowance" benefits that low-income seniors receive are examples. Welfare payments are another example. The only social assistance payments that are specifically excluded from income are payments for foster care (s. 81(1)(h)).

[118]S. 122.5.

[119]S. 122.6.

[120]See heading 14.7(c), "Refundable Credits", below.

[121]*Ibid.*

[122]Ss. 118(1)(a), (b), (c.1) and (d).

[123]S. 118(2). These credits are discussed further under heading 14.7, "Tax credits", below.

[124]See heading 12.3, "Public pensions", above.

ity to pay tax.[125] In the case of workers' compensation payments, there is the additional argument that since the premiums that employers pay are tax deductible, the payments received by former employees should be taxable. The main argument against taxing these payments is that the net cost to the government would be the same: since the level of assistance is predetermined, any amount of tax payment must be covered by an increase in the assistance payment. The Government of Canada treats the non-taxation of social assistance and workers' compensation as a tax expenditure, valued at $875 million for 2009.[126]

(d) — Universal child care benefit

The Universal Child Care Benefit (UCCB) of $100 per month for each child under six years of age. It was promoted in the 2005/2006 federal election campaign as a tax policy alternative to direct funding for additional child care spaces (although, arguably, it is not) as it has the advantage of allowing both working and non-working parents the flexibility to spend it on anything they want to. The election was won and UCCB payments commenced July 1, 2006.

The UCCB is similar to the post World War II Family Allowance program that was discontinued when the income-tested Canada child tax benefit program commenced in 1992: it is paid to all families (it is not income tested)[127] and the payments are taxable in the hands of the lower income parent[128] but it is effectively tax-free (like the Canada child tax benefit) in the hands of a single parent.[129] But a new twist was

---

[125]Workers' compensation payments were initially excluded from income (see s. 81(1)(h), as it read before 1982) until 1982, when the current inclusion-deduction system for these payments became effective (s. 56(1)(v)). The Carter Commission recommended that workers' compensation and social assistance payments be subject to tax.

[126]*Tax Expenditures and Evaluations 2009*, note 26, above, Table 1. The $875 million figure reported above is the sum of three projections for 2010 contained in the report: $85 million for the Guaranteed Income Supplement and spouse's allowance benefits, $115 million for social assistance payments and $675 million for worker's compensation benefits. Expenditures have declined in recent years because of increases to the personal tax credits (which therefore now have a larger reported tax expenditure) as well as the reductions to the lowest personal income tax.

[127]The March 4, 2010 federal budget contains a proposal to allow individuals who have joint custody after a separation or divorce to split the tax-free Child Tax Benefit, UCCB and the child component of the refundable GST/HST Credit if the child lives approximately equally with each individual. (The payments can continue to be received by one individual if the two parties so agree.) This proposal is effective July 1, 2011.

[128]S. 56(6).

[129]The March 4, 2010 federal budget contains a proposal that that will allow UCCB received by a single parent family to be taxed in the hands of the child claimed as a spouse equivalent (eligible dependant) effective 2010. If no child is claimed as a spousal equivalent, the UCCB can be included in the income of any child for whom the taxpayer is receiving UCCB. This change will provide a single parent receiving UCCB with the same tax relief available to a two parent family with one-income earner.

added: it does not affect the calculation of income-tested refundable credits or the claw backs that are based on income because it is excluded from the calculation of adjusted income for these purposes.[130]

(e) — Policy considerations

We have seen that the Act is not consistent in its treatment of government transfer and other payments that increase a taxpayer's ability to pay:

- Scholarships and items listed in section 81 are excluded from income and taxable income.
- Government social assistance and workers' compensation payments are included in income but are excluded from taxable income. This is does so that they impact the calculation of income-tested refundable credits and the claw backs that are based on income so that they are not taxed.
- The UCCB payment is included in the income and taxable income of the lower income parent (in the case of two parent couples) but is specifically exempted from income for the purposes of the same income-tested refundable credits and claw backs.

In all cases, there is a good argument for taxing all these payments: they increase the recipient's ability to pay tax. There is also a good argument against taxing all these payments: the net cost to the government would be the same whether the payments were tax-free or not. The key question is as follows? Why are some payments excluded from income for the purposes of income-tested refundable credits and benefit and the claw backs and some included if income is to be used as a "means test" for this purpose?

Where is the logic and consistency? There is no simpler answer to some of these questions because there appears to be no broad principle behind also these rules. The Act has not been consistent in its treatment of tax exempt items and the reason why (except for the politics at the time) is not at all clear.

12.9 — Moving expenses

(a) — Deduction

Section 62 allows a deduction for "moving expenses". The definition of moving expenses includes travel costs, transportation and storage of household effects, temporary lodging and meals, the costs of selling an old residence and the legal expenses of buying a new residence. The deduction is only available if the move was within Canada, was 40 kilometres or more and was caused by a change in the loca-

[130] That is, it is excluded from adjusted income for the purposes of computing the refundable GST credit, the Canada child tax benefit, the proposed Working Income Tax Benefit, and the refundable medical expense credit. It is also excluded from adjusted income for the purposes of determining the claw back of a taxpayer's Old Age Security and EI payments. See, for example, the references to s. 56(6) in s. 122.5(1), s. 122.6 and Part I.2 of the Act.

tion of the taxpayer's work (or, in the case of a student, a change of university).[131] The deduction can be taken from income from employment at the new location or income from business at the new location or scholarships or research grants at the new location (paragraph 62(1)(c)). Any excess of deductible expenses over qualifying income can be carried forward for one year (paragraph 62(1)(d)).

The deduction for moving expenses is available only for expenses that were not reimbursed by the taxpayer's employer. In chapter 5, Income from Employment, above, the point was made that the rules allowing an employer to reimburse an employee for moving expenses on a tax-free basis are far more generous than the rules in section 62, which allow an employee to deduct only those expenses listed in subsection 62(3).[132] As a result, it is better for an employer to reimburse a taxpayer for non-deductible moving expenses than to pay the taxpayer an allowance for the same amount. For example, if an employee is reimbursed for a $15,000 loss on the sale of a house, the reimbursement need not be reported because it not considered to be employment income.[133] However, if the taxpayer's employer pays the taxpayer a $15,000 allowance in respect of this loss, the allowance would have to be reported as employment income,[134] but no amount would be deductible as a moving expense because a loss on the sale of a house is not one of the deductible moving expenses listed in subsection 62(3). In the second case, the taxpayer would report $15,000 of income for tax purposes whereas, in the first case, the taxpayer would have nothing to report. This is an anomalous result.

(b) — Policy objectives

Moving expenses incurred to start a new job or education at a new location are generally considered to be personal expenses, or at most, mixed expenses, and are not deductible. In order to promote mobility of Canadians within Canada and to recognize the dual nature of moving expenses, section 62 specifically allows the deduction. The conditions and limitations of this deduction reflect these policy objectives. Expenses related to relocation for pure personal reasons are not deductible. The amount of deduction is tied to the income to be derived from employment, business or scholarship at the new location.

---

[131] See definition of eligible relocation in s. 248(1).

[132] The restricted list of moving expenses is set out in s. 62(3). The rules state that a taxpayer deducting moving expenses must include any reimbursement or allowance received in respect of those expenses in his income in order to deduct the expenses (s. 62(1)(g)). Typically, however, any employer-reimbursed expenses would simply be left off the list of moving expenses to be deducted in the employee's tax return whereas any allowances would automatically be included in his or her income under s. 6(1)(b). S. 62(1)(g) ensures that employer-reimbursed expenses are not deducted.

[133] Note that one-half of any reimbursement of housing losses in excess of $15,000 is included in a taxpayer's income. See heading 5.7(c)(ii), "Statutory rules", above.

[134] S. 6(1)(b).

12.10 — Child care expenses

(a) — Deduction

Subsection 63(3) defines "child care expenses" as expenses incurred to enable the taxpayer (or a supporting person) to perform duties of an office of employment, to carry on a business, to carry on research or to attend a designated educational institution. In order to qualify, the services must be provided by someone other than a person who is the child's parent, a dependant claimed by the taxpayer or a related person who is under 18 years of age. The amount that can be claimed for boarding school or camp is also restricted.[135] In essence, child care expenses represent large out-of-pocket costs to families and, as defined above, might not be incurred except to enable parents to work outside the home.

The section 63 deduction is subject to three important limitations: (1) only the lower-income parent can generally claim the deduction, therefore the deduction cannot be claimed at all if one parent has no income;[136] (2) the deduction cannot generally exceed two-thirds of the "earned income" of the lower income parent which is defined to include income from an office or employment, income from a business and income from grants and training allowances;[137] and (3) the deduction cannot generally exceed $7,000 per child under the age of seven and $4,000 per child between the ages of seven and 16, inclusive.[138]

(b) — Policy objectives

The deduction for child care expenses can be seen as a tax expenditure designed to assist parents with the costs of child care and to lower a barrier to the entrance of women to the workforce. This special deduction is necessary because, as discussed in chapter 8,[139] child care expenses have been traditionally regarded as personal or living expenses that are not deductible as income-earning expenses.

---

[135] See definition of child care expenses in s. 63(3) and Interpretation Bulletin IT-495R3, "Child Care Expenses," (2005).

[136] S. 63(1)(b). There are some exceptions to this rule to meet the case where both incomes are equal (in which case a joint election determines eligibility) (s. 63(2.1)), and where the lower-income person is separated from the taxpayer, infirm, confined to a bed or wheelchair, in prison or attends a secondary school or a designated educational institution (in these cases, the higher-income parent may claim a deduction) (s. 63(2)).

[137] See s. 63(1)(e) for the earned income limitation and s. 63(3) for the definition of "earned income". Note that this definition of earned income is different than the one used for the "earned income" RRSP contribution. The RRSP definition is contained in s. 146 and is discussed under heading 12.4(d)(ii), "Contributions based on earned income", above.

[138] There is no deduction for the care of a child after the year of his or her 16th birthday, except in the case of a child with a mental or physical infirmity (s. 63(3) definition of "eligible child"). If a child is eligible for the disability credit (s. 118.3), the annual limit is $10,000 (rather than $7,000 or $4,000) (see s. 63(3) definition of "annual child expense amount").

[139] See heading 8.4(b), "Child care expenses", above.

As a tax expenditure, section 63 is open to criticism. Although it treats employed and self-employed taxpayers equally, it possesses the fundamental disadvantage of all deductions: it delivers a larger benefit to high-income earners than to low-income earners, and no benefit at all to persons without taxable income. Other policy instruments, such as direct provision of day care services, or direct subsidization of low-income parents, might be more effective uses of the amount of revenue foregone by section 63. If the tax system is to be a vehicle of assistance, section 63 would be better targeted as a tax credit, especially a credit that was refundable and income-tested (or vanishing).[140]

Moreover, because the amount of deduction under section 63 is limited, the deduction cannot fully offset the cost of childcare incurred by full-time working parents. In *Symes v. Canada* (1993),[141] the Supreme Court of Canada held that section 63 was the legislative response to help women enter the workforce and it was not necessary for the Court to reconsider whether child care expenses were business expenses in light of the fact that women are an important part of the workforce. In this case, the taxpayer argued that her section 15 right under the Charter was infringed by the Act to the extent that section 63 prevented her from fully deducting her child care expenses as business expenses under section 9. The Court split along gender lines on this issue. The majority (all the male judges) rejected the taxpayer's argument that the section 63 restrictions had a disproportionate impact on women: although women were more likely to bear the social costs of child care, there was no evidence that women were more likely to bear the financial costs of child care; and the restrictions affected only the financial costs of child care. The majority reasoned that section 63 did not draw a distinction on the basis of sex and it did not have an adverse effect upon women.[142] As to the social costs that were born by women disproportionally, the majority regarded it to be "very real", but nonetheless something that "exists outside of the *Income Tax Act*".[143]

---

[140]See heading 14.7(c), "Refundable credits", below.

[141][1993] 4 S.C.R. 695, [1994] 1 C.T.C. 40, 94 D.T.C. 6001 (S.C.C.), discussed further under heading 8.4(b), "Child care expenses", above.

[142]*Symes*, *ibid.*, para. 135-144.

[143]*Ibid.*, para. 143.

13
Income Splitting

13.1 — Whose income?

Previous chapters have discussed two of the crucial questions an income tax law must answer, namely: what items are taxable? (chapter 4) and how is income computed? (chapters 5 to 12). This chapter deals with another crucial question, namely, whose income is it?

Ordinarily, of course, the question "whose income is it?" is easily answered. Income is taxed to the person who earns and receives it, by providing personal services as an employee, by carrying on a business, or by virtue of owning property. However, in some instances the question requires further analysis, both in terms of technical rules and tax policy. One major instance arises in the context of the family. Family members often make gifts to each other, support each other, and some family members (often parents) exercise some control over the economic and personal lives of others (children). Related to this context is the use of family-controlled corporations, trusts and partnerships. Another instance arises in the business world where related corporations enter into transactions with each other to gain maximum after-tax profit for the entire corporate group. In these instances, the economic interest is generally shared, while "legal" interest may be separately owned. So who is to be the taxpayer? The answer to this question is crucial because the *Income Tax Act* (the "Act") taxes each "person" (an individual, corporation or trust) as a taxpayer.

As discussed below, the Act implicitly encourages income shifting in its fundamental design. On the other hand, the Act contains a large number of rules attempting to attribute the right amount of income to the correct taxpayer so as to prevent undue shifting.[1] Overall, the scheme of the Act seems to allow income splitting as long as the specific type of transaction or arrangement does not run afoul of the anti-income splitting rules.

13.2 — Legislative scheme

(a) — Inviting income split

The Act taxes each person separately and taxes individuals at progressive rates. As explained in chapter 14, the first dollar of taxable income is currently taxed at 15% and this rate rises as income rises (currently 29%). The net result is that as taxable income rises, tax liability also rises, both in absolute terms and as a percentage of income. The progressive rate structure encourages high-income individuals to shift income to low-income family members or to lowly taxed entities, such as corporations or trusts. This effort is often referred to as the "splitting" of income.

In addition to taxing individuals as tax units and the progressive rate structure, the Act "invites" income split by respecting the separate identity of corporations and trusts and recognizing the marital unit as a single unit for certain purposes.

(i) — Individual as the tax unit

The taxation unit under the Act is a "person", which includes an individual and a corporation. Therefore, although an individual generally regards his or her immediate family (typically spouse and children) as an economic unit from the standpoint of resources and expenditures, the Act treats each member of the family as a separate taxable person. This means that (subject to the anti-avoidance rules discussed below), if a child owns property in his or her own right, the income from the property is included in the child's taxable income and reported on the child's tax return. The Act does not lump the child's income together with the parents, even though parents and children are obviously members of a single household. The same is true of family-controlled business entities, such as trusts or corporations. Each entity is viewed as a separate taxpayer.

---

[1]Although the concept applies equally to corporations, inter-corporate income splitting is not the focus of this chapter. In the domestic context, corporate income splitting is limited by some of the same sections that regulate family income splitting, namely the s. 67 reasonable requirement and the s. 69 fair market value rule discussed in this chapter. As well, various rules prevent the transfer of losses to other corporations, including the change of control rules which regulate the use of pre-existing losses to shelter future income (discussed under heading 14.5(b)(v), "Change of corporate control", below). Another example of rules that limit corporate income splitting is the rule that requires the annual income limit for the low small business rates of tax to be shared by associated corporations (discussed under heading 15.5(d)(iv), "Limits on the small business deduction", below). There are also many rules that prevent income splitting with offshore corporations, such as s. 247 and the foreign accrual property income (FAPI) rules. It is beyond the scope of this book to discuss these international tax rules in any detail.

(ii) — Progressive rates

Taxing each person as a unit would not necessarily lead to income splitting if every taxpayer were taxed at the same flat rate. That is not the case under the Act. On the contrary, the rates applicable to individuals under the Act are progressive: when an individual receives additional income, he or she not only pays more tax, but also pays the tax at a higher rate. Moreover, each individual is eligible for the basic personal credit which (in 2010) effectively exempts the first $10,382 of income from tax.[2] As a result, the marginal rate varies from one individual to another, depending upon the individual's income bracket and his or her credits. A family whose entire income is taxed to one member — say, the father — would usually pay a higher overall tax than a family with the same income but divided evenly among all the family members.[3]

(iii) — Separate taxation of corporations and trusts

A corporation is a "person" for the purposes of the Act. As such, it computes its own tax liability separately from its owners (the shareholders). Earning income through a corporation thus creates opportunities for taxpayers to split income with the corporation and with other family members who may be shareholders.

Tax savings also arise where income earned by a corporation is taxed at a rate lower than the rate of the individual shareholder. For example, if a taxpayer operates a business as a sole proprietor and earns $500,000 in 2010, the income is subject to tax at progressive rates (with a top combined federal-provincial rate of almost 50 per cent applying to income over $127,021[4]). If the business is operated through a corporation wholly owned by the taxpayer the general tax rate is 30%. But if the corporation is eligible for the "small business deduction" (which is discussed in chapter 15, below), the $500,000 is taxed at a combined federal-provincial rate of approximately 16 per cent.[5] The after-tax income of the corporation is not taxed in the taxpayer/shareholder's hands until it is distributed to him or her by way of dividend. Dividends are taxable only on a cash basis. Dividends are paid at the discretion of the directors of the corporation; there is no mandatory legal requirement to pay dividends. Therefore, tax savings occur due to the rate differentials and the deferral benefits of cash-basis taxation of dividends.

Taxpayers can use closely-held corporations to split income with their family members by having them as shareholders. Different classes of shares can be created to provide different legal rights and obligations for the shareholders. Dividends can be "sprinkled" among the holders of different classes at the choice of the board of directors, who are elected by the shareholders. "There is nothing in the [corporate

---

[2]Tax rates and credits are discussed in ch. 14, "Taxable income and tax for individuals", below.

[3]This is discussed further under heading 13.3(c)(i), "Equity between families", below.

[4]*Ibid.*

[5]See ch. 15, Corporations and shareholders, below.

statute] or at common law that prohibits this dividend allocation technique."[6] Iacobucci J. of the Supreme Court of Canada stated in *Neuman v. Minister of National Revenue* (1998):[7] "[T]axpayers can arrange their affairs in a particular way for the sole purpose of deliberately availing themselves of tax reduction devices in the *ITA*." That, he explained, included the use of "corporate structures which exist for the sole purpose of avoiding tax".[8]

The tax savings through the use of family corporations are sweetened by two special tax treatments of shareholders of small business corporations. One is the dividend tax credit discussed in chapter 15. The use of a corporation to carry on the business effects a change in the character of income for tax purposes. When the after-tax business income is distributed by the corporation to a shareholder, the distribution gives rise to a dividend. Individual shareholders can claim a dividend tax credit, resulting in a lower effective rate for dividends, as opposed to other types of investment income.[9] If the shareholders prefer not to receive dividends and the after-tax business income is instead retained by the corporation, the value of the share will increase to reflect the retained income. The increased share value will be realized as a capital gain when the shareholder sells the share. As discussed in chapter 10, capital gains from the sale of small business corporation shares are not only taxable half, but also eligible for the lifetime capital gains exemption.[10]

Trusts are also used to split income between a taxpayer and his/her family members. Typically, the taxpayer that carries on a business (such as the practice of law or medicine and other professionals) is the settlor and trustee of a family trust whose beneficiaries include the taxpayer's adult children or spouse or common-law partner. The family trust may own the real property that is leased to the taxpayer to be used as his/her place of business. The family trust may also provide management services to the taxpayer. The rent and management fees are deductible to the taxpayer (subject to the reasonable standard test under section 67) and taxable to the trust. As discussed in Chapter 17 in more detail, the trust can distribute the income to the beneficiaries who pay tax at the applicable rates, benefiting (if they are age 18 or over) from lower tax rates and a set of personal credits.[11]

---

[6]*McClurg v. Minister of National Revenue* (1990), (sub nom. *McClurg v. R.)* [1990] 3 S.C.R. 1020, [1991] 1 C.T.C. 169, 91 D.T.C. 5001 (S.C.C.).

[7][1998] 1 S.C.R. 770, [1998] 3 C.T.C. 177, (sub nom. *Neuman v. R.)* 98 D.T.C. 6297 (S.C.C.).

[8]*Ibid.*, para. 63.

[9]See heading 15.4, "Taxation of shareholders", below.

[10]See heading 10.2(f), "Tax subsidies for certain investments", above.

[11]As discussed under heading 13.10, "Kiddie tax", below, the kiddie tax applies if the beneficiary is under 18 years of age at the end of the year.

(iv) — Explicitly permitting income splitting

The Act contains a number of rules to specifically permit family members, especially spouses, to split income. For example, transfers of capital property can be done on a cost (or rollover) basis between spouses or common-law partners.[12] Other examples include the deduction for a contribution to a registered retirement savings plans for a spouse or common-law partner,[13] the pension-income splitting rules,[14] and the exemption of tax-free savings account (TFSA) withdrawals from the rules explicitly prohibiting income splitting discussed below.[15]

(b) — Explicitly prohibiting income splitting

Income splitting is possible because the Act generally relies on private law to determine the ownership of income. A taxpayer can therefore use legally effective arrangements and structures to allocate income to a spouse and children.

In certain circumstances, however, the Act prevents income spliting by ignoring legal arrangements and taxing the person that actually earns the income. These rules include the following:

- limitations on deductions for compensation paid to family members (such as section 67, and paragraph 18(1)(h) and discussed in Chapter 8);
- restrictions for "personal services businesses" which effectively "pierce the corporate veil" in the case of incorporated employment income (i.e., subsection 125(7), which denies the small business deduction, and paragraph 18(1)(p), which limits the expense deductions, which are discussed in Chapter 5);
- substitution of fair market value for transfer price of certain gifts and other non-arm's length transactions (subsection 69(1));
- attribution of income that formally belongs to a spouse or minor child to the taxpayer who loaned or transferred the income-producing property to the spouse or child or to a trust for their benefit (e.g., sections 74.1 and 74.3);
- attribution of capital gains from the disposition of property loaned transferred to a spouse or a spouse trust (sections 74.2 and 74.3);
- imputation of income at the prescribed interest rate to a taxpayer who transfers property to corporation for the purpose of splitting income with a spouse or child (section 74.4);
- assignment of income from the person who formally receives the payment to the taxpayer who actually "earns" it (i.e., subsection 56(2)); and

---

[12]See heading 13.4(b), "Rollovers for transfers to a spouse or common-law partner", below.

[13]See heading 12.4(b), "Tax assistance", above.

[14]*Ibid.*

[15]S. 74.5(12): see heading 12.5(a), "Tax free savings accounts (TFSAs)", above.

- a special "kiddie tax" at the top rate when certain types of income (including dividends from private corporation are earned by minor children (i.e. section 120.4).

In addition, the General Anti-avoidance Rule (GAAR) under section 245 is potentially applicable to income-splitting transactions, especially where the transaction was designed to circumvent the application of any specific anti-avoidance rules.[16]

It is obvious from the above list that the targeted transactions are those that a taxpayer entered into with non-arm's length persons. As explained below, non-arm's length persons include, but not limited to, the taxpayer's spouse or common-law partner and children. Some of these rules are designed to prevent the shifting of capital gains (e.g., subsection 69(1) and section 74.2). Most of the rules are designed to prevent the shifting of income from property (which is inherently more mobile than business income) directly or indirectly through the use of corporations or trusts.

The statutory "anti-split" rules have become increasingly complicated over the years, as more and more loopholes have gradually been plugged. As a result, they now add considerable complexity to the Act. Some anti-avoidance rules even have their own anti-avoidance rules to ensure that they are not abused by crafty tax planning. For example, subsection 74.5(11) provides that the attribution rules do not apply to a transfer or loan of property "where it may reasonably be concluded that one of the main reasons for the transfer or loan" was to use the attribution rules to reduce the tax on the income or capital gain derived from the property.

In the meantime, however, taxpayers and their advisers have developed complicated planning techniques to avoid the anti-split rules. For example, in each of *McClurg v. Minister of National Revenue* (1990)[17] and *Neuman v. Minister of National Revenue* (1998),[18] the taxpayer succeeded in avoiding the application of subsection 56(2) and split income with his wife through the use of a corporation. In *Ferrel v. R.* (1999),[19] the taxpayer split with his minor children through the use of a trust earning business income.

Ironically, as the rules have become more watertight, their importance in preventing income-splitting may have diminished. There are simple ways to income split without running afoul of the attribution rules. For example, a couple can simply arrange their affairs so that consumption expenditures are made by the high earner and funds for savings and investment are provided by the lower-income earner: in that way, future investment income will be derived by the lower-income spouse. Another method used by business owners is to pay a reasonable salary to a spouse or child for services rendered. Finally, a common method for income splitting with

---

[16]One example is the *Lipson v. R.*, 2009 SCC 1, [2009] 1 S.C.R. 3, [2009] 1 CTC 314, 2009 DTC 5015, which is discussed in more detail in chapter 20, below.

[17]Note 6, above.

[18]Note 7, above.

[19][1999] 2 C.T.C. 101, (sub nom. *R. v. Ferrel*) 99 D.T.C. 5111 (Fed. C.A.).

minor children is to transfer funds to them to be invested in securities (such as mutual funds) that earn primarily capital gains. None of these methods are very complicated nor do they run afoul of any specific anti-avoidance rules.

13.3 — Policy

(a) — Progressivity of individual taxation

The personal income tax system is the only element of the Canadian tax structure that is truly progressive. It allocates the tax burden among Canadians on the basis of the ability to pay and helps redistribute social income to achieve equity. Income splitting allows high-income earners to reduce their tax liability, resulting in the overall reduction of progressivity of the tax system. If progressivity is justified, controlling income-splitting is undeniably an important policy objective.

(b) — Fairness

"Fairness" is a fundamental notion of tax policy. It certainly encompasses fair treatment of individual taxpayers. But more importantly, fairness refers to fair treatment of taxpayers as a whole. The distributional effect of income splitting, as in the case of most forms of tax avoidance, is unfair. In terms of opportunities, taxpayers earning only income from employment have virtually no opportunities to split their income before paying income tax. Tax is withheld at source and deductions are limited. Employees cannot simply "incorporate" themselves to avail the benefit of tax deferral and income splitting mentioned above. In contrast, taxpayers earning business or investment income (who often have higher levels of income and wealth) have more choices. They can conduct their activities directly as a sole proprietor or indirectly through a corporation or trust. There is a "sense of injustice and inequity which tax avoidance raises in the breasts of those unable or unwilling to profit by it."[20] The Carter Report stated: "Opportunities of tax avoidance are not equal, for it clearly has little practical meaning to salaried and wage-earning taxpayers from whom tax is deducted at source . . ."[21] In other words, the more you make and the wealthier you are, the more opportunities you have to save tax.

Even among taxpayers who have the opportunities for income splitting may not have the ability or sophistication to actually use them. It is simply unfair that the tax liability of certain taxpayers is "dependent upon the taxpayer's sophistication at manipulating a sequence of events to achieve a patina of compliance with the apparent prerequisites for a tax deduction."[22] Moreover, taxpayers who use devices and schemes to minimize their tax burden unfairly shift the avoided tax to other taxpayers.

---

[20]Canada, *Report of the Royal Commission on Taxation*, vol. 3 (Ottawa: Queen's Printer, 1967), appendix A, at 542.

[21]*Ibid.*

[22]*The Queen v. Bronfman Trust*, 87 D.T.C. 5059, [1987] 1 C.T.C. 117 (S.C.C.).

On the other hand, individual taxpayers have the right to arrange their affairs to minimize their tax. As the Supreme Court noted in *Canada Trustco*, the preservation of "certainty, predictability and fairness" for individual taxpayers is considered a "basic tenet of tax law."[23] Iacobucci J. warned that Courts should not be "quick to embellish" tax avoidance provisions in the Act, but should await "precise and specific" measures from legislators to combat any perceived "mischief".[24]

(c) — Treatment of the family

The Act does not regard the family as a taxation unit. As explained above, this creates income-splitting opportunities. Generally speaking, high income-earners are not willing to divest themselves of any of their income, because, although the divestment would save some income tax, it would also reduce their disposable income and therefore their standard of living. However, when part of a high income can be diverted to a spouse, common-law partner, or child, the divested income will remain available to essentially the same persons or purposes that it would have been spent on anyway. In this way, the high income-earner is able to reduce his or her tax liability without suffering any real loss of command over goods and services. If the family were the taxation unit, the incentive to split income among members of a family would disappear. Many jurisdictions remove the most obvious temptation to income-splitting by aggregating for tax purposes the incomes of spouses (or common-law partners). The Carter Commission's recommended family unit went one step further by including children's income in the aggregation.[25] Canada has rejected these approaches, but the Act recognizes the family in limited instances.

The choice of taxing individuals as opposed to families as taxation units has significant policy implications in terms of tax equity between families with one income-earning spouse and families with two income-earning spouses, as well as tax equity between families and unattached individuals. The differences in treating families also have impact on household labour and women's participation in the paid workforce.

(i) — Equity between families

The discrepancy in tax liability between one large income and two smaller incomes is the inevitable result of a progressive tax system. The higher income-earner has the ability to pay a higher proportion of his or her income in tax than the lower income-earner. Therefore, if ability to pay is the criterion of tax equity, the higher marginal and average rates of tax that the higher income-earner bears are fair. This

---

[23] *The Queen v. Canada Trustco Mortgage Co.* (2005), (sub nom. *Canada Trustco Mortgage Co. v. Canada)* 2005 D.T.C. 5523 (Eng.), (sub nom. *Hypothèques Trustco Canada v. Canada)* 2005 D.T.C. 5547 (Fr.), [2005] 5 C.T.C. 215, [2005] 2 S.C.R. 601, ¶13 [S.C.R.] (S.C.C.).

[24] *Neuman*, note 17, above, para. 63.

[25] Carter Report, note 20, above, vol. 3, ch. 10.

rationale only holds true as long as the comparisons are between financially independent taxpayers.

The fairness of the result may be questioned when families, rather than individuals, are used as the basis of comparison. Assume that family A has one income-earner with an income of $100,000, and family B has two income-earners each with an income of $50,000. Each family has a total income of $100,000, and (assuming that each family is otherwise similarly situated) would seem to have an equal ability to pay tax. Yet family A (with one income of $100,000) pays far more tax than family B (with two incomes of $50,000). The credit for the dependent spouse,[26] which is available to the income-earner in family A, but not available to either income-earner in family B, is worth about $2,000 in 2007 to family A.[27] As a result, the credit only slightly offsets the great advantage of family B's income-split. Under a flat-rate income tax system, of course, there would be no difference between the tax liability of family A and family B.

The Carter Commission argued that it was inequitable that a family with one income-earner should pay more tax than a family with two (or more) income-earners and the same total income. In the Commission's view, the proper measure of ability to pay was the income of a family (spouses and children under 18) rather than the income of individuals within a family.[28] If the family were the taxpaying unit, then two families with the same total income would pay the same amount of tax regardless of how the income was split among individual members of each family. The Commission accordingly recommended that the family become the taxpaying unit. For adult individuals who were not living within a family, the individual would of course remain as the taxpaying unit.

The White Paper that was issued by the federal government after the Carter Report agreed that there was "logic in the argument that the family, or at least the husband and wife together, is the basic spending unit". However, the White Paper went on to say that "the Commission's proposed family unit tax would have imposed a "tax on marriage" — that is, a husband and wife each having an income would together pay more tax than two people with the same income who were not married". The government took the view that such a "tax on marriage" would be "unfair and undesirable", and decided against any change.[29] The Act that was enacted in 1971 therefore continued to recognize the individual, and not the family, as the basic taxation unit in Canada.[30]

---

[26]S. 118(1)(a). See heading 14.7(b), "Non-refundable credits", below.

[27]The federal credit is $1,549 (15% × $10,324). The provincial credit varies by province: in Ontario it is $384 (5.05% × $7,594).

[28]Carter Report, note 20, above, vol. 3, ch. 10.

[29]Benson, *Proposals for Tax Reform* (1969), 14.

[30]In 1999, a House of Commons Finance Sub-committee revisited this issue briefly when it found that most of the difference in the way that single-earner and two-earner families are treated by Canada's tax system is due to the system's progressive rate structure and its recognition of the individual as the basic unit of taxation. The Sub-committee "... concluded

The argument that an individual's marital status and familial relationships are relevant to the determination of his or her ability to pay is based on certain assumptions about families, each of which is controversial. The first assumption is that the family is the basic economic and social unit in society. This assumption is undermined by high divorce rates and the prevalence of a variety of cohabitation arrangements. At the very least, difficult questions of definition would have to be resolved, and it would be hard to avoid investigations into the living arrangements of people who might be cohabiting in lieu of marriage or for other reasons.

The second assumption is that taxation should be based on the benefit derived from income, rather than on legal title to income.[31] Under a legal title test, even if the sole income-earner in a family did typically share the income with the other members of the family, the income-earner's legal title to the income gives him or her a degree of control over expenditure decisions which, it could be argued, makes it reasonable to treat him or her as the sole taxpayer in respect of the income. Under a benefit test, if sharing is typical, then it may be appropriate to share the tax burden by treating the family as the taxation unit. Oddly enough, this particular issue does not arise in other taxation contexts, and it is difficult to derive a principled answer to the question whether it is legal title or benefit that counts.

If the first two assumptions are accepted, the third assumption has to be considered, namely, that the benefit of family income is usually shared among the members of the family regardless of who actually earns the income. Intuitively, it seems obvious that sharing is prevalent and substantial in a family that shares the run of the house or apartment, eats the same food, is clothed to the same standard, and goes on vacations together. For most families, these consumption expenditures would absorb most of the income. On the other hand, there do not seem to be comprehen-

---

that the tax system treats families in an equitable manner because they are taxed as individuals. Any changes to the basic nature of the tax system would constitute broad tax reform, which is well beyond the mandate of this Committee". See *Report 19, For the Benefit of our Children: Improving Tax Fairness*, tabled in the House of Commons on June 9, 1999.

[31] Academics analyze the question of whether the individual or the family is the most appropriate taxation unit with reference to two principles: (1) the legal control principle, which holds that individuals should pay tax on the income they control; and (2) the economic benefit principle, which holds that individuals should be taxed on income from which they benefit. Those who favour the legal control principle support the individual as the unit of taxation. Those who favour the economic benefit principle and assume that families share the income that they earn support the family as the unit of taxation. But the evidence is that many families do not share. Because of this, many argue that income that a taxpayer legally controls is a better measure of ability to pay and that the individual is the better unit of taxation than family in terms of equity, neutrality and gender equality. See, for example, Brooks, "The Irrelevance of Conjugal Relationships in Assessing Tax Liability," in Head and Krever, eds., *Tax Units and the Tax Rate Scale* (1996).

sive empirical studies of the patterns of family expenditures, and those studies that do exist cast doubt on the prevalence of sharing.[32] As Brooks states, however,

> as a conceptual matter, the debate is not really over whether the family or the individual is the correct unit of account. Few people claim that the household is that natural unit to which utility — or anything else that matters for tax purposes — accrues. Instead, the individual is the proper focus of fairness in any social institution; therefore, the proper question is, in determining an individual's tax liability, should that individual's marital status, or other personal relationships, be relevant?[33]

(ii) — Impact on household labour and employment

Whether or not families are taxed as units may have significant impact on household labour and women's participation in the workforce. A possible difference between the one-job family and the two-job family (each with the same total cash income), lies in the amount of "imputed income" derived by each family.[34] Imputed income is the value of the benefit derived by a person from his or her own personal services (such as care-giving, cooking, cleaning, maintenance, repairs or whatever else people do for themselves) or from the use of his or her own property (such as a house, a cottage, or an automobile).

It is arguable that the family with only one spouse working has greater taxable capacity because of the imputed income of the non-earning spouse (or common-law partner), who usually increases the taxable capacity of the family by performing care-giving and other unpaid household services which the two-job family would have to purchase (or forego). The value of this work, like other forms of imputed income, is not directly recognized for tax purposes. The present higher tax on the one-job family could be defended as an indirect recognition of that family's higher imputed income from unpaid household services. However, since the present law is not based on any measurement of this amount, it is therefore a very arbitrary recognition of this imputed income. Should some attempt be made to measure the imputed income from unpaid household services and incorporate it into the tax base? The Carter Commission rejected this approach on the ground that it was unfair to single out and tax one form of imputed income while ignoring other forms of imputed income.[35] Of course, like other forms of imputed income, household labour

---

[32]See, for example, Pahl, "Patterns of Money Management within Marriage" (1980) 9 *J. of Social Policy* 313, 328; Dulude, "Taxation of the Spouses" (1985) 23 *Osgoode Hall L. J.* 67, 94; Woolley, "Women and Taxation: A Survey" (working paper for Ontario Fair Tax Commission's Women and Taxation Working Group Report, 1991), 13; Ontario Fair Tax Commission, "Women and Taxation Working Group Report" (1992); and Ontario Fair Tax Commission, *Fair Taxation in a Changing World* (1993), 269-270.

[33]Brooks, note 31, above, at 47.

[34]See heading 4.8, "Imputed income", above.

[35]Carter Report, note 20, above, vol. 3, 118.

is difficult to value, and it does not bring in any of the cash that would be needed to pay the tax.[36]

Using the family as the tax unit would probably operate as a disincentive to a non-earning spouse (or common-law partner) entering the paid labour force. (It is, of course, hard to know to what extent people take into account tax considerations in making occupational choices, but it seems reasonable to assume that tax considerations have some influence.) Under the present system, when a non-earning spouse (or common-law partner) starts earning income, the new income is taxed as if it were the income of a single individual. The advantage of that income-split would be lost if the family became the unit of taxation: the new income would have to be added to the existing income and would not be taxed at the lower rates appropriate to a separate individual. The possible discouragement of the non-earning spouse (or common law partner) from entering the paid work force has formed the basis for some opposition to the idea of the family as a unit of taxation.[37]

(iii) — Equity between families and unattached individuals

The adoption of the family as the taxation unit implies a decision that families with equal incomes should be treated alike, but it does not decide the question of how tax burdens should be allocated as between families and single individuals. The question remains whether the aggregated family income should be taxed at the same rates as are applicable to the income of a single individual, or at lower rates. There are two polar positions. At one pole (represented in some European systems), the aggregated income of the two spouses is taxed under a rate schedule which is applicable to single taxpayers as well; under this system, a married couple in which H earns $50,000 and W earns $40,000 would pay the same tax as a single individual earning $90,000. At the other pole (represented in the United States from 1948 until 1969), the aggregated income of the two spouses is taxed as if each spouse had earned exactly one-half of it; under this system, a married couple in which H earned $50,000 and W earned $40,000 would pay the same tax as two single individuals each earning $45,000; in other words, the married couple is given the benefit of a perfect income-split. The Carter Commission recommended a middle ground.[38] The Commission recommended that tax should be levied on the family

---

[36]Another problem with the taxation of imputed income from household services is that most home-centred work is performed by women, so that the taxation of imputed income would indirectly place a disproportionate burden on women. This has led to other proposals to reduce the bias in the tax system in favour of unpaid household work, as well as proposals to use the tax system to compensate for the economic disparities between men and women. For a discussion of a variety of proposals, see Lahey, "The Tax Unit in Income Tax Theory", in Pask (ed.), *Women, the Law and the Economy* (1984) 273, 299–302; Maloney, "Women and the Income Tax Act" (1989) 3 *Can. J. Women and the Law* 182, 194–203; Ontario Fair Tax Commission, "Women and Taxation Working Group Report", note 32, above, 24-25; and Ontario Fair Tax Commission (1993), note 32, above.

[37]See *Dulude*, note 32, above; and *Lahey*, *ibid*.

[38]Carter Report, note 20, above, vol. 3, ch. 10.

under a rate schedule which would differ from the rate schedule applicable to a single individual; the two rate schedules should be so designed that a family would pay less tax than one single individual with the same income as the family, but more than two single individuals with the same total income as the family.

(iv) — Limited recognition of the family

While the individual continues to be the basic taxation unit in Canada, the Act does recognize the interdependence of family members in various ways. One example of this is the set of rules that govern a taxpayer's eligibility for tax exemptions, credits and special deductions. For example, the ability to designate a home as a principal residence to obtain an exemption from capital gains is lost if the homeowner's spouse or child under 18 has made a rival designation.[39] The Act also provides for tax credits[40] for a dependent spouse/common-law partner and their medical expenses, and allows the transfer from one spouse/common-law partner to another of the benefit of certain unused tax credits, and the transfer from a child to a parent of the disability credit, and the tuition credit and education credit. In addition, the Act allows a deduction for a contribution to a registered retirement savings plan for the spouse of the taxpayer[41] and taxes the Universal Child Care Benefit (UCCB) for children under seven in the hands of the lower income parent of a two parent family (presumably because the lower income parent is likely to be caring for the children).[42]

The income-tested benefits programs administered by the Act also use family income, rather than individual income, to determine benefit eligibility. A taxpayer's entitlement to receive the child tax benefit or the goods and services tax (GST) credit and the working income tax benefit (WITB) are each dependent on the combined income of the taxpayer and his or her spouse or common-law partner excluding the UCCB[43] and many provinces also have refundable income-tested provincial credits based on this measure of family income. The use of family income as the test of eligibility for these credits is consistent with federal and provincial social security programs which tend to use the same approach, denying benefits to the spouse of the millionaire even if he or she has no personal income. And yet, it is not easy to see why we should pool the shared consumption of poor families be-

---

[39]See heading 10.8, "Principal residence exemption", above.

[40]See heading 14.7(b), "Non-refundable credits", below.

[41]S. 146(5.1), discussed under heading 12.4(d), "Registered retirement savings plans (RRSPs)", above.

[42]Starting in 2010, a UCCB received by a single parent family can be taxed in the hands of the child claimed as a spouse equivalent (eligible dependant). This change will provide a single parent receiving UCCB with the same tax relief available to a two parent family with one-income earner. This change will provide a single parent receiving UCCB with the same tax relief available to a two parent family with one-income earner. See heading 12.8(d), "Universal child care benefit", above.

[43]See heading 14.7(b), "Non-refundable credits", below.

cause that will reduce their entitlement to income support, but we should not pool the shared consumption of more affluent families because that would increase their liability to pay tax.[44]

(d) — Sharing family wealth

Tax-motivated splitting of income among family members may have positive social implications. It may be an incentive to property owners to share their property with their spouses, common-law partners, and children, which might contribute in some small way to a more equitable distribution of wealth, especially to women, who often lack the same opportunity to accumulate wealth as men.

The attribution rules have the effect of discouraging substantial intra-family gifts, because when the rules apply the donor has to be willing not only to give away property, but to continue to pay the tax on the income yielded by the property. Thus, the rules tend to reinforce existing accumulations of wealth by discouraging the sharing of property among family members. For example, one of the main criticisms of the recently introduced pension income splitting rules is that it will discourage taxpayers from making a spousal RRSP contributions which have the effect of legally giving away future pension income.

13.4 — Non-arm's length transfer of property

(a) — The fair market value principle

When a person enters into transactions or makes gifts to his or her family members or a controlled corporation, he or she may charge the highest price available on the market for the property transferred, or charge nothing or a nominal amount for various personal reasons. From a tax perspective, the value for the transaction is crucial to the determination of the tax consequences of the transferor and the transferee. It is the basis for computing the transferor's profit (in the case of a transfer of business assets) and capital gain or loss (in the case of a transfer of capital property). It is also the basis for computing the transferee's cost of the property acquired, which is in turn, key to the determination of the transferee's future profit and capital

---

[44]Moreover, it is arguable that income support and income tax should, as a matter of policy, be treated as two sides of the same coin. The refundable credits provide a limited model for a negative income tax, under which any tax-filer reporting income below a stipulated "poverty line" would receive a payment from the government. A negative income tax is probably the simplest way of implementing a guaranteed annual income, which would replace all existing welfare or income support programs. If a negative income tax were implemented, the poverty line would probably be defined by reference to family income rather than individual income. But if family income becomes the basis for entitlement to tax "refunds" to the poor, it is going to be difficult to explain why it should not also be the basis for tax liability for everyone else.

gain.[45] If left unregulated, a taxpayer can give a property (with an adjusted cost base of $10,000 and fair market value of $16,000) to her child as a gift. Technically, the taxpayer would have zero proceeds of disposition and realize a loss. The child can immediately sell the property to a third party for $16,000 and realize a gain. Shifting the gain in this manner is obviously offensive in terms of tax policy.

Since it is impossible to specify the exact price for an infinite number of transactions, subsection 69(1) adopts the standard of fair market value for transactions between non-arm's length parties. The intention is to use the fair market value as a benchmark in determining the price for those transactions where the parties have the common intention to "manipulate" price to achieve tax savings. Subsection 69(1) reads:

> Except as expressly otherwise provided in this Act,
>
> (a) where a taxpayer has acquired anything from a person with whom the taxpayer was not dealing at arm's length at an amount in excess of the fair market value thereof at the time the taxpayer so acquired it, the taxpayer shall be deemed to have acquired it at that fair market value;
>
> (b) where a taxpayer has disposed of anything
>
> (i) to a person with whom the taxpayer was not dealing at arm's length for no proceeds or for proceeds less than the fair market value thereof at the time the taxpayer so disposed of it,
>
> (ii) to any person by way of gift *inter vivos*, or
>
> (iii) to a trust because of a disposition of a property that does not result in a change in the beneficial ownership of the property; and
>
> the taxpayer shall be deemed to have received proceeds of disposition therefor equal to that fair market value; and
>
> (c) where a taxpayer acquires a property by way of gift, bequest or inheritance or because of a disposition that does not result in a change in the beneficial ownership of the property, the taxpayer is deemed to acquire the property at its fair market value.

Subsection 69(1) applies the fair market principle to inter vivos gifts and transactions between non-arm's length persons. This general principle is subject to the exception for "rollovers" which permit transfers of property to a spouse/common-law partner or a child in limited circumstances to be done on a cost basis.

---

[45]This value also has implications for the capital cost allowance system: it affects the transferor's computation of recapture on the sale of the property and forms the base on which the transferee computes capital cost allowance.

(i) — Fair market value

The term "fair market value" is undefined in the Act. Its determination is a question of fact, not law.[46] The often-quoted common-law definition of fair market value is the following:[47]

> the highest price an asset might reasonably be expected to bring if sold by the owner in the normal method applicable to the asset in question in the ordinary course of business in a market not exposed to any undue stresses and composed of willing buyers and sellers dealing at arm's length and under no compulsion to buy or sell.

In other words, fair market value is the best price a vendor can obtain in an open market. When the courts hear cases with valuation issues, they hear evidence from valuation experts. Because valuation is far from an exact science, a high degree of professional judgment is involved and experts may present different estimates of fair market value.[48] If the court finds the parties to be dealing at arm's length, the valuation may no longer be an issue.[49]

(ii) — Arm's length

Subsection 69(1) applies only to inter vivos gifts and transactions between a taxpayer and "a person with whom the taxpayer was not dealing at arm's length". The notion of "arm's length" refers to a relationship that is "as far away from one as the arm can reach; away from familiarity, at a distance; without fiduciary relations".[50] The determination of whether taxpayers deal at "arm's length" is also important in the application of other rules in the Act.[51] Generally speaking, any dealings between strangers are presumed to be at arm's length.

For the purposes of the Act, subsection 251(1) deems "related persons" not to be "dealing with each other at arm's length." "Related persons" are in turn listed in subsection 251(2). Individuals, for example, are "related" for tax purposes to other

---

[46]*CIT Financial Ltd. v. R.*, [2004] 4 C.T.C. 9, 2004 D.T.C. 6573, para. 3 [D.T.C.] (F.C.A.); leave to appeal refused (2004), 2004 CarswellNat 4370, 2004 CarswellNat 4371 (S.C.C.).

[47]*Henderson v. Minister of National Revenue*, [1973] C.T.C. 636, (sub nom. *Bank of New York v. Minister of National Revenue)* 73 D.T.C. 5471, para. 21 [D.T.C.] (Fed. T.D.); affirmed [1975] C.T.C. 497, 75 D.T.C. 5340 (Fed. C.A.); affirmed [1975] C.T.C. 485, 75 D.T.C. 5332 (Fed. C.A.); recently cited in *Carr v. R.*, [2004] 4 C.T.C. 2280 (T.C.C. [Informal Procedure]). The definition used by the CRA is similar: see Information Circulation IC 89-3, "Policy Statement on Business Equity Valuations", (1989) at para. 3.

[48]In *General Electric Capital Canada Inc. v. Canada*, 2009 TCC 565, a case dealing with the deductibility of a cross border non-arm's length loan guarantee, there was testimony from over ten valuation experts as to what the arm's length price for the guarantee would be for the purposes of ss. 247 and 69. At the time of writing (March 2010), the case is under appeal.

[49]E.g., in *Canada v. McLarty*, 2008 SCC 26, discussed under heading 8.7(b)(ii), Contingent Liabilities, above.

[50]*The Shorter Oxford Dictionary*, 3rd edition, definition of "at arm's length".

[51]E.g. ss. 18(4), 56(4.1), 78(1), 84.1, 118.1, 160, 212, certain definitions in 248(1), 247.

individuals connected by blood relationship, marriage or common-law partnership or adoption[52] and to corporations that either they or "related" persons control.[53] A father, for example, is related to his daughter and his daughter's common-law partner and any corporation that the father, his daughter or his daughter's common-law partner controls.

Paragraph 251(1)(c) further provides that unrelated parties can also be regarded as non-arm's parties based on the facts and circumstances of the case. The criteria that courts generally use in determining whether or not a transaction is at arm's length are as follows:[54] (a) was there a common mind which directs the bargaining for both parties to a transaction, (b) were the parties to a transaction acting in concert without separate interests, and (c) was there *de facto* control? In addition, the court may consider whether the terms of the transactions between the parties reflect "ordinary commercial dealings", but only to "reflect on the soundness" of the conclusions after applying the three tests above.[55]

(iii) — Symmetrical application to gifts

The fair market value principle is applied to both parties to a gifting transaction. Under paragraph 69(1)(b), where a person has made an *inter vivos* gift of property, the donor is deemed to have received proceeds of disposition equal to the fair market value of the property. Thus any accrued gain (or loss) must be recognized by the donor at the time of the gift.[56] Under paragraph 69(1)(c), the donee of the gift is deemed to acquire the property at its fair market value, the intent being to step up the donee's cost base so that the donee never has to pay tax on the gain that was taxed at the time of the gift.

A gift on death is treated in the same manner. Under subsection 70(5), the deceased (the donor) is deemed to have received proceeds of disposition equal to the fair market value of the property and the estate or beneficiary (the donee) is deemed to acquire the property at its fair market value.

---

[52]S. 251(2)(a). Each of these terms is defined in s. 251(6).

[53]S. 251(2)(b).

[54]These three tests are summarized by the CRA in Interpretation Bulletin IT-419R2, "Meaning of Arm's Length", (2004), at para. 23. See, for example, *Peter Cundhill & Associates Ltd. v R.*, [1991] 1 C.T.C. 197, 91 D.T.C. 5085 (Fed. T.D.); affirmed [1991] 2 C.T.C. 221, 91 D.T.C. 5543 (Fed. C.A.), *Gosselin v. R.*, [1997] 2 C.T.C. 2830 (T.C.C.) and *H.T. Hoy Holdings Ltd. v. R.*, [1997] 2 C.T.C. 2874, 97 D.T.C. 1180 (T.C.C.).

[55]See *The Queen v. Remai Estate*, 2009 FCA 340 at para. 34; and *Petro-Canada v. The Queen*, 2004 FCA 158, 2004 DTC 6329 at para. 55. In *Remai*, the Federal Court of Appeal rejected the argument that the "ordinary commercial dealings" test was in addition to the three other tests. The rationale is that arm's length parties may not always have ordinary commercial terms in their dealings.

[56]When a donor makes a gift of property to a registered charity, the donor can claim a tax credit or deduction for the fair market value of the donation; see heading 14.7(b), "Non-refundable credits", below.

Therefore, gifts are generally considered as tax-free windfalls to the recipient.[57] To the donor, however, gifted property is deemed to have been sold for fair market value, which may result in a gain or capital loss, depending on the cost of the gifted property.[58] As discussed below there is an exception to this rule for "rollovers" which permit transfers of property to a spouse/common-law partner or a child in limited circumstances to be done on a cost basis.

(iv) — Asymmetrical application to other transactions

In addition to gifts, subsection 69(1) applies to situations where a taxpayer has acquired "anything" from a non-arm's length person at an amount in excess of the fair market value or has disposed of anything to a non-arm's length person for consideration below the fair market value. Unlike the treatment of gifts, subsection 69(1) provides for asymmetrical treatment of the transferor and transferee in these circumstances. This asymmetrical treatment can be understood as an implicit penalty for non-arm's length transactions that deviate from the fair market value.[59]

When a person has made a non-arm's-length sale for consideration that is less than fair market value, paragraph 69(1)(b) provides that the transferor is deemed to have received proceeds of disposition equal to the fair market value of the property. Therefore, just as in the case of a gift, any accrued gains (or losses) must be recognized by the transferor. However, because paragraph 69(1)(c) makes no reference to a non-arms-length sale for less than fair market value consideration, there is no corresponding step up in the cost base of the property. The cost of the property to the transferee is the amount paid for the property: there is no adjustment. As can be seen in the example below, this leads to eventual double taxation of the difference between the amount paid and the fair market value of the property at the time of the transaction.

Example:

> Father owned a piece of land which he acquired at a cost of $80,000. In year one, he sold the land to his daughter for $100,000 while the fair market value was $120,000. The daughter then sold the property in year two for $130,000. Under subparagraph 69(1)(b)(i), the father is deemed to have received pro-

---

[57]See heading 4.5, "Gifts and inheritances", above.

[58]In the case of charitable gifts of shares or stock options of publicly traded corporations or ecologically sensitive land, there will be no amount included in taxable income because the taxable capital gain is deemed to be nil. This is discussed further at 10.6(c), "Gifts", above.

[59]Some transactions are governed by agreements that contain a price-adjustment clause (that is, a clause which states that if the CRA determines that the fair market value of the property to be greater or less than the price used in the transaction, that parties will adjust the price accordingly). In Interpretation Bulletin IT-169, "Price Adjustment Clauses" (1974), the CRA states that it will respect a price-adjustment clause and allow for a two-sided adjustment in the price (rather than the one-sided adjustment that s. 69 imposes) if the agreement, among other things, reflects a *bona fide* intention to transfer the property at fair market value and arrives at that value for the purposes of the agreement by a fair and reasonable method.

ceeds of disposition equal to $120,000 and a capital gain of $40,000 ($120,000 - $80,000), but the daughter has acquired the property at a cost of $100,000 because section 69 provides no corresponding adjustment to her cost. In year two, when she sells the property for $130,000, she would have a capital gain of $30,000 ($130,000 - $100,000). When the father and daughter are viewed together, they have a total of $70,000 capital gain ($40,000 + $30,000), while the actual gain accrued to the land is $50,000 ($130,000 - $80,000). There is double taxation of $20,000, the difference between the non-arm's length transaction price and the fair market value at the time ($120,000 - $100,000). The $20,000 gain is taxed twice: once to the father and again to the daughter.

Now consider the opposite situation which is not as common: the case of a non-arm's-length sale for consideration that is more than fair market value. Using the facts in the above example, except that, instead of selling the land to his daughter for $100,000, Father sold it for $125,000 (presumably to help daughter minimize her future capital gains tax). In this case, section 69 contains no rule to lower the proceeds received to fair market value. Therefore, Father must report a gain of $45,000. At the same time, paragraph 69(1)(a) applies to deem the transferee to acquire the property at a cost equal to the fair market value rather than the amount paid. When the daughter sold the property in year two, she has a $10,000 gain. When father and daughter are viewed together, they have a total of $55,000 capital gain ($45,000 + $10,000). There is double taxation of $5,000, which is the difference between the non-arm's length transaction price and the fair market value at the time ($125,000 - $120,000). Again, this asymmetrical treatment of the transferor and transferee is the implicit penalty or deterrent in subsection 69(1).

(v) — Rollover exceptions

As the opening words of subsection 69(1) indicate, this provision is subject to other specific rules in the Act that allow transfers of property at a value other than fair market value. One example of such an exception is a transfer to a spouse, which is deemed to occur at cost rather than fair market value, unless an election is made.[60] These exceptions are called "rollovers".

The effect of a rollover is to defer the recognition of gain or loss that has accrued to the property "rolled over" to the transferee until the transferee eventually disposes of the property. The rollover provisions in the Act are intended to encourage certain types of transfers for policy reasons (e.g., providing tax relief to families) or to postpone the taxation of gains when no economic realization has occurred (transfers of property to a corporation).[61] This favourable treatment is accorded to certain

---

[60] S. 73(1).

[61] Rollover treatment is also accorded to transfers of property to a corporation in return for shares of the corporation and certain transfers of property between related corporations. These corporate rollovers are designed to remove tax obstacles to the formation of corporations and the reorganization or amalgamation of corporations. There are comparable roll-

dispositions of property within a family, namely, dispositions of capital property from one spouse to another and dispositions of farm property from a parent to a child. These intra-family rollovers eliminate tax consequences from at least some transactions within a family, and they constitute a rudimentary recognition of the family as a single taxation unit.

(b) — Rollovers for transfers to a spouse or common-law partner

(i) — "Spouse" and "common-law partner" defined

The term "spouse" is defined in subsection 252(3) as including another individual who is a party to a void or voidable marriage with the particular individual. This definition is "inclusive": it extends the term "spouse" without defining it. Clearly, parties to a legally valid marriage are "spouses" for the purposes of the Act, even though they are not part of the definition in subsection 252(3). The term "common-law partner" is defined in subsection 248(1) to mean:

> . . .a person who cohabits at that time in a conjugal relationship with the taxpayer and
>
> (a) has so cohabited with the taxpayer for a continuous period of at least one year,[62] or
>
> (b) would be the parent of a child of whom the taxpayer is a parent, . . .

Because there is no reference to gender, the term "common-law partner" covers both heterosexual and homosexual partners. A taxpayer's common-law partner includes a person of the same or opposite sex who cohabits with the taxpayer "in a conjugal relationship" and who has either cohabited with the taxpayer for a continuous period of at least one year or is a parent of a child of the taxpayer.

(ii) — Inter-vivos transfers

Subsection 73(1) provides for a rollover when capital property is transferred *inter vivos* by a taxpayer to the taxpayer's spouse/common-law partner, a trust for the benefit of the spouse/common-law partner.[63] Consider the following example:

> H transfers to W, his wife, as a gift, a capital property with an adjusted cost base of $20 and a fair market value of $30.

---

overs for partnerships. See heading 16.5, "Rollovers for the formation and dissolution of Canadian partnerships", below.

[62]Former Bill C-10(2007), a technical amendments bill, proposed to change the reference to "with the taxpayer for a continuous period of at least one year" in the definition of common-law partner in s. 248(1) to "throughout the twelve-month period that ends at that time" applicable to 2001 and subsequent years. The March 2010 federal budget documents indicated that this legislation will be re-introduced.

[63]This rollover rule applies only to "qualifying transfers" as defined in subsection 73(1.01). A qualifying transfer is a transfer of property by an individual to the individual's spouse or common-law partner, or to a former spouse or common-law partner in settlement of rights arising out of their marriage or common-law relationship. The rollover also applies on a

Instead of a deemed disposition by H for fair market value of $30, subsection 73(1) deems H to have disposed of the property for proceeds equal to his cost (i.e., $20) so that H would have zero gain or loss. Technically, the rollover is not accomplished by denying that there has been a disposition from H to W. On the contrary, the property is "deemed to have been disposed of . . . by the taxpayer", but for proceeds of disposition equal to the adjusted cost base of the property.[64] The taxation of the accrued economic gain of $10 is thus deferred, but not foregone, because it was "embedded" in the property now owned by the transferee. Under subsection 73(1), the transferee (recipient) of the property is deemed to have acquired the property for an amount equal to the deemed proceeds, that is, the adjusted cost base of the property (that is, $20 in our example).[65] In this way, the transferee steps into the shoes of the transferor, taking over the property at its adjusted cost base to the transferor. Any accrued gain waits in the property until the property is disposed of. The rollover does not eliminate the liability to pay tax on the accrued capital gain; it simply postpones the liability until the transferee-spouse disposes of the property (or is deemed to dispose of it). In our example, where W acquired property with an adjusted cost base of $20 and a fair market value of $30, if W subsequently sold the property for $35 she would have to recognize a capital gain of $15 ($35 — $20 = $15). This capital gain would consist of the $10 gain which had accrued while H owned the property and the $5 gain which had accrued after W acquired the property. The entire $7.50 taxable capital gain (50 per cent of $15) will be attributed to H by virtue of the attribution rule of section 74.2 (as discussed below).

The subsection 73(1) rollover is not confined to gifts. It speaks of property "transferred". A sale from one spouse to another is therefore also eligible for the rollover. Thus, in our example, even if W paid H $30, so that H actually realized the gain of $10, H need not recognize the gain for tax purposes. However, an election against rollover treatment in this case would mean the normal rules in the Act apply. If $30 is the fair market value of the property, then the disposition will take place at $30. However, if $30 is less than or greater than the fair market value and an election against the rollover is made, then the fair market value principle under subsection 69(1) will apply to make one-sided adjustments: if the proceeds are less than fair market value then the proceeds (but not the cost) are adjusted upwards to fair market value. Thus, if the fair market value is $40, section 69 deems H to have received $40 (thus realizing a gain of $20) but does not change the fact that W has acquired a property at a cost of $30. As explained earlier, one-side adjustment rule

---

transfer of property to a "spouse trust", which is a trust created by the taxpayer under which the spouse or common-law partner is the income beneficiary, and no person except the spouse is entitled to the capital of the trust during the spouse's or common-law partner's life. The definition of a spouse trust and the rollover to a spouse trust are discussed in ch. 17, Trusts, below.

[64]Or, in the case of depreciable property, the undepreciated capital cost.

[65]*Ibid.*

results in double tax: if W sells the property tomorrow for its fair market value of $40, W will pay tax on $10 of the gain that H just paid tax on.[66]

(iii) — Transfers on death

A similar rollover is available under subsection 70(6) for a capital property inherited by the spouse or common-law partner of the deceased taxpayer (or testamentary gifts). This rollover overrides subsection 70(5) which deems the transfer to take place for fair market value.

Technically, subsection 70(6) deems the property to have been disposed of by the deceased immediately before death for proceeds of disposition equal to the cost amount of the property, and to have been acquired by the spouse or spouse trust for the same figure. This creates a rollover on death similar in design to that created for *inter vivos* dispositions by subsection 73(1). While the deferred capital gain will be attributed to the transferor in the case of inter vivos gifts, there is no attribution for the capital gain in the case of testamentary gifts.

(iv) — Election

The rollovers under subsections 73(1) and 70(6) are not mandatory. They can be elected out by the taxpayer and the spouse/common-law partner. If the election is made, the fair market value principle under subsection 69(1) or 70(5) will apply. If no election is made, the rollover occurs automatically.

In most cases of *inter vivos* gifts, the transferor will prefer rollover treatment because it permits the postponement of tax on accrued capital gains. In some cases, however, it will be advantageous to elect out of the rollover in order to realize capital gains (to either offset capital losses or benefit from the lifetime capital gains exemption).[67]

In the case of testamentary gifts, subsection 70(6.2) enables the legal representative of the deceased taxpayer to elect against the rollover. In the case of shares that are eligible for the lifetime capital gains exemption,[68] the legal representative should make an election on sufficient shares in order to realize a capital gain to use up the balance of the deceased's available exemption. An election on properties with accrued gains would also be advantageous if the deceased were otherwise in a loss

---

[66]As discussed under heading 13.4(a)(iv), "Asymmetrical application to other transactions", above, there is a second rule that applies when proceeds are greater than fair market value. In this case, the one-sided adjustment is to adjust the cost to the purchaser (but not the proceeds) downwards to fair market value: s. 69(1)(a). If, for example, the fair market value is $25, s. 69(1)(a) deems W to have acquired the property at $25 but does not change the fact that H sold the property at $30. If W holds on to the property and sells it at $30, W will pay tax on $5 of the gain that H paid tax on.

[67]No capital loss can be created on an *inter vivos* transfer to a spouse of property that has declined in value; such a loss is a "superficial loss" (s. 54) and is deemed to be nil by s. 40(2)(g)(i).

[68]Discussed under heading 10.2(f), "Tax subsidies for certain investments", above.

position since it would allow the loss to be used to offset gains that would otherwise be realized by the spouse on the eventual disposition of the property. Even if the deceased had income in the terminal year, if that income was particularly low an election still might be worthwhile to take advantage of the lower marginal rates of tax and/or unused personal tax credits. As well, if the spousal property had accrued losses, but the deceased had income in the terminal year, an election would enable the losses to be used to reduce income in the terminal year.[69]

(c) — Rollovers for transfers of farming or fishing property or woodlots to child

On a transfer of capital property by a parent to a child, there is no general rollover equivalent to those applicable to transfers between spouses. The idea of the family as the taxation unit has not progressed that far yet. However, on a transfer from a parent to a child, there is a rollover provision for three classes of capital property, namely, farming property, fishing property and woodlots.[70] The purpose of these rollovers is to facilitate the retention of these properties (and income sources) within a family. If tax were payable on the accrued gain on a farm, fishing property or woodlot when the property passed from parent to child, the resulting requirement of cash might force the sale of the property. The solution is the rollover, allowing property to pass (either *inter vivos* or on death) from parent to child without the need to recognize any accrued capital gains. This rollover is not essentially different from the spousal rollover, although it includes a more complicated elective provision.

(d) — Rollovers for transfers to corporation

On a transfer of property to a corporation in return for shares of the corporation, section 85 makes a rollover available. The idea is to eliminate any tax cost from the incorporation of a business, which obviously involves the transfer of business assets to the new corporation in return for shares of the corporation. The rollover is also available where property is transferred to an established corporation in return for shares of the corporation. To the extent that the transferor receives from the corporation non-share consideration such as cash or a debt (non-share consideration is often called "boot"), there is a genuine realization of the property transferred which should attract normal capital gains treatment. Section 85 accordingly regu-

---

[69]Capital losses are allowed because a deemed disposition under s. 70 is exempted from the definition of a "superficial loss" described in ch. 10, above. In the terminal year, allowable capital losses and net capital losses are deductible against income from all sources, not just taxable capital gains: s. 111(2). See Interpretation Bulletins IT-510, "Transfers and loans of property made after May 22, 1985 to a Related Minor" (1987) and IT-511R, "Interspousal and Certain Other Transfers and Loans of Property" (1994).

[70]Ss. 70(9)–(11), 73(3)–(4). These rollovers to a child of the taxpayer will not be discussed in detail in this book. Capital gains on farming and fishing property are also eligible for the lifetime capital gains exemption discussed under heading 10.2(f), "Tax subsidies for certain investments", above.

lates how much non-share consideration can be received without losing (or partially losing) the rollover. The section is hedged with other restrictions as well, and is elective. The resulting law is quite complex.[71]

The section 85 rollover is commonly used to incorporate a business (to benefit from the limited liability protection of corporations and the low small business rate of tax[72]) and to reorganize corporate holdings.

13.5 — Attribution of income from property

(a) — Nature of attribution rules

Generally, income from property is treated for tax purposes as owned by the owner of the property and is taxed to that person, at his or her rate. The "attribution rules" change the general rule: income that belongs to one person is deemed for tax purposes to belong to another person. The income is said to be "attributed" to that other person. The attribution rules under section 74.1 apply only to income from a property transferred or loaned, directly or indirectly, by a taxpayer to a spouse/common-law partner or a related minor.

Assume that A and B are common-law partners and A is the high-income earner. A gives $1,000 cash to B, and B invests the money in a bond that earns $100 interest every year. The interest income is taxed to A, even if it is legally received by B. The same rule applies if B were a 5-year old daughter of A.

Section 74.1 addresses the taxation of the income earned from the property after it is loaned or transferred. For all other purposes, the loan or transfer is perfectly valid and effective. In the case of a transfer, for example, the transferee will become the owner of the transferred property and of the income or capital gains which it yields. If the transferor has a non-tax reason for making a gift to a family member, then the transferor may still decide to make the gift; indeed, the transferor may be happy to pay the tax on the transferee's income.

In essence, the attribution rules override the principle of taxing each individual as a separate unit. The logic of individual tax unit arguably demands the elimination of all attribution rules. After all, the tax savings that result from income-splitting are purchased at the price of a legal divestment of the income-earning property in favour of another individual. It is true that the transferee is a member of the transferor's family, but if the arguments in favour of the individual as the tax unit are valid, it seems logical to treat the transferor's loss of legal title to and control over

---

[71]There are other corporate rollovers in addition to the s. 85 rollover: a share-for-share exchange (where one corporation takes over the shares of another in return for treasury shares of the acquiring corporation: s. 85.1), corporate reorganizations and amalgamations (ss. 86, 87), and the winding-up of a corporation's wholly owned subsidiary (s. 88(1)). All of these rollovers are automatic and are provided to remove tax impediments to changes in corporate structure that do not involve a genuine realization of capital assets. These rollovers are outside the scope of this book.

[72]See ch. 15, Corporations and Shareholders, below.

income as having tax consequences, especially if the transfer of the property does takes place on a fair market value basis.

(b) — Income from property or substituted property

The attribution rules apply only to income or loss from a property transferred or loaned by the taxpayer.[73] The term "property" is defined in subsection 248(1) in very broad terms. It means "property of any kind whatever whether real or personal or corporeal or incorporeal", and it includes "unless a contrary intention is evident, money". Of course, "money" by itself cannot yield income or capital gains, but as soon as the recipient of the money invests the money in income-yielding investments, the attribution rules will continue to apply to the investments that have been substituted for the money. This is because the rules apply not only to the property transferred or loaned, but also to the "property substituted therefor".

If the recipient of property to which the attribution rules apply sells the property and reinvests the proceeds of sale, the attribution rules continue to cling to the new investments. Income from the new investments (or capital gains from their disposition) will be attributed in the same way as if the investments were the original subjects of the transfer or loan. However, if the recipient of property to which the attribution rules apply invests the income yielded by the transferred property, the income yielded by the investments representing the income ("income on income" or "second generation income") is not attributed. Investments that represent income from the transferred property are neither property transferred nor property substituted therefor. For the same reason, interest on interest that is allowed to accumulate is also not attributed.[74]

Section 74.1 does not attribute income from a business. It is "income from property" that is attributed.[75] The characterization of income earned from the transferred property is thus crucial. The transfer of an apartment building (yielding pro-

---

[73]As discussed under heading 13.5(e) "Attribution from a minor", below, this chapter uses the term "related minor" as a short hand for minors who are either related (for tax purposes) to the taxpayer or are the taxpayer's nieces or nephews.

[74]This is recognized by the CRA in Interpretation Bulletin IT-511R, note 69, above, para. 6. The CRA used to take the same view of income from investments that represented reinvested capital gains realized by the transferee, but it has repented this position. Now the CRA takes the view that an investment representing the entire proceeds of disposition of property transferred or loaned, including any capital gain, is "property substituted" for the property transferred or loaned: IT-511R, para. 27. Therefore, there is no apportionment of the income of the new investment: all of the income, including the income from the reinvested capital gain, is attributed to the transferor.

[75]Since the Act in its other provisions often distinguishes between income from "property" and income from a "business", it was perhaps inevitable that the attribution rules would be interpreted as not applying to income from a business. See *Wertman v. Minister of National Revenue*, [1964] C.T.C. 252, 64 D.T.C. 5158 (Can. Ex. Ct.); *Robins v. Minister of National Revenue*, [1963] C.T.C. 27, 63 D.T.C. 1012 (Can. Ex. Ct.); Interpretation Bulletin IT-510, note 69, above, para. 3; and Interpretation Bulletin IT-511R, note 69, above, para. 5.

perty income) will therefore attract attribution, while the transfer of an apartment hotel (yielding business income) will not.[76] This gap in the attribution rules may be explained on the basis that income from a business does not flow automatically from the ownership of property but requires activity on the part of the transferee (or his or her employees). In view of the difficulty of apportioning the transferee's income from the business between the assets transferred and the transferee's own efforts, the Act does not attribute any of the income from the business.[77]

(c) — "Transfer" or "loan"

The attribution rules apply to income transferred or loaned by a taxpayer to a spouse/common-law partner or a related minor. A "transfer" typically includes a gift or sale. Gifts are the primary targets of these rules. The gift divests the donor of the income produced by the transferred property, and, since the donor receives no consideration, the divested income is not replaced by income from assets received in return for the transferred property. A sale is a typical form of transfer. However, as explained below, a sale for fair market value is exempted from the attribution rules.

A "loan" is specifically referred to in the attribution rules because the courts held that a loan was not a transfer.[78] Even an interest-free loan was held to be outside the attribution rules;[79] and the interest-free loan became a common method of avoiding the attribution rules. The lender would derive no income from the money lent, because no interest was payable. The borrowing spouse or minor would invest the borrowed money in income-producing investments, and the resulting income would not be attributed back to the lender. In this way, a diversion of income was achieved. To prevent this, the Act was amended in 1985 to treat a loan in the same way as a transfer for purposes of the attribution rules.

Indirect transfers and loans are specifically covered by the attribution rules. The word "indirectly" would enable the court to penetrate to the reality of some hitherto unforeseen device for laundering a transaction the effect of which was to divert

---

[76] For the distinction between business and property income, see heading 6.2(f), "Business distinguished from property", above.

[77] There is a rule, however, that deems income (that would otherwise be business income) earned by a limited partner in a limited partnership or a passive partner in a partnership to be property income: s. 96(1.8). This rule was introduced when it became popular to transfer businesses such as hotels and nursing homes to partnerships and then sell them as passive partnership investments which would otherwise be exempt from the attribution rules.

[78] *Dunkelman v. Minister of National Revenue*, [1959] C.T.C. 375, 59 D.T.C. 1242 (Can. Ex. Ct.).

[79] *Oelbaum v. Minister of National Revenue*, [1968] C.T.C. 244, 68 D.T.C. 5176 (Can. Ex. Ct.).

property income to a spouse or a related minor.[80] In addition, the Act specifically deals with "back-to-back transfers and loans", in which it is the intervention of a third party individual that masks the transfer of property to a spouse, common-law partner, or related minor. For example, Partner A could give Blackacre to a third party, who in turn gives the property to Partner B. Or, A could give Blackacre to Third Party, who in turn gives Greenacre to B. In both these examples, there is no direct transfer or loan from A to B, but Third Party is playing a purely intermediary role in what is in substance a gift from A to B. Both cases are specifically provided for by subsection 74.5(6), which treats the transactions as if the property had been given directly by A to B.

(d) — Attribution from a spouse or common-law partner

In the case of property transferred or loaned to a spouse or common-law partner, the attribution will continue so long as the transferee remains the spouse or common-law partner of the transferor, and the transferor remains a resident of Canada. The attribution will end in the event of the termination of the spousal or common-law relationship, or the death of either party, or the permanent departure from Canada of the transferor. Where spouses or common-law partners are living separate and apart because of a breakdown of their marriage or common-law partnership, subsection 74.5(3) provides that attribution of income under section 74.1 is suspended for as long as the separation continues. If the marriage is ended by divorce, the attribution rules will cease to apply.

(e) — Attribution from a minor

The attribution rule under subsection 74.1(2) applies if property is transferred or loaned to or for the benefit of "a person who was under 18 years of age" and who "does not deal with the individual [transferor] at arm's length, or is the niece or nephew of the individual [transferor]". A niece or nephew of a taxpayer is not "related" to the taxpayer, and thus not automatically included in the definition of arm's length.[81] Therefore, paragraph 74.1(2)(b) specifically includes a niece or nephew. The practical effect is that a transfer (or loan) to a minor attracts attribution only if the minor transferee is the child, grandchild, brother, sister, niece or nephew of the transferor.

---

[80] E.g., *Naiberg v. Minister of National Revenue*, [1969] Tax A.B.C. 492, 69 D.T.C. 361 (Can. Tax App. Bd.), where attribution was applied to a complex scheme involving transfers of property among three married couples.

[81] As discussed under heading 13.4(a)(ii), "Arm's length", above, related persons are deemed not to deal at arm's length (s. 251(1)(a)) and individuals are "related" for tax purposes to individuals connected by blood, marriage or adoption (s. 251(2)(a)). Minor individuals connected by blood would include a taxpayer's sibling or child (or other descendant) but not a niece, nephew or cousin (s. 251(6)). Before 1985, there was no requirement that the minor transferee be related to the transferor.

Attribution of income from a related minor will continue for so long as the transferor remains a resident of Canada, and the transferee remains under the age of 18. In the taxation year in which the transferee attains 18, attribution ceases. The death of either transferor or transferee will also bring the attribution to an end.

(f) — Exception for fair market value transactions

The attribution rules do not apply to a transfer or loan of property for fair market value under subsection 74.5(1). The reason for the exemption is that, if fair market value has been paid by the transferee spouse, common-law partner, or related minor, then the transferor has simply substituted another potentially income-producing asset for the one transferred; there is no income-splitting and the transaction is outside the mischief of the attribution rules. However, paragraph 74.5(1)(a) stipulates that the consideration must be equal in value to the property transferred, and paragraph 74.5(1)(b) stipulates that if the consideration includes indebtedness the purchaser must be obliged to pay a commercial rate of interest and must actually regularly pay the interest.[82] These stipulations ensure that artificial sales for inadequate consideration or for consideration in the form of an interest-free debt cannot be used as devices to divert property income from the "vendor" to a "purchaser" who is a spouse,[83] common-law partner or a related minor.

There is a similar exemption for loans at a commercial rate of interest. Subsection 74.5(2) exempts a loan if the loan is made at a commercial rate of interest and if the borrower actually regularly pays the interest.[84] The reason for this exemption is that, if the debt bears interest, the lender has acquired an income-producing asset (the debt) for the money lent; there is no income-splitting and the transaction is outside the mischief of the attribution rules.[85]

13.6 — Attribution of capital gains

Once a property is transferred to a family member, the transferee can use the property to earn income or sell it for a capital gain (or loss, as the case may be). If the transferee is a spouse or common-law partner of the transferor, however, the capital

[82]More precisely, s. 74.5(1)(b) stipulates that the interest rate must be no less than the lesser of (a) the "prescribed rate" that was in effect at the time that the indebtedness was incurred, and (b) the market rate at that time. The prescribed rate is set quarterly under Reg. 4301. The interest agreed upon must be paid not later than 30 days after the end of the year throughout the term of the indebtedness.

[83]In the case of a spouse or common-law partner, s. 74.5(1)(c) adds the further requirement that, on the sale, the transferor must have elected against the s. 73(1) rollover.

[84]The precise stipulations of s. 74.5(2) are the same as those of s. 74.5(1).

[85]If the borrowing spouse, common-law partner, or minor can obtain a rate of return on the investments purchased with the borrowed money that is higher than the interest rate payable to the lender, then the net income is not attributed and an income-split is achieved.

gain or loss is attributed to the transferor pursuant to section 74.2.[86] If the transferee is a related minor, there is no attribution of capital gains.[87] In other words, while the attribution of income under section 74.1 covers loans and transfers to both spouse/common-law partners and children, the attribution of capital gains under section 74.2 is limited to transfers to a spouse or common-law partner.[88]

What are the technical and policy justifications for attributing capital gains from a spouse/common-law partner, but not a child? Technically, although these rules appear incoherent when viewed as stand-alone rules, they make sense when viewed as part of the scheme of the Act that deals with intra-family transfers. You may recall that the tax treatment of the initial transfer from the taxpayer to a spouse/common-law partner and a child is different: a transfer to the former qualifies for a "rollover" under subsection 73(1), but a transfer to a child does not. In the absence of an attribution, a taxpayer could transfer a property with accrued gains to a spouse/common-law partner and divert not only the gains accrued after the transfer, but also the gains accrued prior to the transfer. That would be a complete shift of the transferor's tax liability to the transferee spouse/common-law partner. On a transfer to a child, because capital gains must be accrued to the transferor by virtue of subsection 69(1) and the child is deemed to acquire the property at its fair market value at the time of the transfer, only gains accrued after the transfer are shifted to the child.[89]

Conceptually, the capital gains attribution rule reflects the recognition of marital unit as a tax unit in respect of property transfers, but not the unit of parents and children. In the case of transfers between spouses/common-law partners, the Act effectively ignores the transfers. No real tax consequences arise until the property finally leaves the marital unit. For example, Partner A buys a rental property in Year 1 for $20,000 and earns $3,000 rental income (characterized as income from property) each year. In year 1, A includes the rent in his income. In Year 2, A gives the property to his partner, B, when the fair market value is $21,000 and B receives

---

[86]The attribution of capital gains to a spouse generally ends when the income attribution ends: on death or divorce (when the taxpayer is no longer a spouse) or departure from Canada (when the taxpayer is no longer resident in Canada): see the preamble to sections 74.1 and 74.2. However, if there is a marital break-down and spouses are living separate and apart, income attribution will automatically be suspended but capital gains will not. Both spouses must jointly elect to suspend capital gains attribution. If the separation is ended by reconciliation, the attribution rules will return to force. See subsections 74.5(3) and (4).

[87]This is because s. 74.1(2), like s. 74.1(1), applies only to income or loss from property, and there is no equivalent of s. 74.2 applicable to transfers to minors.

[88]However, capital gains and losses on the transfer of farming property from a taxpayer to his or her child are attributed to the transferor under section 75.1, but this is a special case (explained in the next paragraph). In general there is no attribution of capital gains or losses on a transfer to a minor.

[89]In the case of farming property, fishing property and woodlots there is a rollover on a transfer from the taxpayer to his or her child under subsection 73(3), and that is the special case in which there is attribution of capital gains and losses (section 75.1).

the $3,000 rent. The accrued $500 gain is not taxable to A because of the rollover and B is deemed to have bought the property at a cost equal to $20,000. The $3,000 rental income is attributed to A under section 74.1. When B sells the property in Year 3 for $24,000, the $4,000 capital gain is attributed to A (so is any rental income earned prior to the sale). Consequently, as far as tax law is concerned, the outcome is exactly the same as if A has owned the property until the sale in Year 3.

In contrast, a child is treated by the Act as a separate taxpayer. Transfers of property (other than farming or fishing property or a woodlot) between a parent and her child are treated like fair market value gifts to total strangers. Income from the property transferred is attributed to the parent under section 74.1 because of anti-avoidance concerns: the assumption is that the parent exercises de facto control over the income received from the investment of the property until the child turns 18 years of age. Taxation of capital gains generally occurs only when the property is disposed of. Because the attribution ceases in the year of the minor's eighteenth birthday, a minor could avoid attribution of capital gains very easily, by not disposing of the transferred property until he or she turns 18. One way of precluding this result would be to provide for a "deemed disposition" of the transferred property at fair market value on the minor-transferee's eighteenth birthday. But the policy decision was evidently taken not to introduce that much complexity into the system. The result is that the Act makes no provision for attribution of capital gains derived by a transferee-minor when logic would dictate it should. When the rule was designed in 1972, very few minors earned capital gains. At that time, there were very few mutual funds which would allow investors to invest to earn capital gains annually on a diversified portfolio of "growth" investments. The situation is quite different today and investing in growth mutual funds which earn capital gains is one of the main ways that parents income split with their minor children.

13.7 — Family trust

In the case of transfers of property directly from a taxpayer to a spouse/common-law partner, the aforementioned attribution rules determine which of the two parties (transferor or transferee) should be taxed on the income or capital gains. Transfers of property to a trust involve three parties who are potential taxpayers. The owner of a property (settlor) transfers it to a trustee to administer, with instructions for distributing the income, currently or at a later date, to one or more beneficiaries. Should the settlor, trustee (or the trust), or one of the beneficiaries be taxed on the income?

As discussed in more detail in Chapter 17, below, a trust is taxed as an individual. Inter vivos trusts are always taxed at the top marginal rate (currently 29%) to prevent the splitting of income between the settlor and the beneficiaries. However, if a trust distributes income to the beneficiaries, the amount of distribution is deductible to the trust, but taxable to the beneficiary.[90]

Where the beneficiary is a spouse/common-law partner or related minor of the settlor, the income from the trust is attributed to the settlor. The attribution rules under section 74.1 specifically include "indirect transfers" through the use of a trust. As such, they cannot be avoided by the interposition of a trust between the transferor and the transferee.[91] The basic attribution rules are supplemented by more specific rules under section 74.3.

Without going into detail, the results could be summarized as follows:

1. Where the trust's property income is paid or payable to a spouse, common-law partner, or a related minor, there will be attribution under subsection 74.1(1) or (2). Where the trust's capital gains are paid or payable to a spouse or common-law partner, there will be attribution under section 74.2. This is so, even if the payment is the exercise of a discretionary power by the trustee.
2. Where income is not paid or payable to a spouse, common-law partner, or related minor, there will be no attribution. This is so, even if the income is being accumulated in the trust for the ultimate benefit of a spouse, common-law partner, or related minor. The income is taxed in the trust at the top marginal rate.

In addition, the trust income may be attributed to the settlor under subsection 75(2). This provision operates to attribute to the settlor income or taxable capital gains from property transferred to a trust in which a settlor has reserved to himself or herself a power to revoke the trust, or a power to change the beneficiaries, or a power to direct or veto dispositions of the trust property. Attribution occurs regardless of who are the beneficiaries of the trust; subsection 75(2) is not confined to trusts for spouses and related minors. The idea is that a settlor should not be able to divert taxable income away to the beneficiaries of a trust while continuing to retain substantial control over the trust.

13.8 — Family corporation

Section 74.4 is an anti-avoidance rule which is designed to deter taxpayers from attempting to income-split by transferring or loaning property to a corporation in cases where the transferor's spouse, common-law partner, or a related minor is a "specified shareholder" (generally speaking, owning 10% or more of the shares). Before 1985, there was a question whether the attribution rules applied in this situa-

[90]The attribution of income from property applies to property settled on trust for a spouse or related minor. This was decided by the courts in 1948: see *Fasken Estate v. Minister of National Revenue* (1948), [1948] C.T.C. 265, 49 D.T.C. 491 (Can. Ex. Ct.). Since then the position has been reinforced by express references to a trust in the rules in the Act.

[91]The pre-1985 rules were not sufficiently specific to provide clear answers to all the attribution issues raised by trusts for the benefit of spouses and minors.

tion, because a corporation is an entity distinct from its shareholders, who have no proprietary interest in property that has been transferred or loaned to the corporation. Section 74.4 now applies to such situations, but only if "one of the main purposes of the transfer or loan [to the corporation] may reasonably be considered to be to reduce the income of the individual [transferor] and to benefit . . . [a spouse, common-law partner, or related minor of the transferor]". This "purpose test" involves an inquiry into the intention of the transferor at the time of making the transfer or loan to the corporation. This inquiry injects into section 74.4 an element of uncertainty that is absent from the other attribution rules; the other rules simply rely on the objective legal effect of the transfer or loan.

Another unique feature of section 74.4 is that it stipulates the amount to be attributed to the transferor, and that amount is derived by applying the prescribed quarterly interest rate[92] to the value of the property transferred or loaned.[93] This arbitrary figure is attributed regardless of whether or not a dividend is paid by the corporation to the spouse, common-law partner, or minor.[94] Indeed, if a dividend is paid to the spouse, common-law partner, or related minor, there is no provision to exclude the dividend from the income of the spouse or minor, and the recipient will have to report the dividend for tax purposes. That amounts to double taxation, because the transferor also has to report the arbitrary attributed figure. Double taxation is scrupulously avoided in the other attribution rules, each of which stipulates that income attributed to the transferor is deemed not to be the income of the actual recipient (spouse, common-law partner, or minor).[95]

Section 74.4 exempts a transfer or loan to a "small business corporation", which is defined in section 248 as a CCPC with assets "all or substantially all" (generally considered to mean 90 per cent or more) of which were "used in an active business carried on primarily in Canada". This exemption reflects the policy of the attribution rules to apply to income from property, and not income from a business.[96]

---

[92]The prescribed rate is set quarterly under Reg. 4301.

[93]This is the maximum amount to be taxed in the transferor's hands. If consideration is received that is not shares or debt, this is deducted from the value of the property transferred or loaned before applying the prescribed rate: see definitions of "outstanding amount" and "excluded consideration" in s. 74.4. If the transferor has received income on the shares or debt, this income — 5/4 × non-eligible dividends, 1.44 (in 2010) × eligible dividends as well as any interest income — is deducted from the amount that must otherwise be attributed: see s. 74.2(2).

[94]The attributed figure is reduced by the amount of any dividends (grossed-up) or interest paid by the corporation to the transferor (but not to the spouse or minor for whose benefit the transfer or loan was made).

[95]Note, however, s. 160 makes the transferee as well as the transferor liable, and empowers the Minister to assess the transferee. Presumably, this power would be invoked only if the tax could not be collected from the transferor.

[96]This policy is explained under heading 13.5(b), "Income from property or substituted property", above.

However, the narrowness of the definition of a small business corporation makes section 74.4 somewhat under-inclusive in its pursuit of this policy. A loan or transfer to a company that was not Canadian-controlled, or was not private, or was using more than 10 per cent of its assets to derive property income, could attract section 74.4 even though the company's income was wholly or mainly derived from carrying on a business.

13.9 — Income diversion

The attribution rules of sections 74.1 through 74.5 are designed to stop income splitting by the transfer of income-producing property from a high-income taxpayer to his or her spouse, common-law partner, and related minor.

They do not apply to transfers of property to other non-arm's length persons (such as parents, adult children or siblings). Neither do these attribution rules apply to transactions that do not involve a transfer or loan of "property". The rules discussed below are intended to address some of the income-diversion arrangements. As with the attribution rules, the income diversion rules override the legally effective arrangements in allocating the income to its "rightful" owner.

(a) — Indirect payment

The first general rule precluding diversion of income from high-income earners to lower-income earnings is subsection 56(2) which provides:

> A payment or transfer of property made pursuant to the direction of, or with the concurrence of, a taxpayer to some other person for the benefit of the taxpayer or as a benefit that the taxpayer desired to have conferred on the other person ... shall be included in computing the taxpayer's income to the extent that it would be if the payment or transfer had been made to the taxpayer.

It is useful to view this provision as having four conditions that must be met in order for it to apply:

1. there is a payment or transfer of property to a person other than the taxpayer;
2. the payment or transfer is at the direction of or with the concurrence of the taxpayer;
3. the payment or transfer is for the taxpayer's own benefit or for the benefit of some other person upon whom the taxpayer wished to have the benefit conferred; and
4. the payment or transfer would have been made to the taxpayer if it had not been made to that other person.[97]

[97] Adapted from the list of conditions set out by Cattanach J. in *Murphy v. R.*, [1980] C.T.C 386, 80 D.T.C. 6314 (Fed. T.D.) which has been applied by the courts in dealing with the application of s. 56(2) in subsequent cases.

When subsection 56(2) applies, it will render diversions of income by a taxpayer to another person ineffective. For example, an employee might direct the employer to pay all or part of the employee's salary to a creditor of the employee. Or a creditor might direct the debtor to make payments of interest to the creditor's mother. Or a consultant might bill clients (for work done by the consultant) in the name of a company controlled by the consultant. All of these arrangements are perfectly legal and effective for other purposes, but subsection 56(2) makes them ineffective for tax purposes because they meet the four conditions.[98] These arrangements will not shift the tax liability away from the person who is entitled to the source of the income. In each case, the taxpayer would have to report the income, even though he or she did not actually receive it.

The application of subsection 56(2) to situations involving shareholders receiving dividends was considered by the Supreme Court of Canada in *McClurg v. Canada* (1990)[99] and *Neuman v. R.* (1998).[100] In *McClurg*, the taxpayer and an associate had incorporated a company to operate a truck dealership. The corporation had three classes of shares, two of which were held entirely by the taxpayer and his associate. The third class was held entirely by the taxpayer's wife and the wife of his associate. The articles of incorporation contained a discretionary dividend clause that entitled each class of shares to dividends only at the discretion of the directors. The taxpayer and his associate, who were the sole directors, exercised their power under this clause to declare a dividend of $10,000 only on the class of shares held by the wives. The corporation accordingly paid this dividend to the wives, and paid nothing to the taxpayer and his associate who held the other classes of shares. In assessing the taxpayer's income, the Minister applied subsection 56(2) and attributed to him a portion of the dividend that had been paid to the taxpayer's wife. The Supreme Court of Canada, by a majority, held that the dividend payment in *McClurg* escaped attribution under subsection 56(2). According to Dickson C.J. for the majority, the exercise by the directors of their power under the discretionary dividend clause in the company's articles of incorporation should not be regarded as a payment caught by subsection 56(2). Had no dividend been declared, the income would have remained in the corporation; it would not have gone to the taxpayer. Because this fourth and last condition in subsection 56(2) was not met, this provision did not apply. Subsection 56(2) was therefore blocked by the corporate veil, and the discretionary dividend clause was held to be successful in diverting income away from the higher-income taxpayer to his lower-income spouse.

In *McClurg*, Dickson C.J., made a puzzling reference to the fact that the taxpayer's wife had been active in the business: he described the dividend payment to her as a

---

[98]The taxpayer must have "desired" to confer a benefit on the recipient. Where there is no evidence of such a desire, as where a company transferred a property to Father at the direction of Son for a price that Son did not realize was less than fair market value, s. 56(2) does not apply: *Ascot Enterprises v. R.* (1995), [1996] 1 C.T.C. 384, 96 D.T.C. 6015 (Fed. C.A.).

[99]Note 6, above.

[100]Note 7, above.

"legitimate *quid pro quo*" for what she had contributed.[101] Since a dividend is income from property — the return on the capital invested in the company by the shareholder — it seems odd to characterize it as a *quid pro quo* for services performed for the company. This statement also seemed irrelevant to the *ratio decidendi* in the case: had no dividend been declared, the income would have remained in the corporation and would not necessarily have gone to the taxpayer. This issue of the relevance of the contribution made to the company by the shareholder was subsequently settled in *Neuman*. In the *Neuman* case, unlike *McClurg*, the recipient wife had made no contribution to the company other than her subscription to the shares on which the dividend was paid and it was held that subsection 56(2) did not apply.[102]

In *Ferrel*,[103] the Federal Court of Appeal considered applying subsection 56(2) to a situation where a trust was set up to earn business income and found that it did not apply. In *Ferrel*, management fees were paid to a trust by a holding company controlled by the taxpayer and in which the trust also owned shares. The beneficiaries of the trust were the taxpayer's children. The taxpayer, the trust and the company had entered into an agreement under which the trust (through the taxpayer) provided services to the company in return for a management fee. In *Ferrel*, the court cited the Supreme Court of Canada's dictum in *Neuman* that "the Courts should not be quick to embellish tax avoidance provisions .... but should await precise and specific measures from legislators to combat any perceived mischief".[104]

(b) — Assignment of income

Subsection 56(4) attributes income to the taxpayer where the taxpayer has assigned the rights to receive income to a person with whom the taxpayer is not at arm's length. For example, an author might assign a right to royalties to his or her child (whether or not that child is a minor); the royalty income will be attributed back to the author by virtue of subsection 56(4).

(c) — Interest free or low interest loans

Subsection 56(4.1) applies to non-arm's length loans that bear little or no interest and the borrower invests the loan in an income-producing property, but only when "it may reasonably be considered that one of the main reasons for making the loan . . . was to reduce or avoid tax". It attributes the income from the property to the lender.

---

[101] Note 6, above, para. 44.

[102] The facts of *Neuman*, note 7, above, arose before 1985, when s. 74.4 was added to the Act. S. 74.4 would now attribute to the husband an amount of income determined by the formula in that section, unless the corporation qualifies as a "small business corporation" throughout the year.

[103] [1999] 2 C.T.C. 101, 99 D.T.C. 5111 (Fed. C.A.).

[104] *Ibid.*, para. 1.

Interest free or low interest loans extended by a taxpayer to his or her spouse/common-law partner and a related minor are governed by the income attribution rules under section 74.1. Subsection 56(4.1) differs from 74.1 in three important respects. First, subsection 56(4.1) applies only where the lender of the money had a tax avoidance reason for the loan; if the loan can be explained by a non-tax avoidance reason, then subsection 56(4.1) will not apply. Subsection 74.1 does not have such a purpose test. Second, subsection 56(4.1) applies to transactions that divert income to *any* non-arm's length individual and not just to spouses, common-law partners and related minors. For example, subsection 56(4.1) will catch a loan to an adult child. Third, subsection 56(4.1) applies only to loans and not to outright gifts. As a result, a loan to an adult child of the taxpayer would be caught by subsection 56(4.1), while an outright gift to an adult child is neither caught by that section nor by any other provision of the Act.[105] This has led one commentator to argue that subsection 56(4.1) favours the wealthy, who can "afford parting irrevocably with their capital by making gifts rather than loans to their children".[106]

13.10 — Kiddie tax

(a) — Rationale

The decline in the number of two-spouse, one-income families has changed the focus of the attribution rules. It has reduced the importance of the rules as they apply to spouses or common-law partners, and increased the importance of the rules as they apply to minor children. This is because where both spouses or common-law partners earn similar incomes, there is little scope for income-splitting between the spouses or partners and it is the diversion of income to minor children that becomes most attractive.[107] Not surprisingly then, it is the diversion of large amounts of investment income to minor children that is the focus of the most recent addition to attribution rules: the special tax on minor children under section 120.4 (the "kiddie tax") that took effect in 2000.

(b) — Application

Over the years, three major tax planning arrangements have allowed taxpayers owning businesses to split substantial amounts of income with their minor children through family trusts with these children as beneficiaries. To stop these arrangements, the "kiddie tax" or tax on "split income" was introduced for 2000 and subse-

---

[105]A sale in return for a non-interest-bearing promissory note probably also avoids the section, because a sale on deferred payment terms has not in the past been treated as a loan for tax purposes: Goodman, Tax Column (1988) 9 *Estates and Trusts J.* 77, 79.

[106]*Ibid.*

[107]Because the personal tax credit for a dependant child that is not reduced by the income that the child earns (as the case for the credit is for a dependant spouse), there is no tax cost to income splitting with a child, except where the child is being claimed as a spouse equivalent or eligible dependant (s. 118(1)(b)).

quent years.[108] The kiddie tax is a special tax at the top rate on "split income" (as defined) received by minor children (section 120.4). No tax credits can be claimed against the "kiddie tax" except for the dividend tax credit or foreign tax credit, if applicable. The tax is similar to what is paid by an *inter vivos* trust: it is at the top rate with no personal tax credit. The rationale is that the tax is intended to equal the tax that the parent who is taxable in the highest tax bracket would have paid on the income if not for the income split.

The four planning arrangements affected are as follows:

1. The first arrangement is similar to the one that we saw in *McClurg* and *Neuman*: an arrangement where a trust established for a minor child's benefit owns shares of a private corporation paying dividends. These arrangements allow dividend income to be diverted to a minor, with substantial savings in tax.

2. The second arrangement is where a trust established for a minor child's benefit owns an interest in a partnership earning business income by providing property[109] or services to a related entity. For example, the trust for the child of a lawyer may be a partner in a limited partnership that provides services to the parent's law firm. The partnership will buy services on behalf of the law firm and then sell them to the law firm charging a management fee with a mark-up (generally 15 per cent).[110] The mark-up is retained as a profit in the limited partnership, allocated to each trust that is a partner and is taxed in the hands of the child by having the trust make the income paid or payable to the child.[111]

---

[108]The idea for this type of tax is borrowed from other countries, such as the United States and Australia, which use a "kiddie tax" instead of attribution rules to prevent individuals from saving taxes by income splitting with minors. Because the Canadian tax is layered on top of other attribution rules, it is more targeted than either of the Australian or U.S. kiddie taxes and simpler in design. The Australian and the U.S. kiddie taxes apply to unearned income in general and are more complex.

[109]The words "property or" are added in accordance with amendments to s. 120.4 proposed to be applicable to taxation years that begin after December 20, 2002. The amendments were contained in former Bill C-10 (2007), a technical amendments bill which, according to the 2010 federal budget papers, is to be reintroduced into Parliament. They are included in the text in the interests of clarity and caution. Assuming these amendments are passed, the kiddie tax would apply to income from property provided to a related entity as well as services. Examples include: (1) rental income earned by a partnership (or trust) owning real estate that is rented to a related entity and (2) interest income earned by a partnership (or trust) loaning money to a related entity. Note that income earned on property provided to other entities would not be subject to kiddie tax but might be subject to the normal attribution rules under 74.1(2) and 74.3.

[110]A mark-up of 15% is generally not challenged by the CRA.

[111]The use of a limited partnership is an improvement over a management corporation because it avoids the imposition of corporate income taxes on the income to be diverted to family members while allowing the family members to maintain limited liability status simi-

3. The third arrangement is one where a trust established for a minor child's benefit operates a business that earns its income from property or services provided to a related entity. This was the arrangement used successfully in *Ferrel.*[112]

4. The fourth arrangement is where the minor child (or a trust established for his or her benefit) owns shares of a private corporation and the minor child receives a shareholder benefit under section 15, such as a loan from a private corporation that triggers a taxable benefit to the shareholder under subsection 15(2).[113]

All four of these income-splitting techniques are still possible starting in the year that a child has his or her eighteenth birthday.

This special tax is layered over the current system of attribution rules. Income that is subject to the kiddie tax will not be subject to the attribution rules and will not be subject to Part I tax. Parents are jointly and severally liable for the kiddie tax.

The kiddie tax only applies to the income earned in the four types of arrangements discussed above. It does not apply, for example, to dividend income earned on shares of public corporations, interest income, employment income, or capital gains. As well, the kiddie tax rules do not apply to situations where a trust or partnership earns business income from services provided to an unrelated entity. The kiddie tax also does not apply to minors who have no Canadian resident parent, to income from property inherited from a deceased parent or to income from property inherited from persons other than a parent if the minor is a full-time student at a post-secondary institution or is eligible for the disability credit.

---

lar to that which they would have as shareholders of a corporation. The taxation of corporations and shareholders, partnerships, and trusts is discussed in chs. 15, 16 and 17, respectively.

[112]Note 19, above.

[113]See heading 5.7(b), "Loans", above.

14
TAXABLE INCOME AND TAX FOR INDIVIDUALS

14.1 — Tax for individuals

(a) — Computation of tax payable

Individuals compute their tax liability (the amount of tax payable) by taking the following steps:[1]

(i) determining "net income";

(ii) determining "taxable income"; and

(iii) determining "tax payable" by multiplying taxable income by tax rates and subtracting applicable tax credits.

The concept of "income", income from each of the enumerated sources and the statutory rules for "other income" and "other deductions" have been the topic of chapters 4 to 13. This chapter shows how the "end result" (positive or negative) of this source-by-source computation is used to determine an individual's tax. If this net income can be imagined as a cake, this chapter discusses the rules that determine the size of the slice for the government. Naturally, fundamental economic and social policies underlie the design of these rules.

The key statutory rules discussed in this chapter include: section 3 of the *Income Tax Act* (the "Act"), which measures a taxpayer's economic income for the year; subsection 2(2) which requires refinement of net income for the purpose of determining a taxpayer's tax base — taxable income — by adding or subtracting items contained in Division C; the basic Division C deductions (sections 110, 110.6, 111 and 114); and the rules for rates and tax credits in Division E and E.1 (sections 117 to 127.55).

---

[1]Corporations compute their tax liability in the same steps and, in many cases, under the same rules. As discussed in Chapter 15, however, the rules in Division C and the tax rates and credits applicable to corporations are very different from those for individuals.

(b) — Staging deductions

Mechanically, the amount of tax payable is the end result of a lengthy process of deductions. In addition to the deductions allowed for expenses incurred for the purpose of earning income (i.e., those discussed in Chapter 5, 8, and 9), there are a variety of deductions allowed for policy reasons. As discussed below, these deductions generally fall into two categories: losses and policy-deductions. The Act allows these deductions to be made at all three stages of computing tax liability.

At the first stage of computing income under section 3, taxpayers can deduct subdivision e amounts (e.g., child care expense and moving expense)[2] and losses sustained in the current year.

At the second stage of computing taxable income, Division C allows deductions for losses sustained in other years (i.e. loss carryovers) (section 111), welfare payments, workers' compensation payments (paragraph 110(1)(f)), benefits from employee stock options (paragraph 110(1)(d)), capital gains from the disposition of qualified properties (section 110.6)), income earned during part of the year when the taxpayer is a non-resident (section 114), and other items discussed below.

At the final stage of computing tax payable, Division E allows a final set of deductions, called "credits" because they are dollar-for-dollar reduction in tax liability. These credits are provided for tuition fees, medical expenses, and a large number of personal expenses.

Why does the Act allow these policy deductions at differing stages? There are perhaps two answers to this question. The first lies in the differing utility of each of the concepts of "net income" and "taxable income". The second is the advantage of using a tax credit over a tax deduction to provide fair and equitable tax relief for individuals. Both are explained in more detail below.

14.2 — Tax policy

(a) — Ability to pay

A taxpayer's ability to pay should be taken into consideration in determining the tax base. Since a loss naturally reduces the taxpayer's ability to pay, it should, therefore, be deductible in computing the tax base. The ability to pay principle may also justify the allowance of certain personal expenses, such as medical expenses, and claims in support of dependents. For example, the credit for medical expenses[3] could be justified on the ground that a taxpayer's ability to pay is reduced by the extraordinary and perhaps crushing, unexpected and largely involuntary financial burden of medical expenses. Another way of looking at the credit is that such expenses are not made for personal consumption but to repair (human) capital. Of course, the credit can also be perceived as a tax relief. Other examples are the cred-

[2] Subdivision e deductions are discussed in ch. 12.

[3] S. 118.2.

its for a spouse and dependent children.[4] The financial obligation to support a spouse, common-law partner, and dependent children reduces a taxpayer's ability to pay.

(b) — Economic efficiency and neutrality

The logic of taxing net income requires that losses be deductible. To earn income from a business or investment, a taxpayer incurs risks which sometimes result in a loss as opposed to a profit. It is a cost of doing business or investing. For this and the reasons explained immediately below, losses realized in a taxation year should be deductible (at some point) in computing taxable income.

To tax a gain but not allow an offset for losses would bias the Act against risk taking. The principle of neutrality requires that tax be "neutral" as to risk and investment decisions and thus a deduction for losses in gain-seeking activities or transactions is required. Otherwise, risky investments will go unmade or will require a much higher rate of return to compensate for the unmitigated risk of loss if unsuccessful. Because the economic or investment cycle rarely coincides with the taxation year, losses incurred in other years are deductible in computing taxable income of a particular year. Thus, the loss carryover rules overcome the arbitrary use of "taxation year" for computing tax liability.[5]

(c) — Stimulation of private activities

Going beyond neutrality, the Act provides assistance to promote certain economic and social activities through tax expenditure rules. An obvious example is investment in an incorporated small business: a Canadian controlled private corporation (CCPC) carrying on active business in Canada. First, active business income earned by a CCPC is taxed at a preferential rate in the hands of the corporation.[6] Second, shareholders are taxed preferentially if they realize capital gains from the sale of qualified small business corporation (QSBC) shares as a result of the lifetime capital gains exemption under section 110.6. Third, the tax system subsidizes capital losses realized by holding debt or shares of a "small business corporation" by allowing the unrestricted deduction of allowable business investment losses (ABIL) under paragraph 3(d).[7] Incorporated small businesses are considered worthy of tax subsidies because of the economic externalities they create (such as employment for Canadians) and the disadvantages they face raising capital.

---

[4]Ss. 118(1)(a), (b).

[5]For a discussion of "taxation year" and its implications for fluctuating income, see heading 1.5(c), "Timing and accounting period", above.

[6]See heading 15.5(d), "Active business income of Canadian-controlled private corporations", below.

[7]See heading 14.4(d)(iii), "Allowable business investment losses," below.

Other examples are the employee stock option deduction,[8] which reduces the net amount included in income to one-half of the stock option benefit, the home relocation loan deduction, which subsidizes the interest benefit related to employee relocation loans,[9] the deduction for working and living in remote regions,[10] and the exemption for scholarship income and the various credits for post-secondary education.[11]

Finally, the Act encourages donations to charities by exempting the gain on the gift of certain property and by providing a tax credit for individuals.[12] The justification for charitable donations can be made on grounds of social policy and cost efficiency. The tax expenditure incidentally relieves government of some welfare costs it otherwise would be called upon to bear and gives taxpayers more control over the type of causes that they consider worthy of support. As a result, the donated dollars may be more efficiently and directly spent on socially desirable activities.

14.3 — Net income

(a) — Utility of "net income" concept

Why are some items deducted under Division C in computing taxable income and others deducted under Division B in computing net income? The reason is that the concept of "net income" is intended to correspond closely to the taxpayer's economic income so that some of the tax subsidies can be based on it. For example, the GST credit, the child tax benefit and the proposed Working Income Tax Benefit (WITB) (as well as certain refundable income-tested provincial credits) are based on the net income of the taxpayer and the taxpayer's spouse or common-law partner[13] Similarly, the tax credits that can be claimed for a dependent spouse or common-law partner or other dependant are reduced dollar for dollar if the dependent has "net income" over a specified amount.[14]

Net income thus includes receipts that are considered to constitute economic income, such as social assistance and workers' compensation. It is this net income amount that determines the taxpayer's eligibility for tax subsidies. Ultimately, the taxpayer is not required to pay tax on social assistance and workers' compensation because paragraph 110(1)(f) (in Division C) allows a deduction for these amounts in computing taxable income.

---

[8]Ss. 110(1)(d) and (d.1), discussed under heading 5.7(b), "Loans", above.

[9]110(1)(j), discussed under heading 5.7(b), "Loans", above.

[10]S. 110.7.

[11]Ss. 118.5, 118.8 and 118.9, discussed under heading 14.7(b), "Non-refundable credits", below.

[12]As discussed in ch. 15, there is a Division C deduction for charitable donations (rather than a tax credit) in the case of corporations: s. 110.1.

[13]See heading 14.7(c), "Refundable credits", below

[14]See heading 14.7(b), "Non-refundable credits", below.

(b) — Aggregation of income from all sources

Section 3 is the closest the Act comes to defining "income". Paragraph 3(a) requires income to have a "source", and paragraph 3(b) specifically includes taxable capital gains from the disposition of property. Therefore, if an individual is employed part-time, carries on a business, and owns some investments, she must first compute her income or loss from each of the employment, business and property. She must add the income from each source under paragraph 3(a) and recognize the losses separately under paragraph 3(d). If she sells some investments and has capital gains or losses, she must compute the amount of taxable capital gain and/or allowable capital losses. If she has both taxable capital gains and allowable capital losses, the losses are offset against the taxable captain gains.

Paragraph 3(c) then aggregates the income amounts from each source and the net taxable capital gains from all dispositions of property, and allows subdivision e deductions (which are not otherwise deductible in computing income under paragraph 3(a) or (b), but are allowed because of policy concerns).[15]

Finally, paragraph 3(d) allows the deduction of current year losses from office, employment, business, or property, and the deduction of allowable business investment losses. Paragraph 3(e) provides that the amount determined under paragraph 3(d) is the taxpayer's "income" for the year. If the paragraph 3(d) amount is negative, paragraph 3(f) will deem the amount of income to be nil; "income" can never be a negative figure. As discussed later, the negative paragraph 3(d) amount is a "non-capital loss" that can be carried over to other years.

Consequently, income under section 3 is "net income" in the sense that current year losses are offset against current year income. Because capital gains are taxed more preferably than income gains, capital losses are "quarantined"; capital losses are deductible only from capital gains. Where capital losses exceed capital gains, the excessive amount is a "net capital loss" that can be carried over to other years.

14.4 — Losses

(a) — Characterization by nature

A "loss" for the purposes of the Act is generally the "negative" figure of computing income pursuant to subdivisions a to c of Division B of Part I of the Act. Specifically, it is the amount under subsection 5(2) (loss from office or employment), subsection 9(2) loss from business or property, and paragraph 39(1)(b) (capital loss).

In the case of an office or employment, however, a loss would be very unusual, because the few available deductions would rarely exceed the income. In the case of a business or property, however, a loss is a common occurrence. This is especially the case with a business, where expenses may exceed expectations or revenue may fall below expectations or both. Even a successful business may incur losses in the early (start-up) years, or for temporary periods; of course many businesses are unsuccessful, consistently incurring losses until they are wound up. Income from

[15] Subdivision e deductions are discussed in ch. 12, above.

property is obviously far less risky than income from business, but property can yield losses, especially where the property has been acquired with borrowed money, in which case the interest expense, when added to other carrying costs, may exceed (for example) the rent from the real estate or the dividends from the shares.

The character of a loss is as important in tax law as the character of income. For the purpose of recognition in computing net income and taxable income, losses are broadly characterized as "non-capital losses" (or losses on revenue account, or regular losses) and "capital losses" (or losses on capital account). Non-capital losses are those arising from the four enumerated sources under paragraph 3(a). Capital losses are losses from the disposition of capital property where the proceeds of disposition are less than the adjusted cost base and any selling expenses. This generally occurs when a property is sold at a price below the cost of acquisition. Capital losses from personal-use property (PUP losses) are denied and losses from listed personal property (LPP losses) are restricted to LPP gains.[16] Business losses from farming are also restricted because of anti-avoidance concerns. In contrast, some capital losses, referred to as "ABILs", are not subject to the quarantine rule and can offset regular income. These rules are discussed below.

(b) — Attribution of losses

Losses are deductible by the taxpayer who incurs the losses. Losses cannot be transferred from one taxpayer to another. The attribution rules discussed in chapter 13 apply equally to losses realized from the transferred property or substituted property.

If an individual taxpayer incorporated a business, and the corporation had a business loss, the individual taxpayer could not deduct the corporation's loss. If the corporation had no positive income to offset the loss, then the loss would not be deductible by the corporation. The loss could be carried over to other years by the corporation, in accordance with the loss carryover rules that are described later. But, if the corporation never became successful, the loss carryover would not be able to be used.[17]

---

[16]See heading 10.7, "Stop-loss rules", above.

[17]The deductibility of losses must be taken into account in determining whether or not to incorporate a business, especially if start-up losses are anticipated. It may be prudent to delay incorporation until it is clear that the business is successful. For the same reason, it is often imprudent for a corporation with more than one business to organize the different businesses as separate (subsidiary) corporations. If the separate businesses are operated within a single corporation, then, if losses are incurred by one of the businesses, the losses can be deducted from the profits of a profitable business. If the unprofitable business was operated by a separate corporation, the losses may be wasted for tax purposes because the Act does not permit the consolidation of the income and losses of related corporations; each corporation is taxed separately. In order for the loss carryovers and losses to be used on a prospective basis, the two corporations must be amalgamated so that the profits and losses can be earned in the same legal entity. If the two companies were a parent and a subsidiary, a wind-up under s. 88 could be used as an alternative to an amalgamation. Certain restrictions apply if control of

(c) — Limitations on deductions for losses

(i) — Personal losses

Personal losses are losses resulting from personal consumption. The Act contains no specific provisions denying the deduction of personal losses but paragraph 3(d) limits the deduction of losses to those incurred from an income source. This is an implicit prohibition against the deduction of personal losses as personal losses are not from any of the income sources. The result corresponds to the rule in paragraph 18(1)(h) disallowing any deduction of personal expenses.

Perhaps the most significant cause of personal losses is the depreciation in the value of household durables and other personal effects (referred to as "personal-use property" under the Act). In this respect, subparagraph 40(2)(g)(iii) deems losses from the disposition of personal-use property, other than listed personal property, to be nil.

(ii) — Quarantined capital losses

Allowable capital losses are "quarantined" in the sense that they can only be deducted from taxable capital gains (paragraph 3(b)). To the extent that the allowable capital losses exceed taxable capital gains (i.e., paragraph 3(b) is negative), the excess is carried back three years and forward indefinitely (as a Division C deduction), but can be used only to offset taxable capital gains. Losses from listed personal property are further restricted: they can only be deducted against gains from the disposition of listed personal property in the year; any excess can be carried back three years and forward seven years.[18]

(iii) — Farm losses

Losses from the business of farming are generally treated in the same way as losses from other businesses. However, the deductibility of farming losses is limited if the taxpayer is a part-time farmer[19] or a hobby farmer.[20] For the part-time farmer, the principal restriction is contained in section 31. A part-time farmer is defined in these terms: "Where a taxpayer's chief source of income for a taxation year is neither farming nor a combination of farming and some other source of income . . .". The phrase "chief source of income" is not defined in the Act, and is rather obscure considering that the question of the recognition of farming losses arises only in the case of a taxpayer who has no income at all from farming, but has

---

the loss corporation has changed since the losses were realized: see heading 14.5(b)(v), "Change of corporate control", below.

[18]S. 41(1). See also heading 10.7(d), "Listed personal property losses", above.

[19]This is the person referred to in s. 31 as having his or her "chief source of income" from farming.

[20]See *Moldowan v. Minister of National Revenue* (1977), (sub nom. *Moldowan v. R.*) [1977] C.T.C. 310, 77 D.T.C. 5213 (S.C.C.); Interpretation Bulletin IT-322R, "Farm losses" (1978).

instead incurred a loss. In *Moldowan v. R.* (1977),[21] the Supreme Court of Canada held that a taxpayer's "chief source of income" was not to be determined solely by comparing the amount of income earned from farming with the amount earned from other sources. It depended as well on the taxpayer's lifestyle. Thus, a taxpayer for whom farming was the main occupation in terms of time and effort would be held to have farming as his or her "chief source of income", even if other sources of income tended to be more profitable. Such a taxpayer would be free of the restrictions of section 31.

The obscure reference in section 31 to a taxpayer whose chief source of income is not "a combination of farming and some other source of income" contemplates the case of the taxpayer whose main occupation is farming, but also has some ancillary sources of income. This was also the decision in *Moldowan*. It renders the combination phrase redundant, since such a taxpayer's chief source of income would be farming anyway.

In the end, section 31 applies to the taxpayer who operates a farm as a sideline business. The typical case is the taxpayer (often in a high tax bracket) whose chief source of income has nothing to do with farming (for example, a city lawyer), but who also owns a farm. If that person could deduct all farming losses, the deduction would enable him or her to shelter from tax some professional income. Of course, even if the losses only cost the taxpayer 50 cents on the dollar, that is still a cost. However, the farm may also be a source of recreation for the taxpayer and it may be appreciating in value (an appreciation which will eventually be taxed only as a capital gain). Section 31 accordingly restricts the deductibility of a part-time farmer's farming losses.

Section 31 permits the recognition of the first $2,500 of losses and one-half of the next $12,500 of losses from farming. The result is that the part-time farmer cannot deduct more than $8,750 of farming losses from his or her non-farming income in any taxation year, and can deduct that much only if the farm suffered a loss of $15,000 or more. For example, a taxpayer who incurs a loss from farming of $5,500 would be entitled to recognize a loss for the current year of $2,500 plus one-half of $3,000 ($5,500 — $2,500 = $3,000), that is, a total of $4,000. The balance of the loss, namely, $1,500, would be disallowed. The portion of the loss from farming that is disallowed by section 31 (in our example, $1,500) is described by the provision as the taxpayer's "restricted farm loss" for the year and can be carried over to other years but only against farming income.[22]

Section 31 applies only where the part-time farming operation is conducted with a reasonable expectation of profit. If there is no reasonable expectation of profit, the losses are completely disallowed as "hobby" losses. It is certainly arguable that, where a farm is operated with a reasonable expectation of profit, any losses should be fully recognized. However, in the case of the part-time hobby farmer, the farm,

---

[21] *Ibid.*

[22] Carryover of farm losses is discussed under heading 14.5(b)(iv), "Farm losses and restricted farm losses", below.

although operated with a reasonable expectation of profit, often serves as a place of recreation as well. If the farm incurs a loss, it is often realistic to attribute part of the loss to the recreational benefit: to that extent, the loss is a consumption expense (personal or living expense) which should not be deductible. Yet it is very difficult to determine on a case-by-case basis what portion of a farming loss is to be treated as a deductible business loss and what portion is to be treated as a non-deductible personal loss. It is this difficulty which has led Parliament to create an arbitrary half-way house between the full-time farmer whose losses are recognized in full and the hobby farmer whose losses are not recognized at all. Section 31, by restricting the recognition of the losses of the part-time farmer, attempts to prevent the use of the tax system to finance what may be partly a hobby.

(iv) — Losses deemed nil

Because losses are not deductible until they are realized, taxpayers who wish to deduct the accrued economic loss on a property without fully parting with it are tempted to trigger a loss for tax purposes by selling it to a related person. The Act contains several provisions (or "stop-loss rules") to prevent this.[23] For example, paragraph 40(2)(g) deems the loss to be nil where it is a "superficial loss", a PUP loss, or a loss from the transfer of property to a registered retirement savings plan (RRSP). In the case of a superficial loss and a loss from transfers to a RRSP, the loss is not ignored, but became embedded in the property, the ultimate disposition of which will trigger a real loss. For example, a superficial loss is added to the adjusted cost base of the property that has been acquired within the specified period.

There are similar rules that deem a terminal loss to be nil when an individual transfers depreciable property to a corporation[24] that he or she controls, and deem a capital loss or terminal loss to be nil.[25] In these cases, the loss stays with the original owner of the property (rather than being added to the cost base of the property and therefore moving with the property as in the case of a superficial loss). The loss can eventually be realized when the property is sold to a third party. If the property is depreciable property, the original owner can continue to claim capital cost allowance on the property.

(d) — Current-year loss

(i) — Loss from a source

Under paragraph 3(d), a loss from an income source, such as business or property, is deductible against income from all other sources, including taxable capital gains, derived in the same taxation year. For example, assume taxpayer A has income from employment of $20,000 (includible under paragraph 3(a)) and a taxable capi-

---

[23]See heading 10.7, "Stop-loss rules", above.

[24]S. 13(21.2). A s. 85(1) election cannot be made in such a situation: s. 13(21.2)(d).

[25]These rules apply to corporations that are affiliated persons as defined in s. 251.1.

tal gain of $10,000 (includible under paragraph 3(b)). If, in the same year, A has incurred a business loss of $30,000, A may deduct (under paragraph 3(d)) the amount of the loss from the combined amount under paragraphs 3(a) and 3(b), resulting in a total income of Nil ($20,000 + $10,000 — $30,000 = zero) under paragraph 3(e).

(ii) — Allowable capital losses

An "allowable capital loss" is one-half of a capital loss. It is deductible under paragraph 3(b) only from taxable capital gains derived in the same taxation year. Assuming in 2007, a taxpayer has income from a business of $50,000 (includible under paragraph 3(a)), a taxable capital gain of $9,000 (includible under paragraph 3(b)) and an allowable capital loss of $30,000. She is only able to deduct (under paragraph 3(b)) $9,000 of the allowable capital loss, because that is the extent of her taxable capital gains for the year. She must report income for tax purposes of $50,000.

The restriction on the deductibility of allowable capital losses stands in contrast to the treatment of losses from an income source. These losses, as noted above, are deductible from income from all other sources, including taxable capital gains. The deduction of allowable capital losses is restricted to taxable capital gains.[26]

The restriction on the deductibility of allowable capital losses also stands in contrast to the treatment of taxable capital gains. A taxable capital gain must be recognized in the year that it is derived, whereas an allowable capital loss is not necessarily deductible in the year that it is incurred. The asymmetrical treatment of gains and losses has been described as creating "a bias against risk-taking".[27] What is the reason for this distinction? The answer is that it is an attempt to reduce the advantage of the realization basis of capital gains taxation. Capital gains that have accrued on a capital property do not have to be recognized for tax purposes until they are realized by the sale or other disposition of the property. This enables tax on capital gains to be postponed until a time of the taxpayer's choosing (a disposition usually being a voluntary act). If there was no restriction on the deductibility of capital losses, a taxpayer could dispose of a property with accrued losses and obtain an immediate deduction despite the fact that the taxpayer was continuing to hold other properties upon which gains had accrued but had not been realized. By restricting the deductibility of capital losses, the Act reduces the incentive to postpone the realization of capital gains and diminishes the ability of taxpayers to manipulate their capital gains income.[28]

---

[26]The Act used to permit an individual (but not a corporation) to deduct allowable capital losses from income other than taxable capital gains, but only up to a limit of $2,000. In 1985, this deduction was repealed, leaving the current deductibility of allowable capital losses entirely dependent on the existence of taxable capital gains in the same taxation year.

[27]Bossons, "Implementing Capital Gains Reforms" (1979) 27 Can. Tax J. 145, 152.

[28]As discussed under heading 5.9, "Employee stock options", above, the Act creates a similar "bias against risk-taking" in its treatment of employee stock options eligible for the

(iii) — Allowable business investment losses

A "business investment loss" is defined in paragraph 39(1)(c) as a "capital loss" on the disposition of shares or debt of a "small business corporation." A "small business corporation" is a Canadian-controlled private corporation (CCPC)[29] that uses "all or substantially all" (90 per cent is the accepted standard) of its assets in "an active business carried on primarily in Canada".[30] An "allowable business investment loss" (ABIL) is one-half of the business investment loss. The allowable portion is thus the same as other capital losses. However, an ABIL, although a type of capital loss, is treated differently from other capital losses in that an ABIL is fully deductible against all other income of the taxpayer. Paragraph 3(d) places an ABIL on the same footing as a loss from income sources by allowing for a full deduction against income from other sources.

The reason for the full deductibility from current income of ABIL is to encourage investment in CCPCs carrying on business in Canada. The theory is that, by making losses deductible on the same basis that gains are includible, the bias against risk-taking which is inherent in the asymmetrical treatment of capital gains and capital losses will be eliminated for investments in CCPCs that carry on business in Canada. This treatment of losses then complements the other tax advantages accorded to the business income of CCPCs.[31] The policy is to encourage the growth of small Canadian-owned incorporated businesses.

(e) — Losses of other years

Losses sustained in other taxation years may be deducted in computing taxable income pursuant to section 111 of the Act. The details of this deduction are discussed below.

$100,000 deferral. This is because the stock option benefit that is deferred is employment income (not a capital gain). There is therefore an incentive to sell the stock (and not defer the benefit) because any future capital losses from holding the stock cannot be used to offset the employee benefit.

[29]S. 125(7), definition of "Canadian-controlled private corporation".

[30]S. 248(1), definition of "small business corporation".

[31]The most important of these are the small business deduction in s. 125 (see heading 15.5(d), "Active business income of Canadian-controlled private corporations", below) and the lifetime capital gains exemption for small business shares in s. 110.6 (see heading 10.2(f), "Tax subsidies for certain investments", below). The tax expenditures for the small business deduction and the lifetime capital gains exemption for small business shares are relatively large: they are projected to be $3,375 and $635 million, respectively, for 2009. The tax expenditure in respect of the allowable business investment losses is much smaller: the projection for 2009 is only $56 million (which is the sum of the figures on Table 1 for the personal tax expenditure and the figure on Table 2 for the corporate tax expenditure). See Canada, *Tax Expenditures and Evaluations 2009*, Tables 1 and 2.

14.5 — Taxable income

(a) — Nature of Division C deductions

Except for loss carryovers which apply to both individuals and corporations,[32] most of the Division C deductions apply either to corporations or individuals — but not both. The more important Division C deductions for individuals have already been discussed in earlier chapters.[33] These include the deductions for:

- the $750,000 lifetime capital gains exemption (section 110.6);[34]
- employee stock options (paragraphs 110(1)(d)and (d.1));[35]
- home relocation loans (paragraph 110(1)(j));[36] and
- social assistance payments (paragraph 110(1)(f)).[37]

The purpose of these Division C deductions is to exempt certain types of income from tax by offsetting all or part of the amount included in net income under Division B. On their own, these deductions make little sense; but when considered with other rules in the Act, these deductions make sense. For example, the deduction for social assistance payments under paragraph 110(1)(f) "neutralizes" the inclusion of such payments in the recipient's income under subsection 56(1) so that such payments are "free of tax".[38] The deduction for employee stock option reduces the net inclusion rate for the stock option benefit to one-half, which is the same fraction as for capital gains.[39]

(b) — Loss carryovers

(i) — Non-capital-losses

The point has been made that, when a taxpayer incurs an income-source loss in a taxation year, the loss is deductible against any income derived by the taxpayer from other sources in the loss year. If the positive income for the loss year is not sufficient to offset the loss, the taxpayer will have no income pursuant to paragraph 3(f). The taxpayer's deficit for the year (the excess of the current loss over the

---

[32]Division C deductions for corporations are discussed in chapter 15, Corporations and Shareholders. These include: charitable donations (s. 110.1(1)); dividends received by Canadian corporations from other Canadian corporations (s. 112); and dividends received by Canadian corporations from foreign affiliates (s.113(1)).

[33]There is also a northern employee travel and housing benefits deduction (s. 110.7) which has not been discussed.

[34]See heading 10.2(f), "Tax subsidies for certain investments", above.

[35]See heading 5.9, "Employee stock options", above.

[36]See heading 5.7(b), "Loans", above.

[37]See heading 12.8(c), "Workers' compensation and social assistance," above.

[38]*Ibid.*

[39]See heading 5.9, "Employee stock options", above.

current income) is the taxpayer's "non-capital loss" for the year under subsection 111(8). For example, a taxpayer who in a taxation year had employment income of $50,000, a taxable capital gain of $9,000 and a business loss of $80,000, would have a non-capital loss for that year of $21,000 ($50,000 + $9,000 - $80,000 = $21,000).

A non-capital loss for a particular taxation year may be carried over to other taxation years and deducted in those years. Paragraph 111(1)(a) provides as follows:

> For the purpose of computing the taxable income of a taxpayer for a taxation year, there may be deducted such portion as the taxpayer may claim of the taxpayer's
>
> (a) non-capital losses for the 20 taxation years immediately preceding and the 3 taxation years immediately following the year;

This provision allows the non-capital loss to be carried back three years and forward 20 years from the year in which the loss was incurred.[40]

Paragraph 111(1)(a) is confusing at first until one realizes that it is drafted from the standpoint of the year in which the non-capital loss may be deducted, not the year in which the non-capital loss was incurred (the loss year). From the standpoint of the loss year, the loss may be carried back three years and forward twenty years. From the standpoint of any other year, a non-capital loss is available as a deduction if it were incurred in the three years immediately following (from which it would have been carried back) or in the twenty years immediately preceding (from which it would have been carried forward).

Paragraph 111(1)(a) allows the deduction of "such portion as the taxpayer may claim" of the non-capital loss for a year.[41] This language gives the taxpayer discretion as to whether or not to deduct an available non-capital loss in a particular year, and discretion to deduct only a portion of the loss in a particular year.[42] This makes it possible for the taxpayer to allocate the loss as advantageously as possible over the years of highest income (which will usually result in the highest tax refund). Of course, holding on to a non-capital loss in anticipation of future high income in-

---

[40]The carry-forward period is ten years in the case of losses incurred in taxation years ending before 2006 but after March 22, 2004 and seven years in the case of losses incurred in taxation years ending before March 23, 2004.

[41]When a taxpayer decides to carry a non-capital loss back to a previous taxation year, this involves re-opening the taxpayer's tax liability for the previous year. In the usual case, the taxpayer will have filed a return for that year; the Minister will have issued an assessment; and the taxpayer will have paid the tax due for the year. In order to deduct a loss carryback in a previous year, the taxpayer files a form entitled "Request for Loss Carryback" with the CRA to claim the deduction. If the request is in order, the Minister reassesses the taxpayer for the previous year (employing that year's rules), and then sends the taxpayer a refund of the tax which, as the result of the new deduction, will be shown to have been overpaid. (Interest on the refund is payable only from the time that the loss is claimed: s. 164(5)(d).)

[42]S. 111(3) provides that the amount of a loss that may be deducted in a particular year is reduced by amounts that have been deducted in previous years.

volves the risk that the income will not materialize before the expiry of the 20-year carryforward period, in which case the loss could be wasted.

(ii) — Net capital losses

If in a taxation year a taxpayer incurs allowable capital losses that exceed the taxpayer's taxable capital gains in that year, the non-deductible excess of the allowable capital losses is described by the Act as the taxpayer's "net capital loss" for the year under subsection 111(8). Our previous example was a taxpayer who in a taxation year has $50,000 of business income and a taxable capital gain of $9,000. If he had an allowable capital loss of $80,000 (instead of a business loss of $80,000), he would have a net capital loss for the year of $71,000 ($80,000 - $9,000).

A net capital loss is not deductible in the year that it is incurred, because the taxpayer has no more taxable capital gains against which the loss could be applied. This is so even if, as in our example, the taxpayer does have positive income other than taxable capital gains in the same year. However, paragraph 111(1)(b) provides that a net capital loss for a particular year may be carried back three years and carried forward indefinitely (for the lifetime of the taxpayer).[43]

Any such carried-over net capital loss is still subject to the same restrictions on deductibility: it is deductible only against taxable capital gains of the year into which the net capital loss has been carried. It is the existence of this restriction that explains why the carryforward period is not restricted to ten years, as it is for a non-capital loss. In the year of death and the immediately preceding year, subsection 111(2) removes the restriction on deductibility. In those two years, net capital losses (as well as allowable capital losses incurred in the year of death) are deductible against income from all sources.[44] The reason for the more generous treatment of the last two years is that the year of death is the end of the carryforward period, and any losses not deducted by then would be wasted.

In other respects, the rules for the carryover of a net capital loss are similar to the rules for a non-capital loss. In particular, the taxpayer has discretion as to the year or years to which the loss is carried, and whether to deduct only a portion of the loss in a particular year.

(iii) — Allowable business investment losses

The hybrid nature of allowable investment losses is reflected in the manner they can be carried forward. Paragraph 111(1)(d) allows these losses to be carried forward like non-capital losses for twenty years. On the other hand, because net capital losses can be carried forward indefinitely (but only against taxable capital

---

[43]The deductibility of a corporation's net capital losses is restricted after a change of control: see heading 14.5(b)(v), "Change of corporate control", below.

[44]This deduction against all sources of income is reduced to the extent that the taxpayer has claimed the lifetime capital gains exemption claims: see the reference in s. 111(2)(b)(iii) to s. 110.6.

gains), the Act effectively treats unused ABIL as net capital losses from the twentieth year onward.[45] As a result, such losses can be carried forward indefinitely.

(iv) — Farm losses and restricted farm losses

A "farm loss" is defined in subsection 111(8) as the non-deductible portion of the taxpayer's loss for the year from a farming or fishing business. Farm losses can be carried back three years and forward twenty years.[46]

A "restricted farm loss" is defined in subsection 31(1.1). It is the amount of a part-time farmer's farming loss that is non-deductible for a particular year by virtue of the formula in subsection 31(1) of the Act.[47] Restricted farm losses can be carried back three years and forward twenty years but only against farming income.[48]

(v) — Change of corporate control

The loss carryover rules are restricted for a corporation that has undergone a change of control.[49] Two of such rules are found under subsections 111(5) and 111(4).

Subsection 111(5) provides that non-capital losses arising before the change of control cannot be deducted after the change of control, unless they are business losses, and the business in which the losses were sustained is continued with a reasonable expectation of profit after the change of control. If those conditions are met, the losses can be deducted after the change of control, but only to the extent of income from the business in which the losses were sustained or from another similar business.[50]

The purpose of this limitation is to stop a market for loss companies, under which unprofitable corporations are taken over solely for the tax value of their unused losses, which could be used to shelter income from the business of the corporation that has taken over the unprofitable business. Where a corporation with unused

---

[45]The definition of "net capital loss" in s. 111(8) provides that a ten-year-old unused allowable business investment loss is to be included in the taxpayer's net capital loss for the tenth year — the year in which the loss would otherwise have expired. In that way, an allowable business investment loss that cannot be deducted in the carryforward period for non-capital losses can be carried forward indefinitely as a net capital loss. Of course, after the tenth-year transformation, the loss can only be applied against taxable capital gains.

[46]S. 111(1)(d).

[47]S. 31 is discussed under heading 14.4(c)(iii), "Farm losses", above.

[48]S. 111(1)(c).

[49]Technically speaking, these restrictions apply only when control of a corporation is "acquired", which will not necessarily occur on a "change of control". Since the terms are synonymous in many cases, however, the use of the more common term "change of control" is sufficient for our purposes.

[50]See CRA Interpretation Bulletin IT-302R3, "Losses of a corporation — The effect on their deductibility of changes in control, amalgamation and winding up" (1993), paras. 14 and 15.

losses is taken over, and the new managers make the acquired corporation's business profitable, then the acquired corporation's unused losses can be applied against the profits from the formerly unprofitable business, even though the profits were earned after the change of control. In that situation, the takeover has accomplished the sound commercial objective of making an unprofitable business profitable, and there is no reason why the unused pre-takeover losses should not continue to be available.

Subsection 111(4) stops the carryover of net capital losses (and non-capital losses arising from losses from property and allowable business investment losses) when a corporation undergoes a change of control. Net capital losses incurred before the change of control cannot be carried forward to the years after the change of control, and net capital losses incurred after the change of control cannot be carried back to the years before the change of control.

There are other rules that deem a company to have a year-end[51] on a change of control and require that a variety of assets be written down to their fair market values[52] thus subjecting any resulting losses to the loss carryover restrictions. The deemed year-ends will often result in a short tax year (or "stub period") ending the day before the change of control. Most of the "writedowns" will add to the business loss for the year and the non-capital loss to be carried forward is subject to the change of control restrictions. However any writedowns of non-depreciable capital property will result in allowable capital losses which will become net capital losses that expire after the change of control.

The corporation is allowed by paragraph 111(4)(e) to treat some or all of its capital properties as having been disposed of immediately before the end of the taxation year preceding the change of control. The corporation has an election, under which it is allowed to stipulate the amount of the deemed proceeds of disposition of each capital property, provided the elected amount is more than the adjusted cost base and not more than the fair market value of the property. This provision enables the corporation with losses that would otherwise expire — unused allowable capital losses and net capital losses[53] — to use up the losses against gains accrued before the change of control.

---

[51]S. 249(4).

[52]Ss. 111(4)(c) and (d) apply to non-depreciable capital property, s. 111(5.1) applies to non-depreciable property, s. 111(5.2) applies to eligible capital property and s. 111(5.3) applies to accounts receivable.

[53]Property losses and allowable business investment losses would also expire.

14.6 — Tax rates

(a) — Rate structure

(i) — Federal rates

The rates of tax payable by an "individual"[54] are set out in subsection 117(2), which employs a graduated rate structure, with four brackets.[55] This means that as income rises, not only does the amount of tax rise, but the tax rate rises so that a greater proportion of the higher income is payable in tax. For 2010, the four income brackets and rates are as follows:

Federal Tax Brackets	Federal Tax Rate
First $40,970	15%
$40,971 to $81,941	22%
$81,942 to $127,021	26%
Over $127,021	29%

As can be seen, the first three brackets are almost equal. The rate structure is progressive because the marginal rate for each bracket is progressively higher;[56] the marginal rate for the first $40,970 of taxable income earned is 15%, the marginal rate for the next $40,971 earned is 22% and the marginal rate for the next $45,080 earned is 26%. The four brackets are also indexed for inflation. This protects taxpayers from paying tax rates just because of inflationary increases.

(ii) — Provincial rates

Provinces also levy income taxes.[57] Alberta is the only province that has a flat provincial tax (10%). Most provinces have progressive rate structures similar to the federal structure. Some provinces have made the progression steeper for provincial purposes allowing credits against provincial tax for low-income taxpayers and by

[54]The definition section (s. 248) defines an "individual" as a person other than a corporation. Thus, s. 117 is concerned only with tax on personal income and that is the topic of this chapter.

[55]The brackets are indexed for inflation. See heading 14.6(d), "Indexing for inflation", below.

[56]Unlike individuals, corporations pay income tax at a proportional rate. The basic corporate federal rate (before the general rate reduction or the small business deduction) is 38%, with an abatement of 10% of the corporation's taxable income "earned in a province". Each province then levies a tax at a rate which may be higher or lower than this 10% abatement. See ch. 15, Corporations and Shareholders, below.

[57]See heading 1.3(f), "Provincial income tax statutes," above.

imposing a provincial surtax on high-income taxpayers. As can be seen below Ontario has three brackets, the first two of which cover $37,106 of taxable income:

Ontario Tax Brackets	**Ontario Tax Rates**
First $37,106	5.05%
$37,107 to $74,214	9.15%
over $74,214	11.16%

In order to obtain an individual's total combined federal and provincial tax rate, the provincial rates have to be added to the federal rates. For example, the highest combined federal-provincial rate of tax in Ontario in 2010 is 46.41%, a figure which includes a 29% federal top rate, an 11.16 provincial top rate, and two provincial surtaxes.[58] In Alberta, on the other hand, the highest combined rate is 39% (the 29% federal top rate and the 10% Alberta flat rate). And in British Columbia, the highest combined rate is 43.70% (the 29% federal top rate plus the 14.70% top British Columbia rate): the rate structure in British Columbia is progressive but there are no surtaxes.

When provinces levy surtaxes, they are calculated on provincial tax, not income.[59] The taxpayer first determines the amount of his or her federal tax, and then calculates provincial tax and then adds the provincial surtax (or surtaxes) to yield the full tax liability. Surtaxes make the rate structure more progressive, which could also be done through the creation of additional tax brackets. Replacing surtaxes by building additional tax brackets would make the actual rates of provincial tax more apparent to taxpayers, and harder for governments to hide tax hikes through changing surtaxes. Changing the rate schedule is considered to be a reform of the tax system whereas introducing or changing a surtax is considered to be a more temporary measure.[60]

---

[58]That is, 46.41% = 29% plus 1.56 x 11.16%. The provincial surtaxes are 20% and 36% and are levied as follows in 2010: 20% of Basic Ontario Tax over $4,006 plus 36% of Basic Ontario Tax over $5,172. Basic Ontario tax is Ontario tax after most tax credits, including the dividend tax credit.

[59]*Ibid.*

[60]There are no federal surtaxes at present but there was a high-income surtax from 1991 to 2000 (it was 5% of basic federal tax over $15,500 in 2000) and a general federal surtax in effect from 1986 to 1999 which applied to all taxpayers (the rate varied between 1.5%, 3% and 5%, depending on the year): s. 180.1. The general federal surtax was introduced as a temporary measure to reduce the deficit and was to be removed when the GST was introduced. Although the GST was introduced in 1991, the state of the federal deficit discouraged previous federal governments from removing this surtax. In 1999, the general surtax was reduced to 1.5% of basic federal tax and eliminated for low and middle-income taxpayers. In 2000, it was removed completely.

(b) — Marginal versus average rates

A marginal rate is the applicable rate of tax at each bracket level, while the rate that is applicable to the taxpayer's total taxable income is called the average or effective rate.

It is important to note that the rates of tax which are applicable within each bracket of income are applicable only to that part of an individual's income which falls within that bracket. For example, an individual who earned over $127,021 of taxable income in 2010 has income that falls within the 29 per cent top federal tax bracket. The rate of 29 per cent is known as the individual's federal *marginal rate*, because it is the rate that is levied at the margin, that is, on the last dollar of taxable income. But the federal marginal rate is not applied to the whole of the taxpayer's income. It is applied only to the income falling within the same bracket as the last dollar.

If we assume that this individual earns only $1,000 more than $127,021 (that is, $128,021), then the 29 per cent federal marginal rate will be applicable to that $1,000.

The rest of the taxpayer's taxable income, namely the first $127,021, will be taxed at the lower federal rates in the chart. The result is that the taxpayer's federal *average rate* (or overall federal rate) of tax will be substantially less than his or her marginal rate, since only $1,000 of taxable income is taxed at 29 per cent and the rest of his income ($127,021) is taxed at an average rate of 21% (the average of the three rates applicable to the first three equal brackets: 15%, 22%, 26%). Thus, the average rate of tax paid by this taxpayer on his total income is around 21 per cent, about 8 points less than his 29% marginal rate.[61]

The marginal rate is often more important than the average rate, because it is the marginal rate that governs a taxpayer's economic decisions. For example, a taxpayer who has a choice whether or not to work overtime at his or her employment would compare the value of the time as leisure with the after-tax earnings from the extra work. It would be the taxpayer's marginal rate that would determine the amount of after-tax earnings that the taxpayer would receive. Similarly, the value to the taxpayer of the deduction for contributing to a registered retirement savings plan (RRSP) would be determined by the marginal rate rather than the average rate.[62]

---

[61] As discussed above, his combined federal-Ontario rate would be 46.41%.

[62] This simple example has been used to illustrate the difference between *average* and *marginal* rates. A more accurate calculation would take into consideration personal tax credits, which would make this taxpayers average tax rate slightly lower. In 2010, for example, the basic credit effectively exempts the first $10,382 of taxable income from taxable income. It is like another tax bracket with a rate of zero.

(c) — Progressive, regressive or flat rates

The rate structure under subsection 117(2) is progressive because as income rises, the tax rate rises as well so that a greater proportion of the higher income is payable in tax. The provincial individual income tax rate structure is also progressive, with the exception of the province of Alberta (which has a flat rate of 10%). Under progressive rates, the marginal rate is higher than the average rate.

In contrast, under a "flat" rate structure, as income increases, the increase in tax would be proportional to the increase in income; the rate would remain constant. Marginal and average rates of tax would be the same.

A progressive tax and a proportionate tax may be contrasted with a "regressive" tax. A regressive tax is the opposite of a progressive tax. The rates of a regressive tax increase as income decreases. The clearest example would be a "poll tax", in which every adult person was required to pay a tax of, say, $1,000. The levy would constitute a higher proportion of a low income than of a high income. Its effective rate would therefore diminish as income rose. In Canada, payroll taxes, real property taxes[63] and sales taxes are regressive because the effective rate of tax increases as an individual's income decreases and decreases as an individual's income increases. This is why the tax system employs income-tested refundable credits to reduce the regressivity of property and sales taxes. This is also why federal and provincial sales taxes do not apply to basic necessities, such as food and (residential) rent.

Progressive, proportionate and regressive are terms that describe the *incidence* of a tax. But there are two kinds of incidence: legal and economic. The legal obligation to pay the tax in the first instance defines the tax's legal incidence, while the tax's economic incidence depends upon who ultimately bears the burden of the tax. Economic incidence measures how progressive a tax is after the reactions of the taxpayers have been factored in. Three studies in 1994 examined the economic incidence of taxes; two studies covered the whole of Canada, while the other focused on Ontario.[64] Although no subsequent studies have been identical to those done in 1994, they have come to the same conclusion on one important point: the personal income tax is the only progressive tax and all other taxes are regressive.[65]A study covering the period 1990 to 2005 also found that the tax system overall "was far

---

[63]Either paid directly or indirectly through rental payments.

[64]Vermaeten, Gillespie, Vermaeten, "Tax Incidence in Canada" (1994) 42 *Can. Tax J.* 348; and Block and Shillington, "Incidence of Taxes in Ontario in 1991" in *Taxation and the Distribution of Income* (1994). Another study was published in the same year, but it examined the position of taxpayers after including the value of government expenditures and so is more properly considered a fiscal incidence study: Ruggeri, Van Wart, Howard, "The Redistributional Impact of Taxation in Canada" (1994) 42 *Can. Tax J.* 417. Kesselman, Chung, "Tax Incidence, Progresssivity and Inequality in Canada", (2004) 52 *Can. Tax J.* No. 3 702 is a literature review of such studies.

[65]Lee, *Eroding Tax Fairness: Tax Incidence in Canada, 1990 to 2005*, Can. Centre for Policy Alternatives, 2007.

more fair in 1990": by 2005, the personal income tax had become less progressive and increases in the other regressive taxes had made them even more regressive.[66] It has also been suggested that the personal income tax may be partially shifted[67] which may make its economic incidence less progressive than its legal incidence.

It is hard to say whether the personal income tax today (in 2010) is more or less progressive than it was in 2005 because there have been some changes made since then which likely increase its progressivity (e.g., increases in non-refundable and refundable credits) and some which likely do not (e.g., pension income splitting). What is clear, however, is that monitoring the progressivity of the personal income tax as well as the inclusions and deductions allowed in computing an individual's taxable income is important and the government publishes personal tax statistics at least annually which show what percentage of tax top income earners pay and, occasionally, who is benefiting from certain provisions in the Act.[68] The personal income tax comprises more than half of federal government revenues and is the only progressive tax in Canada. Its incidence is also more transparent than other taxes even it its cost can be partially shifted to other taxpayers. Its progressive legal incidence at least shows it maximum economic incidence on high-income earners and the government can monitor this with more accuracy than it can other taxes.

(d) — Indexing for inflation

(i) — Effect of inflation

Without indexing, one of the characteristics of a progressive tax system is that when an individual's income rises his or her tax liability rises more than proportionately: the taxpayer becomes liable to pay more tax on the new dollars than the taxpayer was paying on the old dollars. This is obvious if the rise pushes the individual into a new tax bracket (bracket-creeping). But even if the rise does not push the individual into a new tax bracket, the increase in income will be taxed at the individual's marginal rate — and the marginal rate is always higher than the previous year's average rate. From the point of view of the individual taxpayer, a rise in before-tax income of five per cent produces a rise in after-tax income of somewhat

---

[66] *Ibid.*

[67] See Kesselman, Chung, note 64, above and cited in Lee, note 65, above.

[68] For example, the March 4, 2010 budget, which proposed to change the treatment of public employee stock options contained Table A5.3 which showed how high income earners had been benefiting from employee stock option claims. Although taxpayers with total incomes over $500,000 comprised 10% of the taxpayers making such claims, the dollar value of the claims were so high ($393,000 on average) compared to lower income earners, that the claims (by 7,985 individuals) comprised 75% of the dollars deducted under this provision of the Act. See Department of Finance, Budget 2010, Table A5.3. Total income is the subtotal disclosed at the bottom of page 2 on the T1 return and is before various deductions, such as union dues and professional fees (under subdivision a) and child care and RRSP contributions (under subdivision d). See heading 5.9, "Employee stock options", above, for a detailed discussion of this topic.

less than five per cent. Where a rise in income is equal to the rate of inflation, the recipient's purchasing power will actually decline, because of the progressive increase in the related tax liability. From the point of view of the government, a rise in incomes of five per cent produces a rise in income tax revenues of more than five per cent. With a progressive rate structure, tax revenues are bound to grow at a faster rate than incomes. To the extent that the rise in incomes is due simply to inflation, there is a regular but surreptitious increase in the real rates of tax without the necessity of any amendment to the Act.

The increase in the rate of tax which is caused by inflation is exacerbated if personal deductions from income or credits against tax are defined in fixed-dollar terms rather than as a percentage of income. The effect of inflation on income causes the fixed-dollar deductions or credits to become less valuable to the taxpayer. When income rises due to inflation, the fixed-dollar deductions or credits (which would remain unchanged without indexing) constitute a smaller percentage of the inflated income, effectively causing the average rate of tax paid by the taxpayer to rise.

If the tax system is to offset the increase in the rate of tax which is caused by inflation, then the tax brackets and all the fixed-dollar deductions and credits have to be adjusted (or "indexed") so that they will rise with the rate of inflation.[69]

(ii) — Indexation rules

Indexation was first introduced in 1974 when section 117.1 of the Act was enacted. Until 1985, section 117.1 caused the tax system to be indexed by the annual change in the Consumer Price Index.[70] Effective in 1986, section 117.1 was amended so as to exclude from the indexing formula the first 3 per cent of the annual increase in the Consumer Price Index.[71] Full indexing was re-introduced in 2000 and there

---

[69]See Allan, Dodge and Poddar, "Indexing the Personal Income Tax: A Federal Perspective" (1974) 22 *Can. Tax J.* 355.

[70]S. 117.1 provided that each of the principal personal deductions (which had not then been converted into credits) and each of the tax brackets in the rate schedule would be increased for each taxation year by the same percentage as the Consumer Price Index had increased in the 12 months ending in the previous September. In the years of high inflation that followed, the results were dramatic. The basic personal deduction (or exemption) to which every individual taxpayer was entitled rose from $1,600 in 1973 to $4,140 in 1985 — a cumulative increase of 159%. A similar increase took place in the other personal deductions and in the tax brackets.

[71]Because the indexing factor for a taxation year is based on the movement of the Consumer Price Index for the 12-month period ending in the previous year, indexing always lags a year behind reality. Each year's indexing factor is based on the previous year's inflation. The selection of September as the cut-off time to calculate the rate for the next taxation year (which would start on January 1) was driven by the need to ascertain the indexing factor some time before the beginning of the year so as to give time for the printing and distribution of the source-deduction tables that are used by employers to calculate how much income tax they are supposed to deduct from their employees' pay. The system's reliance on the previ-

have also been increases ever since then to increase brackets and credit amounts over and above the indexed amounts.[72]

Full indexation automatically raises the amount of the fixed-dollar deductions and the tax brackets to correspond with the rate of inflation for the previous year ending in September. An increase in income that is exactly equal to that rate of inflation is therefore spread evenly over all the applicable deductions and all the applicable brackets. Instead of being taxed at the taxpayer's marginal rate, and thereby increasing the taxpayer's average rate, the increase in income was taxed at the same average rate as was applicable in the previous year. An increase in income that exceeded the rate of inflation would of course be taxed at the taxpayer's marginal rate, and might even push the taxpayer into a new tax bracket.[73] Either way, the taxpayer's average rate of tax would be increased. But, since indexing would offset the increased rate on the part of the taxpayer's new income that was attributable to inflation, the increase in the taxpayer's rate of tax would be less than it would have been if the system were not indexed. The taxpayer whose income failed to keep pace with inflation would find his or her loss in purchasing power mitigated somewhat by the decline in his or her average rate of tax caused by the expansion of the credits and brackets.

Since 2001 (when tax on income (TONI) was introduced), indexing for inflation has been slightly different for provincial purposes than for federal purposes. In other words, while tax brackets (and credits and other limits) started out the same in 2000, they have changed since then because of the different approaches to indexation taken by the various provinces. Some provinces index by the national or provincial CPI, some use a modified index and some have not indexed at all since 2000 or 2001. Ontario, Manitoba, Alberta and B.C and the three territories, for example use each province's/territory's CPI rather than the national CPI for indexation. The Alberta provincial rate, of course, is not affected because it is a 10% flat tax.[74]

---

ous year's inflation may in fact be a virtue. It provides an answer to the Carter Commission's objection that indexing would "irreparably damage the built-in stability of the system". The answer is that "by applying indexing with a lag, the taxpayers are compensated for past inflation, thereby preserving the current response of revenue flows to the current level of inflation". Allan, Dodge and Poddar, note 69, above, 368.

[72]See heading 2.2(h), "1989 to 2005", above, for a description of these increases.

[73]This is called "bracket-creep". History shows that about 61 per cent of Canadians would have had taxable incomes in the lowest tax bracket in 1996 if the tax system had been fully indexed during the period 1986 to 1996, whereas only 54 per cent did because there was essentially no indexing (because CPI was rarely above 3%). See Perry, "Where Did They Go?" (1999) *Can. Tax Highlights*, Vol. 7, 35. Even today, the increase in rates between the first and second brackets is significant: federal rates rise from 15 per cent to 22 per cent and Ontario rates rise from 5.05% to 9.15%. Preventing bracket creep is important.

[74]For details, see Perry, "Provincial Indexing Variations", *Can. Tax Highlights*, Vol. 13 No. 2, February 2005.

14.7 — Tax credits

(a) — Nature of tax credits

A tax credit reduces tax payable. A tax credit is different than a deduction which reduces income under section 3 or taxable income and avoids the perverse upside down effect of a deduction. The upside-down effect of a deduction results because income tax is levied at progressive rates: as a result, the value of a deduction in computing the tax base (i.e., at the first two stages of computing tax liability) increases when a taxpayer's marginal tax rate increases. For example, in Ontario (in 2010), the combined federal-provincial tax saving arising from a $100 deduction would be $46 for A who is in the highest bracket,[75] $20 for B who is in the lowest tax bracket,[76] and nil for C who has no taxable income.

The tax reform of 1998 converted personal exemptions (which were deductions from taxable income) to credits (which are deductions from tax payable) to avoid the upside-down effect of deductions. The credits under section 118 to 118.9 are set at the rate for the lowest bracket so that the tax savings are the same for A and B in the above example, but still nil for C. However, if the tax system is to be used to provide special assistance to low-income taxpayers who have no tax payable (and to whom a credit would be worthless), tax credits will not work unless they are refundable and income tested.

(b) — Non-refundable credits

The Act provides for a number of "personal credits", including those listed below. There are detailed rules setting out the criteria that a dependant or expense must meet in order to be eligible for a particular credit. The amount of each of these credits is calculated by multiplying the eligible amount by 15 per cent (the rate in the lowest tax bracket).[77] Most eligible amounts and the income limits change each year because they are indexed for inflation. (The pension income, education, textbook and fitness credits are the four exceptions.) For 2010, the eligible amounts are as follows:

	Amount
Basic personal amount, s. 118(1)(c)	$10,382
Spouse/Common-law partner, s. 118(1)(a)	$10,382 (reduced by dependant's income)

[75]The combined rate for thre highest bracket is 46.41%. See note 58, above.

[76]The combined rate for the lowest bracket is 20.05% (15% plus 5.05%). See heading 14.6, "Tax rates", below.

[77]In one of those circumlocutions that make the Act unnecessarily difficult, s. 118 speaks only of "the appropriate percentage". One eventually discovers that this phrase is a defined term in s. 248, where it is defined as "the lowest percentage referred to in s. 117(2) that is applicable in determining tax payable under Part I for the year".

	Amount
Spouse equivalent/Eligible dependant, s. 118(1)(b)	$10,382 (reduced by dependant's income)
Caregiver, s. 118(1)(c.1)	$4,223 (reduced by dependant's income over $14,422)
Infirm dependant over 17, s. 118(1)(d)	$4,223 (reduced by dependant's income over $5,702)
Child, s. 118(1)(b.1)[a]	$2,101
Disability, s. 118.3	$7,239
Disabled supplement under 18, s. 118.3	$4,223 (reduced by child/attendant care expenses over $2,473)
Age, s. 118(2)	$6,446 (reduced by 15% of taxpayer's income over $32,506)
Pension income, s. 118(3)	Eligible income, maximum $2,000[b]
Medical expenses, s. 118.2	Amounts paid in excess of the lesser of 3% of net income and $2,024[c]
Tuition fees, s. 118.5[d]	Amounts paid
Education, s. 118.5(2)[e]	
- Full-time	$400 per month
- Part-time	$120 per month
Textbook, s. 118.5(2)[f]	
Full-time	$65 per month
Part-time	$20 per month
Student loan interest, s. 118.62[g]	Amounts paid
CPP/QPP, s. 118.7	Amount paid (maximum $2,163)
EI, s. 118.7	Amount paid (maximum $747)
Adoption expenses, s. 118.01	Amount paid, maximum $10,975
Employment credit, s. 118(10)	$1,051
Fitness credit, s. 118.03	Amount paid, maximum $500
Public transit credit, s. 118.02	Amound paid

Notes:

a Under 18 at the end of the year.

b Discussed under heading 12.4, "Tax-assisted private pension plans", above.

c This formula applies to amounts paid for medical expenses of the taxpayer, the taxpayer's spouse and minor children. In the case of any other dependent (e.g., a child who is 18 or older), the maximum amount is $10,000 and the formula is different: it is the lesser of the amounts paid in excess of the lesser of the 3% of *the dependent's net income* and $2,024.

d Unused tuition, education and textbook credits to be transferred to a spouse or common-law partner (s. 118.8) or parent or grandparent (s. 118.9) but the amount transferred cannot exceed $5,000 (s. 118.81). Unclaimed tuition, education and textbook credits can be carried forward indefinitely (s. 118.61).

e *Ibid.*

f *Ibid.*

g Unclaimed interest expense can be carried forward for five years. (s. 118.62).

In addition to these credits at 15 per cent, there are the following credits: the charitable donation credit (discussed below), the dividend tax credit (discussed in detail in chapter 15)[78] and the political contributions tax credit.[79]

The charitable donations credit is a two-tier credit. Only the credit on the first $200 of donation claimed in a year is at 15 per cent. The balance of donations claimed qualifies for a credit at 29 per cent. Why? Because it was thought that having the entire credit at 15 per cent would be a disincentive for donors in the top tax bracket. The $200 threshold, in a sense replaces the $100 standard taxable income deduction that all taxpayers could claim for donations without any receipts. The other rules for charitable donations are essentially as follows and are the same for individuals and corporations: only donations to registered charities and registered athletic associations qualify; there is a maximum charitable donation limit of 75 per cent of net income;[80] and donations can be carried forward for five years. There is also a one-year carryback in the year of death and donations made by will qualify for this claim.

The credits above are all non-refundable credits, which means that if the taxpayer pays no tax, the credit cannot be claimed. However, many of the credits exist because a taxpayer who pays no tax will not be eligible for a basic credit: this is part of the reason for the spouse/common-law partner credit, the spouse equivalent (or eligible dependant) credit amount, the caregiver credit and the disable/ infirm dependant credit. If these dependants have income over a certain threshold, these credits cannot be claimed. The medical expense and charitable donation credits can be claimed by either spouse or common-law partner and the medical expenses of minor children can be claimed by parents unless the child has income in excess of the basic credit amount.

The Act also provides for the transfer of certain unused credits. Subsection 118.3(2) allows the disability credit to be transferred from anyone that the taxpayer has claimed as dependant (or could have claimed had their income not been as high). Section 118.8 permits any unused age, pension, mental or physical impair-

---

[78]See heading 15.4, "Taxation of shareholders", below.

[79]The formula is 75% of the first $400, 50% of the next $350 and 33 1/3% of the balance. The maximum credit per year is $650: s. 127(3). Most provinces have similar credits for donations to provincial political parties.

[80]There is an additional limit of 25% of the amount of taxable capital gain and recapture that are realized (by virtue of s. 69) on gifts of capital property to a charity. As well, only one-quarter of the capital gain is taxable on gifts of publicly traded securities to registered charities other than private foundations.

ment, tuition and education credits to be transferred to a spouse. Similarly, section 118.9 allows the unused tuition and education credits can be transferred to a parent or grandparent. Students also have the option of carrying forward unused tuition and education credits to a future year when they might owe tax.

(c) — Refundable credits

A non-refundable tax credit provides little help for those whose incomes are so low that they are outside the tax system altogether and cannot transfer their credits to other taxpayers. The non-refundable tax credit also does not confer a full benefit upon those whose tax liabilities are less than the amount of the credit. These regressive features can be eliminated by making the credit "refundable". The refundable feature requires the CRA to make payments to individuals who qualify for the credit but who have insufficient income to employ (or fully employ) the credit as an offset to their tax liability. Another possible refinement of a tax credit is to make it subject to an income test. An income-tested (or "vanishing") credit declines and eventually vanishes as a taxpayer's income rises above a stipulated level. Both the refundable and the income-tested features steepen the progressivity of a tax credit.[81]

Most of the credits under the Act are neither refundable nor income-tested. However, there are two credits that are income-tested but not refundable: the age credit allowed to persons 65 and older and the medical expense credit. The four credits below are both refundable and income-tested. Each of them has maximum benefits and income thresholds that are indexed each year.

- The goods and services tax (GST) credit under section 122.5 is refundable so that an individual whose tax liability is too low to absorb the credit will still benefit from it. It is paid quarterly. The GST credit is subject to an income test: it starts to reduce when the net income of the family (taxpayer and cohabiting spouse) reaches a stipulated (indexed) threshold. The amount of the GST credit (which is calculated by a formula based on the size of the family) is reduced by 5 per cent of the family income (income of the tax-filer and cohabiting spouse) above the threshold, so that it eventually vanishes altogether.
- The child tax benefit under section 122.61 is calculated by a formula that depends primarily upon the number and ages of the tax-filer's children. It is paid monthly. There is a basic benefit, a supplement and a child disability benefit. All three are income tested and begin to vanish at various rates. The basic and disability benefits vanish at the rate of 4 per cent (or 2 per cent where there is only one child) of family income when family income reaches a stipulated threshold. The supplement, which is for very poor families, vanishes at steeper rates.

---

[81] The difficulty with an income-tested credit is that it creates a spike in the overall progressivity of the tax system. At income levels where the credit is being reduced, the taxpayer's effective marginal rate is increased, sometimes to levels above those applicable to higher income levels.

- The refundable medical expense credit under section 122.51 is available to taxpayers who have a minimum level of income from employment or business ($3,135 in 2010). The credit begins to vanish at the rate of 5 per cent of family income when family income reaches a stipulated threshold ($23,775 in 2010). The purpose of the credit is to give some additional relief for medical expenses to low income working individuals. The credit is paid annually when a tax return is filed.
- The working income tax benefit (WITB) under section is designed to offset costs incurred by low-income workers 19 years of age or older. The WITB is equal to 25 per cent of employment and business income over $3,000 (to a maximum amounts for single individuals and families), with an additional supplement for individuals eligible for the disability tax credit. The credit is phased out at a rate of 15 per cent of net income in excess of a stipulated threshold and is not available to students. The WITB is paid annually when a tax return is filed but it if the estimated WITB is at least $200, taxpayers can apply to have 50 per cent of the WITB paid in advance on a quarterly basis.

An innovative feature of both the GST credit and the child tax benefit and (to some extent as described above) the WITB is the timing of the payment of the "refunds". An ordinary tax refund is paid in one cheque, which is sent out several weeks or months after the filing of the tax return for the taxation year in which tax was overpaid or over-withheld; it is only then that the tax situation of a taxpayer has been finally assessed. Both the GST credit and the child tax benefit are calculated on the basis of earlier year's tax returns, and are paid in advance in instalments. The GST credit and advance payments of the WITB are paid quarterly. The child tax benefit is paid monthly, reflecting the fact that it is an income-support programme.

These credits could be expanded into a negative income tax, under which all tax-filers reporting incomes below a stipulated poverty line would receive regular payments from the government. This would be one way of designing a guaranteed annual income, which would replace a myriad of existing programs, and which would ensure that no Canadian lacked the means to maintain an adequate standard of living.

14.8 — The alternative minimum tax

(a) — Rationale

As discussed in previous chapters, the Act is replete with tax expenditure provisions, providing various tax preferences. As many of the tax preferences are available only to wealthy individuals, higher-income taxpayers are sometimes able to avail themselves of sufficient tax preferences to reduce their tax liability to an extremely low figure. Indeed, it became apparent in the mid-1980s that tax preferences enabled a few wealthy individuals to escape the bite of tax altogether. The ensuing public protest caused the enactment in 1986 of the alternative minimum tax (AMT) under section 127.5.

The AMT is "alternative" because taxpayers must calculate both the amount of their AMT and their "ordinary tax", and then pay whichever figure is greater. The rate of the AMT is 15.5 per cent (the rate applicable to the lowest tax bracket in section 117), which combines with provincial tax to yield a combined rate of approximately 22 per cent. The AMT differs from ordinary income tax in that it is calculated on a broader tax base (one that excludes many tax preferences) than the ordinary income tax. However, if AMT is payable, the amount by which it exceeds the ordinary income tax is available as a credit against ordinary income tax in any of the following ten years. In most cases, therefore, the AMT will not be an additional tax liability, but rather an early payment of a future tax liability.

The political appeal of an AMT can be easily understood, but its tax policy rationale is less easy to fathom. If the tax preferences that are excluded from the AMT base are unfair, then surely the appropriate response is to repeal them. Since it is the policy of the government to retain the provisions, why should some taxpayers be precluded from using them? In any case, the AMT applies to few taxpayers and raises little revenue, so that it is of little practical importance.[82]

(b) — Computation of the AMT

There are four steps involved in determining the amount of the AMT. First, a taxpayer must re-calculate his or her taxable income based on the peculiar rules under section 127.52. This process basically involves the calculation of taxable income in the normal way, followed by the adding back into income of those deductions considered to be tax preferences. For example, a taxpayer who had reported a taxable capital gain would be required to add 30 per cent of the capital gain back into his or her taxable income for the purposes of the AMT so that 80 per cent (rather than 50 per cent) is applicable. Once this "adjusted taxable income" has been calculated, the next step is that the taxpayer is allowed to deduct a "basic exemption" of $40,000 from the adjusted taxable income. The $40,000 exemption ensures that only upper-income taxpayers making extensive use of tax preferences will be subjected to the AMT. The third step is to apply the rate of 15.5 per cent to the figure determined by the previous calculations. Finally, taxpayers are permitted to deduct certain credits from the amount of tax thus far determined. However, many credits that would otherwise be available are not available for the purposes of the AMT on the ground that they are tax preferences.

Having derived the amount of the AMT, the taxpayer must now compare this figure to the ordinary tax otherwise payable, and pay the greater of the two amounts. Only where the amount of the AMT exceeds the amount of tax calculated in the ordinary way is the taxpayer obliged to pay the AMT. If the taxpayer must pay the AMT rather than his or her ordinary tax, the amount by which the AMT exceeds the ordinary tax may be carried forward for up to ten years and used as a credit against tax in any year where ordinary tax payable exceeds the AMT. For example, if in year one a taxpayer has calculated $30,000 of ordinary tax, and $36,000 of AMT,

---

[82] Larins and Jacques, "Is the Alternative Minimum Tax a Paper Tiger?" (1994) 42 *Can. Tax J.* 442, studied the effect of the AMT on Quebec taxpayers in 1988 and answered their own question "yes".

the taxpayer must pay the higher figure of $36,000. However, the $6,000 difference between ordinary tax and AMT may be carried forward for up to ten years. If in year two the taxpayer's ordinary tax payable is $40,000 and his or her AMT is only $30,000, the $6,000 carried forward from the previous year may be applied to reduce the tax liability for year two to $34,000.

The four steps for the calculation of AMT are summarized in Table 14-1, which follows.

Table 14-1

	Taxable income
Step 1	+/- Adjustments (a)
	Adjusted taxable income
Step 2	($40,000 Exemption)
	Net Amount
Step 3	x 15.5% Rate
	Minimum tax before minimum tax credits
Step 4	(Minimum tax credits) (b)
	Minimum tax
Step 5	Compare to basic federal tax and use the greater (c)

Notes:

(a) The adjustments to taxable income include

Add

Losses due to CCA or interest/carrying charges on rental, leasing, film and videotape properties

Losses due to resource deductions

30% of the excess of capital gains over capital losses for the year[83]

60% of the stock option deduction[84]

Losses from united partnerships

Home relocation loan deduction

---

[83]The purpose of the 30% add back is to include 80% of the capital gain in AMT income (80% = 50% + 30%). When the taxable capital gains fraction was 3/4, the entire capital gain was included in AMT income. However, when the fraction changed to one-half, including the entire capital gain was thought to be too severe: 80% was a compromise.

[84]The stock option deduction is normally 50% of the stock option benefit. The purpose of the 60% add back is to reduce the stock option deduction from 50% to 20% of the stock option benefit ([100% - 60%] × 50% = 20%) thereby resulting in 80% of the stock option benefit being included in AMT income. When the stock option deduction was 25% of the stock option benefit, the entire deduction was added back. However, when the fraction was changed to one-half, including the entire stock option benefit was thought to be too severe: like the treatment of capital gains *ibid.*, 80% was a compromise.

Losses from partnerships in which the taxpayer is a passive partner

Losses from tax shelters

Resource-related deductions

Deduct

30% of business investment losses for the year

Dividend gross-up

(b) The credits exclude

Credits transferred from others

Pension and dividend tax credits

Political tax credit

Investment tax credit

(c) There is a similar calculation for most provinces.

Source: *Income Tax Act*, Part I, Division E.1.

15
CORPORATIONS AND SHAREHOLDERS

15.1 — Introduction

(a) — Scope of chapter

This chapter is about the taxation of corporations and shareholders. It will examine the policies and rules which are relevant to the taxation of income earned by corporations and income distributed by corporations to their shareholders. It will cover the most common kinds of Canadian corporations and the most common kinds of distributions. It will not deal with the numerous kinds of corporations that attract special tax treatment, such as non-resident corporations, non-resident-owned investment corporations, investment corporations, mortgage investment corporations, mutual fund corporations, cooperative corporations and insurance corporations. Nor will the chapter deal with the rollovers and other tax rules regarding the transfer of assets to corporations,[1] reorganizations, amalgamations, reductions of capital and the winding up of corporations.

(b) — Incorporation

A corporation or company (for present purposes these terms are synonymous) may be incorporated under either federal or provincial law. Once incorporated, the company is a legal person which is separate from its shareholders. The shareholders have no proprietary interest in the company's underlying assets, that is, the things

[1] For a very brief treatment, see heading 13.8, "Family corporation", above.

that the company has acquired with the funds raised by issuing shares (or borrowing money or retaining earnings). What the shareholders own are shares in the company, a quite different kind of asset. Similarly, the liabilities of the company are its alone and they must be satisfied out of the assets of the company. In a sole proprietorship or partnership business, the proprietor or partners are personally liable to satisfy the liabilities incurred by the business, and in the event of business failure they may lose their own personal assets and become bankrupt. A prime reason for the incorporation of a company is that the shareholder's risk is limited to the sum paid for, or agreed to be paid for, his or her shares. The personal assets of the shareholder are not at risk. This is known as "limited liability".

(c) — Public and private corporations

Anglo-Canadian corporate law has traditionally distinguished between "public" and "private" companies. The private company was one with less than 50 shareholders, with restrictions on the sale of shares contained in the company's constitution, and which was prohibited from offering its shares to the public. This classification of companies was employed in order to exempt the private company from some of the reporting and regulatory requirements that had to be satisfied by a more widely-held company. The public-private dichotomy is still employed by the corporate law of several provinces, but the tendency of recent statutory amendments has been to substitute other nomenclature and qualifications, still with the general purpose of exempting the closely-held corporation (or "close corporation" as the Americans call it) from some of the regulations of the governing corporate statute.

The *Income Tax Act* (the "Act") draws important distinctions between public and private corporations, with private corporations being eligible for a number of tax advantages which are denied to public corporations. However, the terms "public corporation" and "private corporation" are specifically defined by the Act for its purposes. A "public corporation" is defined by subsection 89(1) as a corporation resident in Canada whose shares are "listed on a prescribed stock exchange in Canada". Regulation 3200 lists the following as prescribed stock exchanges for the purpose of this definition: Tiers 1 and 2 of the TSX Venture Exchange, Tiers 1 and 2 of the Canadian Venture Exchange, the Montreal Stock Exchange and the Toronto Stock Exchange.[2] A "private corporation" is defined by subsection 89(1) as a cor-

---

[2]In addition, a corporation whose shares are not listed on a prescribed stock exchange may become a public corporation by (1) election, or (2) designation. As to election, s. 89(1)(g) allows a corporation to elect to become a public corporation if it complies "with prescribed conditions relating to the number of its shareholders, dispersal of ownership of its shares, public trading of its shares and size of the corporation". Those conditions are prescribed by regs. 4801 to 4802. As to designation, s. 89(1)(g) gives to the Minister the power to designate a corporation as a public corporation where it complies with the same conditions as are stipulated for election as a public corporation.

poration resident in Canada which is "not a public corporation", and is not "controlled" by "one or more public corporations".[3]

(d) — Canadian-controlled private corporations

The Act, as well as distinguishing for various purposes between public corporations and private corporations, has a number of important provisions that are applicable to Canadian-controlled private corporations (CCPCs). This term is defined in subsection 125(7) as follows:

> "Canadian-controlled private corporation" means a private corporation that is a Canadian corporation other than a corporation
>
> > (a) controlled, directly or indirectly in any manner whatever, by one or more non-resident persons, by one or more public corporations ... or by any combination thereof. ...

As the name implies, a CCPC is a private corporation. It must also be a "Canadian corporation", which is defined in subsection 89(1) as a corporation that is resident in Canada and was incorporated in Canada. Finally, it must not be "controlled, directly or indirectly in any manner whatever" by non-residents of Canada or by public corporations.

The word "controlled" is used elsewhere in the Act as well, but there is no generally applicable definition of "control" or "controlled". The courts have held that the word "controlled", appearing elsewhere in the Act without the accompanying phrase "directly or indirectly in any manner whatever", means *de jure* control and not *de facto* control.[4] *De jure* control requires ownership of a majority of the voting shares in the corporation enabling election of a majority of the members of the board of directors. Therefore, if a majority of the voting shares of a private corporation are owned by non-residents (or public corporations), the corporation cannot be a CCPC. However, the definition does not require that the corporation be controlled by residents, so long as it is not controlled by non-residents. Therefore, if exactly 50 per cent of the shares are owned by non-residents, the corporation could be a CCPC.

Where non-residents (or public corporations) do not have *de jure* control of a private corporation, but do have *de facto* control, the *de facto* control will suffice to deny the corporation the status of a CCPC. Subsection 256(5.1) provides that the phrase "controlled, directly or indirectly in any manner whatever" (which, it will be recalled, is in the definition of a CCPC) includes the case where "the controller has any direct or indirect influence that, if exercised, would result in control in fact of the corporation". This expands the concept of control in subsection 125(7) to include *de facto* control. An example of *de facto* control would be where a non-resi-

---

[3]The meaning of "controlled" is discussed under heading 15.1(d), "Canadian-controlled private corporations", below.

[4]*Buckerfields v. M.N.R*, [1964] C.T.C. 504, 64 D.T.C. 5301 (Ex. Ct.); *M.N.R. v. Dworkin Furs*, [1967] C.T.C. 50, 67 D.T.C. 5035 (S.C.C.); and *Duha Printers (Western) Ltd. v. R.*, [1998] 1 S.C.R. 795, [1998] 3 C.T.C. 303, 98 D.T.C. 6334 (S.C.C.).

dent person owned only 49 per cent of the voting shares of a corporation, but the remaining shares were "widely dispersed among many employees of the corporation or held by persons who could reasonably be considered to act in respect of the corporation in accordance with his wishes".[5] In that case, the non-resident owner of the 49 per cent block would be in actual (*de facto*) control of the corporation, even though the owner did not have the *de jure* control that would flow from ownership of a majority of the voting shares. *De facto* control can also arise in non-share ownership situations, such as where a non-arm's length person is a major creditor, customer or supplier. Any time non-residents (or public corporations) have *de facto* control, the corporation would not be a CCPC.

(e) — Corporate distributions

While a company is a going concern, it will make various kinds of payments to persons associated with it. The company will pay "dividends" to its shareholders; dividends are declared at the discretion of the directors of the company. Dividends may only be paid out of profits, either current earnings or retained earnings from prior years. The company will pay "interest" to its debt holders. The company will be obliged by its contracts with the debt holders to pay them interest at agreed-upon rates, whether or not the company is earning sufficient money to afford it. Similarly, the company will be obliged by its employment contracts to pay salaries or wages to the company's employees, whether or not the company is earning sufficient money to afford them.

In computing the company's profit (or loss) for a year, interest and salaries or wages will be two of the expenses which are deducted from gross revenue. Any resulting profit is then available for payment to shareholders: it may be paid to the shareholders in whole or in part by declaration of a dividend, and any amount not so paid will be retained in the company as "retained earnings". Any sum retained by the company will be available for use in the company's business or for investment by the company. As such it will increase the value of the common shares, but it will not provide any direct benefit to any of the individuals associated with the company.

Payments received by an individual from a company are of course taxable in the hands of that individual if they constitute income within the meaning of the Act. In the case of interest, or salary and wages, there is no question of double taxation. These are costs which are incurred for the purpose of gaining or producing income, and therefore the company is permitted to deduct these payments from its taxable income, so that they are taxed only in the hands of the debt-holder, employee or other recipient.[6] However, the company is not permitted to deduct dividends paid

---

[5]This example was given in the technical notes to s. 256(5.1) when it was introduced in Bill C-139 on June 30, 1988.

[6]S. 18(1)(a). In addition, most employee benefits must be included in the income of an employee (s. 6, discussed under headings 5.5, "Benefits — general scheme", and 5.6, "Allowances", above) and, with the exception of club dues (s. 18(1)(l)) and entertainment ex-

to shareholders from its taxable income. Dividends are not costs of earning revenue; they are distributions of profits. Profits that are paid out to shareholders as dividends are therefore taxed twice: first at the corporate level as income of the company, and, second at the shareholder level as income of the individual shareholders. We shall see in the next section of this chapter that it is possible to give shareholders credit against their tax liabilities for tax paid by the corporation, so that the total tax liability at both the corporate and shareholder level is no greater than if the income actually earned by the company had been earned directly by the individual shareholders. This "integration" of the corporate and personal income tax was recommended by the Carter Commission, but only partially adopted by the Act of 1971.

Where integration (or other tax relief) is not provided for, corporate-source income is subjected to an element of "double taxation".[7] It is, of course, literally taxed twice, once at the corporate level and again at the shareholder level; but if the shareholder does not receive full credit for the tax paid at the corporate level, then the cumulative burden of the two taxes is heavier than the burden of tax which would be borne by the shareholder if he or she had earned the income directly.

What is the actual incidence of this extra taxation? Who ends up paying it? It is possible that some or all of the "extra" tax is "shifted" to the consumer in the form of higher prices for the corporation's goods and services; to the corporation's employees in the form of lower wages; or to capital generally, by way of lower investment in the corporation and greater investment in other assets, which reduces the economic return of those assets. The extent to which this shifting occurs will depend upon the nature of the corporation's market, how competitive it is and from whom the competition comes. This is because the incidence of the corporate income tax depends upon whether the corporations pass the tax on to their shareholders (in the form of reduced dividends) or their employees (in the form of lower wages) or their consumers (in the form of higher prices for the corporation's goods

---

penses (s. 67.1), discussed under heading 8.4(d), "Entertainment expenses", above, most are fully deductible to the company.

[7]The cost of a benefit provided to a shareholder in his or her capacity as a shareholder (i.e., *qua* shareholder) is subject to "double taxation": such benefits are not deductible at the corporate level (s. 18(1)(a)) and, since they are not dividends, there is no dividend tax credit to reduce the tax at the shareholder level. A shareholder receives a benefit *qua* shareholder (as opposed to *qua* employee) in cases where he or she is not an employee (or is provided with a benefit that other employees do not have). Such benefits are included in a shareholder's income under s. 15(1) (rather than under s. 6). A shareholder who is an individual must also include the amount of any loan or indebtedness provided by the company in income (s. 15(2)), but certain exceptions are provided in cases where the shareholder is also an employee: see ss. 15(2.2) to 15(2.6), discussed under heading 5.7(b), "Loans", below. If all or part of a shareholder's loan that has been included in income under s. 15(2) is subsequently repaid, the amount repaid can be deducted by the shareholder in the year of repayment: s. 20(1)(j). The objective of ss. 15(1) and 15(2) is to prevent shareholders from extracting cash from their companies without paying tax on the amount.

or services). There is a consensus that corporate income tax is ultimately borne by individuals, but no consensus on which groups of individuals bear the tax. Some tax incidence studies assume that the tax was born entirely by shareholders, while others assume that part of the tax was shifted back to employees and forward to consumers.[8] Different assumptions yield different conclusions about the incidence of the tax. To the extent that corporations are successful in passing the tax on to consumers through higher prices for their products, the corporate income tax is, in effect, a sales tax without exemptions, which is a regressive tax.

15.2 — Integration of corporation and shareholder taxes

(a) — Double taxation of corporate income

In an ideal tax system, income passing through an intermediary such as a corporation (or a trust) should not attract any additional (or any less) taxation than income received by an individual directly. In other words, the corporate income tax should be eliminated. However, this is more easily said than done.

One way of eliminating the double taxation of corporate-source income would be to levy no taxes on corporate income at all, and to levy taxes on individual shareholders on the basis of the dividends received by them. The trouble with this simple solution is that, if there were no tax on corporate income, individuals who could arrange to earn income through a corporation would be able to retain their savings untaxed in the corporation. In order to block this mode of tax avoidance without levying a tax on corporate income, it would be necessary to levy taxes on the individual shareholders on the basis not only of dividends received, but of the change in value of their shares during the year, that is, accrued gains or losses. The difficulty with this approach is the practical difficulty of valuing and taxing accrued capital gains, which, it will be recalled, had led the Carter Commission to recommend that in general capital gains should be taxed only when they were realized. The removal of taxes from corporate income would also mean a loss of revenue to Canada from the substantial proportion of corporate income which is attributable to those shares in Canadian corporations that are owned by non-residents of Canada.[9]

A second way of eliminating the double taxation of corporate-source income would be to levy a tax on corporate income at approximately the top individual rate, but to allow the corporation a deduction for dividends paid to shareholders. This would mean that the corporate income tax would apply only to retained earnings. Distributed earnings would bear no corporate income tax; they would be taxed only in the

[8]See, for example, Vermaeten, Gillespie, and Vermaeten, "Tax Incidence in Canada" (1994) 42 *Can. Tax J.* 348; and Block and Shillington, "Incidence of Taxes in Ontario in 1991" in *Taxation and the Distribution of Income* (1994). Another study was published in the same year, but it examined the position of taxpayers after including the value of government expenditures and so is more properly considered a fiscal incidence study: Ruggeri, Van Wart and Howard, "The Redistributional Impact of Taxation in Canada" (1994) 42 *Can. Tax J.* 417.

[9]*Report of the Royal Commission on Taxation* (Carter Report) (1966), vol. 4, 4-5.

hands of individual shareholders. As we shall see, this is essentially the scheme of taxation of trusts.[10] The trust receives a deduction for income distributed to the beneficiaries; the trust itself pays tax only on income retained in the trust. The disadvantage of treating corporations in the same way as trusts is the large proportion of shares of Canadian corporations that are held by non-residents of Canada. If corporations were able to deduct dividends paid to shareholders, the dividends paid to non-residents of Canada would escape ordinary Canadian income tax at the shareholder level (because the shareholder would be non-resident) as well as at the corporate level (because the corporation would deduct the dividends). The dividends would attract the Part XIII withholding tax on payments to non-residents, but under the Act the Part XIII tax is only 25 per cent, and under Canada's tax treaties the rate is normally reduced to 15 per cent and occasionally to a lower rate.[11] Therefore, unless Canada raised the rate of its Part XIII tax, and renegotiated all of its tax treaties, the allowance to corporations of a deduction for dividends paid to shareholders would result in a loss of revenue.

A third way of eliminating the double taxation of corporate-source income would be to levy a tax on the corporation, but not on the shareholder: dividends would be received by individual shareholders free of tax. The difficulty with this idea is that it makes no adjustment for the differing ability of individual shareholders to pay tax. In effect, each shareholder of a corporation would bear a tax at the rate paid by the corporation. If the rate was low, this would be inappropriate for a high-income shareholder. If the rate was high, this would be inappropriate for a low-income shareholder.

A fourth way of eliminating the double taxation of corporate income is to levy taxes at both the corporate level and the shareholder level, but to "integrate" the two taxes so that the total of the two taxes is no greater than the single tax that would be paid by an individual receiving income directly (not through a corporation). Under a system of full integration, a corporation would pay tax on its income, but when the income was distributed to the shareholders they would report as their personal income not only the amount of corporate income received by them as a dividend, but also the amount of corporate income that had been paid by the corporation as tax. Then the shareholders would receive credit against their personal income tax liability for the full amount of tax paid by the corporation in respect of the distributed income. In order to remove any tax advantage from the retention of corporate earnings, the corporate income should be taxed at the same rate as the top rate of personal income tax.[12] An integration system was recommended by the Carter Commission and is explained in the next section of this chapter.

---

[10]Ch. 17, Trusts, below.

[11]See chapter 3, "Residence", above.

[12]Carter Report, note 9, above, vol. 4, 7.

(b) — History

(i) — Carter Commission's proposals

The Carter Commission concluded that the only practical way to eliminate the double taxation of corporate-source income was to integrate the corporate and personal income taxes. To this end, the Commission proposed an imputation (or gross-up and credit) system along the lines described in the previous paragraph.

The Carter proposal may be illustrated by the following example. Suppose that a shareholder receives a dividend of $50. This actually represents $100 of income received by the corporation, because (under the Carter proposals) the corporation would have paid tax at the rate of 50 per cent before it paid the dividend. For tax purposes, the additional corporate income is "imputed" to the shareholder. The shareholder in reporting his or her income for tax purposes "grosses up" the dividend by 100 per cent (the amount of tax paid by the corporation) in order to include the full amount of corporate income in his or her personal income. The shareholder then becomes liable to pay tax on the full $100 at whatever rate of tax his or her personal income attracts. From the resulting tax liability the shareholder receives credit for $50, the amount of the tax paid by the corporation (and also the amount by which the dividend was grossed-up for inclusion in the personal tax return). The result for taxpayers in various brackets is illustrated in the following table:[13]

Table 15-1

		Tax bracket of shareholder*	
		15%	**50%**
1.	Dividend received	$50.00	$50.00
2.	Gross-up for corporate tax paid	50.00	50.00
3.	Taxable income	100.00	100.00
4.	Personal tax	15.00	50.00
5.	Minus tax paid by corporation: line 2	(50.00)	(50.00)
6.	Tax (refund)	(35.00)	Nil
7.	(Tax) refund	$35.00	Nil
8.	Plus cash dividend: line 1	50.00	50.00
9.	Total cash received by shareholder	$85.00	$50.00

* Combined federal-provincial personal tax bracket

If you compare the last figure of each column (total cash received by shareholder) with the shareholder's tax bracket for that year, you will notice that the total cash received by the shareholder is exactly the sum that he or she would have received had the corporate income of $100 been received by him or her directly. Thus the taxpayer with a marginal rate of 15 per cent receives $85 ($100 less 15 per cent) and the taxpayer at 50 per cent receives $50 ($100 less 50 per cent). The gross-up

[13]The table is a modification of Table 19-1 in the Carter Report, note 9, above, vol. 4, 8.

and credit procedure eliminates the ultimate impact of corporate income tax by integrating it with the personal income tax.

The integration of corporate and personal income taxes would satisfy the basic demands of equity and neutrality by ensuring that the ultimate tax on income received through a corporation was the same as if the income had been received directly by individuals. An individual who could arrange to receive his or her income through a corporation would pay tax at the same rate as the taxpayer who received the same amount of income directly. Nor could the shareholder-taxpayer gain any advantage by causing the corporation to retain its earnings, because all corporate earnings were to be taxed at 50 per cent, which under the Commission's recommendations would also be the top rate of personal income tax.

There were some other side effects of the Carter proposal. The gross-up and credit procedure would be available only in respect of dividends received by Canadian residents. This would improve the after-tax rate of return on shares in Canadian corporations for most Canadian residents, but not for non-residents. This would in turn lead to a rise in the price of Canadian shares, which would encourage non-residents (whose after-tax yield would not justify the higher price) to sell their shares to Canadians. The increase in price of Canadian shares would lower the cost of raising share capital in Canada which should increase the total amount of share capital raised in Canada, and encourage Canadian corporations owned by non-residents to raise new capital by issuing shares in Canada.[14] These side effects appear to conflict with Carter's goal of neutrality, but they were simply the inevitable consequences of applying the system of integration to the tax system of Canada but not the United States. In any event, the tendencies of the new system were all in the direction of increased Canadian ownership of Canadian corporations, a result of which most Canadians would presumably approve.[15]

(ii) — Tax reform of 1971

The Act that was enacted in 1971 did not fully accept any of the Carter Commission's proposals. First, the integration of corporate and personal income taxes was only implemented with respect to two classes of corporate income, namely, the Canadian investment income of private corporations and (within limits) the active business income of CCPCs. Second, the taxation of all corporate income at the flat rate of 50 per cent was not implemented, although corporate income other than the Canadian investment income of private corporations and the active business income of a CCPC was taxed at a "standard" flat rate of 50 per cent; the two exceptional categories of corporate income were taxed at a "low" rate of 25 per cent. Third, the top rate of personal income tax (which was 80 per cent in 1971) was not

---

[14] *Ibid.*, at 9.

[15] It would be possible by treaty to extend the benefits of an imputation (gross-up and credit) system of taxing dividends to Canadian-corporation shareholders who are resident in the United States or other countries. However, the rules would involve a complex relationship between two national tax systems and would presumably result in lost revenue to Canada.

brought down to 50 per cent — the same as the standard corporate rate — although it was reduced to a combined federal-provincial rate of approximately 61 per cent.

Although the 1971 Act did not adopt full integration of corporate and personal income taxes, it did adopt an imputation system of taxing dividends. The Act required that the tax on dividends in the hands of individual shareholders be calculated by the gross-up and credit procedure recommended by Carter. However, the gross-up in the 1971 Act was not Carter's 100 per cent but 33 1/3 per cent, and the credit was not Carter's 100 per cent but 33 1/3 per cent. The 33 1/3 per cent gross-up in the 1971 Act and credit "imputed" to the shareholder (i.e., added to the shareholder's income, and credited against the shareholder's tax) assumed a corporate income tax at the rate of 25 per cent. The corporate rate of 25 per cent was the "low rate" of tax which the 1971 Act imposed on the Canadian investment income of private corporations and (within limits) the Canadian active business income of CCPCs. In respect of this income, therefore, corporate and personal income taxes were integrated.

(iii) — Subsequent reforms: 1972 to 2005

After 1971, the Act was frequently amended to alter the corporate tax system. The amount of the dividend gross-up and credit was changed in 1977 from 33 1/3 per cent to 50 per cent, and in 1987 was changed back to 33 1/3 per cent. In 1982, the low rate of tax on Canadian investment income of private corporations was extended to foreign (as well as Canadian) investment income, but the rate could be claimed only by CCPCs (instead of all private corporations). Various other changes were made and unmade in the period up to 1988. It was the tax reforms of 1988, 1994/1995 and 2000, 2006 and 2008 which put into place the rules that are in effect at the time of writing (2010).

(c) — Current rules

The basic rules for 2010 are as follows. The basic federal rate of corporate income tax is 38 per cent. Because a rate reduction of 10 per cent (in 2010) is available on most types of income, the combined federal-provincial net rate on most types of income is 30 per cent in most provinces. [16]This rate reduction takes the form of the "manufacturing and processing credit" for corporations engaged in manufacturing and processing and the "general rate reduction" for corporations earning other types of income.[17] There is no ten per cent rate reduction on investment income and Canadian active business income earned by CCPCs which is eligible for the small business deduction because both are subject to tax at a lower rate.

---

[16]This combined 30% rate assumes that the provincial rate is 12% and is calculated as follows: 38% - 10% abatement — 10% general tax reduction + 12% provincial rate. Provincial rates vary by province and range from 10% to 16% in 2010 for income other than income eligible for the small business deduction.

[17]The rate reduction increases from 10% in 2010 to 11.5% in 2011 to 13% in 2012 and subsequent years.

The combined federal-provincial net rate on the investment income of CCPCs (after the investment income has been distributed to shareholders as a dividend and tax is refunded as a dividend refund) is about 20 per cent in most provinces.[18] The combined rate of tax on the first $500,000 of Canadian active business income of CCPCs earned annually is eligible for the small business deduction is about 16 per cent in most provinces.[19] Dividends paid by CCPCs out of income eligible for the small business deduction and investment income have a dividend gross-up and credit of 25 per cent, which compensates the shareholder for corporate tax at the rate of 20 per cent, which is close to the low rate of corporate income tax on the investment income and the first $500,000 of active business income of CCPCs. For those two categories of income, integration is approximately achieved. More detail on the present system is provided later in the chapter.

The current system is designed to provide integration of the low-rate (16% and 21%) and high-rate corporate income tax (30%) with the personal income tax. The low-rate system works with a 20% low corporate rate. Assume, for example, that a corporation earns income of $100, which is taxed at the low combined rate of 20 per cent (as would be the case for a CCPC earning investment income subject to provincial tax of 12 per cent or a CCPC earning up to $500,000 of Canadian active business income subject to provincial tax of eight per cent). Assume that the after-tax portion of the corporation's income, namely, $80, is paid to a shareholder, who resides in a province where the provincial personal income tax rate is 50 per cent of the federal rate, and whose total income places him or her in the top federal personal tax bracket of 29 per cent, which yields a combined rate (ignoring surtaxes) of 43.5 per cent (29 per cent × 150 per cent = 43.5 per cent). That case is reflected in the first column of Table 15-2, below. The second column assumes that the shareholder is in the first federal personal tax bracket of 15.5 per cent, which yields a combined rate of 23.25 per cent (15.5 per cent × 150 per cent = 23.25%).[20]

---

[18]The 20% results from a 46.67% combined initial tax rate and a 26.67% dividend refund when the income is distributed to shareholders as a dividend. The 46.67% combined initial rate is computed as 38% - 10% (abatement) + 6 2/3% (additional refundable tax) plus 12% assumed provincial rate. This is explained under heading 15.5(c), "Investment income of Canadian-controlled private corporations", below.

[19]The combined 16% rate assumes a 5% provincial rate: 20% = 38% — 10% (abatement) — 17% + 5% provincial rate. Provincial rates vary by province and range from 1% to 16% in 2010.

[20]For individual income tax rates, see heading 14.6, "Tax rates", above.

Table 15-2

		Tax bracket of shareholder*	
		43.5%	**23.25%**
1.	Corporate income before tax	$100.00	$100.00
2.	20% Corporate income tax*	(20.00)	(20.00)
3.	Corporate income after tax	80.00	80.00
4.	Dividend paid to shareholder	$80.00	$80.00
5.	25% Gross-up	20.00	20.00
6.	Taxable amount	100.00	100.00
7.	Personal income tax on $100 taxable amount	$43.50	$23.25
8.	25% Dividend tax credit*	(20.00)	(20.00)
9.	Net personal income tax	23.50	3.25
10.	Total tax paid by corporation and shareholder: line 2 + line 9	$43.50	$23.25
11.	Tax if shareholder had earned $100 directly: line 7	$43.50	23.25

* Assumed combined federal-provincial rates

In Table 15-2, the shareholder is required to report as income $20 more than he or she actually received (the gross-up), and receives a tax credit of the same amount (the dividend tax credit). In this way, the tax paid by the corporation is imputed to the shareholder. In column 1, the result for the shareholder in the 43.5 per cent bracket is that he or she pays $23.50 of personal tax on the dividend; this figure, when combined with the $20 paid by the corporation, yields a total tax paid of $43.50 (line 10). That is precisely the amount of tax that the individual would have paid had he or she earned the $100 directly (line 11). Lines 10 and 11 are again identical in column 2, the result for the shareholder in the 23.25 per cent bracket. This means that, regardless of the personal tax bracket of the individual shareholder, the corporate and personal income taxes are perfectly integrated (in theory). There is no difference in the tax treatment of a person who earns income through a corporation and a person who earns the same amount of income directly. The intervention of the intermediary (the corporation) does not increase (or reduce) the total burden of tax imposed on the income.

Dividends (called "eligible dividends") paid out of corporate income that is taxed at the high-rate of 30 per cent[21] are eligible for a higher gross-up of 44 per cent (in 2010).[22] Table 15-3 shows the effect of the 25 per cent and 44 per cent gross-up

[21]See note 16, above.

[22]The higher gross-up for eligible dividends was 45% when it was introduced in 2006. Because of reductions in federal and provincial corporate rates, the 2008 federal budget reduced the gross-up to 44% in 2010, to 41% in 2011 and to 38% in 2012.

and credit rules on corporate income that is taxed at the high-rate of 30 per cent. The 25% gross-up and credit rule of one-quarter of the dividend produces a serious under-integration for corporate-source income that has borne tax at a standard rate of 30 per cent. An individual taxpayer in the 43.5 per cent tax bracket would receive an after-tax return of $50.79 ($100.00 - $49.21) on $100 of corporate-source income, compared with an after-tax return of $56.50 ($100.00 - $43.50) on $100 of income received directly. Because the gross-up and credit of 25 per cent of the dividend provides compensation to the shareholder for corporate tax of only 20 per cent of the corporate income, when the corporate tax is more than 20 per cent, the compensation is insufficient.

Compare this with the 44 per cent gross-up and mechanism, which improves the situation substantially. There is no difference in the tax treatment of a person who earns income through a corporation and a person who earns the same amount of income directly when the combined corporate tax rate is 30 per cent and the dividend gross-up is 44 per cent. The intervention of the intermediary (the corporation) does not increase (or reduce) the total burden of tax on the income.

Table 15-3

		Tax bracket of shareholder*	
		44%	**25%**
1.	Corporate income before tax	$100.00	$100.00
2.	Corporate income tax at 30%*	(30.00)	(31.00)
3.	Corporate income after tax	70.00	69.00
4.	Dividend paid to shareholder	$70.00	$69.00
5.	Gross-up (44% or 25%)	30.00	17.25
6.	Taxable amount	100.00	86.25
7.	Personal income tax at 43.5%	$43.50	$43.50
8.	Dividend tax credit* (equal to gross-up)	(30.00)	(17.25)
9.	Net personal income tax	13.50	26.25
10.	Total tax paid by corporation and shareholder: line 2 + line 9	$43.50	$57.25
11.	Tax if shareholder had earned $100 directly: line 7	$43.50	$43.50

* Assumed combined federal-provincial rates

15.3 — Sheltering income in a corporation

(a) — The problem

The integration of corporate and personal income taxes would be perfectly achieved if corporate income was free of tax; the only tax would be levied at the individual shareholder level. But this regime would give rise to other problems. One is that corporate income attributable to shares owned by non-residents of Canada would escape Canadian tax, except for the withholding tax on payments to non-residents. Another is that corporations would be encouraged to retain their earnings rather than distribute them to the shareholders (where they would be taxed). Individuals with income in excess of their personal needs would make sure that their investments and their businesses were held by corporations; excess income would be retained in the corporations where it would be sheltered from tax. The only way to overcome this form of avoidance would be to tax the annual accrued gain on the shares held by the individual shareholders, which would present major administrative difficulties. These are the reasons that led the Carter Commission to recommend that taxes be levied at the corporate as well as the shareholder level, and that integration be achieved by the imputation method of taxing dividends.

The problems that would arise from a failure to tax corporate income at all also arise, albeit in less severe form, when corporate income is taxed at a lower rate than the top rate applicable to personal income. High-income individuals then have an incentive to store excess income in corporations where it will be at least partly sheltered from tax. In the absence of remedial provisions, a high-income investor would use a holding company to make his or her investments, leaving the income in the corporation for reinvestment, so that the extra bite of personal income tax that would be triggered by the payment of a dividend is put off (or "deferred") for as long as possible. Even a corporation with a genuine business purpose would be powerfully influenced to retain profits in excess of the personal needs of a controlling shareholder so as to avoid that second bite of tax. As corporations became swollen with retained earnings, shareholders would search for ways of removing the earnings other than through dividends that would attract tax. This would lead to complex "dividend stripping" or "surplus stripping" schemes, which, if successful, would have to be countered by amendments to the Act.

(b) — History

(i) — Carter Commission

All of these problems existed in Canada when the Carter Commission reported in 1966. At that time, there was a "low rate" of tax on corporate income up to $35,000 of only 21 per cent; above that level, the "standard rate" was 50 per cent. Rates of personal income tax, by contrast, rose to 80 per cent. The Carter Commission recommended that there should be no "low rate" of corporate income tax. All corporate income should be taxed at the same rate of 50 per cent, and that rate of 50 per cent should also be the top rate of personal income tax. This would have eliminated any tax incentive for an individual to earn income through a corporation instead of directly, and (when combined with the Commission's scheme of integration) would have eliminated any tax incentive for a corporation to retain its earnings rather than distributing them to its shareholders.

(ii) — Tax reform of 1971

The government did not accept Carter's recommendations. The Act of 1971 did reduce the top rates of personal income tax so that (when combined with the various provincial rates) the top rate fell from its 1971 level of 80 per cent to 61 per cent for residents of Ontario (and somewhat higher for residents of most other provinces). This was a step in Carter's direction, but it left the top personal income tax rate well above the rate of 50 per cent which was established as the standard rate for the income of corporations (section 123). The standard corporate rate was set to decline by one percentage point per year down to 46 per cent in 1976, and that decline increased the discrepancy between the top personal rate and the standard corporate rate. In addition, the 1971 Act introduced the "small business deduction" which had the effect of reducing the standard rate of federal tax all the way down to 25 per cent for Canadian active business income of CCPCs. This was the old "low rate" of tax in a new guise. The discrepancy between a top personal tax rate of over 60 per cent and a low corporate rate of 25 per cent created the same powerful incentive to retain earnings in a corporation, and thereby defer the payment of personal taxes by the shareholders.[23] That low rate persists to this day. The combined federal provincial rate is 20 per cent if provincial tax is 8 per cent (38 per cent - 10 per cent - 16 per cent + 8 per cent).

(iii) — Tax reform of 1988

The tax reform of 1988 narrowed the discrepancy between the top personal rate and the standard corporate rate of income tax. The top personal rate was reduced to 29 per cent federally, which, in a province that levied provincial tax at the rate of 50 per cent of the federal rate, rose to a combined level of 43.5 per cent (29 per cent + 150 per cent = 43.5 per cent). The standard corporate rate was reduced to 38 per cent, with a 10 per cent abatement to allow the provinces room to levy their own corporate income taxes. Ignoring the corporate surtax, this yielded a rate of 38 per cent in a province that levied its tax at 10 per cent (the same level as the abatement). Actual rates depended on the province but the general situation was that the top personal and corporate rates were fairly close.

The tax reform of 1988 did not get rid of the low rate of tax produced by the small business deduction (subsection 125(1)). The tax credit for Canadian active business income earned by CCPCs still reduced their federal tax rate by 16 per cent to 12 per cent (after abatement) (38 per cent - 10 per cent - 16 per cent = 12 per cent) so that, in a province that levied tax on income eligible for the small business deduction at the rate of 8 per cent, the combined federal-provincial rate was 20 per cent (12 per cent + 8 per cent = 20 per cent). We have already noted that the tax reform of 1988 set the rate of gross-up and credit at 25 per cent of dividends. That is the level at which integration of personal and corporate income taxes is achieved for corporate-source income, when tax at the corporate level is 20 per cent. Even with integration, the payment of a dividend out of this low-rate corporate income will generate a considerable personal tax liability for a high-income shareholder. Obviously, in

---

[23]It also led to much litigation of the question of what qualified as active business income. The term is now defined in s. 125(7), although the definition does not solve all problems: see heading 15.5(d)(ii), "Active business income", below.

order to defer that personal tax liability, the incentive to retain low-rate income in a CCPC remains.

(iv) — Reforms in the 1994 and 1995 budgets

After the tax reform of 1988, steep increases in provincial personal income tax rates, as well as federal and provincial surtaxes, brought the top combined federal-provincial personal income tax rates up to above 50 per cent in all provinces except Alberta. At the same time, there were lesser increases in provincial corporate tax rates and federal and provincial corporate surtaxes, so that in most provinces the federal standard rate of 38 per cent rose to a combined federal-provincial corporate tax rate of about 43 per cent (with provincial taxes of around 15 per cent). A gap of seven percentage points between the top personal rate and the combined corporate rate created an incentive for wealthy Canadians to transfer their investments to investment holding companies to have the income at the lower corporate rates.

The federal budgets of 1994 and 1995 increased the tax that a CCPC must pay on investment income not distributed to shareholders. The purpose was to reduce the gap between the corporate tax rate and the top personal tax rate and thus remove the opportunity to defer personal tax by retaining investment income in a corporation. The two budgets did not make any fundamental change in the taxation of the Canadian active business income of CCPCs although the budget of 1994 did tax the low rate caused by the small business deduction away from very large CCPCs. The small business deduction is explained later in this chapter.[24]

With respect to the investment income of CCPCs, the budgets of 1994 and 1995 made two changes. The first was to increase the refundable Part IV tax that private corporations pay on dividends received from other taxable Canadian corporations from the 25 per cent rate that was imposed by the tax reform of 1988 to 33 ⅓ per cent. The rate of 33 ⅓ per cent is much closer to the top rate that individuals pay on dividends after gross-up and credit. (The Part IV tax is explained later in this chapter.[25]) The second change was to increase the tax on investment income other than dividends of CCPCs by a special 6 ⅔ per cent additional refundable tax. When this is added to the average combined federal-provincial corporate rate, which is about 40 per cent in 2010 (with provincial taxes of around 12 per cent but without the general rate reduction), it brings the rate of tax on the investment income of CCPCs up to a level that is close to the top personal tax rate. Both of these tax increases are refundable: they increase the taxes paid initially by an investment holding corporation, but they are refunded when investment income is distributed to individual shareholders. The mechanics of the system of refundable taxes on investment income is discussed later in this chapter.[26]

---

[24]See heading 15.5(d)(i), "Small business deduction", below.

[25]See heading 15.5(c)(iv), "Dividends", below.

[26]See heading 15.5(c), "Investment income of Canadian-controlled private corporations", below.

(v) — Rate reductions from 2000 to 2006

In order to make Canada's corporate tax system more internationally competitive, particularly with the United States,[27] the February 28, 2000 budget and October 18, 2000 federal economic statement introduced a seven per cent general rate reduction which phased in over several years.[28] This rate reduction did not apply to income that was already eligible for reduced rates, i.e., income eligible for the manufacturing and processing deduction, income eligible for the small business deduction and investment income earned by CCPCs. This rate reduction reduced the federal rate (after the 10 per cent abatement) from 28 per cent to 21 per cent and the combined federal-provincial corporate tax rate (with provincial taxes of 14%) from about 42 per cent to 35 per cent.

(c) — Rate reductions for 2007 to 2011

The small business deduction increased from 16 per cent in 2007 to 16.5 per cent in 2008 and 17 per cent in 2009 and subsequent years.

The general rate reduction increased from seven per cent in 2007 to eight and a half per cent in 2008, nine per cent in 2009, ten per cent in 2010 and will increase to 11.5 per cent in 2011 and 13 per cent in 2012. This will reduce the federal rate (after the 10 per cent abatement) from 21 per cent (in 2007) to 15 per cent (in 2012). With the effect of provincial tax reductions, the combined federal-provincial corporate general tax rate has fallen from about 35 per cent (with provincial taxes of 14 per cent) in 2007 to 30 per cent (with provincial taxes of 12 per cent) in 2010. The federal 2010 budget states that the federal-provincial goal is a 25 per cent combined rate in 2012 (with provincial taxes of 12 per cent) which will be the lowest in the G7.[29]

15.4 — Taxation of shareholders

(a) — Integration and imputation

In an earlier section of this chapter it was explained that the corporate-level tax and the shareholder-level tax on corporate-source income could be integrated by notionally imputing to the shareholder the corporate-level tax already paid by the corporation.[30] The Carter Commission popularized the term "integration" in Canada to describe the gross-up and credit system which the Commission advocated. Similar systems have been enacted in Europe (though not in the United States), where they are described as "imputation" systems. The term "imputation" is probably the more useful one to describe a system which gives too little (or too much) credit to shareholders for the tax paid by the corporation and which accordingly leaves some part

[27]Federal Budget, February 28, 2000, Supplementary Information, "Corporate Tax Rate Reduction".

[28]S. 123.4: see discussion under heading 15.5(b)(ii), "General rate reduction", below.

[29]Department of Finance, Budget 2010, March 4, 2010, page 47.

[30]See heading 15.2, "Integration of corporation and shareholder taxes", above.

of the two taxes "dis-integrated".[31] The earlier section of this chapter showed how Canada's imputation system works in principle, but the earlier account omitted many complications. This section of the chapter will examine in more detail how shareholders are taxed, and the next section will examine how corporations are taxed.[32]

(b) — Gross-up and credit procedure

When a shareholder receives a dividend on his or her shares, the dividend is income from property. Paragraph 12(1)(j) (in subdivision b) requires the inclusion in a taxpayer's income of: any amount required by subdivision h to be included in computing the taxpayer's income for the year in respect of a dividend paid by a corporation resident in Canada on a share of its capital stock.

Subdivision h, which is headed "Corporations Resident in Canada and their Shareholders", opens with subsection 82(1), and provides (for 2009 and subsequent years):

> In computing the income of a taxpayer for a taxation year, there shall be included the total of the following amounts:
>
> (a) the amount, if any, by which
>
> (i) the total of all amounts, other than eligible dividends. . .received by the taxpayer in the taxation year from corporations resident in Canada as, on account of, in lieu of payment of or in satisfaction of, taxable dividends,
>
> . . . . .
>
> (a.1) the amount, if any, by which
>
> (i) the total of all amounts. . . received by the taxpayer in the taxation year from corporations resident in Canada as, on account of, in lieu of payment of or in satisfaction of, eligible dividends,
>
> . . . . .
>
> (b) if the taxpayer is an individual, other than a trust that is a registered charity, the total of
>
> (i) 25% of the amount determined under paragraph (a) in respect of the taxpayer for the taxation year, and
>
> (ii) the product of the amount determined under paragraph (a.1) in respect of the taxpayer for the taxation year multiplied by
>
> (A) for the 2009 taxation year, 45%,[33]
>
> (B) for the 2010 taxation year, 44%,
>
> (C) for the 2011 taxation year, 41%, and

---

[31]Gibson, "Imputation Tax Systems" (1979) 27 *Can. Tax J.* 347, 348.

[32]See Kellough and McQuillan, *Taxation of Private Corporations and their Shareholders* (3rd ed.) (1999).

[33]The 45% gross-up also applied for 2006 to 2008.

(D) for taxation years after 2011, 38%;

Paragraph 82(1)(a) refers to "corporations resident in Canada"[34] and "taxable dividends" other than "eligible dividends" Paragraph 82(1)(a.1) refers in turn to "eligible dividends". The terms "eligible dividends" and "taxable dividends" are defined in subsection 89(1). "Taxable dividends" means all dividends except for dividends which are exempt from tax (subsection 89(1))[35] and a dividend is an "eligible dividend" if the corporation designates it as such when it is paid (subsection 89(14)). This text will refer to taxable dividends other than eligible dividends as "ineligible dividends".

Eligible dividends can be designated by public and private corporations. Dividends paid out of active business income eligible for the small business deduction or investment income eligible for refundable tax treatment will not be eligible for designation by CCPCs. Each CCPC will have a general-rate income pool (GRIP) and can designate and pay eligible dividends during the year to the extent that its GRIP has a positive balance at year end.[36] Excess designations are subject to penalty tax.[37]

Paragraphs 82(1)(a) and 82(1)(a.1) requires the inclusion in the shareholder's income of a dividends "received" by the taxpayer. (It will be recalled that the word

[34]See heading 3.4, "Residence of corporations", above.

[35]For practical purposes, taxable dividends are all dividends except those paid out of the capital dividend account of a private corporation. This chapter will be confined to describing the tax situation of taxable Canadian corporations and their shareholders. Dividends from other corporations are included in income from property, but there is no gross-up and credit: ss. 12(1)(j), 12(1)(k), 82(1)(a), 90.

[36]S. 89(1) provides that each CCPC's GRIP account will include the following amounts for each taxation year, starting with the 2006 taxation year:

Eligible dividends received

Plus: 68% of taxable income earned in 2006 and before 2010 (excluding active business income eligible for the small business deduction and investment income eligible for refundable tax treatment). The 68% is the "general rate factor" for 2006 to 2009 (as defined in s. 89(1)). This general rate factor increases to 69% in 2010; 70% in 2011 and 72% after 2011;

Less: eligible dividends paid.

S. 89(7) provides that at the beginning of each CCPC's 2006 taxation year, each CCPC will have a GRIP account balance reflecting taxable income earned and dividends received and paid in the 2001 to 2005 taxation years. The calculation is slightly different than the annual GRIP calculation in s. 89(1).

[37]Corporations making excess designations will pay Part III.1 tax equal to 20% of the excess designation. A corporation that makes an excess designation in error can avoid Part III.1 tax by electing to treat all or part of the excess designation as a separate non-eligible dividend. The election must be filed within 90 days after the mailing of the notice of Part III.1 assessment. A Part III.1 return must also be filed by a corporation resident in Canada paying taxable dividends (eligible or non-eligible).

"received" calls for the cash method of reporting income.)[38] Paragraph 82(1)(b) then requires the shareholder who is an individual to include an additional amount equal to 25 per cent for an ineligible dividend (subparagraph 82(1)(b)(i)) and 44 per cent (in 2010) for eligible dividends (subparagraph 82(1)(b)(ii)). The shareholder is thus required to "gross-up" the dividend actually received by a factor of 25 per cent or 44 per cent (as the case may be) and to include the grossed-up figure of 1.25 or 1.44 in his or her income. The shareholder therefore pays tax not only on the dividend that he or she received, but also on the gross-up that he or she did not receive. However, against his or her total personal tax liability the shareholder is allowed a dividend tax credit which should, in principle, be equal to the gross-up. The simple method of computing the tax liability of a shareholder who receives an ineligible dividend of $100 in a province that levies personal income tax at the rate of 50 per cent is displayed in the following Table 15-4.

---

[38]See heading 6.5(a), "Cash method", above.

Table 15-4

		Tax bracket of shareholder*	
		43.5%	**23.25%**
1.	Dividend received (s. 82(1)(a))	$100.00	$100.00
2.	Gross-up (s. 82(1)(b))	25.00	25.00
3.	Taxable income	125.00	125.00
4.	Personal income tax	$54.38	29.06
5.	Dividend tax credit*	(25.00)	(25.00)
6.	Net personal income tax	$29.38	$4.06

* Combined federal-provincial rates

In principle, in an imputation system, the credit should equal the gross-up. Table 15-4 assumes that the tax credit is equal to the gross-up (one quarter of the dividend). However, this assumption is correct only in a province that levies a personal income tax which is about 50 per cent of the federal tax and provides a provincial dividend tax credit which is about 50 per cent of the federal dividend tax credit. This is because the federal dividend tax credit is provided by section 121, which provides as follows for 2009 and subsequent years:

> There may be deducted from the tax otherwise payable under this Part by an individual for a taxation year the total of
>
> (a) 2/3 of the amount, if any, that is required by subparagraph 82(1)(b)(i) to be included in computing the individual's income for the year; and
>
> (b) the product of the amount, if any, that is required by subparagraph 82(1)(b)(ii) to be included in computing the individual's income for the year multiplied by
>
> (i) for the 2009 taxation year, 11/18,[39]
>
> (ii) for the 2010 taxation year, 10/17,
>
> (iii) for the 2011 taxation year, 13/23, and
>
> (iv) for the 2012 taxation year, 6/11.

It can be seen that section 121 allows the shareholder who receives an ineligible dividend a credit (a deduction from tax) of ⅔ of the gross-up (which is the amount required to be included under subparagraph 82(1)(b)). In order for the system to work when section 121 allows a credit of only ⅔ of the gross-up (rather than the full amount of the gross-up), the provincial tax systems must provide a credit equal to about the remaining ⅓ of the gross-up. The idea is that a taxpayer will get a credit from federal personal income tax of ⅔ of the gross-up (⅔ × 25 per cent gross-up = 16.67 per cent of the actual dividend) and a credit from provincial personal income tax of about ⅓ of the gross-up (⅓ × 25 per cent = 8.33 per cent). In theory, the full effect of the credit would be a reduction in tax about equal to the gross-up. In actual fact, the provincial dividend tax credit varies from province to

[39] The 11/18th fraction also applied from 2006 to 2008.

province, depending upon provincial tax policy and the dividend gross-up and credit system does not work perfectly.

The simple method of computing the tax liability of a shareholder who receives an eligible dividend of $100 in a province that levies personal income tax at the rate of 50 per cent is displayed in the following Table 15-5.

Table 15-5

	Tax bracket of shareholder	
	43.5%	**23.25%**
1. Dividend received (s. 82(1)(a.1))	$100.00	$100.00
2. Gross-up (s. 82(1)(b)(ii))	44.00	44.00
3. Taxable income	144.00	144.00
4. Personal income tax	$62.64	$31.32
5. Dividend tax credit*	(44.00)	(44.00)
6. Net personal income tax	$18.64	$Nil**

* Combined federal-provincial rates

** If the taxpayer owed tax on other sources of income, the excess dividend tax credit of $12.68 ($44 minus $31.32) could be used to reduce it. But if no tax was owing, the excess credit would be lost.

It can be seen that the 44 per cent gross-up and tax credit for eligible dividends in 2010 results in lower net personal tax in Table 15-5 than the 25 per cent gross-up and tax credit for ineligible dividends. In this case, section 121 allows the shareholder who receives an eligible dividend a credit (a deduction from tax) of 10/17 of the gross-up (which is the amount required to be included under subparagraph 82(1)(b)(ii)). In order for the system to work perfectly when section 121 allows a credit of only 10/17 of the gross-up (rather than the full amount of the gross-up), the provincial tax systems must provide a credit equal to about the remaining 7/17 of the gross-up. The idea is that a taxpayer will get a credit from federal personal income tax of 10/17 of the gross-up (10/17 × 44 per cent gross-up = 25.88 per cent of the actual dividend) and a credit from provincial personal income tax of about 7/17 of the gross-up (7/17 × 44 per cent = 18.12 per cent). All provinces have now adopted provincial tax rules that parallel the federal rules for eligible and ineligible dividends but the combined federal-provincial dividend tax credit is never exactly 44 per cent.

(c) — Effect of gross-up and credit

The gross-up and credit and credit procedure reduces the effective personal rate of tax on dividends from taxable Canadian corporations. The credit, when combined with the gross-up, is the same as additional taxable income. The effect of the per cent gross-up and credit is to increase the after-tax yield on dividend income so that it is equivalent to the after-tax yield on other income which is 44 per cent higher (in 2010) in the case of eligible dividends (25 per cent in the case of ineligible dividends). Thus, a dividend from a Canadian public corporation of $100 yields the same after-tax return as interest income of $144 (because it is an eligible dividend). The gross-up and credit therefore provides an incentive for individuals who are Canadian residents (non-residents and corporations are not entitled to the gross-up and credit) to invest in the shares of Canadian public corporations instead of those of foreign corporations.

The encouragement to invest in the shares of Canadian corporations is not, of course, the primary purpose of the gross-up and credit. The primary purpose is to impute to the shareholder all or part of the tax paid by the corporation on the gross income which is represented by the dividend. A tax of 30 per cent paid by the corporation will be wholly imputed by the 44 per cent gross-up and credit. On income which is taxed to the corporation at the rate of 30 per cent, the corporate-level tax (at 31 per cent) and the shareholder-level personal income tax is integrated. This was illustrated by Table 15-3 under heading 15.2(c) of this chapter. Similarly, a tax of 20 per cent paid by the corporation will be wholly imputed by the 25 per cent gross-up and credit. On income which is taxed to the corporation at the rate of 20 per cent, the corporate-level tax (at 20 per cent) and the shareholder-level personal income tax is integrated. This was illustrated by Table 15-2 under heading 15.2(c) of this chapter.

The reason why integration is achieved in each instance is that the gross-up is equal (in theory) to the corporate tax paid. The gross-up therefore restores the amount of the dividend to the figure received by the corporation before corporate tax: $70 (eligible dividend) + $30 tax (44% gross-up) = $100 (if the corporate tax rate is 30%) and $80 (eligible dividend) + $20 tax (25% gross-up) = $100 (if the corporate tax rate is 20%).

The total grossed-up dividend is then included in the shareholder's income and taxed at his or her marginal rate, exacting the same tax as if the individual had received the full amount of the income directly. The dividend tax credit is equal to the corporate tax which has already been paid by the corporation. The result is, therefore, that the individual has paid the same tax as if he or she had received the corporate income directly, minus the tax paid by the corporation.

The gross-up and credit procedure may be explained in another way. The individual shareholder reports as income not only the dividend actually received but also his or her share of the company's pre-corporate-tax distributed profits; he or she then receives a credit for the tax paid by the corporation. The corporate tax is a kind of withholding tax. The net effect is to eliminate "double taxation" of corporate profits.

The gross-up and credit mechanisms for eligible and ineligible dividends achieve integration of corporate and personal income taxes in respect of income which is taxed at general corporate rates and low corporate rates, respectively.

15.5 — Taxation of corporations

(a) — Taxable income

(i) — General rule

Generally speaking, the rules for computing "income" or net income are the same for corporations as they are for individuals. This follows from the fact that a corporation is a "person" as defined under subsection 248(1) and may be a "taxpayer" as defined under subsection 248(1). Division A of Part I of the Act applies to a "person", and most of the provisions of Division B which define net income apply to a "taxpayer". Some of the rules in Division B apply only to individuals and some only apply to corporations, however the general rule is that the computation is the same. Taxable income is different. As discussed in chapter 14, above, there are a considerable number of differences when it comes to Division C deductions and the taxable income computation.[40] The important Division C deductions for corporations are loss carryovers (discussed in chapter 14)[41] and the deductions for intercorporate dividends and charitable corporations, which are discussed below.

(ii) — Intercorporate dividends

We have already considered the problem of double taxation which arises because corporate-source income is subject to (1) the corporate income tax that is applicable when the income is earned by the corporation and (2) the personal income tax that is applicable when the corporation's after-tax income is distributed to the shareholders by the payment of dividends. We have also considered the imputation method (gross-up and credit) of taxing dividend income, which provides a partial remedy to the problem. Up to now, however, our assumption has always been that the shareholders of the corporation would be individuals. Needless to say, this is often not true: the shareholders of a corporation may include other corporations. If a dividend received by a corporation-shareholder were taxable to the recipient corporation, a third layer of tax would be imposed, because the income which the dividend represents has already been taxed in the hands of the payor corporation (which earned the income), and will be taxed again in the hands of the shareholders of the payee corporation when the payee corporation pays it out as a dividend to its own shareholders. Indeed, if the payee corporation itself has some corporate shareholders, then a fourth layer of tax would be imposed and a fifth or sixth layer would be possible. To tax corporate-source income twice is bad enough; to tax it more than twice is ridiculous.

The solution of the Act to the problem of multiple taxation is to effectively exempt from Part I tax (ordinary income tax) dividends received by a corporation (intercorporate dividends). The dividends have to be included in the "income" of the recipient corporation by virtue of subsection 82(1)(a) or (a.1), although they are not grossed-up (paragraph 82(1)(b) applies only "where the taxpayer is an individual"). However, subsection 112(1), which is in Division C of Part I, allows the amount of the dividends to be deducted from the income of the recipient corporation in computing its "taxable income". The net result is that intercorporate dividends are washed out of the taxable income of the recipient corporation.

The effective exemption from Part I tax (ordinary income tax) of intercorporate dividends applies whether the recipient is a "public corporation" or a "private corporation" (the definitions were discussed earlier in this chapter).[42] But dividends received by a private corporation are subject to a Part IV tax of 33 ⅓ per cent,

[40]See heading 14.5, "Taxable income", above.

[41]See heading 14.5(b), "Loss carryovers", above.

[42]See heading 15.1(c), "Public and private corporations", above.

which is refundable when the dividend is passed on to the private corporation's shareholders. The purpose of this tax, which is discussed more fully later,[43] is to discourage a private corporation from sheltering dividend income by not paying it out to the corporation's shareholders. The refund is made regardless of whether the private corporation's shareholder is an individual or another corporation.

(iii) — Charitable donations

Whereas individuals are allowed a non-refundable tax credit for charitable donations, corporations are allowed a deduction in computing taxable income.[44] The other rules are the same: the same types of donations qualify, the same maximum limit of 75 per cent of net income applies[45] and the same five-year carryforward applies. Because corporations do not die, there is no one-year carryback in the year of death.

(b) — Tax rates

(i) — Federal tax

The rules for the computation of tax (as distinct from the computation of income) are quite different for corporations than they are for individuals. Division E of Part I of the Act supplies the rules for the computation of tax. Subdivision a of Division E prescribes the rules applicable to individuals. It will be recalled that the leading features of subdivision a are the graduated rate schedule of section 117 and the indexing provision of section 117.1 which were examined in chapter 14. Subdivision b of Division E then sets out the rules applicable to corporations. They are our present concern.

Corporate income is not taxed at graduated rates. In place of the graduated rate schedule for individuals (section 117), the general rule for corporations is supplied by section 123, which imposes a single rate of 38 per cent. This is the "standard" federal rate, and it is a flat rate which applies regardless of how much taxable income a particular corporation derives. Because a corporation is simply an intermediary, there is no attempt to make the tax on corporate income "progressive".

(ii) — General rate reduction

Subsection 123.4(2) provides for a general rate reduction at the same rate as the manufacturing and processing credit: 10 per cent (in 2010). The general rate reduction applies to "full rate taxable income" which does not include income of a CCPC that is either investment income or income eligible for the small business deduction or the income of any corporation that is eligible for the manufacturing and process-

---

[43]See heading 15.5(c), "Investment income of Canadian-controlled private corporations", below.

[44]S. 110.1(1)

[45]The same rules also apply to exempt capital gains for qualifying donations of publicly traded securities and ecological property made after May 1, 2006: s. 38(a.1) and (a.2).

ing profits credit.[46] As discussed earlier, the general rate reduction and the manufacturing and process credit will increase from 10 per cent in 2010 to 11.5 per cent in 2011 to 13 per cent in 2011 and subsequent years.[47]

Before 2000, lower federal income tax rates were provided to Canada's manufacturing and processing and resource sectors. The purpose of this general rate reduction is to extend these reduced rates to all sectors including "the fast-growing service and knowledge-based firms that are likely to influence the pace of Canada's future economic and social development" in order to make Canada's corporate tax system more internationally competitive.[48]

(iii) — Corporate surtax

Before 2008, section 123.2 imposed a surtax of 4 per cent of corporate income tax. This resulted in a 1.12 per cent additional tax because it was computed as 4 % × 28 % (that is, as if the federal abatement applied to all taxable income.

(iv) — Large corporations tax

The "large corporations tax" was a federal capital tax that was imposed until January 1, 2006. It was computed by applying the Part I.3 rate for the year to the corporation's taxable capital employed in Canada in excess of $50 million.

The large corporations tax was a capital tax rather than an income tax: it based on the size of a corporation's balance sheet (its capital). Unlike provincial capital tax, this federal capital tax was reduced by corporate surtax. As a result, only a large corporation (with taxable capital in Canada in excess of $50 million) that paid no corporate surtax (and therefore has very low taxable income) paid large corporations tax.[49] In essence, it functioned as a "minimum tax" for large corporations that were not paying "enough" income tax.

---

[46]The taxation of these types of income is covered under headings 15.5(c), (d) and (e), below.

[47]Subsection 123.4(2) provides for the general rate reduction by providing a deduction from tax equal to the product obtained by multiplying the corporation's "general rate reduction percentage" by its "full-rate taxable income" which are defined in subsection 123.4(1) contains the definitions of "general rate reduction percentage" and "full-rate taxable income".

[48]February 28, 2000 federal budget, supplementary information, Corporate Tax Rate Reduction. There are still lower corporate rates for manufacturing and processing profits in several provinces and the separate federal manufacturing and processing deduction still exists for this reason. At the federal level, there are higher capital cost allowance rates for equipment and buildings used in manufacturing and processing activities: see heading 9.4(b)(ii), "Rate of CCA", above.

[49]A corporation was permitted to deduct its surtax liability for a particular year against its large corporations tax liability for that year. If the surtax liability was not wholly absorbed in a particular year, it could be carried over to other years (back three and forward seven) and credited against the large corporations tax in those other years.

This tax was repealed because basing a corporate minimum tax on a corporation's balance rather than its income was inherently unfair and penalized corporations in capital intensive industries which weren't earning high profits.

Some provinces also levy capital taxes on a corporation's taxable capital and several plan to reduce them or phase them out. In the text that follows, the corporation surtax, the large corporations tax and the provincial capital taxes will all be ignored for the sake of simplicity.

(v) — Provincial abatement

The rate of tax stipulated by section 123, like the graduated rates of section 117, is of course the rate of federal income tax. We have already noticed how the provincial income taxes correlate with the federal income tax for individuals.[50] The way in which the two levels of government share the field of corporate income tax is different and simpler. The federal rate of tax, namely, the 38 per cent rate under section 123, is subject to an abatement of 10 per cent, which is intended to allow the provinces "room" to levy their own corporate income taxes. The abatement is provided by subsection 124(1), which provides:

> There may be deducted from the tax otherwise payable by a corporation under this Part for a taxation year an amount equal to 10% of the corporation's taxable income earned in the year in a province.

Subsection 124(1) allows a deduction from tax, not income, so that it is preferable to describe it as a credit. The amount of the credit is however expressed as a percentage of income, not tax. It is "10% of the corporation's taxable income earned in the year in a province". (The federal *Interpretation Act* defines a province as including a territory.) The rules for allocating income to a particular province are set out in the *Income Tax Regulations*, Part IV, which were briefly described in chapter 3, Residence.[51]

(vi) — Provincial taxes

Eight of the provinces (and the three territories) levy corporate income taxes which are expressed as a percentage of the corporation's (federally-defined) taxable income earned in the province, and which is collected by the Canada Revenue Agency (CRA). That is because these provinces have entered into tax collection agreements with the federal government,[52] under which the federal government collects each agreeing province's corporate income tax on condition that the provincial tax is levied on the same income base as the federal corporate income tax. At the time of writing, (2010), Quebec and Alberta have not entered into tax collec-

[50]Ch. 14, Taxable Income and Tax for Individuals, above.

[51]See heading 3.6, "Provincial residence", above.

[52]See heading 2.2(d), "Federal-provincial agreements", above.

tion agreements with the federal government regarding corporate taxes.[53] They do levy corporate income taxes, of course, and the abatement is available in respect of corporate income earned in those provinces. However, the two provinces outside the collection agreements collect their own corporate income taxes and require separate provincial returns to be filed with each provincial government. Although Quebec and Alberta are currently free to define the base of corporate income tax as they choose, for the most part taxable income in those provinces is defined by the same rules for provincial tax purposes as for federal tax purposes. For ease of exposition in the rest of this chapter no distinctions will be drawn between Quebec and Alberta, on the one hand, and the remaining eight provinces, on the other.

The standard rates of tax levied by the provinces on corporate income in 2010 generally range between 10 and 16 per cent. Ontario's general rate is 12 per cent effective July 1, 2010. Each province has a lower rate (in 2010, between 2.5 and 8.9 per cent) for income that is eligible for the small business deduction, discussed below.[54] Many provinces also have lower rates for income that is eligible for the manufacturing and processing credit, discussed below.[55]

The rates of provincial tax have no relevance to corporate income earned outside Canada, for no provincial tax is levied on such income, and the abatement does not apply to such income. The rate of tax on such income is therefore the 38 per cent stipulated by section 123. But corporate income earned anywhere in Canada is taxed a rate of 38 per cent minus the abatement (10 per cent) minus the general tax reduction (10 per cent) plus the rate of provincial tax. In a province that levied tax on corporate income at the rate of 12 per cent, the combined rate of tax would therefore be 30 per cent (38 per cent - 10 per cent - 10 per cent + 12 per cent = 30 per cent).

(vii) — Standard corporate rate

The "standard" rate of corporate income tax (namely, 38 per cent minus the abatement minus general tax reduction plus surtax plus the provincial rate) is the rate of tax applicable to corporate income whenever the Act has no provision to the contrary. The two main provisions to the contrary are (1) the refundable tax on the investment income of CCPCs, which adds 6 ⅔ percentage points to the tax rate and then reduces the tax on that class of income after distribution to shareholders by 26 ⅔ percentage point and (2) the small business deduction in respect of qualifying active business income of CCPCs, which reduces the tax on that class of income by 17 percentage points. The manufacturing and processing profits credit is also relevant because income which is eligible for this 10% credit (instead of the 10% general rate reduction) is often eligible for lower provincial rates. These three provisions are our next three topics.

---

[53]The October 2006 agreement with Ontario is effective for taxation years ending after 2008.

[54]See heading 15.5(d)(i), "Small business deduction", below.

[55]See heading 15.5(e), "Manufacturing and processing credit", below.

(c) — Investment income of Canadian-controlled private corporations

(i) — Canadian-controlled private corporations

The statutory definition of a CCPC was examined earlier in this chapter.[56] A CCPC will often be closely held; in fact, the most common case is where the shares are all held by members of one family. Very often, the corporation is controlled by one person, who is the major shareholder and the principal manager of the corporation's investments and business.

(ii) — Policy

The rules concerning the investment income of CCPCs attempt to make the corporation an investment vehicle of little tax significance. This involves, in the first place, taxing the corporation and its shareholders so that the shareholders obtain the same after-tax return on the investments held by the corporation as they would have obtained if they had received the income from the investments directly. This "integration" of personal and corporate income tax is achieved, as we have seen, when the corporate tax rate is 20 per cent. Thus, the idea is to impose corporate income tax of approximately 20 per cent on the investment income of a CCPC that is distributed to the shareholders by the payment of dividends.

Secondly, however, the rules concerning taxation of the investment income of CCPCs try to discourage the retention of income in the corporation, which would of course postpone the tax payable at the individual shareholder level. This second objective is pursued by initially taxing the investment income of a CCPC at the standard corporate rate plus 6 ⅔ percentage points, which gives a rate close to the top personal rate. Tax equivalent to 26 ⅔ per cent of the investment income of the corporation is refunded to it when dividends are paid out to the corporation's shareholders. In general, the refund is designed to reduce the effective rate of corporation income tax to the theoretical rate of 20 per cent that achieves integration. The high initial rate of corporate income tax (before refund) will be an incentive to pay dividends to shareholders whose marginal rate is less than the standard corporate rate plus 6 ⅔ per cent.

The mechanism of the refund is the refundable dividend tax on hand (RDTOH) account which is briefly described next.

(iii) — Refundable dividend tax on hand account

The way in which the refund provisions work is complicated and the details are outside the scope of this book. Briefly, a CCPC will establish a "refundable dividend tax on hand" (RDTOH) account, and will credit the account with 26 ⅔ per cent of its "aggregate investment income". This term comprises, essentially, income from property (except for dividends from taxable Canadian corporations: see

---

[56]See heading 15.1(d), "Canadian-controlled private corporations", above.

next section) and taxable capital gains[57] (subsection 129(4)). The investment income may be Canadian or foreign. This RDTOH account represents money that has been paid to the CRA, but which will be refunded if and when the corporation pays dividends, in accordance with a formula established by the Act. The effect of the formula is that every $3 of dividend will generate a $1 refund from the RDTOH account.

For example, take the case of a CCPC that in a taxation year has investment income of $100. The corporation will pay combined federal-provincial corporate income tax at the rate of 46 ⅔ per cent in a province that levies provincial corporate income tax of 12 per cent (38 per cent + 6 ⅔% - 10 per cent + 12 per cent = 46 ⅔ per cent). The corporation will pay $46.67 of combined income tax, and will credit $26.67 (26.67 per cent of $100) to its RDTOH account. After tax, the corporation has only $53.33 left out of the $100 income, but it can also regard the $26.67 in the RDTOH account as available for payment of dividends, because that sum is refundable to the corporation by the CRA. The corporation can, therefore, pay a dividend of $80 to its shareholders. A dividend of $80 will entitle the corporation to a refund from the RDTOH account of $26.67 (i.e., $1 for each $3 of dividend paid). That refund, paid by the CRA, lowers the tax on the corporation's investment income from 46 ⅔ per cent to 20 per cent. Note that the full refund would only be made if the corporation paid a dividend of three times the amount in the RDTOH account, which in this example requires a dividend of $80 ($26.67 × 3 = $80). This ensures that the low rate of tax is applicable only to income that has been fully distributed by the corporation.

In the example given, after receiving the refund from the RDTOH account, the corporation pays a net tax of 20 per cent (46 ⅔ per cent - 26 ⅔ per cent = 20 per cent). The rate of 20 per cent is, of course, the rate at which perfect integration is achieved by the gross-up and credit rules for the taxation of dividends received by individual shareholders. Unfortunately, the rate of 20 per cent is more theoretical than real, because most provinces levy corporate income tax at rates of 10 to 16 per cent, instead of the 12 per cent that was assumed in the example. In addition, there is a federal corporate surtax of 4 per cent and there are provincial surtaxes which further increase the standard rate of corporate tax. When the standard combined federal-provincial rate of corporate tax (including surtaxes) plus 6 ⅔ per cent is more than 46 ⅔ per cent, then the refund from the RDTOH account will leave the net amount of corporate tax somewhat higher than the magic figure of 20 per cent, and integration will not be fully achieved.[58]

---

[57]The treatment of capital gains is explained under heading 15.5(c)(v), "Capital gains", below.

[58]When the 6 2/3 per cent "additional refundable tax" was introduced in the federal budget of February 27, 1995, the combined federal-provincial rates were even higher because (1) provincial rates in most provinces were higher and (2) the federal rate included 1.12% in respect of the federal surtax of 4%.

(iv) — Dividends

Dividends paid by taxable Canadian corporations are excluded from the definition of aggregate investment income. It will be recalled that dividends paid by taxable Canadian corporations to shareholders that are corporations must be reported by the corporation-shareholder as income from property, but are deductible under subsection 112(1). This deduction means that intercorporate dividends paid by taxable Canadian corporations are effectively exempt from Part I tax.[59] But in order to discourage the use of a private corporation to "store" tax-exempt dividend income, section 186 (which is in Part IV of the Act) imposes a special tax (Part IV tax) on private corporations of 33 ⅓ per cent of the dividends received by the private corporation that were deductible under subsection 112(1). When a dividend is received by a private corporation and the Part IV tax is paid, the full amount of the Part IV tax goes into the RDTOH account. It is therefore potentially refundable in full.[60]

The sole purpose of the Part IV tax is to encourage a private corporation to pass the dividends received by it along to the shareholders, in whose hands of course they will be taxable. In principle, in order to accomplish its purpose, the Part IV tax should be equal to the rate of personal income tax that would be payable on a dividend by an individual shareholder in the top tax bracket. After taking into account the reduction of tax on dividend income caused by the gross-up and credit procedure, the rate of 33 ⅓ per cent is about right for this purpose. Therefore, a high-income individual cannot defer any tax by holding portfolio investments in a private corporation and retaining the investment income in the corporation.

The refundable Part IV tax is payable by all private corporations, not just CCPCs. This means that a private corporation that is not a CCPC will also have an RDTOH account. However, that account will include only the Part IV tax on intercorporate dividends. The tax on other kinds of investment income, including income from property (other than dividends) and taxable capital gains is not partially refundable for a private corporation that is not a CCPC.[61]

(v) — Capital gains

Taxable capital gains come within the definition of aggregate investment income. When received by a CCPC, it is treated in the same way as income from property (other than dividends), that is, it is initially taxed at the standard corporate rate plus 6 ⅔ per cent, but, through the mechanism of the RDTOH account, a portion of the tax equivalent to 26 ⅔ per cent of the taxable capital gains is refundable. When the

---

[59] See heading 15.5(a)(ii), "Intercorporate dividends", above.

[60] If the corporation pays a dividend equal to the entire dividend received, this will produce a full refund from the refundable dividend tax on hand account, which pays a refund of $1 for every $3 of dividend.

[61] Before 1982, the partial refund of corporate tax on investment income other than dividends was available to all private corporations. Since 1982, it has been restricted to CCPCs. However, the Part IV tax on dividends is still payable by private corporations that are not CCPCs, and the tax is still refundable to private corporations that are not CCPCs.

taxable capital gains are distributed to the shareholders as dividends, the refund is obtained, reducing the rate of tax (in a province that levies corporate tax at the rate of 12 per cent) to 20 per cent, the rate that achieves integration.[62]

Taxable capital gains are one-half of capital gains. The non-taxable one-half of the capital gain, which has been received free of tax by the corporation, should not be taxed when it is distributed to the shareholders as a dividend. This would be a violation of integration, for the non-taxable one-half of a capital gain would be free of tax if received by an individual directly. The Act, by subsection 83(2), accordingly allows a private corporation, but not a public corporation, to set up a "capital dividend account" into which the non-taxable half of capital gains are placed. Out of that account, the corporation can "elect" (by filing special forms) to pay "capital dividends" to the shareholders. Capital dividends are tax-free in the hands of the shareholders.

(d) — Active business income of Canadian-controlled private corporations

(i) — Small business deduction

A CCPC pays a "low rate" of corporate income tax on its first $500,000 of Canadian active business income. Section 125 provides a "small business deduction" of 17 per cent of "the income of the corporation for the year from an active business carried on in Canada" up to a "business limit" of $500,000.[63] The deduction is from tax, not income, so that it is really a credit. The 17 per cent credit reduces the federal rate of tax on the qualifying active business income of a CCPC to 11 per cent (38 per cent - 10 per cent - 17 per cent = 11 per cent). This rate, when combined with provincial tax rates, which are also lower for this class of income (around 5 per cent, on average), brings the combined rate to approximately 16 per cent. The rate of 16 per cent is, of course, lower than the 20% rate at which integration of the corporation's tax and the shareholder's personal tax is achieved with the 25 per cent gross-up and dividend tax credit for ineligible dividends, which leads to "over-integration" and tax savings for income earned in a corporation and paid out as a dividend in several provinces.

---

[62]The mechanics of the refundable dividend tax on hand account for investment income are explained under heading 15.5(c)(iii), "Refundable dividend tax on hand account", above. As is acknowledged, several provinces levy corporate tax at rates in excess of 12%, and those higher rates, plus federal and provincial surtaxes, make the net corporate tax (after refund) closer to 25% in some provinces.

[63]The small business deduction was not always as generous. The annual business limit was $200,000 limit for several decades before the 2003 and 2004 budgets increased it to $225,000 in 2003, $250,000 in 2004, $300,000 in 2005 and 2006 and $400,000 in 2007 and 2008: see s. 125(2). The credit rate was 16% until 2008, when it was changed to 17%: see s. 125(1.1)

The small business deduction is available only to a CCPC. The definition of a CCPC was explained earlier in the chapter.[64] It excludes foreign-controlled private corporations, and public corporations, as well as individuals operating unincorporated businesses as sole proprietorships or partnerships. This obviously violates the principle of horizontal equity — namely that equal income should be treated equally. As will be explained, the CCPCs that benefit from the low rate of tax include many large, established, flourishing businesses, which on the face of it do not seem to need the help. New struggling businesses that earn no income after paying salaries, or incur losses, are not helped at all.

(ii) — Active business income

Only income "from an active business" qualifies for the small business deduction. The term "active business" is defined by subsection 125(7) as follows:

> "active business carried on by a corporation" means any business carried on by the corporation other than a specified investment business or a personal services business and includes an adventure or concern in the nature of trade.

The reference to "any business" makes clear that there is no real force to the word "active" in the phrase "active business". If the CCPC's income is business income,[65] then it qualifies for the low rate, provided it does not come within one of the two exceptions. The first exception is a "specified investment business" (defined in subsection 125(7)), which is a business whose principal purpose is to derive income from property.[66] The second exception is a "personal services business" (defined in subsection 125(7)), which covers "incorporated employees";[67] this exception is designed to prevent an employee from converting income from

---

[64]Under heading 15.1(d), "Canadian-controlled private corporations", above.

[65]See heading 6.2, "Characterization of "Business" and "property", as a source", above.

[66]There are two cases when income earned by such a business will be considered to be active. First, if the business employs more than five full-time employees throughout the year, it will be an active business (s. 125(7)); this rule recognizes that, once a company earning property income has a certain level of activity, it should be regarded as active. Second, if the business earns income (e.g., rent, interest) from an associated company and the associated company deducts the amounts in computing its income from an active business, these income items will be considered income from an active business (s. 129(6)); this rule prevents an associated group of companies from reducing its overall active business income by using such intercompany transactions.

[67]There are two cases when income earned by such a business will be considered to be active. First, if the business employs more than five full-time employees throughout the year, it will be an active business (s. 125(7)); this rule recognizes that, once a business has a certain level of activity, it should be regarded as active. Second, if the business earns income from services (e.g., consulting services) provided to an associated company, it will be an active business (s. 125(7)); this rule recognizes that no tax advantage is being gained in such situations since an associated group of companies must share the $500,000 annual limit for the small business deduction in any case.

employment into low-rate active business income by interposing a corporation between the employer and the employee.[68]

(iii) — Investment income compared

It will be recalled that the investment income of a CCPC is also taxed at a rate of approximately 20 per cent, so as to come close to achieving integration of the corporate tax on that income with the shareholder's personal tax on ineligible dividends. There are two important differences, however, between the tax treatment of investment income and that of active business income. First, there is no limit on the amount of investment income that can benefit from the low rate, whereas there is the "business limit" of $400,000 on qualifying active business income. Second, the low rate on investment income is implemented by the device of a refundable portion of the tax, which is initially levied at the standard corporate rate plus 6 ⅔ per cent. The refundable tax is intended to discourage CCPCs from retaining tax-sheltered investment income in the corporation; only after distribution of the income and receipt of the refund does the tax fall to the low rate. The qualifying active business income of a CCPC, by contrast, never bears the full standard rate of corporate tax, let alone the addition of 6⅔ per cent; it is entitled to the small business deduction whether or not the income is distributed to the shareholders. The small business deduction provides an incentive for a CCPC to retain its active business income and thereby avoid the payment of tax in excess of the low rate of 20 per cent. This is a deliberate policy of the Act: by enabling CCPCs to accumulate partially tax-sheltered dollars, it is intended to encourage the expansion of Canadian businesses.

(iv) — Limits on the small business deduction

The "small" business deduction is available to large as well as small CCPCs. However, since 1994, there has been a limit on the size of CCPCs that can claim the deduction. Subsection 125(5.1) reduces the $500,000 business limit for CCPCs with "taxable capital employed in Canada" in excess of $10 million according to a sliding scale which reaches nil for a CCPC with taxable capital of $15 million. Therefore, no small business deduction is available to a CCPC with taxable capital of $15 million, and less than the full deduction is available to CCPCs with capital of less than $15 million but more than $10 million. Even with these limits, the small business deduction continues to be available to relatively large corporations. A corporation with taxable capital of less than $10 million that earns before-tax profits of $500,000 after paying all expenses, including salaries to its managers, is not all that small.

---

[68] As well as the low rate of tax created by the small business deduction, the conversion of income from employment into income from business makes available additional deductions for business expenses. These additional deductions have also been denied to a "personal services business": s. 18(1)(p).

Where a CCPC has active business income in excess of the $500,000 business limit, the excess will be taxed at the standard corporate rate of 30 per cent (or more in most provinces). When that high-rate income is distributed to the shareholders, there is a substantial additional burden of tax compared with the tax that would be payable if the shareholder had earned the active business income directly. This tax penalty creates an incentive for a CCPC to keep its active business income within the annual limit of $500,000.

The Act accordingly strikes at certain devices that might be used to artificially reduce corporate income. One device is to take profits out of the corporation in the form of salaries (which are deductible, of course) rather than dividends. It is in fact common for prosperous CCPCs to pay or accrue substantial salaries (or bonuses) to senior employees (who are usually also shareholders) so as to get the income of the corporation down to $500,000. However, it is clearly established that section 67 (the reasonableness requirement) applies to make such salaries deductible from corporate income only to the extent that they are "reasonable in the circumstances"[69] and any amount accrued must be a true liability.[70] Another device is to create several small CCPCs instead of one large one, or to split a large CCPC into two or more smaller CCPCs. This is met by rules concerning "associated" corporations, which provide that when several CCPCs are "associated" with each other they must share a single limit of $500,000 for the 17 per cent small business deduction. If the corporations cannot agree on the allocations, the Minister has the power to divide up the limit among the associated corporations (subsection 125(3)).

(e) — Manufacturing and processing credit

Section 125.1 of the Act allows a tax credit to reduce corporate income tax on "Canadian manufacturing and processing profits". The credit is not available to unincorporated businesses engaged in manufacturing and processing. It is however available to any corporation, public as well as private, and foreign-controlled as well as Canadian-controlled. The Act (subsection 125.1(1)) and Regulations (Part LII) provide rules for computing a corporation's "Canadian manufacturing and processing profits". The credit is equal to seven per cent of Canadian manufactur-

[69]See heading 8.6, "Reasonable" requirement", above. The CRA says that it will generally not challenge the reasonableness of salaries and bonuses paid to an individual shareholder who is actively involved in the day-to-day business activities of the corporation and is resident in Canada. It does not matter whether the corporation's income is income from an active business or investment business. "The key is that the Canadian resident recipients must be active in the operating business and contribute to the income-producing activities from which the remuneration is paid. The CRA does, however, reserve the right to challenge the reasonableness of any inter-corporate management fees". See CRA Questions and Answers on Shareholder/Manager Remuneration at the 2001 annual conference of the Canadian Tax Foundation (Income Tax Technical News No. 22 (2002).

[70]See, for example, *Earlscourt Sheet Metal Mechanical Ltd. v. M.N.R.* (1987), [1988] 1 C.T.C. 2045, 88 D.T.C. 1029 (T.C.C.) and *Samuel F. Investments Limited v. M.N.R.* (1988), 88 D.T.C. 1106 (T.C.C.).

ing and processing profits that are not eligible for the small business deduction. Income eligible for the small business deduction does not receive the additional relief of the manufacturing and processing credit. The effect of the credit, therefore, is to reduce the standard federal rate of corporate tax by 10 per cent of qualifying income. As explained earlier, this credit and the general rate reduction will both increase to 11.5 per cent in 2011 and 13 per cent in 2012.

The policy behind the manufacturing and processing deduction was to provide encouragement to manufacturing and processing industries, on the theory (which would no doubt puzzle economists) that those industries are more valuable than service industries. Although the introduction of the ten per cent general rate reduction effectively removes any preference in the federal corporate income tax system for manufacturing and processing income, there still are many provinces that provide a reduced provincial rate.

(f) — Conclusion

It is a depressing exercise to review the foregoing chapter and to note that there are four different rates of corporate taxation for ordinary business corporations in Canada today. Ignoring surtaxes and assuming the stated provincial rates,[71] the three rates are listed below.

1. Corporate tax at 30 per cent (38 per cent - 10 per cent - 10 per cent + 12 per cent assumed provincial rate):
   - Business and investment income of public corporations
   - Business and investment income of private corporations other than CCPCs
   - Business income of CCPCs that is not eligible for the small business deduction
2. Corporate tax at 16 per cent (38 per cent - 10 per cent - 17 per cent + 5 per cent assumed provincial rate):
   - Business income of CCPCs that is eligible for the small business deduction
3. Corporate tax at 20 per cent (38 per cent - 10 per cent + 6 ⅔ per cent - 26 ⅔ per cent + 12 per cent assumed provincial rate):
   - Investment income of CCPCs that is distributed to shareholders

Of the three rates, only the last two are close to the 20 per cent figure which is imputed to the shareholder by the 25 per cent gross-up and credit rules for ineligible dividends, and which would yield integration. Income in class 1 is taxed more heavily at 30 per cent which is the imputed rate for eligible dividends which qualify for the 44 per cent gross-up and credit rules. The eligible dividend rules introduced

[71] As explained earlier above, provincial rates for income eligible for the small business deduction are as low as 2.5% and other provincial rates are as high as 17%.

in 2006 have rectified a complex situation that was neither equitable nor neutral. Indeed, it is hard to believe that it could possibly take 40 years to complete a process of tax reform which started with the Carter Commission's Report in 1966.

16
PARTNERSHIPS

16.1 — Introduction

This chapter provides a very brief account of the tax treatment of partnerships.[1] First, it describes the general nature of partnerships and their use, the calculation of partnership income for tax purposes, and the way in which the *Income Tax Act* (the "Act") levies tax on that income. It then goes on to deal with the nature and tax treatment of each partner's interest in a partnership and the rollovers available for the formation and dissolution of Canadian partnerships.

16.2 — Definition of partnership

The provincial partnership acts that have been enacted in each common law jurisdiction define a partnership as "the relation that subsists between persons carrying on business in common with a view to profit".[2] Because the Act contains no special definition of "partnership", a particular business relationship will be considered to be a partnership for income tax purposes if it is a partnership under provincial law.

---

[1]For a more detailed account of the law, see Tobias, *Taxation of Corporations, Partnerships and Trusts* (Carswell, 2006).

[2]E.g., Ontario *Partnership Act*, R.S.O. 1990, c. P.5, as amended, s. 2. The definition of a partnership at common law is not entirely clear, and each of the partnership acts enacted in each common law jurisdiction (following the model of the *English Act*) supply this definition as well as associated rules. The civil law position is similar to the common law, although the civil code does accord more legal personality to a partnership than does the common law: Brierley and Macdonald (eds.), *Quebec Civil Law* (1993), 667. Although partners normally share profits (or losses), the sharing of profits (or losses) is normally neither a necessary nor a sufficient characteristic of a partnership: *Cox and Wheatcroft v. Hickman* (1860), 8 H.L. Cas. 268, 11 E.R. 431 (H.L.) and Ontario *Partnership Act*, *ibid.*, s. 3.

This has been confirmed by the Supreme Court of Canada[3] and is acknowledged by the CRA.[4]

Unlike a corporation, a partnership is not a legal person that is separate from its investors (partners). Property used by a partnership is owned in law by the individual partners. Liabilities incurred by a partnership are owed in law by the individual partners and may have to be satisfied out of the personal assets of the partners. It is the lack of separate legal personality, and the consequent lack of limited liability, that distinguishes a partnership from a corporation. For these reasons, a corporation is usually the preferred form of business organization.

There are two main uses of partnerships. The first is by professionals, such as accountants and lawyers, who have traditionally practised in partnerships because they were not allowed to incorporate.[5] Today, most professional accountants and lawyers practise in limited liability partnerships (LLPs), which give them some limited liability protection. Under provincial LLP legislation, a partner of an LLP is still liable for the professional negligence of another partner except to the extent of his or her capital account (the amount he or she has invested in the firm).

The second use of partnerships is to flow through income and losses to partners. This use is possible because partnership income is computed using a two-step process: the first step is to compute partnership income (or loss) as if the partnership was a separate person and the second step is to apportion the partnership's income (or loss) among the partners in accordance with their shares in the partnership. This special characteristic of partnerships allows them to be used as a conduit to flow out losses for tax purposes.

---

[3]*Continental Bank Leasing Corporation v. R.*, [1998] 2 S.C.R. 298, [1998] 4 C.T.C. 119, 98 D.T.C. 6505 (S.C.C.); *Spire Freezers Ltd. et al. v R.*, [2001] 1 S.C.R. 391, [2001] 2 C.T.C. 40, 2001 D.T.C. 5158 (S.C.C.); and *Backman v. R.*, [2001] 1 S.C.R. 367, [2001] 2 C.T.C. 11, 2001 D.T.C. 5149 (S.C.C.).

[4]See Interpretation Bulletin IT-90, "What is a partnership?" (1973) and GST Policy Statement P-171R, "Distinguishing between a Joint Venture and a Partnership for the purposes of section 273 Joint Venture Election". A "joint venture" is very similar to a partnership, but it does not entail a continuing relationship between the co-venturers, who join together to carry out a specific project. Because a joint venture is not a partnership, it does not have the same tax characteristics as a partnership.

[5]The law in several provinces now allows lawyers and accountants to incorporate but it does not allow them limited liability as they must form special "professional corporations". As a result, the main advantage of "professional corporations" is the low small business rate. Incorporation is usually not attractive to professionals who would otherwise practice in partnerships, because of the income limit of the low small business rate ($500,000) and the limited liability protection afforded by limited liability partnerships (LLPs). As a result, incorporation will usually only be attractive to sole proprietors (who cannot otherwise limit their liability).

The three most recent Supreme Court cases dealing with the issue of what is a partnership (*Continental Bank, Spire Freezers*, and *Backman*[6]) were situations where, in fact, a partnership was being used as a conduit to flow out losses to investors. At issue was whether the partners were "carrying on business in common with a view to profit". In *Continental Bank* and *Spire Freezers*, the Supreme Court of Canada held that passively carrying on a pre-existing business for a couple of days was sufficient for this test. In *Backman*, however, there was no pre-existing business and the purchase of businesses to "window-dress" the partnership failed to characterize the relationship as a partnership.

A limited partnership is a special type of partnership used to flow out deductions and losses to passive investors. Provincial limited partnership acts allow the creation of a "limited partnership", in which a "limited partner" (or partners) has limited liability like that of a shareholder in a corporation, and a "general partner" (usually a corporation with no assets) has unlimited liability. However, the limited partner must be an entirely passive investor: participation in the management of the business exposes the limited partner to the same liability as a general partner. The use of limited partnerships for tax shelters has resulted in restrictions for these partnerships.[7] The LLPs used by lawyers and accountants, discussed earlier, are not limited partnerships and are exempted from these restrictions.[8]

Corporations can enter into partnerships as well as individuals but this chapter, for the most part, will be limited to partnerships of individuals.

16.3 — Taxation of partnership

The Act recognizes the lack of legal personality of a partnership, and does not treat the partnership as a taxpayer.[9] Although it is the individual partners who are liable to pay tax on the partnership's income, the Act does require the income of the

---

[6]Note 3, above.

[7]As discussed in detail under heading 16.4 below, s. 40(3.1) provides that if the adjusted cost base of the partnership interest of a limited partner is negative, the negative amount will be a capital gain. As well, the "at risk" rules set out in ss. 96(2.1) to 96(2.4) and s. 111(1)(e) limit a limited partner's losses to the amount he or she has "at risk" as an investment in respect of the partnership.

[8]Ss. 40(3.14)(a) and 96(2.4)(a) exclude a partner of an LLP from the definition of "limited partner" for the purposes of the negative adjusted cost base rules and "at risk" rules discussed, *ibid.*

[9]As discussed in chapter 17, below, on October 31, 2006 a measure was announced to tax certain publicly traded income trusts and publicly traded limited partnerships like corporations. The tax applies to amounts distributed by a "specified investment flow-through" (SIFT) trust or the income of a SIFT partnership. The tax is effective as of 2007 to new entities, but is deferred until 2011 for SIFTs that were publicly traded as of October 31, 2006. The tax is levied on partnership income (not distributions as in the case of trusts) because (unlike trusts) partnerships do not get a deduction for their distributions.

partnership to be calculated at the partnership level before the income is apportioned among the partners. The partnership does not file a tax return, but it does have to file an annual "information return" setting out the income of the partnership and details of the partners who are entitled to a share of the income (regulation 229).

As mentioned earlier, partnership income is calculated for tax purposes in a two-step process. The first step is to calculate the income of the partnership "as if the partnership were a separate person resident in Canada" (paragraph 96(1)(a)). For this step, the partnership is required to recognize all income and take all deductions that would be applicable to a separate person resident in Canada that uses the calendar year as a fiscal period.[10] The second step is to apportion the partnership's income among the individual partners in accordance with their shares in the partnership (paragraph 96(1)(f)). Each individual partner is then obliged to report his or her share of the partnership income as part of his or her income for the year.

The allocation of partnership income will generally be defined in the partnership agreement. However, if the principal reason for the allocation may reasonably be considered for the purpose of reducing or postponing tax, the share of each partner is deemed to be the amount which is "reasonable" in the circumstances.[11] Further, if non-arm's length persons agree to allocate partnership income in a manner that is not reasonable with regard to the partners' contributions of property, work performed and other factors, the share of income is deemed to be the amount which is "reasonable" in the circumstances.[12]

The income of each individual partner retains the source characterization that it had when it was derived by the partnership. Accordingly, the appropriate share of income that was business income in the partnership is treated as business income in the hands of the partner; property income remains property income; and taxable capital gains remain taxable capital gains. This means that the individual partner is subject to the rules applicable to each source of income. For example, a partner's share of partnership dividends from taxable Canadian corporations is grossed up and eligible for the dividend tax credit in the partner's hands. As another example, although the partnership's business income will be a net figure from which all deductions that were applicable at the partnership level have been taken, the individual partner may have further deductions if he or she incurred expenses personally to earn the partnership income (for example, by using a personal automobile in the business or by attending a business conference). As another example, if an individual partner incurred an allowable capital loss in his or her private investments, the loss will be deductible against his or her share of any taxable capital gains derived by the partnership.

---

[10]A non-calendar year is only allowed if none of the partners are individuals, professional corporations or partnerships: s. 249.1(1)(b)(ii).

[11]S. 103(1).

[12]S. 103(1.1). There is no principal purpose test in the case of non-arm's length partners.

16.4 — Partnership interest

Each partner in a partnership is said to have an "interest" in the partnership. It is the extent of each partner's interest in the partnership that determines his or her entitlement to share in the profits of the business and the extent to which he or she may participate in the distribution of partnership property when the partnership is dissolved. For income tax purposes, each partner's interest in the partnership is treated as a capital property, separate from the assets held by the firm.

Because a partnership interest is capital property, the disposition of the interest gives rise to a capital gain or loss. When a partner disposes of his or her interest for proceeds of disposition that exceed the adjusted cost base of the interest, the partner will have to recognize a capital gain, one-half of which will be taxed. If the proceeds of disposition are less than the adjusted cost base, then the partner will have to recognize a capital loss.

The adjusted cost base of a partnership interest is determined by reference to a set of rules laid out in section 53. Obviously, the cost of the interest to the partner is the primary figure from which the adjusted cost base of the partnership interest is derived. Once this starting figure is ascertained, paragraph 53(1)(e) provides for various additions to be made, and paragraph 53(2)(c) provides for deductions from the cost figure. Under paragraph 53(1)(e), the main figures to be added to the cost base of the interest include the value of any property contributed to the firm by the partner and any amount of partnership income from a prior year to which the partner is entitled.[13] The reason that the amount of income from a prior year to which the partner is entitled must be added to the adjusted cost base of the interest is to ensure that the partner's share of partnership income, which has already been reported by the partner under section 96, is not subject to double taxation by increasing the value of the partner's interest in the firm.[14] Similarly, the partner's share of any losses generated by the partnership in a prior year must be deducted from the partner's adjusted cost base, as these amounts will also have been reported under section 96.[15] The other major deduction from the adjusted cost base of the partner-

---

[13]The income of the current year is not included: see the wording in the preamble of s. 53(1)(e)(i) and the CRA's comments in Income Tax Technical News, No. 5 (1995). This is proposed to change in the case of a disposition of a partnership interest for 1995 and subsequent years (2003 and subsequent years in the case of the death of a partner). If a partnership interest is disposed of during the year, the income earned to the date of sale will now be included in the adjusted cost base of the partnership interest by virtue of proposed s. 96(1.01). See Bill C-10 (2007) which government intends to reintroduce according to the March 4, 2010 Federal Budget.

[14]In order to avoid double taxation, the partner adds to the adjusted cost base the partner's share of the partnership's full capital gain (not just the one-half portion that is a taxable capital gain): s. 53(1)(e)(i)(A).

[15]The treatment of capital losses is similar to capital gains: see previous note. A partner must deduct from the adjusted cost base the partner's share of the partnership's full capital loss, not just the one-half that is an allowable capital loss (s. 53(1)(e)(i)(A)).

ship interest, provided for by paragraph 53(2)(c), is the value of any distribution (or "drawings") of capital or income which the partner has received from the partnership.[16]

If subsection 53(2) deductions exceed (on a cumulative basis) the original cost of the interest and all subsection 53(1) additions, the adjusted cost base of the partnership interest will be a negative amount. A partner with a partnership interest having a negative adjusted cost base may have to recognize a capital gain equal to this amount (subsection 40(3)) and the adjusted cost base of the partnership interest will be adjusted to zero (paragraph 53(1)(a)). Owning a partnership interest with a negative adjusted cost base will not result in an *immediate* capital gain for partners who are active in their partnerships, as is generally the case when accountants or lawyers practise in partnerships or LLPs. Instead, the amount will be added to the partner's capital gain arising in the year that the interest is disposed of (paragraph 98(1)(c)). But owning a partnership interest with a negative adjusted cost base will result in an immediate capital gain when a partner is a limited or passive partner (subsections 40(3.1) to (3.2)) or when the interest is a "residual interest" in a partnership.[17]

16.5 — Rollovers for the formation and dissolution of Canadian partnerships

The Act contains special rollover rules for the formation and dissolution of Canadian partnerships. A Canadian partnership is a partnership whose partners are all Canadian residents.[18]

A partnership usually requires capital in order to operate its business. This will be supplied by the partners, each of whom will usually contribute property to the partnership in exchange for a partnership interest (discussed in the previous section of this chapter). When a partner (or potential partner) transfers property to a Canadian partnership, there is an elective rollover under subsection 97(2) similar to the sec-

---

[16]Similarly, the partner's share of charitable donations and political contributions which have been made by the partnership must be deducted from the adjusted cost base (s. 53(2)(c)(iii)). Since these amounts are eligible for a tax credit or deduction in the partner's income tax return (ss. 110.1, 118.1, 127(4.2)), there is no double taxation.

[17]S. 98.1(1). A person who has ceased to be a partner, but has a right to receive property from the partnership in respect of a partnership interest, owns a "residual interest" in the partnership (s. 98.1(1)(a)) and is not considered to have disposed of a partnership interest (s. 98.1(1)(b)). An example of a person with a "residual interest" in a partnership is a retired partner of a law firm who receives distributions of partnership capital after retirement. The retired partner may also receive an annual distribution of income during retirement. Providing the income amounts are received from a Canadian partnership, they are deemed to be income from a partnership because the former partner is deemed to be a member of the partnership for this purpose (s. 96(1.1)).

[18]S. 102 contains the definition of "Canadian partnership".

tion 85 rollover that is available on the transfer of property to a corporation in return for shares in the corporation.[19]

When a partnership disposes of capital property, the partnership will first recognize a taxable capital gain or allowable capital loss under the same rules that apply to a corporation or an individual. Any resulting gain or loss is then apportioned among the partners in accordance with their shares, and is reported by the partners as part of their personal income. This is the two-step process of calculating each partner's income that was described earlier in the chapter.

On the dissolution of a Canadian partnership, the Act provides for rollovers of capital property where the business is continued by a former partner as a sole proprietorship (subsection 98(5)), or by some of the former partners in a new partnership (subsection 98(6)), or by a corporation in circumstances where the section 85 rollover is available (subsection 85(2)). The policy of the Act in all these cases is to remove tax impediments to what are really changes in the organization of a business. Where a Canadian partnership is dissolved and the property of the partnership is distributed to the partners, there is another rollover (subsection 98(3)),[20] recognizing that the distribution is a return of each partner's share in what is really the partners' own property.

---

[19] The details of the s. 85 rollover are outside the scope of this book.

[20] Under s. 98(3), each partner must take an undivided share in each property equal to his or her share of the partnership.

17
TRUSTS

17.1 — Introduction

This chapter provides an overview of the tax treatment of trusts and beneficiaries. In studying this chapter, it is worthwhile to compare the taxation of trusts with the taxation of corporations and partnerships discussed in chapters 15 and 16, respectively. While corporations are taxed as separate entities and partnerships as "flow-through" or "conduit" entities (that is, income earned through a partnership is not taxed in the hands of the partnership, but that of the partners), trusts are taxed as a hybrid of the two approaches: income is taxed to the trust only if it is not otherwise taxable to the beneficiaries. Therefore, income earned through a trust is either taxed at the trust level or at the beneficiary level, but not both. Because trusts are also intermediaries in earning income, the hybrid taxation of trusts plus the legal characteristics of trusts make them a powerful tool for income tax and estate planning.

17.2 — Nature of trusts

(a) — Definition of trust

A trust exists when the management and control of property is vested in one person or persons (the "trustee") while enjoyment of the property is vested in another person or persons (the "beneficiary"). Normally, the legal forms by which this division between management and enjoyment of property is accomplished are that legal title to the trust property is in the trustee, while equitable (or beneficial) title to the trust property is in the beneficiary. Normally, so long as there is a separation of legal and beneficial ownership, there is a trust.

Trusts are classified into several categories, based on whether the settlor is alive at the time the trust is created, whether the powers of the trustee are discretionary, whether the beneficiary is a spouse, or whether the purpose of the trust is personal or commercial. The main categories are briefly discussed below.

(b) — *Inter vivos* vs. testamentary trusts

A trust may be created by a living person (called the "settlor"), in which case the trust is called an "*inter vivos*" (or living) trust. A testamentary trust is a trust created "as a consequence of the death of an individual".[1] Most testamentary trusts are created by will, which of course becomes operative only on the death of the testator or testatrix (who is the settlor). An *inter vivos* trust is defined as a trust other than a

[1] S. 108(1).

testamentary trust.[2] A major difference in the tax treatment of *inter vivos* trusts and testamentary trusts is the applicable tax rates.[3]

A testamentary trust is a trust arising as a consequence of the death of a taxpayer and the terms of a testamentary trust are generally set out in a taxpayer's will. What is also somewhat confusing, however, is that the *Income Tax Act* (the "Act") draws no distinction between a "trust" and an "estate"; the term "trust" refers to both.[4] For the purposes of the Act, it is immaterial whether a person who is administering property for others is doing so as a personal representative (estate trustee) or as a trustee.

What is an estate? When a person dies, his or her assets and liabilities are known as the deceased's estate. The deceased's estate passes to the personal representative (or legal representative, which is the phrase used in the Act). A personal representative is known in estate law as an estate trustee. An estate trustee is a person who is appointed by the will of the deceased or by the court which occurs if the deceased left no will (died intestate) or if the deceased left a will which failed to appoint an estate trustee or if the appointed estate trustee declined to serve. The duty of the personal representative is to administer the deceased person's estate.[5]

If the deceased died intestate, or if the will directs the immediate distribution of the deceased's property, the personal representative's final act will be to distribute the property to the deceased's successors. But if the will establishes a trust (in which case it is called a trust will), the personal representative's final act will be to transfer the assets given on trust to the person appointed trustee by the will. Thenceforth the trustee will hold the assets on trust for the beneficiaries designated in the will. In practice, a trust will often appoint the same person (or persons) to be both estate trustee and trustee of a particular trust created by the will. If so, at the time when that person has completed the administration of the estate, he or she ceases to be an estate trustee administering an estate and becomes a trustee. It is often difficult to ascertain when that mysterious transformation occurs, but it is rarely necessary to do so because there are so few differences between a personal representative and a trustee that nothing usually turns on the question of whether the person was acting in the capacity of a personal representative or in the capacity of a trustee. For tax

[2] *Ibid.*

[3] See heading 17.3(c), "Rates", below.

[4] S. 104(1).

[5] This involves ascertaining and getting in all the assets, paying the debts, filing tax returns and paying taxes, paying funeral expenses and the expenses of administration, and generally getting the estate into a form in which it can be distributed to the persons who are entitled to inherit it under the terms of the will (if there is one) or provincial intestacy law (if there is no will). Obviously, the relationship between the personal representative and the deceased's successors is very similar to the relationship between a trustee and beneficiaries, but there is authority for the proposition that a personal representative is not a trustee of the property in an unadministered estate. *Commr. of Stamp Duties (Queensland) v. Livingston* (1964), [1965] A.C. 694 (P.C.).

purposes, the definition of a trust includes an estate,[6] so that tax consequences rarely flow from the shadowy distinction between an estate and a trust.

(c) — Personal vs. commercial trusts

A personal trust is defined as a testamentary or *inter vivos* trust in which the beneficiaries did not purchase their interests from the trust or from anyone who had made a contribution to the trust.[7] The term "commercial trust" is not defined in the Act but is generally used to refer to a trust which is not a personal trust. The most common examples of commercial trusts are publicly traded mutual funds (which own a portfolio of securities), real estate investment trusts or "REITS" (which own a portfolio of real estate) and business income trusts or "income trusts" (which own shares and debt of a corporation or businesses). These three types of trusts are all mutual fund trusts under the Act and most have complex structures.[8]

Publicly traded income trusts gained popularity until 2006, because, all things being equal, investors could receive a greater cash flow from holding trust units than they could from holding shares of public corporations because there was no corporate tax reducing the cash flow to investors.[9] These trusts were particularly popular with tax exempt investors (such as pension plans and registered retirement savings plans). Because of the revenue loss to the government, two measures were introduced in 2006 to reduce the attractiveness of income trusts.[10] The first measure announced on May 1, 2006 was the enhanced gross-up and dividend tax credit for eligible dividends which reduced the personal tax on dividends paid out of income taxed at general corporate rates. Because the first measure failed to address tax exempt investors (which are not impacted by changes in gross up and dividends tax credit rules because they do not pay tax), it failed to stem the popularity of income trust structures. A second measure was therefore announced on October 31, 2006 to tax the distributions of a publicly traded "specified investment flow-through"

---

[6] S. 104(1).

[7] S. 248(1).

[8] A mutual fund trust (defined in s. 132(6)) is a type of unit trust resident in Canada (defined in s. 108(2)). Mutual fund status is very important to investors for a number of reasons, such as eligibility for registered retirement savings plans (reg. 4900(1)(d)).

[9] Income earned and distributed as dividends by corporations was taxed in a corporation. See ch. 15, Corporations and their Shareholders, above, for a discussion of the tax treatment of corporations and dividends paid to shareholders.

[10] An earlier measure to prohibit pension funds from investing in business income trusts was proposed in the 2004 budget. It was withdrawn a few months later (on May 18, 2004) after several large pension funds protested.

(SIFT) trust[11] and the income of a publicly traded SIFT partnership.[12] The purpose of the SIFT rules is to tax income trusts and publicly traded limited partnerships like corporations. The rules came into effect in 2007 for new entities, but are deferred until 2011 for entities that were publicly traded as of October 31, 2006. At the time of writing (March 2010), several income trusts have already converted to corporations and it is expected that several more will convert by December 31, 2010, which is when they lose their comparative tax advantage.[13]

Unless otherwise stated, the rules discussed in this chapter apply to personal trusts resident in Canada and with Canadian resident beneficiaries.

(d) — Discretionary vs. non-discretionary trusts

The trust document (or will) sets out the powers and the obligations of the trustee of a trust. Many trusts will allow the trustee some discretion as to the amounts to be paid to beneficiaries or perhaps the date of the termination of the trust. In a non-discretionary trust, the payment of income and capital to beneficiaries is set out in the terms of the trust and there is no flexibility. If a trustee has some discretion as to whether or not to pay income or capital to a particular beneficiary, the trust is called a discretionary trust. Discretionary trusts are more useful for tax and estate planning than non-discretionary trusts.

(e) — Spousal trusts

As discussed earlier in chapter 13, there is a tax-deferred rollover available when a transfer is made to a spouse or a common-law partner (of the same or opposite sex) during a taxpayer's lifetime or on his or her death.[14] The same rollover exists when a transfer is made to a spousal or common-law partner trust (a "spousal trust"). A spousal trust may be either an *inter vivos* or testamentary trust. It is a trust created by a taxpayer under which: (i) the taxpayer's spouse or common-law partner is entitled to receive all of the income of the trust that arises before the spouse's or common-law partner's death, and (ii) no person except the spouse or common-law

---

[11]SIFT trust distributions of "non-portfolio earnings" (generally speaking, Canadian business income) are subject to a tax equal to the federal and provincial general corporate rate for the year (s. 122(1)(b)) and investors receiving such distributions are deemed to have received an eligible dividend from a taxable Canadian corporation rather than a distribution from a trust (s. 104(16)). REITs that do not own businesses such as hotels or retirement homes or foreign real estate are exempt from the SIFT tax.

[12]SIFT partnerships are subject to Part IX.1 tax. The tax is on SIFT partnership income and not distributions because, as discussed in chapter 16, partnerships do not get a deduction for their distributions.

[13]See, for example, Freeman "Analysts expect many income trust conversions in 2010 before 2011 tax reforms" *Investment Executive*, Jan. 3, 2010.

[14]See headings 13.4(b), "Rollovers for transfers to a spouse or common-law partner", above.

partner may, before the spouse's or common-law partner's death, receive or otherwise obtain the use of any of the income or capital of the trust.[15]

In a spousal trust, only the spouse is entitled to the income[16] from the property arising in his or her lifetime, and other beneficiaries (such as children) are not entitled to "the use of" the capital until the spouse's death. If the trustee has a power to encroach on the capital for the benefit of the spouse, the trust would still qualify as a spousal trust. But if the trustee has a power to allocate income or capital to anyone other than the spouse during the lifetime of the spouse, the existence of that power would "taint" the trust.[17] A tainted trust is of course perfectly valid: it simply loses the benefit of the spousal trust's tax privileges, which include a rollover.

A spousal trust enjoys two major tax advantages: (1) a rollover when property is transferred to the trust; and (2) an exemption from the 21-year deemed disposition rule.[18] Note, however, instead of the deemed disposition every 21 years, there is a deemed disposition on the death of the spouse, whether that occurs more or less than 21 years after the creation of the trust.[19] After the death of the spouse, if the trust continues (that is, if the property is not distributed to the capital beneficiaries), there will be a deemed disposition of all capital property every 21 years.

(f) — Alter ego and joint spousal trusts

There is also a rollover available for transfers into two types of *inter vivos* trusts created after 1999: the "alter ego" trust (a trust for oneself) and the "joint spousal trust" (a trust for oneself and one's spouse or common-law partner). Except for the age 65 requirement (see below), the rules for these trusts are simply extensions of the *inter vivos* spousal trust rules, except that the beneficiary of an alter ego trust is the settlor and the beneficiary of a joint spousal trust is the settlor and his or her

---

[15]See ss. 70(6)(b) and 73(1.01)(c)(i). In the case of a testamentary trust, it must be shown, within the period ending 36 months after the death of the taxpayer or, where written application therefor has been made to the Minister by the taxpayer's legal representative within that period, within such long period as the Minister considers reasonable in the circumstances, that the property has become vested indefeasibly in the spouse or common-law partner trust, as the case may be.

[16]The word "income" in the definition of a spousal trust in ss. 70(6) and 73(1) means income in the trust accounting sense, not the tax sense (s. 108(3)). It is not necessary, therefore, for the spouse to be entitled to capital gains: see also heading 17.6(c), "Special rules for capital gains", below. Accordingly, capital gains realized by a spousal trust will be subject to tax in the hands of the trust unless the gains are paid or made payable to the spouse beneficiary. This tax rule is often not understood or forgotten.

[17]A trust is not "tainted" if it merely provides for the payment of estate, succession or income taxes payable by the trust (s. 108(4)). Testamentary spousal trusts also may be "untainted" under s. 70(7) if otherwise qualifying as a spousal trust but for the payment of certain testamentary debts defined in s. 70(8).

[18]See heading 17.5(b), "Deemed disposition of trust property", below.

[19]Ss. 104(4)(a)(iii) and (5).

spouse or common-law partner. The main use of alter ego and joint spousal trusts is as a substitute will in order to avoid the process of probate.

An alter ego trust is a trust created after 1999 by an individual taxpayer who is at least 65 years of age under which the taxpayer is entitled to receive all of the income of the trust that arises before his or her death and no person except the taxpayer may, before the taxpayer's death, receive or otherwise obtain the use of any of the income or capital of the trust.[20] There is a rollover on the transfer of property into an alter ego trust[21] and a deemed disposition on the death of a taxpayer.[22]

A joint spousal trust is defined as a trust created after 1999 by an individual taxpayer who is at least 65 years of age under which, before the later of the taxpayer's or the spouse's (or common-law partner's) death, the taxpayer and his or her spouse (or common-law partner) are entitled to receive all of the income of the trust that arises in the trust, and no person except the taxpayer and his or her spouse (or common-law partner) may receive or otherwise obtain the use of any of the income or capital of the trust.[23] There is a rollover on the transfer of property into a joint spousal trust[24] and a deemed disposition of property owned by a joint spousal trust on the death of the surviving spouse or common-law partner.[25]

17.3 — Special features of taxation

(a) — Legislative scheme

The rules governing the taxation of the income of trusts and their beneficiaries are found in sections 104–108, in subdivision k of Division B of Part I of the Act. As discussed below, the Act draws no distinction between a "trust" and an "estate": the term trust refers to both.[26] For the purpose of subdivision k, it is immaterial whether a person who is administering property for others is doing so as a personal representative (executor or administrator) or as a trustee.

---

[20] S. 248(1).

[21] Ss. 73(1) and 73(1.01)(c)(ii). There is also a tax deferred rollover on the transfer of property out to the settlor/beneficiary under s. 107(2).

[22] S. 104(4)(a)(iv)(A).

[23] S. 248(1).

[24] S. 104(4)(a)(iv)(B)and (c). There is also a tax deferred rollover on the transfer of property out to the settlor/beneficiary under s. 107(2).

[25] S. 73(1) and 73(1.01)(c)(iii).

[26] S. 104(1).

(b) — Taxed as an individual

A trust is deemed to be an "individual" for income tax purposes[27] and an individual is defined as a person other than a corporation.[28] This means that a trust is taxed under the same rules as an individual taxpayer.

The treatment of a trust as an individual has several important implications. The first implication is the potential for income splitting. A trust is an intermediary like a corporation, and it presents opportunities for tax avoidance. These facts have led to some changes in the general rules concerning the computation of income and the rates of tax. Since a trust is taxed as an individual, an obvious measure of tax avoidance would be the creation of multiple trusts, each of which would be taxed at a low rate. However, the Act strikes at this form of income splitting with a number of provisions. As explained below, although trusts are taxed as individuals, *inter vivos* trusts are taxable only at the top marginal rate: this is intended to eliminate the possibility of income splitting by creating trusts for family members.[29] Also, subsection 122(1.1) denies to a trust the personal credits allowed to individuals by section 118 of the Act:[30] the denial of these credits stops taxpayers from creating trusts in order to obtain the advantage of multiple personal credits. Finally, subsection 104(2) provides that, where there are a number of trusts in which:

> (a) substantially all the property of the various trusts has been received from one person, and
>
> (b) the various trusts are conditioned so that the income thereof accrues or will ultimately accrue to the same beneficiary, or group or class of beneficiaries,
>
> the Minister has the power to lump all the trusts together and tax all of the income as the income of a single trust.[31]

Because the top rate of tax is applicable to all *inter vivos* trusts, the main effect of this multiple trust rule is to prevent tax avoidance through the creation of multiple testamentary trusts for the same beneficiary (or group or class of beneficiaries).

Another implication arising from the deemed status of a trust as an individual is that a trust is a separate taxpayer from its settlor or beneficiary. That means that

---

[27]S. 104(2).

[28]S. 248(1).

[29]The attribution rules and the kiddie tax limit a taxpayer's ability to save tax by income splitting with spouses and minors during his or her lifetime. See heading 13.5, "Attribution of income from property" and heading 13.10, "Kiddie tax", above.

[30]The $40,000 basic exemption from minimum tax is also denied: s. 127.53(1)(b).

[31]This does not prevent taxpayers from setting up different trusts for different beneficiaries: see *Mitchell v. M.N.R.* (1956), 16 Tax A.B.C. 99, 56 D.T.C. 521 (T.A.B.). In *Mitchell*, the settlor had four children and he created a separate trust for each of them. It was held that, because the beneficiary of each trust was different, the multiple trust rule in s. 104(2) was inapplicable (Ss. 104(2) was 63(2) at that time.) After this decision, until the enactment of s. 122(1) in 1971, the use of separate *inter vivos* trusts for children became a popular means of income splitting.

where a property is transferred to or from a trust, there is a disposition of the property. That disposition may give rise to tax consequences.[32]

(c) — Rates

With respect to rates of tax, the general rule is derived from the premise that a trust is deemed to be an individual for tax purposes.[33] This means that the trust will be taxed in accordance with the graduated rate schedule in subsection 117(2), and that provincial taxes and surtaxes will also apply.[34]

Section 122 creates an exception for *inter vivos* trusts created after June 18, 1971.[35] Section 122(1) imposes on *inter vivos* trusts a flat rate of federal tax of 29 per cent, which is the top rate in the individual rate schedule of subsection 117(2).[36] The purpose of the imposition of the highest rate is to discourage income splitting by creating a trust for each family member. The use of an *inter vivos* trust to divert income away from the settlor cannot be advantageous with respect to income taxed to the trust, because the trust will be taxed at the same rate as that applicable to the top personal tax bracket.

Section 122 does not apply to testamentary trusts, presumably because these are operative only on the death of the settlor and are not effective vehicles for a living person to divert income to a lower-tax-paying entity. Of course, it would be possible for a living person to contribute property to a pre-existing testamentary trust. But the Act's definitions of "testamentary trust" and "*inter vivos* trust"[37] make clear that any *inter vivos* contribution of property to a testamentary trust (however small) will convert the trust into a deemed *inter vivos* trust for tax purposes.[38] As

[32]For a discussion of the tax consequences arising on the transfer of property to a trust, see heading 17.4, "Creation of trust", below. For a discussion of the tax consequences arising on the transfer of property from a trust to a beneficiary, see heading 17.8, "Termination of trust", below.

[33]S. 104(2).

[34]Ch. 14, Taxable Income and Tax for Individuals, above.

[35]The budget date when the terms of the 1971 Act were officially announced.

[36]That rate has to be grossed-up by the applicable provincial rate in order to ascertain the combined federal-provincial rate, and the rate will be further increased by applicable federal and provincial surtaxes. In most provinces, the federal rate of 29 per cent grows to a combined rate of almost 50 per cent.

[37]Both definitions are in s. 108(1).

[38]For trust taxation years ending after December 20, 2002, proposed paragraph (d) of the definition of testamentary trust in s. 108(1) sets out the circumstances when a non-arm's length loan will also convert a testamentary trust into an *inter vivos* trust for tax purposes. See Bill C-10 (2007) which had received second reading in the Senate when the 39th Parliament was dissolved on September 7, 2008. These proposals must be reintroduced in the 40th Parliament in order to become law.

an *inter vivos* trust, all of its income would become subject to the high, flat rate imposed by section 122.[39]

(d) — Conduit treatment of trusts

As mentioned at the beginning of this chapter, trusts are treated as "conduits" for tax purposes in certain circumstances. This conduit treatment of income earned through a trust is manifested in two ways: (1) income earned by a trust is taxable to the trust to the extent that the income is not taxable to the beneficiary; and (2) in certain circumstances, the character of income earned by a trust "flows through" the trust and is retained in the hands of the beneficiary, which is important because the Act accords differential treatment of different types of income.[40]

17.4 — Creation of trust

(a) — Methods of creation

A trust may be created *inter vivos* in two ways, namely, by transfer or by declaration. A trust by transfer is created when a property-owner, the settlor, transfers property to a trustee (or trustees) to hold upon trust for certain beneficiaries. A trust by declaration is created when a settlor declares himself or herself to be a trustee of property for certain beneficiaries. The mode of transfer is more common than the mode of declaration.

(b) — Transfer of property

(i) — General

A transfer of property by a settlor to a trust may be a gift or a sale, depending upon whether the trust gives consideration. It may constitute a new trust or add to the assets of an existing trust, depending upon whether the trustee was already holding property on the terms stipulated by the settlor. In all of these situations, the transfer is a "disposition" for tax purposes, because the definition of disposition in subsection 248(1) includes "any transfer of property to a trust". Where the transfer of property by the settlor to the trust is by way of a gift or a sale for inadequate con-

---

[39]S. 122 does not have retrospective effect: it does not apply to *inter vivos* trusts created before June 18, 1971. However, these pre-1972 *inter vivos* trusts avoid the minimum rate only so long as they continue to satisfy a set of stipulations in ss. 122(2), of which the most important is that the trust "has not received any property by way of gift since June 18, 1971". Any gift to a pre-1972 *inter vivos* trust will therefore "contaminate" it. This result cannot be avoided by the time-honoured device of a sale in return for a promissory note, because another of the criteria of s. 122(2) is that the trust has not since June 18, 1971 incurred a debt to a non-arm's length person. Even a gift by will after June 18, 1971 will contaminate a pre-1972 *inter vivos* trust.

[40]See heading 17.6(d), "Flow-through character of income", below.

sideration, the proceeds of disposition is generally deemed to be the fair market value of the property.[41]

Where a trust is created by the settlor declaring him or herself to be a trustee, it is obvious that the tax consequences should be the same as where a trust is created by transfer. Although the definition of disposition refers to a "transfer of property to a trust", it is likely that the courts would give a sufficiently broad reading to the word "transfer" to enable both modes of creating an *inter vivos* trust to attract the same tax consequences.

With the exception of rollovers, the creation of a trust by transfer, and any subsequent transfer of property to the trust, may give rise to a taxable capital gain (or loss) in the hands of the settlor.[42]

(ii) — Transfer of property on death

On death, all capital property of a deceased taxpayer is deemed to have been disposed of, immediately before death, for proceeds of disposition equal to the fair market value of the property.[43] Any resulting taxable capital gains (or allowable capital losses) have to be recognized as income (or loss) of the deceased for the taxation period ending at his or her death (the deceased's terminal year). The estate is thus deemed to acquire the property of the deceased at a cost equal to the fair market value of the property. These rules apply to all of a deceased person's capital property, including property left on trust.

(c) — Rollovers

As discussed earlier, the spousal trust, the alter ego trust and joint spousal trusts are exceptions to the deemed disposition and acquisition on death rules because there are tax-free rollovers of assets into these trusts. Capital property which is transferred to a qualifying trust on a rollover basis, either *inter vivos* or on death, is deemed to have been disposed of for proceeds of disposition equal to the adjusted

---

[41] S. 69(1)(b), discussed under heading 13.4(a), "The fair market value principle", above. If the property transferred to the trust is capital property to the settlor, then, to the extent that the proceeds of disposition of the property exceed the adjusted cost base of the property, the settlor will have to recognize a capital gain on the disposition, one-half of which is taxable as income. See generally ch. 10, Capital Gains, above. In the case of depreciable property, the disposition may also cause a recapture of capital cost allowance, which is taxable as income (s. 13(1)). See generally ch. 9, Income from Business or Property: Capital Expenditures, above.

[42] Besides the rollovers available for property transferred to a spousal trust, alter ego trust and joint spousal trust discussed above, there is also a rollover available where the transfer of property to a trust does not result in a change in the beneficial ownership of the property: see ss. 107.4(1) and (3).

[43] S. 70(5)(a).

cost base of the property.[44] This creates a rollover, because it means that no capital gain or loss is caused by the transfer of property to the trust.[45] The trust acquiring property on a rollover is deemed to acquire the property at its adjusted cost base (cost to the settlor), not at its fair market value, so that any tax liability is deferred until the property is actually disposed of by the trustee or until the beneficiaries of the trust die (when there is a deemed disposition). The general idea is to eliminate income tax consequences from transactions between spouses.

The spousal rollover can be elected against by the settlor in the case of an *inter vivos* trust[46] and by the legal representative in the case of a testamentary trust.[47] The election makes the normal rules applicable, which will cause a deemed disposition at fair market value on the transfer of the property to the trust.[48] The election would be advantageous if the settlor or the deceased had capital losses or other deductions available to offset any capital gain caused by the deemed disposition, or if the property consisted of shares of a qualified small business corporation or farming property qualifying for the lifetime $750,000 capital gain exemption.[49]

There is a rollover on the transfer of property into an alter ego trust[50] and a deemed disposition on the death of a taxpayer.[51] Similarly, there is a rollover on the transfer of property into a joint spousal trust[52] and a deemed disposition of property owned by a joint spousal trust on the death of the surviving spouse or common-law partner.[53]

17.5 — Income taxed to the trust

(a) — Computation and designation of trust's income

A trust is treated as an individual for tax purposes and, is therefore taxable on its income earned during the year. However, because a trust is allowed to deduct the amount of income that is taxable to the beneficiary, the trust is a conduit in terms of

[44] Ss. 70(6) and 73(1). In the case of depreciable property, the deemed proceeds of disposition is normally the undepreciated capital cost of the property.

[45] See heading 13.4(b), "Rollovers for transfers to a spouse or common-law partner", above.

[46] S. 73(1).

[47] S. 70(6.2).

[48] If the transfer is *inter vivos*, s. 69(1)(b) applies. If the transfer is testamentary, s. 70(5) applies. See heading 13.4(a), "The fair market value principal", above.

[49] See heading 10.2(f), "Tax subsidies for certain investments", above.

[50] Ss. 73(1) and 73(1.01)(c)(ii).

[51] S. 104(4)(a)(iv)(A).

[52] Ss. 73(1) and 73(1.01)(c)(iii).

[53] S. 104(4)(a)(iv)(B) and (C).

income.[54] In other words, a trust is taxed only on income accumulating in the hands of the trustee. The amounts of income taxable to the beneficiary are discussed under heading 17.6, below. For present purposes, it is suffice to summarize that these amounts typically include: (1) income paid or payable to a beneficiary, and (2) amounts subject to a preferred beneficiary election.[55]

When income is taxable to the beneficiary, the trust's deduction[56] and the beneficiary's inclusion[57] will divert the income from the trust to the beneficiary for tax purposes. The only income that is taxed to the trust (as opposed to the beneficiary) is income that is earned by the trust in a taxation year that is not paid or payable in the year to a beneficiary[58] and income that is subject to a designation under subsection 104(13.1) or 104(13.2).

The designations referred to above make it possible to have income or capital gains that are paid or payable to beneficiaries taxed in the trust.[59] The Act provides the trustees with the discretion to deduct less than the full amount paid or payable to each beneficiary ("such amount as the trust claims")[60] and a mechanism for these designated amounts to be excluded from the beneficiary's income. Subsection 104(13.1) allows income which is payable to a beneficiary to be designated to be taxed in a trust and subsection 104(13.2) allows capital gains which are payable to a beneficiary to be designated to be taxed in a trust. The beneficiary then receives such items tax-free. The stated purpose of these rules is to allow a trust that has to distribute all of its income to take advantage of losses realized in the trust.[61] However, in practice, it provides an important opportunity to split income between the trust and the beneficiary, which is advantageous in the case of a testamentary trust that might be in a lower tax bracket than that of a beneficiary. It may be recalled that in order to qualify for the rollover on death, all the income of a testamentary spousal trust must be paid or payable to a beneficiary.[62] As a result, this is a key income splitting opportunity for spouses who are the beneficiaries of testamentary spousal trusts.

---

[54]Note that a trust is not a conduit in terms of a loss. A trust may not allocate a non capital loss or a net capital loss for a year to a beneficiary. Non capital and net capital losses are retained in the trust and are subject to the normal carryover rules for individuals.

[55]This election is discussed in detail under heading 17.6(b), "Preferred beneficiary election", below.

[56]S. 104(6)(b).

[57]S. 104(13).

[58]This assumes that the income is not subject to a preferred beneficiary election of an infirm or disabled beneficiary.

[59]See heading 17.6, "Income taxed to the beneficiary", below.

[60]S. 104(6)(b).

[61]See technical notes accompanying the 1988 Federal Budget's amendments to s. 104(13.2).

[62]See heading 17.2(e), "Spousal trusts", above.

(b) — Deemed disposition of trust property

Capital gains earned by a trust are generally taxed in a trust in the same way as they are taxed in the hands of an individual: that is, the disposition of capital property by the trustee will produce capital gains (or losses) one-half of which are taxable (or allowable). However, in addition, subsection 104(4) provides for a periodic deemed disposition at fair market value of all capital property held by a trust. For trusts other than spousal trusts, alter ego trusts and joint spousal trusts, the deemed disposition occurs every 21 years.[63] It is immaterial whether a particular capital property has been held for 21 years; the 21-year periods relate to the duration of the trust. Spousal trusts, alter ego trusts and joint spousal trusts are not subject to these deemed dispositions during the lifetime of the spouse or settlor beneficiaries (as the case may be)[64] but there is a deemed disposition on the death of these persons and (if the trust continues) every 21 years thereafter.[65]

On the date of a particular trust's deemed disposition, all capital property held by the trust has to be given a fair market value. The property is then deemed to have been disposed of and reacquired at fair market value,[66] thereby forcing the trust to recognize for tax purposes all accrued capital gains and losses.[67] Unless the terms of the trust provide that capital gains are payable to the spousal beneficiary, the deemed gains and losses are subject to tax in the trust.

The reason for the 21-year deemed realization is to preclude the indefinite deferral of capital gains (and recaptures) through the use of a long-term trust. An individual taxpayer can only defer capital gains for the period of his or her lifetime, because there is a deemed disposition of all capital property on death. A settlor who transfers capital property to a trust avoids that deemed disposition, but the trust will be subject to the 21-year deemed dispositions.

If a trust consists of portfolio investments which are being frequently changed, the 21-year deemed disposition will not have particularly serious tax consequences since the turnover of investments will result in the regular recognition of any capital gains and will keep the adjusted cost base of the trust property relatively up to date. But the 21-year deemed disposition would be very serious for a trust which held longstanding assets with substantial accrued gains. Where it is possible for a

---

[63]The 21-year periods are measured from the creation of the trust, or, in the case of trusts in existence at the beginning of 1972, from January 1, 1972 (s. 104(4)(b) and (c)). In 1991, ss. 104(5.3) to (5.7) were enacted, which enabled a trust with at least one "exempt beneficiary" (a family member only one generation removed from the settlor, e.g., a child of the settlor) to elect to postpone the deemed disposition until the death of the exempt beneficiary. This election is not available after 1998 (s. 104(5.3)). Trusts that made the election had a deemed disposition on January 1, 1999 of any property they own on that date (s. 104(5.3)(a)(i)).

[64]Ss. 104(4)(a)(iii) and (iv).

[65]Ss. 104(4)(b) and (c).

[66]S. 104(4).

[67]In the case of depreciable property, the deemed disposition is required by s. 104(5), and of course it may also cause a recapture of capital cost allowances.

trust to last for longer than 21 years, it is often good practice to confer upon the trustees the power to distribute all or some of the assets at any time. This enables the trustees to avoid the 21-year deemed disposition by distributing appreciated capital property to the beneficiaries before the expiry of the 21-year period. As will be explained later,[68] a distribution of property to capital beneficiaries is a tax-free transaction.

17.6 — Income taxed to the beneficiary

(a) — Income paid or payable in the year

Income which is "payable" to a beneficiary in a taxation year and deducted from the income of the trust for tax purposes[69] must be included in the income of the beneficiary to whom it was payable.[70] As discussed earlier, there is an exception for income that is payable to a beneficiary but is not deducted by the trust and is designated by the trustee(s) to be taxed in the trust.[71]

Income is "payable" in a taxation year to a beneficiary if it is "paid" in the year to the beneficiary, or, if, although it was not actually paid, the beneficiary "was entitled in that year to enforce payment thereof".[72] If a beneficiary is an infant or minor and cannot enforce payment solely for that reason, the income is still deemed to be payable to the beneficiary.[73]

If the trustee has no discretion as to the payment of income, that income will automatically be "payable" to the income beneficiary as soon as it is earned by the trust. Where the trustee has a discretion as to whether or not to pay income to a particular beneficiary, the best way to make sure that the income is payable to the beneficiary is for the trustee to exercise the discretion and pay the income to the beneficiary before the end of the year. If the actual payment cannot be made before the end of the year, the next best thing is for the trustee to make sure that the beneficiary has become entitled to enforce the payment. This could be done by signing a written resolution before the end of the year, resolving to pay the desired amount, and issuing a demand promissory note to the beneficiary (or, preferably, paying the amount), as soon as it can be quantified.

---

[68] See heading 17.8, "Termination of trust", below.

[69] S. 104(6)(b).

[70] S. 104(13).

[71] S. 104(13.1).

[72] S. 104(24).

[73] S. 104(18) applies to income held in trust for minors up until 21 years of age; if the minor cannot enforce payment because of trustee discretion to retain trust income, trust can still deem the amount payable to the beneficiary, and thus, the income will be taxable to the beneficiary even though retained in trust.

The CRA considers amounts paid to third parties for expenses incurred for the benefit of beneficiaries to be income payable to a beneficiary.[74] Amounts considered as expenses incurred for the benefit of beneficiaries include the cost of tuition fees, medical expenses, clothing and holidays but not general household expenses.[75] Proper accounting records supporting the expenses must be kept.[76]

(b) — Preferred beneficiary election

A preferred beneficiary election is an election[77] which can be made to have income that is not paid or payable to a beneficiary ("accumulating income") to be taxed in the hands of certain beneficiaries ("preferred beneficiaries"). "Preferred beneficiaries" must meet the eligibility criteria for the credit for mental or physical impairment (or the disability tax credit)[78] or must be dependent on another individual because of a mental or physical infirmity.[79] In addition to the infirmity requirement, "preferred beneficiaries" must meet a relational requirement. Preferred beneficiaries are restricted to the settlor of the trust, the spouse or common-law partner of the settlor, and the child, grandchild or great grandchild of the settlor or the spouse or common-law partner of any such person.[80]

Before 1996, the preferred beneficiary election was not so restricted and this allowed trust income which had not in fact been distributed to be split among family members (including minors) for income tax purposes. The effect of the change is that accumulating trust income can no longer be diverted to beneficiaries for tax

---

[74]S. 105(1). The value of these benefits is included in the income of a taxpayer, whether a beneficiary or not, and such amounts are not deductible by the trust.

[75]S. 105(2) excludes income of the trust used for the upkeep, maintenance or taxes of property used by a life tenant beneficiary as is reasonable in the circumstances. *Cooper v. M.N.R.* (1988), [1989] 1 C.T.C. 66, 88 D.T.C. 6525 (Fed. T.D.) held that interest-free loans to beneficiaries are excluded from s. 105(1).

[76]See CRA Technical Interpretations in 1993 and 1997 on this issue (Document Nos. 9233505 and 9722465, respectively). See also *Ken & Jesie Degrace Family Trust v. R.* (1998), [1999] 1 C.T.C. 2807, 99 D.T.C. 453 (T.C.C.).

[77]The preferred beneficiary election is set out in s. 104(14). The deduction in computing the trust's income is provided for under s. 104(12).

[78]For the criteria, see ss. 118.3(1)(a) and (b).

[79]That is, individuals eligible to be claimed as dependants under ss. 118(1)(b) or (d). The criteria that an individual must meet to be considered a dependant because of a mental or physical infirmity are far less onerous than those outlined in ss. 118.3(1)(a) and (b). In Interpretation Bulletin IT-513R, "Personal Tax Credits", (1998), Appendix A, the CRA states the term "mental or physical infirmity" takes on its ordinary meaning, that the dependency must be brought about solely by reason of the infirmity, that the degree of the infirmity must be such that it requires the person to be dependent on the individual for a considerable period of time and that a temporary illness is not an infirmity.

[80]S. 108(1) definition of "preferred beneficiary".

purposes. Only if the income is paid or payable to the beneficiaries will it be taxed to the beneficiaries.

(c) — Special rules for capital gains

The tax treatment of capital gains will often reflect a difference between the concept of income for tax purposes and the concept of income for trust accounting purposes. Taxable capital gains are, of course, income for tax purposes, but they are capital for trust accounting purposes (unless the trust instrument provides otherwise). Accordingly, capital gains which are earned by a trust will not normally be payable to the income beneficiary of the trust, but will be added to the capital of the trust. Even if all of a trust's income (for trust accounting purposes) is payable each year to an income beneficiary, capital gains will not be payable to the income beneficiary. Capital gains will ultimately be payable to the capital beneficiary, but not until the time comes to distribute the capital of the trust. It follows that capital gains earned by a trust in a taxation year will often not be payable to a beneficiary in the year and will therefore be treated for tax purposes as accumulating income of the trust. If so, the trust will be obliged to report the capital gains as its income.

If capital gains are payable to a beneficiary, a designation under subsection 104(13.2) can be made to have them taxed in the trust. If capital gains are not payable to a beneficiary, a preferred beneficiary election may be available (in respect of an infirm or disabled beneficiary) to have the capital gains taxed in the beneficiary's hands.

(d) — Flow-through character of income

The Act gives different tax treatment to income from different sources. When a beneficiary reports income from a trust, because it was paid or payable to the beneficiary, the general rule is that the income must be reported as income from property under subdivision b of Division B of Part I of the Act.[81] This is the general rule, laid down by paragraph 108(5)(a), and it means that income derived by a trust from a variety of sources loses its differentiated character when it flows through to the beneficiaries.

The general rule is subject to important exceptions, where the Act stipulates that income flowing through a trust retains its character in the hands of the beneficiary. The most important of these ancillary conduit provisions are as follows. Dividends from Canadian corporations received by the trust retain that character when so designated by the trustee:[82] this enables the beneficiary to take advantage of the Act's preferential treatment of Canadian dividend income. Similarly, capital gains received by the trust retain that character when so designated by the trustee:[83] this enables the beneficiary to take advantage of the Act's preferential treatment of cap-

[81]S. 12(1)(m).

[82]Ss. 104(19) and (20).

[83]Ss. 104(21) and (21.2).

ital gains. Finally, foreign-source income received by the trust retains that character when so designated by the trustee:[84] reported by a beneficiary; this enables the beneficiary to claim the foreign tax credit.

(e) — Tax-free payments to beneficiaries

A beneficiary may become liable to pay tax on income which has been retained in the trust and which he or she has not received for two reasons: (1) because it was payable to him or her in the year but was not actually paid;[85] or (2) because, although it was not payable to him or her in the year, it was the subject of a preferred beneficiary election.[86] In both cases, when the income is subsequently paid out, it is not taxable to the recipient in the year of payment because tax on the income has already been paid.[87] It should be noted that the ultimate recipient of the income might not necessarily be the beneficiary who paid the tax on the income when it was accumulating. That beneficiary may have died, or become disqualified for some other reason; but in these cases the subsequent distribution is still free of tax.

Income which is not paid or payable to a beneficiary or is paid or payable to a beneficiary but is subject to a designation under subsection 104(13.1) or (13.2) will of course be taxed in the trust and not as income of the beneficiary. When this after-tax income is subsequently paid to a beneficiary, it is distributed on a tax-free basis because it is (at that point) capital of the trust: tax on the income has already been paid. Curiously, the Act does not expressly say this, but it is clear that the subsequent distribution to the beneficiary is free of tax.

17.7 — Income taxed to the settlor

(a) — Anti-avoidance concerns

Under the general scheme of the Act, income earned through a trust is taxed either to the trust or to the beneficiary, not the settlor. However, as discussed below, in certain circumstances, income earned by the trust or the beneficiary may be attributed to the settlor.

---

[84]Ss. 104(22) and (22.1).

[85]S. 104(6).

[86]S. 104(14).

[87]Ss. 104(13) and (14).

(b) — Trusts for spouses or related minors

Section 74.1 provides that when property is transferred (or loaned)[88] to a spouse or common-law partner of the transferor or to a related minor,[89] the income from the property is deemed for tax purposes to be the income of the transferor and not the transferee. Section 74.2 provides that when property is transferred (or loaned) to a spouse or common-law partner of the transferor, any capital gain or loss on the disposition of the property by the transferee is deemed to be a capital gain or loss of the transferor and not of the transferee. These attribution rules have already been examined in chapter 13, Income Splitting, above.[90] The purpose of the rules is to preclude income splitting among members of a family. The rules expressly apply to transfers (or loans) to a spouse or related minor by means of a trust.[91]

Where a person transfers (or loans) property to a trust, and the income from the property is payable by the trust to the transferor's spouse, or to a related minor, then the income will be attributed to the transferor (or lender). This result is produced by subsection 74.1(1) (in the case of the spouse) and subsection 74.1(2) (in the case of the minor). If the transferred property is disposed of by the trust, and if any capital gain is payable to the transferor's spouse, then the capital gain will be attributed to the transferor. This result is produced by subsection 74.2(1). Note that section 74.2 applies only to spouses: there is no attribution of capital gains on a transfer to a related minor.

---

[88]Before 1985, a trust funded by a loan escaped the attribution rules. At that time, the attribution rules applied only to a "transfer" of property, and it was decided in *Dunkelman v. M.N.R.*, [1959] C.T.C. 375, 59 D.T.C. 1242 (Ex. Ct.) that a loan was not a transfer. The attribution rules were revised in 1985, and ss. 74.1 and 74.2 now expressly apply to a loan as well as a transfer. Because s. 74.5(2) exempts a loan at a commercial interest rate, one current practice is to settle a trust with a nominal amount (which was never invested to earn income) and provide the investment funds in the form of a loan at the commercial rate of interest. If the funds are invested in shares in a private corporation, it is possible for the trust to earn a large dividend which will give it the means to pay back the loan and then distribute future dividends to trust beneficiaries for the purpose of income splitting. This practice can no longer result in tax savings if the beneficiaries receiving the dividends are minor children after 1999 due to the introduction of the kiddie tax which is a tax at the top rate on "split income" which includes dividends from private corporations: see heading 13.10, "Kiddie tax", above.

[89]That is, a person under 18 years of age who is related to the transferor as a child or other descendant, brother or sister, niece or nephew.

[90]See headings 13.5 to 13.7. Where a person loans (rather than transfers) property to a trust and income is payable by the trust to other related persons, the income will also be attributed to the lender (s. 56(4.1)): see heading 13.9, "Income diversion", above.

[91]See also s. 74.5(9). S. 74.3 provides a formula, for the purposes of ss. 74.1 and 74.2, for calculating what amount of income is attributed to whom in the circumstance where a trust has received property from more than one individual or where a trust has distributed income to several beneficiaries not all of whom are a spouse or related minor to whom attribution would apply.

Where payments of income or capital gains from transferred (or loaned) property are made to a spouse or related minor (in the case of income only) in the exercise of a discretion conferred upon the trustee by the trust instrument, attribution will still apply. Payments made pursuant to a discretion attract the same attribution consequences as payments made pursuant to a duty.[92]

Income accumulating in a trust for the ultimate benefit of a spouse or related minor is not subject to attribution. This was decided in *Pichosky v. M.N.R.* (1964)[93] and is now confirmed by statute (section 74.3). It will be recalled that *inter vivos* trusts are subject to a flat rate of tax equal to the top personal marginal rate so that no tax savings can be achieved at least in the case of an *inter vivos* trust. Testamentary trusts, on the other hand, are not subject to the flat rate of tax, but there is no attribution of income of testamentary trusts in any event because the transferor of the trust property is deceased, and attribution ceases with the death of the transferor.

(c) — Trusts with reserved power of revocation or control

Subsection 75(2) of the Act provides as follows:

> Where, by a trust created in any manner whatever since 1934, property is held on condition
>
> (a) that it or property substituted therefor may
>
> (i) revert to the person from whom the property or property for which it was substituted was directly or indirectly received (in this subsection referred to as "the person"), or
>
> (ii) pass to persons to be determined by the person at a time subsequent to the creation of the trust, or
>
> (b) that, during the lifetime of the person, the property shall not be disposed of except with the person's consent or in accordance with the person's direction,
>
> any income or loss from the property or from property substituted therefor, any taxable capital gain or allowable capital loss from the disposition of the property or of property substituted therefor, shall, during the lifetime of the person while the person is resident in Canada be deemed to be income or a loss, as the case may be, or a taxable capital gain or allowable capital loss, as the case may be, of such person.

---

[92] See also *Murphy v. M.N.R.*, [1980] C.T.C. 386, 80 D.T.C. 6314 (Fed. T.D.) (a result that is confirmed by s. 74.3, which yields an amount to be attributed in this situation).

[93] [1964] C.T.C. 177, 64 D.T.C. 5105 (Ex. Ct.). The reasoning of the case was that the rules only apply to income that would otherwise be taxable to a spouse or related minor. Although this reasoning was far from compelling, the result is now confirmed by s. 74.3, as noted above. Accumulating income that is allocated to a spouse or related minor by a preferred beneficiary election is also attributed: see *Sachs v. R.*, [1980] C.T.C. 358, 80 D.T.C. 6291 (Fed. C.A.) and s. 74.3, which confirms this result.

Subsection 75(2) is, of course, another of the attribution provisions.[94] It operates to attribute income from a trust in which the settlor has reserved to himself or herself a power to revoke the trust, or a power to change the beneficiaries, or a power to direct or veto dispositions of the trust property, or a reversionary interest in the trust property. Thus, the section operates as a powerful disincentive to the creation of revocable trusts or trusts in which the settlor retains substantial control. However, it is not clear whether the subsection will apply to the income of a trust of which the settlor is a trustee. In that situation, the settlor in his or her capacity as trustee would possess controls over the trust of the kind contemplated by the section. It is obviously prudent to avoid creating a trust in which the settlor is the sole trustee. Indeed, even if the settlor were just one of several trustees, if the trustees' decisions must be unanimous, there is a risk that subsection 75(2) would apply. In the common case where the settlor does want to be a trustee, it is good practice to have two additional persons as trustees and for the three trustees to be empowered to act by a majority.

Where a settlor has funded a trust, in whole or in part, by loan, and the loan is secured by a promissory note payable on demand, the settlor's ownership of the note gives him or her a power over the trust that is akin to a power of revocation. Since this power is derived from the settlor's position as creditor, rather than from the trust instrument, it is probable that subsection 75(2) does not apply, although no case has considered the point.[95]

17.8 — Termination of trust

A trust is brought to an end by the distribution of its property to the beneficiaries. In many cases, in order to make an equitable distribution, it will be necessary to realize some or all of the trust property. Any such sales will of course be dispositions which may give rise to taxable capital gains or allowable capital losses. These gains or losses will be brought into the income of the trust, unless they are paid or payable to a beneficiary in the year, as they may well be, if the realization was for purposes of distribution. Where taxable capital gains (or losses), are paid or payable in the year to a beneficiary, then they are brought into the income of the beneficiary who is entitled to payment. It will be recalled that while capital gains are income for tax purposes, they will normally be capital for trust accounting pur-

---

[94]It is also important to note that the general rule that property is transferred on a tax-free basis to a beneficiary in satisfaction of his or her capital interest in a trust (s. 107(2), discussed under heading 17.8, below) will not apply if s. 75(2) was applicable at any time to any property of the trust (s. 107(4.1)(b)). Instead, the transfer will take place at the property's fair market value in cases where (1) the property is distributed to a beneficiary who is neither a contributor of the particular property to the trust nor his or her spouse (or common-law partner) (s. 107(4.1)(c)), and (2) the contributor of the particular property is still alive (s. 107(4.1)(d)).

[95]The attribution rules in ss. 74.1, 74.2 and 56(4.1) would apply: see heading 17.7(b), "Trusts for spouses or related minors", above.

poses, so that they will be brought into the income for tax purposes of the capital beneficiary of the trust, not the income beneficiary.

When property is transferred *in specie* out of a trust in satisfaction of an *income* interest, that is, to a beneficiary who is an income beneficiary for trust accounting purposes, subsection 106(3) provides that the trust is deemed to have disposed of the property at its fair market value. A distribution of property in satisfaction of an income interest is not a common occurrence, but it may occur if a trust is brought to an end prematurely. It would occur, for example, if a trust were terminated during the life of the life tenant (income beneficiary), and the capital property of the trust were divided *in specie* between the life tenant and remainderperson (capital beneficiary) in proportion to the values of their interests. The property that is distributed to the income beneficiary in satisfaction of his or her interest will be deemed to have been realized at fair market value, and will force recognition of any accrued capital gain (or loss).[96] Is the deemed income of subsection 106(3) taxable to the trust or to the person to whom the property has been distributed? The gain has, of course, been transferred *in specie* to the beneficiary. Does that mean that it has been paid to the beneficiary,[97] and is therefore deductible by the trust[98] and includible in the beneficiary's income?[99] The answer to this question is likely yes, although the position is not clear.[100]

When property is transferred *in specie* out of a trust[101] in satisfaction of a *capital* interest, that is, to a beneficiary who is a capital beneficiary for trust accounting purposes, the trust is deemed by subsection 107(2) to have disposed of the property

---

[96]On a sale by an income beneficiary of his or her income interest in the trust, s. 106(2)(a) requires the vendor to bring the entire proceeds of the disposition into income. But s. 106(3) is expressly exempted from the operation of s. 106(2)(a). Under s. 106(3), when the income beneficiary gives up his or her interest to the trust in return for trust property, the income beneficiary is not required to bring into income the value of the trust property received. The only tax consequence to the income beneficiary may be the recognition of any capital gain (or loss) accrued on the trust property received by him or her.

[97]S. 104(24).

[98]S. 104(6).

[99]S. 104(13).

[100]The same question arises in respect of the deemed income created by s. 104(4)(a) (death of a spouse or settlor beneficiary in the case of a spousal trust, alter ego trust or joint spousal trust, as the case may be) and s. 107(4) (distribution of spousal trust property to someone other than a spouse), but in these two cases the flow-through to the beneficiary is specifically denied by s. 104(6)(b), which however makes no reference to s. 106(3).

[101]S. 107(2) was amended in 1988 to apply only to a "personal trust" and a "prescribed trust". A prescribed trust is defined in reg. 4800.1 as one that falls within three categories: (1) a trust to hold employer shares; (2) a trust to secure debts; and (3) a voting trust. A trust that is neither a personal trust nor a prescribed trust suffers a deemed disposition at fair market value when property is distributed to a beneficiary in satisfaction of a capital interest (s. 107(2.1)).

for proceeds equal to its "cost amount" to the trust.[102] The result is that the property rolls out of the trust to the capital beneficiary and the trust recognizes no capital gain or loss (and no recapture or terminal loss) on the distribution. An election out of the rollover is available on the winding up of a trust.

The beneficiary to whom the distribution is made is deemed to acquire the property at its cost amount to the trust plus an additional amount.[103] In the usual case where the beneficiary acquired his or her interest in the trust for a cost of nil on the original creation of the trust,[104] then the additional amount will be inapplicable, and the beneficiary will acquire the property at its cost amount to the trust. The additional amount applies only in those cases where the beneficiary purchased the interest from a former beneficiary or inherited the interest on the death of a former beneficiary.[105] In those cases, the beneficiary's interest in the trust will have an adjusted cost base, namely, the price for which it was purchased, or the fair market value at the time it was inherited;[106] and that adjusted cost base could be higher than the cost amount to the trust. In that case, the net effect is to step up the cost amount of the property distributed to the beneficiary to the price he or she paid for the purchased capital interest or was deemed to pay for the inherited capital interest. Without this step-up there would be an element of double taxation when the beneficiary later disposed of the property.

The tax-deferred roll-out which is available for capital property provides a powerful tax incentive for trustees to distribute capital property to the beneficiaries *in specie*. That way, recognition of accrued capital gains is deferred until the beneficiary disposes of the property. However, if the trust directs a distribution among several beneficiaries in equal (or otherwise defined) shares, it may not be possible to accomplish that result by a *specie* distribution. Even when assets can be distributed *in specie* in accordance with the trust instrument, there may be difficulties in equalizing the shares of the beneficiaries since the adjusted cost base of each asset will have to be considered as well as its fair market value.

Take the case of a trust which at the time for distribution has two capital beneficiaries, both equally entitled, and two properties, Blackacre and Whiteacre, both of equal value. This looks like an easy case for a *specie* distribution. But now suppose that Blackacre, with a fair market value of $100,000, has an adjusted cost base of $40,000, and Whiteacre, also with a fair market value of $100,000, has an adjusted

---

[102]The cost amount of properties of various kinds is defined in s. 248(1). In the case of capital property other than depreciable property, the cost amount is the adjusted cost base of the property; in the case of depreciable property, the cost amount is the undepreciated capital cost.

[103]S. 107(2)(b).

[104]S. 107(1.1).

[105]Neither of these circumstances would cause the trust to lose its character as a "personal trust", because the beneficiary would not have bought the beneficial interest from the trust or from anyone who had made a contribution to the trust.

[106]S. 107(1.1).

cost base of $90,000. In that case, the recipient of Blackacre faces a much larger future capital gain than does the recipient of Whiteacre. Even if the trust also has some cash to make an equalizing payment to the recipient of Blackacre, it will not be obvious how much that payment should be, because the present value of the future tax liabilities inherent in the two properties will not be obvious. Unless an agreement can be reached with the two beneficiaries, and releases obtained from them, a *specie* distribution in this situation is unsafe from the point of view of the trustees, who could be liable for a failure to make an "equal" distribution. The trustees can avoid these headaches by selling the trust assets and making an equal distribution in cash. If they do that, however, the disposition of capital property by the trustees will require the immediate recognition of any accrued capital gains so that the tax postponement allowed by subsection 107(2) will be lost.

The roll-out under subsection 107(2) on the distribution *in specie* of trust assets also applies to a spousal trust, an alter ego trust and a joint spousal trust. (There is one exception to this rule, which is discussed in the next paragraph.) However, it will be recalled that paragraph 104(4)(a) imposes a deemed disposition of all capital property on the death of the spouse (or common-law partner) or settlor beneficiary. If the assets of the trust are distributed soon after the death of this beneficiary (which would commonly occur), the trust will not benefit from the subsection 107(2) roll-out: since its capital property will have recently suffered the deemed disposition under paragraph 104(4)(a) on the death of the spouse (or common-law partner) or settlor beneficiary that the property is unlikely to have any accrued capital gains. Of course, if there is a substantial lapse of time between the death of the spouse or settlor beneficiary and the termination of the trust, then the trust's capital property might well have accrued gains, and the subsection 107(2) roll-out would be a benefit, enabling the recognition of those gains to be deferred.

The roll-out on the distribution *in specie* of trust assets does not apply to a spousal trust, alter ego trust or a joint spousal trust in one exceptional situation. If the trust is terminated prematurely during the beneficiary spouse or settlor's lifetime, and if capital property is distributed to someone other than the spouse or settlor beneficiary, then there is a deemed disposition of the capital property for proceeds equal to the fair market value of the property.[107] This provision is necessary to prevent these types of trusts (which receive property on a rollover basis) from being used to divert property to other beneficiaries on a tax-free basis by terminating them prematurely in order to avoid the deemed disposition on the death of the spouse or settlor beneficiary. As well, any property distributed to the spouse in satisfaction of his or her income interest will suffer an immediate deemed disposition.[108]

---

[107] S. 107(2.1), (4).

[108] S. 106(3).

17.9 — Tax planning with trusts

(a) — Reasons for creating trusts

The majority of family trusts, especially testamentary trusts, are created for reasons that have nothing to do with tax. Some of those reasons are:

- management is separated from enjoyment, which enables the settlor to appoint an experienced trustee to manage property for beneficiaries who may be too young or otherwise incapable of managing the trust property;
- control over the settlor's property can be projected over two or more generations by the creation of a life interest (or interests) followed by remainder interests;
- beneficial interests can be created for minors, or persons not yet born (such as future grandchildren), or persons not yet ascertained (such as future spouses of unmarried children or grandchildren);
- beneficial interests can be made subject to postponed vesting so that interests do not vest until the holder has reached a stipulated age;
- the trustee can be given discretion with respect to distributions of income and capital so that the future circumstances of the beneficiaries can be taken into account; and
- *inter vivos* trusts (such as alter ego trusts and joint spousal trusts) can be used as will substitutes in order to avoid the process of probating the will and the resulting loss of privacy and the imposition of probate fees.

Tax considerations are still important for trusts that are created for non-tax reasons, because the settlor or testator will want to steer clear of as many as possible of the tax disadvantages that the Act now visits on trusts. Where there are tax advantages to be gained, the settlor or testator will want to consider them, and decide whether any tax-driven suggestions for the structure of the trust are compatible with the non-tax objectives. In some cases, a trust is created primarily for a tax reason, which is usually to accomplish the splitting of income among children or other relatives of the settlor. The rest of this chapter will try and draw together some of the previously described tax doctrine that is relevant to planning the creation of a trust.

(b) — Planning a trust

An initial disadvantage of the trust is that there are no general rollover provisions to facilitate its creation. The formation of corporations and partnerships is addressed by provisions that enable capital property to be rolled into the new organizations without tax costs. In the case of trusts, only the spousal or common-law partner trusts, alter ego trusts, and joint spousal trusts have the benefit of a rollover on its creation. In many cases, a spousal or common-law partner trust will not fit the settlor's non-tax objectives. If it does fit, in order to take advantage of the rollover, care must be taken not to taint the trust, for example, by creating a power of encroachment in favour of persons other than the spouse. The rollover is available to both *inter vivos* and testamentary spousal or common-law partner trusts (subsections 73(1) and 70(6) respectively).

Another disadvantage of the trust instrument, again in comparison with a corporation or partnership, is that the trust generally suffers a deemed disposition at fair market value of all its capital property every 21 years (subsection 104(4)). The only way to escape from the deemed disposition rule is to distribute the trust's property to the capital beneficiaries (taking advantage of the subsection 107(2) rollover on distribution) before the 21-year period has expired. This cannot be done if the trust does not authorize such a distribution, and so consideration should be given to include in a trust that may last for 21 years a power that allows the trustees to terminate the trust within 21 years. If there is no such power, the trustees must obtain court approval for a variation of the trust to permit the distribution.

The spousal trust, alter ego trust and joint spousal trust are exempt from the 21-year deemed disposition during the lifetime of the spouse or settlor beneficiary (as the case may be), but these trusts suffer a deemed disposition on the death of the spouse or settlor beneficiary, that may occur before the 21-year period has expired. Moreover, the deemed disposition on the death of the spouse or settlor beneficiary cannot be avoided by an early termination of the trust, because a distribution to anyone other than the spouse during the lifetime of the spouse gives rise to a deemed disposition at fair market value.[109]

In order to preclude the use of a trust to split income, an *inter vivos* trust is taxed at the top individual rate regardless of the amount of its income.[110] However, income that is paid or payable to the beneficiaries is washed out of the trust and is taxed in the hands of the beneficiaries.[111] This does offer some opportunities for income splitting if the income beneficiaries are adult children of the settlor or are unrelated to the settlor. Payments of income to a spouse (who must be the income beneficiary of a spousal trust) or a related minor trigger the attribution rules of section 74.1 and result in the income being attributed back to the settlor. Payments of capital gains to a spouse (but not to a related minor) also attract attribution (section 74.2). From a tax standpoint, it is desirable that income be payable to persons who will not attract the attribution rules (such as adult children); that there be a power to pay out capital gains (to a person other than a spouse) as well as ordinary income (to persons other than a spouse or related minors); and that the trustees have a discretion as to whom to pay income (so that tax considerations as well as non-tax considerations can be taken into account). However, these kinds of powers cannot be included in a spousal trust without tainting it, and they may be inconsistent with the settlor's non-tax objectives (which may include providing for a spouse or minor children).

---

[109]Ss. 107(2.1), (4).

[110]S. 122(1).

[111]Ss. 104(6), (13).

A testamentary trust offers more potential for income splitting. The trust is taxed at the graduated rates that are applicable to individuals, so that capital gains or other income accumulating in the trust are not taxed at a high rate (unless there is a lot of accumulating income). If the testator wishes to postpone payments of income to children, for example, a separate trust could be set up for each child, and each trust would be taxed on its accumulating income as a separate individual.[112] Income that is paid or payable to beneficiaries is taxed in the hands of the beneficiaries. Because the donor of the property is deceased, there is no attribution; therefore, payments to spouses and related minors are taxed in their hands.

One of the problems with using an *inter vivos* trust (such as an alter ego or joint spousal trust) as a will substitute is the fact that it precludes the settlor from setting up a testamentary trust for those assets on his or her death. Another problem is that when the settlor or spouse beneficiary dies, the accrued capital gain on the assets in the trust is taxed in the trust at the top marginal rate[113] rather than in the beneficiary's hands where the tax rate might be lower.

(c) — Income splitting

Just as loans and transfers can be made directly to family members for income splitting purposes (as long as the attribution rules and the kiddie tax are avoided), an *inter vivos* trust can also be used for income splitting. In fact, when minor children are involved, a trust should always be used because minors cannot contract. The use of discretionary trusts also allows more flexibility with income splitting plans.

(d) — Estate freeze

An *inter vivos* trust is usually one element of an "estate freeze", which is a tax-driven transaction designed to "freeze" accruing capital gains on "growth assets", and transfer the future growth of the assets to the next generation. The simplest case, which will be described in the text that follows, is that of the settlor who owns all of the common shares of a small business corporation.[114] The settlor is concerned about the tax liability on the capital gains that have already accrued on his or her shares, and about the liability on the capital gains that (he or she hopes) will accrue in the future; therefore an estate freeze may be attractive.

The freeze can be carried out in a variety of ways. The simplest type is accomplished by the settlor causing the corporation (that he or she controls) to undergo a reorganization where the settlor's common shares are exchanged for preference shares, and new common shares are issued to the settlor's children (and/or other

---

[112] *Mitchell*, note 31, above.

[113] S. 104(4).

[114] A small business corporation is a Canadian-controlled private corporation, with all or substantially all of its assets employed in an active business in Canada: s. 248(1).

relatives), at a nominal cost. The preference shares issued to the settlor would possess the following characteristics:

- they would be fixed at their face value and would not be entitled to share in any surplus assets if the corporation were wound up;
- they would not be entitled to dividends in priority to the common shares; the directors would have the power to declare dividends on the common shares but not the preference shares;
- they would be retractable (redeemable at the option of the holder), so that they are worth their full face value even though they will not necessarily receive dividends; and
- they would carry voting rights so that the settlor retains legal control of the corporation (in addition to the *de facto* control conferred by the right to require redemption of the shares).

The corporation's newly issued common shares would be entitled to any surplus assets on the winding up of the corporation. However, the new common shares would not carry voting rights. The new common shares could be issued to the settlor's children and/or other relatives. Because the face value of the settlor's preference shares will represent the entire value of the corporation (the fair market value of the common shares for which the preference shares were exchanged), the common shares have little value at the time of the reorganization, and they can be issued for a nominal consideration. The subscribers for the common shares should themselves supply the consideration for their shares. The settlor must not supply the consideration for any shares purchased by a spouse or related minor, because this would cause the attribution rules to apply to future dividends and (in the case of a spouse only) future capital gains.[115] In any event, dividends or shareholder benefits on private corporation shares received by minor children will be taxed at the highest rates under the "kiddie tax" provisions in section 120.4.

This reorganization of the company is known as a freeze, because the settlor's interest in the company is frozen at its value at the date of the freeze. Because the settlor's preference shares are fixed in value, it is the common shares that will increase in value if the company's business increases in value. This means that the settlor knows that his or her capital gains are limited to the amount of his or her capital gains on the common shares that were exchanged for the preference shares. He or she need not recognize the gains at the time of the freeze, because a section 86 rollover is available to shelter the share exchange. But, having frozen his or her capital gains, the taxpayer is in a good position to plan for the tax liability that will arise upon death with the deemed disposition at fair market value of the preference shares that are currently sheltering the gains. For example, the settlor might purchase life insurance to fund the future tax liability.

---

[115] Ss. 74.1 and 74.2.

The simplest form of estate freeze (as described above) need not make use of a trust. But, in many cases, the settlor will prefer the post-freeze common shares to be held by a trust for his or her children (and/or other relatives). If the settlor wishes to benefit minors, or persons not yet born (such as future grandchildren), or persons not yet ascertained (such as the spouses of children or grandchildren not yet married), or if the settlor wishes to create some discretion as to who receives income and how much, then a trust is required. In that case, it will be the trust that subscribes for the post-freeze common shares, borrowing the small sum ($10 or $50 would be usual) that would be required. If the trust borrows the money from the settlor, the loan must be made at a commercial rate of interest and the interest must in fact be regularly paid in accordance with the rules of section 74.5(2) (so as to prevent the application of the attribution rules). The small loan would be repaid, with interest, as soon as the corporation pays a dividend on the common shares. Apart from the retirement of the loan, when the corporation pays dividends on the common shares held by the trust, the income is available for distribution to the beneficiaries. If the income is distributed and the kiddie tax is inapplicable, and the beneficiaries have little or no other income, there will be substantial tax savings in comparison to the total income being received by the settlor.[116]

With respect to the future growth of the corporation, the effect of the freeze is to cause all future growth to be reflected in the value of the common shares that are held by the trust. If the common shares of the trust are distributed *in specie* to the beneficiaries before the 21st anniversary of the trust, the 21-year deemed disposition will be avoided and the taxable capital gains will not have to be recognized until the individual beneficiaries dispose of the shares. When the taxable capital gains do have to be recognized, it will be in the hands of the individual beneficiaries, each of whom is entitled to the $750,000 lifetime exemption. The settlor is also entitled to the $750,000 lifetime exemption, and may decide to recognize the accrued capital gains at the time of the freeze if he or she has room in his or her lifetime exemption to shelter the gain.[117] The effect of the freeze is to multiply the lifetime exemptions that are available to shelter future capital gains.

---

[116]Because the income paid to the beneficiaries is dividend income, the beneficiaries will be entitled to the gross-up and credit by virtue of the ancillary conduit rule of s. 104(19).

[117]To do this, the settlor and the corporation would jointly elect under s. 85(1) to transfer the settlor's common shares of the corporation to the corporation (in exchange for new preference shares of the corporation) at a price which is sufficient to trigger capital gains of $750,000 in the settlor's hands. If such an election is made, the automatic s. 86 rollover rules will not apply.

18
Tax Administration and Ethics

18.1 — Filing of tax returns

We have already noted in chapter 1 that the collection of tax is the responsibility of the Canada Revenue Agency (CRA). The process of collection is started by the filing of a return by the taxpayer. Subsection 150(1) requires that every individual who is liable to pay tax in a particular taxation year must file a tax return for that year. In most cases, the obligation to file a return applies only if the individual has received enough income to become liable to pay tax.[1] However, the Minister has the power, under subsection 150(2) of the *Income Tax Act* (the "Act"), to demand the filing of a return by an individual who is not liable to pay tax. Subsection 150(1) requires corporations to file returns whether or not they are liable to pay tax.

[1]S. 150(1) also requires taxpayers who do not owe tax but who have disposed of capital property during the year or who have capital gains to file a return. This requirement was introduced in 1985 at the same time as the lifetime capital gains exemption (s. 110.6). The purpose of the change was to enable the CRA to keep track of a taxpayer's capital gains even in situations where no tax was owing because the taxpayer claimed the exemption. Since 1994, the lifetime exemption has applied only to farming property and qualified small business corporation shares. There seems no point in reporting other capital gains if the taxpayer is not liable to pay any tax. However, the requirement has not been repealed.

Returns by individuals must generally be filed no later than April 30 of the following year but the deadline is extended to June 15th if either the taxpayer (or his or her spouse or common-law partner) has income from a business.[2] Corporate returns must be filed within six months of the end of the taxation year, which is the corporation's fiscal period.[3] Individuals may file a return by mailing it,[4] by filing electronically (e-file or Netfile using approved software), or (in the case of simple returns) by telephone (Telefile).[5] Corporations with gross revenues in excess of $1 million must generally e-file their returns.[6]

The return is in a form prescribed by the Minister. It not only requires the reporting of all relevant income and expenses with supporting documentation, it also requires the taxpayer to estimate the amount of tax payable,[7] and payment of the tax must accompany the filing of the return.[8]

18.2 — Payment of tax

Payment of unpaid tax must accompany a taxpayer's income tax return. An assessment by the Minister also generates an obligation to pay the unpaid part of the amount assessed. In general, however, taxes are paid either by way of withholding at source or instalments.

(a) — Withholding at source

We have already noted that individual taxpayers are obliged to pay any tax estimated to be due at the time of filing their returns, that is, by April 30 of the year following the taxation year. However, those taxpayers receiving income from employment (and some other sources) have their tax withheld at source: the tax is deducted by the employer from each pay cheque and remitted by the employer to the CRA.[9] For a taxpayer with little or no income other than tax-withheld employment income, there is unlikely to be any tax unpaid at the time of filing the return, and therefore there would be no obligation to pay anything by April 30. Indeed, there is no obligation even to file a return if there is no further tax payable. However, a taxpayer in this situation should normally file a return, because the with-

---

[2]S. 150(1)(d).

[3]S. 150(1)(a). Under certain conditions, Canadian resident corporations are allowed to report their results in their functional currency (e.g. the currency used for accounting purposes) rather than translating the results into Canadian dollars: s. 261.

[4]The return is mailed to the taxation centre for the region in which an individual taxpayer lives.

[5]S. 150.1.

[6]Effective for taxation years ending after 2009. S. 150.1(2.1)

[7]S. 151.

[8]S. 156.1(4).

[9]S. 153(1).

holdings are often too high (for example, because they do not take account of all the deductions or credits to which the taxpayer is entitled), in which case the taxpayer will be entitled to a refund of the overpaid tax.[10]

Section 227 establishes penalties for failure by an employer to withhold tax at source, and for failure to remit to the CRA any tax that was withheld; the delinquent employer is liable for the amount that should have been withheld or remitted, plus penalties, and interest. Where a corporation has failed to withhold or remit tax, section 227.1 imposes personal liability on the directors of the corporation, subject to a defence of due diligence. The employee is also liable for tax that was never withheld, but the employee is not liable for tax that was withheld but not remitted to the CRA.[11]

(b) — Instalments

The general rule is that an individual who derives income from which tax has not been withheld at source (for example, income from business or property) must pay tax by quarterly instalments[12] throughout the calendar year according to a formula[13] and then pay any balance due on April 30 of the following year.[14] The general rule is subject to this exception: if the individual's total federal and provincial tax liability, apart from tax withheld at source, is less than $3,000,[15] then no instalments need to be paid; any tax liability is not payable until April 30 of the following year.[16] The exception is designed to cover the common case where an individual derives most of his or her income from employment, which is subject to withholding by the employer, and derives some additional income from investments (property) or business, which is not subject to withholding. Provided the additional income is not so great as to generate an additional tax liability of $3,000 or more, the individual need not pay instalments; the tax on the additional income

---

[10]Low-income taxpayers should also file in order to establish their entitlement to the GST/HST credit, the child tax benefit and any refundable provincial credits.

[11]*Lalonde v. M.N.R*, [1982] C.T.C. 2749, 82 D.T.C. 1772 (Fed. C.A.).

[12]Tax instalments are payable quarterly, approximately two weeks before the end of each quarter, on March 15, June 15, September 15 and December 15 of each year. The general requirement is that four equal payments be made, even though the taxpayer's income may not be received evenly throughout the year. Farmers and fishermen do not pay quarterly instalments. They must pay a single instalment of two-thirds of their liability (provided it exceeds $3,000) on or before December 31, and the balance on or before April 30 of the following year: s. 155.

[13]Reg. 5300.

[14]S. 156.1(4). S. 248(1) defines the "balance-due day for individual taxpayers as April 30 of the following year.

[15]S. 156.1(4).

[16]More precisely, under s. 156.1, an individual is required to make instalment payments if the difference between total (federal and provincial) tax payable and tax withheld at source is greater than $3,000 in the current year and one of the previous two years.

need not be paid until April 30 of the following year. The $3,000 exemption would also apply to a person who is self-employed or retired, and who has such a low total income that it attracts a combined federal-provincial tax liability of less than $3,000. That person would not have to pay tax by instalments, but could wait until April 30 of the following year.

The general rule is that corporations are required to pay tax in 12 monthly instalments[17] throughout the taxation year subject to a similar $3,000 exemption. Eligible small Canadian controlled private corporations (CCPCs) with a perfect compliance history may make quarterly instalments.[18] The same formula is used for the calculation: the only difference is the frequency of the instalments.[19] Any balance is due within two months or (in the case of a small CCPC) three months[20] of the end of the taxation year.

Because interest is charged on late and insufficient payments, individuals and corporations must ensure that their instalments are correct and made on time.[21] Although corporations and individuals with a June 15th filing deadline do not need to file their returns until after the balance-due day,[22] they do need to make an accurate estimate of the tax owing by the balance-due day because interest will accrue on any amounts owing after that date.

The obligation of individuals and corporations to pay instalments throughout the taxation year combined with the obligation for the withholding of tax means that income tax is paid as taxpayers earn the related income.

18.3 — Assessment

(a) — Notice of assessment

The Minister is required by subsection 152(1) to assess the tax payable by the taxpayer. This task must be accomplished "with all due dispatch".[23] When the return

---

[17]S. 157(1). The instalments are due on the last day of each month.

[18]S. 157(1.1). The criteria are set out in s. 157(1.2).

[19]Reg. 5301 and s. 157(1.1).

[20]The period is three months for a Canadian-controlled private corporation claiming the small business deduction that had taxable income less than or equal to the business limit for the small business deduction in the preceding year: s. 157(1)(b).

[21]S. 161.

[22]S. 150(1)(a) and (d).

[23]S. 152(1). The courts have given a flexible meaning to the phrase "with all due dispatch", defining it as meaning no more than a reasonable period in all the circumstances. With this definition, the courts have accepted as valid assessments issued after quite lengthy delays: e.g., *Hutterian Brethren Church of Wilson v. R.*, [1979] C.T.C. 1, 79 D.T.C. 5042 (Fed. T.D.) (15 months), *Lipsey v. M.N.R.*, [1984] C.T.C. 675, 84 D.T.C. 6192 (Fed. T.D.) (2 years); and *Weih v. M.N.R.*, [1988] 2 C.T.C. 2013, 88 D.T.C. 1379 (T.C.C.) (15 months). However, the limits of tolerance were exceeded by a six-year delay in *J. Stollar Construction v. M.N.R.*, [1989] 1 C.T.C. 2171, 89 D.T.C. 134 (T.C.C.); in that case the court vacated the

is received at the taxation centre (whether by mail or electronically) the process of assessment takes place. The return is checked by officials at the taxation centre to ensure that the arithmetic is correct, that all required documentation has been supplied, and that the return is, on its face, otherwise in order. This process may involve obtaining more information from the taxpayer, and may result in additions to or subtractions from the income reported by the taxpayer. When the process is complete, the taxation centre issues a notice of assessment which is mailed to the taxpayer demanding payment of any tax still owing. That tax must be paid "forthwith".[24] If tax has been overpaid, a refund will be paid to the taxpayer.[25]

The assessment will include interest on overdue taxes.[26] The "prescribed rate" of interest is set quarterly, and consists of the average yield on 90-day treasury bills sold in the first month of the previous quarter, rounded up to the nearest percentage point, plus four percentage points.[27] The prescribed rate of interest that is paid by the CRA on refunds of overpaid taxes to individuals is the same treasury-bill rate plus two (instead of four) percentage points. There is no two percentage point increase for interest owing to corporations with overpaid taxes after July 1, 2010.

Section 222 establishes a 10-year limitation period for the collection of federal taxes unpaid as at March 4, 2004.[28] This rule was introduced in response to the Supreme Court of Canada decision in *Markevich v. Canada* (2003)[29] which limited the collection of federal taxes to the 6-year limitation period set out in the Crown Liability and Proceedings Act because there was no specific limitation period set out in the Act.

(b) — Examination

Because the review of tax returns by the taxation centre is only a limited one, a more thorough examination of some returns is conducted by the taxation centre after the notices of assessment have been issued. That examination takes place within the centre and involves cross-checking the information provided by related taxpayers, for example, employers and employees, companies and shareholders, lenders and borrowers, and the like.

---

assessment. An assessment will not be vacated for failure to assess with all due dispatch unless the taxpayer goes through the objection and appeal process described under headings 18.4(a) and 18.4(b), below: *R. v. Ginsberg*, [1996] 3 C.T.C. 63, 96 D.T.C. 6372 (Fed. C.A.).

[24]S. 158.

[25]No refund will be paid until all returns due under the *Excise Tax Act* and the *Air Travellers Secruity Charge Act* have been filed (s. 164(20.1)) and the Minister may, at the taxpayer's direction, re-appropriate funds to amounts owing under other Acts (s. 221.2).

[26]Ss. 152 and 161.

[27]Reg. 4301.

[28]March 4, 2004 is the date on which these changes were originally announced.

[29][2003] 2 C.T.C. 83, 2003 D.T.C. 5185, 2003 SCC 9 (S.C.C.).

(c) — Audit

A small number of returns are selected for "audit" by the district offices. The audit programme is mainly directed at those categories of taxpayers who are most likely to have under-reported their income. Wage and salary earners, who comprise about 80 per cent of the taxpaying population, are rarely audited. Their taxes are deducted at source and their income is readily cross-checked against information in returns filed by employers. Taxpayers who have sources of income other than salary or wages, such as self-employed individuals, corporations and trusts, are the most likely candidates for audit, but less than five per cent of the returns in these categories are in fact audited each year. An audit usually occurs at the taxpayer's place of business, where the CRA's auditor will inspect the books and records kept by the taxpayer.

The power of the auditor to inspect the books and records of the taxpayer is contained in subsection 231.1(1), which also permits the auditor to enter business premises without a warrant and requires the owner or manager of the premises to provide "all reasonable assistance" and to answer "all proper questions". Entry to a dwelling-house without the consent of the occupant requires a warrant issued by a judge under subsection 231.1(3). Section 231.2 empowers the Minister to demand information or documents from the taxpayer and from others.

When the audit is complete, the CRA may reassess the taxpayer in light of the auditor's findings. Most audits do result in an upward adjustment of the taxpayer's tax liability.

(d) — Reassessment

An examination or audit, which has been conducted after the original assessment, may lead the Minister to reassess the taxpayer. A taxpayer may also seek reassessment. For example, after receiving the notice of assessment, the taxpayer may discover that he or she omitted some reportable item, in which case he or she should write to the taxation centre seeking an adjustment of the tax payable. Another example is where a taxpayer in a later year incurs a loss that under the Act's loss carryover rules can be carried back and deducted from the income of an earlier year. In that case, the taxpayer should file the prescribed form to claim the loss carryback, which of course involves the reassessment of the tax for the earlier year.

Section 152(4) confers on the Minister the power to reassess a return that has already been assessed, but imposes limits on that power. The general rule for individual taxpayers is that a reassessment must be made within three years of the date of mailing of the original assessment (the period is four years in the case of a corporation other than a Canadian controlled private corporation). This time limit may be waived by the taxpayer by filing a prescribed form of waiver within the normal reassessment period, in which case the Minister can reassess at any time. The taxpayer might wish to file a waiver in order to obtain time to produce more information, for example. If the taxpayer fails to file a waiver within the normal period of reassessment for a given taxation year, the Minister is generally powerless to reassess the taxpayer's return for that year once the normal reassessment period of three years has elapsed.[30] The Minister does, however, have power to refund an overpayment of tax after the expiry of the three-year deadline where an application is made by an individual for a reduction in taxes or waiving interest or penalties in the case of taxpayer hardship.[31] The Minister can also reassess beyond the normal reassessment period in cases of misrepresentation or fraud, or where a reassessment within the normal reassessment period affects a taxation year outside the period.[32]

A reassessment will, of course, include interest on overdue taxes.[33] It will also include the civil penalties (see below) if the Minister concludes that a breach of the Act has been committed by the taxpayer.

18.4 — Dispute resolution

(a) — Objection

A taxpayer who disagrees with a notice of assessment should initially contact the nearest office of the CRA for an explanation. Many disputes of a minor nature are resolved informally without recourse to the formal process of objection.

The formal means of initiating an appeal from an assessment (or reassessment) is by serving a notice of objection on the Minister. The deadline is the later of one year after the filing-due date (which for most individuals is April 30 following the relevant taxation year) and 90 days from the mailing of the notice of assessment.[34] The Minister has the discretion to extend the deadline.[35] There is no prescribed form of notice of objection, but the Act provides that the taxpayer must set out in the form "the reasons for the objection and all relevant facts".[36] The notice of objection is served by mailing it or delivering it to the CRA. The taxpayer will be contacted and given an opportunity to make representations during this process. At the end of the process, the Minister will decide whether to confirm, vary or vacate the assessment, and will notify the taxpayer of the decision.

(b) — Appeal

If the taxpayer is unhappy with the Minister's decision on the notice of objection, the taxpayer has the right of appeal. All appeals lie to the Tax Court of Canada, which is a federal court established for the purpose of hearing tax appeals. (The Court replaced the Tax Review Board in 1983, which in turn replaced the Tax Appeal Board in 1971.) Taxpayers have 90 days from the day of the mailing of the Minister's notice of objection decision to appeal to the Tax Court of Canada.

---

[30] *R. v. Canadian Marconi Co.*, [1991] 2 C.T.C. 352, 91 D.T.C. 5626 (Fed. C.A.).

[31] Ss. 164(1.5), 152(4.2), 220(3.1) or (3.4).

[32] Ss. 152(4.3) and (4.4).

[33] Ss. 152, 161.

[34] S. 165(1).

[35] S. 166.2(1).

[36] S. 165(1).

There are two alternative procedures for appeals heard by the Tax Court of Canada. The first is an "informal procedure", which can be elected by the taxpayer for cases where the amount of federal tax and penalties in issue is no more than $12,000, or the amount of loss in issue is no more than $24,000, or where only interest is in issue. Under the informal procedure, the taxpayer may appear in person or be represented by an agent who need not be a lawyer; no special form of pleadings or other formalities are required; the Court is not bound by technical rules of evidence; costs may not be awarded against the taxpayer; and (unless there are exceptional circumstances) judgment must be rendered within 60 days. However, the decision of the Court under the informal procedure is final: there is no further right of appeal.[37]

The other procedure for an appeal to the Tax Court of Canada is the "general procedure". This procedure is to be used for cases where the amount of federal tax and penalties in issue is more than $12,000 or the amount of loss in issue is more than $24,000. The general procedure also applies in cases where the amount of tax or loss in issue is less than the prescribed amounts but the taxpayer has not elected for the informal procedure. Under the general procedure, a taxpayer may not be represented by a non-lawyer; the proceedings are more formal; costs may be awarded against the taxpayer; and there is no time-limit on the rendering of judgment. The decision of the Court under the general procedure is subject to appeal to the Federal Court of Appeal, and from there (with leave) to the Supreme Court of Canada.

The foregoing appeal procedures apply only to those cases that originate as an objection by a taxpayer to an assessment. Prosecutions of taxpayers who are alleged to have evaded tax in violation of the penal provisions of the Act are a different matter entirely. Neither the Tax Court nor the Federal Court has jurisdiction over criminal matters. Prosecutions occur in the courts of the provinces in accordance with the procedure laid down by the *Criminal Code*.[38] Prosecutions are discussed later in this chapter.

(c) — Burden of proof

When the taxpayer appeals to the Tax Court of Canada, there is a trial in which both sides adduce evidence on issues of fact and make submissions on issues of law. It has been held by the Supreme Court of Canada in *Johnston v. M.N.R.* (1948)[39] that the burden of proof lies on the taxpayer to establish that the factual findings[40] upon which the Minister based the assessment were wrong. In that case, the Minister's position that the taxpayer did not support his wife was sustained on

[37]The Court's decision is, however, subject to judicial review by the Federal Court of Appeal under s. 28 of the *Federal Court Act*, R.S.C. 1985, c. F-7, which permits review of the decisions of federal tribunals for breach of the rules of natural justice, error of law, or perverse error of fact.

[38]R.S.C. 1985, c. C-46.

[39][1948] C.T.C. 195, 48 D.T.C. 1182 (S.C.C.).

[40]The doctrine is sometimes expressed with reference to the Minister's rulings of law as well as his or her findings of fact, but there can be no burden of proof on issues of law.

the ground that the taxpayer had not discharged the onus of proving that he did support his wife. A variety of reasons have been suggested for imposing the burden of proof on the taxpayer. One is the wording of subsection 152(8) which provides, rather cryptically, that an assessment is "deemed to be valid and binding notwithstanding any error, defect or omission in the assessment". A second reason is that the taxpayer is the appellant, who ought to affirmatively establish the propositions upon which he or she relies. A third reason, perhaps the most persuasive one, is that the taxpayer has the best access to the facts.

The taxpayer's burden of proof does not require the taxpayer to rebut every imaginable set of facts that would justify the Minister's assessment. The Court in *Johnston* made clear that the Minister was under a duty to disclose to the taxpayer the findings upon which the assessment was based, and it was only those findings that the taxpayer came under a duty to rebut. The standard of proof that must be satisfied by the taxpayer is, of course, the civil standard of the balance of probability.

Sections 163 and 163.2 impose civil penalties in three cases: (1) repeated failure by a taxpayer to report income; (2) knowingly or negligently making a false statement or omission on a return by a taxpayer; and (3) misrepresentation of a taxpayer's tax matters by a third party.[41] If the Minister considers that section 163 or 163.2 is applicable, the penalty will be assessed. If the taxpayer appeals the imposition of the penalty to the Tax Court of Canada, the normal burden of proof is reversed by subsection 163(3), which provides that "the burden of establishing the facts justifying the assessment of the penalty is on the Minister". This special burden is confined to the facts that justify the imposition of a penalty under section 163 or 163.2. The burden of establishing that the underlying assessment of tax is wrong remains with the taxpayer.[42]

Another provision that imposes a special burden of proof on the Minister is subsection 152(4), which is the provision that permits the Minister to reassess a taxpayer outside the usual three year time-limit. This power arises where the taxpayer has been guilty of misrepresentation or fraud. The section does not say anything express about the onus of proof in such a case. However, it has been held that where a taxpayer appeals from a reassessment that has been issued outside the three year limit in reliance on this power, the onus of proving the misrepresentation or fraud that is the pre-condition of the power of reassessment rests on the Minister.[43]

Where a taxpayer is prosecuted for a criminal offence under section 238 or 239 of the Act, the prosecution is conducted in the provincial court system under the rules of criminal procedure of the *Criminal Code*. In a prosecution, the normal criminal rules as to the burden of proof apply. Therefore, the burden of proving all elements

---

[41] See headings 18.6, "Civil penalties", below, and 18.9(b), "Ethical regulation of the tax profession", below, regarding the third party civil penalties in s. 163.2.

[42] *De Graaf v. R.*, [1985] 1 C.T.C. 374, 85 D.T.C. 5280 (Fed. T.D.).

[43] *M.N.R. v. Taylor*, [1961] C.T.C. 211, 61 D.T.C. 1139 (Ex. Ct.).

of the offence charged rests on the Crown, and the standard of proof is proof beyond a reasonable doubt.[44]

(d) — Settlement

The CRA is willing in certain circumstances to settle a dispute with a taxpayer, and many such settlements are in fact made. Typically, of course each side gives up some part of what had originally been claimed in return for a similar compromise by the other side.

It is essential that both sides be bound by a settlement agreement. In *Smerchanski v. M.N.R.* (1976),[45] the Supreme Court of Canada held that a taxpayer, who had agreed to waive a right of appeal from an assessment as part of a settlement agreement, could not later change his mind and exercise that right of appeal. But, in *Cohen v. R.* (1980),[46] the Federal Court of Appeal held that a settlement agreement, under which the Minister agreed to assess a taxpayer's profit as a capital gain while the taxpayer agreed not to object to other assessments, could not bind the Minister. "The Minister has a statutory duty to assess the amount of tax payable on the facts as he finds them in accordance with the law as he understands it"; it followed that an agreement by the Minister to assess otherwise than in accordance with law would be "illegal".[47] The Court accordingly upheld the Minister's assessment, even though it did not comply with the agreement, and even though the taxpayer had complied with his part of the agreement.

The effect of the *Smerchanski* and *Cohen* cases is that the taxpayer is bound by a settlement agreement, but the Minister is not.[48] Of course, a settlement of litigation that was implemented by a formal entry of judgment would then have the force of a court judgment, which is binding on both parties. However, in *Galway v. M.N.R.* (1974),[49] the Federal Court of Appeal refused an application for a consent judgment to implement the terms of a settlement agreement between the Minister and a taxpayer. According to the Court, the Minister has no power to assess in accordance with a "compromise settlement", and the Court should not sanctify an *ultra vires* act. The Minister's duty is to assess in accordance with the law, and the only kind of settlement that the Court would be prepared to implement by a consent judgment would be one in which the parties were agreed on the application of the law to the facts.[50]

---

[44] *Medicine Hat Greenhouses v. R.*, [1981] C.T.C. 141, 81 D.T.C. 5100 (Alta. C.A.).

[45] [1976] C.T.C. 488, 76 D.T.C. 6247 (S.C.C.).

[46] [1980] C.T.C. 318, 80 D.T.C. 6250 (Fed. C.A.).

[47] *Ibid.*, 319, 6251.

[48] See also *Consoltex Inc. v. R.*, [1997] 2 C.T.C. 2846, 97 D.T.C. 724 (T.C.C.).

[49] [1974] C.T.C. 454, 74 D.T.C. 6355 (Fed. C.A.).

[50] As Smith, "Reassessments, Waivers, Amended Returns, and Refunds" [1988] *Corp. Management Tax Conf.* 8:1, 8:14, points out, some compromises are possible within this doctrine. An issue of valuation could be compromised because value is a matter of opinion. Where

The attitude of the Federal Court of Appeal in *Cohen* and *Galway* is far too rigid and doctrinaire. If the Minister were really unable to make compromise settlements, he or she would be denied an essential tool of enforcement. The Minister must husband the CRA's limited resources, and it is not realistic to require the Minister to insist on every last legal point, and to litigate every dispute to the bitter end. Most disputes about tax are simply disputes about money which are inherently capable of resolution by compromise. Presumably, the Minister would agree to a compromise settlement only on the basis that it offered a better net recovery than would probably be achieved by continuance of the litigation. It seems foolish to require the Minister to incur the unnecessary costs of avoidable litigation in the name of an abstract statutory duty to apply the law.[51] It seems obvious that the Act should be amended to give the Minister express authority to settle cases.[52]

(e) — Remission order

Generally speaking, liability for income tax does not depend upon administrative discretion.[53] There is, however, one exception to this proposition, and that is the

---

there are several issues of law in dispute, a compromise could be achieved by the Minister accepting the taxpayer's position on some issues, while maintaining his or her own position on others. What cannot be compromised is a single issue to which there can only be one answer, e.g., is a particular profit a capital gain or ordinary income? In that case, the Minister cannot make a compromise settlement of the "split-the-difference" kind.

[51]Compare the ruling in *Optical Recording Laboratories v. Canada*, [1990] 2 C.T.C. 524, 90 D.T.C. 6647 (Fed. C.A.), where it was held that the Minister did have the power to negotiate postponed-payment arrangements with a taxpayer who was unable to pay in full. This power stemmed from the Minister's authority over "the management of taxes".

[52]Smith, note 50, above, points out (8:14) that in the United States the Internal Revenue Service is given express authority to settle cases: *Internal Revenue Code*, ss. 7121, 7122, and regulations thereunder. In the United Kingdom, there is similar authority: *Taxes Management Act* 1970 (U.K.), c. 9, s. 54.

[53]The Act provides the Minister with discretion to provide relief from the deadlines and interest and penalties in the case of taxpayer hardship, but none of these rules authorize any change in the liability to pay tax. For example, the Act permits the Minister to extend the deadline for filing a return (s. 220(3)); reassess an income tax return beyond the normal reassessment period if requested by an individual (s. 152(4.2)); accept various late-filed, amended, or revoked election (ss. 220(3.2) to 220(3.7)); and waive or cancel penalties or interest (s. 220(3.1)). For administrative reasons, the 2004 federal budget introduced changes to limit adjustments to taxation years that end in any of the ten preceding calendar years. See amendments to s. 220(3.1) (for the waiver of penalties and interest) and s. 220(3.2)(b) (for late, amended or revoked elections). See also Information Circular IC 07-1, "Taxpayer Relief Provisions".

power to make a remission order, which is conferred by section 23 of the federal *Financial Administration Act*.[54] Subsection 23(2) provides that:

> The Governor in Council, on the recommendation of the Treasury Board, whenever he considers it in the public interest, may remit any tax, fee or penalty.

This power cannot be used to impose any new liability on a taxpayer; it can only be used to forgive a liability imposed by the Act (or any other taxing statute). This power is exercised sparingly, in order to relieve against cases of hardship. For example, complex provisions of the Act may have unexpectedly produced double taxation, or a taxpayer may have been misled by the CRA, or a taxpayer may have fallen ill and lost the financial capacity to meet a tax liability.

By the terms of the *Financial Administration Act*, the power of remission is exercised by the Governor in Council on the recommendation of the Treasury Board. In practice, however, most remissions of income tax are determined by the CRA. Requests for remission orders are considered, first, by a district office and, second, by a remission committee at the CRA's head office. If the remission committee were to recommend in favour of a remission order, the Minister of National Revenue would normally recommend to the Treasury Board that the order be made, and the order would normally be made.

Like other orders in council, remission orders are published in Part II of the *Canada Gazette*. They are also required to be reported to the House of Commons in the Public Accounts,[55] and they are also reported by the commercial tax services. The CRA has published the guidelines developed by its remission committee to identify cases worthy of remission.[56] There is, therefore, a reasonable information base upon which a tax professional may determine whether or not it is worthwhile to apply for a remission order to correct a particular perceived injustice.

18.5 — Confidentiality

Section 241 of the Act prohibits the use or release of "taxpayer information" by an "official". "Taxpayer information" is defined in subsection 241(10) as including information of any kind relating to one or more taxpayers that was "obtained by or on behalf of the Minister for the purposes of this Act". The prohibition applies only to an "official", who is defined as a person "in the service" of the Crown or a person formerly in the service of the Crown. No provision of the Act attempts to protect taxpayer information that is in the hands of persons who are not civil servants. For example, there is no protection for the taxpayer's own copy of his or her tax return.

---

[54] R.S.C. 1985, c. F-11.

[55] *Ibid.*, s. 17(8).

[56] Sherman and Sherman, "Income Tax Remission Orders" (1986) 34 *Can. Tax J.* 801, set out the guidelines and analyzes the orders that have been made.

Subsections (3) through (5) of section 241 create more than 30 exceptions to the prohibition on the release or use of taxpayer information. Subsection 241(3) provides that the prohibition does not apply in respect of "criminal proceedings" or "legal proceedings relating to the administration or enforcement of this Act". Accordingly, income tax returns may be subpoenaed, and officials are free to testify or otherwise release taxpayer information in such proceedings.[57] Subsection 241(3.1) provides that officials may release taxpayer information to the appropriate persons in situations where an individual is in imminent danger. Subsection 241(4) provides for the use of taxpayer information in a variety of circumstances, such as where the information is required in formulating government policy, or where the information is needed for the enforcement or administration of various federal or provincial laws. Subsection 241(5) allows the release of taxpayer information where the taxpayer concerned has given his or her consent.

18.6 — Civil penalties

Sections 162, 163 and 163.2 provide civil penalties for a variety of delinquent acts and omissions, including (for example) the late filing of a tax return, the failure to file a return, the repeated failure to file a return, the failure to provide information on a prescribed form, the failure to report an item of income, the making of a false statement or an omission in a return, and the misrepresentation of another person's tax matters by a third party.

The acts and omissions that are the subject of civil penalties under sections 162 and 163 may also be the subject of criminal penalties under sections 238 and 239 (see below). The civil penalties are imposed on taxpayers by the Minister as part of the assessment process, and so when a criminal charge is laid against a taxpayer, the taxpayer has usually already been assessed for the applicable civil penalty. When this is the case, any punishment imposed on conviction for the criminal offence is in addition to the civil penalty. (The criminal court would of course take the civil penalty into account in fixing the punishment.) The decision to prosecute in such a case involves a judgment by the CRA and the Department of Justice that the civil penalty is an inadequate punishment for the taxpayer's conduct. In the unusual case where the taxpayer has not been assessed for a civil penalty at the time when the criminal charge is laid, then the punishment imposed on conviction for the criminal offence is the exclusive sanction, and no civil penalty can be imposed for the same conduct.[58]

---

[57]The phrase "legal proceedings relating to the administration or enforcement of this Act" has received a broad interpretation by the courts. In *Slattery (Trustee of) v. Slattery*, [1993] 2 C.T.C. 243, 93 D.T.C. 5443 (S.C.C.), the Supreme Court of Canada held that in a bankruptcy initiated by the Minister of National Revenue, proceedings by the trustee in bankruptcy for the recovery of assets were proceedings concerning the administration of the Act within the meaning of s. 241(3).

[58]Ss. 238(3), 239(3).

18.7 — Criminal prosecutions

(a) — Tax evasion

Sections 238 and 239 make tax evasion a criminal offence.[59] Section 238 makes it an offence to fail to file a tax return or to break various other provisions of the Act. Section 238 offences are ones of strict liability, that is to say, there is no requirement of *mens rea* (a guilty mind), although a taxpayer may be exculpated by proving that he or she acted with due diligence.[60] Section 239 makes it an offence to falsify records or to evade compliance or payment in other ways. Section 239 offences are ones of which *mens rea* is an essential ingredient.[61]

(b) — Investigatory powers

The special investigations division of each district office of the CRA investigates suspected cases of tax evasion, and when it obtains evidence, prepares the case for prosecution. The Act provides officials of the CRA with investigatory powers.[62] In the earlier discussion of audits, we noted the power conferred by section 231.1 to enter business premises without a warrant, and to enter a dwelling-house with a warrant, in order to inspect the books and records of a taxpayer. We also noticed the power conferred by section 231.2 to demand documents or information. These powers are available to an investigator as well as to an auditor. Where material has not been surrendered voluntarily or cannot be found, section 231.3 empowers a judge to issue a search warrant authorizing the investigator to search premises for evidence and seize the evidence. Where all these measures have apparently not yielded full information, section 231.4 authorizes an "inquiry" to be held by a "hearing officer", who is appointed by the Tax Court of Canada, and who has the power to compel the attendance of witnesses and the giving of testimony under oath.

(c) — Prosecution

Where evidence is obtained that the CRA considers is sufficient to justify the preferring of a criminal charge, the case is handed over to the Department of Justice for prosecution. Prosecutions are conducted in the provincial court system under the criminal procedure stipulated by the *Criminal Code*.[63]

---

[59] See generally Innes, *Tax Evasion in Canada* (1987).

[60] *Ibid.*, 13.

[61] *Ibid.*, 101–125.

[62] *Ibid.*, ch. 2.

[63] *Ibid.*, ch. 3.

18.8 — Rectification

There is an obvious corollary to the general rule that tax is imposed according to the legal relationships or transactions established by the parties. The corollary is that a legal relationship or transaction will not be recognized for tax purposes if that relationship or transaction has not been validly established under the rules of the general law. For example, if a particular tax outcome depends upon the fact that a company or a trust or a partnership has been formed, or a sale of a gift has been made, then it is obviously essential that the taxpayer has complied with the general law of corporations, trusts, partnerships, sales or gifts in order to bring the claimed legal relationship into existence.[64] If under the general law the claimed legal relationship has not been validly established, then tax liability (like any other legal consequence) will depend upon the true legal position. Typically, the problem here is that some essential legal formality has not been carried out, or has not been carried out in time to achieve the desired tax result; for example, a trust may not have been validly created,[65] or may not have been created in time.[66]

Cases where a tax advantage is lost by reason of a failure of legal formality do not rest on any doctrine peculiar to tax law. However, such cases are so common in the tax reports that it is necessary to conclude that the courts tend to scrutinize very closely indeed the formal documentation and other facts which are relied upon to achieve some reduction of tax. A minor defect which in another context might have been dismissed as a sufficient compliance with general law formalities may in the tax context be held to vitiate the transaction.[67]

There have recently been a number of cases dealing with a provincial rectification orders, which, as most law students know, is an order from the Provincial Court that retroactively corrects a written agreement that does not record what the parties intended. Of these decisions, the *Juliar v. Canada (Attorney General)* [68]decision is the most important because the rectification order was granted based on the intention of the parties to avoid the immediate tax consequences of an unanticipated deemed dividend.

---

[64]See *Continental Bank Leasing Corporation v. R.*, [1998] 2 S.C.R. 298, [1998] 4 C.T.C. 119, 98 D.T.C. 6505 (S.C.C.) (a valid partnership existed even though it was a violation of the *Bank Act* for the taxpayer to have invested in one of the corporate partners).

[65]E.g., *Atinco Paper Products v. R.*, [1978] C.T.C. 566, 78 D.T.C. 6387 (Fed. C.A.).

[66]E.g., *M.N.R. v. Ablan Leon*, [1976] C.T.C. 506, 76 D.T.C. 6280 (Fed. C.A.).

[67]In *Stubart Investments Ltd. v. R.*, [1984] C.T.C. 294, 84 D.T.C 6305 (S.C.C.), there were some minor technical deficiencies in the formalities associated with the transfer of assets between the sister corporations, but the Supreme Court of Canada held they were insufficient to render the transfer incomplete.

[68]*Juliar v. Canada (Attorney General)* (1999), [2000] 2 C.T.C. 464, 99 D.T.C. 5743 (Ont. S.C.J.); affirmed (2000), [2001] 4 C.T.C. 45, 2000 D.T.C. 6589 (Ont. C.A.); leave to appeal refused (2001), 272 N.R. 196 (note) (S.C.C.).

In *Juliar*, the taxpayers had intended that their holding company be transferred to a new holding company under the rollover provisions of subsection 85(1) without triggering immediate tax consequences. Normally this is possible, however, if an individual taxpayer takes back debt in excess of a certain amount, a deemed dividend is triggered under section 84.1. The taxpayers in *Juliar* had taken back too much debt (and too few shares) and were not aware of these tax consequences until the transaction was the subject of a tax audit. The taxpayers applied to the Ontario Superior Court of Justice for a rectification order. Four requirements must be met before a rectification order is granted: a prior agreement; common intention; a document that properly records the intention of the parties; and a common or mutual mistake. The CRA contested the application on the basis that the taxpayers had not initially intended to acquire shares. The Court, however, disagreed with the CRA and granted the rectification order on the basis that the taxpayer's intention was to avoid immediate tax consequences. This decision was upheld on appeal to the Ontario Court of Appeal and the CRA's request for leave to appeal to the Supreme Court of Canada was refused.

It should be no surprise that the CRA is concerned about rectification orders becoming a way of fixing aggressive tax plans that are uncovered on audit and retroactive tax planning. They are not as concerned about correcting documentation that is in error because it does not reflect the true intention of the parties involved because that is what they believe the doctrine of rectification contemplates. In any event, they want to be informed of rectification orders so that they can contest them. The CRA says that it will contest rectification orders in situations where it believes that there is no evidence as to the taxpayer's initial common intention or where it believes that the taxpayer is not asking the court rectify the transaction back to its intended form but instead to replace the intended transaction with a new one.[69]

18.9 — Professional responsibilities of tax practitioners

(a) — Importance of professional ethics

Tax practitioners are specialists. It often takes years to acquire the necessary level of knowledge, skill and wisdom to render sophisticated tax advice. Such level of expertise generally commands the trust of clients and the confidence of the public. By and large, tax practitioners in Canada have served their clients and the public well. In recent years, however, there has been increasing attention to ethical issues. Tax lawyers have been sued by their clients[70] and by third parties who have relied on a tax opinion in making investment decisions.[71] "Tax schemes" devised by lawyers have been considered "shams" by courts.[72] Minimum standards of tax practice

[69]See "Rectification Orders" in *Income Tax Technical News* No. 22 (2002).

[70]E.g, *Strother*, note 83 below.

[71]E.g., *Lipson v. Cassels Brock*, note 82, below.

[72]*Faraggi et al v. R.*, 2004 F.C.A. 15, 3 C.T.C. 152, 2004 DTC 6523.

have been imposed by the Act.[73] Respected members of the tax profession have opined on ethical standards and the duties of tax practitioners.[74]

The price to be paid for unethical practice is high. No tax practitioner would wish to be associated with tax evasion, be disciplined for professional misconduct, or be a defendant in a civil lawsuit. Even if a lawyer is acquitted or not disbarred, his or her reputation may be irreversibly damaged. More importantly, the public interest is not well served if confidence is lost in tax professionals and the system.

While some countries, such as the United States, have published a code of conduct for tax practitioners,[75] Canada has not. The absence of published standards makes it difficult for tax students and young tax practitioners to grasp the ethical issues. That is the main reason why we added the following headings to the chapter: to provide an overview of the ethical problems in tax practice and some insights on navigating some difficult terrain.

Although tax practice is shared between lawyers, accountants and others, the roles and responsibilities of the tax lawyer are the main concerns of this chapter. Similarly, ethical issues arise in the practice of income tax law as well as other tax laws, but the focus of this chapter is primarily on federal income tax law.

(b) — Ethical regulation of the tax profession

Ethical standards for tax practitioners, as for all practitioners, are regulated primarily by the profession and, to a much lesser extent, by government. In addition, tax practitioners owe fiduciary duties to the client under common law. The main goal of ethical regulation is to protect the public interest.

---

[73]See heading 18.13(b) (iii), "Third party civil penalties," below.

[74]See L. Chapman, M.J. O'Keefe, D.W. Smith and W.L. Tunney, "The Evolving Nature of Tax Practice" (Canadian Tax Foundation, 2006) 2005 Conference Report, 2:1-22; R. J. Hogan and F. Brassard, "Standards of Practice and Duties of Tax Advisors in the Post Enron Environment" 2002 CR, 34:1-47; Silver, Ethical Considerations in Giving Tax Opinions" 1994 CR 36:1-16; and Bruce S. Russel, "Avoiding Evasion: Tax Advisers' Professional Responsibilities" 2004 Conference Report 35:1-10.

[75]United States, IRS Circular 230 establishes standards in various areas, including minimum levels of accuracy for tax return advice given to clients, the diligence required of practitioners, prohibition on representation of conflicting interests, and minimum quality standards for tax shelter opinions. See L. Chapman et al., ibid., at 2:1.

The Rules of Professional Conduct of the provincial bar[76] impose a duty of competence,[77] a duty of *honesty* and *candour*,[78] a duty of *confidentiality*,[79] and the duty of *loyalty*.[80] Like other lawyers, tax lawyers are subject to the disciplinary sanctions under the Rules of Professional Conduct for "professional misconduct" or "for conduct unbecoming a lawyer."[81] In reality, perhaps the more powerful enforcement weapon lies with a client who can bring a civil action against the lawyer for breach of fiduciary duties. One example is a pending class action lawsuit filed by a group of investors against a law firm and one of its senior partners for negligence in providing legal opinions regarding charitable donations.[82] Another example is the *Strother* case[83] in which the lawyer was found to be in breach of his fiduciary duty for his failure to advise a client that his earlier tax advice was no longer correct because of a conflict of interest.

In addition to regulation of lawyers by the profession and common-law fiduciary duties, Parliament has enacted rules to impose civil penalties on tax professionals. The third-party civil penalties rules in section 163.2 of the Act[84] constitute a minimum standard of conduct for tax practitioners. They are disciplinary rules rather than aspirational goals.

[76]E.g., Law Society of Upper Canada (LSUC), *Rules of Professional Conduct* (June 2009), available at *http://www.lsuc.on.ca/media/rpc.pdf.* (hereinafter "LSUC Rules"). See also Canadian Bar Association, Code of Professional Conduct (adopted by Council, August 2004 and February 2006, amended Resolution 09-02-M), available at *http://www.cba.org/CBA/activities/code* (hereinafter "CBA Code"). Similar rules are found in the rules of professional conduct or codes of the ethics applicable to other tax professionals.

[77]LSUC Rule 2.01, *ibid.*

[78]LSUC Rule 2.02, *ibid.*

[79]LSUC Rule 2.03, *ibid.*

[80]LSUC Rule 2.04, *ibid.*

[81]LSUC Rule 6.11, *ibid.*

[82]*Lipson v. Cassels Brock* (2009). This class action was filed with the Ontario Superior Court of Justice on April 15, 2009 on behalf of individuals who participated in a charitable donation program operated and promoted by the Athletic Trust of Canada. The plaintiffs' claims for donation tax credits were mostly denied by the CRA. The plaintiffs allege that the lawyer negligently prepared a tax opinion leading them to believe that they could both support amateur athletics and reduce their tax liability. They claim that the defendants failed to exercise the care and skill to be expected of a reasonably competent tax solicitor.

[83]*Strother v. 3464920 Canada Inc.*, 2007 S.C.C. 24, [2007] 2 S.C.R. 177.

[84]For further information on the application of these rules, see heading 18.13(b)(iii), "Third party civil penalties," below.

18.10 — Duties to the client

(a) — Nature of relationship with the client

Clients seek tax advice from both lawyers and accountants in any of three types of matters: compliance, dispute resolution, and planning. Accountants tend to be more involved in compliance and lawyers more in dispute resolution. Only lawyers can represent clients in courts, with the exception of "informal procedure" in the Tax Court. Tax planning is generally shared.

The lawyer-client relationship is governed by both contract and fiduciary law. When a client retains a lawyer, the scope of the retainer is governed by contract. In this contract, the parties determine the scope of the services the lawyer is to perform and other contractual terms of the engagement. In addition, the lawyer-client relationship is "overlaid with certain fiduciary responsibilities, which are imposed as a matter of law."[85] As discussed in more detail below under heading 18.12, "Fiduciary Duties," the engagement letter or retainer contract generally describes "what" it is that the lawyer must do on behalf of the client. The fiduciary obligation indicates "how" the lawyer must do it: the lawyer must act in the best interests of the client at all times. The core of fiduciary duty is loyalty.

To act in the best interests of the client at all times is at the heart of the lawyer's fiduciary obligation and underscores the rules of professional conduct. The main fiduciary duties owed to the client — competence, honesty and candour, confidentiality and loyalty — are summarized below.

(b) — Competence

All lawyers owe the clients the duty of competence. A "competent lawyer" means "a lawyer who has and applies relevant skills, attributes, and values in a manner appropriate to each matter undertaken on behalf of a client including . . . knowing general legal principles and procedures and the substantive law and procedure for the areas of law in which the lawyer practices . . ."[86]

Tax lawyers are held out as lawyers possessing special knowledge and skills in tax law. A client is thus entitled to assume that the tax lawyer has the ability and capacity to deal adequately with tax matters to be undertaken on the client's behalf.[87] In some situations this will require that the client be referred to a more expert lawyer.

(c) — Honesty and candour

"When advising clients, a lawyer shall be honest and candid."[88] This rule requires that the advice be "open and undisguised, clearly disclosing what the lawyer hon-

---

[85] *Strother*, note 83, above para. 34.

[86] LSUC Rule 2.01(1), note 76, above.

[87] LSUC Rule 2.01(1), *ibid.*

[88] LSUC Rule 2.02, *ibid.*

estly thinks about the merits and probable results."[89] The lawyer has the duty to disclose to the client any material information within his or her mandate in order to adequately equip the client to properly instruct the lawyer. It also requires the lawyer "to inform the client promptly of the facts, but without admitting liability, upon discovering that an error or omission has occurred in a matter for which the lawyer was engaged and that is or may be damaging to the client and cannot readily be rectified."[90] In other words, if the mistake may be harmful to the client's interest, the lawyer must promptly inform the client of the mistake.

This duty also requires a lawyer to disclose any conflict of interest.[91] If a client is kept in the dark, the advice given cannot be, by nature, candid.

(d) — Confidentiality

Rules of professional conduct require that the lawyer must hold in strict confidence all information about the client's affairs that was acquired as the result of the professional relationship.[92] This duty of confidentiality covers not only confidential communications, but also all information that the lawyer obtains relating to the representation of the client.

This duty is of fundamental importance as lawyers cannot advise to the best of their abilities unless the client shares with them crucial information without reserve. Keeping such information confidential helps foster such open communication. At common law, the scope of the duty is defined broadly:[93]

> Whether founded on contract or equity, the duty to preserve confidentiality is unqualified. It is a duty to keep the information confidential, not merely to take all reasonable steps to do so. Moreover, it is not merely a duty not to communicate the information to a third party. It is a duty not to misuse it, that is to say, without the consent of the former client to make any use of it or to cause any use to be made of it by others otherwise than for his benefit.

Confidential information may be disclosed only with the consent of the client or in the rare cases where disclosure is required by law.[94]

(e) — Solicitor-client privilege

In addition to the duty of confidentiality, lawyers must be mindful of privilege.[95]

---

[89] LSUC Commentary on Rule 2.02, *ibid.*

[90] CBA Code, C.III, Commentary 11, note 77, above.

[91] CBA Code, c. V, commentary 4 and LSUC Rule 2.04., *ibid.*

[92] CBA Code, c IV and LSUC Rule 2.03, *ibid.*

[93] *Bolkiah v. KPMG*, [1999] 1 All ER 517, at 527 (HL).

[94] LSUC Rule 2.03 (2)-(5), note 77, above.

[95] The *Quebec Charter of Human Rights and Freedoms*, RSQ, c. C-12, section 9 extends this privilege to a client's information communicated to professionals bound by a professional secrecy law, including accountants.

The solicitor-client evidentiary privilege protects the client's information by prohibiting the state from compelling the lawyer to disclose confidential communications between the lawyer and the client. It is restricted in scope to those communications treated as confidential by the client. The client can waive the claim of privilege under section 232 of the Act. This privilege is related to the lawyer's role as an officer of the court charged with facilitating the administration of justice. It is not extended to communications between an accountant and the client.

The solicitor-client privilege applies only in the context of controversies and serves only to limit the information that can be extracted from the lawyer about communications between him or her and the client. It is different from the ethical duty of confidentiality, which precludes only voluntary disclosure by a lawyer. If a court or tribunal orders disclosure, the lawyer must disclose the information, unless the information is protected by the solicitor-client privilege.

(f) — Loyalty

Loyalty is fundamental to the lawyer-client relationship, which is one of trust and confidence. "Loyalty includes putting the client's business ahead of the lawyer's business."[96] The duty of loyalty requires the lawyer to prevent any conflicts of interest. Conflicts of interest are discussed in more detail under heading 18.12 below.

18.11 — Duties to other parties

(a) — Duties to the tribunal

In litigation, where the lawyer is representing a client in a dispute with the Minister, there do not seem to be any ethical issues that are unique to the tax context. In tax litigation, as in other litigation, the lawyer's duties of honesty and candour require that the lawyer be scrupulous never to mislead his or her opponent or the court by misstating the facts or the law, or by failing to inform the court of a relevant authority. The failure to inform the court of a relevant authority is a breach of legal ethics, even if the authority is adverse to the client and has been overlooked by the opponent's lawyer. This is an example where the lawyer's obligation to the system trumps or mitigates his/her duty of loyalty to the client.

Within these constraints, a lawyer is free to urge on behalf of the client any position that is fairly arguable, even if the lawyer believes that position to be unmeritorious. In the role of an advocate (as opposed to an adviser), the lawyer is not asserting his or her opinion as to the correct legal position, but is simply submitting arguments on behalf of the client. The lawyer leaves to the court the task of evaluating the strengths of the competing arguments, and determining what is the correct legal position.

---

[96] *R. v. Neil*, [2002] 3 S.C.R. 631, 2002 SCC 70, para. 24.

(b) — Relationship with the CRA

Tax practice differs from other types of law practice in that the opposing party is always the government, which through the CRA, assumes a variety of roles with respect to the lawyer. Overall, the relationship between the CRA on the one hand, and the lawyer and client on the other hand, is adversarial or potentially adversarial. The CRA also assumes a quasi-judicial role in issuing rulings in response to taxpayers' requests for guidance in particular situations and in hearing taxpayer appeals from an assessment (or reassessment). Although the CRA is not technically a "tribunal," one would expect that a lawyer to treat the CRA with an appropriate level of candour, fairness, courtesy, and respect.

Lawyers may represent a client in a controversy with the CRA at the stage of audit, administrative appeal within the CRA, or in courts. In this context, the lawyer serves as advocate. Candour towards the tribunal and the duty of confidentiality to the client[97] are critical to the lawyer's role as an advocate.

(c) — Third parties

Tax lawyers sometimes render opinions that affect third parties or the public at large. This is typically the case in which third party investors rely on a legal opinion in making their investment decisions. For example, investors may agree to participate in a corporate reorganization only when a lawyer has provided a legal opinion on the tax consequences of the proposed transactions.

Canadian courts have ruled that a corporate lawyer may owe a duty of care to an investor in the corporation by which the lawyer has been retained.[98] The lawyer may be held liable for negligence or fraudulent misrepresentation or for breach of the fiduciary duty of care. Both ethical and liability considerations may force tax practitioners to adopt a reasonably elevated standard of care in rendering their opinions.[99]

(d) — Duty to the system

Traditionally, the ethical obligations of tax lawyers do not differ much from the ethical obligations of other lawyers. The same rules of professional conduct apply to the practice of tax law. In recent years, however, there has been a trend in Canada and elsewhere to impose additional obligations on tax practitioners, who by virtue of their expertise, are viewed as gatekeepers for the tax system. This trend is discussed further under heading 18.14 below.

---

[97]See heading 18.10(d), "Confidentiality", above.

[98]E.g., *Filipovic v. Upshall*, [1998] O.J. No.2256 (Gen. Div.) (QL), in which it was held that the lawyers stood in a sufficient relationship of proximity with the plaintiffs to engender a duty of care on their part. It required the lawyers to carry out their duties in a reasonable professional and competent manner and with the utmost good faith.

[99]Silver, at 36:8, note 74, above.

18.12 — Fiduciary duties

(a) — Fiduciary duties and public interest

(i) — Fiduciary relationship

The very basis of the lawyer-client relationship is that the lawyer will use his or her special skills to act in the best interests of the client. This relationship has all the core characteristics of a fiduciary relationship: (a) the lawyer has scope for the exercise of some discretion or power; (b) the lawyer can unilaterally exercise that discretion or power so as to affect the client's legal or practical interests, and (c) the client is particularly vulnerable to or at the mercy of the lawyer holding the discretion or power.[100] As Binnie J. stated in *Strother*, "fiduciary duties provide a framework within which the lawyer performs the work and may include obligations that go beyond what the parties expressly bargained for."[101] The core of fiduciary duty is loyalty.

The Supreme Court of Canada has also emphasized that courts will enforce fiduciary duties in the context of all professional advisory relationships:[102]

> The very existence of many professional advisory relationships, particularly in specialized areas such as law, taxation and investments, is premised upon full disclosure by the client of vital personal and financial information that inevitably results in a "power-dependency" dynamic. . . [T]he type of disclosure that routinely occurs in these kinds of relationships results in the advisor's acquiring influence which is equivalent to a discretion or power to affect the client's legal or practical interests. . .. In the advisory context, the advisor's ability to cause harm and the client's susceptibility to be harmed arise from the simple but unassailable fact that the advice given by an independent advisor is not likely to be viewed with suspicion; rather it is likely to be followed.

Under the current Canadian law, therefore, given the level of trust, disclosure of information, and reliance on the skills and knowledge of the tax professionals, the relationships between tax practitioners and their clients are generally fiduciary.

(ii) — Public interest

Why is it important to impose fiduciary duties on tax practitioners? The answer lies in public interest. The public interest is served by protecting "the integrity of the administration of justice"[103] and by maintaining public confidence in tax professionals. It is in the public interest to have truth ascertained by an adversarial judicial system that "function[s] clearly and without hidden agendas."[104] It is important

[100]*Frame v. Smith* (1987), 42 DLR (4th) 81 at 99 (SCC).

[101]*Strother*, note 83, above, para 35.

[102]*Hodghinson v. Simms* (1994), [1994] 3 S.C.R. 377, 95 D.T.C. 5135 (SCC), para. 61.

[103]See *Strother*, note 83, above, Binnie J. citing *MacDonald Estate v. Martin*, [1990] 3 SCR 1235 (SCC), para. 34.

[104]*Neil*, note 96, above, para. 24.

for the law to foster public confidence in lawyers and other professionals in order to preserve a trustworthy image of the judicial system as a whole.

There are other competing values underlying fiduciary law. These include the freedom of the client to secure the counsel of his or her choice, the need for mobility in the legal profession, and the need for lawyers to serve multiple clients. But public confidence in the judicial system prevails over all these other values.[105]

(b) — Loyalty

(i) — Core duty

The fiduciary relationship between the tax lawyer and his or her client is associated with certain duties, such as the duties of care, confidentiality, disclosure, and loyalty. Loyalty is the core of fiduciary duties: the lawyer must act in the best interests of the client. The judgment as to what are the client's best interests is, of course, entrusted to the lawyer. So, how can the lawyer know if his or her duty of loyalty has been fulfilled? "The law's solution is to require that the fiduciary's judgments be made in a "sterile" environment, where even the slightest appearance of impropriety is not tolerated."[106] The parameters of the sterile environment are largely drawn along the line of the conflict of interest rules. These rules build a zone of protection around the possibility of disloyalty. They prevent the fiduciary from being in situations where the duty of loyalty is in danger of being breached.

(ii) — Notion of "conflict of interest"

The term "conflict of interest" was defined by the Supreme Court of Canada in *Neil* as an interest that gives rise to a "substantial risk that the lawyer's representation of the client would be materially and adversely affected by the lawyer's own interests or by the lawyer's duties to another current client, a former client, or a third person."[107] This definition contemplates two kinds of conflicts:

(1) A conflict of the lawyer's self-interest and the lawyer's duty to act in the best interests of the client (self-interest and duty conflict). This may occur when the lawyer's personal interests may have an impact on the substance of the advice given to the client, leading in turn to situations that could prejudice the client's own interest. Fiduciary law prohibits the tax adviser from abusing his or her position to reap a personal gain.

(2) A conflict of the lawyer's duty to different clients (duty-to-duty conflict). The lawyer's duty to provide candid and proper legal advice to one client is in conflict with his or her duty of confidentiality to another client.

---

[105] See *MacDonald Estate*, note 103, above, at 1265 (per Cory). As, McLachlin C.J.C. noted in her dissenting decision in *Strother*, note 83, above, para. 140, there is also a public interest in lawyers' ability to serve multiple clients.

[106] R. Valsan and L. Smith, "The Loyalty of Lawyers: A Comment on *3464920 Canada Inc. v. Strother*" (2008) v.87 *The Canadian Bar Review* 247, at 263.

[107] *Neil*, note 96, above, at para. 31.

The conflict of interest definition above emphasizes "substantial risk" or the appearance of substantial risk, not necessarily "actual conflict". "Conflict" means that the two things point in opposite directions. In the case of conflict of self-interest and duty, the conflict arises merely because the two things (i.e., self interest and duty to the client) point in opposite directions. The lawyer's personal interest could have an impact on the substance of the advice provided, thereby creating a situation that could prejudice the client's own bests interests. The lawyer must therefore avoid being in a situation of conflict.

In the case of duty-to-duty conflict, the rules are not concerned with clients' business interests, but with their interests in even-handed legal representation. The business interests of two clients in the same industry or in the same marketplace may be adverse, but that alone does not create a risk of impairment in even-handed legal presentation. As Binnie J. remarked:[108]

> The clients' respective "interests" that require the protection of the duty of loyalty have to do with the practice of law, not commercial prosperity. Here the alleged "adversity" between concurrent clients related to business matters. This is not to say that commercial interests can never be relevant. . . .However, commercial conflicts between clients that do not impair a lawyer's ability to properly represent the legal interests of both clients will not generally present a conflict problem. Whether or not a real risk of impairment exists will be a question of fact.

The ability to serve multiple clients is important in tax practice. The skills of tax lawyers and accountants often take years to develop. They are entitled to make a living by offering their services to multiple clients who compete commercially within a given industry as long as their legal interests are not in conflict.

(iii) — Avoidance of conflicts

The rules against conflicts exist to protect the client's interest, and not to condemn the professional. The cardinal rule for lawyers to follow is to avoid being in the situation of conflict. The way out of a conflict is to disclose the conflict of interest. With the client's consent, the lawyer can continue to serve the client notwithstanding such conflict.

(c) — The *Strother* case

The *Strother* case is interesting. The facts of this case provide students with a glimpse into tax practice involving tax shelters and the associated ethical issues. By a narrow margin of five judges to four, the Supreme Court of Canada provided some clarification on the scope of the lawyer's duty of loyalty.

(i) — Facts and issues

Monarch was a corporation in the business of selling tax–assisted production services funding ("TAPSF") investments which were tax shelter investments in the

---

[108] *Strother*, note 83 above, para. 55.

Canadian film industry.[109] Strother, a tax lawyer and partner in the firm, Davis & Co ("Davis"), had special expertise in the structuring of these investments. He also had expertise in obtaining favourable advance tax rulings in connection with these tax shelters, which was an important precondition for selling them.

Monarch was a client of Strother and Davis and, effective October 1996, had a written retainer which prohibited them from acting for others in relation to TAPSF investments (with limited exceptions). In the mid-1990's, Monarch paid Davis more than $5 million in legal fees in connection with the $13 million of profits from the sale of TAPSF. Strother was the highest billing Davis partner, with the fees from Monarch representing more than half of his billings.[110]

In November 1996, the federal government announced the introduction of the matchable expenditures rules (MER). These rules meant that Monarch's TAPSF structure would no longer work after October 1997. Strother advised Monarch that he did not have a "fix" to avoid the effect of this legislation.[111] In 1997, Monarch executives sought Strother's advice about what could be done to salvage their business, but Strother suggested that they defer that discussion until 1998. Strother's advice was candid and consistent with the advice given by other tax professionals at that time. By the end of October 1997, Monarch's business was winding down and its written retainer with Strother and Davis was terminated at the end of 1997.

In late 1997 or early 1998, Darc, a former employee of Monarch, approached Strother to discuss another structure which took advantage of an exception in the new rules. Strother drafted an advance tax ruling request and submitted it to Revenue Canada in March 1998. Strother and Darc had agreed in January 1998 that, if a favourable ruling was granted, Strother would receive 55 percent of the first $2 million of profit of Sentinel (the corporate entity used to promote the tax shelters) and 50 percent thereafter.

After terminating the written retainer at the end of 1997, Monarch verbally retained Strother and the firm to continue to do work for Monarch in 1998 and 1999. Monarch executives testified that they met with Strother several times in 1998 and asked him what business opportunities might be available in light of the new tax

---

[109] "In outline, the tax shelter worked like this. Limited partnerships were established. The investors would notionally produce a film for a studio in return for a fee, paid over time, that was contingent on the success of the film. The contingency of the payment introduced a substantial element of risk, and the right to receive such speculative income at some future date was considered by Revenue Canada not to be a capital asset. Therefore, expenditures for the film production were treated as deductible from other income in the year the expenditures were incurred. The scheme yielded a loss to the partnership in the early years because of the mismatch between the front-end expenses in the year the film was made and the delayed and uncertain return. The loss was deducted by investors from their unrelated income — thereby sheltering this income from immediate taxation. If the film was a success, the tax collector's cut would at least be deferred." *Strother*, note 83, above, para. 3.

[110] *Strother*, note 83, above, paras. 5 and 6.

[111] *Ibid.*, para 14.

rules.[112] Strother did not at any time advise them that there might be a "way around" the new rules. Nor did he advise Monarch of the favourable ruling Sentinel received after it was issued in October 1998.

In August 1998, Strother told Davis about a possible conflict of interest. Davis's managing partner told Strother that he would not be permitted to own any interest in Sentinel. Effective March 1999, Strother resigned from the firm. In April 1999, he became a 50 percent shareholder of Sentinel.

By September 2001, when tax law was changed to eliminate the advantages of schemes used by Sentinel, Sentinel and its affiliates had reaped profits of almost \$130 million and Strother's share in profits was estimated to be \$32 million.

After learning of Sentinel's tax ruling in early 1999, Monarch sued Strother and Davis for breach of fiduciary duty, but never continued its film tax shelter business.

The British Columbia Court of Appeal held that Strother had conflicts of interest — a conflict between the interests of his two clients (Monarch and Darc/Sentinel) and a conflict between his own personal financial interests and those of Monarch — and ordered Strother to disgorge to Monarch all profits derived from Sentinel and its affiliates. The majority of the Supreme Court of Canada held that Strother breached his fiduciary duty to Monarch but ordered him to disgorge only the profits made during the period of conflict.

(ii) — Majority judgment

The majority of the Court found that Strother owed fiduciary duties to Monarch in addition to the duties stipulated in the post-1997 oral retainer. A core fiduciary duty is the duty of loyalty, an element of which is the avoidance of conflicts of interest.

According to Binnie J., who authored the majority decision, Strother breached his duty when he took a personal financial interest in the Darc/Sentinel venture during the critical period when Monarch was looking to him for advice about what tax-assisted business opportunities were open. Binnie J. stated:[113]

> The difficulty is not that Sentinel and Monarch were potential competitors. The difficulty is that Strother aligned his personal financial interest with the former's success. . . . Strother put his personal financial interest into conflict with his duty to Monarch. The conflict compromised Strother's duty to "zealously" represent Monarch's interest (*Neil*, at para.19), a delinquency compounded by his lack of "candour" with Monarch "on matters relevant to the retainer" (*ibid.*), i.e., his own competing financial interest.

As a client, Monarch was entitled to candid and complete advice from a lawyer who was not in a position of conflict. Strother's personal interest in Monarch's competitor "gave Strother a reason to keep the principals of Monarch in the dark, in breach of his duty to provide candid advice on his changing views of the potential for film production services tax shelters." In Binnie J.'s view, Strother breached his

---

[112] *Ibid.*, para 15.

[113] *Ibid.*, para. 67.

duty to Monarch twice. The first breach occurred when he failed" to revisit his 1997 advice in 1998 at a time when had a personal, undisclosed financial interest in Sentinel." The second breach happened "when he did not advise Monarch of the successful tax ruling when it became public on October 6, 1998."[114]

Unlike "used car salesmen or pawnbrokers whom the public may expect to operate on the basis of "didn't ask, didn't tell", [the] lawyers' relationship with clients is one of "trust and confidence". Strother owed Monarch a duty of disclosure:[115]

> Why would a rainmaker like Strother not make rain with as many clients (or potential clients) as possible when the opportunity presented itself (whether or not existing retainers required him to do so)? The unfortunate inference is that Strother did not tell Monarch because he did not think it was in his personal financial interest to do so.

According to Binnie J., Strother could not rely on his duty of confidentiality to Darc as a defense for such breach:[116]

> Of course, it was not open to Strother to share with Monarch any confidential information received from Darc. He could nevertheless have advised Monarch that his earlier view was too emphatic, that there may yet be life in a modified form of syndicating film production services expenses for tax benefits, but that because his change of view was based at least in part on information confidential to another client on a transaction unrelated to Monarch, he could not advise further except to suggest that Monarch consult another law firm. Moreover, there is no excuse at all for Strother not advising Monarch of the successful tax ruling when it was made public in October 1998. . .. I therefore conclude that Davis (and Strother) failed to provide candid and proper legal advice in breach of the 1998 retainer.

Acting for clients with competing commercial interests does not, by itself, impair a lawyer's ability to properly represent the legal interests of both clients in an even-handed way:[117]

> There is no reason in general why a tax practitioner such as Strother should not take on different clients syndicating tax schemes to the same investor community, notwithstanding the restricted market for these services in a business in which Sentinel and Monarch competed. In fact, in the case of some areas of high specialization, or in small communities or other situations of scarce legal resources, clients may be taken to have consented to a degree of overlapping representation inherent in such law practices, depending on the evidence. The more sophisticated the client, the more readily the inference of implied consent may be drawn. The thing the lawyer must not do is keep the client in the dark about matters he or she knows to be relevant to the retainer.

---

[114] *Ibid.*, paras. 69 and 70.

[115] *Ibid.*, para. 70.

[116] *Ibid.*, para. 47.

[117] *Ibid.*, para. 55.

Whether or not a conflict of interests exists is a question of fact. It existed in the *Strother* case because "Strother could not with equal loyalty serve Monarch and pursue his own financial interest."[118]

Binnie J. also found that the impact of Strother's breach on Monarch's interest (i.e., in obtaining proper legal advice) was "material and adverse." He noted:[119]

> While it is sufficient to show a possibility (rather than a probability) of adverse impact, the possibility must be more than speculation. . . . That test is met here, for the reasons already discussed. Once the existence of Strother's personal financial interest in Sentinel was established, it was for Strother, not Monarch, to demonstrate the absence of any material adverse effect on Monarch's interest in receiving proper and timely legal advice. . .

On the question of remedies, the majority held that Strother was required to account to Monarch for the profits that he acquired from the moment of the initial breach until the time when the solicitor-client relationship ended.[120] Davis was not in breach but was vicariously liable pursuant to the B.C. Partnership Act.

(iii) — Dissenting judgment

The dissenting decision, authored by McLachlin C.J.C., took a much narrower approach to determining the scope of duties owed by Strother to Monarch and the existence of conflict of interest.

The Chief Justice opined that fiduciary duties should be "moulded to, and should not exceed" the contractual terms.[121] The investigation of a possible conflict of interest should be limited to the provisions of the retainer agreements. She found that there was no conflict between what Strother agreed to do for Monarch and what he was doing for Darc and himself with Sentinel. She also found no conflict between Strother's personal interest and what he agreed to do for Monarch under the retainer. The Chief Justice's approach "would be destructive of a basic underlying principle of the fiduciary relationship."[122]

(iv) — Summary of key points

Based on the majority decision in *Strother* and other cases, the principles governing conflict of interest can be summarized as follows:

(1) The terms of a retainer contract between a lawyer and the client specify the concrete services to be performed by the lawyer, but they are not exhaustive of the duties owed to the client. Fiduciary law imposes on the lawyer fiduciary duties that may not have been expressly included in the retainer.

---

[118] *Ibid.*, para. 70.

[119] *Ibid.*, para. 61.

[120] *Ibid.*, para. 95.

[121] *Ibid.*, para. 141.

[122] Valsan and Smith, note 106, above, at 248.

(2) Fiduciary responsibilities include the duty of loyalty, of which an element is the avoidance of conflicts of interest.

(3) The rules against conflicts are strict, but they do not require lawyers to have superhuman abilities; they require the careful exercise of judgment, something that can always be demanded of a professional.

(4) It is always possible to be candid without disclosing confidential information.

(5) As a fiduciary, a lawyer's duty is to avoid situations where he or she has, or potentially may, develop a conflict. However, this rule does not prevent the lawyer from acting for multiple clients. A lawyer can represent multiple clients with conflicting business interests as long as the lawyer can provide even-handed representation to both clients.

(6) There is always a way out of conflict: either by taking the necessary steps to remove the conflict or by obtaining informed consent to it. Informed consent requires disclosure. "The client cannot be taken to have consented to conflicts of which it is ignorant."[123]

18.13 — Ethical considerations in tax practice

(a) — Roles of tax practitioners

Tax lawyers and accountants share the practice of advising clients in respect of compliance and tax planning. When acting as tax advisors, lawyers and accountants owe the clients the duty to disclose, the duty of confidentiality and the duty to avoid conflicts of interest. However, because of the different professional roles of lawyers and accountants, there are some notable differences in the scope of responsibilities of these two professions.

The practice of law, as distinct from the practice of tax, is preserved exclusively to lawyers. Only lawyers are involved in tax litigation and the preparation of legal documents that create rights and obligations between parties and that have tax consequences. Only lawyers can prepare legal opinions. As an advocate, a lawyer is subject to the strict obligation of loyalty to the client and must present the client's position in the best possible light. The lawyer is a "legal fighter" or "a knight in armour" (whether or not shining) for the client. When acting as an advocate, "the lawyer must treat the court or tribunal with courtesy and respect and must represent the client resolutely, honourably and within the limits of the law."[124] The solicitor-client privilege applies only to communications between a client and a lawyer.

The accounting profession enjoys a statutory monopoly in the performance of the audit of public companies. The price to be paid for this monopoly is the preservation of independence. The provision of non-audit services, such as tax advice, to an audit client may create a conflict with the duty of independence. This is particularly true when accountants are involved in designing and promoting tax-planning prod-

[123] *Strother*, note 83 above, at para. 55.

[124] CBA, c.IX, note 76, above.

ucts aimed at exploiting perceived loopholes in the law in order to generate "tax savings". Since the corporate scandals associated with the collapse of such companies as Enron and WorldCom, accountants have been subject to much public scrutiny and regulation.[125]

In this section, we discuss the various ethical considerations in the main areas of practice, that is, compliance, planning, and dispute resolution.

(b) — Compliance

(i) — Primarily a role of accountants

Compliance is the preparation of the client's income tax return or any other form that must be filed with the Canada Revenue Agency (CRA). A lawyer may be instructed to prepare the return or form, although this task is almost always entrusted to an accountant. The lawyer may be instructed to provide advice to the client or the client's accountant on a tax or non-tax legal issue arising in the preparation of the return or form. In this role, the lawyer is primarily a legal adviser. However, if controversy is anticipated, the lawyer may advise on strategies to avoid the controversy, which may give rise to ethical issues.

The duty to comply with tax law rests on the shoulders of the taxpayer. In the course of the preparation of a complex return, there may be judgment calls to be made as to the characterization of a transaction or expenditure which affects the inclusion of an income item or the deductibility of an expense. A practitioner can advise a client to take a position favourable to the client when there is a reasonable and defendable basis for that position.

(ii) — Lawyer's duty of honesty and candour

In considering ethical issues surrounding compliance, it is important to remember that the integrity of the system depends upon honest self assessment. The CRA cannot audit more than a tiny proportion of the returns filed, and relies heavily on the information supplied by the taxpayer. In these circumstances, compliance is quite unlike litigation, where each position advanced by a lawyer on behalf of the client is opposed by a lawyer on behalf of an opponent, and ruled upon by a judge. The reality of compliance is that positions taken in a tax return can easily be buried and immunized from any scrutiny short of an (unlikely) audit. In these circumstances, the tax lawyer's ethical duty of honesty and candour requires him or her to counsel adequate disclosure.

In providing a legal opinion as to a position to be taken on a return, the lawyer should frankly disclose his or her opinion as to whether a debatable and defendable position is likely to be sustained in court if challenged by the CRA; and, if not, whether there is sufficient support for the position (a reasonable basis) to enable it to be asserted at all, but with adequate disclosure to the CRA. There is no reason

---

[125] For further discussion, see Hogan and Brassard, note 74, above.

why lawyers cannot advise taxpayers to resolve honest doubts in their own favour, provided the circumstances are adequately disclosed.

(iii) — Third party civil penalties

As mentioned above, the duty to comply with tax law rests with the taxpayer. A tax preparer's duties are thus derivative. Nevertheless, the practitioner who either prepares a client's return or advises a taxpayer is liable for the so-called "preparer" penalty under subsection 163.2(4). The preparer penalty is applicable to tax return preparers or advisors who counsel or assist others in making false statements or who are wilfully blind to obvious "errors" when preparing, filing or assisting a taxpayer in filing a return. It could also be applicable in situations where the tax preparers or advisors "assent to or acquiesce in" the making of a false statement. The standard applied is "culpable conduct".[126]

A "good faith reliance" defence is available under subsection 163.2(6). It provides that the preparer penalty will not apply if the advisor relied in good faith on information provided by or on behalf of the client. This good faith reliance defence can be claimed "when the information used by the advisor or tax return preparer is not on its face, clearly false, or obviously unreasonable to a prudent person or does not raise obvious questions in the mind of the advisor or tax return preparer."[127] For example, a new client provides a list of expenses which appear to relate to the client's business and seem to be reasonable but turn out to be fabricated.[128]

A second third party civil penalty, the so-called "planner penalty" under subsection 163.2(2) applies to those who prepare, promote or sell tax shelters or tax shelter-like plans or arrangements that contain false statements. The "good faith" reliance defence does not apply if the advisor is involved in the promoting or selling of a tax shelter arrangement[129] and there is no maximum penalty.

(c) — General tax planning and advice

(i) — Nature of the practice

The bulk of most tax practitioners' time is spent in tax planning and advice. Planning differs from compliance and advocacy in that planning looks to the future rather than the past. The tax practitioner may be instructed to provide advice on how to structure a proposed transaction so as to minimize or defer the tax liability arising from the transaction, or the tax practitioner may be instructed to provide more general advice as to the most favourable way to organize and operate a client's business or personal investments. They may provide an opinion on the tax benefits of a transaction and advise the client about the risks that such benefits will be realized. They may also need to seek an advance ruling from the CRA on the tax

---

[126]S. 163.2(1).

[127]See CRA, Information Circular IC-01-1, "Third Party Civil Penalties" (2001), para. 35.

[128]*Ibid.*, Appendix, Example 1.

[129]See s. 163.2(7) and the definition of "excluded activity" in s. 163.2(1).

consequences of certain transactions. In addition, a tax practitioner may be involved in designing, developing and marketing "tax products" or "tax shelters".

Planning is a field in which accountants as well as lawyers play an important role, but the provision of legal advice on some difficult issues and the drafting of legal documents can only be undertaken by lawyers. As a planner, the tax lawyer is an adviser and not an advocate.

(ii) — The "audit lottery" issue

No ethical issues arise with respect to tax planned transactions that are within the spirit as well as the letter of the Act. Obviously, the tax lawyer may, indeed must, lend his or her aid to the client who seeks to minimize or defer taxes by means that are contemplated by the Act.

No real ethical problem arises with respect to an illegal or deceptive (sham) scheme. Obviously, the tax practitioner cannot advise the client to engage in illegality or deception. If the client decides to do so anyway the lawyer must stop acting for the client. It may well be the case that there is only a small risk that the CRA will detect and attack the scheme, but that factor does not justify engaging in illegality or deception. If the client decides to play the audit lottery, and take the risk, the lawyer should withdraw his or her representation.

(iii) — Advising multiple clients

The issue of a conflict of interest, which was discussed under heading 18.12(b)(ii), above, may arise in circumstances involving tax planning for more than one person. Examples are cases where a lawyer provides advice as to the organization (or reorganization) of a business for two or more clients or where a lawyer mediates a disputed issue between two or more clients. Similarly, where a lawyer acts as an estate planner, often both spouses approach the lawyer together to ask for assistance in planning their estates. Sometimes the client is accompanied by a potential beneficiary, such as a child.

Conflicts of interest may also exist when the lawyer has clients who are business competitors or have adversarial financial interests. The law requires that there be informed consent by the parties to the concurrent representation. Informed consent by a client requires disclosure. In *Neil*, the Supreme Court of Canada stated:[130]

> The bright line is provided by the general rule that a lawyer may not represent one client whose interests are directly adverse to the immediate interests of another current client — *even if the two mandates are unrelated* — unless both clients consent after receiving full disclosure (and preferably independent legal advice), and the lawyer reasonably believes that he or she is able to represent each client without adversely affecting the other.

As discussed earlier, the duty to disclose does not, however, require a lawyer to disclose confidential information concerning one client to another.

---

[130] *Neil*, note 96, above, para. 29.

In some cases, the duty of confidentiality and duty of undivided loyalty may mean that the lawyer cannot act for more than one client. This is the case where the tax advice is crucial to the success of the business transactions. In the case of *Strother*, for example, the Supreme Court of Canada recognized that the new tax shelter structure created for Sentinel was confidential and Strother could not disclose it to Monarch. Instead, the Court suggested that Strother should have advised Monarch that there may be "a way around the new rules" and to consult another lawyer.[131] The proprietary nature of the tax advice implies an exclusive relationship between the tax advisor and the client.[132]

(d) — "Aggressive" Tax Planning

(i) — "Tax" is the "business"

Tax planning may be considered "aggressive" when chasing after the tax savings is the real or dominant reason for the business opportunity. Aggressive tax planning is often associated with tax shelters. For example, the film tax shelters designed by Strother were referred to by Binnie J. as a "tax business."[133]

While some tax professionals make a living out of selling such schemes to taxpayers (just as one might sell any financial product), there is an increasing recognition by most tax professionals of the ethical considerations involved as well as their role as gatekeepers to the system. It is this area of practice that raises the most ethical issues because of a possible conflict between the lawyer's duty to the client and his or her duty to the tax system. Canadian jurisprudence on tax ethics primarily concerns legal advice in aggressive tax planning transactions.

Aggressive tax schemes are designed to comply with the letter of the Act, but generally contrary to the object and spirit of the Act. In other words, they exploit the legislative loopholes in the law. There is always a risk that an aggressive tax planning scheme will be ineffective, either because the provisions of the Act will be interpreted as not according the claimed tax benefit, or because the GAAR will be invoked by the CRA to nullify the claimed tax benefit. But even if the taxpayer eventually prevails in court, as many have, there are financial and reputational costs at risk for those who undertake as well as those who promote such transactions.

(ii) — Shades of grey

Aggressive tax planning deals with the "grey" area of tax law: it is not illegal in the sense of tax fraud, but it is not clearly consistent with the spirit of the law. There are different shades of grey.

If, in the judgment of the tax practitioner, a tax planning scheme, if challenged, is more likely than not to prevail in court, then it is clearly ethical to advise the client

---

[131] See the text around note 116, above.

[132] See Hogan and Brassard, note 74, above.

[133] *Strother*, note 83, above, para. 55.

to undertake the scheme (or help the client to implement the scheme).[134] The notion of "more likely than not" indicates that there may be some risk of being wrong or some room for different conclusions, but a court will likely uphold the scheme.

If the tax practitioner advises a client not to carry out the tax planning scheme because it fails the "more likely than not" threshold, he or she can still assist the client with the transaction as long as there is a reasonable and defendable basis for that position. The lawyer has no obligation to disclose the scheme to the CRA. The public policy reasons for opposing aggressive tax planning are not sufficiently specific and powerful to overcome the lawyer's duty to act in the interests of the client.

In the "big lie" cases where the lawyer is presented with a clearly fraudulent scheme, the lawyer's choice is straightforward — the client must be advised that his/her conduct is fraudulent. If client persists in it, the lawyer should withdraw from the representation. The lawyer also should be on guard against becoming the tool or dupe of an unscrupulous client.[135]

(iii) — Legal opinion

In advising clients on tax matters, the lawyer is often required to provide a legal opinion. A legal opinion is typically a lawyer's expression of his or her judgment as to how the legal issues considered would be resolved if presented for decision to the appropriate legal forum. It is different from a one-sided work of advocacy. The client can best make his or her decision if the opinion is balanced and reasoned.

A legal opinion may be prepared only for the client's eyes or prepared for third parties as well. In the former, the lawyer owes the client all of the duties previously discussed in the context of the lawyer's role as an advisor. If the lawyer prepares an opinion that will be relied upon by third parties, due diligence requires a higher standard of care because the lawyer has access to information that may be available to the client but not to the third parties. Some good practices to follow in the preparation of opinions are as follows:[136]

- Communicating clearly in writing with the client regarding the terms of the engagement.
- Establishing the facts, determining which facts are relevant and evaluating the reasonableness of any assumptions or representations. It is not enough to simply rely on the information provided by the client: the material facts and circumstances upon which the opinion is based should be independently obtained or verified to avoid legal liability.[137]

---

[134]For further discussion, see Chapman et al; Silver, note 74 above.

[135]LSUC Rule 2.02(5), note 76, above, states; "When advising a client, a lawyer shall not knowingly assist in or encourage any dishonesty, fraud, crime, or illegal conduct, or instruct the client on how to violate the law and avoid punishment."

[136]See Chapman et al; Hogan and Brassard; Silver; Russel, note 74, above.

[137]A U.S. court has held that "when a law firm knows or has good reason to know that the factual description of a transaction provided by another is materially different from the ac-

- Making reasonable inquiry about the issues critical to the matter in respect of which an opinion is being given. These issues should not be assumed away. Examples are valuation issues and timing and dating issues. Many tax consequences turn on valuation, and generally the tax practitioner will turn to a qualified appraiser. In some cases, due diligence requires the tax practitioner to identify factors that may affect the fair market valuations. Similarly, the timing of a transaction affects the tax consequences. A tax practitioner must examine documentation that raises difficult timing and dating issues and may, in some circumstances, need to conduct an independent investigation in order to avoid rendering any opinion that would be misleading.
- Documenting and demonstrating that all relevant legal issues have been researched and analyzed and the legal conclusions are backed up by appropriate due diligence.
- Relating the applicable law to the relevant facts. The "law" includes not only the specific provisions of the Act directly applicable to the issue, but also the GAAR and judicial doctrines. A GAAR analysis is crucial in legal opinions about tax planning in general, and aggressive tax planning or tax shelters, in particular. In light of the growing body of jurisprudence and the general shift toward contextual and purposive interpretation, lawyers need to do a sophisticated legal analysis about whether a proposed tax structure violates the object and spirit of the relevant provisions of the Act or the Act read as a whole.
- Arriving at a conclusion supported by the law and facts. Since the term "opinion" connotes a lawyer's conclusion as to the likely outcome of an issue if challenged and litigated, the lawyer should, if possible, state his or her opinion of the probable outcome on the merits of each material tax issue. The lawyer may also need to opine on the position that the CRA is likely to take on the issue and to set forth the risks associated with the proposed tax structures.

(iv) — Advance Tax Rulings

An advance tax ruling is a written statement issued by the CRA to the taxpayers that interprets the law and applies it to a specific set of assumed facts. It is often used when the client desires greater certainty about the tax consequences of the proposed transactions. In some cases, such as complex corporate reorganizations or tax shelters, obtaining a ruling is critical to the client.

When a lawyer seeks a ruling on behalf of a client as to a particular proposed transaction, the lawyer is generally involved in a phase of tax planning. An interesting question is whether the lawyer steps beyond his or her role as advisor and becomes an advocate in dealing with the CRA. Based on Information Circular IC 70-6R5 (which contains the CRA's procedural rules for obtaining rulings), the CRA expects to be treated like a tribunal when a ruling is being requested. The Circular

---

tual transaction, it cannot escape liability simply by including in an opinion letter a statement that its opinion is based on provided facts." Canadian courts may share this view. See Chapman et al; Silver, note 74, above.

requires a "complete description of the facts and a complete description of each proposed transaction". Where the ruling request concerns the application of the GAAR to a transaction, the taxpayer's submissions must "establish that the transaction would not result directly or indirectly in a misuse of the provisions of the Act or an abuse having regard to the provisions of the Act read as a whole." The Circular goes on to state that "where relevant to the ruling request, [the request must include] an analysis of authorities (including case law citations, published commentaries, etc.) known to the taxpayer or the authorized representative which support the taxpayer's position, and those that do not, with submissions why the authorities in support of the taxpayer's position should prevail". Failure to comply with this reqirement may result in the CRA refusal to issue a ruling.

(e) — Advocacy and litigation

A controversy or dispute with the CRA typically starts when the Minister issues an assessment or reassessment that rejects a position taken on the client's income tax return. The lawyer may be instructed to prepare and file a notice of objection or to prepare and file an appeal to the Tax Court, the Federal Court of Appeal or the Supreme Court of Canada, or to represent the client as counsel at hearings before CRA officials or courts.[138] In this context, the tax lawyer serves as advocate before the CRA or courts. Because the government is generally represented by lawyers, especially in court proceedings, the lawyer's duty to the client is paramount.

When acting as an advocate, a lawyer will face situations in which the lawyer and the client differ as to the advisability of disclosure of confidences and secrets. Examples of such situations are where: a lawyer learns that her client has provided false information to the CRA; a lawyer discovers errors made by her client or by the CRA that favour the client; or the lawyer becomes aware of the fact that her client has not complied with the tax law. In these situations, the duty to keep a client's information confidential may be in conflict with the lawyer's duty of honesty and candour. If the lawyer feels strongly about disclosure and the client disagrees, what course may (must) the lawyer pursue? Clearly, lawyers should not make false information or advise clients in doing so. If they do, they may be subject to the third-party civil penalties as well as disciplinary action by the provincial law society to which they belong.[139] But there are no rules requiring the lawyer to reveal confidential information in these circumstances.

---

[138]Accountants as well as lawyers engage in advocacy before CRA officials and in the "informal procedure" of the Tax Court. Only lawyers can appear in the "general procedure" of the Tax Court and in the Federal Court of Appeal and Supreme Court of Canada.

[139]Under LSUC Rule 2.02, note 76, above, "a lawyer shall not knowingly assist in or encourage any dishonesty, fraud, crime, or illegal conduct, or instruct the client on how to violate the law and avoid punishment."

18.14 — Gatekeepers of the Tax System

(a) — Public role of tax professionals

Do tax practitioners owe any *additional* duty to protect the tax system? Because the tax system not only collects revenues to finance public expenditures but also "spends" public money to promote socially and economically desirable activities and serves as a major mechanism of social justice, the integrity of the system is of fundamental importance to all Canadians. The sheer number of taxpayers makes it impractical for the government to directly assess the tax liability of each taxpayer. The proper functioning of our tax system is largely dependent upon the quality and responsible involvement of well-trained tax practitioners. The integrity and standards of these tax professionals have a direct impact on taxpayer compliance and the self-assessment concept itself. Our tax system, in fact, relies on tax lawyers and other professionals acting as "gatekeepers".

There is a growing recognition that tax practitioners likely act as gatekeepers of the system, along with others, such as the courts, government, and employers. In the case of lawyers, this "gatekeeper" idea combines the notions of society,[140] the profession,[141] and the law.[142]

(b) — Legislative changes

Recent developments in Canadian tax law reinforce this notion of tax professionals as gatekeepers. On the legislative front, Parliament has enacted: (a) third-party civil penalty rules in section 163.2;[143] (b) the general anti-avoidance rule (GAAR); (c) rules to eliminate loopholes used by tax shelters[144] and other aggressive tax plan-

---

[140]Commentary on LSUC Rule 4.06(1), note 76, above: "The admission to and continuance in the practice of law implies on the part of a lawyer a basic commitment to the concept of equal justice for all within an open, ordered, and impartial system. However, judicial institutions will not function effectively unless they command the respect of the public, and because of changes in human affairs and imperfections in human institutions, constant efforts must be made to improve the administration of justice and thereby maintain public respect for it."

[141]LSUC Rule 6.01, note 76, above: "A lawyer shall conduct himself or herself in such a way as to maintain the integrity of the profession."

[142]Commentary on LSUC Rule 4.06(1), note 76, above: "A lawyer, by training, opportunity, and experience is in a position to observe the workings and discover the strengths and weaknesses of laws, legal institutions, and public authorities. A lawyer should, therefore, lead in seeking improvements in the legal system, but any criticisms and proposals should be *bona fide* and reasoned."

[143]See heading 18.13(b)(iii), "Third party civil penalties," above.

[144]These include a number of rules, including the "at risk" amount adjustments for limited recourse debt in s. 143.2 and the matchable expenditure rules in s. 18.1 which defeated the shelters promoted by Monarch in *Strother*, note 83, above.

ning techniques; and (d) rules that require promoters and operators of tax shelters to register with the government.[145]

The most significant legislative development is the introduction of the GAAR, which is discussed in more detail in Chapter 20. Under the GAAR, legitimate tax minimization is assumed to involve business arrangements or economic activities that are primarily to produce income and involve an economic cost, which is consistent with the fundamental framework underlying the income tax system (i.e., that tax is imposed on net income and deductions are allowed only for the cost of activities that are aimed at generating income.)

Québec has recently introduced new measures effective October 15, 2009 which include enhanced disclosure requirements and GAAR penalties.[146] Mandatory disclosure rules apply to all transactions providing a tax benefit of at least $25,000 or a reduction of income of at least $100,000 if either (1) the adviser requires the taxpayer to respect a confidentiality agreement with regard to third parties, or (2) the remuneration of the adviser is contingent, in whole or in part, upon the realization of the tax benefit. Voluntary preventative disclosures can also be filed to avoid the possibility of GAAR penalties. Taxpayers and promoters of transactions to which GAAR applies are subject to new penalties unless the taxpayer has filed a mandatory or voluntary preventative disclosure of the transaction with Revenue Québec. An enhanced disclosure and GAAR penalty regime is expected to be introduced federally in the near future. At the time of writing (March 2010), the federal government is consulting on a proposal contained in the 2010 federal budget that is different than the regime in place in Québec.

(c) — Judicial developments

Canadian courts have recently adopted a textual, contextual and purposive interpretation of tax statutes (see Chapter 19). Aggressive tax schemes can be countered by the more purposive interpretation of the provisions of the Act as well as under the GAAR.

Abusive tax avoidance transactions that are subject to the GAAR are transactions that are undertaken to achieve results which constitute an abuse or misuse of the Act. The application of the GAAR requires a "value" judgment about whether an

---

[145]S. 237.1. A "tax shelter" is defined if the property that meets a two-pronged test: (a) would the amounts deductible within the first four years of acquisition of the property be equal to or in excess of, the cost of the property as reduced by certain "prescribed benefits"? (b) Were statements or representations made, or proposed to be made, in connection with the property that an acquisition of the property would result in such amounts being deductible? Promoters are subject to a penalty if they do not obtain a tax shelter identification number before selling a tax shelter.

[146]Revenue Québec, *Information Bulletin 2009-5*, "Fighting Aggressive Tax Planning" at *http://www.finances.gouv.qc.ca/documents/bulletins/en/BULEN_2009-5-a-b.pdf*

avoidance transaction is "legitimate" or "abusive"[147] which can only be made by considering the spirit, object and purpose of the rules in the Act. The GAAR requires practitioners to shift away from a strict, literal interpretation of the Act — which reduces the provisions of the Act to "bright line rules", permitting the delineation of limited spheres of prohibited activity outside of which all activities are permitted and the gatekeepers' role was minimal — to a contextual and purposive interpretation which requires tax practitioners to understand statutory rules in light of the object and purpose of these rules.

(d) — CRA's efforts

The CRA has increased its efforts in fighting tax shelters and aggressive tax planning in terms of audits and has also enjoyed some success in courts. There have been three GAAR cases heard by the Supreme Court of Canada and the CRA has had one clear win (*Mathew*), one loss (*Canada Trustco*) and a win by a 4/3 slim majority (*Lipson*). The CRA has also won some tax shelter cases in courts, such as *Baxter*[148] and *Maege*,[149] which denied the tax benefits sought by investors in tax shelters,[150] and has revoked the tax exempt status of charitable organizations for promoting a tax shelter arrangement which was for the private benefit of the tax shelter promoters.[151]

All these legislative, judicial and administrative developments place a heavier onus on tax practitioners to make value judgements concerning the true nature of transactions proposed by their clients and the object and purpose of the tax provisions.

(e) — International influences

For some time now, the CRA and provincial tax authorities have been working in partnership with tax authorities around the world to share best practices, identify aggressive tax planning strategies, and enhance compliance by gathering and sharing information on taxpayer transactions. This, in turn, has led to improvements in enforcement and legislative responses around the world. Several jurisdictions have introduced additional measures to target unethical conduct and aggressive tax planning and these measures affect tax practitioners with clients who operate globally.

---

[147] It could even be said that there is a concept of morality inherent in the word "abuse." See Silver, note 74 above, at 36:15.

[148] *R. v. Baxter*, [2006] 3 C.T.C. 2427, 2006 D.T.C. 2642 (Eng.) (T.C.C. [General Procedure]); reversed 2007 D.T.C. 5199 (Eng.), [2007] 3 C.T.C. 211 (FCA); leave to appeal refused [2007] 3 C.T.C. 211.

[149] *Maege v. R.*, [2006] 3 C.T.C. 2234, 2006 D.T.C. 3193 (Eng.) (T.C.C. [General Procedure], affirmed, [2007] 5 C.T.C. 67, 2008 D.T.C. 6263 (Eng.).

[150] The *Lipson v. Cassels Brock*lawsuit referred to in note 22, above, was triggered by the denial of charitable tax credits to the plaintiffs.

[151] E.g., CRA, "The Canada Revenue Agency Revokes the Charitable Status of The Millennium Charitable Foundation", see *http://www.cra-arc.gc.ca/nwsrm/rlss/2009/m01/nr090112-eng.html*.

In the United States, for example, the Secretary of the Treasury is authorized to regulate tax practitioners and to suspend or disbar any practitioner found to be incompetent or disreputable or who violates these regulations (which are known as IRS Circular 230). These regulations establish standards in various areas, including minimum levels of accuracy for tax return advice given to clients, the diligence required of practitioners, prohibition on representation of conflicting interests, and minimum quality standards for written tax advice and opinions.[152] There is currently no equivalent of IRS Circular 230 in Canada, which may reflect better practices.

U.S. disclosure requirements are also more onerous. The U.S. also requires specific aggressive tax planning transactions to be disclosed[153] and is proposing to require a schedule with the details of uncertain tax positions and their potential tax exposure.[154] Any position that does not meet the "more likely than not" standard (of prevailing in court) must be disclosed or the preparer is subject to penalties.[155]

U.S. general anti-avoidance rules and related penalties are also more onerous. In March 2010, the U.S. common law "economic substance doctrine" was strengthened when it was codified as section 7701(o) of the *Internal Revenue Code*. This rule imposes a subjective non-tax purpose test and an objective non-tax profit test. The subjective non-tax purpose test looks at the substantial purpose for entering the transaction. The objective non-tax profit test looks at whether the transaction changes a taxpayer's economic position "in a meaningful way "ignoring any tax benefits. Transactions must meet both of these tests in order to have "economic substance" and transactions lacking economic substance are not respected for tax purposes. The March 2010 legislation also includes a 20 percent penalty for underpayments of tax attributable to transactions lacking economic substance that are disclosed to the IRS and a 40 percent penalty for undisclosed transactions. The penalties are expected to raise revenue for the U.S. government.

(f) — Advancing public interest

Well-educated tax professionals who understand the policies and principles underlying our tax system as well as the ethical standards of their profession have an edge over others in light of recent developments. Their in-depth knowledge of the

---

[152]See Chapman et al., note 75 above, at 2:12 to 14.

[153]See, for example, the list of reportable transactions in Revenue Québec, Working Paper on Aggressive Tax Planning at 60 to 61 at http://www.finances.gouv.qc.ca/documents/Autres/en/AUTEN_DocCons_PFA.pdf

[154]According to the IRS, "The goals of our proposal are simple: to cut down the time it takes to find issues and complete an audit. . . ensure that both the IRS and taxpayer spend time discussing the law as it applies to their facts, rather than looking for information. . .and to help us prioritize selection of issues and taxpayers for examination." See *http://www.irs.gov/newsroom/article/0,,id=218705,00.html*

[155]All tax positions, disclosed or not, must meet a "substantial authority test" or the preparer is subject to penalties: IRS 6694.

Act and case law will enhance their ability to advise clients while advancing the integrity of the tax system. Ideally, they can end up "doing well and doing good at the same time."[156] Some leaders of the tax profession recognize that the "legal profession is not simply a business; it is a calling. It is more than a vocation; it is a public trust."[157]

---

[156]E. Freidson, *Professionalism: The Third Logic (2001)*, at 197-222, discussing the "soul" of professionalism.

[157]Chapman et al, note 74, above, at 18, citing Irwin Cotler's address to the Canadian Bar Association, "The Constitutional Revolution, the Courts, and the Pursuit of Justice," August 15, 2005.

19
STATUTORY INTERPRETATION

19.1 — Interpretation of the Act

Statutory interpretation is an important issue in income tax law because tax liability is created solely by statute. The *Income Tax Act* (the "Act") is the primary tax statute. The goal of statutory interpretation is to find the meaning of words in a statutory provision in relation to particular facts. The process of statutory interpretation involves the determination of the meaning of a statutory provision, the characterization of facts for tax purposes, and the application of the appropriate meaning to the facts.

(a) — Meaning of words

Statutory interpretation begins with the words in the Act. Words are the most basic components of legislation. Establishing the meaning of words is often challenging because it is rare for a word to have a single meaning. This is particularly true with the provisions of the Act that are often litigated by taxpayers. Taxpayers rarely go to court with clear cases. Why waste time and money? When more than one meaning can be implied, whether a judge takes a liberal or restrictive interpretation can have fundamental implications for our tax system.

(b) — Characterization of facts

How to characterize a transaction for tax purposes is important because different types of transactions attract different tax treatment. For example, in the *Duke of Westminster* case," payments under an "employment contract" with a household servant were not tax deductible, but payments under an "annuity contract" were.[1] The nearly unlimited range of transactions must be categorized in terms of the provisions of the Act. The Act necessarily has a limited number of terms, many of

[1] See heading 19.2(b)(iii), "The *Duke of Westminster* (1935) case", below.

which are imported into it with their meaning established in private law (e.g., contracts, property, etc.). The challenge is whether the legal rights and obligations created under private law should be respected for tax purposes.

Very often, the legal rights and obligations created in private law are determinative for tax purposes. Unless the legal relationship is a sham or invalid, in most cases, the legal forms must inevitably be controlling. The courts would assume an extraordinary power if, for taxation purposes, they could ignore such basic matters as the obligations of a deed of covenant, the legal and beneficial ownership of property and the separate legal personalities of different companies. Therefore, the courts will not disregard legal relationships genuinely created. Indeed, tax law would become intolerably uncertain if courts felt unconstrained by the legal form of the taxpayer's arrangements, and felt free to impose tax on a different basis. However, if a transaction is structured for no other reason but to "game" the tax system, that is, to exploit textual ambiguities without regard to the scheme and purpose of the Act, should courts overlook the legal form and apply the provisions of the Act according to the economic reality of the transactions?

The question of whether a transaction should be characterized for tax purposes according to its legal form or according to its economic substance is obviously a different question from whether the Act should be given a strict or a purposive interpretation. But the two questions are intimately related. As you can see from the discussions in the next section, under a regime of strict interpretation, the courts are less likely to read the Act as authorizing an inquiry that goes beyond a legal form than they are under a regime of purposive interpretation. Under a regime of purposive interpretation, the argument that the Act imposes liability on a practical, economic result, as opposed to a legal form, becomes more appealing.

(c) — Judicial doctrines

Rules of statutory interpretation are found in case law as statutory interpretation is very much the province of the judiciary. The Act does not contain a general interpretation rule. Parliament is generally reluctant to tell judges how to interpret legislation. In fact, even when Parliament has spoken on the issue of interpretation, its instructions are often ignored.[2]

This chapter provides an overview of the main interpretation doctrines before examining in more detail the prevailing "textual, contextual and purposive" doctrine.

19.2 — Evolution of interpretation principles

(a) — Evolution

The present state of law on statutory interpretation is unsettled. There has been a lack of coherent theory or guidelines on statutory interpretation. The Supreme Court of Canada is often split in its decisions, making statutory interpretation a fascinating area of study for students.

---

[2]Sullivan, *Statutory Interpretation* (1997), at 27.

Canadian courts have adopted various approaches to the interpretation of the Act. Chronologically speaking, these include the strict interpretation, the "plain meaning," and the so-called "modern rule" or the "textual, contextual and purposive" approach. The general trend has been to move from a literal, formalistic approach to a more liberal, substantive approach.

(b) — Strict Interpretation

(i) — Literal meaning

The old rule that tax legislation must be interpreted strictly is perhaps best articulated in a dictum of the House of Lords in 1869:[3]

> . . . as I understand the principle of all fiscal legislation, it is this: if the person sought to be taxed comes within the letter of the law he must be taxed, however great the hardship may appear to the judicial mind to be. On the other hand, if the Crown, seeking to recover the tax, cannot bring the subject within the letter of the law, the subject is free, however apparently within the spirit of the law the case might otherwise appear to be.

Under this approach, if the language of the statute is not literally apt to catch the transaction at issue, then it escapes. There is a presumption that if there is doubt or ambiguity in provisions that levy a tax, the ambiguity should be interpreted in favour of the taxpayer.

From the taxpayers' perspective, the strict interpretation could be a double-edged sword. It not only leads to a narrow (strict) interpretation of charging provisions in a taxing statute, it also leads to a narrow interpretation of relieving provisions, such as exemptions or deductions. For example, in *Whitthum v. Minister of National Revenue* (1957)[4] the taxpayer was denied a medical expense deduction for the expense of a full-time attendant for his spouse. The Act allowed this deduction only if a person was "necessarily confined by reason of illness . . . to a bed or wheelchair." The court found that his wife did not qualify because she was confined to a "rocking chair."

(ii) — Form over substance

Courts adhering to the strict or literal approach to interpreting tax statutes have generally adopted the "form over substance" doctrine in constructing the facts. The character of the relationship for tax purposes is determined by the "true nature of the legal obligation and nothing else is the substance."[5] As long as the contract is a genuine document (i.e., not a sham), the "true legal relationship is determined by

---

[3] *Partington v. Attorney General* (1869), L.R. 4 H.L. 100 (U.K. H.L.), 122, per Lord Cairns.

[4] (1957), 17 Tax A.B.C. 33, 57 D.T.C. 174 (Can. Tax App. Bd.).

[5] (1935), [1936] A.C. 1 (U.K. H.L.), 19.

the legal rights and obligations of the parties ascertained upon ordinary legal principles.[6] In the absence of a sham, the form of the legal relationship generally dictates.

(iii) — The Duke of Westminster (1935) case[7]

The facts in this famous case were straightforward. The Duke of Westminster had a number of household servants. The then British *Income Tax Act* did not allow a deduction of wages of household servants, but allowed a deduction of annual payments made in pursuance of a legal obligation other than remuneration of servants (this is similar to modern day "annuity" or "pensions"). The Duke accordingly entered into deeds of covenant with each of his servants under which he undertook to pay each of them annual sums for a period of seven years. The payments were to be made irrespective of whether any services were performed by the promisee, and were without prejudice to the promisee's entitlement to remuneration if he or she did perform any services to the promisor. However, it was established by evidence that the understanding between the Duke and his servants was that they would rest content with the provision made for them by deed, and would not assert any right to remuneration. In this way, the Duke converted his non-deductible wages obligation into a deductible annuity obligation. The issue was whether the "annual payments" under the covenants fell within the meaning of this term as used in the tax statute.

The House of Lords ruled in favour of the Duke. More importantly, this case established a set of principles which have been profoundly influential in Canada today. These principles are:

1. A tax statute is to receive a strict or literal interpretation;
2. A transaction is to be judged not by its economic or commercial substance but by its legal form;
3. A transaction is effective for tax purposes even if it has no business purpose, having been entered into solely to avoid tax; and
4. Taxpayers are entitled to arrange their affairs to minimize their tax liability.

The principle of strict interpretation was articulated by Lord Russell of Killowen as follows:

> I confess that I view with disfavour the doctrine that in taxation cases the subject is to be taxed if, in accordance with a Court's view of what it considers the substance of the transaction, the Court thinks that the case falls within the contemplation or

---

[6]Lord Russell of Killowen (at pages 24-25) stated: "If all that is meant by the [substance] doctrine is that having once ascertained the legal rights of the parties you may disregard mere nomenclature and decide the question of taxability or non-taxability in accordance with the legal rights, well and good. . . . If, on the other hand, the doctrine means that you may brush aside deeds, disregard the legal rights and liabilities arising under a contract between parties, and decide the question of taxability or non-taxability upon the footing of the rights and liabilities of the parties being different from what in law they are, then I entirely dissent from such a doctrine."

[7]*Inland Revenue Commissioners v. Duke of Westminster* (1935), [1936] A.C. 1 (H.L.), 19.

> spirit of the statute. The subject is not taxable by inference or by analogy, but only by the plain words of a statute applicable to the facts and circumstances of his case.

In this case, the meaning of the terms "annuity" and "salary" were given their literal meaning. None of the law lords made any inquiry about the purpose or spirit of the legislation.

The principle of "form over substance", that is, to characterize the Duke's relationship with his servants in accordance with the contract, not its real commercial substance or purpose, was crucial to the Duke's success in court. There was no doubt that the deeds were legally effective in that all legal formalities had been carried out. Nor were the deeds shams: the Duke had covenanted to pay the annuities for seven years, and had thereby assumed the risk of having to continue to pay an annuitant who had stopped working for him or who had insisted upon additional remuneration for working for him. Of course, the understanding that the faithful retainers would continue to work for him, and would do so without extra charge, virtually eliminated this risk. But the risk was genuinely assumed, and none of their lordships regarded the deeds as shams. The form of the transaction (that is, the "annuity contract") was thus regarded as the "substance" of the transaction. Lord Atkin, the sole dissenter, was the only law lord who found the device unsuccessful in avoiding tax. For Lord Atkin, "the substance of the transaction was that what was being paid was remuneration".[8] But for the other law lords, the legal form of the transactions was controlling and the Duke was entitled to deduct the payments. The substance doctrine was rejected because it involved substituting "the incertain and crooked cord of discretion" for "the golden and straight metwand of the law."[9]

The principle that a taxpayer is entitled to order his affairs so as to minimize his tax liability is found in the often-quoted words of Lord Tomlin:

> Every man is entitled if he can to order his affairs so as that the tax attaching under the appropriate Acts is less than it otherwise would be. If he succeeds in ordering them so as to secure this result, then, however unappreciative the Commissioners of Inland Revenue or his fellow taxpayers may be of his ingenuity, he cannot be compelled to pay an increased tax. This so-called doctrine of "the substance" seems to me to be nothing more than an attempt to make a man pay notwithstanding that he has so ordered his affairs that the amount of tax sought from him is not legally claimable.[10]

(iv) — Outdated presumptions about tax law

The strict interpretation of tax statutes reflects some outdated presumptions about tax law. Traditionally, tax law in England was compared to criminal law and the

---

[8] *Ibid.*, above, at 24-25.

[9] *Ibid.*, at 19-20.

[10] *Ibid.*

confiscation of property.[11] This tradition has been followed in Canada.[12] As a result, if the meaning of words of a tax statute is doubtful, the doubt must be resolved against the government and in favour of the taxpayer as it is for criminal law. This strict interpretation was aimed at protecting the taxpayer's property rights from government claims that were not clearly prescribed in advance. In other words, it was "not only legal but moral to dodge the Inland Revenue."[13]

In recent times, however, taxes have begun to be viewed somewhat differently. True, the immediate economic effect of paying a criminal fine or a tax may be similar, as the payer parts with property in both cases. However, a criminal fine is assessed in order to punish wrongdoing, whereas a tax is collected to apportion the costs of government among those who presumably benefit from it. As explained in Chapters 1 and 2, the main purpose of an income tax is to raise revenue, but subsidiary objectives are also pursued.

Estey J. recognized the Act's fiscal and economic objectives in *Stubart Investments Ltd. v. R.* (1984):[14]

> Income tax legislation, such as the federal Act in our country, is no longer a simple device to raise revenue to meet the cost of governing the community. Income taxation is also employed by government to attain selected economic policy objectives. Thus, the statute is a mix of fiscal and economic policy.

---

[11]Stevens, *Law and Politics: The House of Lords as a Judicial Body*, 1800-1976 (1978), 170–71.

[12]Grover & Iacobucci, *Materials on Canadian Income Tax*, 5th ed, (1981), 62-65, cited by Estey J. in *Stubart*, note 11, below, para. 57.

[13]Willis, 51 *Canadian Bar Review* 1, 26, cited by Estey J. in *Stubart*, note 14, below, 315, 6323 (Willis was referring to *Levene v. Inland Revenue Commissioners*, [1928] A.C. 217 (U.K. H.L.) at 227).

[14]*Stubart Investments Ltd. v. R.*, [1984] C.T.C. 294, 84 D.T.C. 6305 (S.C.C.), 298 [C.T.C.], 6308 [D.T.C.], para. 55. In *Québec (Communauté urbaine) c. Notre-Dame de Bonsecours (Corp.)* (1994), (sub nom. *Notre-Dame de Bon-Secours (Corp.) v. Quebec (Communauté urbaine))* [1995] 1 C.T.C. 241, 95 D.T.C. 5017, 95 D.T.C. 5091 (Fr.) (S.C.C.), the Supreme Court of Canada also recognized that a taxing statute "serves other purposes and functions as a tool of economic and social policy." (para. 33)

(c) — Modern rule

(i) — Purposive interpretation

Stubart[15] is a landmark case that signalled the change towards a more purposive interpretation of the Act. Estey J. held that the "modern rule" applied to taxing statutes just like it did to other statutes:[16]

> The words of an Act are to be read in their entire context and in their grammatical and ordinary sense harmoniously with the scheme of the Act, the object of the Act, and the intention of Parliament.

The modern rule differs from the traditional strict interpretation by requiring statutory provisions be interpreted in a broader context and in harmony with the object and spirit of the legislation. One year after the *Stubart* decision, the Interpretation Act[17] was enacted, codifying the modern rule. Section 12 the Interpretation Act provides: "Every enactment is deemed remedial, and shall be given such fair, large and liberal construction and interpretation as best ensures the attainment of its objects."

Why did the Court feel the need to reject the strict interpretation in *Stubart*? Estey J. attributed part of the reason to the changing role of tax law: "the introduction of [tax] exemptions and allowances was the beginning of the end of the reign of the strict rule."[18] He also regarded the replacement of strict interpretation with purposive interpretation as a blow to tax avoidance and a way of reducing legislative complexity. According to Justice Estey, purposive interpretation would "reduce the attraction of elaborate and intricate tax avoidance plans, and reduce the rewards to those best able to afford the services of the tax technicians"[19] and "reduce the action and reaction endlessly produced by complex, specific tax measures aimed at sophisticated business practices, and the inevitable, professionally guided and equally specialized taxpayer reaction".[20]

These are all admirable sentiments, but the fact is that formulating legislative purpose and determining when it should be applied have been very difficult. Even in *Stubart*, "object and spirit" did not seem to play a role in the final outcome of the case. Subsequent courts have given various degrees of consideration to the relevance of the "object and spirit" of the Act.

(ii) — "True commercial and practical nature" of transactions

The modern rule of statutory interpretation requires a more liberal and purposive approach to interpreting statutory provisions. It would be logical to apply a similar

---

[15] *Ibid.*

[16] *Ibid.*, para. 61.

[17] R.S.C. 1985, c. I-21.

[18] *Ibid.*, para. 59.

[19] *Ibid.*, para. 56.

[20] *Ibid.*, para. 66.

approach to the construction of facts, or at least, it would be more appealing to argue that the Act imposes liability on an economic result, as opposed to a legal form. In fact, Dickson C.J. anticipated in *Bronfman Trust* (1987) that there was to be a trend in Canadian tax cases "towards attempting to ascertain the true commercial and practical nature of the taxpayer's transactions."[21]

The trend anticipated by Dickson C.J. did not occur. Even in the *Stubart* case, the Court accepted the legal forms (sale and agency agreement), although the commercial substance of the arrangement was that Stubart had not divested itself of the business.

(iii) — The Stubart (1984) case

In *Stubart*, a parent company had two subsidiaries. One subsidiary, Stubart Investments Ltd. (Stubart), operated a profitable business, manufacturing food flavourings. The other subsidiary, Grover Cast Stone Co. Ltd. (Grover), operated an unprofitable business, manufacturing concrete products. Because Stubart and Grover were two separate companies, the losses incurred by Grover could not be used to offset the profits earned by Stubart. So long as Grover remained unprofitable, it had no income that would enable it to take advantage of the loss carryforward rules under the Act, which permit losses accumulated in prior years to be used as a deduction against current income.

Distressed by the prospect of losses going to waste, the parent company devised and executed the following plan for the two subsidiaries: Stubart sold the assets of its profitable food flavouring business to Grover. Stubart did not actually relinquish the operation of the business, because Grover appointed Stubart to continue to operate the business as Grover's agent. For three years, Stubart operated the business as Grover's Agent and paid its profits to Grover, the legal owner of the business, at the end of each year. Grover reported this income for tax purposes, and used its accumulated losses from the unprofitable concrete business to create a loss carryforward deduction that effectively sheltered the income from tax. The Minister refused to accept that the profits of the food flavouring business belonged to Grover. The Minister therefore reassessed Stubart on the basis that Stubart was required to report the income that it had transferred to Grover under the agency arrangement as its own. Stubart appealed from this assessment, and the issue reached the Supreme Court of Canada.

The Court rejected the position of the Minister, and accepted the position of the taxpayer. According to Estey J., who wrote the majority opinion, Stubart's food flavouring business assets had been legally transferred to Grover; the operation of the business had been conducted by Stubart under a legal agency agreement with Grover; and, under the terms of that agreement, the income of the business belonged in law to Grover. The income was properly reported by Grover, and the loss carryforward provisions of the Act permitted Grover to take advantage of its accu-

---

[21] *The Queen v. Bronfman Trust*, 87 D.T.C. 5059, [1987] 1 C.T.C. 117 (S.C.C.), at 5067, [D.T.C.], at 128 [C.T.C.].

mulated losses as current deductions. Nothing in the Act directed or empowered the Minister to disregard the legal consequences of the taxpayer's arrangements. Nor did the Act expressly or implicitly impose a business purpose test on tax avoidance transactions: it was irrelevant that the taxpayers' arrangements had no business purpose other than the avoidance of tax. Therefore, the arrangements were successful in sheltering the food flavouring business income from tax.

(d) — Plain meaning

(i) — "Clear and unambiguous" meaning

The so-called "plain meaning" approach to statutory interpretation means that the court must apply the clear and unambiguous meaning of provisions of the Act without the need to resort to the general object and spirit of the provision. For example, McLachlin J. (as she then was) stated in *Shell Canada Ltd. v. R.* (1999):[22]

> [I]t is well established in this Court's tax jurisprudence that a searching inquiry for either the "economic realities" of a particular transaction or the general object and spirit of the provision at issue can never supplant a court's duty to apply an unambiguous provision of the Act to a taxpayer's transaction. Where the provision at issue is clear and unambiguous, its terms must simply be applied.

In a number of cases, including *Antosko* (1994),[23] *Singleton* (2001)[24] and *Ludco* (2001),[25] the Supreme Court, while reiterating the modern rule of statutory interpretation, clearly limited the relevance of legislative purpose or intent to instances where the legislative provision is ambiguous. As discussed below, the Court did not find the provision at issue ambiguous, thus felt no need to go beyond the plain meaning. In essence, the plain meaning approach is not much different from that of "strict interpretation".

The *Antosko* case[26] was one of the first post-*Stubart* cases in which the Supreme Court of Canada formulated the plain meaning approach. In that case, as an attempt to rehabilitate a failing company, the taxpayer acquired for a nominal consideration from a provincial government agency some debt obligations (a debenture and promissory notes) that had been issued by the company to the agency (which had been lending money to the company). The taxpayer also acquired the shares of the company, and became responsible for running the business. The tax issue arose

---

[22] [1999] 4 C.T.C. 313, 99 D.T.C. 5669 (Eng.), 99 D.T.C. 5682 (Fr.) (S.C.C.), para. 40 [D.T.C.]. See also heading 8.9, "Interest expense", above.

[23] [1994] 2 C.T.C. 25, 94 D.T.C. 6314 (S.C.C.).

[24] (2001), 2001 SCC 61, [2002] 1 C.T.C. 121, 2001 D.T.C. 5533 (Eng.), 2001 D.T.C. 5545 (Fr.) (S.C.C.) (discussed under heading 8.9, "Interest expense", above, and heading 19.2(d)(iii), The *Singleton* (2001) case, below.

[25] *Ludmer c. Ministre du Revenu national* (2001), [2002] 1 C.T.C. 95, (sub nom. *Ludco Enterprises Ltd. v. R.)* 2001 D.T.C. 5505 (Eng.), 2001 D.T.C. 5518 (Fr.) (S.C.C.), discussed under heading 8.9, "Interest expense", above.

[26] Note 23, above.

when the company made interest payments on the debt obligations to the taxpayer. The taxpayer reported the full amount of the interest income for tax purposes, but claimed a deduction for the portion of the interest that had accrued prior to the transfer of the debt obligation from the provincial agency to the taxpayer. The deduction was authorized by the literal language of subsection 20(14) of the Act, which provided that, on the transfer of a debt obligation, any unpaid interest accrued to the date of the transfer was to be included in the transferor's income, and deducted from the transferee's income. In this case, the transferor, being an agency of the provincial government, was exempt from tax, so that it did not report or pay tax on the interest accrued up to the date of transfer. The Minister took the position that it was contrary to the object and spirit of the Act to allow the transferee taxpayer to deduct the accrued interest in the circumstances of this case, when the transferor was not taxable on the interest. The Supreme Court of Canada rejected the Minister's argument and allowed the taxpayer to take the deduction. Iacobucci J., who wrote for the Court, held that the taxpayer was entitled to rely upon the terms of the statute, which clearly entitled the transferee of a debt obligation to a deduction for the interest accrued to the date of transfer. Where the words of the statute were "clear and plain", and where the legal and practical effect of the taxpayer's transaction brought the taxpayer within the words of the statute, then the statute had to be applied according to its terms regardless of the object and purpose of the provision.

The decision in *Antosko* is sound in that it would introduce intolerable uncertainty into the Act if clear language in detailed provisions of the Act were to be routinely qualified by unexpressed exceptions derived from a court's view of the object and purpose of those provisions. However, *Antosko* may go too far in implying that one can rely on plain meaning *to the exclusion* of legislative purpose. After all, language can never be interpreted independently of its context, and legislative purpose is part of the context. It would seem to follow that consideration of legislative purpose may not only resolve patent ambiguity, but may, on occasion, reveal ambiguity in apparently plain language.[27]

The plain meaning approach may result in an interpretation that contradicts fundamental principles of income tax law. For example, in *Friesen v. R.* (1995)[28] the issue was whether vacant land held in an adventure or concern in the nature of trade constituted "inventory" for purpose of subsection 10(1) of the Act. If the land was inventory, the taxpayer could deduct the accrued but unrealized loss by writing down the value of the land under the lower of fair market value and cost valuation

---

[27]In *Canada Trustco Mortgage Corp. v. Port O'Call Hotel Inc.* (1996), (sub nom. *Pigott Project Management Ltd. v. Land-Rock Resources Ltd.)* [1996] 1 C.T.C. 395, (sub nom. *R. v. Alberta Treasury Branches)* 96 D.T.C. 6245 (S.C.C.), at 403-404 [C.T.C.], at 6248 [D.T.C.] per Cory J. for majority ("even if the ambiguity were not apparent, it is significant that in order to determine the clear and plain meaning of the statute it is always appropriate to consider the 'scheme of the Act, the object of the Act, and the intention of Parliament'.")

[28][1995] 2 C.T.C. 369, 95 D.T.C. 5551 (S.C.C.) For more discussion on inventory, see heading 8.8, Inventory, above.

method permitted by subsection 10(1). Subsection 248(1) defines "inventory" to mean "a description of property the cost or value of which is relevant in computing a taxpayer's income from a business for a taxation year". The majority of the Supreme Court of Canada held that the plain meaning of the definition in subsection 248(1) is that an item of property need only be relevant to business income in a single year to qualify as inventory because the key word used in the definition is "a", not "the" (as argued by the Minister). As a result, the taxpayer could deduct the paper loss. This result was contrary to the fundamental principle of realization in income tax law and had to be overruled by amendment to subsection 10(1) and the introduction of subsection 10(1.01).

(ii) — No recharacterization of "bona fide legal relationships"

The shift towards the plain meaning approach was accompanied by a more explicit recognition of "legal" substance and virtual rejection of the "economic" substance doctrine. For example, McLachlin J. stated in *Shell:*[29]

> . . . this Court has never held that the economic realities of a situation can be used to recharacterize a taxpayer's bona fide relationships. To the contrary, we have held that, absent a specific provision of the Act to the contrary or a finding that they are a sham, the taxpayer's legal relationships must be respected in tax cases. . . .

The principle in *Shell* is, therefore, that bona fide legal relationships created by the taxpayer cannot be recharacterized to reflect the economic realities. Since this principle applies only to "*bona fide* legal relationships," it is necessary to make a normative inquiry into whether or not such relations are created *bona fide*. The Court has not provided any guidelines for such inquiry. In fact, there seems to have been no cases in which the Court found the taxpayer's relationships not to be bona fide. The *Shell* principle resonates well with the *Duke of Westminster* principles. The substance of taxpayer's legal relationships, especially those created with professional advice, is generally consistent with the form of the legal arrangements.

In cases where the tax avoidance purpose is achieved through a series of transactions or multiple legal steps, the *Shell* principle requires each transaction or step be characterized separately without looking at the overall purpose or effect of these transactions. This is illustrated in the *Singleton* case.

(iii) — The Singleton (2001) case

In this case, the taxpayer was a partner of a law firm and had at least $300,000 in his capital account at the firm before October 27, 1988. On October 27, 1988, he did the following transactions:

- Borrowed $298,750 from a bank and used the house he was going to purchase as mortgage;

---

[29]Note 22 above, paras. 39-40.For an excellent overview of the form over substance doctrine, see Chief Justice Bowman's decision in *Continental Bank v. R.*, [1995] 1 C.T.C. 2135, 94 D.T.C. 1858 (T.C.C.)

- Paid $300,000 (the $298,750 borrowed money along with $1,250 of his own money) into the taxpayer's capital account at the firm;
- Received a $300,000 cheque from the firm and deposited it into his personal bank account;
- Issued a cheque of $300,000 drawn on his personal bank account to pay for the purchase of the house.

The exact sequence of the above transactions was disputed. Unfortunately, it is the sequencing of the transactions that determines the outcome of the case.

The issue is whether the taxpayer could deduct the interest paid on the money borrowed from the bank under paragraph 20(1)(c) of the Act. The Minister denied the interest deduction on the ground that the borrowed money was used to finance the purchase of the house (an ineligible use of the borrowed money). Bowman J.T.C.C. of the Tax Court of Canada upheld the Minister's assessment. He took a "realistic" view of the transactions and concluded that, on October 27, 1988, the borrowed money was channelled through the firm and immediately went to the taxpayer for the purchase of the house. He remarked:[30]

> On any realistic view of the matter it could not be said that the money was used for the purpose of making a contribution of capital to the partnership. The fundamental purpose was the purchase of a house and this purpose cannot be altered by the shuffle of cheques that took place on October 27, 1988.

Bowman J.T.C.C. added that the steps of the transaction were "conterminous and interdependent". Even if the legal validity of the steps was accepted and the tax motivation treated as irrelevant, he concluded that ". . . one is still left with the inescapable factual determination that the true economic purpose for which the borrowed money was used was the purchase of a house, not the enhancement of the firm's income earning potential by a contribution of capital."[31]

Adhering to the *Shell* principle, the majority of the Federal Court of Appeal and Supreme Court of Canada overruled Bowman J.T.C.C.'s decision. Major J., writing for the majority of the Supreme Court, held that the taxpayer was entitled to deduct the interest expense. Paragraph 20(1)(c) of the Act requires, among other conditions, *the borrowed money be used for the purpose of earning non-exempt income from a business or property* and a direct link be drawn between the borrowed money and an eligible use. Investment in the firm by paying into the capital account is an "eligible use". Given that the taxpayer had at least $300,000 of his own money in the law firm and he was free to use his own money or borrowed money to finance the business of his law firm, Major J. found a direct link between the borrowed money and financing the law firm. He stated:[32]

> In reviewing what the respondent did, it is clear that the relevant cheques were deposited and honoured. There is no suggestion that the transaction was a sham. Giv-

---

[30] *Singleton v. R.*, [1996] 3 C.T.C. 2873, 96 D.T.C. 1850 (T.C.C.), para. 12.

[31] *Ibid*, para. 16.

[32] *R. v. Singleton*, 2001 SCC 61, 2001 DTC 5533, [2002] 1 CTC 121, para. 32.

> ing effect to the legal relationships in this case, it is clear that the respondent used the borrowed funds to refinance his capital account.

Major J. further stated that the characterization of the use of the funds is not altered by the fact that the transactions occurred on the same day.[33]

> In my respectful opinion, it is an error to treat this as one simultaneous transaction. In order to give effect to the legal relationships, the transactions must be viewed independently.

(e) — Textual, contextual and purposive interpretation

(i) — Contextual and purposive interpretation

The "textual, contextual and purposive" principle was adopted by the Supreme Court in *Canada Trustco v. R.* (2005):[34]

> The interpretation of a statutory provision must be made according to a textual, contextual and purposive analysis to find a meaning that is harmonious with the Act as a whole. When the words of a provision are precise and unequivocal, the ordinary meaning of the words plays a dominant role in the interpretive process. On the other hand, where the words can support more than one reasonable meaning, the ordinary meaning of the words plays a lesser role. The relative effects of ordinary meaning, context and purpose on the interpretive process may vary, but in all cases the court must seek to read the provisions of an Act as a harmonious whole.

This textual, contextual and purposive principle is in essence a restatement of the "modern rule". There is no coincidence that the Court articulated this principle in *Canada Trustco*, its first general anti-avoidance rule (GAAR) case. As discussed further in Chapter 20, section 245 of the Act specifically requires a contextualized purposive interpretation of the Act in determining whether an avoidance transaction is "abusive" for the purposes of GAAR. The Court applied this principle in its second GAAR case, *Mathew* (2005),[35] which was heard at the same time as *Canada Trustco*. The Court has also applied this principle in subsequent non-GAAR cases, such as *Placer Dome* (2006)[36] and *Imperial Oil* (2006).[37]

These four landmark decisions (i.e., *Canada Trustco*, *Mathew*, *Placer Dome*, and *Imperial Oil*) indicate that the Court is prepared to slowly move away from the

---

[33]*Ibid*, para. 34.

[34]*Canada Trustco Mortgage Co. v. R. (2005), [2005] 5 C.T.C. 215, (sub nom. Canada Trustco Mortgage Co. v. Canada)*, 2005 D.T.C. 5523 (Eng.), (sub nom. *Hypothèques Trustco Canada v. Canada)* 2005 D.T.C. 5547 (Fr.) (S.C.C.), para. 10 and 11.

[35]*Mathew v. R.*, [2005] 2 S.C.R. 643.

[36]*Placer Dome Canada Ltd. v. Ontario (Minister of Finance)*, 2006 D.T.C. 6532 (Eng.), [2006] 1 S.C.R. 715, 2006 SCC 20 (S.C.C.), para. 111.

[37]*Imperial Oil Ltd. v. R.* (2006), 2006 SCC 46, [2007] 1 C.T.C. 41 (S.C.C.) and (2006), (sub nom. *Imperial Oil Ltd. v. Canada)* 2006 D.T.C. 6639 (Eng.), 2006 D.T.C. 6660 (Fr.) (S.C.C.). For a discussion of this case, see heading 19.4(c), The *Imperial Oil* (2006) case, below.

plain meaning approach towards a more contextualized and purposive approach. In each of these cases, the Court emphasized the importance of textual interpretation following the citation of the modern rule. For example, the Court stated in *Canada Trustco* that:[38]

> There is no doubt today that all statutes, including the *Income Tax Act*, must be interpreted in a textual, contextual and purposive way. However, the particularity and detail of many tax provisions have often led to an emphasis on textual interpretation. Where Parliament has specified precisely what conditions must be satisfied to achieve a particular result, it is reasonable to assume that Parliament intended that taxpayers would rely on such provisions to achieve the result they prescribe.

The Court also qualified the modern rule with the principle of certainty, predictability and fairness and the respect for the right of taxpayers to legitimate tax minimization. Nonetheless, the Court has taken the first step in moving beyond pure textual (or plain meaning) interpretation.

(ii) — Potential relevance of economic substance of transactions

The shift towards a contextualized purposive interpretation of tax provisions revives the debate about the relevance of "economic substance" or "commercial reality." In fact, the Court recognizes in *Canada Trustco* that the economic substance of the transaction "may be relevant at various stages of the [GAAR] analysis."[39] It refers to the statement by the Department of Finance "that the provisions of the Act are intended to apply to transactions with real economic substance."[40] The Court has not provided much guidance on the scope of "economic substance" and the circumstances in which economic substance prevails. The relevance of this doctrine in the anti-avoidance context is discussed further in Chapter 20.

(iii) — The Placer Dome (2006) case

This is an excellent case in illuminating the relevance of legislative context and purpose in interpreting tax statutes. The taxpayer in this case was engaged in the international exploration, production and sale of gold. In 1995 and 1996, the taxpayer operated mines in Ontario and was subject to Ontario's *Mining Tax Act*. It realized over $17 million in profits from hedging transactions in those two years, but these transactions did not involve delivery of output of mine in Ontario. The issue in this case was whether the hedging profits were taxable under the *Mining Tax Act*.

For the purpose of the *Mining Tax Act*, profits are calculated by subtracting allowable deductions from *proceeds*. The word "proceeds" is defined to include "all consideration received or receivable from *hedging* and future sales or forward sales of

---

[38] Note 34 above, para. 11.

[39] *Ibid*, para. 76.

[40] Canada, Department of Finance. *Explanatory Notes to Legislation Relating to Income Tax*. Ottawa: Queen's Printer, 1988, at 464-5. The Supreme Court of Canada quoted the above paragraph in *Canada Trustco* (paras. 48-49).

the output of the mine [in Ontario]." "Hedging" is defined to mean "the fixing of a price for output of a mine before delivery by means of a forward sale or a futures contract on a recognized commodity exchange," "the purchase or sale forward of a foreign currency related directly to the proceeds of the output of a mine," and "does not include speculative currency hedging."

The taxpayer took a narrow interpretation of "hedging" to mean "setting the price that will be paid upon delivery of the output of a mine." The Minister took a broader interpretation of "hedging" to encompass contracts which have as their subject matter something other than the output of a mine, but which can nevertheless be said to fix the price for the output of a mine. The broad interpretation does not require the delivery of output of a mine in Ontario.

LeBel J., writing for a unanimous Court, upheld the Minister's broad interpretation. He recognized that taxpayers are entitled to rely on the clear meaning of taxation provisions in structuring their affairs. In this case, though, because the meaning of the word "hedging" is ambiguous in the context of the *Mining Tax Act*, legislative context and purpose become relevant in determining the meaning.

LeBel J. started with the textual or ordinary meaning of "hedging" by referring to the Generally Accepted Accounting Principles (GAAP) and Canadian jurisprudence and found that hedging transactions are seldom settled by the physical delivery of goods. Instead, they are more commonly settled by either cash or an offsetting contract. For GAAP purposes, the method of settlement is irrelevant to the characterization of a transaction as a "hedge."[41] Furthermore, financial transactions that are not settled by physical delivery of the output of an Ontario mine may "fix the price" for that output and act as a hedge.

The statutory context was then considered to shed light on the interpretation of the term "hedging." LeBel J. considered the statutory definition of the term, its relationship with the definition of "proceeds," and the legislative history of the statutory definition of "hedging." He concluded that the taxpayer's narrow interpretation was not consistent with the context of the statutory definitions of "proceeds" and "hedging." He stated:[42]

> It is significant that futures contracts are seldom settled by physical delivery. Similarly, a sale or purchase forward of foreign currency is a separate transaction from the sale of an underlying commodity and would not itself be settled by physical delivery of the commodity. In short, the other elements in the statutory definition of "hedging" are consistent with the [Minister's] broader interpretation.

---

[41]Under GAAP, a transaction is a "hedge" where a party has assets or liabilities exposed to a particular financial risk and that risk is mitigated by the transaction. For example, to mitigate the risk of fluctuating prices, a party may agree to sell a good in the future at a fixed price (a party looking to buy a good may enter into that transaction for the same reason). There are two basic categories of transactions — forward contracts and options. A forward contract obligates both parties to complete the transaction, whereas an option gives one party the right to complete the transaction.

[42]Note 36, above, para. 47.

If the narrower interpretation was accepted, the Court reasoned, all consideration from hedging would fall into the second and third components ("future sales and forward sales of the output of the mine") of the term "proceeds", leaving the first component ("all consideration from hedging") unnecessary. According to LeBel J., "[to] the extent that it is possible to do so, courts should avoid adopting interpretations that render any portion of a statute meaningless or redundant."[43]

In spite of the illumination by LeBel in this case and *Imperial Oil* (discussed below), there are many questions remain about the relevance of context and purpose in interpreting provisions of the Act. If "context" and "purpose" play second fiddle to the "textual" meaning, is "textual, contextual and purposive" interpretation much different from "textual" or "plain meaning" interpretation? Under what circumstances should the courts examine the context and purpose of the particular provisions or the Act as a whole? What constitutes "context"? Where can the courts find legislative purpose or intent? We will turn to these questions in the next few sections.

19.3 — Statutory text

The fundamental task in statutory interpretation is to establish the meaning of words used by Parliament in the statute. Therefore, statutory interpretation begins with the words of the Act. This is the case under all of the above-discussed doctrines of statutory interpretation.

Words often have multiple meanings, both in their everyday usage and legal usage. Some words in the Act are defined by Parliament, some are "terms of art", and majority of words are common words. There are some interpretation conventions about which meaning takes precedence.

(a) — Statutory definitions

Subsection 248(1) and other sections of the Act define the meaning of certain words and phrases. Statutory meaning takes precedence over the ordinary meaning. In fact, in interpreting the Act, one should always refer first to the statutory definitions.

There are three types of statutory definitions in the Act: exhaustive, inclusive, and deemed. The Act uses the word "means" or "is" to indicate an exhaustive definition. For example, an "individual" "means a person other than a corporation." [44] A "taxation year" for individuals "is . . . a calendar year."[45] An exhaustive definition is a complete definition and is the most authoritative.

The Act uses the word "includes" to indicate an inclusive definition. For example, a person is defined under subsection 248(1) to include "any corporation." An inclu-

[43] *Ibid*., para. 45.

[44] S. 248(1).

[45] S. 249(1).

sive definition is not complete; it simply specifies a specific meaning to be added to the ordinary meaning of the defined word or phrase. Thus, the ordinary meaning is implicitly included. Because individuals are generally understood to be persons, they are implicitly included in the definition of "persons" so that both individuals and corporations are taxed as "persons" under the Act.

The Act uses the phrase "shall be deemed" in defining some concepts. For example, under paragraph 70(5)(a), a taxpayer shall be deemed to have disposed of each of his or her capital property and received proceeds of disposition therefore equal to the fair market value of the property immediately before his or her death. The deemed meaning is often artificial or even counterintuitive, but it is useful in achieving a particular legislative purpose. The deemed disposition rule under paragraph 70(5)(a) ensures that capital gains (or losses) are realized and taxed in the year of death.

(b) — Ordinary, technical, or legal meaning

The ordinary meaning of words is their ordinary, everyday meaning or idea conveyed by the word. It is often the meaning found in dictionaries. In the absence of statutory definitions or overriding legal meanings, it makes sense to interpret words used in the Act according to their ordinary meaning. "Most taxpayers are not (and likely have no desire to be) learned in the law."[46] In assessing their income tax liability, it is the everyday meaning of words to which these taxpayers refer. Drafters of the statute can be presumed to have adopted such meaning in the statute.

However, where a word has a technical or legal meaning, the technical or legal meaning should be preferred to the ordinary and grammatical meaning, especially where such an interpretation is justified by the statutory context in which the word appears. In *Will-Kare Paving & Contracting Ltd. v. R.* (2000),[47] the issue was whether the words "goods for sale," when used for purposes of two tax incentives (the investment tax credit and accelerated capital cost allowance), have their ordinary meaning or their legal meaning. The Court held that although the word "sale" has an everyday meaning, its settled legal meaning as established under private commercial law prevails. The legal meaning was more consistent with the purpose of the two tax incentive provisions.

(c) — Ambiguous meaning

When cases go to court, they often involve statutory provisions whose meaning is open to different interpretations. It does not matter whether the impugned term is statutorily defined (such as "hedging" in *Placer Dome*) or undefined (such as "cost" in the Act in *Canada Trustco*).

---

[46] *Will-Kare Paving & Contracting Ltd. v. R.*, 2000 S.C.C. 36, [2000] 3 C.T.C. 463, 2000 D.T.C. 6467 (Eng.), 2000 D.T.C. 6479 (Fr.) (S.C.C.), para. 39, per Binnie J. (dissenting).
[47] *Ibid.*

Since there is no metric to measure ambiguity, it is really up to the judge to decide how ambiguous a statute must be to be "ambiguous." In *Placer Dome*, two justices of the Ontario Court of Appeal found the meaning of "hedging" in the Ontario *Mining Tax Act* to be "clear, unambiguous and precise," while the Supreme Court disagreed.

19.4 — Context

(a) — Statutory context

Words must be interpreted within the context in which they are used. This is particularly important when a word has more than one meaning, or the meaning is ambiguous. The context includes the particular section of the Act in which the word is used (immediate context), other related sections of the Act and the Act as a whole. The presumption underlying contextual analysis is that the provisions of the Act work together towards a common purpose and are internally coherent, consistent and logical.[48]

Very often, the immediate context is sufficient to establish the ordinary meaning. For example, the meaning of the phrase "other benefits of any kind whatever" in paragraph 6(1)(a) of the Act is apparently broad, but its scope is limited by its immediate context to mean economic benefits received in respect of employment. In other cases, the broader context as established by the scheme of the Act must be examined.[49]

(b) — Legislative scheme

The Act has a well-structured scheme that addresses five basic questions: (1) who is liable to tax; (2) what is income and whose income is it? (3) when is tax payable? (4) how much is payable by a taxpayer; and (5) how is the tax collected. Presumably, each provision of the Act has a purpose. For example, the purpose might be to accurately measure economic income, to provide a subsidy to taxpayers for engaging in a particular activity in a specific way, or to exclude or defer certain items from income for a variety of reasons.

Depending on the policy objective to be met, a provision of the Act can be a "technical" provision that answers the five questions above, a "tax expenditure" provision that provides relief to taxpayers out of social or economical concerns, or an "anti-avoidance" provision that ensures the integrity of the technical provisions and the tax expenditure provisions. In interpreting the Act, it is important to be aware of the type of the provision to be interpreted and to apply the proper policy analysis when necessary.

---

[48]See *Sullivan and Driedger on the Construction of Statutes*, (4th ed), 261 to 262.

[49]See ch. 5, Income from Employment, above.

The scheme of the Act is important in establishing the purpose or intent of the provisions of the Act.[50] In *Imperial Oil*, LeBel J. gave significant weight to legislative scheme in interpreting paragraph 20(1)(f) of the Act.[51]

(c) — The *Imperial Oil* (2006) case

(i) — Text of paragraph 20(1)(f)

The issue in *Imperial Oil*[52] was whether pararagraph 20(1)(f) should be given a "narrow" interpretation to allow a deduction for only "original issue discount" or a "broad" interpretation to permit a deduction for "original issue discount that is computed in a manner to include foreign exchange losses." Before discussing the case per se, it is perhaps helpful to provide an overview of this provision.

The text of paragraph 20(1)(f) is highly technical. It provides that when computing income from business, a deduction is allowed where:

> (f) an amount paid in the year in satisfaction of the principal amount of any bond, debenture, . . . issued by the taxpayer . . . on which interest was stipulated to be payable, to the extent that the amount so paid does not exceed,
>
> (i) in any case where the obligation was issued for an amount not less than 97% of its principal amount, and the yield from the obligation . . . does not exceed 4/3 of the interest stipulated to be payable on the obligation, . . . the amount by which the lesser of the principal amount of the obligation and all amounts paid in the year or in any preceding year in satisfaction of its principal amount exceeds the amount for which the obligation was issued, and
>
> (ii) in any other case, ¾ of the lesser of the amount so paid and the amount by which the lesser of the principal amount of the obligation and all amounts paid in the year or in any proceeding taxation year in satisfaction of its principal amount exceeds the amount for which the obligation was issued.

The essence of this provision can be expressed in a formula that looks like the following: X = [lesser of A or B] - [C]

where

X is the amount of the deduction (often referred to as "discount");

A is the principal amount of the obligation;

B is all amounts paid in the year or in any preceding year in satisfaction of the principal amount; and

C is the amount for which the obligation was issued.

---

[50]See *Canada Trustco*, note 34, above, para. 10. "The relative effects of ordinary meaning, context and purpose on the interpretive process may vary, but in all cases the court must seek to read the provisions of an Act as a harmonious whole."

[51]Note 37, above, para. 17.

[52]See also heading 8.10(c), "Foreign Exchange Losses,"above, for a brief discussion of the issues.

If all amounts are in Canadian dollars, the calculation is straightforward. For example, if A is $1,000, B is $1,000, C is $960, then X is $40. Subparagraph 20(1)(f)(i) permits a deduction of a "shallow" discount (up to 3% of the principal amount), i.e., $30. The remaining $10 is a "deep" discount, 75% of which (i.e. $7.5) is deductible under subparagraph 20(1)(f)(ii), and the remaining $2.5 is a capital loss under subsection 39(2).

If the debt is issued in a foreign currency, then all amounts must be converted into Canadian dollars. In applying paragraph 20(1)(f), the issue is whether the amount denominated in foreign currency is converted at the exchange rate on the date of issue or the date of redemption. When the foreign currency appreciates against the Canadian dollar, the exchange rate on those two dates can be very different. Assuming the exchange rate on the date of issue is US$1,000 = C$1,100, but US$1,000 = C$1,150 on the date of redemption, it takes C$50 extra to pay off US$1,000 debt. Is this additional C$50 part of "discount"? That was the question in *Imperial Oil* case.[53]

(ii) — Facts of the case

In 1989, Imperial Oil issued 30-year debentures with a face amount of US$300 million at a discount. In 1999, it redeemed a portion of those debentures at a loss (consisted of original issue discount as well as foreign exchange losses) because the United States dollar had appreciated against the Canadian dollar from 1989 to 1999. Imperial Oil sought to deduct the entire loss under paragraph 20(1)(f)(i) of the Act. In the alternative, it took the position that it was entitled to deduct 75% of the "loss" under paragraph 20(1)(f)(ii) and that the remaining 25% as a capital loss under subsection 39(2). The Minister denied the deduction under paragraph 20(1)(f), considering the entire loss as predominantly a capital loss under subsection 39(2), 50% of which is deductible against taxable capital gains.

The Supreme Court was split four to three. LeBel J. wrote the majority decision. Binnie J. authored the dissenting judgment. Both the majority and the dissent purportedly followed the approach of textual, contextual and purposive interpretation. The majority's reasoning is contextualized, reflecting the internal logic of the scheme of the Act, whereas the dissenting decision seems more "pragmatic" and "result oriented", relying on materials extrinsic to the Act to establish "legislative purpose."

(iii) — Majority decision

Starting with the text of paragraph 20(1)(f), LeBel J. noted that the word "discount" was absent and there was no express mention of foreign currency exchanges in the text of paragraph 20(1)(f). However, the opening words of subparagraph 20(1)(f)(i) (or the formula A or B minus C) set out what is commonly accepted as the definition of a discount. The text of this provision thus suggested that the "*primary referent* of s. 20(1)(f) is something other than foreign exchange losses, namely, pay-

[53]This case involved two corporate taxpayers — Imperial Oil and Inco.

ments in the nature of discounts."[54] He then considered whether the phrase "in any other case" in subparagraph 20(1)(f)(ii) referred to "any case in which the obligation was issued for an amount less than 97 percent" (which is consistent with the wording in subparagraph (i)) or to "any case in which the cost of repaying the principal amount exceeds the amount for which the debt was issued"? The taxpayers argued the latter. LeBel J. opined that the "better reading of the opening words of s. 20(1)(f)(ii) is the one that preserves a higher degree of parallelism of expression (i.e., any case in which the obligation was issued for an amount less than 97%)."[55] He concluded that paragraph 20(1)(f) addressed the deductibility of original issue discounts.

LeBel J. also considered the definition of "principal amount" in subsection 248(1), which contemplates the possibility that the principal amount can be the amount payable in Canadian currency at the time of issue or the time of redemption. If it is the latter, foreign exchange losses would be included. To resolve this ambiguity, LeBel J. found it necessary to determine whether Parliament intended foreign exchange losses to be covered by paragraph 20(1)(f) in the same way as discounts.

In LeBel's view, paragraph 20(1)(f) was never intended to apply to foreign exchange losses. He gave several reasons for his conclusion. First, the scheme of subsection 20(1) indicates that only expenses arising directly out of the borrower-lender relationship are deductible because other costs enumerated in pargraph 20 are intrinsic costs of borrowing, such as interest payments and premiums. Since a foreign exchange loss is a cost of borrowing only where the thing borrowed is *foreign currency*, it is not an intrinsic cost of borrowing, and thus not deductible.

Second, an interpretation of paragraph 20(1)(f) that allows the deduction of foreign exchange losses means that this section "would operate quite differently in relation to obligations denominated in foreign currency than it does in relation to obligations denominated in Canadian dollars." In the context of foreign currency obligations, the deduction would reflect the appreciation or depreciation of the principal amount over time, whereas in the context of Canadian dollar obligations, the deduction would reflect a point-in-time expense. In the context of foreign currency obligations, the paragraph 20(1)(f) deduction would accordingly be available even where there was no original issue discount. This approach also has the effect of altering the distinction between the two branches of paragraph 20(1)(f). Therefore, Parliament could not have intended such a differential tax treatment as it would create incentives to structure obligations in a particular way.

Third, the broader context of the Act, such as subsection 39(2), sheds light on legislative intent. LeBel J. appreciated the fact that the Act has separate schemes for capital gains (and losses) and income gains (and losses):

> Despite its undeniable — and growing — complexity, the current federal *ITA* displays some fundamental structural characteristics. One of these characteristics,

---

[54]Note 37, para. 62.

[55]*Ibid.*, para. 64.

which is provided for in s. 3, is the distinction between income and capital. Capital gains are only partially brought into income for taxation purposes.[56]

Because subsection 20(1) is part of the income regime, allowing deductions against income, only capital amounts that are specified under subsection 20(1) (such as interest and capital cost allowance) are deductible. Permitting a deduction for foreign exchange losses, which are on capital account, in the absence of expressed authorization under subsection 20(1), would lead to "conflicts with the general treatment of capital gains and losses in the *ITA*." LeBel J. correctly stated that the taxpayer's argument "indicates a failure to properly appreciate the role of s. 39", which is a statement of Parliament's intent to treat foreign exchange losses as capital losses."

Fourth, the broad statement that "Parliament encourages companies to raise capital by allowing them to deduct virtually all costs of borrowing under the provisions of s.20(1)"[57] was not persuasive enough. Paragraph 18(1)(b), for example, provides that payments on account of capital may not be deducted from business income unless the deduction thereof is expressly permitted. Therefore, not all costs of borrowing are deductible under paragraph 20(1)(f). Otherwise, this provision would be turned into a broad provision allowing for the deductibility of a wide range of costs attendant upon financing in foreign currency, in the absence of any mention of such costs in the text of the Act, and despite the fact that such costs are usually regarded as being on capital account.[58]

(iv) — Dissenting decision

Binnie J. described the provisions of the Act as the "rules of engagement" for the "battlefield on which over 21 million Canadian taxpayers engage with the Minister of National Revenue."[59] This characterization of the tax system as a "battlefield" provides an interesting context for understanding his decision.

Technically, Binnie J. put a great deal of weight on the definition of "principal amount" in subsection 248(1) and noted that this expression "principal amount" was used nine times in the course of paragraph 20(1)(f). Subsection 248(1) defines "principal amount" to mean the amount that "is the maximum amount or maximum total amount, as the case may be, payable on account of the obligation by the issuer." In the context of debt issued in a foreign currency, since Canadian dollars must be used for the purposes of the Act, the maximum amount payable can only be determined on the date of redemption, not the date of the issuance of the debt. Thus, the relevant exchange rate is the rate prevailing at the date of redemption. Therefore, exchange losses are included in the calculation of the deduction under paragraph 20(1)(f).

---

[56] *Ibid.*, para. 17.

[57] *Ibid.*, para. 65.

[58] *Ibid.*, para. 67.

[59] *Ibid.*, para. 73.

Binnie J. did not examine the meaning of other words used in paragraph 20(1)(f). He did not find the legislative scheme, including section 39, to be of any help to the interpretation of paragraph 20(1)(f). He stated:

> It all comes back to the simple proposition that in Canadian tax terms foreign currency is a commodity, and its fluctuations will inevitably carry costs (or benefits). Had the Canadian dollar appreciated against the U.S. dollar in the relevant period of time, for instance, the taxpayers would have *lost* the original issue discount to which they might otherwise have been entitled. What the taxing authority loses on the swings it will make up on the roundabouts. At the end of the day it will have its just desserts.[60]

This statement is problematic. Foreign exchange gains and losses are generally on capital account to *Imperial Oil* and other taxpayers who are not currency traders. As such, capital expenditures are not deductible in the absence of a specific provision under section 20. Even if paragraph 20(1)(f) was interpreted to allow a deduction for foreign exchange losses, there is no equivalent provision to tax foreign exchange gains as income. Therefore, foreign exchange gains are not the "just desserts" to offset the deduction for foreign exchange losses. While taxpayers will argue for a full deduction for the loss under paragraph 20(1)(f), they will surely not argue for full inclusion of the gain. Instead, foreign exchange gains will be treated on capital account, partially taxable. The differential treatment of full deduction for the loss and partial inclusion for the gain can be appreciated only when one appreciates the scheme of the Act.

According to Binnie J. "finding unexpressed legislative intentions under the guise of purposive interpretation runs the risk of upsetting the balance Parliament has attempted to strike in the Act." On the other hand, he relied on the "unexpressed" legislative purpose to resolve the textual ambiguity. Since "Parliament encourages companies to raise capital by allowing them to deduct virtually all costs of borrowing under the provisions of s. 20(1)", allowing the deduction of foreign exchange losses advance such purpose. Given the modest size of the Canadian capital market, "it would be counterproductive in a global economy to discourage foreign borrowings."[61]

The way that Binnie J. pit "legislative intent" against "legislative purpose" is unfortunate. Many provisions in the Act originate from the 1917 Act or subsequent amendments. Given the change in the complexity of business today and the sophistication of tax advisors, it is likely that these provisions are used in ways that Parliament never intended. Perhaps out of this concern, LeBel J. did not see legislative intent and purpose to be mutually exclusive.

---

[60] *Ibid.*, para. 104.

[61] *Ibid.*, para. 103.

19.5 — Legislative purpose and intent

(a) — Growing relevance

The legislative purpose or intent is an important element of the "textual, contextual and purposive" interpretation. Ideally, courts interpret the meaning of a provision to best reflect its underlying purpose and the intention of Parliament.[62] In practice, however, it may be difficult to discern statutory purpose and/or legislative intent by simply reading the Act. As such, the extent that legislative purpose or intent affects the outcome of statutory interpretation largely depends on the willingness of the courts to go beyond the "plain meaning" of the text of a specific provision.

Since the Act rarely expressly state the purpose or intent of a particular provision, such intent or purpose must be discerned from materials intrinsic to the Act (e.g. the text of the particular provision and scheme of the Act), materials extrinsic to the Act (such as legislative history and other statutes) or resorting to cannons of statutory interpretation (such as presumptions).

(b) — Purpose or Intent

The terms "purpose" and "intent" were used interchangeably in *Canada Trustco*[63] and *Mathew*. In *Imperial Oil*, however, the distinction between "purpose" and "intention" is apparently important. The majority referred to the intention of Parliament in enacting paragraph 20(1)(f), whereas Binnie J. (writing for a three-justice minority) focused on the "purpose" of subsection 20(1) in general. LeBel J. framed the question as follows:[64]

> In the end, the question is still whether s. 20 (1)(f) was intended by Parliament to apply to the appreciation or depreciation of the obligation, in which case the calculation would be analogous to the computation of a capital gain, or whether it was intended to apply to an income expense or, more accurately, a point-in-time expense that would, but for that section, be a payment on account of capital.

Binnie, J. was uncomfortable with the reliance on unexpressed Parliament's intention:[65]

> My colleague concludes that s. 20(1)(f) is designed "to address a specific class of financing costs arising out of the issuance of debt instruments at a discount" (para. 67). Such a narrow focus, as stated earlier, is nowhere expressed in the Act, although it would have been a simple thing to say so if that was Parliament's intent.

Given that the purpose of subsection 20(1) was to encourage "companies to raise capital by allowing them to deduct virtually all costs of borrowing," Binnie J. opined that interpreting paragraph 20(1)(f) more broadly "advance[s] Parliament's

---

[62] *Ibid.*

[63] Note 34, above, para. 74.

[64] Note 37, above, para. 56.

[65] *Ibid.*, para. 102.

purpose whereas the conclusion reached by my colleague would act as a deterrent."[66]

The Court provides no principled basis for determining "purpose" or "intent." As can be seen from above, the term "intent" is often used to refer to the meaning that Parliament would have given to a specific provision in a given fact situation whereas the term "purpose" is broader and more dynamic by allowing the court to address issues that were not totally anticipated by the drafters. It is debatable whether Parliament's actual intention can be clearly established, especially in cases where there are new problems that were unanticipated by the drafters of the statute. Nonetheless, the textual, contextual and purposive principle requires the textual interpretation be consistent with the intention of Parliament.

In some cases, there maybe more than one legislative intent or purpose. For example, the Court in *Notre Dame* (1994)[67] found that the purpose of the statute as a whole was to raise revenue, but it also "serves other purposes and functions as a tool of economic and social policy." In this particular case, the taxing statute also pursued "a secondary policy of exempting social works."[68] This secondary policy goal was advanced by giving a broader interpretation of the exemption provision at issue.

(c) — Inferences from text of the statute

Legislative intent or purpose can be inferred from the text of the provisions, the absence of specific rules and legislative context. The text and the scheme of the Act sometimes indicate the purpose of a provision, at least at a general level. For example, paragraph 6(1)(a) uses extremely broad language to convey the intention of taxing various forms of compensation for employment.[69]

In *Imperial Oil*, LeBel J. referred to the text of paragraph 20(1)(f) and the scheme of the Act before reaching his conclusion that paragraph 20(1)(f) was not intended to allow the taxpayer to deduct foreign exchange losses associated with a debt issued in a foreign currency. Legislative context was also helpful in establishing the

---

[66] *Ibid.*, para. 103.

[67] Note 14, above. In this case, the question arose whether an old age home was entitled to a full exemption from Quebec's municipal property tax. There was no doubt that 11 per cent of the home, which was a shelter section in which the residents received special care, qualified for the exemption. The question was whether the remaining 89 per cent of the home, which consisted of apartments, also qualified for the exemption. Since the language of the exemption did not provide a clear answer, the Supreme Court of Canada had to settle the question by reference to the purpose of the provision.

[68] *Ibid.*, 250, 5022.

[69] The Supreme Court held that the purpose of paragraph 20(1)(c)(i) is "to encourage the accumulation of capital which would produce taxable income" (*Bronfman Trust v. R*, note 21, above). Subsequent decisions endorsed this conclusion: *Shell Canada* (1999), *Ludco* (2001), *Gifford v. R.*, 2004 SCC 15, [2004] 2 C.T.C. 1, 2004 D.T.C. 6120 (Eng.), 2004 D.T.C. 6128 (Fr.) (S.C.C.) and *Imperial Oil* (2006).

purpose or legislative intent of the impugned provision in *Mathew*.[70] The Supreme Court opined that "the legislative context surrounding s.18(13) and s.96 of the *Income Tax Act*, while perhaps not in itself conclusive, suggests that Parliament would not likely have intended arm's length parties to be able to buy losses generated by s. 18(13) transfers."[71]

Inferences about statutory purpose may be made from the absence of specific provisions. In *Canada Trustco*, for example, the Court found that the purpose of the CCA provisions "emerges clearly from the scheme of the CCA provisions within the Act as a whole"[72] which did not limit CCA deductions to amounts bearing real financial risk or "economic cost." The Court stated:[73]

> The applicable CCA provisions of the Act do not refer to economic risk. They refer only to "cost". Where Parliament wanted to introduce economic risk into the meaning of cost related to CCA provisions, it did so expressly, as, for instance, in s. 13(7.1) and (7.2) of the Act, which makes adjustments to the cost of depreciable property when a taxpayer receives government assistance.

Similarly, in *65302 British Columbia Ltd.* the Court found the lack of a specific provision prohibiting the deduction of fines and penalties to be an indication of Parliament's intent to permit their deduction.[74]

(d) — Relevance of extrinsic materials

Extrinsic materials sometimes explain the object and purpose of a provision of the Act. These are viewed as "interpretive aids" and can only be used with caution. In *Imperial Oil*, LeBel J. expressed this point by saying that he "would be loath to rely on one" and "will return to the text of the statute itself" for inferring legislative purpose.[75] These extrinsic materials include:

- Technical Notes issued by the Department of Finance to explain the introduction of or amendments to a provision (referred to in *Canada Trustco*, *Mathew*, and *Imperial Oil*);
- The interpretive practice adopted by the Minister. In *Placer Dome*, LeBel J. stated that "It is well established that in resolving doubt about the meaning of a tax provision, the administrative practice and interpretation adopted by the

---

[70] *Mathew*, note 35, para. 48.

[71] *Ibid.*, para. 50.

[72] *Ibid.*, para. 74.

[73] *Ibid.*, above, para. 75.

[74] *65302 British Columbia Ltd v. R.*, [2000] 1 C.T.C. 57, 99 D.T.C. 5799 (Eng.), 99 D.T.C. 5814 (Fr.) (S.C.C.), para. 63. He also regarded the design of the tax collection system to be based on self-assessment was evidence of Parliament's intention to allow the deduction of all income-earning expenses, including fines and penalties (para. 57).

[75] Note 37, para. 57.

Minister, while not determinative, are important factors to be weighed."[76] When the administrative practice changed, the new practice was considered as reflective of the ambiguity that inheres in the statute itself and deserve more weight.[77] In *Imperial Oil*, on the other hand, LeBel J. found the Minister's practice (i.e., allowing certain foreign exchange losses to be deducted as expenses) "troubling" and did not give it much weight.[78]

- The historical context of a statutory provision is often very telling about the purpose of the provision. Clear examples are some recent provisions enacted to override a specific court decision, such as section 245 (in reaction to *Stubart*), section 20.3 (in reaction to *Shell Canada*), section 67.6 (in reaction to *65302 British Columbia Ltd.*), section 56.4 (in reaction to *Fortino* and *Manrell*) and proposed section 3.1 (in reaction to *Ludco*, *Stewart*[79] and *Walls*[80]).
- Other statutes may define the meaning of a term that may be relevant to the interpretation of the Act. In *Will-Kare* the meaning of "sale" under the Sale of Goods Act, 1893"[81] was adopted for the purposes of the Act.
- Academic texts sometimes help the courts identify legislative purpose. In each of its recent decisions, the Supreme Court cited some texts, including earlier editions of this book.
- Case law in other countries. As a common-law jurisdiction, Canadian courts draw inferences from the case law of other common-law jurisdictions, particularly the United Kingdom, United States and Australia. One of the most important common law principles in Canadian tax law — The *Duke of Westminster* principle — is derived from a British decision.

---

[76] *Ibid.*, para. 10. LeBel J. cited the following cases as precedence *Harel v. Quebec (Deputy Minister of Revenue)* (1977), [1978] 1 S.C.R. 851, [1977] C.T.C. 441, 77 D.T.C. 5438 (S.C.C.), at p. 859 [S.C.R.], per de Grandpré J.; *Will-Kare Paving & Contracting Ltd. v. R.*, note 46, above, para. 66, per Binnie J. (dissenting, but not on this point).

[77] *Ibid.*, above, para. 40.

[78] Note 37, above, para 59.

[79] *Stewart v. R.*, 2002 SCC 46, 2002 D.T.C. 6969 (Eng.), 2002 D.T.C. 6983 (Fr.), [2002] 3 C.T.C. 439 (S.C.C.), discussed under heading 6.2 (b), "Business" or "property" defined", above.

[80] *Walls v. R.*, [2002] 2 S.C.R. 684, [2002] 3 C.T.C. 421, *(*sub nom. *R. v. Walls)* 2002 D.T.C. 6960 (Eng.), *(*sub nom. *R. v. Walls)* 2002 D.T.C. 6964 (Fr.) (S.C.C.), discussed under heading 6.2 (b), ""Business" or "property" defined", above.

[81] *Will-Kare*, note 46, above, para. 59.

(e) — Presumptions

In certain cases, it may be necessary to impute legislative intent when the "actual" intention is difficult to discover. The Supreme Court has relied on a number of canons of statutory construction or presumptions. These include:

- The presumption against a Parliamentary intention to encourage violations of other laws. In *65302 British Columbia Ltd.*, Bastarache J, writing for the dissent, was persuaded by the presumption and Iacubocci J. was not, but both found it relevant.[82]
- The presumption against tautology. LeBel J. stated in *Placer Dome*: "A court should avoid adopting an interpretation that renders any portion of a statute meaningless or redundant and, in this case, the presumption against tautology carries considerable weight."[83]
- The presumption in favour of the taxpayer in cases where application of the ordinary principles of interpretation does not resolve the issue. In *Placer Dome*, LeBel J. emphasized that this is a residual presumption only. "Any doubt about the meaning of a taxation statute must be reasonable, and no recourse to the presumption lies unless the usual rules of interpretation have been applied, to no avail, in an attempt to discern the meaning of the provision at issue."[84]

There may be more than one intention that can be inferred from the text of the Act, extrinsic materials and the above presumptions and, in the case of differing intentions, the Court must decide which intention is the overriding one. Thus far, the intention derived from the scheme of the Act tends to override others. In *65302 British Columbia Ltd.*, for example, five out of seven justices of the Supreme Court favoured Parliamentary intention to permit the deduction of fines and penalties based on the scheme of the Act over the presumption against Parliamentary intention to encourage violations of other laws.

19.6 — Navigating between text and purpose

When the Court restated the modern rule as the textual, contextual and purposive interpretation principle in *Canada Trustco*, it was unclear whether this principle applied merely to the interpretation of the GAAR or other provisions of the Act as well. In *Placer Dome* and *Imperial Oil*, the Court clarified that it was a general interpretation principle and all provisions of the Act should be interpreted contextually and purposively. It is a welcome shift from the court's previous interpretation stance that emphasized plain meaning of the text. However, unless appropriate

---

[82] *65032 British Columbia Ltd.*, note 74, above, paras. 9 to 13 (Bastarache J.) and paras. 52 and 68 (Iacobucci J.).

[83] *Placer Dome*, note 36, above; paras. 3 and 43 to 46.

[84] *Ibid.*, para. 24.

weight is accorded to "context" and "purpose", this principle may be reduced to the "textual" approach. Navigating from text to purpose poses significant challenges.

(a) — Special characteristics of tax statutes

One factor that is intrinsic and unique to the Act is its high-level technical detail, precision, and complexity. The Supreme Court stated in *Canada Trustco* and subsequent decisions, that the text of the Act has often been given "greater emphasis" in the interpretation "because of the degree of precision and detail characteristic of many tax provisions."[85] The Court further stated that clear, precise, and unequivocal words play a dominant role because taxpayers are entitled to certainty in planning their affairs.[86] LeBel J. states:[87]

> The interpretive approach is thus informed by the level of precision and clarity with which a taxing provision is drafted. Where such a provision admits of no ambiguity in its meaning or in its application to the facts, *it must simply be applied.* Reference to the purpose of the provision "cannot be used to create an unexpressed exception to clear language." . . . Where, as in this case, the provision admits of more than one reasonable interpretation, greater emphasis must be placed on the context, scheme and purpose of the Act. Thus, legislative purpose may not be used to supplant clear statutory language, but to arrive at the most plausible interpretation of an ambiguous statutory provision.

In the meantime, the Court also acknowledges that statutory context and purpose may reveal or resolve latent ambiguities of apparently clear statutory language.[88]

The fact of the matter is that the Act is an intimidating statute to interpret. Since its introduction in 1917, the Act has been amended constantly and grown to be a gigantic statute, occupying thousands of pages and weighing more than a kilogram. The statutory language has become more technical and detailed. Many provisions are drafted in a formulaic style. The following passage,[89] written over 60 years ago, succinctly describes the state of complexity of the Act today:

> In my own case the words of such an act as the Income Tax, for example, merely dance before my eyes in a meaningless procession: cross-reference to cross-reference, exception upon exception — couched in abstract terms that offer no handle to seize hold of — leave in my mind only a confused sense of some vitally important, but successfully concealed, purport, which it is my duty to extract, but which is within my power, if at all, only after the most inordinate expenditure of time. I know that these monsters are the result of fabulous industry and ingenuity, plugging up this hole and casting out that net, against all possible evasion; yet at times I cannot help recalling a saying of William James about certain passages of Hegel: that they were no doubt written with a passion of rationality; but that one cannot help wonder-

---

[85] *Ibid.*, para. 21.

[86] *Ibid.*.

[87] *Ibid.*, para. 22.

[88] *Canada Trustco*, note 34, above, para. 10.

[89] Learned Hand, "Thomas Walter Swan," (1947) 57 *Yale L.J.* 167, at 169.

> ing whether to the reader they have any significance save that the words are strung together with syntactical correctness.

The complexity of the statute attracts different reactions from reasonable and well-intentioned judicial minds:

> Legislation weighing more than a kilogram does not have much room in it for liberal, general interpretation, particularly when the road to the resolution of a specific issue is well-marked and the voyage is undertaken in accordance with a detailed map and a handy guidebook.[90]

> It is quite true that as the articulation of a statute increases, the room for interpretation must contract; but the meaning of a sentence may be more than that of the separate words, as a melody is more than the notes, and no degree of particularity can ever obviate recourse to the setting in which all appear, and which all collectively create.[91]

It is important to note that the traditional approach to statutory interpretation is in part responsible for the increasing complexity of the Act. Under strict interpretation or the plain meaning approach, taxpayers are entitled to benefit from any ambiguity in the legislation or unintentional glitches in the law that they (or their tax advisors) find by applying a literal reading of the law until the ambiguity or glitches are addressed through legislation. New provisions of the Act are drafted as detailed and air-tight as possible. The Act can only become inexorably longer and more complicated as Parliament must overturn decision after decision by statutory amendment. As the Act becomes more detailed and complex, it breeds more aggressive tax planning and leaves less room for "liberal" interpretation, causing yet more amendments. The cycle perpetuates itself.

It is also important to keep in mind the fact that despite its size and complexity, the Act is just like any other statutes. It has objectives and a legislative scheme. At a general level, the Act has a well-structured scheme designed to meet its various social and economic policy objectives. The provisions of the Act are organized to address three major issues: (1) the normative system of taxation, that is to determine who is taxable, what is taxable, when and how much is tax payable and how tax is paid (the "technical provisions"); (2) the tax expenditure system, that is to determine who is entitled to receive a tax relief and how much is the relief; and (3) anti-avoidance regime, that is to ensure the integrity of the technical provisions and the tax expenditure provisions. Each provision of the Act constitutes part of a coherent whole. As such, the common law presumption against tautology and the presumption of coherence and consistency make good sense in interpreting the Act as well as other statutes.

---

[90] *Ipsco Inc. v. R.*, [2002] 2 C.T.C. 2907, 2002 D.T.C. 1421 (T.C.C. [General Procedure]), para. 26. [D.T.C.].

[91] *Halvering v. Gregory*, 69 F.2d 809 (U.S. C.C.A., 1934), at 810-811.

(b) — Common law traditions

While income tax law is statutory law, its interpretation is a matter of common law. With the exception of those trained in the Quebec civil law system, judges generally possess the so-called "common-law mentality". A great common law judge is described as the person "who has the intelligence to discern the best rule of law for the case at hand and then the skill to perform the broken-field running through earlier cases that leaves him free to impose that rule."[92] To the mind-set of a common-law judge, the key questions are "what is the most desirable resolution of this case" and "how can any impediments to the achievement of that result be evaded?"[93] This mind-set is not appropriate in statutory interpretation. The judge must work with the text produced by Parliament, not common law broken-field running toward the end zone of good policy.[94] The precision and specificity of the language of the Act represent the starkest contrast to the traditional common-law mind-set. The frequent amendments to the Act to specifically overrule the common law do little to encourage judges to adjust their mind-set to work with the legislative purpose and intent.

This inherent challenge for common-law judges in working with the tax statute may explain some judicial interpretation practices. One is the judicial preference for getting the "right result" in a given case (which often means that the taxpayer gets the benefit of the doubt in case of any ambiguity in the text) over finding the purpose of the text or the intention of Parliament. For example, in determining whether strike pay is taxable in the *R. v. Fries* (1990), Sopinka J. wrote the shortest decision in the Supreme Court's recent history (72 words), stating:[95]

> We are not satisfied that the payments by way of strike pay in this case come within the definition of "income . . . from a source" within the meaning of section 3 of the *Income Tax Act*. In these circumstances the benefit of the doubt must go to the taxpayers.

The context and purpose of section 3 are not mentioned and the clear wording — "from a source inside or outside Canada, including, without restricting the generality of the foregoing, the taxpayer's income for the year from each office, employment, business and property" — was ignored.

A second judicial practice is to follow a precedent or common-law principle instead of giving a purposive interpretation of the statutory provision. For example, in *Tsiaprailis v. R.* (2005), the issue was whether a lump-sum settlement received by the taxpayer from her employer's insurer under a disability policy must be included in her income under paragraph 6(1)(f). Charron, J., writing for the majority, held

---

[92]Antonin Scalia, "Common-Law Courts in a Civil-Law System: The Role of United States Federal Courts in Interpreting the Constitution and Laws," in *A Matter of Interpretation* (Gutmann, ed., 1997), at 9.

[93]*Ibid.*, at 13.

[94]*Ibid.*

[95]*R. v. Fries*, [1990] 2 C.T.C. 439, 90 D.T.C. 6662 (S.C.C.).

that settlements were taxable and to conclude otherwise would "render the surrogatum principle meaningless."[96] The context and purpose of paragraph 6(1)(f) are not even mentioned.

The doctrine of precedent at common law poses a significant challenge to the movement towards a more purposive interpretation of the Act. With minor deviations, the courts have largely adopted a textual interpretation. There is a paucity of precedence on the contextual and purposive interpretation.

(c) — Divergent theories

In traditional common law, the judges make the law and interpret the law. In statutory law, it takes two branches of the government — the legislature and the courts — to make and interpret the law. In income tax law, the administrative agency (Canada Revenue Agency) also plays an important role in not only administering the law, but also interpreting it as its interpretation is one source of interpretive aids. The Act is perhaps the most pervasive federal statute on the books, and has become an important governmental tool for influencing many aspects of modern Canadian life. As such, it is not surprising that there are divergent views on the role of the courts in giving meaning to the text of the Act.

(i) — Role of judges

The textual, strict interpretation approach is closely associated with the restrictive theory of statutory interpretation and the doctrine of Parliamentary supremacy. Judges want no or minimal role in the making of tax law. McLachlin J. states in *Shell Canada*:[97]

> The Act is a complex statute through which Parliament seeks to balance a myriad of principles. This Court has consistently held that courts must therefore be cautious before finding within the clear provisions of the Act an unexpressed legislative intention. . . . Finding unexpressed legislative intentions under the guise of purposive interpretation runs the risk of upsetting the balance Parliament has attempted to strike in the Act.

Iacobucci J. makes a similar point in *65302 British Columbia Ltd.*:[98]

> The law of income tax is sufficiently complicated without unhelpful judicial incursions into the realm of lawmaking. As a matter of policy, and out of respect for the proper role of the legislature, it is trite to say that the promulgation of new rules of tax law must be left to Parliament.

This narrow view of the role of the courts is problematic. While easy cases do exist, for the most part the disputes that reach the courtroom involve ambiguous statutory

---

[96] *Tsiaprailis v. R.*, [2005] 2 C.T.C. 1, 2005 D.T.C. 5119 (Eng.), 2005 D.T.C. 5126 (Fr.) (S.C.C.), para. 16. [D.T.C.]. For a discussion of this case, see heading 4.7(a) The "surrogatum principle", above.

[97] Note 22, above, para. 43.

[98] Note 74 above, para. 62.

language. If judges simply interpret with the use of a dictionary or with reference to the ordinary plain meaning of the words, they can certainly resolve the particular dispute. However, it is highly questionable whether they have discharged the duty reposed on them. Chief Justice McLachlin writes about the changing role of the judges:[99]

> Resolving disputes is still the primary and most fundamental task of the judiciary. But for some time now, it has been recognized that the matter is not so simple. In the course of resolving disputes, common law judges interpreted and inevitably, incrementally, with the aid of the doctrine of precedent or stare decisis, changed the law. The common law thus came to recognize that while dispute resolution was the primary task of the judge, the judge played a secondary role of lawmaker, or at least, law-developer. In the latter part of the twentieth century, the lawmaking role of the judge has dramatically expanded. Judicial lawmaking is no longer always confined to small, incremental changes. Increasingly, it is invading the domain of social policy, once perceived as the exclusive right of Parliament and the legislatures.

The Chief Justice's view of a more active role for judges in general stands in contrast to her restrictive view of the judicial role in tax cases. Since the Act is arguably one of the most important instruments of social policy in Canada, a more purposive interpretation of the Act is more consistent with her vision of the role of judges.

(ii) — Legislative supremacy

The doctrine of legislative supremacy provides the conceptual basis for statutory interpretation as it means how much, if any, policymaking discretion is left for those interpreting and implementing the legislature's statutes. It supports both the strict, textual interpretation and the more liberal, purposive interpretation. The strict textual interpretation reflects the value of this doctrine: the legislature is supreme and it enacts laws into statutory text. Judges are the "honest agents" of the legislature and "carry out decisions they do not make."[100] Under such theory, judicial discretion to make law is suspect in statutory interpretation.

A more liberal and purposive interpretation of statutes also finds support in the legislative supremacy doctrine. It was argued that "purposive interpretation . . . better accords with the principle of legislative supremacy,"[101] "intelligent judicial co-operation" is important in a parliamentary democracy in the "fulfilment of the aims

---

[99]See "Remarks of the Right Honourable Beverley McLachlin, P.C.: The Role of Judges in Modern Society" May 5, 2001, published on http://www.scc-csc.gc.ca/aboutcourt/judges/speeches/role-of-judges_e.asp.

[100]See, for example, Easterbrook, *The Supreme Court, 1983 Term — Foreword: The Court and the Economic System*, 98 Harv. L. Rev. 4, 60 (1984); and Easterbrook, *The Role of Original Intent in Statutory Construction*, 11 *Harv. J.L. & Pub. Pol'y* 59 (1988) (arguing that honest agent will look only to statutory language in discharging her responsibilities).

[101]Willis, J. "Statute Interpretation in a Nutshell" (1938), 16 Can. Bar. Rev. 1, at 14.

and objects of parliament."[102] The Supreme Court of Canada recognizes this view in *Mathew*:[103]

> To resolve the dispute arising from the combined operation of s. 18(13) and s. 96 of the *Income Tax Act*, it is necessary to determine Parliament's intention in enacting these provisions by interpreting them purposively, in light of their context.

Chief Justice McLachlin acknowledges that judges play "a secondary role of lawmaker, or at least, law-developer.[104]

The cooperative relationship between Parliament and the courts is particularly important in certain areas of tax law where it is inherently difficult for Parliament to use precise language in the statute in order to achieve its legislative goals. As discussed in more detail in Chapter 20, taxpayers minimize tax by taking advantage of legislative gaps in the Act or by taking advantage of its provisions by structuring transactions that arguably come within the textual interpretation of its statutory language. Anti-avoidance rules are intended to prevent such tax avoidance and the Act has specific anti-avoidance rules for specific types of transactions as well as the GAAR, which is a general rule. The purpose of these rules is clear. If these anti-avoidance rules are interpreted literally, this would obviously defeat the clear intention of Parliament.

[102] J.A. Corry, "Administrative Law and the Interpretation of Statutes" (1936), 1 U.T.L.J. 286 at 289.

[103] Note 35, above, para. 40.

[104] McLachlin, note 99, above.

20
TAX AVOIDANCE

20.1 — Introduction

In the modern world, virtually everything a taxpayer does takes into account tax consequences. Tax planning leads to tax avoidance. Tax avoidance "is not a dirty word"[1] and it is not illegal. If left uncontrolled, however, aggressive tax planning amounts to "gaming" the tax system and offends fundamental tax policies. Drawing the line between legitimate tax planning and offensive tax avoidance is the key. In theory, the line should be drawn on the basis of whether the avoidance transaction violates Parliament's legislative intent or purpose. In practice, however, the line-drawing is often difficult because such legislative intent or purpose may be unclear.

Tax avoidance is one of the most difficult topics in income tax law. It involves a variety of complex issues, including statutory interpretation, the use of tax incentives in the *Income Tax Act* (the "Act"), the effectiveness of the general anti-avoidance rule (GAAR), the role of the judiciary, and the role of Parliament. This chapter discusses the types of tax avoidance transactions and the judicial and legislative responses to tax avoidance.

(a) — Tax evasion distinguished

Tax "avoidance" must be distinguished from tax "evasion". Evasion involves a deliberate breach of the Act, by, for example, failing to file a return, failing to report all taxable income, deducting non-existent expenses, or concealing or falsifying

[1] *Canada Trustco Mortgage Co. v. R.*, [2003] 4 C.T.C. 2009, 2003 D.T.C. 587, ¶57 [D.T.C.] (T.C.C. [General Procedure]); affirmed [2004] 2 C.T.C. 276, 2004 D.T.C. 6119 (F.C.A.); leave to appeal allowed (2004), 2004 CarswellNat 1925, 2004 CarswellNat 1926 (S.C.C.); affirmed [2005] 5 C.T.C. 215, (sub nom. *Canada Trustco Mortgage Co. v. Canada)* 2005 D.T.C. 5523 (Eng.), (sub nom. *Hypothèques Trustco Canada v. Canada)* 2005 D.T.C. 5547 (Fr.) (S.C.C.). This case is described under heading 20.4(f)(i), "*Canada Trustco*", below.

other relevant information. Evasion is illegal, and is subject to both civil and criminal penalties under the Act.[2] The process of audit, investigation, search, seizure and prosecution has been described in an earlier chapter.

Avoidance differs from evasion in that it is legal. It does not involve fraud, concealment or any other illegal measure. What it does involve is the ordering of one's affairs in such a way as to reduce the tax that would otherwise be payable. Avoidance presupposes that the taxpayer has a choice as to the ordering of his or her affairs, and the taxpayer chooses the course that would minimize tax liability. Where the course of tax-minimization is taken for predominantly personal or business reasons, with tax-saving only a subsidiary consideration, then the taxpayer's action can hardly be objected to; and, indeed, it may not be appropriate to describe it as "avoidance" at all. For example, a taxpayer who transfers a business to a family-owned corporation on a tax-deferred basis will be able to defer tax and split income with family members who are shareholders and employees of the corporation. When this offers commercial or personal advantages, as well as tax advantages, it is difficult to see upon what basis the move could possibly be criticized.

When a taxpayer orders his or her affairs primarily to avoid or reduce tax, then there is a true case of tax avoidance. Even here, however, the morality of the case depends upon the circumstances. A person with sufficient investment income may stop working in order to avoid paying tax on the extra income. Or, alternatively, he or she may continue to work, but give the investments away to adult children or their families. People who deliberately choose leisure instead of work, or divest themselves of income-producing assets, may be engaged in tax avoidance, but they hardly seem open to moral criticism since they have also reduced their after-tax income.

At the other end of the spectrum are people who design and market "tax products" and "tax shelters" aimed at exploiting the textual loopholes of the Act to produce tax savings for other taxpayers. These are people who have been able to increase their after-tax income by selling products that "game" the system.

(b) — Goals of tax avoidance

The ultimate goal of tax avoidance is a reduction of tax liability. This can be achieved through deferral, re-characterization of transactions, and the shifting of the income or loss to another taxpayer.

"Deferral" involves the postponement of the payment of a tax liability. The extent of tax savings depends on the time value of money.[3] Taxpayers can structure their transactions to take advantage of the timing rules by advancing deductions or postponing income recognitions.[4] They can also achieve deferral through the use of a corporation, which is taxed separately from its shareholders and is not required to

[2]See ch. 18, Tax Administration and Ethics, under headings 18.6 and 18.7, above.

[3]For further discussion of deferral, see heading 1.6(c), "Tax deferral".

[4]Timing rules have been discussed in chapters 5–10 of this book.

distribute dividends every year. Taxpayers can also use the tax incentives provided in the form of tax deferrals, such as savings for retirement (including registered retirement savings plans or RRSPs).[5]

"Re-characterisation" involves the conversion of the legal character of an item or transaction from a highly taxed item (such as income from business or property) to a tax-free or less heavily taxed item (such as windfalls or capital gains). In *Fortino v. R.* (1999)[6] and *Manrell v. R.* (2003),[7] for example, the taxpayers converted a portion of the capital gains from the sale of shares to "non-compete payments" that were held to be tax-free. In the so-called "surplus stripping" transactions discussed below, such as *McNichol v. R.* (1997)[8] and *Evans v. R.* (2005),[9] distributions of corporate profits (normally in the form of dividends) are converted into capital gains eligible for the lifetime capital gains exemption. Achieving re-characterization is also the goal of tax arbitrage transactions.

"Shifting income" from a highly-taxed person to a less-heavily taxed family member naturally achieves tax savings without causing the reduction of economic income of the family unit.[10] "Shifting losses" in a reverse direction (i.e., from an entity that has no tax liability to a highly taxed, related entity) equally achieves a reduction of the overall tax liability of the related corporate group. An example is the *Stubart Investments Ltd. v. R.* (1984).[11] Shifting losses from a stranger (arm's length party) has been considered in several GAAR cases, including in *Mathew v. R.* (2005)[12] and *MacKay v. R.* (2008).[13] Both are discussed below.

Achievement of any or all of these goals is possible because of the inconsistencies and gaps that exist within the Act (and across national tax systems in the case of international transactions), tax expenditure provisions, the creativity and aggressiveness on the part of taxpayers and their advisors, and judicial attitudes towards tax avoidance.

---

[5]See heading 12.4, "Tax assisted private pension plans", above.

[6](1999), [2000] 1 C.T.C. 349, 2000 D.T.C. 6060 (Fed. C.A.), discussed under heading 4.3(d), "Unenumerated sources", above.

[7][2003] 3 C.T.C. 50, 2003 D.T.C. 5225 (Fed. C.A.).

[8][1997] 2 C.T.C. 2088, 97 D.T.C. 111 (T.C.C.).

[9](2005), 2005 D.T.C. 1762 (Eng.), [2006] 2 C.T.C. 2009 (T.C.C. [General Procedure]).

[10]Chapter 13.

[11][1984] C.T.C. 294, 84 D.T.C. 6305 (S.C.C.).

[12][2005] 5 C.T.C. 244, 2005 D.T.C. 5538 (Eng.), 2005 D.T.C. 5563 (Fr.) (S.C.C.).

[13]2007 TCC 94, 2007 D.T.C. 425 (Eng.) (T.C.C. [General Procedure]), reversed by the FCA, [2008] 4 C.T.C. 161, 2008 D.T.C. 6238, [2008] 4 F.C.R. 616.

(c) — Types of avoidance transactions

(i) — Using a tax relief

Taking advantage of a relief provision of the Act is technically a form of tax avoidance, although it is clearly acceptable. Indeed, Parliament wants many tax relief schemes to be used by taxpayers in order to achieve the desired policy objectives. For example, a person may give to charity, or to a political party, or contribute to a registered retirement savings plan (RRSP), in order to increase credits or deductions allowed by the Act. These credits and deductions are available for the very purpose of encouraging private provision for charitable objects and political parties and private saving for retirement. One can argue about the wisdom of the statute's policy, but one can hardly question the moral right of a taxpayer to do what the statute manifestly approves. In addition to tax expenditure provisions, the Act contains "favourable" treatment of certain transactions, such as inter-spouse transfers of property, corporate rollovers, etc. Naturally, there is nothing wrong when a taxpayer engages in these transactions.

Is there anything wrong when a taxpayer uses an elaborate and contrived scheme to take advantage of a tax relief? In *Canada Trustco Mortgage Co. v. R.* (2005),[14] the Supreme Court held that a complex cross-border finance lease transaction to benefit from the capital cost allowance deductions was not abusive. Even when a series of transactions was designed to solely benefit from tax relief provisions and in the absence of such relief the transaction would not have taken place, the court may not find the transactions offensive under the GAAR (e.g., *Univar Canada Ltd. v. R.* (2005)[15]).

Canada's tax treaties also provide tax relief in the form of exemptions or reductions to residents of treaty countries. Because Canada does not have a treaty with every country, notably tax haven countries, residents in non-treaty countries sometimes structure transactions in order to formally qualify for treaty relief. This is called "treaty shopping". It remains controversial about whether treaty shopping is abusive. In some recent cases[16] however, Canadian courts have held that treaty shopping does not violate the GAAR.

(ii) — Tax-efficient structures

A common type of avoidance transaction is to use a more tax-efficient structure in arranging one's economic affairs when the Act treats economically similar transactions differently. For example, because the Act treats the cost of financing (i.e., dividends and interest) differently, the taxpayer might take advantage of the interest

---

[14][2005] 5 C.T.C. 215, (sub nom. *Canada Trustco Mortgage Co. v. Canada)* 2005 D.T.C. 5523 (Eng.), (sub nom. *Hypothèques Trustco Canada v. Canada)* 2005 D.T.C. 5547 (Fr.) (S.C.C.). See also note 1, above.

[15](2005), 2005 TCC 723, 2005 D.T.C. 1478 (Eng.), [2006] 1 C.T.C. 2308 (T.C.C. [General Procedure]).

[16]See *R. v. MIL (Investments) S.A.* (2007), 2007 FCA 23.

deduction through debt financing rather than equity financing. Because business income earned by a sole proprietor is taxable at progressive rates, but business income earned through a corporation is taxable at a lower flat rate, the very decision to incorporate a business often entails a choice between these two tax treatments. Similarly, the decision to retain corporate profit to enhance the value of its shares rather than to distribute the profits to shareholders by way of dividends leads to different tax treatment because capital gains are taxed differently from dividends. In these cases, it is difficult to argue that avoiding of tax by simply using a more tax-efficient structure is offensive.

However, the more aggressive type involves taxpayers exploiting the differential treatment through the use of intermediate steps. For example, a person who tries to take the retained earnings out of a closely held corporation as a capital gain instead of a dividend is prevented from doing so by various rules designed to prevent "surplus stripping"[17] and must go through various other steps to avoid the specific rules. Surplus stripping was the issue in *McNichol v. R.* (1997)[18], the very first case to apply the GAAR. In that case a holding company ("Holdco"), owned by four shareholders, sold its only asset which was an office building. After all tax-free distributions had been made to the shareholders, the company was left with cash of approximately $318,000. Since the company had no business and no other reason for existence, the natural next step would be for the shareholders to wind the company up. However, because subsection 84(2) provides that, on the winding-up of a company, the property distributed to shareholders in excess of the paid-up capital is deemed to be a taxable dividend, this would have forced each of the four shareholders to report and pay tax on a dividend of $79,500 ($318,000 divided by 4). In order to avoid this result, the four shareholders found a purchaser for the shares. The purchaser was an arm's length inactive company and agreed to purchase all the shares of Holdco for $300,000. The purchaser company had virtually no assets (it had a bank account with $63 in it) and borrowed the $300,000 purchase price from a bank. Then, as soon as the transaction closed, the purchasing company repaid the loan using Holdco's cash and was left with a profit of $18,000, which was the difference between the value of Holdco's assets and the purchase price.[19] The four shareholders of Holdco each received $75,000, which constituted a capital gain for each of them. Before the application of GAAR, two of the shareholders paid no tax and the other two shareholders paid only a small amount of tax because of the lifetime capital gains exemption.[20]

---

[17]These rules include ss. 84(2) and (3), 84.1 and 245(2).

[18]Note 8, above.

[19]Holdco also had a balance in its refundable dividend tax on hand account, which represented a possible future tax refund.

[20]The Tax Court held that the transactions were abusive in this case. As discussed later in this chapter under heading 20.5(e)(iii), "Abusive transactions", however, there is some doubt as to whether the same conclusion would be reached today.

(iii) — Tax arbitrage

Tax arbitrage takes advantage of inconsistent provisions of the Act or gaps that exist in the legislative scheme. The transactions in *Ludco Enterprises Ltd.* (2001)[21] (an investment in shares of offshore companies) and *Stewart v. R.* (2002)[22] (an investment in rental properties) are examples of arbitrage. These transactions are designed to take advantage of the different treatment of capital gains and income from property and the different timing rules for the deduction of interest expense and the realization of capital gains. When the current full deduction of expenses (typically interest expense) exceeds the current income (from rent or dividends), the resulting loss can be used to shelter income from other sources. Overall, the taxpayer will derive a profit if the investment property appreciates in value each year, but the capital gains are only partially taxed. Because interest expense is deductible on a current basis and the recognition of capital gains can be deferred until the property is sold, the mismatch results in tax savings.[23] The fact that the interest is normally deductible in full and capital gains are partially tax-free further increases the tax savings.

The *Shell Canada Ltd. v. R.* (1999)[24] case is another example. In this case, the taxpayer, through weak-currency loans and forward contracts, achieved a current deduction of interest expense payable at a higher than normal rate (to compensate for risks associated with a weak currency), while at the same time, realizing capital gains from the forward arrangements that covered these risks. In effect, the taxpayer's capital gain was equal to his excess interest expense. Mismatching was involved in *Shell* because the gains were taxed at the end of the term of the loan, while interest expense was deducted on a current basis. Additional tax savings were available because capital gains are partially tax-free.

(iv) — Tax shelters

A "tax shelter" can be simply described as an investment vehicle that "shelters" taxes. When used in a general sense, it includes a tax-favoured investment that is clearly sanctioned by the Act, such as an RRSP and other registered plan.[25] It can also describe tax arbitrage transactions or schemes designed to "trade" or "manufacture" tax attributes (e.g., a tax deduction or exemption). At a technical level,

---

[21](2001), 2001 SCC 62, (sub nom. *Ludco Enterprises Ltd. v. R.)* 2001 D.T.C. 5505 (Eng.), (sub nom. *Ludco Enterprises Ltd. v. R.)* 2001 D.T.C. 5518 (Fr.), [2002] 1 C.T.C. 95 (S.C.C.).

[22]2002 SCC 46, 2002 D.T.C. 6969 (Eng.), 2002 D.T.C. 6983 (Fr.), [2002] 3 C.T.C. 439 (S.C.C.).

[23]The situation in *Canderel Ltd. v. R.*, [1998] 2 C.T.C. 35, 98 D.T.C. 6100 (S.C.C.) is also an example of mismatching because the lease inducement was deducted up front while the income was earned over the term of the lease.

[24][1999] 4 C.T.C. 313, 99 D.T.C. 5669 (Eng.), 99 D.T.C. 5682 (Fr.) (S.C.C.).

[25]See ch. 12, Other income and deductions, above, for a description of RRSPs and other registered plans, for example: deferred profit sharing plans, registered pension plans, Registered Educational Savings Plans, Registered Disability Savings Plans.

however, a "tax shelter" is defined to be an investment that can be written off over four years and must be registered for tax purposes under section 237.1 of the Act. This chapter uses the term "tax shelter" in its general sense.

Tax shelters are legal. Some tax shelters are totally legitimate in that they involve tax-favoured investments clearly sanctioned by the Act. Examples are RRSPs and other registered plans.[26] Arbitrage-based transactions, such as those in *Shell, Ludco, Stewart* have been sanctioned by the Supreme Court. As discussed in more detail below, however, the tax shelter transaction in *Mathew* was found "abusive" under the GAAR.

(v) — Anti-avoidance karate

"Anti-avoidance karate" is a term coined by Lord Walker of Gestingthorpe to refer to a situation in which taxpayers attempt to use a statutory anti-avoidance provision to their advantage.[27] One example of this is the *Mathew* case. In *Mathew*, the taxpayers attempted to take advantage of the "stop-loss" rule in subsection 18(13) to acquire the loss of another taxpayer. As the Supreme Court stated:[28]

> Section 18(13) preserves and transfers a loss under the assumption that it will be realized by a taxpayer who does not deal at arm's length with the transferor. . . . To use these provisions to preserve and sell an unrealized loss to an arm's length party results in abusive tax avoidance under s. 245(4).

Another example is *Lipson v. R.* (2008)[29] in which the taxpayers turned an attribution rule under subsection 74.1(1)[30] on its head and used it as part of scheme to obtain interest deductions. Bowman C.J.T.C. remarked:[31]

> The purpose of section 74.1 is to prevent income splitting. . . . Here the attribution rules are being used in essence to allow the attributed dividend income to carry back with it to [the transferor] the interest deduction [to cloak a non-deductible interest expense with an income-earning purpose].

Not surprisingly, the Court had no difficulty ruling against the taxpayers in both *Mathew* and *Lipson*.

---

[26]See ch. 16, Partnerships, above, on the taxation of partnerships and their use. The Act requires promoters of "tax shelters" to register under s.237.1. Similar requirements can be found under provincial legislation; see section 1079.1 to 1079.8 of Quebec Taxation Act. The Federal Budget, March 4, 2010 announced a public consultation on proposals to require reporting of certain types of "aggressive" transactions, similar in some respects to measures previously proposed in Quebec.

[27]Robert Walker, "Ramsay 25 Years On: Some Reflections on Tax Avoidance" (2004) *LQR* 412 at 422.

[28]Note 12 above, para. 58.

[29][2006] 3 C.T.C. 2494, 2006 D.T.C. 2687 (Eng.) (T.C.C. [General Procedure]); affirmed 2007 CarswellNat 640, 2007 FCA 113, [2007] 3 C.T.C. 110 (F.C.A.).

[30]See heading 13.5, "Attribution of income from property, above".

[31]Note 12, above, para. 22.

(d) — Abusive avoidance distinguished

Not all tax avoidance is unacceptable. Until the enactment of the GAAR, the line between legitimate tax minimization and abusive tax avoidance was drawn by the courts through statutory interpretation or by Parliament through specific anti-avoidance rules. Now the "GAAR draws a line."[32] Because the GAAR is a general rule, its effectiveness depends on the judicial interpretation. As such, the line-drawing exercise is a joint-venture between the judiciary and Parliament. Abusive transactions are generally avoidance transactions that violate the object and purpose of the specific provision of the Act or the Act read as a whole. At the moment, "the line is far from bright."[33]

(e) — Moral and tax policy implications

Tax avoidance, in the strong sense of taking advantage of loopholes to avoid the general intent of the statute, is not, of course, subject to any legal penalty. So long as it falls short of evasion it is, by definition, legal. For the taxpayer, the only question is one of morality. On the moral question, there is no general agreement. Certainly, tax avoidance is not universally condemned, as witnessed by the famous dictum of Lord Tomlin in the *Duke of Westminster* case: "Every man is entitled if he can to order his affairs so that the tax attaching under the appropriate Acts is less than it otherwise would be".[34] The underlying assumption is that the tax laws are confiscations of private property, interferences with the natural order of the free market, and violations of civil liberty: the oppressed taxpayer is morally entitled to get around tax laws if it can be done legally.[35]

As explained in Chapter 19, because the roles of the income tax are no longer limited to raising revenue, the above assumption is thus somewhat outdated. The GAAR signals Parliament's disapproval of abusive tax avoidance.

In terms of tax policy, aggressive tax avoidance results in loss of tax revenue, inequity in sharing the tax burden among taxpayers, and a threat to the integrity of the system. The exact amount of revenue lost to aggressive tax planning is difficult to determine. On the basis of the amount of additional taxes uncovered by the CRA through its efforts in fighting against tax shelter planning schemes, the loss is in the billions.[36] The lost revenue to the government presumably shifts the burden onto other taxpayers through the need to maintain tax rates at higher levels than would otherwise be needed. The equities of the situation are further impaired by the fact

---

[32] Note 14, above, para. 16.

[33] *Ibid.*

[34] *Inland Revenue Commissioners v. Duke of Westminster* (1935), [1936] A.C. 1 (U.K. H.L.), 19. The case is described under heading 19.2(b)(iii), below.

[35] For more discussion, see heading 19.2(b)(iv), "Outdated presumptions about tax law", above.

[36] CRA, 2006-2007 Canada Revenue Agency Annual Report to the Parliament of Canada in January 2008, p.59.

that, generally speaking, opportunities for tax avoidance are unavailable to those whose income is derived from employment, which is reported by their employer and for which there are limited deductions; only those with substantial investment or business income are usually able to profit from tax avoidance. It has even been suggested that widespread tax avoidance may lead to a deterioration of tax morality in that taxpayers who see others avoiding taxes legally and are unable to do the same may feel justified in resorting to illegal methods; this kind of attitude is, of course, fatal to the system of self-assessment. Finally, it may be said that tax avoidance leads to a substantial expenditure of effort by lawyers, accountants and administrators which is economically unproductive.[37]

20.2 — Judicial approach to tax avoidance

(a) — Role of the court

As can be seen from the discussion of the landmark tax decisions in Chapter 19 and this chapter, Canadian judges see themselves as referees in the battlefield between taxpayers and the government.[38] As true referees, they take no sides and ensure both sides play properly. In Rothstein J.'s words, "the role of the court is solely to adjudicate disputes between the Minister and the taxpayer. It is not a protector of government revenue."[39]

In the "battle" between law-abiding taxpayers desiring to avoid tax by whatever means available to them and Parliament that intends to limit the scope for avoidance, Parliament has often been worsted by the skill, determination and resourcefulness of its opponent. The only weapon available to Parliament is words. As powerful as words can be, there are limits to the power of the "blunt instrument of legislation": whatever a statute may provide, it has to be interpreted and applied by the courts.[40]

During the past few decades, the taxpayers' hand seems to have been strengthened by a number of factors, including a growing "tax engineering industry" that design, package and market "tax products" to exploit legislative loopholes in Canada and across borders.[41] There is a growing tax culture that rewards cleverness in devising tax avoidance schemes and regards aggressive tax planning as legitimate. The glob-

---

[37]*The Report of the Royal Commission on Taxation* (Carter Report), (1966), vol. 3, Appendix A, includes a public policy analysis of tax avoidance.

[38]*Imperial Oil v. R.*, 2006 D.T.C. 6639 (Eng.), 2006 D.T.C. 6660 (Fr.), [2007] 1 C.T.C. 41, 353 N.R. 201, 273 D.L.R. (4th) 450, [2006] 2 S.C.R. 447 (per Binnie J., para.73): "The *Income Tax Act* is the battlefield on which over 21 million Canadian taxpayers engage with the Minister of National Revenue ("the Minister") and his or her various tax assessors, adjudicators and collectors."

[39]*R. v. McLarty*, 2008 SCC 26, para.75.

[40]*Furniss v. Dawson*, [1984] AC 474, Lord Scarman at 513.

[41]For further discussion, see Quebec, Aggressive Tax Planning: Working Paper, January 2009, heading 1.2, "Proliferation of ATP [aggressive tax planning] schemes.

ally integrated market place has enabled taxpayers to take advantage of the gaps among national tax laws. In the face of these changes, however, the role of the court has not changed much.

Since 1935, when the *Duke of Westminster* case was decided, the scope and sophistication of tax avoidance have increased significantly. The courts in the United Kingdom and elsewhere began to realize their important role in controlling avoidance. Lord Wilberforce remarked in *W.T. Ramsay Ltd. v. Inland Revenue Commissioners* (1981):[42]

> While the techniques of tax avoidance progress and are technically improved, the courts are not obliged to stand still. Such immobility must result either in loss of tax, to the prejudice of other taxpayers, or to Parliamentary congestion or (most likely) to both. To force the courts to adopt, in relation to closely integrated situations, a step by step, dissecting, approach which the parties themselves may have negated, would be a denial rather than an affirmation of the true judicial process. In each case the facts must be established, and a legal analysis made: legislation cannot be required or even be desirable to enable the courts to arrive at a conclusion which corresponds with the parties' own intentions.

The House of Lords also decided that it is time to move away from the *Duke of Westminster* doctrines. In *Furniss v. Dawson* (1984),[43] Lord Roskill opined:

> The ghost of the *Westminster* case . . . has haunted the administration of this branch of the law for too long. I confess that I had hoped that that ghost might have found quietude with the decisions in *Ramsay* and in *Burmah*. Unhappily it has not. Perhaps the decision of this House in these appeals will now suffice as exorcism.

While the *Duke of Westminster* may have been reduced to more or less a ghost in his home country, he is very much alive in Canada. Canadian courts continue to adhere to the *Duke of Westminster* principles. Wilson J. stated in *Stubart*: "Lord Tomlin's principle is far too deeply entrenched in our tax law for the courts to reject it in the absence of clear statutory authority."[44] The *Duke of Westminster* principles co-exist with the GAAR and taxpayers remain entitled to engage in legitimate tax minimization.[45]

(b) — Attitude towards tax avoidance

At the risk of oversimplification, judicial attitude can be described as "occasionally distasteful" for artificial tax schemes, but generally highly sympathetic to tax planning. In *Stubart*, Estey J. remarked that the modern rule of interpretation would "reduce the attraction of elaborate and intricate tax avoidance plans, and reduce the rewards to those best able to afford the services of the tax technicians."[46] In *Mathew*, the Court was not impressed by the "the vacuity and artificiality" of the

[42](1981), [1982] A.C. 300 (U.K. H.L.), 326.

[43]Note 40, above, para 515.

[44]Note 11, above, para 72.

[45]Note 14 above, para. 13-16.

[46]*Stubart*, note 11, above, para.56.

relationships underlying the tax schemes. The strongest expression of distaste for artificial tax schemes came from Rip (A.C.J. as he then was) in *Farragi* (2007):[47]

> Mr. Langlois and Mr. Faraggi started off with a clean sheet of paper, with no past history, and created a set of facts for their own purposes. Everything done in Series 1 and 2 [of the transactions to create capital dividend accounts] was artificial. The appellants exploited provisions of the Act to achieve a result they hoped would not be discovered by the tax authorities.

(c) — Interpretive principles

(i) — Strict interpretation

The interpretive principles derived from the *Duke of Westminster* case were highly sympathetic to tax avoidance. Under strict or literal interpretation of statutes, if the language of the statute is not literally apt to catch the transaction in issue, then the transaction escapes taxation. In other words, where there is doubt or ambiguity in provisions that levy a tax, the interpretation most favourable to the taxpayer should be adopted. This doctrine is crucial to the success of tax planning. It casts upon the drafters of tax legislation the burden of finding language that would squarely catch every transaction that ought to be taxable. This forced Parliament to define the rules with great specificity and to pass amendments adding more and more detail as avoidance techniques emerged and had to be blocked to protect the revenue. The resulting complexity tended to reinforce the courts in their literal approach. The frequency of amendment had the same effect: judicial creativity was suppressed by the knowledge that Parliament could and would act quickly to repair gaps in the Act that a more purposive judicial interpretation might have filled.

There is perhaps no coincidence that the "modern rule" or the "textual, contextual and purposive" rule of statutory interpretation was adopted by the Supreme Court of Canada in the landmark tax avoidance cases, i.e., *Stubart* and *Canada Trustco*. But, the legacy of strict interpretation remains much evident.

(ii) — Form over substance

In the discussion of the *Duke of Westminster* case in Chapter 19, we noticed that the success of the Duke's tax avoidance plan depended upon the Court's willingness to characterize the agreements entered into with his servants as annuity contracts rather than employment contracts. The Court's acceptance of the legal form (annuity) rather than the commercial substance (employment) was critical to the success of the plan. Similarly, in the *Stubart* case, the Court accepted the legal forms (sale and agency agreement), although the commercial substance of the arrangement was that Stubart had not divested itself of the business.[48]

While the courts should not freely disregard the taxpayer's legal relationships in general, it does not mean that the courts should always be bound by such relation-

---

[47] *Farragi*, note 77, below, para.80.

[48] Note 11, above.

ships, especially where the actual legal relationships were different from legal substance[49] or "true character."[50] Expressing the idea more colourfully, "calling a horse a dog does not make the horse a dog."[51] There are some examples where the courts find the legal form mischaracterizes the legal substance.[52]The Court stated in *Shell* that "[r]echaracterization is only permissible if the label attached by the taxpayer to the particular transaction does not properly reflect its actual legal effect".[53] In determining whether the "label" (i.e., the legal relationships existing between parties to a transaction as evidenced by the words of the documents used to label the transaction) reflects the actual legal rights and obligations agreed to by the parties, the courts may examine the actions taken by the parties. In *Backman v. R.* (2001),[54] for example, a "partnership" was found not to exist because the evidence did not show that the parties intended to carry on business with a view to profit.[55]

In general, however, a rigorous logical analysis would conclude that properly legally documented transactions will not have a legal substance that is different from its form. The "form over substance" or the "legal substance" doctrine is a natural fit

---

[49]*Continental Bank of Canada v. R.* (1998), (sub nom. *Continental Bank Leasing Corp. v. Canada)* [1998] 2 S.C.R. 298, 98 D.T.C. 6505, [1998] 4 C.T.C. 119, ¶21, per Bastarache J. (S.C.C.); affirming the decision by Bowman J. (as he then was) (1994), [1995] 1 C.T.C. 2135, 94 D.T.C. 1858 (T.C.C.).

[50]*Purdy v. Minister of National Revenue*, [1985] 1 C.T.C. 2294, 85 D.T.C. 254, per Christie C.J.T.C. (T.C.C.).

[51]*Gillette Canada Inc. v. The Queen*, [2001] 4 C.T.C. 2884, 2001 D.T.C. 895, per Rip, J. (T.C.C. [General Procedure]); appeal dismissed [2003] 3 C.T.C. 27, 2003 D.T.C. 5078 (Fed. C.A.).

[52]For example, a contract for independent services was recharacterized as a contract of employment (see *CCLI (1994) Inc. v. The Queen*, 2006 D.T.C. 2695 (Eng.), [2006] 4 C.T.C. 2001 (T.C.C. [General Procedure]); reversed 2007 D.T.C. 5372 (Eng.), [2007] 4 C.T.C. 19, per Miller J. (F.C.A.) at para. 26 [D.T.C.] ([General Procedure]); a "retiring allowance" was recharacterized as consideration for the surrender of a share (see *Milne v. R.*, [1994] 2 C.T.C. 2190 (T.C.C.)); consulting fees" were recharacterized as payments for goodwill (see *Bowens v. R., (*sub nom. *Bowens v. Canada)* [1994] 2 C.T.C. 2404, 94 D.T.C. 1853 (T.C.C.); affirmed [1996] 2 C.T.C. 120, 96 D.T.C. 6128 (Fed. C.A.)); and a lump sum payment made by a lessee to a lessor was characterized as income rather than capital on the basis that its substance was a pre payment of rent, causing the lessor to agree to receive (and pay tax on) a lower rate of rent (see *Front & Simcoe Ltd. v. Minister of National Revenue*, [1960] C.T.C. 123, 60 D.T.C. 1081 (Can. Ex. Ct.)).

[53]Note 24 above, para. 39.

[54]Sub nom. *Backman v. Canada* [2001] 1 S.C.R. 367, [2001] 2 C.T.C. 11, 2001 D.T.C. 5149 (S.C.C.). The Court stated at para.25: "[T]o ascertain the existence of a partnership the courts must inquire into whether the objective, documentary evidence and the surrounding facts, including what the parties actually did, are consistent with a subjective intention to carry on business in common with a view to profit."

[55]*Ibid.*, para. 25.

with strict interpretation doctrine. Both doctrines favor a literal construction of the law or facts that are highly accommodating to aggressive tax planning.

(d) — Judicial anti-avoidance doctrines

Judicial anti-avoidance doctrines refer to those doctrines created in common law that discourage tax avoidance. Examples are the "business purpose" doctrine, the "economic substance" doctrine, and the "sham" doctrine. Until recently, the "reasonable expectation of profit" test functioned as an judicial anti-avoidance doctrine.[56]

(i) — Business purpose

The "business purpose" doctrine has been applied by courts in the United States and United Kingdom, but rejected by the Supreme Court of Canada in *Stubart*. As discussed later in this chapter, a broader, "non-tax purpose" test has now been codified into the GAAR.

A "business purpose" test has been adopted by Courts in the United States as either a stand-alone anti-avoidance doctrine or part of the economic substance doctrine. Under this doctrine, tax benefits with respect to a transaction are not allowable if the transaction does not have economic substance or lacks a business purpose. [57] Whether a taxpayer has a substantial business (or non-tax) purpose for entering into a transaction is determined on the basis of objective facts, such as whether the transaction was structured and implemented to make a profit. In a recent case, *Klamath v. USA* (2009) the Fifth Circuit Court of Appeals denied the taxpayer's "head in the sand" defense: "[Taxpayers cannot] profess a profit motive but agree to a scheme structured and controlled by parties [investment advisor and a bank] with the sole purpose of achieving tax benefits for them." [58]

In the United Kingdom, a business purpose test has been applied by the House of Lords to a "step transaction". In *Furniss v. Dawson* (1984),[59] the House of Lords charged the vendor of property with a capital gain, although the capital gain had actually been received by a company owned and controlled by the vendor that was incorporated in the Isle of Man (a tax haven). Their lordships held that the transaction was to be regarded as a sale and purchase between two United Kingdom parties, which was the commercial reality. The intermediate step of transferring the property to the controlled Isle of Man company (which then sold the property to the

---

[56]See heading 6.2, "Characterization of "business" and "property" as a source, above.

[57]This common-law doctrine was codified as section 7701(o) of the *Internal Revenue Code* in March 2010.

[58]*Klamath Strategic Investment Fund v. United States*, 568 F.3d 537 (5th Cir. 2009). In this case, the individual taxpayer invested US$1.5 million of his ownmoney in Klamath, a partnership formed by the taxpayer and an investment advisor, and "generated" a US$25 million loss from the partnership. This loss was denied by the courts on the ground that the transactions lacked economic substance.

[59]Note 41, above.

true purchaser) had been undertaken solely to divert the capital gain to the Isle of Man and avoid its recognition in the United Kingdom. Their lordships held that this "inserted step", because it had "no business purpose apart from the deferment of tax", was to be disregarded for tax purposes.[60]

The business purpose test of *Furniss v. Dawson* has been confined to "step transactions", or "composite transactions", as they are known in the United Kingdom.[61] Even so, the case obviously constitutes a radical change in the approach of the House of Lords to artificial tax avoidance schemes. As Lord Roskill noted, the *Duke of Westminster* case was seriously undermined by *Furniss v. Dawson*[62] in the United Kingdom.

In Canada, however, the *Duke of Westminster* case remains good law. In that case, the deeds of covenant that the Duke entered into with his servants were effective for tax purposes despite the fact that they had been brought into existence solely to avoid tax. The case thus became authority for the important proposition that there was no business purpose test in tax jurisprudence. The courts had no power to disregard a transaction for tax purposes simply because the transaction lacked an independent business purpose. Before *Stubart*, there had been occasional cases in which Canadian courts had applied a business purpose test in order to defeat artificial tax avoidance schemes, but these cases ran against the general current of authority, which remained faithful to the *Duke of Westminster* case. This issue was fully argued before the Supreme Court of Canada in the *Stubart* case, where counsel for the Minister argued that the transfer of assets between the two subsidiaries should be disregarded for tax purposes on the ground that it lacked any business purpose other than the avoidance of tax. Estey J. for the majority of the Supreme Court of Canada reviewed the American, English and Canadian authorities, and rejected the business purpose test for Canada: "I would therefore reject the proposition that a transaction may be disregarded for tax purposes solely on the basis that it was entered into by a taxpayer without an independent or bona fide business purpose."[63] Parliament introduced the GAAR in 1988, principally in response to the *Stubart* decision.

(ii) — Economic substance

The economic substance doctrine has been applied by courts in the United States and, to lesser extent, in the United Kingdom to attack aggressive tax avoidance

---

[60]Note 41, above, 527. The gain would eventually have to be recognized in the United Kingdom, but only when the shares in the Isle of Man company (whose value reflected the capital gain) were sold

[61]*Furniss v. Dawson* followed two earlier decisions of the House of Lords, namely, *Inland Revenue Commissioners v. Burmah Oil Co.* (1981), [1982] S.T.C. 30 (U.K. H.L.) and *Ramsay*, note 12, above. The later case of *Craven v. White* (1988), [1989] A.C. 398 (U.K. H.L.) confined *Furniss* to step transactions.

[62]Note 41, above.

[63]Note 11 above, para. 55.

transactions.[64] The U.S. courts have long held that if a business transaction has no value except to create tax losses, then it can be disallowed by the government. "Otherwise, tax lawyers could just move symbols around pieces of paper, and their clients would never pay taxes."[65]

The U.S. courts developed a two-prong test for determining whether a transaction lacks economic substance: the objective prong looks at whether the taxpayer has shown that the transaction has effected meaningful change to the taxpayer's economic position beyond the creation of tax benefits; and the subjective prong looks at whether the taxpayer has shown that it had a business purpose for engaging in the transaction other than tax avoidance.[66] In March 2010, this test was strengthened when it was codified as section 7701(o) of the *Internal Revenue Code*

To meet the U.S. economic substance test, a transaction must change a taxpayer's economic position in a meaningful way, ignoring any tax benefits. To demonstrate a meaningful change in economic position, the taxpayer must rely on such factors as business or regulatory realities, the fact that the transaction was "imbued with tax-independent considerations" and that the transaction was "not shaped solely by tax avoidance features that have meaningless labels attached."[67] A taxpayer can also rely on profit potential to prove economic substance, but "only if the present value of the reasonably expected pre-tax profit from the transaction is substantial in relation to the present value of the expected net tax benefits that would be allowed if the transaction were respected".[68] The notion of "pre-tax profit" refers to profit before considering the tax benefits. In computing the pre-tax profit, transaction fees and other expenses must be taken into account as expenses.

In *Altria Group, Inc. v. United States* (2010), [69] U.S. courts found transactions similar to those in *Canada Trustco*[70] lacked economic substance and denied the taxpayer the tax benefits of ownership (that is, the depreciation deduction associated with the cost of acquiring the assets). In this case, Altria entered into four transactions to "acquire" leasehold interests in large infrastructure assets (that is, a railroad's maintenance facility in New York, a Dutch wastewater treatment plant, and

---

[64]The economic substance doctrine is part of the American and UK common law, although both countries have attempted to enact statutory general anti-avoidance rules that would include this doctrine. In Australia, South Africa and Spain, the doctrine has been codified in the statutory GAAR. For more discussion, see J. Li, "Abusive Tax Avoidance versus Legitimate Tax Minimization: Economic Substance Draws the Line" (2006) vol.54, no.1 *Canadian Tax J.* 23-56.

[65]D. C. Johnston, "A Tax Shelter, Destructed," *New York Times*, July 13, 2003.

[66]*Frank Lyon Co. v. United States* (1978), 435 U.S. 561 is considered to be the leading case that created this test.

[67]Note 66, above 583-84.

[68]See s. 7701(o)(2) of the *Internal Revenue Code*

[69]2010 U.S. Dist. LEXIS 25160 (S.D.N.Y.2010).

[70]Note 14, above, discussed under heading 2.4(f)(i) "*Canada Trustco*", below.

two power plants in Georgia and Florida). Each of the counterparties was indifferent to U.S. federal income tax in the sense that the ability to depreciate the assets would not substantially affect the entities' tax liability. In each transaction, Altria immediately leased the asset back to its original owner, the rent to Altria was prepaid, and the original owner/lessee had the option to repurchase the asset. About 4/5 of the capital was financed by a non-recourse financing from a bank. The financial risks for the bank and Altria were minimal.

After paying sizeable transaction fees (and setting aside an amount less than the tax benefits created by the transactions), the lessee (the original owner) was required to immediately transfer the money it received from Altria from the "acquisition" transactions into two bank accounts: a "debt" defeasance account and an "equity" defeasance account. The debt defeasance account was established at an affiliate of the bank and was governed by agreements whereby the "rental" payment due to Altria was paid on the same day when Altria's interest payment to the bank was due. As such, the rent payment offset a corresponding interest payment. The equity defeasance account held, in essence, Altria's equity (ie, 1/5 of the total cost) and the funds were invested in U.S. treasury bonds. The lessee was prohibited from accessing the money in these two accounts.

From the persepective of the U.S. Treasury, these and similar transactions entered into by Altria created billions of dollars of tax-defferral benefits out of thin air. The Internal Revenue Service concluded that the transactions had no purpose, substance, or utility apart from their anticipated tax consequences and disallowed the deductions for depreciation, interest expenses and other expenses.

The U.S. courts examined whether Altria actually "owned" the asset to enable it to depreciate the cost of acquisition and whether the up to 3.8% rate of return on the investment was sufficient economic substance. On the issue of ownership, the court acknowledged that there is no single test ofownership determination, and found that Altria did not retain significant and genuine attributes of traditional owner status on the ground that:

- Altria did not have the actual command or control over the asset. The asset was critical to the lessee (original owner).
- The purchase price did not reflect the fair market value. The appraisals had the 'trappings of a serious inquiry into the assets' commercial value, but they were little more than window dressing designed to bolster Altria's tax position.
- Altria did not bear the cost of various expenses in connection with the property including repairs, insurance and taxes (the lessee was required to bear these expenses).
- Altria did not bear any risk of loss in the event of the destruction of the asset as it was "insulated from any meaningful economic risk of loss or potential for gain."

The court also found that these seemingly complex transactions appeared to be similar to the traditional "leveraged lease" (which entitled the "lessor" to depreciate the cost of the asset), but they were not. The asset was unique and had no viable secondary market. The lessee's rent and purchase option price were fully defeased and the lessee received no additional liquidity aside from an amount that was directly traceable to the tax benefits created by the transactions.

On the issue of economic substance, the court recognized that taxpayers are entitled to structure their transactions in such a way as to minimize tax. But, the court found Altria lacked a legitimate business purpose and that as non-tax based return of up to 3.8% was insignificant compared to the billions of dollars of tax benefits.

(iii) — Sham

In Canada, the sham doctrine is the only doctrine that has been invoked by courts to defeat blatant, artificial tax structures. This doctrine allows the court to ignore the "façade" created by the taxpayer and to impose tax in accordance with the true facts.[71] If an entire transaction is a sham, the transaction will be completely ineffective. For example, parties may create false documentation for the sale of an asset when no such sale occurred (the motive could be to create a capital loss for the pretended vendor). If only part of the transaction was a sham, then the transaction will be effective in accordance with the actual rights and liabilities created. For example, if an asset is actually sold for $1, but the parties inserted a figure of $150 for consideration in the documentation (perhaps, to increase the purchaser's capital cost allowance deduction), the tax consequences would be determined based on the actual consideration of $1.

A sham was defined in the *Snook v. London & West Riding Investments Ltd.* (1967) case[72] as:

> . . . acts done or documents executed by the parties to the "sham" which are intended by them to give to third parties or to the court the appearance of creating between the parties legal rights and obligations different from the actual legal rights and obligations (if any) which the parties intend to create.

The *Snook* definition makes clear that a sham always involves an element of deceit. A transaction is not a sham merely because it is artificial, contrived or lacking in an independent business purpose.[73] There is no sham where the legal formalities accurately reflect the true relationship between the parties. In the *Duke of Westminster* case, for example, the deeds of covenant entered into by the Duke with his servants were bona fide instruments under which the Duke genuinely undertook an enforce-

[71]Justice McLachlin stated in *Shell* that taxpayer's legal relationships must be respected, unless they are a sham. Note 24, above, para. 40.

[72][1967] 2 Q.B. 786 (Eng. C.A.), 802.

[73]From time to time the word "sham" is broadened to include any artificial tax avoidance transaction: see e.g., the *obiter dictum in Bronfman Trust v. R.*, [1987] 1 C.T.C. 117, 87 D.T.C. 5059 (S.C.C.), 129-130, 5068. If this were a merely semantic issue, it would not matter, but the classification of a transaction as a sham carries the legal consequence of invalidity for tax purposes. The broader usage should therefore be avoided. The Snook definition, with its requirement of deceit, has been approved by the Supreme Court of Canada in *Minister of National Revenue v. Cameron* (1972), [1974] S.C.R. 1062, [1972] C.T.C. 380, 72 D.T.C. 6325 (S.C.C.) and in *Stubart*, note 11, above.

able obligation to pay the annuities. The deeds were not deceptive, and could not be disregarded as shams.

Canadian courts have adopted the *Snook* definition of "sham"[74] but have applied it "sparsely."[75] In the *Stubart* case, the Court concluded that there was a genuine sale of assets and agency agreement between the sister corporations. There was no sham because there was no attempt to create "a false impression" for tax purposes: the "appearance" was "precisely the reality", and fully enforceable obligations were genuinely created. The deceit which is "the heart and core of a sham" was entirely absent.

Faraggi v. R. (2007)[76] is the most recent case that applies the sham doctrine. Mr. Faraggi and his partner, Mr. Langlois, were lawyers specialized in corporate and tax law. They applied their expertise to creating an elaborate tax plan. Justice Rip describes the plan as follows:[77]

> The plan contemplated using newly formed corporations with nominal assets to subscribe for shares in other newly formed corporations and then create [capital dividend account] CDA through a combination of share subscriptions, redemption of shares, capital gains by sale of shares and purported elections under subsection 83(2) of the *Income Tax Act* ("*Act*"), among other things. Then, through another sequence of share subscriptions and share redemptions, third parties at arm's length to the appellants would receive capital dividends.
>
> In short, after the "creation" of capital gains several corporations would make elections under subsection 83(2) of the *Act* and declare tax-free dividends on classes of preferred shares. Near the end of the exercise the aggregate CDAs of these corporations would find their way to an appellant corporation. A third-party corporation would subscribe for shares in an appellant corporation. These shares would have a nominal par value, say $0.01 per share, and a high redemption amount, say $1,000 per share. The third-party corporation would pay $1,210 per share and an appellant corporation would redeem the share for $1,000, electing under subsection 83(2) of the *Act* that the deemed dividend of $999.99 (subsection 84(1) of the *Act*) be paid out of the appellant company's capital dividend account. The third-party corporation would then have a capital dividend account and pay its shareholders, after making its own subsection 83(2) election, $1,000 tax-free. Before the transaction, the third-party corporation had no amount in a capital dividend account and could only pay its

---

[74]See *Minister of National Revenue v. Cameron* (1972), [1974] S.C.R. 1062, [1972] C.T.C. 380, 72 D.T.C. 6325 (S.C.C.); and Stubart, note 11, above.

[75]*Central Supply Co. (1972) Ltd. v. R.*, [1997] F.C.J. No. 751, [1997] 3 C.T.C. 102, (sub nom. *R. v. Central Supply Co. (1972) Ltd.)* 97 D.T.C. 5295 (Fed. C.A.); leave to appeal refused (1997), (sub nom. *Minister of National Revenue v. Central Supply Co. (1972) Ltd.)* 226 N.R. 393, [1997] 3 S.C.R. vii (S.C.C.); leave to appeal refused (1997), 226 N.R. 317 (S.C.C.) (per Linden J.);*Susan Hosiery Ltd. v. Minister of National Revenue (No. 2)* (1969), [1969] C.T.C. 533, 69 D.T.C. 5346 (Can. Ex. Ct.).

[76]sub. nom 2530-1284 *Québec Inc. et al v. The Queen*, 2007 TCC 286; [2008]1 CTC 2425, 2008 DTC 3245 confirmed by 2529-1915 *Québec Inc. et al v. The Queen*, 2008 FCA 398, 2009 DTC 5023.

[77]*Ibid*, paras. 2 and 3.

shareholders a taxable dividend of $1,210; the tax rate in Quebec for individual shareholders was 41.87 per cent. After the transaction the shareholders received $1,000 tax-free; the third-party corporation effectively paid $210 for the tax-free $1,000 dividend. The effective cost to the third-party corporation and its shareholders for the $1,000 dividend was 21 per cent, an economic saving of 20.87 per cent.

The taxpayer corporations created by Farraggi and Langlois were assessed on the basis that they earned a profit of $4.6 million and $8.1 million, respectively, in their 1987 taxation years from carrying on businesses of selling fictitious CDA to third parties. The taxpayers' appeal to the Tax Court was dismissed with costs.[78]

Rip, A.C.J. found the scheme to be a sham. He had little difficulty finding a common intention to deceive to be present in each step of the series of transactions. Faraggi and Langlois knew that corporations never had any capital gains nor, consequently, any CDA; the bank and potential arm's length subscribers for shares were each informed as to the nature of the prospective transactions. The maker of each promissory note and the creditor had no intention of ever paying the money promised. They created an appearance of legal relations to mask the purpose of the real intended transactions: to carry on a business for profit. These two sophisticated lawyers "concocted the scheme and controlled the corporate appellants to effect transactions that were shams and abuses of provisions of the *Act*. All the appellants knew the score."[79]

20.3 — Specific anti-avoidance rules

(a) — General features

The Act contains numerous provisions that are designed to counter tax avoidance techniques. Some of these are directed at particular practices. For example, the rules in subsections 56(2) to 56(5) and sections 74.1 to 75.1 and the "kiddie tax" under section 120.4 each prevent a taxpayer from saving tax by using a particular technique to split income with a family member.[80] Other provisions are more general in nature, such as the requirement of section 67 that expenses are only deductible to the extent that they are "reasonable",[81] or the many provisions that provide special treatment for transactions entered into between parties that are "not at arm's length" (related persons or corporations who may have a common interest in saving tax).[82]

A common feature of the specific anti-avoidance rules is that they are highly technical and detailed. Some judges have openly complained about this drafting style.

[78]The court also upheld the assessment of tax penalty under s. 163(2) of the Act for lie on their tax returns.

[79]Note 76, above para. 96.

[80]The attribution rules are examined under heading 13.5, "Attribution of income from property", above.

[81]S. 67 was discussed under heading 8.6, ""Reasonable" requirement", above.

[82]See heading 13.4, "Non-arm's length transfers of property", above.

For example, Mogan J. referred to the definition of "term preferred shares" (which is part of the anti-avoidance scheme in respect of after-tax financing transactions) as follows:[83]

> The definition of "term preferred shares" is prolix in the extreme. The persons who drafted that definition did not practise any economy of words or language. One may ask how many members of Parliament understood the definition when it was made law by amendment to the Act. . . . It is so detailed; so particularized; so long and tedious and excessive in its use of language.

Many specific anti-avoidance rules have been proposed or introduced in reaction to an unsatisfactory decision of the court. For example, section 20.3 deals with weak-currency loans and was introduced in response to the Supreme Court decision in *Shell*; [84] subsection 10(1.01) prohibits taxpayers from using the "lower of cost and fair market value" method in inventory accounting and was introduced in response to the Supreme Court decision in *Friesen*;[85] proposed section 56.4 ensures that a payment for a non-competition payment covenant is included in taxable income and was introduced in response to the Federal Court of Appeal decisions in *Fortino v. R.* and *Manrell v. R.* (2003);[86] section 67.6 denies the deduction of fines and penalties and was introduced in response to the Supreme Court decision in *65302 British Columbia Ltd. v. R.* (2000);[87] and draft section 3.1 was proposed in 2003[88] to deny the deduction of losses where the taxpayer has no reasonable expectation of earning cumulative profit from a business or property and was released in response to the Supreme Court decision in *Ludco*,[89] and *Stewart* and *Walls*.[90]

---

[83]*Citibank Canada v. R.*, [2001] 2 C.T.C. 2260, 2001 D.T.C. 111 (T.C.C. [General Procedure]); affirmed [2002] 2 C.T.C. 171, 2002 D.T.C. 6876 (Fed. C.A.), para. 29 [D.T.C.].

[84]*Shell Canada*, note 24, above.

[85][1995] 2 C.T.C. 369, 95 D.T.C. 5551 (S.C.C.), discussed under heading 8.8(d), "Valuation methods", above.

[86]*Fortino v. R.*, Note 6, above, discussed under heading 4.3(d), "Unenumerated sources", above.

[87](1999), [2000] 1 C.T.C. 57, 99 D.T.C. 5799 (Eng.), 99 D.T.C. 5814 (Fr.) (S.C.C.), discussed under heading 8.5(b), "Fines and penalties", above.

[88]In reaction to the widespread concern raised by the private sector that the proposal would inappropriately apply to ordinary commercial ventures, the government withdrew the proposal on February 23, 2005 and stated that it would replace it with a more modest proposal. At the time of writing (September 2007), no replacement proposal has been released.

[89]Note 21, above

[90]*Stewart v. R.*, note 22, above; *Walls v. R.*, [2002] 3 C.T.C. 421, 2002 D.T.C. 6960 (Eng.), 2002 D.T.C. 6964 (Fr.) (S.C.C.). These cases were discussed under heading 6.2(b)(ii), "Common law", above.

The history of specific anti-avoidance rules testifies to the fact that tax law promulgation is like a game described as follows:[91]

> The government has the first move, in which it must determine the content of the law. The taxpayer then determines her transactions. The government has the pen; the taxpayer has the plan. Given this game, the taxpayer has a distinct advantage over the government, because the taxpayer acts with complete knowledge of the government's decisions while the government can only guess at the taxpayer's decisions. One-way [anti-avoidance] rules level the playing field by reducing the taxpayer's ability to take advantage of the situation.

(b) — Targeted transactions

By nature, specific anti-avoidance rules are designed to address specific types of avoidance transactions. These transactions include: timing of transactions (e.g., subsection12(4) and some of the deemed disposition rules); income splitting (e.g., subsection 56(2), 74.1 and the "kiddie tax"); and surplus stripping (e.g., sections 84 and 84.1). Some rules override the "form-over-substance" doctrine, such as paragraph 12(1)(g) and subsection 16(1). Some expressly recognize the notion of "economic profit" or "substance" (e.g., subsection 126(7))[92] or authorize recharacterization of transactions (e.g., subsection 247(2)).[93]

Some specific anti-avoidance rules are designed to curtail abuse in the area of tax shelters. Examples are: section 31 restricts the use of farming as a tax shelter;[94] subsection 40(3.1) provides that if the adjusted cost base of the partnership interest of a limited partner is negative, the negative amount will be a capital gain; regulations 1100(11) to (14) do not allow taxpayers to increase or create a rental loss with capital cost allowance;[95] subsection 96(2.2) limits the business or property losses by a limited partner to the extent of the partner's "at risk" amount in the partnership in the year;[96] subsection 96(1.8) deems the income of a business (such as the running of a hotel or a nursing home) earned by a limited partner in a limited partnership or a passive partner in a partnership to be property income for the purposes of

---

[91]Weisbach, "Costs of Departures from Formalism: Formalism in the Tax Law," (1999) 66 *U. Chi. L. Rev.* 860, 878.

[92]This provision effectively denies the foreign tax credit to transactions that lack economic profit.

[93]Subsection 247(2) authorizes the Minister to redetermine the nature and quantum of transfer pricing transactions.

[94]See heading 14.4(c)(iii), "Farm losses", above.

[95]See heading 9.4(i)(ii), "Rental property", above.

[96]A partner's "at risk" amount is the partner's investment in the partnership and share of the partnership's profit in excess of any amount owing to the partnership by the partner and any guaranteed return in respect of the partnership interest, or guaranteed buy-back of the partnership interest.

the attribution rules; subsection 162(7) requires certain tax shelters[97] to be registered and that the promoter of a tax shelter must file a special tax shelter information; and the alternative minimum tax (AMT) rules[98] add back losses created by using certain tax shelters.[99]

(c) — Effectiveness

Specific anti-avoidance rules are not always effective in preventing tax avoidance when the courts adhere to the strict interpretation of the rules and refuse to examine the economic substance or business purpose of the transactions. Taxpayers structure their transactions on the basis of the literal meaning of the provisions. For example, in *Stubart*, Estey J. relied on the number and variety of these specific anti-avoidance measures that were in existence at the time to buttress his conclusion that the Court of its own motion should not create a business purpose test that had not been enacted by Parliament. Since none of the specific anti-avoidance measures caught the situation in that case, he reasoned that the Court should not assume the power to disregard genuine legal arrangements simply because of their tax avoidance motivation. The lesson that the Department of Finance drew from the reasoning in *Stubart* was that the Act ought to include a general anti-avoidance rule, which would cover such a broad range of tax avoidance activity that an unforeseen device such as that employed in *Stubart* would not fall through the cracks again.

Under the contextual and purposive interpretative principle, specific anti-avoidance rules are presumably more effective. Taxpayers cannot simply argue that their avoidance transaction is not caught by the strict wording of a provision, they must also argue why it does not violate the object and spirit of the rule. [100]

(d) — Co-existence with the GAAR

Specific anti-avoidance rules are useful, even under the GAAR. As discussed below, the GAAR is a measure of last resort that can be invoked to control tax avoidance transactions that are otherwise successful. If a tax avoidance scheme does not

---

[97]The Act defines the terms "promoter" and "tax shelter" in s. 23.1. A tax shelter is defined to be an investment that can be written off over four years and must be registered for tax purposes. A promoter is defined to be the person who sells the tax shelter.

[98]Heading 14.8, "The alternative minimum tax", above.

[99]Losses resulting from MURB and film CCA resource property deductions, limited partnership losses, losses from a partnership in which the taxpayer is a passive partner, tax shelter losses and carrying charges (interest expense) relating to the losses listed above.

[100]When an anti-avoidance rule is introduced to close a loophole in a pre-existing provision, the taxpayers that took advantage of the loophole may not be able to argue that the loophole was previously intended by Parliament. See *Water's Edge Village Estates (Phase II) Ltd.* (2003), [2003] 2 F.C.25, para. 47: "The amendment demonstrates that Parliament moved as quickly as it could to close the loophole exploited by the appellants" precisely because the result achieved was anomalous having regard to the object and spirit of the relevant provisions of the Act."

work independently of the GAAR, there is no need to invoke it.[101] If no specific anti-avoidance rule applies to a particular avoidance transaction, GAAR can be used to "fill the gap".[102] The GAAR can apply to abusive transactions that circumvent the application of a specific anti-avoidance rule or transactions that use the specific rule to achieve tax avoidance results.

The enactment of the GAAR has not stopped the introduction of new specific anti-avoidance rules. Once introduced, a new specific rule cannot be used to block the application the GAAR on the grounds that that the specific rule covers a situation that was not specifically prohibited. The Minister seems to have leeway in invoking the GAAR, the specific anti-avoidance rule, or both.[103]

20.4 — General anti-avoidance rule (GAAR)

(a) — Section 245

Section 245 was introduced to the Act in 1988 and amended once in 1998 with retroactive effect to 1988. The current text reads as follows:

> (1) In this section,
>
> "tax benefit" means a reduction, avoidance or deferral of tax or other amount payable under this Act or an increase in a refund of tax or other amount under this Act or an increase in a refund of tax or other amount under this Act, and includes a reduction, avoidance or deferral of tax or other amount that would be payable under this Act but for a tax treaty or an increase in a refund of tax or other amount under this Act as a result of a tax treaty;
>
> "tax consequences" to a person means the amount of income, taxable income, or taxable income earned in Canada of, tax or other amount payable by or refundable to the person under this Act, or any other amount that is relevant for the purposes of computing that amount;
>
> "transaction" includes an arrangement or event.
>
> (2) Where a transaction is an avoidance transaction, the tax consequences to a person shall be determined as is reasonable in the circumstances in order to deny a tax benefit that, but for this section, would result, directly or indirectly, from that transaction or from a series of transactions that includes that transaction.

---

[101] *Geransky v. The Queen*, [2001] 2 C.T.C. 2147, 2001 D.T.C. 243 (T.C.C. [General Procedure]), para. 25 [D.T.C.].

[102] *OSFC Holdings Ltd. v. The Queen* (2001), [2001] 4 C.T.C. 82, 2001 D.T.C. 5471 (Fed. C.A.); leave to appeal refused (2002), 2002 CarswellNat 1388, 2002 CarswellNat 1389 (S.C.C.).

[103] In *Lipson v. Canada*, 2009 SCC 1, [2009] 1 S.C.R. 3 Rothstein J. wrote in para.108: "If there is a specific anti-avoidance rule that precludes the use of an enabling rule to avoid or reduce tax, then the GAAR will not apply." The other judges did not rule on the application of s. 74.5(11), a specific anti-avoidance rule, because both parties to the dispute maintained from the beginning that it did not apply having regard to the facts. See also note 29, above.

(3) An avoidance transaction means any transaction

(a) that, but for this section, would result, directly or indirectly, in a tax benefit, unless the transaction may reasonably be considered to have been undertaken or arranged primarily for bona fide purposes other than to obtain the tax benefit; or

(b) that is part of a series of transactions, which series, but for this section, would result, directly or indirectly, in a tax benefit, unless the transaction may reasonably be considered to have been undertaken or arranged primarily for bona fide purposes other than to obtain the tax benefit.

(4) Subsection (2) applies to a transaction only if it may reasonably be considered that the transaction

(a) would, if this Act were read without reference to this section, result directly or indirectly in a misuse of the provisions of any one or more of

(i) this Act,

(ii) the Income Tax Regulations,

(iii) the Income Tax Application Rules,

(iv) a tax treaty, or

(v) any other enactment that is relevant in computing tax or any other amount payable by or refundable to a person under this Act or in determining any amount that is relevant for the purposes of that computation; or

(b) would result directly or indirectly in an abuse having regard to those provisions, other than this section, read as a whole.

(5) Without restricting the generality of subsection (2), and notwithstanding any other enactment,

(a) any deduction, exemption or exclusion in computing income, taxable income, taxable income earned in Canada or tax payable or any part thereof may be allowed or disallowed in whole or in part,

(b) any such deduction, exemption or exclusion, any income, loss or other amount or part thereof may be allocated to any person,

(c) the nature of any payment or other amount may be recharacterized, and

(d) the tax effects that would otherwise result from the application of other provisions of this Act may be ignored,

in determining the tax consequences to a person as is reasonable in the circumstances in order to deny a tax benefit that would, but for this section, result, directly or indirectly, from an avoidance transaction.

(b) — Purposes

(i) — Preventing abusive tax avoidance

The historical context in which the GAAR was enacted and the wording of section 245 clearly indicate that the GAAR is a necessary response by Parliament to the problem of tax avoidance. In *Canada Trustco*, the Supreme Court accepted the government's statement about the purpose of the GAAR:[104]

> The new section 245 . . . is intended to prevent abusive tax avoidance transactions or arrangements but at the same time is not intended to interfere with legitimate commercial and family transactions. Consequently, the new rule seeks to distinguish between legitimate tax planning and abusive tax avoidance and to establish a reasonable balance between the protection of the tax base and the need for certainty for taxpayers in planning their affairs.

The Court also stated that the GAAR's purpose is "to deny the tax benefits of certain arrangements that comply with a literal interpretation of the provisions of the Act, but amount to an abuse of the provisions of the Act. But precisely what constitutes abusive tax avoidance remains the subject of debate."[105]

(ii) — Attenuating the Duke of Westminster principle

The GAAR provision was enacted to impose some constraints on the application of the common law doctrine that taxpayers are entitled to arrange their affairs in order to minimize their tax liability — the *Duke of Westminster* principle. The extent of the constraint is currently unclear. Some judges worry about the "health" of the *Duke of Westminster*.[106] How to strike a balance between the statutory anti-avoidance rule and the common law principle that encourages tax avoidance may reflect a philosophical divide among judges about the role of the judiciary in controlling tax avoidance. Judges who see themselves as "arbiters" of the tax battlefield would be hesitant in "siding" with the government. Those who consider the role of the judiciary is to properly construct tax law, including the GAAR, may be more inclined to avoid "gutting" the GAAR. "A desire to avoid uncertainty cannot justify ignoring a provision of the ITA that is clearly intended to apply to transactions that would otherwise be valid on their face."[107]

(iii) — Measure of last resort

Unlike specific anti-avoidance rules, the GAAR is expressed in more general language. It is an extraordinary provision and is applicable only after all of the other provisions of the Act. On the basis of the GAAR jurisprudence, it seems clear that the courts have been extremely cautious in applying the GAAR. Some Tax Court judges have described the GAAR as an "extreme sanction",[108] an "ultimate

---

[104] Note 14, para. 15.

[105] *Ibid.*, para. 16

[106] *Lipson*, note 103, above, para. 54, per Binnie J.

[107] *Ibid.*, para. 52, per LeBel J.

[108] Bowman, A.C.J. in *Jabs Construction Ltd. v. R.*, [1999] 3 C.T.C. 2556, 99 D.T.C. 729 (T.C.C. [General Procedure]), para. 48 [D.T.C.].

weapon",[109] a "heavy hammer",[110] or a "blunt instrument".[111] In *Lipson* (2008), however, LeBel J. clarified that the "GAAR is neither a penal provision nor a hammer to pound taxpayers into submission."[112]

(c) — No down-side risk for taxpayers

The description of the GAAR as "extreme sanction" is not really accurate in terms of the consequences of the application of the GAAR. It merely denies the tax benefit of an avoidance transaction. It does not impose any penalty (other than interest for the taxes owing). Where a transaction is characterized as an "avoidance transaction" (discussed below), subsection 245(2) requires that the tax consequences to the taxpayer be determined "as is reasonable in the circumstances in order to deny a tax benefit that, but for this section, would result, directly or indirectly, from that transaction or from a series of transactions that includes that transaction." Consequently, the GAAR applies to discourage taxpayers from taking the chance that they might get away with abusive tax avoidance transactions. There is no down-side risk to the taxpayer. The cost of failure is no more than a loss of the tax benefit sought. The taxpayer is in no worse position than not having undertaken the transaction in the first place.[113]

A draft version of section 245 (in the 1987 white paper) stipulated that the tax consequences should be designed "ignoring the transaction". This phrase is not in the current version, but there is no doubt that, in most cases, the reasonable tax consequences will be constructed by ignoring the transaction. For example, if the deeds of covenant entered into by the Duke in the *Duke of Westminster* case were caught by GAAR, this would result in the payments made to the servants becoming nondeductible, as if the deeds did not exist. The Duke would be no worse off than not if he had not entered into the covenants in the first place.

(d) — Minister's discretion

The GAAR is a relatively new development in Canada's income tax law, and the breadth and vagueness of the controlling concepts could make its potential applica-

---

[109]Miller T.C.J. in *Hill v. R.* (2002), [2003] 4 C.T.C. 2548, 2002 D.T.C. 1749 (T.C.C. [General Procedure]), para. 63 [D.T.C.].

[110]Note 1, above, para. 58.

[111]Bowman A.C.J. in *CIT Financial Ltd. v. R.* (2003), [2004] 1 C.T.C. 2232, 2003 D.T.C. 1138, ¶30 [D.T.C.] (T.C.C. [General Procedure]); reconsideration refused (2003), [2004] 1 C.T.C. 2992, 2003 D.T.C. 1545 (T.C.C. [General Procedure]); affirmed (2004), [2004] 4 C.T.C. 9, 2004 D.T.C. 6573 (F.C.A.); leave to appeal refused (2004), 2004 CarswellNat 4370, 2004 CarswellNat 4371 (S.C.C.).

[112]Note 103, para. 52.

[113]In contrast, Québec's anti-avoidance regime provides for penalties for taxpayers and third parties; see Québec Working Paper on Aggressive Tax Planning (2009) at section 2.2.4. Penalties are also imposed under the tax legislation in the United States, Australia, New Zealand and some other countries.

tion somewhat unpredictable. It should be noted, however, that the provision does not take the easy route of leaving the issue to the discretion of the Minister. In practice, of course, much will depend upon the Canada Revenue Agency's (CRA's) interpretation and its policies with respect to its application. The CRA's GAAR committee, comprised of officials from Finance and Justice as well as from the CRA, helps standardize the application of the GAAR. The committee reviews all files where GAAR might apply, including requests by taxpayers for advance rulings and referrals from the CRA's audit division, and decides whether or not a GAAR-based ruling or reassessment should be issued.

Needless to say, the CRA's decisions that emerge from this careful process will not be decisive. The ultimate forum of interpretation remains the courts. The taxpayer can use the objection and appeal process to secure a review by a court of any determination made by the Minister under the GAAR, and the court will not be obliged to defer to the Minister's findings of fact or law or to the Minister's decision as to the tax consequences. There is a growing body of GAAR jurisprudence that sheds light on the interpretation of the GAAR.

(e) — Interpretation guidelines

In *Canada Trustco* (2005) and *Mathew* (2005) the Supreme Court ruled for the first time on the application of the GAAR. Chief Justice MacLachlin and Justice Major wrote for the unanimous court and articulated a textual, contextual, and purposive approach to statutory interpretation and the following set of guidelines for the interpretation and application of the GAAR.[114]

1. Three requirements must be established to permit application of the GAAR:

   (1) A *tax benefit resulting from a transaction* or part of a series of transactions (s. 245(1) and (2));

   (2) that the transaction is an *avoidance transaction* in the sense that it cannot be said to have been reasonably undertaken or arranged primarily for a bona fide purpose other than to obtain a tax benefit; and

   (3) that there was *abusive tax avoidance* in the sense that it cannot be reasonably concluded that a tax benefit would be consistent with the object, spirit or purpose of the provisions relied upon by the taxpayer.

2. The burden is on the taxpayer to refute (1) and (2), and on the Minister to establish (3).

3. If the existence of *abusive tax avoidance* is unclear, the benefit of the doubt goes to the taxpayer.

4. The courts proceed by conducting a unified textual, contextual and purposive analysis of the provisions giving rise to the tax benefit in order to determine why they were put in place and why the benefit was conferred. The goal

[114] *Canada Trustco*, note 14 above, para. 66.

is to arrive at a purposive interpretation that is harmonious with the provisions of the Act that confer the tax benefit, read in the context of the whole Act.

5. Whether the transactions were motivated by any economic, commercial, family or other non-tax purpose may form part of the factual context that the courts may consider in the analysis of abusive tax avoidance allegations under s. 245(4). However, any finding in this respect would form only one part of the underlying facts of a case, and would be insufficient by itself to establish abusive tax avoidance. The central issue is the proper interpretation of the relevant provisions in light of their context and purpose.

6. Abusive tax avoidance may be found where the relationships and transactions as expressed in the relevant documentation lack a proper basis relative to the object, spirit or purpose of the provisions that are purported to confer the tax benefit, or where they are wholly dissimilar to the relationships or transactions that are contemplated by the provisions.

7. Where the Tax Court judge has proceeded on a proper construction of the provisions of the *Income Tax Act* and on findings supported by the evidence, appellate tribunals should not interfere, absent a palpable and overriding error.

(f) — GAAR jurisprudence

It took 17 years for the first GAAR case to be heard by the Supreme Court. By March 2010, there had been only three GAAR cases: *Canada Trustco*, *Mathew*, and *Lipson*. The Court was unanimous in holding that the GAAR applied in *Mathew* but not in *Canada Trustco* and was split *Lipson*. These cases serve as guideposts for determining whether an avoidance transaction is subject to the GAAR.

(i) — Canada Trustco

Canada Trustco involved a factually complex but conceptually straightforward type of leveraged lease. The Supreme Court summarized the facts as follows:[115]

> Briefly stated, on December 17, 1996, the respondent, with the use of its own money and a loan of approximately $100 million from the Royal Bank of Canada ("RBC"), purchased trailers from Transamerica Leasing Inc. ("TLI") at fair market value of $120 million. CTMC [*Canada Trustco*] leased the trailers to Maple Assets Investments Limited ("MAIL") who in turn subleased them to TLI, the original owner. TLI then prepaid all amounts due to MAIL under the sublease. MAIL placed on deposit an amount equal to the loan for purposes of making the lease payments and a bond was pledged as security to guarantee a purchase option payment to CTMC at the end of the lease. These transactions allowed CTMC to substantially minimize its financial risk. They were also accompanied by financial arrangements with various other parties, not relevant to this appeal.

For Canadian tax purposes, *Canada Trustco* treated the stated cost of the trailers as their capital cost and deducted capital cost allowance (CCA) in computing its profit. From the taxpayer's perspective, "[t]he transaction provides very attractive

---

[115] *Ibid.*, para. 3.

returns by generating CCA deductions which can be used to shelter other taxable lease income generated by Canada Trust."[116] The Minister invoked the GAAR in denying the CCA deductions.[117]

At the Supreme Court, the Crown argued that (1) the object and spirit of the CCA provisions is "to provide for the recognition of money spent to acquire qualifying assets to the extent that they are consumed in the income-earning process"; and (2) the circular sales-leaseback transaction involved "no real risk" and the taxpayer did not actually spend $120 million to purchase the trailers. Because the taxpayer created a "cost for CCA purposes that is an illusion" without incurring any "real" expense, the arrangement contravened the object and purpose of the CCA provisions and constituted abusive tax avoidance. The Crown's economic substance argument was framed as follows:[118]

> In this case, the pre-ordained series of transactions misuses and abuses the CCA regime because it manufactures a cost for CCA purposes that does not represent the real economic cost to CTMC of the trailers. . . *There was no risk at all that the rent payments would not be made.* Even the $5.9 million that CTMC apparently paid in fees was fully covered as it, along with the rest of CTMC's contribution of $24.9 million in funding, will be reimbursed when the $19 million bond pledged to CTMC matures in December 2005 at $33.5 million.

In contrast, *Canada Trustco* relied on the Tax Court's conclusion that "the transaction was a profitable commercial investment and fully consistent with the object and spirit of the Act."[119] *Canada Trustco* argued that the policy of the Act is that "cost" means the price (the amount) that the taxpayer gave up in order to get the asset (except in specific circumstances not applicable to the case at issue), and that "[a] cost is not reduced to reflect a mitigation of economic risk."[120] Thus, the transaction was not abusive. *Canada Trustco*'s position prevailed.

The Supreme Court found that the purpose of the CCA provisions, as applied to sale-leaseback transactions, was to permit deduction of CCA based on the cost of

---

[116] *Ibid.*, para. 2.

[117] The taxpayer's appeal to the Tax Court of Canada was upheld (2003 D.T.C. 587, [2003] 4 C.T.C. 2009 (T.C.C. [General Procedure])). The Tax Court's decision was affirmed by the Federal Court of Appeal (2004 D.T.C. 6119, [2004] 2 C.T.C. 276 (F.C.A.); leave to appeal allowed (2004), 331 N.R. 395 (note) (S.C.C.); affirmed (2005), 2005 D.T.C. 5523 (Eng.), (sub nom. *Hypothèques Trustco Canada v. Canada)* 2005 D.T.C. 5547 (Fr.), [2005] 5 C.T.C. 215 (S.C.C.)). The Minister of National Revenue sought leave to appeal to the Supreme Court of Canada, which was granted.

[118] Note 14, para. 70.

[119] *Ibid.*, para. 71. This is a factual determination. The Tax Court considered whether, as an evidentiary matter, the taxpayer had behaved in a fashion that reflected reliance on the legal formulation and concluded that transactions of this nature are normal commercial transactions. Since the Supreme Court regarded this as a question of fact, it simply adopted the Tax Court's characterization.

[120] *Ibid.*, paras. 71 and 72.

the assets acquired. "This purpose emerges clearly from the scheme of the CCA provisions within the Act as a whole."[121] The provisions of the Act do not refer to "economic risk" but only to "cost;" moreover, the court found the Crown's submission on "economic substance" to be "narrow":[122]

> It did not focus on the purpose of the CCA provisions read in the context of the Act as a whole, to determine whether the tax benefit fell outside the object, spirit or purpose of the relevant provisions.

Overall, the Supreme Court's analysis of subsection 245(4) in the context of this case is disappointing. A "textual, contextual and purposive" interpretation of the concept of "cost" was effectively reduced to a mere "textual" interpretation. The court did not shed much light on how to establish the legislative purpose of the CCA provisions; it simply declared that the purpose "emerges clearly from the scheme of the CCA provisions within the Act as a whole." To back up its conclusion that "cost" refers only to "legal" cost, and not "economic" cost, the Court drew a negative inference from the fact that Parliament introduced economic risk into the meaning of cost in subsections 13(7.1) and (7.2) of the Act (which adjust the cost of depreciable property when a taxpayer receives government assistance), but not in the context of CCA provisions. Presumably a taxpayer can only deduct CCA in respect of assets acquired or owned by the taxpayer. But what constitutes ownership? Did Canada Trust "own" the trailers? In *Altria*,[123] a U.S. case with similar facts, the Court looked at this issue in examining the economic substance of the transaction. In *Canada Trustco*, the Supreme Court of Canada did not consider economic substance of the transaction and adopted the "legal substance" analysis:[124]

> Here the documents detailing the transaction left no uncertainty as to the relationships between the parties. CTMC paid $120 million to TLI for the equipment, partly with borrowed funds and partly with its own money. Having become the owner of the equipment, it leased it to MAIL. MAIL then subleased it back to the vendor, TLI. The relationships between the parties as expressed in the relevant documentation were not superfluous elements; they were the very essence of the transaction.

The Supreme Court upheld the Tax Court's characterization of the transaction as being "not so dissimilar from an ordinary sale-leaseback [as] to take it outside the object, spirit or purpose of the relevant CCA provisions."[125] As noted above, the Supreme Court also relied on the Tax Court's conclusion that "the transaction was

---

[121] *Ibid.*

[122] *Ibid*, para.76. The specified leasing property rules implicitly reflect decisions about the economic implications of certain sale-leaseback transactions. In the context of CCA, cost is a well-understood legal concept. The court stated, *ibid.*, at paragraph 75, "Like the Tax Court Judge, we see nothing in the GAAR or the object of the CCA provisions that permits us to rewrite them to interpret 'cost' to mean 'amount economically at risk' in the applicable provisions."

[123] See note 69, above. The Altria case is discussed in the text surrounding this note.

[124] Note 14, at paragraph 77.

[125] *Ibid.*, at para. 78.

a profitable commercial investment and fully consistent with the object and spirit of the Act." It did not mention the fact that the transaction was "profitable" likely because of the tax savings (CCA deductions).

(ii) — Mathew

The *Mathew* case involved a transfer of business losses from a corporation to unrelated persons through the use of a partnership. Standard Trust Company was in the business of lending money on the security of mortgages of real property. As a result of financial difficulties, Standard Trust was wound up in 1991. Standard Trust's assets included a portfolio of mortgage loans ("the STIL II portfolio") with a total cost of $85 million and a fair market value of $33 million, and thus accrued losses of $52 million. These losses were of no value to Standard Trust because of its insolvency. In order to maximize the amount realized by Standard Trust on liquidation, the liquidator devised a plan to sell the portfolio. The following steps were taken:

- Standard Trust incorporated a wholly owned subsidiary.
- Standard Trust entered into a partnership with the subsidiary ("partnership A"). The interests of Standard Trust and its subsidiary in partnership A were 99 percent and 1 percent respectively.
- The STIL II portfolio was transferred to partnership A at a cost of $85 million pursuant to subsection 18(13) of the Act.[126]
- The liquidator carried out an intensive campaign to market Standard Trust's 99 percent interest in partnership A and, after difficult and protracted negotiations, eventually sold it to OSFC Holdings Ltd.
- OSFC assigned its partnership interest to a general partnership ("partnership B").
- OSFC retained an interest in partnership B but sold interests in the partnership to a number of individuals and entities (the taxpayers in the *Mathew* case). On the eventual sale or write-down of the STIL II portfolio, partnership B allocated the portfolio losses to its partners, including the taxpayers, who claimed their proportionate shares of the losses as a deduction against their own incomes.

As a result of these transactions, Standard Trust's accrued losses of $52 million were transferred to various arm's-length taxpayers through the use of subsection 18(13) and the partnership vehicle.[127]

---

[126]By virtue of subsection 18(13) of the Act, the $52 million in accrued losses was disallowed on the transfer of the portfolio to the partnership; instead, the amount of the losses was added to the fair market value of the portfolio, resulting in a cost to the partnership of $85 million.

[127]The taxpayers in *Mathew* had a tough case even before they reached the Supreme Court. In *OSFC Holdings Ltd. v. The Queen*, 2001 D.T.C. 5471, [2001] 4 C.T.C. 82 (Fed. C.A.); leave to appeal refused (2002), 2002 CarswellNat 1388, 2002 CarswellNat 1389 (S.C.C.),

A textual, contextual, and purposive interpretation of subsection 18(13) and the partnership rules in section 96 led the Supreme Court to conclude that the purpose of these provisions is "to prevent a taxpayer who is in the business of lending money from claiming a loss upon the superficial disposition of a mortgage or similar non-capital property"[128] — not to facilitate the transfer of losses to arm's-length persons.

The court held that allowing the appellants to deduct the losses would frustrate this purpose and the transaction was not of the type contemplated by Parliament:[129]

> A purposive interpretation of the interplay between s. 18(13) and s. 96(1) indicates that they allow the preservation and sharing of losses on the basis of shared control of the assets in a common business activity.

The lack of such common business activity presumably renders the transaction abusive. In reaching its decision, the court found the following facts relevant:[130]

- The losses originated from the failure of a third party (Standard Trust).
- Partnership A served as a "holding vehicle" for the unrealized losses that Standard Trust planned from the outset to sell to arm's-length parties.
- Partnership B was relatively passive; its purpose was simply to realize and allocate the tax losses without any other significant activity.
- Even though the partners of partnership B paid substantial amounts to acquire their partnership interests and sought to minimize their exposure to risk, these facts cannot negate the above conclusions.
- Neither partnership A nor partnership B ever dealt with real property, apart from the original mortgage portfolio from Standard Trust.
- Standard Trust was never in a partnership relationship with either OSFC or any of the taxpayers.
- The purported non-arm's-length relationship between partnership A and Standard Trust was vacuous and artificial.

The Court did not provide any illumination for distinguishing this case from the *Canada Trustco* case. It did not explain why it took a broader, and more purposive interpretation of the relevant provisions in this case, but not the CCA provisions in the other case.

---

the Federal Court of Appeal ruled against the taxpayer and held that the transactions constituted an abuse of the provisions of the Act read as a whole. In *Mathew*, not surprisingly, the taxpayers lost at both the Tax Court ((2002), 2002 D.T.C. 1637, [2003] 1 C.T.C. 2045 (T.C.C. [General Procedure])) and the Federal Court of Appeal ((2003), (sub nom. *Kaulius v. R.)* 2003 D.T.C. 5644, [2004] 1 C.T.C. 115 (F.C.A.); leave to appeal allowed (2004), 332 N.R. 199 (note) (S.C.C.); affirmed (2005), (sub nom. *Mathew v. Canada)* 2005 D.T.C. 5538 (Eng.), 2005 D.T.C. 5563 (Fr.), [2005] 5 C.T.C. 244 (S.C.C.).

[128] Note 12 above, para. 53.

[129] *Ibid.*, at para. 62.

[130] *Ibid.*, at paragraphs 61 and 62.

(iii) — Lipson

The facts of this case can be simply described as "Singleton with a twist" because the transactions undertaken by Mr. and Mrs. Lipson were similar to those in the *Singleton* case.[131]

- On April 24, 1994, the taxpayers entered into an agreement to purchase a house for $750,000 with a closing date of September 1, 1994.
- On the day before the closing date, Mrs. Lipson borrowed $562,500 from a bank and used the money to purchase certain shares that Mr. Lipson held in a family company. Mrs. Lipson did not have enough income to pay the interest on this loan (the "share loan") and the bank would not have lent it to her on an unsecured basis but for the fact that Mr. Lipson had agreed to repay the loan in its entirety the following day.
- On the closing date, the proceeds from the sales of the shares were used to pay for the purchase of the house.
- The next day, the Lipsons mortgaged the house (the "house loan") and used the money to repay Mrs. Lipson's original share loan.

These transactions were designed to enable Mr. Lipson to deduct the interest expenses in respect of the "house loan". They relied on the following provisions of the Act:

- Subsection 73(1) allows a transfer of property between spouses on a rollover basis. The Lipsons relied on this provision so that the shares were transferred to Mrs. Lipson without triggering any immediate capital gain to Mr. Lipson.
- Section 74.1 attributes any income or loss from property transferred from one spouse to another back to the transferor for tax purposes. Any income or loss earned by Mrs. Lipson from the shares acquired from her husband was deemed to the income or loss of Mr. Lipson.
- Paragraph 20(1)(c) permits the deduction of interest on money borrowed for the purpose of earning income from a property. The shares in Lipson family company were income-producing property. Interest on the share loan was thus deductible.
- Subsection 20(3) allows a deduction for interest on money borrowed to repay previously borrowed money if the interest on the original loan is deductible. Because the Lipsons used the house loan to repay the share loan, the house loan is treated as having funded the share purchase.

Mrs. Lipson deducted the interest on the house loan pursuant to paragraph 20(1)(c) in computing her income from owning the shares. Depending on the amount of dividend received from the family company and the interest expense, she may have a net income or loss from owning the shares. Such income or loss is attributed to Mr. Lipson.

---

[131] See heading 19.2 (d)(iii), "The *Singleton* (2001) case," above.

The Minister invoked the GAAR to deny the interest expense deduction. The parties conceded that the transactions were avoidance transactions for purposes of the GAAR. Therefore the sole issue before the court was whether the transactions constituted an abuse or misuse.

The Tax Court applied the GAAR, holding that the "overall purpose" of the transactions was to make interest on the house loan deductible and that resulted in a misuse of the relevant provisions of the Act. The Federal Court of Appeal upheld that decision. The Supreme Court was unanimous that *Singleton*-type planning remains acceptable under the GAAR, but split on the application of the GAAR to the spousal twist.

The majority of the Supreme Court (4:3), written by LeBel J., held that the "spousal twist" was abusive because the Lipsons turned to the anti-avoidance rules under subsections 73(1) and 74.1 to obtain the tax savings. The dissent written by Binnie J. held that the transactions did not result in an abuse of those provisions, but fulfillment of them. Preventing spouses from reducing their tax burden through non-arm's length transactions as abuse would give GAAR too large a field of operation. Rothstein J. disagreed with both LeBel and Binnie on the ground that the specific anti-avoidance rule in section 74.5 should be applied in stead of the GAAR.

This split decision of the Supreme Court in this case speaks to the uncertainty about the application of the GAAR. It also reveals the philosophical divide among the justices. According to LeBel J., one cannot read the GAAR out of the Act out of concerns with certainty for tax planning. The "GAAR may introduce a degree of uncertainty into tax planning, but such uncertainty is inherent in all situations in which the law must be applied to unique facts."[132] Binnie J. called the majority's fears for GAAR "apocalyptic"[133] while it is the *Duke of Westminster* principle that is ailing: "The GAAR is a weapon that, unless contained by the jurisprudence, could have a widespread, serious and unpredictable effect on legitimate tax planning."[134] According to the majority, however, "Binnie J. essentially guts the GAAR and reads it out of the ITA under the guise of an exercise in legal interpretation."

20.5 — Application of the GAAR

(a) — Tax benefit

The first step in applying the GAAR is to determine whether there is a tax benefit arising from a transaction or series of transactions of which the transaction is part. A "tax benefit" is defined in subsection 245(1) as including not only the avoidance or reduction of tax, but also the deferral of tax. A tax benefit may be the result of a deduction of an expense, exclusion of an income, the time value of money from deferral, obtaining a tax relief under the tax expenditure provisions, using a tax-

[132] *Lipson*, note 103, above para. 52.

[133] *Ibid.*, para. 96.

[134] *Ibid.*, para.55.

efficient structure to earn less-taxed income item (such as capital gains as opposed to business income), or deduction of losses.

There are several important principles guiding the determination of whether a tax benefit exists. The first principle is that the determination is a factual one.[135] As such, the Minister will initially make a determination on the basis of the available information or assumptions of facts. The taxpayer has the onus of refuting the Minister's determination. The court will decide whether the taxpayer has met the onus of refuting the existence of a tax benefit.

The second principle is that the magnitude of the tax benefit is not relevant.[136] "If a deduction against taxable income is claimed, the existence of a tax benefit is clear, since a deduction results in a reduction of tax."[137] The value of the tax benefit could be in millions or several dollars. In most GAAR cases, the amount of tax benefit is quite significant because of the costs of litigation. In *Canada Trustco*, the existence of the tax benefit was easily found as the taxpayer had purchased and leased the trailers in order to generate over $80 million of CCA deductions ($36.2 million in 1996 and $46.3 million in 1997). The CCA deductions effectively "sheltered" *Canada Trustco*'s income from other investment operations. The evidence of internal correspondence within Canada Trust clearly indicated that the key to the transaction were the CCA deductions. In *Mathew*, the tax benefit was the over $10 million losses that were deducted by the taxpayers against other income.

The third principle is that in cases other than a reduction in taxable income, the existence of a tax benefit can be established by comparison with an alternative arrangement. The Court stated in *Canada Trustco*:[138]

> For example, characterization of an amount as an annuity rather than as a wage, or as a capital gain rather than as business income, will result in differential tax treatment. In such cases, the existence of a tax benefit might only be established upon a comparison between alternative arrangements.

This principle is particularly helpful in identifying the existence of tax benefit in transactions involving tax efficient structures or tax arbitrage. For example, in an earlier surplus-strip case, *McNichol v. R.* (1997),[139] the Tax Court said:

> There is nothing mysterious about the subsection 245(1) concept of tax benefit. Clearly a reduction or avoidance of tax does require the identification in any given set of circumstances of a *norm* or *standard* against which reduction is to be measured. (Emphasis added.)

---

[135] Note 14, above, para. 19.

[136] *Ibid.*

[137] *Ibid.*, para. 20.

[138] *Ibid.*

[139] See note 8, above. In *Evans* (2006), note 9 above, Bowman C.J.T.C. also had no difficulty finding the tax benefit to be the tax otherwise payable on dividends. He said (at para. 17): "I think there was a tax benefit. Had Dr. Evans simply received a dividend of over $267,000 from 117679 he would have paid tax on it."

In that case, the shareholders of a corporation sought to distribute the funds in the corporation in a manner other than by way of dividend. That manner resulted in an arrangement producing capital gains that were eligible for the lifetime capital gains exemptions.

But what if the alternative is "doing nothing"? In *Univar Canada Ltd. v. R.* (2005)[140] the taxpayer (Univar Canada) was a subsidiary of Univar Corp., a U.S. corporation. Univar Corp. also owned all of the outstanding shares of Dutch corporations and Univar Europe. Univar Corp. had previously loaned about US $27 million to Univar Europe. A tax strategy was developed to address financial problems within the Univar group and to improve Univar Corp.'s U.S. tax position (regarding its excess foreign tax credits and other factors). Under this strategy, Univar Canada used about C $12 million of cash as well as borrowed funds to subscribe for about US $27 million of common shares of a newly formed Barbados subsidiary (Barbadosco). Barbadosco then acquired the loan owed by Univar Europe to Univar Corp. Univar Europe paid interest on its loan (now owed) to Barbadosco. After paying a 2.5 percent tax in Barbados, Barbadosco distributed the funds received from Univar Europe to Univar Canada as dividends which were tax exempt in Canada.[141]

The Minister sought to deny the tax benefits by relying on the GAAR and the specific anti-avoidance rule under paragraph 95(6)(b). The interest deduction by Univar was clearly a tax benefit. However, the CRA argued the case on the basis that the transaction should be compared with an alternative transaction of Univar Canada (rather than Barbadosco) acquiring the Univar Europe loans). The Tax Court rejected the Minister's argument. The court held that the test for determining "tax benefit" was not to look for an alternate transaction that would have resulted in the greatest amount of tax, but rather an alternate transaction that the taxpayer may have actually otherwise done. In this case, the Court found that the taxpayer would simply not have entered into the alternate transaction suggested by the CRA (i.e., acquiring the loans owed by Univar Europe directly). The only alternate arrangement that can be considered is the possibility of the alleged avoidance transaction not having occurred at all. According to the Court, had the shares of Barbadosco not been acquired by the taxpayer, there would be no tax otherwise payable which could be avoided, reduced or deferred. With respect, the court erred in not finding the existence of tax benefit because the interest deduction (that existed only because of the borrowing to fund the purchase of the shares of Barbadosco) is clearly a "reduction in taxable income". Finding an alternative transaction was not the only way to establish a tax benefit in this case.

---

[140]Note 15, above.

[141]In international tax parlance, this is a typical "double dip" because the interest expense is deducted in Canada and in a foreign country. By virtue of paragraph 113(1)(a) of the Act, the dividends received by Univar Canada are tax exempt in Canada.

Finally, a transaction cannot be recharacterized for the purpose of determining whether there is a tax benefit.[142] Recharacterization is allowed only at the final stage of the GAAR analysis under subsection 245(4). The person who obtains the tax benefit does not necessarily have to be the person that undertook or arranged the transaction in question. In other words, "subsection 245(3) does not say that the person who undertakes or arranges the transaction must be the one who obtains the tax benefit".[143]

The threshold for finding whether there is a tax benefit has been set relatively low. In the majority of cases, a tax benefit is not difficult to find in the form of a reduction in tax payable. The GAAR analysis moves to the next step, that is, whether the transaction is an "avoidance transactions".

(b) — Avoidance transaction

Once it is determined that there is a tax benefit from a transaction or series of transactions, the second step in applying the GAAR is to determine if the transaction is an "avoidance transaction" within subsection 245(3). Subsection 245(3) specifically defines "avoidance transaction" as a transaction that results in a tax benefit, either by itself or as part of a series of transactions, "unless the transaction may reasonably be considered to have been undertaken or arranged primarily for bona fide purposes other than to obtain the tax benefit". "The function of this requirement is to remove from the ambit of the GAAR transactions or series of transactions that may reasonably be considered to have been undertaken or arranged primarily for a non-tax purpose."[144]

(i) — Transaction

A "transaction" is defined under subsection 245(1) to include an arrangement or event. It is generally not a contentious issue. The meaning of "serious of transactions" and the purpose test are the two key elements.

(ii) — Series of transactions

The meaning of the expression "series of transactions" under subsections 245(2) and (3) is not clear on its face."[145] What kind of link is required to "string" the transactions together for the purpose of the GAAR analysis?

At common law, the link is "preordained" and "pre-planned": "[A] series of transactions involves a number of transactions that are "pre-ordained in order to produce

---

[142]See *Canadian Pacific Ltd. v. R.* (2001), 2002 D.T.C. 6742, [2002] 2 C.T.C. 197, ¶33 [D.T.C.] (Fed. C.A.); reconsideration refused (2002), [2002] 2 C.T.C. 150 (Fed. C.A.) and *Canada Trustco*, note 14 above, para. 30.

[143]See *OSFC*, note 101, above, para. 43. In *OSFC*, the avoidance transaction was arranged by another taxpayer (Standard Trust).

[144]Note 14, above, para. 21.

[145]*Ibid.*, para. 25

a given result" with "no practical likelihood that the pre-planned events would not take place in the order ordained."[146]

Subsection 248(10) extends the meaning of "series of transactions" to include "related transactions or events completed in contemplation of the series". This occurs where the parties to the transaction "knew of the . . . series, such that it could be said that they took it into account when deciding to complete the transaction".[147] The phrase "in contemplation" can be read in a broader sense of "because of" or "in relation to", and be applied to events either before or after the basic avoidance transaction.[148] For example, the *OSFC* case involved the same transactions as those in *Mathew*. OSFC was a partner in Partnership B described in the *Mathew* case. As mentioned above, the Supreme Court adopted Rothstein J.A.'s (as he then was) interpretation of the meaning of "series of transactions". Rothstein J.A. had little difficulty finding that the incorporation of the subsidiary corporation, the formation of the partnership, and the transfer of the STIL II portfolio to the partnership constituted a preordained series of transactions. However, the purchase by OSFC from Standard Trust of the partnership interest was the result of arm's-length negotiations and not preordained. It would not be part of the series in the absence of the deeming rule under subsection 248(10). He concluded that OSFC knew about the series of transactions by which Standard Trust had transferred STIL II portfolio to a partnership and took that series into account in acquiring the interest in the partnership. In fact, the prior series of transactions was fundamental to effect the sale of the accrued tax losses to any arm's length persons acquiring interests in the partnership.[149] Therefore, he found that OSFC's acquisition of the partnership interest was part of series of transactions that resulted in a tax benefit.

(iii) — Non-tax purpose test

Having determined that a transaction or series of transactions resulted in a tax benefit, the next question is whether the primary purpose of the transaction or any transaction in the series was to obtain the tax benefit, as opposed to achieve some bona fide non-tax purpose. Subsection 245(3) excludes a transaction from being an "avoidance transaction" if it "may reasonably be considered to have been undertaken or arranged primarily for bona fide purposes other than to obtain the tax benefit".

---

[146]*Craven v. White* (1988), [1989] A.C. 398 (U.K. H.L.), at p. 514, per Lord Oliver; see also *W.T. Ramsay Ltd. v. Inland Revenue Commissioners*, [1981] 1 All E.R. 865 (U.K. H.L.). The Supreme Court endorsed the test for a series of transactions in *Canada Trustco*, note 14 above, para. 25.

[147]*OSFC*, note 101, above, para. 36.

[148]Note 14 above, para. 26.

[149]The taxpayer in OSFC argued that GAAR requires that the person who arranges the transactions or series of transactions must be the same person who obtains the tax benefit from those transactions. The Court rejected that argument for the reason that this requirement was not found in the wording of subsection 245(3).

"Non-tax purpose" is obviously broader than "non-business purpose". Section 245 does not use the phrase "business purpose", which was the controlling concept under the 1987 white paper version of section 245. The main difficulty with the phrase "business purpose" is that "many legitimate transactions are carried out for non-tax reasons, such as family, personal, or investment reasons, that cannot be characterized as business reasons".[150] The non-tax purpose test is able to accommodate all purposes other than tax avoidance.[151]

Subsection 245(3) uses the word "reasonably" to suggest an objective, not subjective, standard of inquiry. It gives primacy to the objective facts available to an outside observer as opposed to the evidence as to the taxpayer's subjective intention. It is a factual determination falling within the jurisdiction of the Tax Court. In the absence of a palpable and overriding error, the Tax Court's decision cannot be overruled by the appellate court. A high premium is thus paid for meticulous documentation during the planning and execution of a tax plan and careful presentation of the facts at the Tax Court.

Subsection 245(3) uses the word "primarily" to suggest a comparative evaluation in cases where a transaction has both a non-tax and tax-avoidance purpose. It mandates "an objective assessment of the relative importance of the driving forces of the transaction."[152] The non-tax purpose being primary cannot be ruled out simply because the tax benefit is significant.[153] Some factors have been considered relevant in such objective assessment, including:

- Quantitative comparison of the "tax savings" and non-tax benefit of the transaction;
- Transitory nature of the arrangements;
- Tax drove the deal;
- Choice of one method of accomplishing transaction over another.

A comparison of the amount of the estimated tax benefit and the estimated business earnings may be relevant to the determination of the primary purpose of a transaction. In *Water's Edge Village Estates (Phase II) Ltd.*[154], a group of taxpayers purchased a 93.5 per cent interest in an American partnership ("Klink") on December 20, 1991 for $320,000. Klink held a capital asset, a mainframe computer with a fair market value of US$7,000, which was leased to a third party for profit. Klink acquired the computer in 1981 for US$3.7 million. On December 20, 1991, Klink contributed the computer to a partnership in British Columbia in return for a 50 per

[150] Arnold and Wilson, note 57, above, 1155.

[151] Nevertheless, the test is really nothing more than "an expanded version of the business purpose *test*". *Ibid.*, 1159.

[152] Canada Trustco, note 14 above, para. 28.

[153] *Ibid.*, para. 58.

[154] [2002] 4 C.T.C. 1, (sub nom. *Water's Edge Village Estates (Phase II) Ltd. v. R.*) 2002 D.T.C. 7172 (Fed. C.A.); leave to appeal refused (2003), (sub nom. *Water's Edge Village Estates (Phase II) Ltd. v. Minister of National Revenue*) 311 N.R. 198 (note) (S.C.C.).

cent interest in the partnership. The taxpayers purportedly tried to lease the obsolete computer in a foreign market. In computing its income for 1991, Klink treated the computer as a depreciable property and claimed a large terminal loss under subsection 20(16) as a result of the disposition of the computer to the B.C. partnership. The terminal loss deduction led to a net loss of $4.4 million in Klink. The taxpayers claimed their share of the loss against their incomes. The taxpayers accepted that they received a tax benefit, but argued that the transactions were undertaken for a purpose other than to obtain this tax benefit. Noël J.A. found that "the quest for the tax benefit was the only reason why the transactions unfolded as they did." He contrasted the value of the tax loss in the hands of the taxpayers with the income earning prospects of the obsolete computer, noting that the former was much larger. He found that the difference between the cost of the Klink partnership interest (i.e., $320,000) and the value of the computer (i.e., US$7,000) indicated that first and foremost, the taxpayers paid to acquire a tax loss.

"Transitory arrangements", such as the creation of a corporation or a partnership, followed within a short period of time by its elimination, or being a partner of a partnership for a short period of time, ordinarily would not be considered to have been carried out primarily for bona fide non-tax purposes. For example, in *MacKay* (2008), a bank was planning to foreclose on its interest in shopping centre. The taxpayers, who were real estate developers, agreed to purchase the shopping centre from the bank for $10 million through the following series of transactions:

- On November 5, 1993, the bank incorporated a wholly owned subsidiary and formed a partnership with this subsidiary: the subsidiary was the general partner and the bank was the limited partner;
- On November 23, 1993, the bank assigned its $16 million mortgage receivable to the partnership in exchange for 10,000 limited partnership units. The transaction was structured to fall within subsection 18(13) so that the bank was denied the loss on the transfer of the mortgage to the partnership and the $6 million denied loss was added to adjusted cost base of mortgage inside the partnership.
- The partnership foreclosed on the mortgage and acquired the shopping centre (cost base: $16 million plus interest and foreclosure expenses; fair market value $10 million)
- On December 29, 1993, the taxpayers became general partners in the partnership by purchasing 2,000 partnership units for $2 million
- On December 30, 1993, the partnership redeemed the bank's limited partnership units for $8.6 million, using the money the bank had lent to the partnership. The bank ceased to be a partner of the partnership.
- On December 31, 1993 (the partnership's year end), the partnership wrote down the cost base of the land to its then fair market value ($10 million) under subsection 10(1), resulting in a $6 million loss.

The primary purpose of the transactions by which the bank became a partner of the partnership at the outset, transferred the mortgage receivable to the partnership before any of the respondents became partners, and remained a partner for more than 30 days after the transfer was to obtain the tax benefit (transferring the tax loss through the partnership to the taxpayers). The court concluded that "[n]othing the record suggests that the non-tax business objectives of the respondends required those steps to be taken."[155]

When evidence indicates that "the tax benefit drove the deal",[156] such as was the case in *Canada Trustco*, the primary purpose of the transaction is clearly to obtain the tax benefit. In *Canada Trustco*, the taxpayer hired an arranger to put together the plan that can generate CCA deductions and interest expense deductions in a way to shelter its leasing income. The deal was recommended to the Board as a transaction that "provides very attractive returns, by generating CCA deductions which can be used to shelter other taxable lease income generated by Canada Trust."[157] Canada Trustco's own banker, RBC, referred to the transaction in their Transaction Outline as a Canadian Cross-Border Leveraged Tax Lease. Miller T.C.J. had no difficulty in concluding that "this was a profitable investment in a commercial context, but such a finding does not outweigh the primary purpose of obtaining the tax benefit from the investment — the tax benefit drove the deal."[158]

When there is a legitimate business or non-tax objective for undertaking a transaction and there are alternative methods of achieving that objective, the use of a most tax-efficient method does not necessarily make the transaction an avoidance transaction.[159] The Explanatory Notes[160] adopted by the Supreme Court of Canada in paragraph 30 of *Canada Trustco* state:

> Subsection 245(3) does not permit the "recharacterization" of a transaction for the purposes of determining whether or not it is an avoidance transaction. In other words, it does not permit a transaction to be considered to be an avoidance transaction because some alternative transaction that might have achieved an equivalent result would have resulted in higher taxes.

---

[155]*MacKay*, note 13, FCA at para. 22.

[156]Note 1, para. 57.

[157]*Canada Trustco* (TCC), note 1, above, para. 52.

[158]*Ibid.*, para. 57.

[159]See, for example, in *Evans v. R.* (2005), 2005 D.T.C. 1762 (Eng.), [2006] 2 C.T.C. 2009, the taxpayer used a series of transactions to take advantage of the lifetime capital gains exemption in respect of qualified small business corporation shares under section 110.6 as well as the exemption from the attribution rules in paragraph 74.5(1)(b) to remove corporate surplus from a corporation virtually tax-free. Bowman C.J.T.C. held Bowman T.C.C.J. found as a matter of fact that the primary purpose of the series of surplus stripping transactions was to put the corporate funds in Dr. Evans' hands. The method chosen was one designed to enable him to do so at the least tax cost.

[160]Canada. Department of Finance. *Explanatory Notes to Legislation Relating to Income Tax*. Ottawa: Queen's Printer, 1988.

In the case of a series of transactions, is it the primary purpose of *each* transaction in the series or the *entire series* that is relevant to the determination whether there is an avoidance transaction? The answer is the former:[161]

> If at least one transaction in a series of transactions is an "avoidance transaction", then the tax benefit that results from the series may be denied under the GAAR. This is apparent from the wording of s. 245(3). Conversely, if each transaction in a series was carried out primarily for bona fide non-tax purposes, the GAAR cannot be applied to deny a tax benefit.

This question is important as many avoidance transactions involve a series of transactions that are carefully planned and everything was supposed to work like clockwork. Even if the primary purpose of the series is not tax avoidance, a particular transaction in the series may still constitute an avoidance transaction. The GAAR may apply to deny the tax benefit if the transaction is abusive under subsection 245(4). There is no need for every transaction in the series to be an avoidance transaction.[162]

(c) — Abuse or misuse

A tax avoidance transaction is subject to the GAAR only if it may reasonably be considered that the transaction would result directly or indirectly in a misuse of the provisions of a taxing statute or an abuse having regard to those provisions read as a whole. The wording of subsection 245(4) refers to both "misuse" and "abuse" in the English version, and only "abus" in the French version. The Supreme Court found the concept of "abuse" broad enough to include "misuse."[163]

The abusive analysis under subsection 245(4) is the key and most difficult issue in the application of the GAAR. It is the only issue before the Supreme Court in the three GAAR cases.[164] Several general principles can be discerned from the GAAR jurisprudence.

First, an avoidance transaction is abusive if it defeats or frustrates the *purpose*, not necessarily the overarching policy,[165] of the statutory provisions. In *Canada*

---

[161] *Canada Trustco*, note 14, above, para. 34.

[162] However, the Supreme Court in *Canada Trustco* did not clearly reject the principles set out in *Canadian Pacific Ltd. v. R.* (2002): (1) that the overall purpose of the series determines the primary purpose of each transaction in the series for the purposes of subsection 245(3); and (2) that, if the primary purpose of the series is not tax avoidance, taxpayers are entitled to use the more tax-efficient structure.

[163] Note 14, above, para. 43.

[164] The fact that the Court was unanimous in applying the GAAR in *Mathew*, but not *Canada Trustco* indicates a line between abusive tax avoidance and acceptable tax minimization. The split decision in *Lipson* highlights the challenges in applying the abusive analysis in *Singleton* type of transactions that were considered acceptable before the GAAR.

[165] See "Clear and unambiguous policy test", heading 20.4(f)(iv) of the 5th edition of this book. That test requires the identification of a clear and unambiguous policy underlying or overarching the provisions of the Act in order to justify a finding of abuse.

Trustco, the Supreme Court made it clear that policy remains relevant. However, the "search for an overarching policy . . . that is not anchored in a textual, contextual and purposive interpretation of the specific provisions that are relied upon for the tax benefit would run counter to the overall policy of Parliament that tax law be certain, predictable and fair, so that taxpayers can intelligently order their affairs."[166]

Second, the GAAR mandates a purposive interpretation of the Act. The Supreme Court identified a two-stage test for determining abuse.[167] The first stage involves a textual, contextual and purposive interpretation of the provisions relied upon by the taxpayer to obtain the tax benefit. It is a question of law. The second stage is to determine whether the avoidance transaction falls within or frustrates that purpose. The Court regarded this to be a question of fact. The overall abuse analysis under subsection 245(4) is thus a mixed question of fact and law.[168]

Third, the GAAR was intended to prevent abusive tax avoidance as well as to preserve taxpayers' right to tax planning under the *Duke of Westminster* principle. It applies only when the abusive nature is clear.[169]

Fourth, the lack of economic substance in an avoidance transaction does not necessarily mean that the transaction is abusive.[170] "Motivation, purpose and economic substance are relevant under subsection 245(4) only to the extent that they establish whether the transaction frustrates the purpose of the relevant provisions".[171] In *Canada Trustco*, the Court found that the CCA provisions of the Act (e.g., paragraph 20(1)(a)) require "cost" to mean "legal cost", not "economic cost", and the avoidance transaction at issue was not abusive. On the other hand, the existence (or lack) of economic substance plays a role, either implicitly or explicitly in some GAAR cases. In *Mathew*, the Court found the avoidance transactions to be abusive and the abusive nature is confirmed by the "vacuity and artificiality" the transactions.[172]

Fifth, in a case where the series of transactions at issue result in more than one tax benefit, "the individual tax benefits must be analyzed separately, but always in the context of the entire series of transactions that bearing in mind that each step may have an impact on the others, in order to determine whether any of the provisions relied upon for each tax benefit was misused and abused."[173] For example, the Majority in *Lipson* found that the tax benefit conferred on Mrs. Lipson by para-

---

[166]Note 14, above, para. 42.

[167]*Ibid.*, paras. 44 and 55.

[168]*Ibid.*, para. 44.

[169]*Ibid.*, para. 50.

[170]*Ibid.*, para. 57.

[171]Canada Trustco, note 14, above, paras. 57-60; Lipson, per LeBel J., note 103 above, para. 38.

[172]*Mathew*, note 12, above, para. 62.

[173]*Lipson*, per LeBel, para. 40.

graph 20(1)(c) and subsection 20(3), that is, the entitlement to deduct the interest, did not result in a misuse or abuse of these provisions. The tax benefit conferred by subsection 73(1) and section 74.1, namely the rollover and attribution of income or loss, results in an abuse because "a specific anti-avoidance rule is being used to facilitate abusive tax avoidance."[174]

To sum up, a transaction can result in an abuse and misuse of the Act where the result of the avoidance transaction is an outcome that the provisions relied on seek to prevent, defeats the underlying rationale of the provisions relied on, or circumvents certain provisions in a manner that frustrates the object, spirit or purpose of those provisions.[175]

(d) — Abusive tax avoidance versus legitimate tax minimization

The GAAR is about drawing a line between acceptable tax planning and abusive tax avoidance. The generally-worded legislation delegates the line-drawing task to the courts, albeit within some guideposts. One guidepost is that the GAAR provision as well as the specific provisions of the Act that conferred the tax benefit must receive a textual, contextual and purposive interpretation. It mandates a rejection of the traditional literal interpretation. Another guidepost is that series of transactions must be examined and a specific transaction in the series must be analyzed in the context of the series. Courts cannot look at a document or transaction in blinkers, isolated from any context to which it properly belongs. However, the GAAR does not overrule the *Duke of Westminster* principle and the legal form determines the substance in most cases.

The courts have provided some guidance on distinguishing between abusive tax avoidance and acceptable tax planning. At one end of the spectrum, an avoidance transaction is not abusive if: (a) it involves the use of a more tax-efficient structure for carrying out ordinary commercial transactions; (b) it is designed to take advantage of the "tracing" rule for interest deductibility (the entire court in *Lipson* found Singleton-type of transactions acceptable under the GAAR); (c) or even if it is part of the series of transactions that are circular and self-canceling, structured through a third-party arranger to achieve tax results (e.g., the transactions in *Canada Trustco*). At the other end of the spectrum, an avoidance transaction is abusive if it is structured to take advantage of anti-avoidance rules in order to achieve the results of tax avoidance (i.e., *Mathew*, *Lipson* and *MacKay*).

20.6 — The future of the GAAR

The introduction of the GAAR was a landmark event in Canadian income tax history. It demonstrated that Parliament had perceived tax avoidance to have become a major issue and that specific anti-avoidance rules and judicial anti-avoidance approaches were inadequate. It was also evidence of Parliament's and the CRA's

---

174 *Ibid.*, para.42.

175 *Ibid.*

growing public acknowledgement of the inability of the tax administers to combat tax avoidance with their existing administrative and statutory tools. Through the GAAR, Parliament instructs courts to take a more "holistic" and "realistic" approach to statutory interpretation as opposed to the traditional "technical" and "formalistic" approach. More importantly, while recognizing the fundamental principle of taxpayers' entitlement to minimize taxation, Parliament introduces a statutory limitation on this principle by requiring that such minimization does not result in an abuse of the provisions of the Act read as a whole.

The Supreme Court has correctly stated in *Canada Trustco* that "there was abusive in the sense that it cannot be reasonably concluded that a tax benefit would be consistent with the object, spirit or purpose of the provisions relied upon by the taxpayer." The Court has also correctly acknowledged that the GAAR was intended to ensure that the provisions of the Act apply to transactions with real economic substance. At the same time, the Court stated that economic substance is not a stand-alone doctrine and must be grounded in statutory interpretation.[176]

> While the"economic substance" of the transaction may be relevant at various stages of the [s.245] analysis, his expression has little meaning in isolation from the proper interpretation of the specific provisions that are relied upon for the tax benefit.

The future of the GAAR thus lies in the proper interpretation of the provisions of the Act that are relied upon for the tax benefit. The question is whether the tax benefit was consistent with the object, spirit or purpose of the provision of the Act. Unfortunately, the jurisprudence on contextualized purposive interpretation is at an early stage of development in Canada. Courts will surely benefit from thoughtful and vigorous arguments on statutory interpretation from counsel representing the Crown and the taxpayer.

The fate of the GAAR largely depends on the judicial appreciation of the basic income tax logic and attitudes towards aggressive tax planning. It is trite to say that income tax is a tax on income. The concept of income is used to measure a taxpayer's ability to pay, which is the basis for measuring vertical and horizontal equity. Income is an economic concept. It is thus logical that transactions lacking economic substance should be ignored when the Act is applied, unless Parliament intended otherwise. Furthermore, income is taxed to the person who earns (or owns) it. It is unthinkable to tax a person on another person's income. Similarly, it is illogical to allow a deduction for a loss or expense belonging to another person. Ownership is a fundamental concept.

Judicial attitude towards agressive tax planning has been evolving in Canada. The Supreme Court has clearly recognized in *Canada Trustco* that the common-law doctrine that taxpayers are entitled to minimize taxation is subject to limitation. However, in order for the limitation to be reasonable, courts must be prepared to consider not only the rationale for protecting taxpayer's right to tax minimization, (that is, respect for private property and freedom of contract), but also the rationale for the limitation (that is, public interest in sharing the burden of financing the

---

[176]Note 14, above, para.76.

government fairly and efficiently by all taxpayers). In other words, worrying about the "health of the Duke" without worrying about the health of the tax system is worrisome. It is hoped that future jurisprudence will shed more light on defining the limitation.

INDEX

U